Life Understood

---◆---

From a Scientific and Religious Point of View

Life Understood

From a
Scientific and
Religious
Point of View

FREDERICK L. RAWSON

NEW YORK

Life Understood: From a Scientific and Religious Point of View
Cover © 2007 Cosimo, Inc.

For information, address:

Cosimo, P.O. Box 416
Old Chelsea Station
New York, NY 10113-0416

or visit our website at:
www.cosimobooks.com

Life Understood: From a Scientific and Religious Point of View was originally
published in 1912.

Cover design by www.kerndesign.net

ISBN: 978-1-60206-196-5

Sin, sickness, troubles, limitations, and even matter,
are a non-reality, merely false concepts, and capable of being
easily and effectually destroyed, bit by bit, through a knowledge
of how to think rightly. All over the world troubles of every
kind are being got rid of, and extraordinary results are being
obtained by all classes; so extraordinary that people do not care
to speak of them, except to those whom they find have
had similar experiences...

—from "The So-Called Evolution of the Material World"

CONTENTS

PAGE

SECTION I

FOREWORD 1

THE MYSTERIES OF OUR WORLD ... 4
"Occult" Phenomena 4
Scientific Difficulties 4
Medical Difficulties 6
Physiological Difficulties ... 7
Unaccounted-for Human
Capacity 8
Unaccounted-for Animal
Wonders 8
Philosophic Difficulties... ... 9
The Mystery of God 10
This Mystery "Finished" ... 11

THE SOLUTION OF ALL MYSTERIES 11
"No-mind" and "Non-mental" 12
The False Spiritual World ... 12
The Real Mind, God 12
Matter "Non-mental" 12
Matter the Manifestation of
False Impressions 13
A Correct Basic Theory ... 14

EVIL AND THE MATERIAL WORLD 14
Evil 14
The Illusion 15
The Devil and Hell 15
Hell an Individual State of
Wretched Consciousness ... 16
The Non-reality of Evil and
therefore of Matter 16
What Origin has Evil? ... 18
The Illusory Cause of Evil ... 19
"No-mind" 19
Sin the Cause of Disease ... 20
The Arraignment of the So-called
Man 20
The Ignorant Man a Helpless
Victim 21
The Death Struggle of Nature... 21
Wonders of the World ... 22
The Arraignment of the So-called
God 23
Good 24

EVOLUTION OF OUR SENSE OF GOD 25
The Religion of One God ... 26
The Definition of God 27
The Trinity 28
Origin of Good 29
The Religion of Many Gods ... 29

IS THE REAL MAN MATERIAL OR
SPIRITUAL? 30

PAGE

The Material or Carnal Man as
Described in the Bible ... 30
The Apparent Duality 31
False Spirituality 32
The True Man 32
Sons of the Living God ... 34
In Christ 34
The "Second Coming of
Christ" 35
Three Points of View 36
Choice of Words 37

ADVANCING HUMAN KNOWLEDGE... 37
Theology 39
Dogma 40
New Truths Hateful to the
Sluggard 42
Philosophy 43
Science 43
True Science Includes True Re-
ligion 45
Ethics 46
Miracles 46
The World's Awakening ... 48

WHAT IS HEAVEN? 49
The Kingdom of God that is
Within 49
Individuality 50
The Unfolding of God's Ideas... 50
Creation 51
Heavenly Happiness 51
Reality of Good 52
Proof of Our Knowledge of
Heaven 52
Movement Instantaneous ... 53
Practical Results an Undeniable
Proof 53
Perfect Sequence of Thought ... 54
Indication of Spiritual Realities 54
A World of Four Dimensions ... 55
Counterfeits and Symbols ... 58
Natural Laws Merely *Memoria
Technica* 60

SECTION II

A CONSISTENT THEORY OF MATE-
RIAL PHENOMENA 62
Scientific Forecasts 62
"Exposure is Nine Points of Des-
truction" 63
Cinematographic Pictures ... 63
So-called Thinking Merely
"Picturing" 64
Material Phenomena 64

PAGE

A Consistent Theory a Safe
Temporary Guide   64
The Ether   65
Material "Thoughts"—Lines of
Force   68
Human "Thoughts" Merely Ex-
ternal Beliefs   68
"Thoughts" Intensify Them-
selves   69
Pain a Mental Effect   69
The Human Mind   70
A Mechanical Concept   71
A Chemical Concept   71
The Basic False "Mentality"   ...   71
The "Subconscious Mind"   ...   72
The Material Body   73
The Electron   73
Matter   74
Matter Merely Ethereal Pheno-
mena   76
Motion   76
Gravity   76
Time   77
The Scientific "Now"...   ...   78
The Metaphysical View of Time
and Space   79
The Ethereal Chart   80

THE NON-REALITY OF MATTER   ...   80
Scientific Views   80
Philosophic Views   84
This   Suppositional   Opposite
World a Dream   85
Cause Must be Good   86

THE SO-CALLED EVOLUTION OF
THE MATERIAL WORLD   ...   86
Birth and Death   87
Lines of Force   87
Electrons   87
Aqueous Vapour...   87
The Constellations   88
So-called Solid Matter   88
Material Man   89
The Idea of God Evolving   ...   89
The Inevitable End of Matter ...   89
Meaning of the End of the World   90
The Power of Truth   91
Be of One Mind   92
The End Unexpected   92
Troubles at the End   93
The Power of United Right
Thinking   93
The Darkest Hour   93
The Loosing of the Devil   ...   94
Satan Loosed for Destruction ...   95
Signs of the End   96
Education   98

HEAVEN   99

PAGE

SECTION III

THE HUMAN "MIND" THAT IS
"NO-MIND"   103
The Subconscious Mind or Basic
False Mentality   103
Sense Impressions   104

HUMAN SO-CALLED "POWERS"   ...   104
Memory is Mental   105
Thought Sequences Repeated ...   105
Sight is Mental   107
Clairvoyance   107
Seeing with the Nose and Ear   108
Paintings   109
Hearing is Mental   109
Rapid Transmission of News   110
Speech is Mental   111
Smell is Mental   112
Reading the Past and Future   ...   112
Scientific Explanation   112
Inventions   113
The Divining Rod   114
Evil Effects when Reading   ...   114
Scientific Method of Working ...   114
Thought-Reading   115
Lack of Knowledge Results in
Trouble   116
Early Experiences   116
Work Mentally Only by Think-
ing of God and Heaven   ...   116
Foretelling the Future   116
Genius   118
Calculating Boys   119
Trance Speaking   119
Somnambulism   120
Ghosts and Visions   120
The Apparent Power of the "No-
Mind" to Move Instantly   ...   121

DANGER AHEAD   123
Dangerous and Useless Experi-
ments   123
Harmful Results   124

THE SAFE WAY TO WORK...   ...   125
The Appearance of Jesus when
the Doors were Shut   ...   125

DIVINE POWERS   126
A Scientific Remedy   126
The Denial or "Michael"   ...   127
The Affirmation or "Gabriel"...   127
Constant Conscious Communion
with God   128
Reverse Every Wrong Thought
Instantly   129
Wrong Thoughts   130
The Two-edged Sword of Truth   131
Man the Male and Female of
God's Creation   133

PAGE

Striving a Joyous Realisation ... 133
Scientific Working Restful ... 134
Man Cannot Retrograde ... 134
Treatment 135
Personal Treatment 136
Impersonal Treatment ... 137
The Rod of Iron 138
The Practitioner 139
Dematerialisation 139

SECTION IV

PHILOSOPHIC APPROACH TO TRUTH 142
Evil is of No Value 142
Process of Self-Destruction of
Evil 144
A Present Devil and a Future
God ! 144
What is Truth? 145
The Truth of Being 145
Two Horns of a Dilemma ... 145
The Only Alternative 145
Man's Better Understanding of
God 146
Two Impossibilities 146
God Finite if not Omnipotent ... 146
Is God Unwilling or Unable to
Abolish Evil? 147
The Evolution of Philosophy ... 147
The New Theology 148

HOW TO UNDERSTAND ADVANCED
WRITINGS 148
Misinterpretations of Truth ... 148
Definition of "The Scriptures" 149
Fear of Criticism Betrays Doubt
of Truth 149
The Bible the Book of Books ... 150
Difficulties in Understanding the
Bible 150
Numbers and Names 153
Anglo-Israelites 153
Bible Symbolism 153
Symbols 154

INSPIRATION 154
Madness 156
Inspiration Scientific 156
Proofs of Its Truth 157

PRACTICAL DEMONSTRATIONS ... 158
The Ether and Matter 158
Disappearance of Matter ... 159
"The Earth Helped the Woman" 159
Crookes's Berlin Lecture ... 159
Non-Reality of Matter ... 160
"Correct" and "Accurate" ... 161
Short-circuiting 161

PROPHESYING, PREDESTINATION,
FATALISM 162
Value of Historical Evidence ... 162
Spiritual Significance 163

PAGE

The Value of Prophecy ... 163
Vibration the Cause of the
Apparent Unity 164
Astrology 164
Numerical Value of Names ... 165
Predestination Correct 166
"Appointments" not to be Kept 167
The Hopeless Injustice of the
Material World 168
Fatalism Untrue 168
The Prophecies of Moses ... 169
The Covenant 170
The Book of Revelation ... 170
Value of the Book of Revelation 171

FELLOW-SOLDIERS 172
Impersonality of Evil 172

SECTION V

SO-CALLED MENTAL EFFECT ... 175
Medical Needs 175
The Effect of So-called Thought 175
Confidence 178
Psychotherapy 179
The King's Touch 183

CONTEMPORARY VIEWS ON MENTAL
EFFECT 183
Changed Mental Conditions
Create Chemical Changes ... 185
A Purely Metaphysical Basis Re-
quisite 187
Medical Recognition 188
Admitted Ignorance 190
Practical Experience 191
So-called Mental Effect on
Muscles 191
On Animals... 192
On Human Beings 192
On Inert Matter 192
On Watches 193
On Vegetable Life 193
Platform Displays 194
A Warning 194

MENTAL HEALING 194
The Bible Testimony 194
Our Present Duty 195
Raising of the Dead 196

ACTION OF THOUGHT 197
Homœopathy 197
The Cause of Disease 198
Poison 198
All Action in the Material Seem-
ing World only Apparent ... 199
Cancer and Humanity 199
"Some Ray of Hope" 199
Hope Fulfilled 200
Appearance and Disappearance
of Matter 200
"There is Nothing but God" ... 201

                                PAGE   PAGE
Two Methods of Working   ... 201   The Mighty Purpose to be Ac-
Alteration of Electrical Tension 202   complished   236
Short-circuiting Particles   ... 203   Joy   237
Reappearance of the Disease   ... 203   Beauty   238
Synchronous Vibration 204
The Beam in the Eye   204
Startling Home Truths   ... 204   SECTION VI
Sin and Its Punishment   ... 205
The Freeing from Sin 205   ETHEREAL "NO-MIND"   240
The Way of Escape   206   Good is Absolute, Evil Relative   240
"Greater Works"   207   Conscience   241
                                            Sin   241
THE EVOLUTION OF PRAYER   ... 207   Persecution   242
  Material Gods   207
  Semi-human Gods   208   THE ABSOLUTE STANDARD OF GOOD   242
  Anthropomorphic God 208   The Unfailing Action of the
  The One God   209   Principle of Good   242
  The One True God   210   Apparent Two Worlds   243

FAITH-HEALING 211   COLLECTIVE FORCE OF FOOLISH
  Return of Trouble   213   BELIEFS   243
  No Real Healing with the   The Action of Food   244
    Human So-called "Mind"   ... 213   Be a Law of God, Good, unto
  Supplicatory Prayer 214   Yourself   244
  Suggestion   215   Sleep a Waste of Time   245
  "Mental" Suggestion 217
  The Real Test 218   DANGEROUS FALSE BELIEFS   ...   245
                                            Hypnotism   245
DIVINE HEALING 218   Hypnotic Prayer   246
  The Key to the Miracles of Jesus 219   Unfortunate Workers   247
  God Destroying Matter   ... 220   Napoleon   247
  Results of True Prayer 220   False Christs   248
  Results According to Law   ... 221   Occultism   249
  Early Instantaneous Results ... 223   Spiritualism 249
  The Holy Ghost...   223   So-called Proofs   251
  All Can Heal 224   Stages in the Formation of
  The Medical World   225   Matter   251
  The Man in Authority 226   The Explanation of Its Seem-
  Main Points in Instantaneous   ing Mystery   252
    Healing   227   Objections and Dangers 252
  Love   228   Terrible Results 253
  The Power of Love   230   Deterioration of Moral Charac-
  The Protective Power of Love... 230   ter   253
  Three Phases of Love   ... 230   Planchette   255
  Purity 232   Grief for a "Departed"
                                                Friend   256
                                              Theory Unsound   256
THE FALSE DIVISION OF THE   Magicians and Wizards   257
  SEXES 233   Divination   257
  The Union of Mental Qualities... 233   Extraordinary Powers of Animals 258
  Platonic Friendship 233
  Dangerous Whirlpools 234   DISASTROUS SELF-MADE LAWS   ...   259
  God's Protection   234   Tiredness   259
  A Warning   234   Disease   259
  The Marriage Tie   234   Fear 260
  Unity with Spiritual Advance-   Will-Power   261
    ment 235   "Mental" Malpractice   261
  Spiritual Consecration Necessary 235   "Drawing Fire"   262
  Need for Fulfilment of the   Malicious "Mental" Malpractice 262
    World's Highest Standard   ... 236   Preventive Legislation   263
  Practical Results the Only Proof 236

PAGE

Matter Refined up to Demateri-
alisation 263
Death 263
Death Unnecessary 265
Raising from the Dead 266
No Spiritual Advancement or
other Gain by Death ... 267
Suicide No Release 268
Victory Over Death 268
What Happens at Death ... 269

BIRTH, ITS MYSTERY SOLVED ... 270
Counterfesance 271
Fleeting Dream Pictures ... 272
Nicodemus 273
Unprejudiced Hearing Necessary
to Gain Truth 274
" History Repeats Itself " ... 274
A Mechanical World 275
Scientific Confirmation 276
The Darwinian Theory of Evo-
lution 278
Unnatural Science 280
Unnatural Religion 280
World's Preparatory School ... 283

SECTION VII

OUR DUTY 285
Man's Dominion 286
Humility 287
Glorify God 287
Progress Necessary 287
Be Selfless 288
Pride 289
Criticism 290
Talking of Others 290
Friends 291
Be Unselfish 292

OUR RESPONSIBILITY 293
Judgment-Day 293
" Choose You This Day " ... 294
The Apparent Law of Evil ... 295
The Law of Good 295

LEARN TO PRAY RIGHTLY 296
The Habit of Reversal 297
Think Rightly 297
Man One with God 298
Sign-posts on the Way 299
Demonstration the Only Proof... 299
Give Tithes to God 299
"Pray Without Ceasing" ... 300
Here Lies Safety 300
Do Not Waste a Second ... 300
Consecration of Self 301
Better Beliefs 302
Trust in God 302

PAGE

Do Not Limit God 303
Pray until Fear is Destroyed ... 303
Nothing too Difficult 303

OUR WORK 303
Have No Doubt 306
Let God Lead You 306
A Cup of Cold Water 307
Give Thanks 307
Payment 307
A Call to Every Man 308
Truth Attracts Those Ready ... 308
Truth the Lamp of Understand-
ing 308
The Morning Star 309
Demonstrable Truth 309
The Heralds of the Day... ... 309

NOTA BENE 310
Reality 310
Man is Spiritual 310
Unreality 311
Material So-called " Thoughts " 311
Predestination and Fatalism ... 311
Death 312
Evolution 312
Demonstrable Truth 313
The End of Evil 313
Eminent Desirability of the End 313
Always Follow a Denial of Error
with Affirmations of Truth ... 314
No Loss of Pleasure 314
Truth is Essentially Demons-
trable 314

CHRISTIAN SCIENCE OR SCIENTIFIC
CHRISTIANITY 315
Truth in Literal and Physical
Terms 316
An Exact Science 317
An Exposure of Fallacies ... 317
Spiritual Accuracy 318
False Brethren 318
A Needful Warning 318
True Christian Science ... 319
Mary Baker Eddy 320

APPENDIX

SUMMARY OF INTELLECTUAL DEVEL-
OPMENT 323
ON THEOSOPHY 347
ON REINCARNATION 348
MAHATMAS 348
COUNTERFESANCE 349
ON SOCIALISM 350
ON WOMEN'S RIGHTS 352
ON BUSINESS 353

	PAGE
THE DIFFERENT WAYS OF LOOK-ING AT LIFE	355
From the Religious Point of View	356
From the Metaphysical Point of View	356
From the Scientific Point of View	357
The Most Accurate View—Cinematographic Pictures ...	357
Successive Periods of History	357
The So-called Evolution of the Material World ...	358
Intellectual Meaning of First Chapter of Genesis ...	359
How to Check Prophecies of the Future	361
Confirmatory Evidence ...	361
Gradually Improving Human Presentations of the Christ	361
The Commencement of Each Period an Escape from Evil	362
The Final Film	363

	PAGE
FORESHADOWINGS OF HEAVEN ...	363
The Radiation of God's Ideas ...	363
Spiritual Reality of Food ...	364
Of Animals	365
Other Spiritual Realities ...	367
The Christ Capacity	368
Summary...	369

	PAGE
TREATMENT OR TRUE PRAYER ...	369
How to Gain a Working Knowledge of God	370
How to Reverse Wrong Thoughts	371
LETTER TO AN ARTIST	374
THE CHRIST	376
Jesus the Christ	377
The Second Coming of the Christ	379
TO WHOM IT MAY CONCERN ...	379
Denial of Material Intelligence is Necessary	380
Knowledge of Truth is Necessary	381
Love is Necessary	381
Knowledge of what the Material World Claims to be is Necessary	382
Knowledge of Underground Working is Necessary ...	383
Assimilation of Mrs. Eddy's Writings is Necessary ...	384
Knowledge of Language is Necessary	385
Knowledge of God is Necessary	387
Knowledge of Evil is Necessary	387
Charity is Necessary	390
Beware of Jealousy	393
The Grave-Clothes of the Letter	394
Take Heed	395
Personality	396
Safety is at Hand	397
The Manner and Period of the End	399
INDEX	401

LIFE UNDERSTOOD FROM A SCIENTIFIC AND RELIGIOUS POINT OF VIEW

and

The Practical Method of Destroying Sin, Disease, and Death

SECTION ONE

FOREWORD

All over the world, not only in scientific circles, but through the daily press, the attention of thinkers is being drawn to the fact that our old ideas are fundamentally wrong, and that some great truth surely remains undiscovered which is likely soon to bring about a great change for humanity at large.   5

Lord Kelvin has written: "One word characterises the most strenuous efforts for the advancement of science that I have made perseveringly during fifty-five years—that word is 'failure.' I know no more of electric and magnetic force, or of the relation between ether, electricity, and ponderable matter, or of chemical affinity than I knew and tried to teach 10 my students of natural philosophy in my first session as a professor." This was because Lord Kelvin, whilst a religious man, endeavoured to find truth in matter.

One of the leading and most practical chemists of the day, in mentioning a new discovery which has not yet been given to the world by its learned 15 discoverers on account of the impossibility of fitting it in with any known theory of matter, made the following statement to me: "It is an extraordinary thing that every science is now coming to a head. This position has been reached before in different sciences, but it is the first time in the known history of the world that all the sciences have come to the same 20 conclusion together, namely, that their old ideas are absolutely wrong." Another, recognised all over the world as a giant in research said: "We do not know whether we are standing on our heads or on our heels."

The consecutive statement in the following pages contains a collection 25 of facts and logical deductions therefrom, which having been learnt and demonstrably proved, are gladly presented to suffering humanity. The facts given will, it is believed, be found of fascinating and vital interest to all.

The aim has been, not to present a theory, but first to expose the 30 foundationless fallacies of material so-called laws on which alone rests all the seeming mystery of human experiences. Secondly, to draw attention to the only practical, universal, and unfailing method of instantaneously

overcoming every kind of sin, disease, and trouble, including death, by a
right understanding of Life as God. To understand God is the work of
eternity, but a grasp of this method will at once revolutionise the life of
the reader. To obtain such a grasp, it is better to read steadily through the
5 sections in the order given, instead of merely taking the most interesting
parts first.

The truths declared are not mere arbitrary statements. They can be
proved by each and all of those who study the laws herein stated. The
main points brought out are as follows :—

10   i. Sin, disease, and even death itself, are merely crude mistakes,
        resulting from ignorance of the law of Life, eternal Mind,
        omnipotent good.
     ii. God is not a distant potentate, but an ever-living, ever-active,
        and unalterable Principle—Mind, Soul, Spirit, Life, Truth, and
15   Love; the omnipotence and omnipresence of which can be
        instantly utilised at any moment and for any good purpose.
    iii. Man's possibilities, resting on a scientific, mental foundation, are
        found to be limitless, for he reflects divine Principle. These, even
        as humanly discerned, are so marvellous that they enable us to
20   form an approximate, and continually improving, conception of
        absolute spiritual realities.
     iv. The mysteries of birth and death are explained, the latter being
        merely a transition into another material state of human con-
        sciousness, which can be entirely avoided.
25   v. The changing and fading fallacies with regard to material evolution
        are laid bare, and the eternal facts of spiritual evolution stated.
     vi. A logical and consistent statement of the theories of material
        phenomena, exposing the fallacies that have hitherto, through
        ignorance, bound mankind, is set forth.
30 vii. Last, and not least, each reader, as he discerns the truths declared,
        can at once put into practice himself, an easy, scientific, and there-
        fore infallible and instantaneous method of obtaining the follow-
        ing revolutionary results :—

        (a) Deliverance from sin, disease, and the last grim enemy,
35   death itself.
        (b) Ability to relieve his fellow-man instantaneously of any
        kind of sin or disease, and, in fact, help him out of any possible
        difficulty.
        (c) The overcoming of limitations of all kinds in every right
40   direction.
        (d) Freedom from all worries and troubles, and the attain-
        ment of perfect peace of mind, with continued increasing
        happiness.

"Slumber not in the tents of your fathers; the world is advancing, advance
45 with it" (Mazzini). Ten years ago I was retained by the *Daily Express* to
make a professional examination into mental working, the vital subject
that is now engaging the attention of the deepest thinkers and greatest

humanitarians throughout the world. In consequence of this I was asked by the Rev. J. Bruce Wallace, under special circumstances, which will be referred to later, to give a lecture, the amplification of which has led to this book.

In the course of this examination the facts came to my knowledge that are now to be presented to you. These facts, however surprising they may appear to you, were, I assure you, no less so to me. I am convinced, however, that anyone who examines them with even a little care and patience, and with an open mind, will come to the same conclusion as I have done, and reap a rich reward. I would emphatically echo the words of Uriel to Esdras, who asked for understanding of some of the most important subjects dealt with in this work, and was answered as follows: "The more thou searchest, the more thou shalt marvel" (II Esdras 4: 26).

"Scepticism is ignorance," writes Victor Longheed, and a sign of wisdom is to keep our minds open and our mouths shut when scientific wonders are put before us. "Disbelief is easier than belief, if in accordance with environment or custom, and is usually due to indolence, and is never a thing to be proud of" (Romanes).

"Psychical research is by far the most important work that is being done in the world" (W. E. Gladstone). Remember that hardly anything is known scientifically about psychology. It is only recently that it has been deemed worthy of being studied and taught. Professor James, one of the leading psychologists of modern times, writes in *Psychology* as follows: "Psychology is but a string of raw facts, a little gossip and a wrangle about opinions, a little classification and generalisation on the mere descriptive level, a strong prejudice that we have states of mind, and that our brain conditions them, but not a single law in the sense in which physics shows us laws. At present psychology is in the condition of physics before Galileo and the laws of motion, or of chemistry before Lavoisier." We should, as Sir William Crookes has said, "keep our minds, like the windows of a lodging-house, with a notice written thereon, 'Rooms to let.'"

"If . . . And ye shall know the truth, and the truth shall make you free" (John 8: 32). It is my intention to present, in accordance with the most recent scientific knowledge, a correct word picture; in other words, by the presentation of up-to-date natural science and latter-day practical metaphysics to enable you to understand better what this material world assumes to be, and how through the exposure of all its hidden workings, and therefore seeming mystery, it is possible to emerge from the mists of shifting appearances into the sunlight of eternal facts.

A. J. Balfour, in his presidential address to the British Association a few years ago, pointed out the necessity of not limiting ourselves to material facts alone, but of coming out of the realm of the unreal, that is, the material world, into that which has hitherto been termed abstract, namely, the spiritual world or world of reality.

It is certain that every honest, unprejudiced seeker will find, as I have proved for myself, that the substitution of metaphysical working, or deep, systematic thinking, produces practical effects, as far exceeding those obtained by physical methods as sunlight exceeds rushlight.

The theory or explanation [1] of material phenomena now put before you has been gradually evolving, and includes and accounts for every known so-called fact of the material world, whether physical or so-called mental, accepted by science, or of the class called occult. This theory 5 is daily, although sometimes unknowingly, being corroborated by leaders in natural science all over the world. Many of the most important facts have been confirmed since they were first brought to my knowledge.

THE MYSTERIES OF OUR WORLD

"*But we speak the wisdom of God in a mystery, even the hidden wisdom,* 10 *which God ordained before the world unto our glory*" (I Cor. 2 : 7).

Our planet is full of mystery, and of the universe only enough is known to make those who are thought to know a great deal, partially recognise their ignorance. "And if any man think that he knoweth any thing, he knoweth nothing yet as he ought to know" (I Cor. 8 :2).

15 Professor Drummond, in *Natural Law in the Spiritual World*, writes : "The one subject upon which all scientific men are agreed, the one theme upon which all alike become eloquent, the one strain of pathos in all their writing and speaking and thinking, concerns that final uncertainty, that utter blackness of darkness bounding their work on every side." This 20 darkness is ignorance, the mystery of evil, the only cause of the apparent limitation in every direction. This darkness has now been dissipated.

"Occult" Phenomena.—Amongst the phenomena known to in-vestigators for which it has hitherto been manifestly impossible to account in any rational way, are those connected with thought-reading, prophesy-25 ing, clairvoyance, clairaudience, second sight, psychometry, somnam-bulism, duplicated personality, suggestion, hypnotism, spiritualism, theosophy, the ancient temples, faith-healers, the Indian Yogis, Moham-medan fakirs, and the witches and sorcerers of olden days. So ignorant have we been of such matters that until quite recently their investigation 30 was tabooed by scientific men on the ground that there was no method of obtaining exact knowledge concerning them. There are many other mysterious phenomena, such as ghosts and visions, miracles and enchant-ments, and marvellous powers that various men have exercised, of which there are many instances recorded in the oldest known writings, in the Bible, 35 and throughout all history. These phenomena are now no longer mysterious, and by reversal of the many falsities in connection with them they serve as waymarks to better, and ultimately to permanent things, the ideas of God.

Scientific Difficulties.—Even if we put on one side all that may be considered "miraculous," those facts which are called "scientific" are 40 just as bewildering. Take, for instance, the ether, which is full of para-doxes. Is a material earth, as stated, flying at the rate of about eighteen miles per second through this ether, the density of which is believed to be

---

[1] "To make hypotheses, to verify them by experiments, then to attempt to connect, by the aid of generalisations, the facts discovered, represents the stages 45 necessary for the building up of all our knowledge" (*The Evolution of Matter,* Dr. G. Le Bon).

four hundred and eighty times greater than that of the densest matter on the earth? To what are due the deviations in the movements of the moon and Mercury? Why does the ninth satellite of Saturn revolve in a direction contrary to the others, and contrary to the general rotation of our solar system? Why do the projections of the western hemisphere corre- 5 spond to the indentations of the eastern? Why does not the sun get appreciably cooler? Why is a comet attracted, and the particles of its tail apparently repelled, by the sun? Why is the view of so-called natural laws constantly being altered? Why, according to Professor Jevons, can only about one mathematical problem out of a million be solved? Why does 10 chemical affinity work in different ways on different substances? What is electricity? What indeed is vibration or force? What is heat? Why is a bar of steel magnetised under a shock if held in one position and not in another? Why does matter sometimes repel and sometimes attract matter? Why at the temperature of liquid air does phosphorus lose its violent 15 affinity for oxygen and sulphuric acid no longer turn litmus paper red? Why does aluminium, which does not decompose water when cold or oxidize at ordinary temperatures, decompose water violently and visibly oxidize with water containing the slightest trace of mercury? Why do extreme heat and cold produce similar effects? Why does a gyroscope 20 running at a very high speed present a strong resistance to any force used to alter its position? Why does every substance, including water, contract upon cooling, while water and bismuth alone expand just before freezing? What is the cause of the movements of the planets and their satellites? What is gravity? To what are the varying cohesive, elastic, frictional, 25 viscous, electric, and magnetic properties due? What are the laws underlying the freedom and mutual constraints of molecules? Such questions have been puzzling both physicists and chemists for centuries.[1]

It is a remarkable thing that the more the materialist has investigated such matters, and the greater his experience of them, the more uncertain 30 has appeared his knowledge and the further he has seemed from any fixed laws. Take, for instance, astronomy. Until recently it was thought the laws governing the movements of the solar system were absolutely fixed and well known. It is now being found that we had practically no real knowledge of them. Astrologers, who laugh at what they speak of as the 35 ignorance of western astronomers, will tell you wonderful things that they have learned from applying the facts brought to light by the astronomers, who, confining themselves to the evidence of their five senses, have failed to reap the reward of their discoveries. "Astronomy is the most perfect science, because we know least about it" (*Modern Science: A Criticism*, 40 Edward Carpenter).

All these difficulties can now be demonstrably accounted for by the real metaphysician, who alone has perfect control over the seeming laws of physics.

---

[1] "All the facts of this order [early evolution of matter] belong to the category 45 of unexplained phenomena of which nature is full, and which become more numerous as soon as we penetrate into unexplored regions. The complexity of things seems to increase the more they are studied" (*The Evolution of Matter*, Dr. Le Bon).

Medical Difficulties.—When we come to the subject about which we should know most, namely, man, how little we find is generally known! He is a mass of mystery and contradictions. Take medical practice, for instance. The only certain thing about it is its uncertainty, and yet some of the greatest men have given up their lifetime to its study and almost broken their hearts at different times over their apparent inability to help a sufferer. Few professions have given, and are giving the world up to the present day, such noble examples of self-sacrifice as the medical profession and those connected with it. Yet, is disease lessen-

10 ing? Dr. James Johnson, surgeon to King William IV, said: "I declare my conscientious opinion, founded on long observation and reflection, that if there was not a single physician, surgeon, apothecary, man-midwife, chemist, druggist or drug on the face of the earth, there would be less sickness and less mortality." Why, according to Sir Victor Horsley, do

15 over ten thousand patients die annually in London alone after operations? Why did the Metropolitan Asylums Board recently report in one year alone over three thousand cases of mistaken diagnosis admitted to their isolation hospitals? Why did the well-known Dr. Abercrombie write: "Medicine is the science of guessing"? Why does a person apparently die of fright?

20 In fact, when is he really dead, since, as will be shown, he does not really die—that is, pass into another state of consciousness—for several days after the appearance of death? Why does a man's hair turn white in a night—in the case of a Bengalee criminal, in front of the spectators? Why does sea-sickness almost invariably disappear in moments of danger? Why does one

25 person catch a disease and another under similar circumstances escape it? In fact, what is the cause (so-called) of many diseases? Sir John Forbes, M.D., F.R.S., F.R.C.P., said: "No systematic or theoretical classification of diseases or of therapeutic agents ever yet promulgated, is true, or anything like the truth, and none can be adopted as a safe guide in practice." Why

30 is the practice of medicine so different in different countries and at different periods?

Dr. Mason Goode, a well-known Professor, writes: "The effects of medicine on the human system are in the highest degree uncertain; except, indeed, that it has already destroyed more lives than war, pesti-

35 lence, and famine, all combined. Why did Dr. Benjamin Waterhouse write: "I am sick of learned quackery," and Oliver Wendell Holmes say, in a lecture before the Harvard Medical School: "I firmly believe that if the whole materia medica could be sunk to the bottom of the sea, it would be all the better for mankind and the worse for the fishes"? Why in allopathy

40 is a large amount of a drug given that causes opposite symptoms to those of the disease, and in homœopathy a small amount of a drug that produces the same symptoms, and why do both contrary systems produce a seem-ing cure? One of the latest ideas is to give drugs to increase fevers, on the ground that a fever is nature's method of supplying increased blood to

45 parts affected, so as to get rid of local disease. Why is this so when ice is freely used, and previously the temperature was kept up, both methods producing like results? Why is it that "what is one man's meat is another man's poison"? To what is the effect of infinitesimal homœopathic doses due? Why does a harmless draught surreptitiously substituted for a narcotic

mixture equally send a patient to sleep? Why have the drugs used been so constantly changed? In fact, why in civilised countries is the use of drugs being given up altogether? Sir Almroth Wright informs me that "it is useless to expect from the drugs with which we are at present acquainted, destruction of the bacteria in the interior of the organism," and that "the 5 method of extinguishing bacteria by the knife will be finally given up."

Why are talismans so believed in? What is the explanation of the deaths and cures of sickness produced at a distance by the witch doctors in Central Africa, and of the wonderful facts related by thoroughly credible travellers in Siberia, Abyssinia, and elsewhere? Why did the Aissouan 10 Arabs, who a little time ago visited London, devour venomous snakes, and allow themselves to be stung by scorpions without harm, after being apparently hypnotised by their chief? To what may the mysterious results be ascribed for which five hundred people were burnt in Zürich in one day, and ten thousand in Germany in a year, with the object of stamping 15 out witchcraft? What sustains the army of so-called quacks? What caused Lavoisier to say: "Medicine came into the world with a twin-brother called Charlatanism," and Voltaire to say: "The art of medicine consists in amusing the patient while nature cures the disease"? Why did Sir James Paget write to Sir Henry Acland, in 1866, as follows: "What 20 unsatisfactory . . . cases these are! This clever, charming, and widely known lady will some day disgrace us all by being juggled out of her maladies by some bold quack, who, by mere force of assertion, will give her the will to bear, or forget, or suppress all the turbulences of her nervous system"? 25

Why do we believe more in the power of drugs to heal than in the power of God? Is God incapable or is He unwilling to heal our sin and sickness? What do we mean by the term God when we say that God heals? What is the cause of the apparent healing done by numerous sects, and of that done at Bethshan, at the holy baths of Lourdes, and elsewhere? How is it 30 that such circumstantial records of the healing of various diseases by the touch of English kings have been handed down to us? What is the explanation of King Menelik's healing of snake bites at a distance, and of the many varieties of faith-healers and other different forms of what appears to be mental healing? None of this apparent healing is of any permanent 35 value, as will be seen hereafter. There is only one method of healing that rests upon a scientific basis. On the same scientific basis rest substantial replies to all questions that can arise.

Physiological Difficulties.—What is the connection, if any, between mind and brain? Why did Sir J. Crichton-Browne, M.D., LL.D., F.R.S., 40 writing of important physiological and pathological discoveries, say that they "have not, it will be found, brought us one hair's breadth nearer the comprehension of the way in which the physical basis of mind is related to mind at all"?[1] How are "nerve stimuli" transmuted into sensation or ideas? How do the nerves affect the muscles, either to contract or release 45 them? Why do nerves seem to ache after they are no longer there, for

[1] "The Hygienic Uses of Imagination." Address on Psychology, delivered at the Annual Meeting of the British Medical Association, 1889.

instance, when a leg has been amputated? How is the inverted image at
the back of the retina transmitted to the brain? Why do we not see everything upside down? What is the process whereby the likeness of the parent
is transmitted to the offspring? How is it that such great physical changes
5 suddenly take place in a child just before the moment of birth? What is
the medium between the so-called mental and physical systems?

There is an extensive literature on the subject which sets forth many
different theories and speculative explanations, and yet no one has ever
pretended to understand such matters until recently.

10   **Unaccounted-for Human Capacity.**—Here again there have been
numerous mysteries. How did Bidder, the eminent civil engineer, seem,
as his grand-daughter told me, to see in the air the answer to any mathematical question, without calculating? Others, called "calculating boys,"
have done the same. What is the source from which Moses, Isaiah,
15 Jeremiah, Daniel, and Huldah the prophetess, with such people as Jacob
Boehme, Andrew Jackson Davis, and many others, have drawn their surprising knowledge? To what were the wonderful powers of Emanuel
Swedenborg due? By what means did the natives know at once in the
Egyptian bazaars of the death of the heroic Gordon? How does news travel
20 so quickly in Central Africa and other places? Why does one speaker
electrify an audience, and another produce no effect, and, as is a matter of
common knowledge, the speeches of one member of Parliament sound well
and read badly, and vice versa? Why does a "rot" sometimes set in at
cricket? Why is one man lucky and another man unlucky? What was
25 Rarey's secret for taming horses, and what was that of Major Wood? Why
did not the tiger spring upon Sir Charles Napier, but slink away when
gazed at fearlessly? [1]

What were the laws known and utilised by Daniel in the lions' den, and
by his three co-religionists in the fiery furnace? It can now be proved that
30 all men have latent within them marvellous powers, and can successfully
apply the same laws for their own benefit and that of others.

Unaccounted-for Animal Wonders.—There are many things here
that no one hitherto has been able to explain. How is it that a dog or cat
will find its way straight home, after having been taken away one hundred
35 miles by train? Why do cubs of wild animals, for instance, in moments of
danger, obey the dam without a sound being uttered or a movement
apparently taking place? How do ants convey to each other a whole series
of instructions concerning places to be visited and work to be done, as
far as one can tell, by merely momentarily touching each other's antennæ?
40 Where does a cat find the fulcrum whereby it falls on its paws even if held
only just above the ground with its feet upwards? How do soft insects,
such as the smaller death watch and the book louse make their sounds?

We now find that the only difference between the material man and
material animal is one of degree, and man has unconsciously limited the
45 powers of animals, instead of improving them.

---

[1] One who faced a tiger in the jungle until it slunk away, on being asked how he
was able to exercise such control, replied: "Because I have conquered the tiger in
my own nature."

Philosophic Difficulties.—There are also other things of vital importance that have puzzled all thinkers for ages. For instance, why is evil permitted to come into the world? This, until recent times, has been the greatest puzzle to all schools of thought. Why have most of us apparently found ourselves aimlessly wandering "on the shores of time, 5 disappointed travellers tossed to and fro by adverse circumstances, inevitably subject to sin, disease, and death?" Why in this world, on the one hand, is there sometimes, without any apparent reason, such wonderful happiness, though always temporary, while, on the other hand, all nature teems with instances of the most diabolical ferocity and awful misery, 10 making a living hell for countless millions of the seeming lower forms of life, patient, tortured sufferers?

What is the reason of so-called evolution? Is there anything besides Darwin's natural selection, or, as Wallace puts it, the struggle for existence? Huxley spoke of predetermined lines of modification, and since then 15 some biologists, endeavouring to explain evolution, have suggested what they provisionally called Bathmism, that is, a tendency towards progress inherent in organisms. All these great thinkers have acknowledged that there must be some further explanation which some day would be discovered. 20

Finally, why has the world appeared full of mysteries for so long, and why is it that, until recently, the more we learned the more difficulties appeared, and the less we found we really knew? "Knowledge is proud that he has learned so much. Wisdom is humble that he knows no more" (Cowper). The following words of Professor Jevons show our previous 25 lamentable ignorance: "It might be readily shown that in whatever direction we extend our investigations and successfully harmonise a few facts, the result is only to raise up a host of other unexplained facts." "Even religion and therapeutics need regenerating" (Mary Baker Eddy). No one admits this more fully than the leading exponents of these two great would- 30 be benefactors of mankind.

> "At thirty, man suspects himself a fool,
> Knows it at forty and reforms his plan;
> At fifty chides his infamous delay,
> Pushes his prudent purpose to resolve." 35

We might add that at sixty he regrets his lost opportunities, and at seventy thinks that it is too late to do anything. One can readily imagine an intelligent, well-informed visitant to this earth for the first time, reporting nearly the whole of its inhabitants to be afflicted with an ignorance of the truth about their own affairs that amounted to insanity. 40

Such a pitiable state of ignorance does the mass of mankind appear to be in, that we find a well-known writer, E. W. Maunder in *The Astronomy of the Bible*, saying: "Science therefore cannot go back to the absolute beginnings of things, or forward to the absolute ends of things. It cannot reason about the way matter and energy came into existence, or how they will 45 cease to exist; it cannot reason about time or space, as such, but only in the relation of them to phenomena that can be observed. . . . Science cannot inquire into them [the facts that are stated in the first chapter of Genesis]

for the purpose of checking their accuracy; it must accept them as it accepts
the fundamental law that governs its own working, without the possibility
of proof." This shows something fundamentally wrong in the line of
research. Surely we have forgotten the injunction, "Open thou mine eyes,
5 that I may behold wondrous things out of thy law" (Ps. 119:18).

Dr. J. W. Heysinger, in *Spirit and Matter before the Bar of Modern
Science*, has said: "What is wanted is to see science put on her spectacles,
and get honestly down to hard work on these difficult but universal and
most important subjects. When that time comes, and it is rapidly coming,
10 psychism, in its broadest sense, will be tried by a jury of its peers, and the
verdict will be in accordance with the evidence of all mankind, everywhere
and from the beginning, and will not represent merely a self-sufficient
ignoring of the whole testimony, and an a priori judgment of the whole
case. The facts will not be superciliously thrown aside, the evidence will
15 not be perverted nor garbled, inconvenient facts will not be suppressed, the
truth will be elicited as it would be by skilled lawyers, and the opinion
rendered as it would be by able and impartial judges, and science will then
win a crown of imperishable glory. Nay, more, in that day the judgment
will be found reflected upon and applicable to many other great problems,
20 now the despair of science, and solid achievements will come in all
directions. Science is clearly moving in the direction of the spiritual;
nothing can be more certain."

This prophecy is of interest, as it is now fulfilled, and "solid achievements" are coming in all directions.

25 **The Mystery of God.**—"*Amid the mysteries which become more
mysterious the more they are thought about, there will ever remain the one
absolute certainty, that man is ever in the presence of an infinite and eternal
energy from which all things proceed*" (Herbert Spencer). "*It is difficult to
attain and dangerous to publish, the knowledge of the true God*" (Cicero).[1]
30 It is well known, and referred to in the Bible, that what the early
Christians taught, was looked upon as a mystery, and that there were
various grades of learners. St. Clement of Alexandria mentions the "minor
mysteries, which have some foundation of instruction . . . and the great
mysteries, in which nothing remains to be learned of the universe." He
35 also says that the Gnosis "has descended by transmission to a few, having
been imparted unwritten by the Apostles" (*Anti-Nicene Library*, Vol.
XII). There are numerous references of this kind in the writings of the
early Fathers. "Without controversy great is the mystery of godliness"
(I Tim. 3 : 16). What is the difference, if any, between Jesus the Christ and
40 the ideal Christ that Paul taught us was the wisdom and power of God?
Why are we told to have only one God in the Bible and yet told in the
Prayer Book that "the Father is God, the Son is God, and the Holy Ghost
is God. And yet there are not three Gods, but one God"? Why does our
Prayer Book, which is a schedule to an Act of Parliament, speak through-
45 out of us as the Children of Israel, of Abraham, or of Isaac? Why does the
preface of the only book in England of which the perpetual copyright is
retained, the authorised translation of the Bible, couple England with

---

[1] *De Natura Deorum*, Abbé d'Olivito translation.

Zion, both words being in italics? "We speak the wisdom of God in a mystery, even the hidden wisdom, which God ordained before the world unto our glory" (I Cor. 2 :7).

This Mystery "Finished."—*"In the days of the voice of the seventh angel, when he shall begin to sound, the mystery of God should be finished, as* 5 *he hath declared to his servants the prophets"* (Rev. 10 :7). *"Ignorance of truth is the cause of all misery"* (Gautama Buddha). *"Ye shall know the truth, and the truth shall make you free"* (John 8 : 32).

This mystery, which is thus referred to by the great Apocalyptic reader of thought, is the mystery of good which arises from ignorance of the 10 laws of eternal Mind, the fact being that God, good, is never absent. "The light shineth in darkness; and the darkness comprehended it not" (John 1 : 5). This mystery is now solved, reason and revelation reconciled. The only practical solution of this "perplexing problem of human existence" may be found in the simple teachings, and is illustrated in the 15 little understood life of Jesus the Christ. When intelligently considered, even the mysticism shrouding the Godhead disappears, leaving a practical knowledge of God. All mystery disappears as we gain the scientific practical understanding of his statements. "There is nothing covered, that shall not be revealed" (Luke 12 : 2). We appear gradually to obtain, not 20 only a knowledge of material things, but the scientific understanding of God that gives life everlasting. The prayer, "Give us, dear God, again on earth the lost chord of Christ," is being divinely answered, and again the song, "Peace on earth, goodwill toward men," floats o'er the earth.

THE SOLUTION OF ALL MYSTERIES   25

"But the Comforter, which is the Holy Ghost, whom the Father will send in my name, he shall teach you all things" (John 14 : 26).

The solution of all these seeming enigmas lies in the fact that this so-called material world is only a world of constantly shifting appearances, false illusions, so-called mental phenomena; and every form of matter, 30 every form of sin, every form of disease and trouble, even the form itself of so-called man, can be caused to appear and disappear by what is falsely termed "thinking." This is because all matter is ethereal,[1] that is, merely supposititious mechanical vibrations in a theoretical ether. "The one certainty of science is the existence of a mental world" (Huxley).   35

The only reality is God and His mental or spiritual manifestation, perfect man and universe, a perfect state of consciousness, called heaven. Having a false sense of existence, viewed from a false standpoint, a belief of life in matter, the material so-called man has an equally false sense of substance, and sees this perfect world only through a false material sense of 40 it. He has been fooled, self-hypnotised, into believing his material self and the ether-world to be real and true; whereas the material part of it is simply a temporary misconception of the real man and universe, a false belief of

[1] The term "ethereal" throughout this work is to be taken in its litereal meaning as applying to matter in its primary form. It means "of the ether," the ether con- 45 sisting of lines of force at right angles to each other, these lines being usually spoken of as "thoughts."

substance in matter, an illusionary effect, cinematographic pictures hiding
heaven, the real world, from us. We must voice the truth and "make all
men see what is the fellowship [R.V., 'dispensation'] of the mystery, which
from the beginning of the world hath been hid in God" (Eph. 3 : 9).

5   **"No-mind" and "Non-mental."**—Mortals have hitherto been
utterly deceived as to the definition of the word "mental." What has
hitherto been dignified by the terms "mind" and "mental" turns out to
be purely ethereal matter in varying degrees, from its most tangible and
ponderable forms to the ethereal lines of force originally advanced by
10 Faraday. It should be spoken of as "no-mind" and "non-mental."
Human "mind" turns out to be human matter, a mechanical counterfeit
of true consciousness, the result of electrical stresses in the ether, and
therefore, purely ethereal. The only power is Love, alias Mind or God, and
we cannot control matter scientifically by a negative "mind."

15   **The False Spiritual World.**—Being utterly ignorant of the ethereal
conditions of the final yet elementary state of matter, and knowing that
there must be consciousness and therefore reality, mortals have mistakenly
conceived of the invisible, ethereal conditions as a spiritual world, and
against all logical deductions their buoyant sense of hope has led the
20 majority to think that on death they reach a far-distant "life eternal," in a
hypothetical perfect world.

    The Real Mind, God.—God, good, is infinite, eternal Mind, and is
of necessity eternally good, and good only. Now this is demonstrable.
The knowledge of God, heaven, and our real selves is a true mental
25 science, demonstrable through application of the rule of right thinking.
So-called "mental" science, which is limited to mere mechanical change
of human phenomena, is an entire misnomer, and utterly misleading, and
should at best be distinguished as "non-mental" science, because it is
not mental and not scientific.

30   **Matter "Non-mental."**—Numberless quotations might be given
here which show that deep, logical thinkers have recognised that matter
cannot possibly be solid fact, but must be merely a form of material
impression, false mental or, more accurately, "non-mental" phenomena.
The following are instances, and more are given later.
35   Professor Herbert says: "The common supposition, then, that the
material universe and the conscious beings around us are directly and
indubitably known, and constitute a world of 'positive' fact, . . . is
an entire mistake, based upon astonishing ignorance of the essential
limitations of human knowledge."
40   John Fiske, the well-known historian and professor of philosophy,
writes: "It was long ago shown that all the qualities of matter are what the
mind makes them, and have no existence as such, apart from the mind.
In the deepest sense, all that we really know is mind, and as Clifford
would say, what we call the material universe is simply an imperfect picture
45 in our minds of a real universe of mind-stuff." [1]

----

[1] *The Idea of God.*

Kant also writes to the effect that this world's life is only an appearance. a sensuous image of the pure spiritual life, and the whole world of sense only a picture swimming before our present knowing faculty like a dream, and having no reality in itself, for if we should see things and ourselves as they are, we should see ourselves in a world of spiritual natures, with 5 which our entire real relation neither begins at birth nor ends with the body's death.

The practical value to the world of this truth, which has been enunciated by many other logical thinkers of equally world-wide reputation, has never been grasped by the majority. Until recently no one has ever followed it 10 up to its logical conclusion, namely, that if the material universe is simply an imperfect false impression, then all that is necessary, in order that we should behold the real and perfect universe, is to change our thoughts to the standard of perfection, and so see the perfect picture, when the imperfections must disappear and heaven appear.   15

Matter the Manifestation of False Impressions.—"*Matter, like space and time, cannot be defined.*" [1]

Matter is merely the manifestation of false impressions of truth; Lord Kelvin expressed it as "made up of thought forces"; Leibnitz defined matter as a momentary mind, an instantaneous consciousness. 20 Matter can be made to appear and disappear by so-called thought, and this in two different ways: one temporary because unscientific, the other disappearance permanent because scientific. Consequently the material world, as long as it has its apparent existence, is subject to continual changes, and has no fixed laws; so-called "thought," literally electric 25 vibration, being the essence of material apparent action. Matter is simply a series of cinematographic pictures.

Carpenter says: "The source of all power is mind." Professor Huxley says: "If the hypothetical substance of mind is possessed of energy, I for my part am unable to see how it is to be discriminated from the hypothe- 30 tical substance of matter." His philosophic position he has summed up as follows: "The key to all philosophy lies in the clear comprehension of Berkeley's problem—which is neither more nor less than one of the shapes of the greatest of all questions, 'What are the limits of our faculties?' And it is worth any amount of trouble to comprehend the exact nature of the 35 argument by which Berkeley arrived at his results, and to know by one's own knowledge the great truth which he discovered—that the honest and rigorous following up of the argument which leads us to materialism inevitably carries us beyond it. The more completely the materialistic position is admitted, the easier it is to show that the idealistic position is 40 unassailable, if the idealist confines himself within the limits of positive knowledge." And he adds in conclusion: "And therefore if I were obliged to choose between absolute materialism and absolute idealism, I should feel compelled to accept the latter alternative,"

Locke, another thinker misunderstood by materialists, writes: "Bodies, 45 by our senses, do not afford us so clear and distinct an idea of active

---

[1] *Mathematical Recreations and Essays*, by W. W. Rouse Ball, Fellow and late Tutor of Trinity College, Cambridge.

2

power as we have from reflection on the operations of our minds. . . . Of thinking, body affords us no idea at all, it is only from reflection that we have that. Neither have we from body any idea of the beginning of motion. . . . I judge it not amiss to direct our minds to the consideration of God, 5 and spirits, for the clearest idea of active powers. . . . God having fitted men with faculties and means to discover, receive, and retain truths, according as they are employed" (*On Human Understanding*).

A Correct Basic Theory.—"*Our scientific theories are perfectly legitimate as long as they are formed as a means towards practical applica-* 10 *tions*" (*The Science of the Future*, Edward Carpenter).

Hitherto we have tried to fit our facts into our theories, and have had to change our theories so as to explain our new facts. In the correct basic theory now brought to your notice, we can account for our real facts, the facts of good, and the spiritual universe, and at the same time test and 15 account for our so-called facts, which are really only final and foundation-less beliefs with reference to the material world. In this way we check our knowledge by means of our theory, and prove it later by demonstration. Probed to the bottom, and laid bare, this correct material theory enables us to account rationally for the first time for our so-called facts. We must 20 not, however, dwell on this theory, and build it up in imagination as permanent fact. We have to reverse the illusive truth of this theory, and so give everlasting place to a knowledge of the absolute facts and the spiritual universe. This true knowledge is a revealed and practical science, the science of God as divine Principle, with intelligent, living good as its 25 manifestation.

Every thought is followed by a similar effect, to a greater or lesser extent. Millions now recognise this and are trying to learn how to control illusionary impressions, mis-called thoughts. "Our thoughts are the rudder of our life," says the Rev. I. R. Shannon. Let us then always steer dead 30 straight. "Let the wicked forsake his way, and the unrighteous man his thoughts: and let him return unto the Lord, and he will have mercy upon him" (Isa. 55:7). This is not so easy to do until you know how to do it. It can only be properly done in a scientific way. Let us proceed to advance fearlessly along this way, proving each step as we go.

35   **EVIL AND THE MATERIAL WORLD**

Evil.—"*He that committeth sin is of the devil; for the devil sinneth from the beginning*" (I John 3:8).

Everything in the material world is more or less bad or limited. "Christian theology has not been able to make up its mind whether 40 sin is a defect, or a transgression, or a rebellion, or a constitutional here-ditary taint, or whether it is all these combined" (W. R. Inge, M.A., D.D., Professor of Divinity, Cambridge[1]).

> "Our life is a false nature—'tis not in
>   The harmony of things—this hard decree,
45   This ineradicable taint of sin" (*Byron*).

---

[1] Later Dean of St. Paul's.

The Illusion.—*"Before a rigorous logical scrutiny, the Reign of Law will prove to be an unverified hypothesis, the uniformity of Nature an ambiguous expression, the certainty of our scientific inferences to a great extent a delusion"* (*Principles of Science*, Stanley Jevons).

Whence therefore comes this material world, and what is it? The Greeks taught that the source of sin is delusion or disease—a perverted condition of the mind. Sin, and therefore everything material, everything unlike God, is only delusion, deception, illusion, but not an illusion that the perfect spiritual beings, our true selves, are suffering under, for, being perfect, we could not in reality suffer from any illusion. "He cannot sin, because he is born of God" (I John 3:9). Sin exists only as a false claim, an utterly false conception, and this is no true existence. The whole of the material world, with its material phenomena, is an elaborate mechanical counterfeit of the spiritual realities of all things, and is at best merely a dream, ethereal, illusionary phantasies, a mesmeric sleep, but without even a real dreamer. As Schopenhauer said, it is a disordered dream of humanity.

The following illustration may enable you to understand the position better. Hold up your hand between your eyes and a light. Then put a sheet of paper between the hand and eyes, and throw some mud on the paper. Let your hand symbolise the real man, the shadow on the paper the material man, while the mud represents sickness and sin. The shadow on the paper is not the real hand, and if the dirt is rubbed off the paper, then the shadow represents the material man, well and free from sin. Go on rubbing, and the paper will ultimately disappear, and you will see the hand, symbolising the real man.

Again the real man in heaven may be symbolised by a human being in bright sunlight. The shadow then symbolises the material man. As the sun becomes more central the shadow decreases, until ultimately it disappears.

The Devil and Hell.—*"The wicked . . . will not seek after God: God is not in all his thoughts"* (Ps. 10:4).

This material world, this "waste howling wilderness" (Deut. 32:10), is therefore simply a terrible illusion, a grouping of false impressions, the devil's world, "the very devil," the only devil there is. This self-imposed agony, this devil or evil, will continue until scientifically disposed of by denying the existence of all wrong thought, and thinking rightly instead. The only devils [1] are the devilish thoughts that attack us. The word "devil" is derived from the Greek "diabolos," which means merely "slanderer." The slander is that man is material and that there is life in matter.

Marlowe, writing in the sixteenth century, makes Faustus say to Mephistopheles: "Where are you damned?" Mephistopheles replies: "In hell." And on Faustus asking: "How comes it, then, that thou art out of hell?" he replies: "Why, this is hell, nor am I out of it

> Hell hath no limits, nor is circumscribed
> In one self place; for where we are is hell,

---

[1] The word "devil" does not occur in the King James translation of the Old Testament. The only devil there is, is the false concept of being, termed in the Bible, "carnal mind."

And where hell is, must we ever be:
And, to conclude, when all the world dissolves,
And every creature shall be purified,
All places shall be hell that are not Heaven."

5   **Hell an Individual State of Wretched Consciousness.**[1]—Dean
Farrar, in one of his sermons, has said: "I say, unhesitatingly; I say,
claiming the fullest right to speak with the fullest authority of knowledge; I
say, with the calmest and most unflinching sense of responsibility—I am
standing here in the sight of God and my Saviour, and it may be of the
10 angels and the spirits of the dead—that not one of these words: 'damnation,' 'hell,' and 'everlasting punishment,' ought to stand any longer in
our English Bible, for, in our present acceptation of them, they are simply
mistranslations."

Heaven and hell are not future states awaiting us at death. We make
15 our own hell and our own heaven by the way in which we think; and we
have to wake up as fast as we can and get out of hell—the hell of the wrong
thoughts that attack us—into heaven, a perfect state of consciousness, the
world of perfect thoughts, perfect ideas, the real world that is here round
us, if we could only see it. "Love . . . builds a heaven in hell's despair"
20 (W. Blake). The only way to escape the suffering which is always the result
of sin is to stop sinning; and the only way to do this is to stop entertaining
wrong thoughts, as will be explained later. To the mistaken teaching that
God made sin, sickness, worries, and troubles, that is, the material world
and material man, is due much so-called atheism and agnosticism.

25   "The world is stamped with no more than a footprint of the Divinity.
Its goodness and wisdom are but caricatures of the Divine, blasphemous
because of their very traces of likeness, mimicking the Creator as a
marionette mimics its living maker. The conception of nature as being
. . . a direct expression or self-manifestation of the Divine character, is
30 responsible for the moral and spiritual perversions that are everywhere
associated with polytheistic or pantheistic nature-worship. To worship the
caricature of Divinity there revealed to us, is really to worship the devil"
(*Lex Orandi*, Tyrrell).

The Non-reality of Evil and therefore of Matter.—"*As for the
35 other people, which also come of Adam, thou hast said that they are nothing*"

[1] A lady, criticising a lecture given by Edward Kimball, c.s.d., said: "Well, I
think that the lecturer spoke very disrespectfully concerning hell." Mr. Kimball
later said, "The lady was right; I have no respect whatever for hell. I have been in
it and through it, and know it to be an abomination and a fraud, entitled only to the
40 execration of mankind. It is an individual state of wretched consciousness, utterly
unlike God, or His nature, or the conceded essentials of His being. It is an illegitimate monstrosity which has no verity, no immortality, nor right to exist. After 'the
pangs of hell' had seized me and impinged upon me their torments, I was rescued
through the operative efficacy of Christian Science. Then the tears began to dry,
45 the tension of fear to relax, the gloom was dispelled, despair lost its hold, the pain
decreased and at last vanished. I 'would not overstate my woe,' for, be that as it
may, I know that a mighty, satisfying impulsion extricated me from as outrageous
a hell as anyone need know, and ushered me into the vestibule of heaven by means
of a transformation of consciousness whereby existence seemed more fair and the
50 obduracy of distress gave way to a certain measure of peace to which man is law-
fully entitled."

(II Esdras 65:6). "*For if a man think himself to be something, when he is nothing, he deceiveth himself*" (Gal. 6:3).

The human problem of evil is at length solved. Mathematically we know that anything that ever was nothing, or ever ceases to exist, cannot be real, whatever it may seem to be; therefore evil must be unreal, however real it may appear, for no logical mind could believe it to be everlasting. Nothing evil, or even imperfect, can possibly last, as it is self-destructive. It always disappears sooner or later. It cannot even harm you when you realise its non-reality. "They that war against thee shall be as nothing, and as a thing of nought . . . their works are nothing" (Isa. 41:12, 29).

The non-reality of matter has now been proved. So fixed has been our belief in its reality that the majority still believe it is something real and permanent. As this belief changes, so we shall see a changing world, until the mist of matter disappears, with its attendant evils, sin, sickness, worries, troubles, and limitations of every kind. "The things which are seen are temporal; but the things which are not seen are eternal" (II Cor. 4:18).

God, as the Principle of good, is very different from the god whom we have been taught to fear, the god who not only allows but uses evil to punish the human beings that he is supposed to have made. How can the Principle of good even know of evil? If God knows evil He must have known of it beforehand, and therefore must have intended it or ordered it, for God, being infinite Mind and eternal cause, must necessarily be omniscient and omnipotent. Habakkuk says: "Thou [God] art of purer eyes than to behold evil, and canst not look on iniquity" (Hab. 1:13). How could God know of evil and not instantly destroy it? As all sin and trouble are simply a hypnotic effect, if God could be conscious of it, "His infinite power would straightway reduce the universe to chaos" (*Unity of Good*, Mary Baker Eddy). This is one of the proofs of its non-reality, for God is Mind, and Mind must be all-knowing. "All nations before him are as nothing; and they are counted to him less than nothing" (Isa. 40:17). Nebuchadnezzar saw this, and said: "All the inhabitants of the earth are reputed as nothing" (Dan. 4:35). "Seeing evil nowhere exists, for God is all things, and to him no evil is near" (Origen, about A.D. 125). All evil is merely a false appearance, produced by wrong thoughts. "Its ['the last enemy'] mind and hostile will, which came not from God, but from itself, are to be destroyed" (Origen).

"Now the sin of which I speak is this, when a man abandons that which really exists and serves that which does not really exist, there is [still] that which really exists, and it is called God" (Melito to Antonius Cæsar, about A.D. 150).

If as John said: "All things were made by him; and without him was not anything made that was made" (John 1:3), it is clear that evil is not a thing; that is, it is nothing.

In the *Timæus*, Plato depicts the material world as essentially vile; he is unable to think of the pure and holy Deity as manifested in it, and accordingly separates the Creator from His creation [so called] by the whole breadth of infinity.

St. Augustine said that "without Him was nothing made; for without

the sovereign good there is no good. But that is evil, in which there is no
good, and consequently it is nothing, because evil is nothing, but the
absence of good." He also made other statements of the kind, for instance,
"evil is therefore nothing; because it was made without the Word, without
5 whom nothing was made." Both St. Augustine and Luther taught that
evil was not real. The latter regards "the visible world as an illusion,
essentially evil and misleading." "For thou art not a God that hath pleasure
in wickedness : neither shall evil dwell with thee" (Ps. 5:4).

The root meaning of the Hebrew word "awen," translated in the Bible
10 "sin," is "deceit, falsity," in other words, that which is not true. God,
Truth, or good, is and must be reality; therefore evil is the absence or
opposite of good, and therefore the opposite of reality, a non-reality. This
is seen also from the fact that at some time or other all evil must disappear,
"the terrible one is brought to nought" (Isa. 29:20). Evil must by its nature
15 eventually destroy itself. The word "naughty" means "of the nature of
naught," like nothing; "wicked" only means "bewitched." We have all
been bewitched, alias hypnotised, into a belief in evil, we "rejoice in a
thing of nought" (Amos 6:13). Tolstoi says : "All the evil of our life only
seemingly exists, because it has been there so long."

20   **What Origin has Evil ?**—"*Behold, ye are of nothing, and your work of
nought*" (Isa. 41:24).

If evil is a dream or illusion, what was the origin of this illusion? This
is the constantly recurring question that has puzzled the leaders of mankind from the earliest days, namely, What is the origin of evil? This is
25 practically the same question as, What is the origin of matter? Is it conceivable that God created evil?

The answer is absolutely logical. As evil is a non-reality it never began.
No one ever created it, because it does not exist. If you could find out who
created it then it would be real. If evil is said to be real it is the business of
30 those who say it is real to find out how it began, and who created it. The
impossibility of finding this out is one of the many proofs of its non-
reality. "Matter is a misstatement of Mind" (Mary Baker Eddy). "In
truth, no thing is contrary to God" (*Theologia Germanica*).

"The 'problem of evil' is manifestly insoluble : we have to make
35 our choice between theories, none of which is free from grave difficulties
and objections" (*Personal Idealism and Mysticism*, W. R. Inge, M.A., D.D.).

At one time there was a belief that there was a flat earth, and the
mediæval Church burned those who denied the so-called fact. Who
created the flat earth? It never existed. No one ever created it. It was an
40 entire illusion, a lie—a lie about the round earth, and when it was known
to be a lie, the belief in its reality, which was the only sense of existence it
ever had, was gone. So, the belief in a material world is a lie about the real
world. As you find out the truth the lie disappears, and you gradually
appear to become conscious of the glorious reality, which has always
45 existed here, around us, the kingdom of heaven, a perfect world.

Truth and the truth about Truth alone is knowable. There may be
countless lies about the truth, but only one truth. We may believe a lie,
but we know the truth. Truth is demonstrable.

"Thou shalt have no other gods before me," means you shall believe only in the existence of good, God and His manifestation, and not believe in evil or matter. If you do you will experience the sense of evil and limitation, sin, sickness, worries, and troubles. "Since there is no being outside God, what we call separation from God, fall, or sin, is but a negative reality, 5 a defect or privation. Evil has no substantial existence. A thing has real existence only so far as it is good, and its excellence is the measure of its reality. Perfection and reality are synonyms . . . evil is the absence of good, life, and being" (Scotus Erigena).

The Illusory Cause of Evil.—In the light of our present know- 10 ledge that all is Mind and mental, it must be remembered that in searching for the origin of evil there can only be a false suppositional mentality, a basic false mentality, to deal with. It being now agreed that matter is merely what is called force or electricity, it is obvious that any seeming material phenomena are entirely secondary, and consequent on this false 15 mentality, which is thus the author of itself, and all its manifest apparent phenomena. "A mad world indeed, my masters !" (Shakespeare).

If Mind can maintain its own phenomena it is self-proved to be eternal cause. If the so-called "mind" fails to maintain its own phenomena it is self-proved to be unreal and illusive, a false mental basis for whatever 20 may apparently be built upon it as its manifestation. "Mind is its own great cause and effect" (Mary Baker Eddy). The Mind that thus proves itself to be eternal cause must be God and infinite. This statement includes of necessity the further recognition that the Mind that is God must be wholly good. Herein will be found conclusive proofs that material sense impres- 25 sions are not permanent. The continually disappearing, sick, sinning, and consequently dying phenomena that are spoken of as "human beings" are proved by their disappearance to rest solely upon the aforesaid false mental basis. "You cannot even be mathematically sure that I, who am speaking to you at this mement, possess a consciousness. I might be a well-con- 30 structed automaton—going, coming, speaking—without internal consciousness, and the very words by which I declare at this moment that I am a conscious being might be words pronounced without consciousness" (*Life and Consciousness*, Henri Bergson). This turns out to be the case as far as the material man is concerned. The only reality is God and the 35 spiritual man and world.

"No-mind."—This false mental basis, hitherto called mind, and now designated "no-mind" (not mind), and the false mental or "nonmental" impressions, called thoughts, are but the suppositional opposites of God or Mind, and God's thoughts, which constitute the only mentality 40 and the only true mental impressions.

The personification of this false mentality, that has been called human mind and body, is self-destructive. Cursed from its supposed startingpoint of a material conception, it is but "a pet nest for devils," a home for evil thoughts of every kind and description, "the habitation of devils, and 45 the hold of every foul spirit, and a cage of every unclean and hateful bird" (Rev. 18:2). All evil conditions come from wrong thoughts, a belief in the power of evil, owing to a want of the scientific knowledge that there

is only one God, and that good. One of the wise sayings of the celebrated
Dr. Abernethy was that "when a man begins seriously to dissect himself,
he will soon be a fit subject for the undertaker." In Jeremiah 6, verse 19,
we read: "Behold, I will bring evil upon this people, even the fruit of their
5 thoughts, because they have not hearkened . . . to my law," the law of
good, the only really existing law. "Be not overcome of evil, but overcome
evil with good" (Rom. 12:21). The only way to do this is to practise the
scientific method of thinking. In Psalm 23, verse 4, we read: "I will fear
no evil, for thou art with me." This "thou" is God, divine Principle, the
10 law of good, which, if only we think rightly is found never to fail to effect
the permanent disappearance of any particular evil.

Sin the Cause of Disease.—A large proportion of the interminable
trouble and myriad forms of disease in this world are acknowledged
to be due to sin; perhaps forty per cent. A medical specialist in diagnosis
15 told me that he thought about seventy-five per cent. of disease was due
either to sin in the individual or sin in his parents. We now find that all
disease is due to sin; but in probably sixty out of a hundred cases the sin
is the lesser one of what would be popularly called merely wrong thinking,
belief in a power other than that of God. This, as will be shown, is the
20 primary cause of all disease and sin. This wrong thinking is due to ignorance. Hence all disease is mental. Socrates said that sin was ignorance. Sin
is ignorance of Truth, ignorance of God. Dr. Thompson, surgeon to H.M.
Prisons in Scotland, after observation for eighteen years, says: "I have
never seen such an accumulation of morbid appearances as here. Scarcely
25 any die of any one disease, for almost every organ of the body is more or
less diseased or degenerated."

The Arraignment of the So-called Man.—*"Man that is born of
woman is of few days, and full of trouble. He cometh forth like a flower,
and is cut down: . . . Who can bring a clean thing out of an unclean? not
30 one"* (Job. 14:1, 2, 4).
The five material miscalled senses condemn themselves. They cannot
feel, taste, smell, see or hear God. Has God created these "senses" that
do not enable us to understand Him in the slightest? Most people have
formed the habit of talking of the human body as something wonderful.
35 It seems to me that it is wonderfully bad. Even a schoolboy could point
out many possibilities of improvement. The eye is, I believe, supposed to
be the most wonderful part of the human frame. Professor Helmholtz, one
of the leading scientific men of modern times, referring to the human eye,
of which he had made a special study said: "Of all our members the eye
40 has always been held the choicest gift of nature—the most marvellous
product of her plastic force." Then, after commenting on its details, he
adds: "If an optician would sell me an instrument which had all these
defects, I should think myself quite justified in blaming his carelessness in
the strongest terms, and giving him back his instrument" (*Lectures on
45 Scientific Subjects*). Every other part of the human body is equally defective
and does not even rival a lobster, which so easily reproduces a lost limb.
If a material man had the different powers of vision apparently possessed
in part by the different animals, his sight, although incomparably better

than that of human beings, would be quite imperfect in comparison with the power of sight of which, as will be seen hereafter, man is capable. The physical eye, however, as will be shown later, is unnecessary for the exercise of this power.

The Ignorant Man a Helpless Victim.—*"Therefore my people are* 5 *gone into captivity, because they have no knowledge: . . . Therefore hell hath enlarged herself, and opened her mouth without measure"* (Isa. 5:13, 14).

It has been stated that man is born free. This is absolutely untrue of the human being. This so-called man is born a helpless babe, and remains 10 helpless, the victim of circumstances, "the football of chance," until he gains some faint idea of what God is, and learns how to think rightly. What poor things mortals are, bound together in this bundle of so-called life. Monkeys on a stick, pulled about by conflicting emotions, creatures of impulse, we are swayed by every passing thought whilst we are learning 15 how to control these thoughts. This lamentable position can only continue until we know how to think rightly, and thus exercise our rightful dominion.

The Death Struggle of Nature.—*"For the earnest expectation of the creature waiteth for the manifestation of the sons of God. . . . For we know that the whole creation groaneth and travaileth in pain together until* 20 *now"* (Rom. 8:19, 22).

Darwin showed the fierce struggle that lies beneath the seeming peace of nature. Many sensitive natures have been overwhelmed, and are daily being overwhelmed, by this universal unrelenting nature, "red in tooth and claw." 25

Dr. Macpherson, of Edinburgh, says that "a mere segment of an earwig will fight with a segment of an Australian ant, under the unmistakable influence of rage, until exhaustion or death ensues." Even with the smaller animal life one sees this. Romanes, in *Animal Intelligence*, gives particulars of a conflict between a small rotifer and a larger one, and Sir 30 William Dawson states that "an amœba shows volition, appetite, and passion." The pious Jacobi is stated to have said: "Nature conceals God; man reveals God." Haeckel writes: "The raging war of interests in human society is only a feeble picture of the unceasing and terrible war of existence which reigns throughout the whole of the living world" (*Confession of* 35 *Faith*). No wonder Philip Mauro, who speaks of this world-system as "stupendous, gigantic, remorseless, terrifying!" says: "Though composed apparently of human beings, and existing presumably for human beings, it nevertheless devours men, women, and children, placidly, and for trifling considerations." 40

Goethe, with all his prosperity and riches, states that he had not had five weeks of genuine pleasure in his whole life; and Caliph Abdulrahman said that in fifty years he had had only fourteen days of pure happiness. Many have not had this small amount. How different it is when one knows how to think rightly. 45

Fiske, the well-known historian, says: "In every part of the animal world we find implements of torture surpassing in devilish ingenuity anything that was ever seen in the dungeons of the Inquisition. We are

2*

introduced to a scene of incessant and universal strife, of which it is not
apparent on the surface that the outcome is the good, or the happiness of
anything that is sentient. If the Creator of such a world is omnipotent, He
cannot be actuated solely by a desire for the welfare of His creatures, but
5 must have other ends in view, to which this is in some measure sub-
ordinated. Or if He is absolutely benevolent, then He cannot be omnipotent, but there is something in the nature of things which sets limits to
His creative power" (*The Idea of God*).

On the other hand, with the lowest there is a sense of good. A friend of
10 mind recently heard a miserable, poverty-stricken wretch, slouching along
in the cold, soliloquising as follows: "Gawd 'elp the poor swines as 'ave
no 'ome of their own this weather." Few of us are thankful enough for
what we have.

Wonders of the World.—Most people are ignorant of the immensity
15 and diversity of the universe, or else they could not possibly have thought
of God as they have done. Our solar system, which itself appears to be
rushing through space at about twelve miles per second—the velocity of
one star is 200 miles a second—is a mere speck in the heavens, and yet the
orbit of Neptune, the farthest planet of this system, is, on an average,
20 2,791 millions of miles from the sun. A train running at sixty miles an
hour would take over 5,000 years, nearly the whole of historical time, to
traverse the distance. Alpha, in Centaur, the nearest fixed star to the sun,
is about 25 millions of millions of miles from it, yet the great Nebula in
Orion has been stated to be 250 times the distance from the sun of the
25 nearest fixed star. The speed of light would enable it to travel round the
equator seven times in a second; yet it could travel round 1,000 million
times during the four and one-third years it takes to come from Alpha
Centauri. The number of the stars perceptible by means of the great
telescopes is estimated at 400 millions, red, orange, yellow, green, lilac,
30 purple, etc. Over 100 million stars are now capable of being photographed.
Many of these are of an enormous size; for instance, Rigel in Orion and
Arided in the Swan, are at an immeasurable distance away, and must
exceed our sun many thousands of times in volume, in mass, and in
splendour. The great southern sun, Canopus in Argo, is estimated by Carl
35 Snyder as having a volume more than 1,000,000 times that of our sun.
"The size of the universe . . . is quite appalling when we comprehend it, for it seems really to be infinite, to have no boundary. Space and
the worlds in space—inhabited worlds many of them, no doubt—extend
beyond the reach of the longest telescope" (Sir Oliver Lodge, D.SC., LL.D.,
40 F.R.S.).

Robert Blatchford, in *God and My Neighbour*, writes as follows: "On
earth there are forms of life so minute that millions of them exist in a
drop of water. There are microscopic creatures more beautiful and more
highly finished than any gem, and more complex and effective than the
45 costliest machine of human contrivance." In *The Start of Creation*, Mr.
Edward Clodd tells us that one cubic inch of rotten stone contains 41,000
million vegetable skeletons of diatoms. "Talk about Aladdin's palace,
Sindbad's valley of diamonds, Macbeth's witches, or the Irish fairies! How

petty are their exploits, how tawdry are their splendours, how paltry are their riches, when we compare them to the romance of science. Do you believe that the God who imagined and created such a universe could be petty, base, cruel, revengeful, and capable of error? I do not believe it."

The Arraignment of the So-called God.— The national attitude of ignorance regarding God is shown by the phrase in legal contracts referring to unavoidable disasters as " acts of God." Even so-called civilisation has its devilish side. According to Victor Longheed, in the United States 12,000 people are annually killed and 70,000 injured by railway traffic. Mr. C. R. Enock, in a paper read before the Institution of Electrical Engineers, stated that in 1907 no less than 150,051 people were killed or injured in Britain and the United States.

Richard Baxter in *Saints' Everlasting Rest*, actually states that God himself will take infinite pleasure in the eternal torments of the damned. The Rev. M. Baxter told me that we should literally see all the scenes depicted in the Apocalypse.

The lie that God made matter, this mist that hides from us the real and glorious spiritual world, has brought forth such statements as the following : " It is His world, remember. He made it, and He is omnipotent . . . . why did not He make it better? If it is wayward and intractable, it can be no more than He expected, or ought to have expected. Wherein consists His right to punish us for our transgressions? Suppose we challenge it; what will He say in defence?" Benson writes : " The essence of God's omnipotence is that both law and matter are His and originate from Him; so that if a single fibre of what we know to be evil can be found in the world, either God is responsible for that, or He is dealing with something He did not originate and cannot overcome. Nothing can extricate us from this dilemma, except that what we think evil is not really evil at all, but hidden good." This is obviously impossible. Under no circumstances can evil be good, and it can never be less nor more than evil; but it has only recently been discovered that evil, as manifested illusion, will temporarily hide from us the permanent good, until this good is understood and acknowledged to be spiritual, tangible, the only reality.

Could a God of even the human standard of morality have made this material evil world of rampant injustice, or could such a hellish wilderness of tangled dreams form part of an original perfect conception? Read William Watson's arraignment of the Powers of Europe at the time of the Armenian massacres, and then think :—

> "Yea, if ye could not, though ye would, lift hand—
> Ye halting leaders—to abridge Hell's reign.
> If such your plight, most hapless ye of men !
> But, if ye could, and would not, oh, what plea
> Think ye shall stand you at your trial, when
> The thundercloud of witnesses shall loom
> At the Assizes of Eternity?"

Haeckel truly writes : " If the one God is really the absolutely good perfect Being they proclaim, then the world which He has created must also be perfect." An organic world so imperfect and full of sorrow as exists on this earth He could not possibly have contrived.

Now God is the greatest friend and guide that a man can have, "a very present help" in every kind of trouble. Poor, deluded humanity! What a terrible penalty it pays for ignorance of God. How fatally it is deceived.

Good.—"*Moreover it* [goodness] *needeth not to enter into the soul, for*
5 *it is there already, only it is unperceived*" (*Theologia Germanica*).

God, the Principle of good, never made the material world, nor ever could have made, or even know of, such a horrible nightmare. If so He is unquestionably responsible. Sin, disease, and death are absolutely unnatural. The true God made the real world, and we find the Bible
10 statement scientifically accurate: "And God saw every thing that he had made, and, behold, it was very good" (Gen. 1:31). The material world is only a false sense of the real or spiritual world, which is here now and everywhere, and which, to those who look for it, shines through the visible world in glimpses of eternal verities. "I expect that the great mass of the
15 beauty around us is hidden from us, even from the highest at present" (Sir Oliver Lodge).

> "For so the whole round earth is every way
> Bound by gold chains about the feet of God" (*Tennyson*).

The material world is fortunately not a fact. It is only a series of illusory
20 false beliefs about the real world which is here around us if we could only perceive it and be conscious only of perfection. "Men, who hold the truth in unrighteousness . . . changed the truth of God into a lie" (Rom. 1:18, 25). "Other world! There is no other world. God is one and omnipresent; here or nowhere is the whole fact" (Emerson). "The world
25 constructed with the impressions of our senses is a summary translation, and necessarily a far from faithful one, of the real world which we know not" (*The Evolution of Forces*, Dr. Le Bon).

"Theism . . . recognises an Omnipresent Energy, which is none other than the living God. The presence of God is the one all-pervading fact
30 of life, from which there is no escape" (*The Idea of God*, John Fiske). Consequently, the love, the life, the beauty, the joy, the wisdom, realities of God's creation, in fact, all the good of which we, unfortunately, only get indications in this so-called material world, is real, made by God. "Lo, this only have I found, that God hath made man upright; but they have
35 sought out many inventions" (Eccles. 7:29). The man that God made is perfect, sinless, and eternal. Paul said: "Neither death, nor life . . . nor things present, nor things to come, nor height, nor depth, nor any other creature, shall be able to separate us from the love of God" (Romans 8:38, 39). He knew well enough that the real man was "in Christ," and never
40 could be separated from God, divine Love. "The earth is full of the goodness of the Lord" (Ps. 33:5). This is spoken of the permanent and perfect, spiritual earth.

Matter while *held in its place by ignorance and false belief*, merely hides from us the real spiritual earth, with all its spiritual beauty and goodness,
45 so that we get a limited, material sense of it, instead of seeing it as it really is. How fortunate it is that we get even gleams of reality, intuitional, significant, timely foreshadowings of the truth. "O world as God has made it! All is beauty; and knowing this is love, and love is duty" (Robert

Browning). Sir Oliver Lodge says : "Everything sufficiently valuable, be it beauty, artistic achievement, knowledge, unselfish affection, may be thought of as enduring henceforth and for ever . . . as part of the eternal Being of God."

> "And all that is at all, 5
> Lasts ever, past recall;
> Earth changes, but thy soul and God stand sure" (*Robert Browning*).

EVOLUTION OF OUR SENSE OF GOD

"Every human institution, therefore, religion itself, so far as man can affect it—is exposed to inevitable decay. Accordingly, a religion which is not 10 *waiting for a revival is waiting only till it be swept away. Christianity has always reformed itself, and will to the end of time continue to reform itself, by going back to the words and to the life of Christ"* (*Chips from a German Workshop*, Max Müller).

When mortal so-called man was a mere brute beast he had no God; 15 he did not even understand what good was, and probably ate his children if he could get at them. This stage of ignorance is alluded to in the second verse of the first chapter of Genesis as "darkness."

This first chapter can be looked upon as a symbolic description of the real or spiritual world, referred to by John in chapter one verse three 20 of his Gospel, when he said, "All things were made by him." The second chapter of Genesis, commencing at the sixth verse, gives a symbolic description of how the material world started. The first chapter may also be taken as a description of the false belief in the evolution of the material, or so-called man from materiality or absolute ignorance and bestiality, up to the 25 true knowledge of God, and dematerialisation. By this term is meant the entire disappearance both of the material body and so-called mind, spoken of by Paul as the carnal body and the carnal mind, which constitute what is called the material man, and is "enmity against God," or good. The former, the material body, was dematerialised by the great Way-shower, 30 the man Christ Jesus, in the silent precincts of the tomb, and the latter was dematerialised at what is called his ascension, this being the disappearance of the material form of the man Jesus of Nazareth to the limited human senses of those who failed to be able to perceive his more perfect form. The spiritual body, his real self, the son of God, imperceptible to the five 35 limited senses, always existed in the real, spiritual world, heaven, which, in fact, is here around us, only we see it falsely. Sooner or later, we all have to get rid of our so-called human mind and body. "Even we ourselves groan within ourselves, waiting for the adoption, to wit, the redemption of our body" (Rom. 8:23). 40

The experience of Jesus the Master-metaphysician understood, will bring a repetition of his attainments, including all his miracles, but without the accompanying crucifixion or tomb, which were the incidental outcome of general ignorant and malicious opposition.

The deep significance of the Master's life, of his words, and of his 45 works, is only just beginning to dawn upon a world waiting in expectation for its release from the overwhelming burdens, which to so many make

life now the hell that we were falsely taught we might find to be awaiting
us only in the future.

"I have laboriously and freshly examined every single passage in the
New Testament bearing upon the subject of God's Will, and I have also
5 examined freshly every single passage in the New Testament bearing upon
suffering and affliction. I fail to find one which warrants the belief that
sickness and death are the will of God, sent directly by His hand upon us.
If sickness and suffering are according to the will of God, then every
physician is a law-breaker, every trained nurse is defying the will of God,
10 every hospital is a house of rebellion instead of a house of mercy. All the
conditions which increase suffering and breed sickness are therefore ful-
filments of the will of God, and sanitation is blasphemy. This tradition
quickly reasons itself out into impossibility" (*Does God Send Trouble?*
Rev. Charles Cuthbert Hall).

15   **The Religion of One God.**—"*Thou shalt have no other gods before
me*" (Ex. 20:3).

When the primeval savage prayed to one of his gods, for instance
to his club lying over the exit from his dwelling-house, he got on better
than the man next door who did not, because it was his best idea of God,
20 and he had greater confidence when fighting, thinking that he was helped
by some other power than himself. It has been truly said: "Man makes
God in his own image." Xenophanes said that if horses, lions, etc., could
paint, they certainly would make gods in their own image.

The idea of God gradually evolved, until we come to the "jealous
25 God" of the Hebrews.[1] This race, strong-thinking, strong-headed, and
determined, looked upon Jehovah as a supernatural being, who not only
told them to slay their enemies, but actually slew them himself, and
required sacrifices of innocent animals—such sacrifices, taken literally,
being very little better than human sacrifices to the heathen's idea of God,
30 called Moloch, Baal, etc.

"The Lord said unto Moses, Take all the heads of the people, and
hang them up before the Lord against the sun, that the fierce anger of the
Lord may be turned away from Israel. . . . And the Lord spake unto
Moses, saying, Vex the Midianites and smite them: For they vex you with
35 their wiles" (Num. 25:4, 16, 17, 18). "The Lord met him [Moses], and
sought to kill him" (Ex. 4:24). "Saul . . . enquired not of the Lord:
therefore he slew him" (I Chron. 10:13, 14). "Er, the firstborn of Judah,
was evil in the sight of the Lord; and he slew him" (I Chron. 2:3).

The idea of God gradually evolved until we see in Psalm fifty-one, verse
40 seventeen, that God required, not the sacrifice of innocent animals, but
the sacrifice of "a broken and a contrite heart." A still higher concept is

---

[1] The Hebrew names descriptive of God have been called "lenses through which
to see the character of God." They are El, Eloah, Elah, Elohim, Jehovah-Elohim,
Gelyon, El Shaddai, Jehovah-Jireh, Jehovah-Nissi, Jehovah-Raphai (The Lord our
45 Healer), Jehovah-Shammah, Jehovah-Shalom, Jehovah-Rohi, Adon, Adonai, Yah,
and Yahveh or Jehovah. The Hebrew language had many words of various meanings which, when the Scriptures were first translated into Greek, about 300 B.C.—
the Septuagint—were translated "theos," which means either the true God or
a false god, and "kurios," which means either heavenly or earthly lord or master.

the later prophets' idea of God, exemplified in the following words: "I desired mercy, and not sacrifice; and the knowledge of God more than burnt offerings" (Hosea 6:6).

Later on we reach a widely held orthodox view of God impossible for any logical person to understand who has thought deeply on the 5 subject. Conscious matter must imply Pantheism, and it is the false conception of God that makes men Christians only in name, spiritual only in empty theory, whilst material in daily practice. A merciless god, who allowed a majority to be eternally punished, who permitted the inhuman torture of his beloved Son, who created beings capable of sin, who per- 10 mitted cruelties inconceivable, was the necessary outcome of an ignorance that was as extraordinary (when we really think logically) as it was universal. Believing man to be the victim of his Maker, eternally punished "for the sins of a few tired years," no wonder God was more feared than loved. No wonder so-called Christians made their religious beliefs a 15 source of fiendish cruelties towards those who differed from their conception of such a devilish god. In the light of the teachings of Jesus, the true understanding of which is now spreading all over the world, we find that this idea of God is little better than that of a magnified human conception of man, and that not even of a noble man. "After nineteen cen- 20 turies of propagandism, Christianity is now compelled to apologise for Christendom" (Prof. R. D. Hitchcock).

The Definition of God.—*"Let not him who seeks . . . cease until he finds, and when he finds he shall be astonished; astonished he shall reach the kingdom, and having reached the kingdom he shall rest "* (*New Sayings* 25 *of Jesus,* from *The Oxyrhynchus Papyri*).

As people's idea of God has become more spiritual, so has their sense of Deity become better. The ideas of primitive Christianity are again elevating mankind. We learn the essence of all goodness, and reach the true, because scientific, concept of this that Jesus demonstrated—the God who 30 is All-in-all, the God who is good and infinite, leaving no room for anything else; not a personal tyrant, but Love itself, Life itself, Truth itself, one infinite Mind. This Mind is the cause of all love, all life, and all truth, and is "reflected in the intelligent, compound idea," man, made in the image or likeness of God, "showing forth the infinite divine Principle" 35 of good, Life, Truth, and Love, called God.[1] Synonymous terms for Mind as God are: Spirit, the essence of all holiness; Soul, the foundation of all wisdom and knowledge; all substance (real and permanent substance, not our false sense of substance); intelligence, the Principle of all Science, and, consequently, the first and only cause, and the only reality. "The 40 remnant shall return, even the remnant of Jacob, unto the mighty God" (Isa. 10:21). This great turning-point of the recognition of the omnipotence and omnipresence of good has now been reached.

"For I am God, and there is none else" (Isa. 45:22). God, being All-in-all, is not a separate person, He is the only Person. Archdeacon 45 Wilberforce in *Mystic Immanence* writes: "Beautiful and consoling as is Isaiah's conception of God as Universal Mother ['As one whom his

---

[1] See *Miscellany,* p. 269, Mary Baker Eddy.

mother comforteth, so will I comfort you'], it is still Deistic, it still leaves the Infinite Intelligence as a Person, which He is not." God is the only Person, the one and only Ego.

If our mind models become less spiritual we deteriorate morally,
5 physically, and what is wrongly termed mentally. We must therefore drop our sense of a finite, personal, changeful God, and get a better conception of the quality and quantity of universal, infinite good.[1] This more perfect idea held to constantly, in our thoughts of things and people, must alter, not only our churches, but our physique, both of which depend upon our
10 ideals. Of man it has truly been said : "For as he thinketh in his heart, so is he" (Prov. 23:7).

"Speak to Him, thou, for He hears, and spirit with spirit can meet,
　　Closer is He than breathing, and nearer than hands and feet" (*Tennyson*).

The Trinity.—Theology has long tried to obtain some simple and
15 logical explanation of the Trinity. Life, Truth, and Love constitute the Trinity of God, Mind, Soul, Spirit; namely, God the Father; Christ, the spiritual idea of sonship, the manifestation of God; and the Holy Ghost or Comforter, Divine Science, the action of God on man—the ideal man, the reflection of God—that makes man what he is, namely, the knowledge or
20 consciousness of God, by means of which God acts and works.[2] Of the Logos Archdeacon Wilberforce, in *Mystic Immanence*, writes : "The Logos is the quality of Originating Mind that forms, upholds, sustains all that is. 'Without the Logos was not anything made that was made.'"

Instead of the many gods that weak mortals now have, we must have
25 only one God, and that triune God must be good and All-in-all. It is not possible that two opposite concepts of God can both be true. If we break the First Commandment and have more than one god, evil must punish us for this sin and keep on punishing us until we return to the Father, whom Paul describes as the "Father of all, who is above all, and
30 through all, and in you all" (Eph. 4:6). Haeckel writes : "To this triune Divine Ideal shall the coming twentieth century build its altars. I conclude my monistic Confession of Faith with the words : May God, the Spirit of Good, the Beautiful, and the True, be with us."

I doubt whether even infidels have no god. Their god they probably
35 call cause or nature. Is their god far removed from the god who used sickness to punish the beings he had so badly created that they were capable

---

[1] The Greek words "*epignosis tou theou*," translated in the epistles both of Peter and Paul as "knowledge of God," should be translated "full or exact knowledge of God," as opposed to the word "*gnosis*," meaning "ordinary knowledge." "*Epi-*
40 *gnosis*" is also used in Rom. 10:2, and Col. 1:9.

[2] See *Science and Health*, pp. 331, 332, Mary Baker Eddy. The word Trinity was first introduced in the apologetic work of Theophilus, Bishop of Antioch, in Syria, who wrote between A.D. 168 and 183. All the ancient nations had their trinity of gods, and the Jews carefully kept free from this heresy. In India there were Brahma,
45 Vishnu, and Siva—Creator, Preserver, and Destroyer. Vishnu is said to have had nine incarnations, with the object of helping the human race; the tenth is said to be about to come at the end of this age. Some Jews have taught that God has descended nine times to the Earth, and that the forthcoming tenth appearance as the Messiah would be final. In Persia the Trinity was Oromasdes, Mithra, and
50 Arimanius; in Babylon, Anu, Bel, and Hea; in Egypt, Osiris, Isis, and Horus. This idea was introduced into Christianity by the Gnostics.

of sin and its punishment, sickness? The more purified the human nature, as a rule, the higher the idea of God. That extraordinary character, Napoleon, said: "Since ever the history of Christianity was written, the loftiest intellects have had a practical faith in God."

> "All are but parts of one stupendous whole,   5
> Whose body nature is, and God the soul" (*Pope*).

Origin of Good.—"*Whatsoever God doeth, it shall be for ever*" (Eccles. 3:14). "*He is the Rock, his work is perfect*" (Deut. 32:4).

All the good that we ever received or ever shall receive, must come from the action of this ever-active Principle, the Principle of good. "Every 10 good gift and every perfect gift is from above [above any limited human conception], and cometh down from the Father of lights [absolute infinite good], with whom is no variableness" (James 1:17). Good is permanent, evil is illusionary.

When dining together, a well-known and religious medical man and 15 a leading clergyman were discussing the great wave of spirituality now flooding the world, and its inevitable results. The medical man turned to the clergyman and, referring to a mutual friend of theirs, said: "It is a curious thing that this is not so much affecting men like you and me, but scientific men like ——, who has been brought up all his life as a practical 20 and scientific man, yet what is your knowledge of God and my knowledge of God as compared with his?" This he said because their friend had been able to prove his knowledge of God by the instantaneous healing of sin and the sickness resulting therefrom.

In Hebrews 8, verse 11, it is foretold that in the latter days mankind 25 will not need to be taught the knowledge of God, "for all shall know me [God], from the least to the greatest." St. Augustine says: "God is present everywhere in His entirety, and yet is nowhere. He dwells in the depths of my being, more inward than my innermost self, and higher than my highest." The scholastic mystics say that God has His centre everywhere, 30 His circumference nowhere. Such teaching deals only in spiritual abstractions. We have now a practical knowledge of God and man, something that will help us over every difficulty that can possibly present itself, an understanding of both as co-existent and co-eternal, spiritual and perfect.

The Religion of Many Gods.—"*God forbid that we should forsake* 35 *the Lord, to serve other gods*" (Josh. 24:16).

Simultaneously, side by side with the evolution of the idea of one God, was what might almost be called an evolution of a religion of many gods. This began with the worship of the constellations and multitudinous natural objects. It developed into the worship of relics, images, etc., the 40 deification of human beings, alive and dead, and now ends with the attempt to make each man a god for himself. This is evidenced by the false "mental science" now being taught by those who, unfortunately for themselves and their followers, know no better, and suffer bitterly for their fatal and needless ignorance. This so-called "mental science" rests entirely upon a false 45 material basis, and is only the modern and final development of the so-called black art, which has been recognised, but not understood, from the earliest ages.

IS THE REAL MAN MATERIAL OR SPIRITUAL?

"Call no man your father upon the earth; for one is your Father, which is in heaven" (Matt. 23:9).

For ages man has been cajoled and generally hypnotised into the
5 belief that he is a material being, liable to sin, sickness, worries, troubles, and ultimate death. There is not a word of truth in it. It is a misapprehension of existence, absolutely false. "For if a man think himself to be something, when he is nothing, he deceiveth himself" (Gal. 6:3). "It is, then, as it appears, the greatest of all lessons, to know one's self. For if a
10 man knows himself, he will know God" (Bishop Clement, Pædag. 111). "There is no question more important to solve than that of knowing what human knowledge is, and how far it extends" (*Œuvres XI*, Descartes). For the earnest expectation of the creature waiteth for the manifestation of the sons of God" (Rom. 8:19). Jesus said, "Ye neither know me, nor
15 my Father: if ye had known me, ye should have known my Father also" (John 8:19). The message of Jesus through Mary to his "brethren" is equally ours by right of inheritance to-day: "I ascend unto my Father, and your Father" (John 20:17). This ascent is mental.

The Material or Carnal Man as Described in the Bible.—*"Ye are
20 of your father the devil, . . . He . . . abode not in the truth [reality], because there is no truth in him . . . he is a liar, and the father of it"* (John 8:44).

The material man is simply an ethereal individualisation of a theoretical human structure; a mere mechanical apparatus manifesting imaginative
25 theories, and bad at that. He is the misformation or misrepresentation of spiritual being. He is dead to Spirit, buried in matter.

It is instructive to see how accurately the Bible description of the material or carnal man supports the so-called facts with reference to his history put forward in this work. The first man mentioned in the Bible as
30 born to human parents became a murderer (Gen. 4:8), and the last time that man is mentioned is in connection with penalties to which he is liable (Rev. 22:19).

"For we are born at all adventure: and we shall be hereafter as though we had never been" (Wisdom of Solomon 2:2). "Dust thou art, and unto
35 dust thou shalt return" (Gen. 3:19). "A man hath no pre-eminence above a beast: . . . All are of the dust, and all turn to dust again" (Eccles. 3:19, 20). "Yet hath he seen no good: do not all go to one place?" (Eccles. 6:6). "The carnal mind is enmity against God . . . they that are in the flesh cannot please God" (Rom. 8:7, 8). "There is none that doeth
40 good, no, not one" (Ps. 14:3). "The heart of the sons of men is full of evil" (Eccles. 9:3). "There is none righteous, no, not one" (Rom. 3:10). "He that committeth sin is of the devil; for the devil sinneth from the beginning. For this purpose the Son of God was manifested, that he might destroy the works of the devil. Whosoever is born of God . . . cannot sin,
45 because he is born of God" (I John 3:8, 9). "To him that knoweth to do good, and doeth it not, to him it is sin" (James 4:17). "They which are the children of the flesh, these are not the children of God" (Rom. 9:8).

"In me . . . dwelleth no good thing : . . . how to perform that which is good I find not. For the good that I would I do not : but the evil which I would not, that I do. . . . It is no more I that do it, but sin that dwelleth in me. . . . For I delight in the law of God after the inward man" (Rom. 7:18, 19, 20, 22). "As for man, his days are as grass : as a flower of 5 the field, so he flourisheth. For the wind passeth over it, and it is gone" (Ps. 103:15, 16). "The grass withereth, the flower fadeth," says Isaiah. He adds, however, "but the word of our God shall stand for ever" (Isa. 40:8).

Mr. Arthur Balfour, former Prime Minister of Great Britain, tells us 10 that, as far as natural science is concerned, man's "very existence is an accident, his story a brief and discreditable episode in the life of one of the meanest of planets." But this cannot be God's intelligent manifestation, though it might well describe the kind of man of whom Huxley was speaking when he said that he would "neither affirm nor deny the immortality 15 of man."

> "For good ye are and bad, and like to coins,
> Some true, some light, but every one of you,
> Stamped with the image of the King" (*Tennyson*).

The Apparent Duality.—"*No man living hath yet seen Man*" (Bishop 20 Foster).

"Man begins to hear a voice that fills the heavens and the earth, saying that God is within him, that there is the celestial host. I find this amazing revelation of my immediate relation to God a solution of all the doubts that oppressed me. I recognise the distinction of the outer and the inner self; 25 the double consciousness that within this erring, passionate, mortal self, sits a supreme, calm, immortal mind, whose powers I do not know; but it is stronger than I, it is wiser than I; it never approved me in any wrong; I seek counsel of it in my doubts; I repair to it in my dangers; I pray to it in my undertakings. It seems to me the face which the Creator uncovers 30 to his child" (Emerson).

Michael Faraday, who spent his lifetime in the forefront of experimental research, declared in a lecture on education, delivered in the Royal Institution, London, that, "High as man is placed above the creatures around him, there is a higher and more exalted position within his view. 35 . . . I believe the truth of that future . . . is made known to him by other teaching than his own, and is received through simple belief of the testimony given."

Something deeper than mere belief is needed. A practical and demonstrable understanding of truth is necessary for intelligent, 40 harmonious existence.

Had there been added to a character such as that of Faraday, the priceless scientific knowledge of to-day, many years of painful waiting for the end of evil might have been saved the world.

"Things of to-day ! What is a man ? A dream of shadow is mankind. 45 Yet when there comes down glory imparted from God, radiant light shines among men" (Pindar). "We feel we are nothing—for all is Thou and in Thee; we feel we are something—that also has come from Thee" (Tennyson). "It is well men should be reminded that the very humblest of them

has the power to fashion after a Divine model" (Maeterlinck). Herbert
Spencer, though regarding the ego as "the transitory state of the moment,"
yet suggests the existence of a permanent ego which cannot be known.

The following statements are scientific when rightly understood.
5 "Ye are not in the flesh, but in the Spirit" (Rom. 8:9). "We know that
we are of God, and the whole world lieth in wickedness" (I John 5:19).
"God sent forth his Son . . . To redeem them that were under the law
. . . And because ye are sons, God hath sent forth the Spirit of his Son
into your hearts . . . Wherefore thou art . . . a son . . . an heir of
10 God through Christ" (Gal. 4:4–7). This being so we must therefore without delay, "Put off the old man which is corrupt . . . and be renewed in
the spirit of your mind" (Eph. 4:22, 23). We must rise from "the burial
of mind in matter, into newness of life as Spirit" (see *Science and Health*,
p. 35. See also Rom. 6:4).

15   **False Spirituality.**—Let us here clear up a misconception that
has misled many, especially earnest religious people. The spiritual
man is not a human being who is constantly thinking of spiritual things;
that is, a material person "spiritually minded." The spiritual man is the
real permanent man now and always in heaven, the son of God. When
20 you think of God you are praying; but this is only the material sense, the
false consciousness, awakening to a better sense of the spiritual world.
This right method of praying is the endeavour to rise in consciousness to
the true sense of heaven, now and here. The effect of this is the elimination
of the material human sense, hitherto thought to be man. Even when the
25 material counterfeit, hitherto thought to be you, is apparently conscious of
evil, your real self is always thinking God's thoughts.

    The True Man.—"*The kingdom of Heaven is within you; and whoever
shall know himself shall find it. Strive therefore to know yourselves, and ye
shall be aware that ye are the sons of the almighty Father, and ye shall know
30 that ye are in the city of God, and ye are the city*" (General interpretation of
New Sayings of Jesus from *The Oxyrhynchus Papyri*).

    You are not sinful and material. "God created man in his own image.[1]
. . . And God saw every thing that he had made, and, behold, it was very
good" (Gen. 1:27, 31). You are a perfect being in a perfect, spiritual
35 world, in heaven, the kingdom of harmony, one with the infinite Mind, as
an individualised expression of that Mind, an individualisation of the
Christ, a spiritual divine emanation, governed by a perfect God, for ever
perfect, imaging forth the infinite perfection of Mind, and with limitless
powers. Act up to this perfect ideal. Mentally identify yourself always with
40 your real self. "We have a building of God, an house not made with hands,
eternal in the heavens" (II Cor. 5:1). "The kingdom of God is within
you"[2] (Luke 17:21), within your present capacity of conscious realisation. We are glorious children of a King, spiritual, eternal, and divine.

    "It alters the whole outlook on life to know you personally are an
45 idea in the mind of God" (*Mystic Immanence*, Archdeacon Wilberforce).

    [1] "Image—an essential, substantial, real and adequate resemblance of another"
(*Wilson's Christian Dictionary*).
    [2] A.V., margin "among you"; R.V., margin, "in the midst of you."

"Never have I not been, never hast thou, and never shall time yet come when we shall not all be" (L. D. V. Barnett's Translation of *The Song Celestial—The Bhagavad Gîtâ*).

We have to recognise clearly the distinction between this real perfect man, the Son of God, and the son of man, the material thing that we have 5 hitherto thought to be ourselves. The Bible speaks throughout of man as the Son of God, and yet Jesus said, "Ye are of your father the devil" (John 8:44).

"The ungodly said, reasoning with themselves, but not aright: . . . Let us oppress the poor righteous man, . . . because he is not for our 10 turn, and he is clean contrary to our doings: . . . He professeth to have the knowledge of God: and he calleth himself the child of the Lord. . . . We are esteemed of him as counterfeits: he abstaineth from our ways as from filthiness: he pronounceth the end of the just to be blessed, and maketh his boast that God is his father. Let us see if his words be true: 15 . . . For if the just man be the son of God, he will help him. . . . Such things they did imagine, and were deceived: for their own wickedness hath blinded them. . . . For God created man to be immortal, and made him to be an image of his own eternity" (Wisdom of Solomon 2:1, 10, 12, 13, 16, 17, 18, 21, and 23). The exactness of this statement has scarcely even 20 been conceived of, much less tested and proved, until recently. "Be ye therefore perfect, even as your Father which is in heaven is perfect" (Matt. 5:48). "Ye are the temple of the living God" (II Cor. 6:16), "in him we live, and move, and have our being" (Acts 17:28). "The Spirit of God hath made me" (Job. 33:4). "For we are also his offspring" 25 (Aratus, quoted in Acts 17:28).

In the 8th Psalm, verse 5, it is said that God made man "a little lower than Elohim" (R.V. margin) or God, and elsewhere in the Psalms and in many other places the statement occurs that we are the "sons of God." In the Authorised Version the word "Elohim" has been translated 30 "angels," for the translators, being so misled by matter, could not see that the real man is and always has been spiritual, and that, being made by God in His image and likeness, he never could fall nor be material.

> "Thou madest man, he knows not why,
> He thinks he was not made to die; 35
> And Thou hast made him: Thou art just" (*Tennyson*).

Jesus, as recorded in John 10, verses 34, 35, not only quoted Psalm 82, verse 6, "Ye are gods," but also drove it home by adding, "and the scripture cannot be broken." The full statement in the Psalm is, "I have said, Ye are gods; and all of you are children of the most High." 40 This definition shows the absolute unity of God and the real man, man not being God, but the manifestation of God, the compound idea of God. The word used in the Psalm is "Elohim," and in John "Theoi," both words referring to the higher sense of God.

Nearly all great men who have lived their religion have recognised 45 and taught that man is divine. St. Athanasius wrote: "He became man that we might be made God." [1] St. Augustine said: "He called men

[1] *Orat. de Incarn. Verbi.*

gods, as being deified by his grace, not as born of his substance." [1] It is
a false sense of life, substance, and mind that hides the divine possibilities
(see *Science and Health*, p. 325).

Zechariah, with prophetic foresight, based upon a knowledge of the
one true God, when speaking of the final battle in the latter days, writes:
"The house of David shall be as God, as the angel of the Lord
before them" (Zech. 12:8). "And it shall come to pass, that in the place
where it was said unto them, Ye are not my people; there shall they be
called the children of the living God" (Rom. 9:26). This prophecy is now
being fulfilled. "Behold, the tabernacle of God is with men, and he will
dwell with them, and they shall be his people, and God himself shall be
with them, and be their God" (Rev. 21:3).

"The essence of our being, the mystery in us that calls itself 'I'—ah,
what words have we for such things?—is a breath of heaven; the Highest
Being reveals Himself in man. . . . We are the miracle of miracles—the
greatest inscrutable mystery of God. We cannot understand it, we know
not how to speak of it, but we may feel and know, if we like, that it is
verily so" (Thomas Carlyle).

Sons of the Living God.—"*Now are we the sons of God*" (I John
3:2). "*Ye are the sons of the living God*" (Hosea 1:10).

Having found the true idea of God, which dawns upon human thought
with the advancing light of spiritual understanding, man learns what he
really is, and always has been, namely, the son of the living God; in other
words, a perfect spiritual being in heaven, a permanent individualisation of
spiritual, scientific consciousness. "We are in infinity now just as we shall
ever be" (Sir Oliver Lodge).

The following quotations are instructive:—

"I have said, Ye are gods; and all of you are children of the most
High" (Ps. 82:6). "Worship him, all ye gods" (Ps. 97:7). "The Lord
hath said unto me, Thou art my Son" (Ps. 2:7). "Which were born, not
of blood, nor of the will of the flesh, nor of the will of man, but of God"
(John 1:13). "There is but one God, the Father . . . and we in him"
(I Cor. 8:6). "Ye are of God, little children" (I John 4:4). The Godhood
of man is the fact which spiritual evolution is bringing to light. "Man is
the noblest work of God." "Himself from God he could not free"
(Emerson). In this material world man should so recognise his noble
destiny, his oneness with God, that holiness be found in him, and he should
live the Christ life.

"In Christ."—Both John and Paul have pointed out that we are in
Christ. "We are in him that is true, even in his son, Jesus Christ" (I John
5:20). "Blessed . . . with all spiritual blessings in heavenly places in
Christ" (Eph. 1:3). This does not mean that we are in the man Jesus.
"Jesus of Nazareth is plainly terrestrial. His advent was the glory, his
reception the shame of the human race" [2] (Sir Oliver Lodge). "Jesus . . .
unveiled the Christ, the spiritual idea of divine Love" (*Science and*

---

[1] Aug. in Psalm 49. Ex. Bened.
[2] *Christian Revelation from a Scientific Point of View*. Address before the National
Free Church Council, at Portsmouth, March 9, 1911.

Health, p. 38). Few grasp the far-reaching and glorious signification of Peter's reply to our Master, "Thou art the Christ, the Son of the living God" (Matt. 16:16).

Each of us is an individualisation of that consciousness, an individualisation of the Christ. "In him is no sin" (I John 3:5). All the spiritual beings together are the Christ,[1] "We, being many, are one body in Christ" (Rom. 12:5); "we are in . . . Jesus Christ" (I John 5:20); "Your bodies are the members of Christ" (I Cor. 6:15); "In Christ shall all be made alive" (I Cor. 15:22); "Your life is hid with Christ in God" (Col. 3:3); "the church, which is his body, the fulness of him that filleth all in all" (Eph. 1:22, 23). Remember that "church" means originally, "an assembly."[2] It is held together by the power of Love alone. "Union with Christ must be something real and substantial, and not merely a metaphor and a flower of rhetoric" (Rev. Charles Kingsley). St. Augustine says: "Let us rejoice and return thanks that we have been made, not only Christians, but Christ."

Dr. Inge writes: "Union with the glorified Christ is the essence of Christianity."[3] Professor Wallace, of Oxford, says: "The great deed that seems to emerge as the life of Christ is the bringing into one of God and man."[4] The Christ is as infinite as God, the true idea of God, "of whom are all things, and we in him" (I Cor. 8:6). We therefore, individualise the power or activity of God, for God is seen to work by man, the Christ by reflection. "Christ the power of God, and the wisdom of God" (I Cor. 1:24). "His eternal power and Godhead" (Rom. 1:20). This is "the mystic Christ" of the early Fathers (see Eph. 3:3-5, 9), which now is no longer hidden and misunderstood by those who can prove their knowledge of God, by demonstration of the Christ-power. "When we recognise . . . that the mystic Christ is in all, and that every human being is a potential Jesus, we have realised what it is to be 'in the Lord.' If only we could stand fast in this truth!" (*Mystic Immanence*, Archdeacon Wilberforce).

The " Second Coming of Christ."—" *Do not be afraid of an idea because it has several times striven to make itself appreciated. Every great revelation is likely to have been foreshadowed in more or less imperfect forms so as to prepare our minds and make ready the way for complete perception hereafter. It is probable that the human race is quite incompetent to receive a really great idea the first time it is offered. So it was with the idea of the Messiah which was abroad in the land, and had been for centuries, before Christ's coming; and never has He been really recognised by more than a few*"[5] (Sir Oliver Lodge).

God must be absolute good, Life itself, Truth itself, Love itself, and the perfect world must be governed by the Principle of all good. The manifestation of good must be made in the image and likeness of good, of

[1] "The oneness of all men with one another in Christ, and their oneness with God through Christ, is the foundation of all practical and effective religion" (Father Tyrrell in *The Way of Truth*).
[2] Smith's *Dictionary of the Bible*.
[3] *The Paddock Lectures* for 1906.
[4] *Lectures and Essays*.
[5] *Christian Revelation from a Scientific Point of View*.

God. The account of the Creation in Genesis 1, verses 26, 27, bears witness to this. Man, therefore must manifest Life, Truth, and Love, having life eternal, and being absolutely truthful and loving. He must thus be found active, energetic, and absolutely joyous, having all know-
5 ledge of what he requires, all wisdom, all intelligence, with an infinite vista of infinite variety before him.

You are now and ever have been, in reality, a perfect spiritual being, "the same yesterday, and to-day, and for ever" (Heb. 13:8). To the human consciousness this truth of our unity with God comes as the
10 birth of a new idea. In reality it is as old as eternity. This is the second coming of Christ, which comes to each of us when ready, lifting us into heaven, into the kingdom of God that is within, when, with glorious possibilities daily unfolding, our hearts go out to every man, and joyously manifesting the Christ, life, love, and truth are spread around, filling the
15 hungry with good things.

> "Thy soul must overflow, if thou
> Another's soul wouldst reach;
> It needs the overflow of heart
> To give the lips full speech.

20
> Think truly, and thy thoughts
> Shall the world's famine feed;
> Speak truly, and each word of thine
> Shall be a fruitful seed;
> Live truly, and thy life shall be
25
> A great and noble creed" (*Horatio Bonar*).

"Before the immense possibilities of man, all mere experience, all past biography, however spotless and sainted, shrinks away" (Essay on *The Oversoul*, Emerson).

Three Points of View.—Throughout history there have been three
30 great classes of thinkers, who, approaching the knowledge of this so-called material universe from different points of view, have always been more or less antagonistic. These are the theologians, who look at things from a religious point of view; the natural scientists, who look at things from a material point of view; and the philosophers, who have until recently
35 looked at things chiefly from a human and therefore semi-metaphysical point of view.

During the last few years a great change, a splendid and glorious change, pregnant with meaning, has been taking place among the advanced workers in these three schools of thought; the least being among the
40 metaphysicians, and the greatest among the natural scientists. For genera-tions these three classes of thinkers, starting from a slough of ignorance, have been climbing up the mountain of knowledge and emerging from the mist into the bright sunlight. Nearing the peak the theologian looks round and is staggered to find on one side the scientific man close within reach,
45 and on the other the metaphysician likewise emerging from his wilderness of theories into practical metaphysics. "I will proceed to do a marvellous work among this people, even a marvellous work and a wonder: for the wisdom of their wise men shall perish" (Isa. 29:14).

Paley says, "We believe what we are taught," and as Bishop Westcott, in his *Gospel of the Resurrection* puts it: "We receive the facts and the dogmatic interpretation of the facts simultaneously." We have to change all this and learn how to learn. Then we shall commence to give up our multitudinous false ideas. "Where is the wise? where is the scribe? where 5 is the disputer of this world? hath not God made foolish the wisdom of this world?" (I Cor. 1:20). "There are things which the intellect can seek, but by herself will never find. These things instinct can find, but will never seek them unprompted by the intellect" (Henri Bergson).

Choice of Words.—At the present time the difficulty in understanding 10 the relative views of these three great classes is largely a question of terms. There will now be put forward some ideas which cannot fail to enable those belonging to different schools of thought to understand each other better and so change opposition into co-operation.

It is always more or less difficult to express metaphysical truths in literal 15 or physical terms. This is why in all religions there is such a wonderful variety in their methods of expressing such concepts. Plato felt this, for as James Martineau says: "His speculations present the liveliest image of a mind struggling with the inadequacy of language to shape into consistent expression relations which nevertheless consist in reality." 20

Expanding thought has to find expression and define its use of terms. Various religious phrases, which may possibly appear to have a hackneyed significance, are used in this book in their scientific sense, and with definite purpose. For instance, "wake up" is used as it would be to awaken one under the influence of hypnotism. "Now it is high time to awake out 25 of sleep: for now is our salvation nearer than when we believed" (Rom. 13:11). A treatise on an inversion of false ideas must include truer meanings of words in general use.

ADVANCING HUMAN KNOWLEDGE

"*Knowledge the wing wherewith we fly to heaven*" (Shakespeare). 30

Good, not what we have hitherto called good, but absolute good, is Truth. God and good are synonymous terms. All religion is a question of man's conception of God, of good; and to find out a man's religion you must find out what he thinks of God. The only real test of a religion is: Are its doctrines demonstrable? It must be proved in every department 35 of life. "A religion that will teach us how to live, that will hold up clear and high the laws of life, and win us to obedience to them—this is the religion the world needs, and it is the only true religion" (W. M. Salter). "For a righteous man thinketh that which is righteous. And whilst he does so, and walketh uprightly, he shall have the Lord in heaven favourable 40 unto him in all his business" (I Hermas, Vis. 1:10).[1]

The only perfect religion must be scientific Christianity, as was that of Jesus the Christ. His innate spirituality enabled him in his boyhood to utilise the powers that God had given him, and to put aside the limitations

[1] Irenæus quotes Hermas as Scripture, and Origen thought it divinely inspired. 45 Eusebius and Jerome say that it was read publicly in the churches.

that appeared to fetter those around him. John Smith, the Cambridge
Platonist, truly said : "Such as men themselves are, such will God appear
to them to be." Dr. W. R. Inge writes : "So closely do gods resemble their
worshippers that we might almost parody Pope's line and say that an honest
5 God is the noblest work of man."

We have made God manlike instead of man Godlike. "Men . . .
changed the glory of the uncorruptible God into an image made like to
corruptible man" (Rom. 1:23). Religions differ according to their amount
of spirituality. This is the essential difference. Some are so material that
10 they are not worthy to be even called religions. The higher the religion the
more spiritual it is and the more it rests on right thinking and its resultant
right acting. What thought is so right and so high as thinking of God?
Now "God is Spirit"—this is a more correct translation than "God is a
Spirit" (John 4:24)—consequently true thoughts are not material, but the
15 opposite, namely, spiritual, or of Spirit, God.

Having found our God we have to find out how to apply this sacred
knowledge rightly, and therefore scientifically. "Acquaint now thyself
with him, and be at peace : thereby good shall come unto thee"
(Job. 22:21). "And this is life eternal, that they might know thee the only
20 true God." (John 17:3). We have to gain a true conception of God and man,
the divine man. In proportion as we gain a better understanding of the
"spotless selfhood" of God, so do we become more like Him, and more
like our real selves, which are created "in the image of God," good, and
"in the likeness of God" (Gen. 1:27, and 5:1). "An acknowledgment of the
25 perfection of the infinite Unseen confers a power nothing else can"
(Unity of Good, p. 7, Mary Baker Eddy). Man is the reflection of the Ego,
co-existent with God, being the eternally divine idea. "The one Ego, the
one Mind or Spirit called God, is infinite individuality," [1] one living
Principle, for God is Life and God is All. Can one say more?

30   "All is of God that is and is to be,
               And God is good, let this suffice us still" (Whittier).

The beginner, in his path upwards, may at one time think that he has
lost his God, when he recognises that God is Principle; but soon after he
will joyfully admit that he has found the Christ, Truth : Life, Truth, and
35 Love.

Browning makes Paracelsus say : "By intuition genius knows and I
knew at once, what God is, what we are, what life is. Alas ! I could not use
the knowledge aright." Now we can use this knowledge, which, as a lens,
magnifies the divine powers that are a present possibility to all, until so
40 recognised that we use them to the full extent, for the benefit of all mankind. What a glorious life then appears before us, enabling us to step out
into the sunlight of Truth, "God-crowned."

Wisdom is "knowledge practically applied to the best ends" (New
Century Reference Library Dictionary). To know Truth we require wis-
45 dom. In the Wisdom of Solomon occurs a scientifically accurate statement
of man's inherent ability to attain to true knowledge. He says : "He hath

---

[1] Science and Health, p. 281, Mary Baker Eddy.

given me certain knowledge of the things that are, namely, to know how
the world was made, and the operation of the elements: The beginning,
ending, and midst of the times: . . . And all such things as are either
secret or manifest, them I know. For wisdom, which is the worker of all 5
things, taught me: for in her is an understanding spirit, holy, one only,
manifold, subtil, lively, clear, undefiled, plain, not subject to hurt,. . . .
she is the breath of the power of God, and a pure influence flowing from
the glory of the Almighty: . . . I perceived that I could not otherwise
obtain her, except God gave her me; and that was a point of wisdom also
to know whose gift she was; I prayed unto the Lord, and besought him" 10
(Wisdom of Solomon 7:17, 18, 21, 22, 25, and 8:21).

Theology.—"*The science that treats of the evidence, nature, and attributes of God, especially of man's relations to God*" (*New Century Reference
Library Dictionary*). Of the three classes of thinkers endeavouring to
ascertain truth, referred to earlier, let us take first the theologian, as his 15
work is the endeavour to gain and teach the knowledge of God. Whether
Truth passes under the theologian's names of God, Elohim, or Jehovah,
under the scientific man's name of cause or nature, or under the metaphysician's name of Mind, we find that religion, which we may almost
define as the endeavour to understand and practise the law of God, or 20
good, has, taken as a whole, presented a steady evolution. Such an idea,
for instance, as eternal punishment, or aimless torture, and "eternal
roasting amidst noxious vapours," as it has been described, is now almost
given up by the more spiritual and cultured classes. Views about the
Atonement are now altering. No longer does a view of God as a jealous, one 25
may almost say a savage God, sacrificing his dearly beloved Son, appeal
to us.

Absolute good or Truth is the Mind that includes all life, truth, love,
wisdom, and joy, in fact, all the good. The statement that God cannot
know evil, and therefore cannot know the material world, excited as much 30
hostility ten years ago as the assertion of universal salvation did fifty years
ago, when men thought that salvation was their reward for being as good
as they could be, not recognising that material thought is the instrument
of all reward or punishment in a material world. "Behold, the righteous
shall be recompensed in the earth: much more the wicked and the sinner" 35
(Prov. 11:31).

To think that God can know evil is equal to saying that eternal consciousness of infinite goodness can at the same time be conscious of evil,
an obvious impossibility, even for a moment, as it is equivalent to saying
that black is white. So many have been the hopeless inconsistencies in the 40
material world, that we have quite calmly fallen into the habit of accepting
as true such absolutely illogical statements. Soon there will be no further
cause for Carlyle's scathing remarks: "Quackery and dupery do abound in
religion; above all, in the more advanced decaying stages of religion they
have fearfully abounded; but quackery was never the originating influence 45
in such things; it was not the health and life of religion, but their disease,
the sure precursor that they were about to die." The only real test of a
religion is: Are its doctrines demonstrable? "It should seem rational that

the only perfect religion is divine Science, Christianity as taught by our
great Master" (*Message for 1900*, p. 4, Mary Baker Eddy). His teachings
are now at last becoming understood, and as they become understood so
do they become demonstrable. This is because they are founded on an
5 unfailing underlying Principle, the Principle of good, an active, living
Principle.

Thomas Aquinas, whom Huxley spoke of as possibly the most subtle
of the world's thinkers, states in his *Summa* that theology, "the word of
God," is the only absolute science known, and shows that every phase of
10 natural science is purely relative. This is correct, as it is solely based upon
mere human knowledge. If Christianity is not scientific and science
Christian, one or other is untrue.

Dogma.—"That which seems to one, opinion, tenet, decree" (*Oxford
Dictionary*).
15 How can we attach much weight to dogma, which has been the cause
of constant demoniacal religious contests in the past? It rests upon the
balance of probabilities, on man's authority. "Custom doth make dotards
of us all." Every age and nation makes and unmakes, each sect tampers
with the prevalent dogma, and the individual modifies it to suit himself.
20 Heaven keep us from the broken reeds of dead rites.[1] "Creed, dogma,
and traditionalism in the Church are fast forcing the best men out, and as a
prominent theologian has well said, are fast making the Church an asylum
for drones and imbeciles" (Stephen Hasbrouck). "Full well ye reject the
commandment of God, that ye may keep your own tradition" (Mark
25 7:9).
In the old days of rigid dogma, knowledge "revolved like a squirrel in a
cage," and intellect "was chained in thrilling regions of thick-ribbed ice."
Those who put forward new religious ideas were burnt. Those who
enunciated new scientific truths were treated as heretics. There is but one
30 heresy—belief in the possibility of separation from God. There is no necessity to give the names of religious martyrs, "earth's luminaries." There
have been hundreds of thousands tortured in the name of religion. In the
thirteenth century one hundred and eighty-three so-called heretics and
their pastor were burned alive together before the Archbishop of Rheims
35 and seventeen prelates.[2]
The scientific martyrs are also numerous, although less known. Pietro,
the great philosopher and physician of the thirteenth century, was held
to be a wizard and condemned to be burnt alive. Copernicus, who, in the
sixteenth century, elucidated the action of the solar system, but thought
40 that the planets moved round the sun in a circle, instead of in a kind of
ellipse, "because God could only choose a perfect figure," was excom-
municated for heresy. Galileo, because he declared that the earth moved,
was imprisoned. Bruno, who declared the stars to be suns, was burnt at
the stake as late as A.D. 1600. Franklin's electrical experiments with kites

45   [1] "Dogmas become dangerous as soon as they commence to grow old" (*The
Evolution of Matter*, Dr. Le Bon). See Matt. 15:9; Gal. 1:14; Col. 2:8; Titus 1:14;
I Peter 1:18.
    [2] Draper's *History of Intellectual Development*.

were ridiculed, and his papers on lightning conductors ignominiously thrown out by the French Academy. Newton was accused by Leibnitz of introducing "occult qualities and miracles into philosophy," the law of gravity being "subversive of natural, and inferentially of revealed, religion." Darwin was denounced and then "whitewashed by being buried in Westminster Abbey." Jesus himself, the great Exemplar, and the most scientific man who ever lived, met a felon's fate. So is the path of human progress strewn with the pitiable evidences of the inhuman battle that has been waged throughout the ages. To-day there is almost the same un-reasoning conflict of creed, the same antagonism of sectarian bitterness.

"Brave men have dared to examine lies which had long been taught, not because they were freethinkers, but because they were such stern thinkers that the lie could no longer escape them" (John Ruskin). "Gods and dogmas do not perish in a day" (Dr. G. Le Bon). What originally was blasphemy or infidelity is now orthodox. "Orthodoxy is my doxy, hetero-doxy is other people's doxy." Many of our clergymen, three centuries ago, would have been burnt for teaching what is already considered practically antiquated dogma by those most earnestly reaching out for spiritual truth. The miracles of yesterday are the scientific discoveries of to-day. Our present beliefs are simply the heresies of previous days. Paracelsus truly wrote: "That which is unexpected will in future prove to be true, and that which is looked upon as superstitious in one century will be the basis for the approved science of the next."

Dr. Heysinger recently has written: "A clergyman of one of our largest Protestant denominations, returning, a few years ago, from one of their general assemblies, and who spent a few days with me, said that, 'If a clergyman had risen and stated what three-fourths of them honestly believed, he would have been expelled by a two-thirds vote.'" [1] No wonder someone has said: "Get on, get honour, get honest."

Dean Farrar, in *The Bible and the Child*, writes: "There are a certain number of persons who, when their minds have become stereotyped in foregone conclusions, become obtrusives, and not unfrequently bigoted obtrusives. As convinced as the Pope of their own personal infallibility, their attitude towards those who see that the old views are no longer tenable is an attitude of anger and alarm. . . . Those whose intellects have thus been petrified have made themselves incapable of fair and rational examina-tion of the truths which they impugn. They think that they can, by mere assertion, overthrow results arrived at by the lifelong inquiries of the ablest students, while they have not given a day's serious or impartial study to them."

Père Hyacinthe, the well-known Roman Catholic priest, writes as follows: "For myself, the more I consider it, the more I am persuaded that Catholic Christianity is approaching a transformation. It seems as if the Lord were saying a second time, as once to the prophet, 'Behold, I create new heavens and a new earth; and the former things shall not be remembered, nor come into mind.' Nor is the Biblical revelation the only revelation, though it be the highest. There is something of God in all the

---

[1] *Spirit and Matter before the Bar of Modern Science.*

great religions which have presided over the providential development of
humanity. It is not true that all religions are equally good; but neither is it
true that all religions except one are no good at all. Science, again, must
not be ignored. It also is a revelation, at once human and divine, and no
5 less certain than the other. Some day will be realised the daring forecast
of Joseph de Maistre, 'Religion and science, in virtue of their natural
affinity, will meet in the brain of some one man of genius—perhaps of
more than one—and the world will get what it needs and cries for; not a
new religion, but the revelation of revelation.'"

10   "Aggressive scepticism is absolutely fatal to any sort of scientific
progress. It warps everything it touches, and vitiates every result obtained.
It is no more defensible or tolerable than the simple and unquestioning
faith of those who accept everything that turns up at a séance" [1] (J. W.
Heysinger, M.D.).

15   "Unbelief is usually due to indolence, often to prejudice, and never a
thing to be proud of; doubt may be scientific, pending investigation, but
denial on *a priori* never" (Romanes). Archbishop Whateley has said
"That man will never change his mind who has no mind to change."
Emerson has said, "A foolish consistency is the hobgoblin of little minds."
20 Huxley has said, "Clear knowledge of what one does not know is just as
important as knowing what one does know."

Even philosophy has its paralysing dogma. The celebrated Auguste
Comte actually proposed the creation of a committee to limit the scientific
researches which should be permitted.

25   Both scientific and religious dogma is fast fading. Dr. Campbell Morgan,
possibly the most "orthodox" Evangelical among leading Congregational
ministers, said recently in one of his sermons, "Ten years ago, when I
began my ministry (*ætat. 40*) in this pulpit, there were things in theology
upon which I would have dogmatised as I cannot dogmatise now."

30   Professor Agassiz says: "Every great scientific truth goes through three
stages. First, people say it conflicts with the Bible. Next, they say it has
been discovered before. Lastly, they say they had always believed it."
T. J. Hudson amplifies this, and says: "First, it is met by a universal
shout of derision. When that fails to disprove it, as it sometimes does,
35 everybody claims it as his own. When that is disproved, as it sometimes is,
each claimant proceeds to cover himself with a dust of old libraries in an
effort to prove that it was always known." Indifference, as Lawrence
Wetherill says, is a "robber of opportunities," and I am not sure that it
does not keep a man back more than aggressive scepticism.

40   **New Truths Hateful to the Sluggard.**—A Baptist minister of
Arkansas is said to have told some members of his congregation, on his
return from a summer visit to Port Smith, that he had seen men making
ice a foot thick. The congregation, who were "sound orthodox believers,"
received this statement with amazement, being doubtful whether he was
45 not mad. The giant intellects of the deacons quickly settled the question,
for, "As the Lord could not make ice more than three-and-a-half inches
thick in that country, in the winter, to say that a man could make it a foot

---

[1] *Spirit and Matter before the Bar of Modern Science.*

thick in the summer was a tale so contrary to reason and experience as to be preposterous," and the preacher was turned out of the church for his scandalous lying.

H. Croft Hillier, in *Heresies*, writes: "New truths are hateful to the public—the public of science included. All is a case of wriggling in familiar 5 mud-holes. Science will have nothing to do with so-called occultism, and snubs metaphysics because the truths of occultism and metaphysics are not in the parish of science."

Throughout the world the exponents of physical science have been held up to scathing ridicule by those familiar with occult matters, now 10 recognised as merely having to do with shifting forms, ethereal phenomena. Many of the truths now put forward, although new to the natural scientist, or only recently admitted, have been, as a matter of fact, known and taught for years.[1] Fortunately, this habit of burying our heads in the sand has now passed, and all workers are on the look-out for higher 15 truths. "Strive for the truth unto death, and the Lord shall fight for thee" (Eccles. 4:28).

At the same time, as Huxley has said, "Take nothing for truth without clear knowledge that it is such."

W. M. Salter says: "The Mighty Power hid from our gaze by the thin 20 screen of nature and of nature's laws . . . is with our struggles after a perfect right." "If God be for us, who can be against us?" (Rom. 8:31).

Philosophy.—"*The knowledge of the causes of the phenomena both of mind and matter*" (*New Century Reference Library Dictionary*).

Philosophy, like a moth fluttering round an incandescent electric 25 lamp, has, as will be shown hereafter, continually touched the fringe of the truth, that truth Plato so desired to know. Sankaracharya, a noble representative of Hindu thought, taught that perfect knowledge was perfect bliss. Knowledge of God is eternal life, and at last Philosophy is on the threshold of truth, with the door opening wide to the glorious light 30 which has always been shining.

The great merit of such men as Descartes is that they are open-minded enough to view as doubtful what up to their time had been considered uncontested truths. We all have to maintain this position, which is really the outcome of logical reasoning. As Dr. Le Bon, in *The Evolution of* 35 *Forces*, says: "Too often do we forget that the scientific idols of the present day have no more right to invulnerability than those of the past." Truth must be demonstrably true.

Science.—"*Knowledge; the comprehension of truth or facts; truth ascertained*" (Webster). 40

"If the time is ever to come in the religious history of the human race when what may be called God's Science of Man is to supersede

---

[1] Mrs. Eddy, forty years ago, gave the world the details of what is now beginning to be accepted as the correct explanation of the universe. Col. Olcott, lecturing on April 26, 1882, at the Patchiappah's Hall, Madras, made the following statement: 45 "Electricity cannot, except under prepared conditions, be seen; yet it is matter. The universal ether of science no one ever saw; yet it is matter in a state of extreme tenuity." This now turns out to be correct.

theology, which is man's Science of God, that time is already here."
(*Spirit and Matter before the Bar of Modern Science*, J. W. Heysinger, M.D.).
At last we begin to understand the Science of Mind.

Science, which Mrs. Eddy describes as "the atmosphere of God," is
5 eternal, and includes all truth. Natural science, like theology, has also been
hampered by its dogma. "Scientific ideas which rule the minds of scholars
at various epochs have all the solidity of religious dogmas" (Dr. Le Bon).
Dr. Heysinger writes: "The dogmatism of theology finds a full counterpart and co-worker in her newer sister, dogmatic science. The scientific
10 pursuit is a noble one to espouse, the work is grand beyond comparison,
the fruits are already priceless and vast; but specialities always narrow the
field of vision of the specialist, and the time for dogmatism has not yet
come, and will not come for ages, if at all." Writing of the extraordinary
phenomena that natural scientists are now admitting must point to some
15 great underlying facts of life, he also says: "I do not fully understand these
things, but that is no reason why I should allow others, who understand
them very much less, or not at all, to do the understanding for me. I
agree with Professor De Morgan that . . . the physical explanations
I have seen are easy, but miserably insufficient. . . . I merely cite the
20 facts, however, leaving to other skilled psychologists the interpretation of
the phenomena" (*Spirit and Matter before the Bar of Modern Science*).

Natural science has, however, presented a steady evolution, checking
the statements put forward by the metaphysicians; and plodding on, by
the gradual elimination of falsities, to the recognition of the non-reality
25 of matter, which soon all leaders in science will accept and acknowledge
to the world as an absolute fact. Our present spiritual understanding is
"the fruit tree yielding fruit after his kind, whose seed is in itself" (Gen.
1:11). We are waking up out of our "learned and happy ignorance"!
Scientific statements change. What is true in one age is out of date in the
30 next.

Natural science is essentially a matter of observation, weighing, measur-
ing, etc. It is now coming to the end of its powers in this direction, for the
simple reason that so attenuated has the thought of matter become, that
we cannot obtain apparatus sufficiently delicate to deal with so ethereal a
35 conception.[1] Who can weigh an electron? Who can measure a line of force?
Its arguments and deductions are now based on mathematical formulæ,
and we have to fall back on reason and logic, for Mind is the Alpha and
Omega, not the human, falsely called mind, but the Mind that is All-in-
all.

40 Natural science has come back now to the knowledge possessed by
Paracelsus, nicknamed "the other Luther," the first teacher who ever
held a Chair of physical science. Striking at the monopoly in learning, by
teaching in German instead of Latin, he produced a revolution in science
as great as the one Luther produced in the Church, and even before
45 Luther's first public denouncement of Papacy, began his lectures at Basle
by lighting some sulphur in a dish and burning a Papal bull with the books

---

[1] Yet our instruments are wonderful. A bolometer, for instance, will register
a rise or fall in temperature of one-millionth of a degree, and will register the heat
from a lighted candle a mile-and-a-half away.

of his great predecessors in the medical art, Avicenna, Galen, and others, saying: "Sic vos ardebitis in gehenna."[1] So far advanced was he in the hidden knowledge of the material world that many, even of those who scoff at the knowledge of the scientific man of the present day, are unable to follow him in his explanations. For fear of punishment for sorcery he had to conceal his doctrines, and used fanciful names. Even those who have recognised and testified to his ability have not recognised the depth of knowledge that he had sounded. It always appeared as though he must have been able to obtain knowledge inspirationally, and I recently found that Dr. Hartmann had testified as follows: "Paracelsus was a Christian in the true meaning of that word, and he always attempted to support the doctrine he taught by citations from the Bible. He asks, 'What is a philosophy that is not supported by spiritual revelation?'"

Edward Berdoe, M.R.C.S., in his *Life of Paracelsus*, writes: "He was called a quack and impostor because he cured sick folk by unaccustomed methods. We have baptised these methods now, and given them orthodox names. Thus does the quackery of to-day, like its heresy, become the orthodoxy of to-morrow. We know how this man's character has been misrepresented in so many ways—we can see that much of his so-called arrogance was inspiration, and inspiration so far beyond the conception of the narrow, bigoted, grossly ignorant, monkish minds about him, that the inspiration of genius was probably mistaken ofttimes for that of wine." "Behold a man gluttonous, and a winebibber: . . . But wisdom is justified of her children" (Matt. 11:19).

A recent writer says of him: "Into the tangled undergrowth of theosophy, mysticism, magic, and theology, he burst with the pioneer's hatchet." This path was narrow and dangerous. Fortunately, he seems to have steered clear of its leading pitfalls, although he, like others, made the mistake of thinking that it was the "soul-powers" of the spirit in man that, by occult means, produced material things, and gave him exceptional powers. He recognised, however, that in "black magic," or when these powers were used to harm, or to interfere with others, they were demoniacal. We now know that "white magic," or when these powers are apparently used to further the wishes of others, is almost as bad.

Before his time, religion and science of the day were one. Working from a material, false basis, each harmed the other, religion strangling science, science putting religion on a false pedestal. The genius of Paracelsus was so far beyond that of those around him, that he was slandered and misrepresented universally, and ultimately he is supposed to have been, to all intents and purposes, murdered in 1541 by those who were jealous of him.

This is the history, more or less, of all those who have been before their time and have had sufficient moral courage to put forward their views.

True Science Includes True Religion.—"*Give us not only angels' songs, but Science vast, to which belongs the tongue of angels and the song of songs*" (Mary Baker Eddy).

---

[1] "So you, too, will burn in hell."

3

Huxley has said: "True science and true religion are twin-sisters, and the separation of either from the other is sure to be the death of both. Science prospers exactly in proportion as it is religious, and religion flourishes in exact proportion to the scientific depth and firmness of its
5 basis." He also has said: "The antagonism of science is not to religion, but to the heathen survivals and bad philosophy under which religion herself is often well-night crushed."

Herbert Spencer writes: "To reach that point of view from which the seeming discordance of religion and science disappears and the two
10 merge into one, must cause a revolution of thought fruitful and beneficial in consequences."

M. Flammarion's forecast of the religion of the future is that it will be "scientific, founded on a knowledge of psychical facts. . . . This religion of science will have one great advantage over all that has gone before it—
15 *unity.*"

Henry Drummond, in the Preface of *Natural Law in the Spiritual World*, writes: "Theology must feel to-day that the modern world calls for a further proof. Nor will best Theology resent this demand; it also demands it. Theology is searching on every hand for another echo of the
20 Voice of which Revelation also is the echo, that out of the mouths of two witnesses its truths should be established . . . Science . . . speaks to Religion with twofold purpose. In the first place, it offers to corroborate Theology; in the second, to purify it. If the removal of suspicion from Theology is of urgent moment, not less important is the removal of its
25 adulterations . . . the artificial accumulations of centuries of uncontrolled speculation . . . they mark the impossibility of progress without the guiding and sustaining hand of Law."

We are in the midst of a mental revolution. Sir Oliver Lodge has written: " The region of religion and a complete Science are one." This
30 complete knowledge is divine, and is now at hand. For years science has been separating itself from the falsities of religion, and the greatest intellects of the twentieth century have been slowly divorcing themselves from it. Now the light has come, and again the two are wedded together, this time with an indissoluble band, the band of the knowledge of truth.
35 "Science is clearly moving in the direction of the spiritual; nothing can be more certain." (J. W. Heysinger, M.D.). Weary of matter, science would endeavour to give the meaning of Spirit.

Ethics.—"*The science that treats of the principles of human morality and duty*" (*New Century Reference Library Dictionary*).
40 "Ethical Science is already for ever completed, so far as her general outline and main principles are concerned, and has been, as it were, waiting for physical science to come up with her" (*Paradoxical Philosophy*). Physical science has now come up.

Miracles.—No miracles could have been exceptions to any law. They
45 must have been scientific and divinely natural, due to the inevitable action of a universal spiritual law. God, being Principle, is the Principle of all law and order, and a perfect Principle could not possibly allow of any deviation from its essential rules.

"The region of the miraculous, it is called, and the bare possibility of its existence has been hastily and illegitimately denied. . . . Miracles are no more impossible, no more lawless, than the interference of a human being would seem to a colony of ants or bees" (Sir Oliver Lodge). As Professor Drummond says in *Natural Law in the Spiritual World*: "Science can hear nothing of a Great Exception." The word miracle merely means marvel. The work of Jesus was marvellous. Now we can confidently assert, indeed prove, and that with overwhelming evidence, that we know the laws governing these scientifically normal occurrences.[1]

Professor H. Langhorne Orchard, in reading the Gunning Prize essay for 1909 at a meeting of the Victoria Institute, held at the Royal Society of Arts, stated that Science set herself to take account, not of some facts only, but of all. The aversion to "miracles" which was cherished by some scientists, did not rest, he said, upon a scientific basis; it might now be stated as a truism that belief in the fact of miracles was thoroughly compatible with the true scientific temper. As to the question whether miracles had actually occurred, science answered in the affirmative. Bible miracles were *a priori* probable from the nature of the phenomena and the conditions under which they were said to have taken place. They were inseparably bound up with Revelation, and explained what was otherwise inexplicable. The exodus of the Israelites from Egypt was unintelligible if the attending miracles did not really take place. Miracles, he said, explained Christianity, and nothing else did; they gave the key to its doctrines, they accounted for its wonderful rise and spread, and the divine vitality of its continuous history.

In *The Decline and Fall of the Roman Empire*, Gibbon, whose views on the subject make him a safe authority, writes: "During the age of Christ, of his Apostles, and of their first disciples, the doctrine which they preached was confirmed by innumerable prodigies. The lame walked, the blind saw, the sick were healed, the dead were raised, demons were expelled, and the laws of Nature were frequently suspended for the benefit of the church."

Mr. George Rawlinson, Tutor of Exeter College, writes as follows: "There is good evidence that the ability of working miracles was not confined to the apostolic age. . . . Papias related various miracles as having happened in his own lifetime, among others, that of a dead man who was restored to life. Justin Martyr declares very simply that in his day men and women were found who possessed miraculous powers. Quadratus, the apologist, is mentioned by a writer of the second century as exercising them. Irenæus speaks of miracles as still common in Gaul when he wrote, which was nearly at the close of the second century. Tertullian, Theophilus, and Minucius Felix, authors of about the same

---

[1] "The word miracle has no supernatural meaning, and never had any. It is the arbitrary translation of two Greek words, one of which means an act of power, and the other a sign; . . . and it is a mere abuse of the Greek language to give it a supernatural significance" (Frederick Dixon in the *Birmingham News*, February, 1914). Jerome, in his translation of the Bible known as the Vulgate, used the Latin words meaning an act of power and a sign. Later on, when the Church had to account for the reason why its followers could not prove the truth of its teachings by acts of power and signs, he used the word "miraculum."

period, are witnesses of the continuance in their day of at least one class
of miracles" (*The Historical Evidences of the Truth of the Scriptures*).
The Prayer Book of Edward VI contains a service of healing and the
journals of Fox and Wesley contain numerous stories of healing by
5 prayer.
   The world wants to know the laws that govern these miracles, so as to
apply them. It has a right to the benefits that are attainable. Men (by this
expression is meant throughout this work both men and women, as there
is no essential difference) are now thirsting for knowledge. All men worthy
10 of the name have, as Browning calls it, "a wolfish hunger after knowledge."
They will no longer accept a stone for bread, nor the creeds and dogmas of
others; they want something definite, something logical; they want proof
of everything advanced, practical proof, something to make them better
men and women. They want men to live what they teach, and openly
15 teach what they live, without fear of criticism or aiming at reward. Like
William Law—according to Gibbon—men should believe all they profess
and practise all that they enjoin. H. C. King, President of Oberlin College
and author of *Reconstruction in Theology*, writes as follows : "There are
laws in the spiritual world; we can find them out; we can know their
20 implied conditions; these conditions we can fulfil; and we can so count
confidently upon results" (*Rational Living*).

   The World's Awakening.—"*Religion is a great reality and a great
truth—nothing less than an essential and indestructible element of human
nature*" (Herbert Spencer).
25   True religion is helping our fellow-man. For this it is necessary to
obtain a better knowledge of God. The world is fast waking up to the true
knowledge of God and all that this means. We are seeing that we cannot
be pushed into heaven at the last moment by a blind belief in an inhuman
sacrifice of a dearly-beloved Son, but that we receive day by day, moment
30 by moment, only the results of the right and wrong thinking of ourselves
and others. Fortunately, we are now recognising that by right thinking
we rise into a consciousness of complete dominion over the evil that
hitherto may have appeared irresistible. "For since by man came death,
by man came also the resurrection" (I Cor. 15:21). "Blessed and holy
35 is he that hath part in the first resurrection" (Rev. 20:6). The Greek word,
"Anastasis," translated resurrection, means primarily, "an arousing from
sleep."
   "Come now, and let us reason together, saith the Lord" (Isa. 1:18).
For the first time in the world's history every man's highest reasoning
40 faculty can be satisfied by the demonstrable truth that is now flooding the
world, proving beyond all cavil the omnipotence of good, at all times, and
under all circumstances. "Awake thou that sleepest, and arise from the
dead, and Christ shall give thee light" (Eph. 5:14). "The entrance of thy
words giveth light" (Ps. 119:130). "The true Light, which lighteth every
45 man that cometh into the world" (John 1:9). This is the light of the knowledge of God and His manifestation, heaven.

WHAT IS HEAVEN?

"Eye hath not seen, nor ear heard, neither have entered into the heart of man, the things which God hath prepared for them that love him. But God hath revealed them unto us by his Spirit" (I Cor. 2:9, 10).

The material, seeming man, gradually waking up, progressing towards a better recognition of the real and therefore spiritual existence, finds out that heaven is not a local habitation, but a perfect state of consciousness in which his real self exists at the present time. He also finds that this sense of a material world, including his apparent selfhood, is only a false sense which, when corrected by the true knowledge of God, disappears.[1] That is to say, the human being gradually loses a false sense of the world as material, and appears ultimately to see things as they really are. The human body and so-called "mind" will, yea, must, be ultimately entirely dematerialised, for "flesh and blood cannot inherit the kingdom of God; neither doth corruption inherit incorruption" (I Cor. 15:50). Then it will be universally demonstrated that man has never actually existed in a material body or been dependent upon such an imperfect organisation. "That which is born of the flesh is flesh; and that which is born of the Spirit is spirit" (John 3:6).

The Kingdom of God that is Within.—*"It is given unto you to know the mysteries of the kingdom of heaven"* (Matt. 13:11).

The following statements with regard to heavenly realities are neither speculative nor arbitrary, but logical conclusions, drawn from scientific premises, and proved by illustrative demonstrations over limitations of material laws.

"Heaven is not," a noted preacher once said in a sermon, "an eternal sitting in damp clouds, playing on harps, and singing praises to God, as so many seem to think." It has recently been recognised that we make our own hell and our own heaven here, and few men are fiends enough to want a worse hell for anyone than many men are temporarily in at the present moment, the hell of their own wrong thoughts, due to their not knowing how to think rightly. "The mind is its own place, and in itself can make a Heaven of Hell, a Hell of Heaven" (Milton). Again, who has not tasted, if not of heaven, of a wonderful sense of heaven, at some time during his lifetime?

> "Love rules the court, the camp, the grove,
> And men below and saints above;
> For love is heaven, and heaven is love" (*Sir Walter Scott*).

"The kingdom of God cometh not with observation: Neither shall they say, Lo here! or, Lo there! for, behold, the kingdom of God is within you" (Luke 17:20, 21). "The further a man goes in search of it, the less likely he is to find it" (Lao-Tze). In other words, heaven is a perfect state of consciousness, or divine state of Mind, consisting of what

[1] Kant pointed out that the material world was wholly different from the real, and that by the nature of our minds we could never know reality. This is true of the material man, but not true of the real man, who is spiritual.

the three classes of thinkers before referred to, call respectively, God and heaven, cause and its manifestation, Mind and its ideas; that is to say, it consists of the real people, the real planets, the real things, of which we appear to see the false concepts round us. Consequently, each of us is, and

5 always has been, in reality, a perfect being, in a perfect world, governed by a perfect God. "Every mystic tells us that heaven is around us all the time" (W. R. Inge).

In the light of present-day knowledge of man as spiritual, we cease to blame God for our own shortcomings, and a man soon begins to find that

10 under the worst circumstances, by turning in thought to God, he can get a faint sense of heaven, and along this scientific high road gain a clearer and increasing sense of its perfection, here and now. In this way he gradually gets rid of his troubles and the troubles of those around him, and so proves his knowledge of God, good.

15 **Individuality.**—The remark has sometimes been made: "It would be very uninteresting if everyone were alike, however perfect they might be." Sir Oliver Lodge even has written, "a mechanically perfect, thoroughly finished world would perhaps be rather dull," and puts into the mouth of an imaginary inhabitant the following words: "Good

20 heavens, I cannot stand this; I am going to put a bit of grit into some of these too-well-oiled machines, as I want to see an explosion or an earth-quake, or something interesting. I do not know what a burglary is, but even a burglary would be a change to this sort of Sunday-school existence. Do not any of you fellows know a wild animal that we might try to kill, or

25 a serpent that might try to bite us, and give us some relief from the monotony; or is there no young person with an apple who would tempt us to have a bite? It is true I was made good—utterly, hopelessly good—but I believe, alas! that it is possible for me to be obstreperous—I propose to try" (*The Clarion*, November 5, 1906).

30 In the present spiritual reality all men are perfect, but this does not prevent spiritual progress. To every individual comes a constant succession of different ideas, each absolutely perfect, consequently each person with whom you come in contact has new beauties of infinite variety to which he calls attention. The difference between men, that is, their

35 individuality, is the difference in the succession of God's ideas that unfold, and are reflected by them, and by this they are distinguished. Even in the seeming material world, as you increase in intelligence, you differentiate between people, not by their appearance, but by what they have mentally presented to you.

40 **The Unfolding of God's Ideas.**—To all of us, now in heaven, there has throughout eternity come a constant succession of perfect ideas. This is the unfolding of the only good ideas, they come from God and return to God, for all Being is God, individually and collectively. God as Life sends these ideas, God as Truth enables us to understand, and there-

45 fore enjoy them, and God as Love causes us to re-present them, that is, call the attention of our fellow-man to them, or pass them on, so giving him the joy that we have received from them, and receiving the happiness that this gives us. In other words, in heaven we are always exchanging

perfect ideas with our fellow-men. Everything in heaven has to do with this perfect interchange of ideas, this revolution in "God's orbits" that is constantly taking place. In the material consciousness, so called, we are simply apparently receiving a counterfeit impression of these perfect spiritual realities, false views of the permanent ideas of God.   5

Creation.—"*God . . . hath in these last days spoken unto us by his Son* [we individualise the Christ], *whom he hath appointed heir of all things, by whom also he made the worlds*" (Heb. 1:1, 2).

We have the power of grouping together any number of these perfect ideas that come to us, into new combinations, spiritual and tangible 10 bouquets of lovely ideas and combinations of them. These also we re-present, pass on, in the way of God's appointing, for the benefit of our fellow-men. We do not, however, lose them ourselves, as they form part of our definite individuality. This fresh grouping of ideas is the only creation in heaven, because all the ideas of which these combinations are 15 formed have always existed, and are perfect and infinite; they cannot be increased in number. This is the only evolution, spiritual evolution.

This is illustrated in the highest plane of human consciousness. Here "we find that wherever joy is, creation has been, and the richer the creation the deeper the joy. . . . He who is certain, absolutely certain, 20 that he has brought a living work to the birth, cares no more for praise, and feels himself beyond glory" (*Life and Consciousness*, Henri Bergson). Such joy can only accompany the unfolding of further good to humanity.

Heavenly Happiness.—

> "Pave with love each golden mile,   25
>   And thus have Heaven here this minute,
>   And not far off in the after while" (Nixon Waterman).

It is obvious that in this kingdom of heaven, the kingdom of harmony, a perfect understanding, which is the basis of happiness, reigns between all. Desire and fulfilment are one. This implies a continual harmonious 30 interchange of ideas. We are eternally re-presenting God's ideas, expressing our ideals in new creations or groupings. This redistribution of God's thoughts is the source of infinite happiness, individual and universal.

Happiness can be differentiated into four principal divisions :—

First, every spiritual being loves his fellow-man, even one met for the 35 first time, with a love of which the material man can hardly form even a faint conception, because it is the perfect love of God.

Secondly, we are always interchanging perfect ideas with those we love, either individually or otherwise.

Thirdly, we are continually manifesting God's power of grouping 40 together new combinations of glorious ideas, so giving our fellow-men fresh happiness, and consequently gaining the highest happiness ourselves.

Fourthly, we can wander with those we love amongst infinite worlds of incalculable beauty.

These four chief sources of real happiness are counterfeited by four 45 in the material world. First, we have the love towards our fellow-man ; secondly, the interchanging of ideas with those we love; thirdly, even the making of a rag doll for a child gives us a sense of happiness that would not follow many a greater action prompted by a lesser motive; and, fourthly, who has not been lifted heavenwards by the beauty and grandeur lying behind Nature's handiwork?

5 The reason for this is, that all the love and happiness, of which we get only glimpses in this material world, is real, though our sense of it is limited.

> "Souls that are gentle and still
> Hear the first music of this
> 10 Far off, infinite bliss" (*Edwin Arnold*).

Reality of Good.—"*For all that must be called good belongeth to none but the true eternal goodness which is God only*" (*Theologia Germanica*).

Now all that this material world indicates of good is real; the love, the life, the beauty, the joy, etc.[1] We get at times glorious glimpses of this 15 reality through the mist; wonderful love, marvellous beauty, unspeakable joy. "For now we see through a glass darkly" (I Cor. 13:12), and "through every grass-blade the glory of the present God still beams" (Carlyle). "Earth's crammed with heaven and every common bush afire with God," Mrs. Browning has said. As we progress, the mist gets thinner, and with 20 the millennium dawns a foretaste of God's world. To limit future good is unquestionably to limit God. Matter, apparently hinting the existence of the spiritual realities, only hides their perfection from us, giving us a false sense of the real world, and as the matter is dematerialised the glorious realities of these perfect ideas gradually appear clearer and clearer.

25 "The ideal is the real well seen" (Carlyle). "The realities of existence can be conceived, and they are probably assisting us, stimulating and guiding us in ways of which we are only half conscious, and some of us not conscious at all" (Sir Oliver Lodge).

> "A thing of beauty is a joy forever;
> 30 Its loveliness increases; it will never
> Pass into nothingness"   (*Keats*).

Pope little knew the depth that lay behind his words "One truth is clear, whatever is, is right."

Proof of Our Knowledge of Heaven.—"*That one who, outside pure 35 mathematics, pronounced the word* impossible, *is wanting in prudence. Reserve is above all a necessity when he is dealing with the animal organisation*" (Arago).

The way to prove whether or not your knowledge of heaven [2] is true is this: if anything is going wrong in the material world, and you realise

---

40 [1] "We do not see much of the real man here, for he is God's man; while ours is man's man" (*Unity of Good*, p. 46, Mary Baker Eddy).

[2] Jesus gave seven parables explanatory of the kingdom of heaven, and in reply to the question of the disciples, "Why speakest thou unto them in parables? He answered and said unto them. Because it is given unto you to know the mysteries 45 of the kingdom of heaven, but to them it is not given" (Matt. 13:10, 11). At the end "Jesus saith unto them, Have ye understood all these things? They say unto him, Yea, Lord. Then said he unto them, Therefore every scribe which is instructed unto the kingdom of heaven is like unto a man that is a householder, which bringeth forth out of his treasure things new and old" (Matt. 13:51, 52).

clearly enough the spiritual perfection of the reality, of which that "wrong" is the counterfeit, the instantaneous disappearance of the trouble will indicate your realisation to have been correct. This means that the difficulty in the material world is immediately put right. This is one important difference between true knowledge and that put forward by the 5 various schools of religious thought; namely, that you are now able to prove your theory by direct experiment, and have not to rely solely upon logical deduction.

Another important difference is that, if the mortal called "you" is thinking scientifically, realising constantly that you—your real spiritual 10 self, not a material "you"—are led by God, then, through the action of God in destroying evil, the mortal "you" appears to be led by God, the Principle of good, just in the way that a young child is taught and protected by its mother when learning first to walk. The "you" may have its troubles and difficulties, but there is steady progress, and every now and 15 then "you" will pause and recognise with satisfaction the progress made, of which "you" were not conscious at the time of the struggle, when the mental faculties were clouded as the "you" passed along, battling its way through a seeming mist of wrong thoughts.

Movement Instantaneous.—"*All stars and mountain peaks are* 20 *thoughts of the Eternal Mind*" (Paracelsus).

Being a mental world, man can go instantly from what, to use material symbols, may be called place to place, in heaven. There is no necessity for such apparent bodily action as accompanies physical movement from place to place. A man moves mentally. For instance, one spiritual being 25 can draw the attention of another spiritual being to the spiritual reality of what is in the material world called the planet Mars. Instantly both have all the effect of what may be called being in Mars; that is to say, without any other movement but the mental one, they are conscious of some of the perfect ideas of the spiritual reality of the planet Mars. When 30 the thought of this spiritual planet or "compound idea" [1] comes to a man, it does not appear as something distant. He is fully conscious of, and shares with his fellow-man, all the beauties that are delighting him, to an infinitely greater degree than the human being does when in the midst of beautiful surroundings. 35

When the enjoyment has been obtained from being conscious of these lovely ideas, the other spiritual being, desirous of returning the happiness that he has received, and being reminded of past enjoyment of heavenly beauties, can draw the attention of his fellow-man to the spiritual reality of some ideas in another planet, say Jupiter. All that is necessary, then, is 40 to think of those ideas, and at once they are both conscious of the new ideas connected with the spiritual reality of Jupiter.

Practical Results an Undeniable Proof.—"*Let us not reject experience on the ground of dogmatic assertion and baseless speculation*" [2] (Sir Oliver Lodge). 45

---

[1] *Science and Health*, p. 585, Mary Baker Eddy.
[2] "Christian Revelation from a Scientific Point of View." Address delivered before the National Free Church Council at Portsmouth, March 9, 1911.

3*

The proof of the above being true is found through its practical application. If in the material world you find that you have lost your train or apparently have not time to go from one place to another, you can get over the difficulty by turning in thought to God, denying the reality of the
5 trouble and realising that in heaven man goes instantly from one idea to another, or you can realise that man is always in the right place. Then, through this reversal of thought and your recognition of the action of God as taking place in heaven, the wrong ethereal thoughts that appear as forms of trouble are destroyed, and you find yourself out of the difficulty,
10 although you cannot be certain that what usually happens will occur. For instance, sometimes you will find on going to the station that there is another train that you knew nothing about, sometimes that a slip-coach has been put on to a later express, or the difficulty disappears in some other way. Sometimes the unrecognised action of God results in your finding that
15 there has been no need to go at all, and that the object of your going has been effected in some unexpected way.

Perfect Sequence of Thought.—In heaven an individual called, never says he cannot come, but it is always exactly the thing most desirable, as there is always a perfect sequence of thought, and the two with mutual
20 rejoicings blend in true unity of joint appreciation of the wonderful ideas of God. To indicate the perfect sequence of thought it may be stated that when you have finished listening to, for instance, a glorious sonata—we have to use material expressions—and are called to admire a beautiful piece of scenery, this scenery is an exact visual (we must again,
25 unfortunately, use a material expression) representation of the sonata, and a further unfoldment of perfection. Whatever one does, it brings infinite happiness to all concerned. In this material world we move with trouble and even danger from one place to another, and often, whilst thinking of something totally inconsequent, politely cover a yawn with our
30 hand whilst our neighbour points out what he thinks the beauties of nature.

Indication of Spiritual Realities.—

" *What if earth,*
Be but the shadow of heaven, and things therein,
Each to each other like, more than on earth is thought" (Milton).

35 Everything in the material world only counterfeits and "hints the existence of spiritual reality." For instance, the spiritual reality of the hand is the power to grasp an idea. The reality of the teeth is the *capacity* to analyse and dissect the ideas; your material digestive organs counterfeit the power with which you digest, assimilate, and understand the ideas, and
40 the arm counterfeits the power with which, in the reality, you re-present them, that is, call the attention of your fellow-man to them, or pass them on. The spiritual reality of the lower limbs is the power to move in thought from idea to idea. That is, as mentioned, you can call the attention of your fellow-man to lovely ideas, even the spiritual reality of any planet or
45 star, and directly you think of them you have all the effect of being there and enjoying them together.

Man being made in the image and likeness of God, every aspect of God has its reflection in him. Consequently, the reflection of every aspect is counterfeited by some portion of the material man. These are all the portions inside the body. The limbs counterfeit the different powers of the spiritual man, and the different parts of the head the various capacities.

There are three great aspects of God—Life, Truth, and Love. So, there are three important organs in man which counterfeit the real organs 5 of the spiritual man. The real spiritual lungs are the reflection of God as Life, through which man receives the ideas of God; the liver, the reflection of God as Truth, through which man arranges the ideas, and groups them together into new combinations, to be re-presented to his fellow-man; the heart, the reflection of God as Love, through which the circulation of the 10 ideas goes on as man calls the attention of his fellow-man to the ideas he is enjoying, so that he participates in such enjoyment. This is an indication from which each person can himself work out the other details as occasion demands. Further details are given in the Appendix (p. 367).

A World of Four Dimensions.—"*And I saw a new heaven and a* 15 *new earth: . . . the holy city, new Jerusalem, . . . Having the glory of God: . . . and the city lieth four-square, . . . And there shall be no more curse: but the throne of God and of the Lamb shall be in it*" (Rev. 21:1, 2, 11, 16; and 22:3).

For some years, reasoning from the analogy of an imaginary two- 20 dimensional being, conscious only of length and breadth, and unable to recognise height or depth, or anything above or below him, and therefore unconscious of the appearance of this three-dimensional world, various thinkers have suggested that there might be a world of four dimensions, of which the seeming three-dimensional man was equally 25 unconscious.[1] It has been suggested that this fourth dimension is "time." It may be more accurately expressed as spiritual infinity. Now heaven may be described mathematically as a world of four dimensions, wholly spiritual.[2] Everything that we see now as three-dimensional is only ethereal, namely, the real four-dimensional world seen wrongly from a 30 false material standpoint, since the material man is only conscious of three dimensions of it, and that consciousness itself is false and absolutely misleading. "The eye is not made to see everything. It picks out of the ocean of forms that which is accessible to it and believes this artificial limit to be the real limit. What we know of a living being is only a part of 35 its real form" (*The Evolution of Matter*, Dr. Le Bon).[3]

---

[1] See *Flat Land*, by Dr. Abbot; *Another World*, by A. T. Schofield, M.D.; *Scientific Romances* by C. H. Hinton; *Nature*, May 1, 1873, by G. F. Rodwell; *Messenger of Mathematics*, 1891, Vol. XXI, p. 20, by W. W. Rouse Ball; *American Journal of Mathematics*, 1880, Vol. III, p. 1, by Stringham. See also article in the 40 *Wintonian*, February, 1910, by R. A. T.; *The Art of Creation*, by E. Carpenter; *A New Era of Thought*, by C. H. Hinton; Professor Caley's Presidential Address to the British Association; Cajori's *History of Mathematics*; *Mathematical Recreations and Essays*, by W. W. Rouse Ball; *Modern Views of Matter*, by Sir William Crookes. 45

[2] "Christian Science translates Mind, God, to mortals. It is the infinite calculus defining the line, plane, space, and fourth dimension of Spirit" (*Miscellaneous Writings*, p. 22, Mary Baker Eddy). See also *Science and Health*, p. 575, l. 21.

[3] In Dr. Gustave Le Bon's book, *The Evolution of Matter*, over 12,000 copies of which were sold in France in the first two years, and the English translation of 50

"If, therefore, we find the subject becomes more thinkable by assuming, say, a fourth-dimensional being than by following the ramifications of 'matter and force' into infinite space and time, we are quite justified in adopting the former method" (*The Art of Creation*, E. Carpenter).
5 Though doubtful assumption is better than nothing, definite knowledge is an absolute necessity for true progress.

In the same way that an imaginary two-dimensional being, appearing like a small, flat object, and only seeing the soles of your boots on the floor, would describe you as a straight line, say, 11 inches long, 3 inches
10 wide, black, sometimes muddy, going about with a twin-brother—the fellow sole—and constantly appearing and disappearing; so does the three-dimensional man describe his neighbour quite wrongly until he knows the truth. Should the two-dimensional being describe "the soles of the boots" as having no intelligence, no feeling, and being of little use, he
15 would make the same mistake that we do if, talking of our fellow-man, we describe him as an ignorant fool, or otherwise, as it is called, malpractise, that is, "think" in a derogatory way of him.

If the sharpened point of a pencil, held vertically, point upward, were placed by the side of this two-dimensional being, he would see it as a very
20 short line. As the pencil was raised he would see this line increasing in length, and might speak of it as "growing." When the pencil had been sufficiently raised, he would see nothing, and might speak of it as dead. So in this three-dimensional world do we get a false sense of birth, growth, and death. Every tree, for instance, as it apparently grows, is merely an
25 exhibition of certain phenomena, preconceived as material so-called facts, and self-raised by the universal thought on the subject of vegetable growth.

In his Presidential Address to the British Association, Professor Caley, the famous mathematician, declared his belief that every mathematical
30 truth has an objective correlative in the world, that is, may actually describe a state of equilibrium. Taking, for instance, a suspension bridge, you can mathematically set out the tension of a wire, the pressure of the wind, the elasticity of the metal, etc. The truth at the back of Professor Caley's statement is one of the proofs that the fourth dimension exists,
35 for this mathematical theory has been developed to a very considerable degree.

In the *Wintonian*, of February, 1910, is an article on the Fourth Dimension, by R. A. T. He states: "To put it very briefly, the knowledge is a real and working knowledge, and the fourth dimension would enable
40 us to move in defiance of the present known limitations of space." So-called occult results are not, however, due to action in four-dimensional

which was published in 1907, were put forward various original theories. These at the time met with a perfect storm of obloquy, which has long since died away in the light of advancing knowledge. Many valuable papers of his have been communi-
45 cated by him to the Royal Academy of Belgium, of which he is a Member, and elsewhere, between the years 1901 and 1906, when he published his paper on "black light." It will be found that he confirms many of the statements now made, which a few years ago would have been thought absolute impossibilities. The most important points are his confirmation of the details of the dematerialisation of
50 matter and energy, first put forward publicly in a lecture given by me in 1901.

space, as they merely exhibit the phenomena of a three-dimensional world that are not generally cognised by the limited physical senses. Such results are solely concerned with matter in its finest ethereal form, invisible under normal human conditions, and have nothing to do with the real world, heaven.

It is significant that C. H. Hinton, in his recent book, *A New Era of Thought*, suggests that the birth, growth, life, and death of animals are explainable by suggesting that an animal's life is simply the pheno-menon of a four-dimensional being passing through a three-dimensional world. This is interesting, because there is nothing to show that an animal may not be a limited sense of a real, spiritual being. He also says: "After many years of work, during which the conception of four-dimensional bodies lay absolutely dark, at length, by a certain change of plan, the whole subject of four-dimensional existence became perfectly clear and easy to impart."

The writer of the article in the *Wintonian* says: "I may say that I devoted no little time some years ago to an effort to comprehend the fourth dimension, according to Hinton's directions, but it was a failure."

All such efforts must prove failures whilst there is any confusion, as in the case of Hinton, between (1) The human, material, three-dimensional thought-forms that Hinton recognised were all around us, although unseen by those who are not psychic, that is, whose sight is not sufficiently devel-oped, and (2) The spiritual reality, of which these and all other material "thoughts" are but counterfeits.

The following short quotation from Cajori's *History of Mathematics* will express briefly some results of the fourth dimension, showing that the four-dimensional world cannot possibly be subject to material limitations. "Newcomb, the American astronomer, showed the possibility of turning a closed material shell inside out by simple flexure, without either stretch-ing or tearing; Klein pointed out that in the fourth dimension knots could not be tied; Veronese showed that a body could be removed from a closed room without breaking the walls; C. S. Peirce proved that a body in four-dimensional space either rotates about two axes at once, or cannot rotate without losing one of its dimensions."

W. W. Rouse Ball puts forward some interesting views with regard to a four-dimensional world, which he says "affords an explanation of some difficulties in our physical sciences."[1] William Sidis, a boy aged 10, who appears to be a mathematical prodigy, delivered a lecture before the Harvard Mathematical Club, in which he put forward some new theories regarding the fourth dimension. Sir William Crookes, F.R.S., writes: "To show how far we have been propelled on the strange new road, how dazzling are the wonders that waylay the researcher, we have but to recall—Matter in a fourth state. . . ."[2]

These references will show how mathematicians are endeavouring to gain a knowledge of a four-dimensional world.

[1] *Mathematical Recreations and Essays.*
[2] "Modern Views of Matter." Address before the Congress of Applied Chemistry at Berlin, 1903.

Counterfeits and Symbols.—"*The invisible things of him* [God] *from the creation of the world are clearly seen, being understood by the things that are made, even his eternal power and Godhead*" (Rom. 1:20.) "*For Christ is not entered into the holy places made with hands, which are*
5 *the figures of the true; but into heaven itself*" (Heb. 9:24).

Man is spiritual and four-dimensional. The apparent material man is not real, but is purely illusionary. "The ideal, after all, is truer than the real, for the ideal is the eternal element in perishable things; it is their type, their sum, their *raison d'être*" (Amiel). "And things are not what
10 they seem" (Longfellow). "Matter, motion, and force, are not the reality, but the symbols of reality" (Herbert Spencer).

A material world of three dimensions only, is visible to the material senses,[1] consequently everything about you is simply something connected with your spiritual self seen falsely, seen materially, a counterfeit of the
15 spiritual reality.[2] "There is a natural body, and there is a spiritual body. . . . The first man is of the earth, earthy: the second man is the Lord from heaven" (I Cor. 15:44, 47). "We have a building of God, an house not made with hands, eternal in the heavens" (II Cor. 5:1).

Charles Kingsley said: "The belief is coming every day stronger with
20 me that all symmetrical objects are types of some spiritual truth or existence. Everything seems to be full of God's reflex, if we could but see it. Oh! to see, if but for a moment, the whole harmony of the great system; to hear once the music that the whole universe makes as it performs His bidding." Plato, in the *Phædras*, says: "The higher qualities
25 which are precious to souls . . . are seen through a glass dimly; and they are few who, going to the images, behold in them the realities, and they only with difficulty." St. Paul says: "For now we see through a glass darkly" (I Cor. 13:12). Professor Drummond said: "Nature . . . is a working model of the Spiritual." It is a very poor counterfeit model.
30 "The world constructed with the impressions of our senses is a summary translation, and necessarily a far from faithful one of the real world which we know not" (*The Evolution of Forces*, Dr. G. Le Bon).

All must gain the knowledge of the real man, of our real selves. "So in man's self arise august anticipation, symbols, types, of a dim splendour,
35 ever on before" (R. Browning). The Revelator, seeing in advance what is about to happen, writes: "The kingdoms of this world are become the

---

[1] In the poem known as the *Odes of Solomon*, which the Bishop of Ossory states was composed between A.D. 150 and 200 for the ritual use of newly-baptised Christians, the following appears: "The likeness of what is below is that which is
40 above; for everything is above; what is below is nothing but the imagination of those who are without knowledge."
"To my sense, we have not seen all of man; he is more than personal sense can cognise, who is the image and likeness of the infinite" (*Miscellaneous Writings*, p. 97, Mary Baker Eddy).
45 [2] "Every creation or idea of Spirit has its counterfeit in some matter belief. Every material belief hints the existence of spiritual reality; and if mortals are instructed in spiritual things, it will be seen that material belief, in all its manifestations, reversed, will be found the type and representative of verities, priceless, eternal, and just at hand. The education of the future will be instruction in spiritual
50 Science, against the material symbolic counterfeit sciences" (*Miscellaneous Writings*, p. 60).

kingdoms of our Lord" (Rev. 11:15). "Upon the heights we see that every act and every thought are infallibly bound up with something great and immortal" (Maeterlinck).

"For anything that may be proved to the contrary, there may be a real something which is the cause of all our impressions; that sensations, 5 though not likenesses, are symbols of that something; and that the part of that something, which we call the nervous system, is an apparatus for supplying us with a sort of algebra of fact, based on these symbols" (Professor Huxley). This something that Huxley so indefatigably searched after has been proved to be God, the Principle of all good "the great I 10 AM; Principle; Mind; Soul; Spirit; Life; Truth; Love; all substance; intelligence"; [1] and the only cause.

Swedenborg spoke of correspondences, but confused heaven with a false belief in "spirit" appearances, as it is clear from his writings that he thought the spiritual world was visible around us under certain material 15 conditions. He had not learned that the things seen by him, which he thought were spiritual, were merely materialised "thoughts" in their more ethereal and less tangible form, and he imagined that there were at least three worlds, the material, the spiritual, and the divine. Plato said that the Ideas were the real things, while mundane objects were only 20 illusive forms, and wrote: "For nothing can have any sense except by reason of that of which it is the shadow." As is well known, he gave to Ideas the greatest import, and said: "They existed before the world [the material world] and the world was created after their pattern" (*Timaeus*). 25

Edward Carpenter writes in *The Art of Creation* as follows: "With Plato the great ruling ideas were Justice, Temperance, Beauty, and the like. But he also considered that there were ideas or patterns, eternal in the heavens, of all tribes and creatures in the world, as of trees, animals, men, and the lesser gods; and he even went so far as to suppose ideas of 30 things made by man's artifice, such as beds and tables (see *Republic*, Book X). Certainly it sounds a little comic at first to hear the 'absolute essential Bed' spoken of, and Plato has been considerably berated by many folk for his daring in this matter. He has been accused of confounding the idea of a bed with the concept of a bed; it has been said, too, that 35 if there are ideas of beds and tables, trees and animals, there must also be archetypes in heaven of pots and pans—absolutely essential worms, beetles, and toadstools, and so forth. Plato, however, had no doubt considered these difficulties, and it may be worth while for our purpose to pause a moment over them." "Man himself and his nature is rooted deep 40 in the nature of God, from whom he springs—and so may we not say that in some sense the idea of bed is rooted in the ultimate reality and nature of things? . . . But anyhow, it is an attempt to show how the Platonic ideas may be brought into some sort of line and harmony with modern science and philosophy. And it enables us dimly to see how the great 45 panorama of creation has come forth, ever determining and manifesting itself from within through the disclosure, from point to point and from

[1] *Science and Health*, p. 587, Mary Baker Eddy.

time to time, of ever-new creative feelings or ideas—the whole forming an
immense hierarchy, culminating in the grandest, most universal, Being
and Life."

This quotation shows how advanced thinkers of the present day are
5 endeavouring to get at the truth, which daily gleams brighter through the
mist of matter.

Natural Laws merely Memoria Technica.—"*If nothing is to be
called science but that which is exactly true from beginning to end, I am afraid
there is very little science in the world outside mathematics. Among the physical
10 sciences I do not know that any could claim more than that each is true within
certain limits, so narrow that, for the present at any rate, they may be
neglected*" (Professor Huxley).

Our views of so-called natural laws, and of our so-called ascertained
facts, have constantly been changing, and such laws must be looked upon
15 as merely a gigantic system of *memoria technica*, made use of to arrive
rapidly at conclusions. A scientific man working from a material basis, can,
by deduction, answer innumerable questions, merely because he has a
recognised system of so-called natural laws, to which he has recourse, and
by which he deduces his results. He could not recollect even a small
20 percentage of these results if he had to rely upon his memory for them.
Every now and then he ascertains a new fact, or series of facts, and then
has to alter his theories in order to fit in these facts. Otherwise he would
not be safe in drawing conclusions from such theories.

Professor Drummond writes: "The Laws of Nature are simply state-
25 ments of the orderly conditions of things in Nature, what is found in
Nature by a sufficient number of competent observers. What these Laws
are in themselves is not agreed. That they have any absolute existence even
is far from certain. . . . But that they have any causal connection with
the things around is not to be conceived." Natural science and its material
30 laws are merely objective states of a false mentality. Professor S. P.
Langley believed that the "Laws of Nature" are merely mental conceptions, and wrote: "The so-called 'Laws of Nature' are from within—
laws of our own minds" (*Smithsonian Report*).

Signor Marconi, at a banquet given in his honour by the American
35 Institute of Electrical Engineers, said: "Whenever matter had to be
considered there could be no exact law of action." [1] Professor Jevons has
said: "The utmost successes which our scientific method can accomplish
will not enable us to comprehend more than an infinitesimal fraction of
what there doubtless is to comprehend."

40 Only a short time ago Faraday said that if even a straw could be moved
by will-power,[2] then his conception of the universe would be altered, but
he considered such a thing as absolutely incredible. Yet Sir Oliver Lodge,

---

[1] From article entitled "The End of Matter" in the *New York Evening Sun*
of March 24, 1906.
45 [2] Recently I was taken to see a lady who was able to cause a suspended cylinder
to rotate rapidly merely by means of her "mind." She thought that the action was
magnetic through electricity passing from her finger tips, until I proved to her that
the movement could be stopped directly I realised that there was "nothing but
God." See also page 192, line 44.

speaking to the British Association recently, asked how do we know that "a body may not be moved without material contact by an act of will? . . . I venture to say that there is something here not provided for in the orthodox scheme of physics, that modern physics is not complete."

These so-called laws of matter are merely "modes of material motion," 5 the individual's false sense of the real laws of God; and they therefore vary with individuals. God's laws are invariable and inviolable because God is Principle, the foundation of all law and order, and God always works through moral and spiritual law, the immutable and eternal law of good, and by none other. 10

Only those who have made a study of the subject, and are in constant touch with advanced thinkers, recognise what a marvellous change is at the present time taking place all over the world. Old ideas are fast disappearing. Natural science stands expectant, awaiting developments. The Science of God awaits us. 15

SECTION TWO

A CONSISTENT THEORY OF MATERIAL PHENOMENA

"We are, it appears, on the very verge of the discovery of a greater inte-
gration, as Professor Richet, the learned President of the Society for Psychical
5 *Research, believes, which shall include all the psychical classes of phenomena*
which I have mentioned, but which shall not yet itself be any single one of them.
It will include spiritualism, it will include clairvoyance, and telepathy, and
prevision, but yet not be any one of these things. It will harmonise, and sur-
round, and interpret all these mysteries and many more; and this is the trend
10 *of psychology to-day, and is the apology for these chapters"* (*Spirit and Matter*
before the Bar of Modern Science, J. W. Heysinger, M.D.).

In making public the elaborate detail of the human consciousness and
its undreamed-of possibilities, a serious question confronts us at the
outset. Whilst scarcely one-millionth part of possible good is known, it
15 is equally true that only a small fraction of the possible practice of evil has
ever been dreamed of, and much less attempted. It is impossible to state
the truth adequately without exposing the possibilities of evil. We lie
between Scylla and Charybdis. Are we to suppress the knowledge of good
on account of the fear of evil? The present condition of the world renders
20 it essential to expose false mental working, and show how harmful it is to
all concerned, even at the risk of mistakenly being thought to bring about
a certain amount of evil. All mystery surrounding phenomena must be
thoroughly cleared up to prevent a far greater danger. As the power of
evil, even in its highest apparent seething activity, is but as darkness before
25 the sun of omnipotence, the needful throwing of light on hidden evil will
never be feared by those who understand enough to avail themselves of
the omnipotence of Truth.

"Even now we are only beginning to understand; for we are in the
morning of the times. The human race is a recent comer to the earth,
30 and its palmy days lie in the future. There is an immense amount still
to be discovered. Science [material science] is modern, a thing of yesterday, full of hope and promise, rather than of achievement. Much has been
done, but we are still only, as it were, scratching the surface. There are
things even now being dreamed of in philosophy, which were once out-
35 side its pale altogether. Philosophy is becoming a far more comprehensive thing than it used to be" (Sir Oliver Lodge, D.SC., LL.D., F.R.S.).

Scientific Forecasts.—Huxley's prophecy, that the next great
discovery would be in the realm of mind, has been fulfilled. It is certain
that it would be comparatively easy to fulfil another of his prophecies,
40 namely, that soon it would be possible to measure the strength of a thought
as we measure the power of a steam engine.

The following wonderful prophecy of another of the world's greatest
thinkers and searchers after truth, Charles Darwin, has already been fulfilled: "In the future I see open fields for far more important researches.

Psychology will be securely based on the foundation already well laid by Mr. Herbert Spencer, that of the necessary acquirement of each mental power and capacity by gradation. Much light will be thrown on the origin of man and his history" (*Origin of Species*).

All over the world are little knots of people studying the apparent 5 action of the so-called human "mind" and getting results of almost every description. All sorts of incorrect and incomplete theories have been put forward, and such theories are getting nearly as numerous as the religions of the present day. Professor Lombroso's recent book, *After Death— What?* is an instance of the utter fog in which many of the really able men 10 of the world are seemingly enveloped. It is time that the light of Truth should be turned upon these conflicting false theories, so that men may know how to act intelligently.

"Exposure is Nine Points of Destruction."[1]—Having undertaken to prove the *truly* scientific foundation, upon which everything of importance 15 in this book is based, there is now placed before you a consistent theory of the web of illusory material phenomena. This exposes the fallacies that have bound us, discloses the final and fundamental so-called basis of this material world and its hitherto inexplicable phenomena, and clears away all doubt as to its inevitable total disappearance by the recognition of 20 spiritual reality. "A bare fact is nothing, or little, till it is clad in theory" (Sir Oliver Lodge). "Whatever the difficulties in discerning new truths, there are still greater ones in getting them recognised" (Lamarck).

In the forthcoming explanation of the so-called action of the material world, it should be clearly understood that this theory, whilst giving a 25 system of sufficiently legitimate *memoria technica* to help us to arrive rapidly at conclusions, is correct but not true, being simply the logical outcome of the theories generally accepted as true, when forced to their ultimate conclusion. The real position is, that there is no material movement of any kind or description, no action, reaction, or interaction of 30 particles; in fact, there are no material particles in this seeming world. It is not sufficient to state this. The fact must be proved that these seemingly moving pictures, with all their discordant detail, are not real, and therefore can be made to disappear. These pictures are hypothetical, ethereal impressions, which seem to be flitting through the human 35 consciousness, and are only the real or spiritual world seen falsely, seen materially, by counterfeits or suppositional opposite beings in a suppositional opposite world. Professor William James suggests, in speaking of the "stream of consciousness," that "the thoughts themselves are thinkers." This is true; the thinker and the thoughts are one.   40

Cinematographic Pictures.—The whole of this material world is simply a series of cinematographic pictures, the men, animals, trees, in fact, all so-called life, being merely ethereal counterfeits. These forms have no more life or intelligence in them than the pictures on a cinematographic screen. They are merely shifting appearances. Such so-called material 45 beings have apparently powers of thinking, reasoning, deducing and acting

[1] *No and Yes*, p. 24, Mary Baker Eddy.

upon such deductions; whereas, as a matter of fact, these so-called material
personalities are merely individualisations of illusory, basic false mentality,
and counterfeits of the spiritual perfect beings.

So-called Thinking Merely "Picturing."—One cannot correctly
5 speak of a so-called human being as "thinking." "Picturing" would be a
more accurate expression. The true people are perfect spiritual beings in a
perfect world, governed by a perfect God, eternally manifesting divine
wisdom.

Material Phenomena.—The word "phenomenon" has been used
10 for ages by philosophers to express that which is apparent to the senses
or human consciousness—and which is ever changing in appearance—as
distinguished from its substance or actual constitution, called
"noumenon," that is, what really exists.

The only object in giving publicity to the following theory is to educate
15 false thought out of itself—falsely called man—and show how
"phenomena" are merely fleeting ethereal impressions capable of instantaneous destruction, either before, after, or during the moment that they
appear to impinge upon the consciousness. In this way we prove the non-
reality of all so-called matter, and the present eternal reality of God, good.
20 "Every great advance in the sciences consists of a vast generalisation
revealing deep and subtle analogies" (Jevons).

A Consistent Theory a Safe Temporary Guide.—There will now
be put before you a complete theory, evolved by following to their definite
ultimate conclusions the scientific premises to which for many ages a
25 universal assent has been given, and by the grouping together of ideas,
some not yet presented to the world, which are the result of the latest work
of leading thinkers. Into this theory you will find that all the new so-called
material facts recently brought to light will fit. So far, this theory has been
a safe guide when new material phenomena, and hitherto unknown so-
30 called causes, have had to be dealt with. It will also be of value to others
who have not as yet had an opportunity of investigating such matters, and
find themselves in a difficulty, as we are all liable to do when facing
seeming mystery.

But little of this theory is new. Nearly the whole of it you will find
35 has been given to the world, at one time or another, by theologians,
philosophers, scientific men, and seers. My work has only been the
winnowing of the chaff by the light of the knowledge of God. "For it is
not ye that speak, but the Spirit of your Father which speaketh in you"
(Matt. 10:20).
40   The purpose of modern science has been defined as "The intellectual
unification of the mind of man and the mind of God." Emerson expressed
it as "The extension of man on all sides, into Nature, till his hands should
touch the stars, his eyes see through the earth, his ears understand the
language of beast and bird, and, through his sympathy, heaven and earth
45 should talk with him." But even such a development of a material consciousness, apart from an increasing study and knowledge of God, would
only extend man's present material and mortal experience. It would in no

way lessen sin, disease, or death. This has been evidenced by many abnormal individual developments in the history of the world.

It is necessary that an accurate view of the so-called material world be formed, instead of the present almost universally accepted fallacious view, *in order that we may all learn how properly to reverse false thoughts of it and* 5 *so gain dominion over it,* and obtain the power to destroy all evil as it enters our consciousness. Mrs. Eddy, under the marginal heading "Fallacious Hypotheses," says, "Science must go over the whole ground, and dig up every seed of error's sowing" (*Science and Health*, p. 79).

Every false sense of the action of Mind must be uncovered before it 10 can be universally destroyed by the action of Truth. Every seed that has been falsely conceived of and implanted in the human consciousness, will assuredly have to be exposed by someone as having been a lie from the beginning, before universal salvation can be achieved. The more we understand of the power of thought, the more we shall recognise the importance 15 of this. It is a mistake to imagine that every individual has to "dig up every seed," which the whole, as a whole, is responsible for spreading. Each man fills his niche, and one intelligent exposure of even one generally accepted mistake may bring its opposite truth to the comprehension of a world. God apportions to each his work and each is individually blessed 20 only as he fulfils it.

At the commencement of my examination into metaphysical healing I found a number of results that were quite inexplicable, according to the ordinary theory of matter. The atomic theory, propounded by Epicurus, and elaborated by the poet Lucretius, was still accepted by the majority 25 of people, although Thomson and others had seen that the ordinarily accepted idea of the atom could not be correct.[1] I remember, after reading Professor Rücker's defence of the atom in his Presidential Address to the British Association, about seven years ago, saying to myself, "Good-bye, atom." 30

The doctrine of a material evolution and the Darwinian theory,[2] although incomplete, were accepted by scientists, and were largely approved of by theologians. This theory of evolution assumes that in the primal nebula from which this planet evolved, everything potentially existed which in time would visibly belong to it. If you leave out the word 35 "potentially," this will be absolutely accurate, supposing that the material universe had a real existence.

The Ether.—"*Scientific method must begin and end with the laws of thought*" (Professor Jevons).

The first thing that came to me of any importance was that the ether 40 is most accurately viewed from a natural science point of view as consisting of lines of force (high-tension electric currents) at right angles to

---

[1] "The material atom is an outlined falsity of consciousness" (*Unity of Good*, p. 35, Mary Baker Eddy). "The atom of matter is composed of electrons, and nothing else" (*Æther and Matter*, Sir Joseph Larmor). 45
[2] The Darwinian theory is not, as many think, the theory of evolution, which was put forward long before Darwin's time, but his belief in the causes of evolution.

each other[1] (see "Inspiration Scientific," pp. 156–162). Professor Faraday, I learned afterwards, knew this, but did not publish it.[2] Each of these lines of force is so-called vibration, miscalled a thought; their action one upon the other forms matter.[3]

5   Sooner or later an invention will be worked out for utilising the so-called power of the ether. Several have been brought to me to advise upon, but none of the inventors understood really what the power was that they were endeavouring to utilise. Each had different ideas of it. The action and re-action of the lines of force one upon the other tends to cause a particle to 10 revolve. So one day it will be found that there is a hypothetical etheric force always tending to make matter revolve, and this will be what is called utilised.

Thomas A. Edison, when interviewed by the *New York Times*, gave as seventh in a list of probable discoveries, "A new force in nature of 15 some sort or other will be discovered, by which many things not now understood will be explained. We unfortunately have only five senses; if we had eight, we'd know more."

Nikola Tesla in 1891 foresaw that the power of the ether would soon be utilised as a source of ordinary motive power. He wrote: "The time will 20 soon be when it will be accomplished, and the time has come when one may utter such words before an enlightened audience without being con-sidered a visionary. We are whirling through endless space with incon-ceivable speed, all around us everything is spinning, everything is moving, everywhere is energy. There must be some way of availing ourselves of 25 this energy more directly."

Sound is supposed to travel at about 1,100 feet per second. The Hertzian waves, according to Maxwell, have a rate of transmission, but not by means of the atmosphere, of from 100,000,000 to 300,000,000 yards per second. Sight and sound are both transmitted, not by the vibration of the atmos-30 phere, but by the vibration of the lines of force of which the ether is composed. In the transmission of light the ether is supposed to vibrate up to at the very least 1,000,000,000,000 oscillations per second to produce violet light. Sir William Crookes says that such statements go to show the infinite power that in reality lies at the back of all so-called force.

35   Dr. Le Bon has commenced to probe the bay of mystery. He says, for

---

[1] "The looms of crime, hidden in the dark recesses of mortal thought, are every hour weaving webs more complicated and subtle . . . they ensnare the age into indolence" (*Science and Health*, p. 102, Mary Baker Eddy).

[2] It is to Faraday that we owe the idea of "lines of force." He was the first 40 to advance in a very cautious manner the ideas regarding them which are now held by many scientists (see *On Faraday as a Discoverer*, by Tyndal. Weekly Evening Meetings, January 17 and 24, 1868. *Proc. Roy. Inst.*, Vol. V). In his Presidential Address to the British Association (1913), Sir Oliver Lodge said that Sir J. J. Thomson's statement as to the ether suggested that it may be fibrous in 45 structure, and a wave run along lines of electric force, as the genius of Faraday surmised might be possible in his *Thoughts on Ray Vibrations*.

[3] "All mass is mass of the ether; all momentum, momentum of the ether; and all kinetic energy, kinetic energy of the ether" (*Electricity and Matter*, Professor J. J. Thomson). "Atomic elements . . . only seem to be nuclei of condensation in the 50 ether. . . . What was to be one day the universe was then only constituted of shapeless clouds of ether" (*The Evolution of Matter*, Dr. Le Bon).

instance, that the sending of a pencil of parallel Hertzian waves to a distance would render war impossible, as not only all the shells and torpedoes
stored in the holds of the enemies' ironclads could be exploded, but also
the stores of powder in the fortresses, and even in the metal cartridges
of the soldiers. He also says that the ship or fortress could not be pro- 5
tected from the action of the Hertzian waves. Now we find that
"thought," being only a high-tension current, the powder could be
exploded also "mentally." This shows to what a crisis the world is now
coming.

It is as a result of a theoretical vibration of the ether that the material 10
man appears to gain knowledge. It is from this vibration of the ether that
we get our material sense of movement. All phenomena are merely
apparent vibration of the ether. "Colour is in us, not in the rose," said
Professor Langley.

Dr. Heysinger, in *Spirit and Matter before the Bar of Modern Science*, 15
writes: "The transmission of light alone, for example, requires a substance so dense or rigid that, in the mass, face to face, as it were, it will
quiver from a state of absolute quiescence into a velocity or rapidity up
to at least 1,000,000,000,000 oscillations in each second of time. It requires
that rapidity to produce the sensation of violet light on the retina, and, in the 20
case of the sun, that this oscillation shall be continuous along a line nearly
a hundred million miles long; for us to see the planet Neptune requires that
the line from the sun to that planet as a relay station must be three thousand
million miles long, and as long again for the wave of reflected light to
travel back to our telescopes. Yet the distance of Neptune is a mere infini- 25
tesimal fraction of the distance from our planet to many of the so-called
fixed stars. The ether, while the substance of all substances in actual
density and resistance, lacks one, and, so far as we know, only one,
property of matter, and that is gravity; . . . to our physical tests it is
without gravity." This is a good illustration of the inconsistency of the 30
present material theory of the universe, which is now believed to be
dependent upon a property found lacking in its original element.

Sir John Herschel, in his paper on *Light*, states that a cubic inch
of this ether, if confined, and relieved from outside pressure, would
have a bursting pressure of more than seventeen billions of pounds to 35
the square inch, and adds: " Do what we will—adopt what hypothesis we
please—there is no escape, in dealing with the phenomena of light, from
these gigantic numbers; or from the conception of enormous physical force
in perpetual exertion at every point through all the immensity of space."
Strike out the word "physical" and change "exertion" to "action," 40
and the latter portion of the statement is correct.

This ether is the theoretical foundation of a supposed material world,
and of all its troubles, and has to be self-destroyed by being short-circuited.[1] Professor Poincaré, a learned French mathematician, and a
member of the Academy of Sciences, writes in *Science and Hypo-* 45
thesis: "A day will come when the ether will be rejected as useless."

[1] "Error, urged to its final limits, is self-destroyed," owing to the action of
"Truth, which sweeps away the gossamer web of mortal illusion" (*Science and
Health*, p. 476, Mary Baker Eddy).

This day has come, and we find the ether not only useless but the suppositious cause of all trouble.[1] Fortunately, this illusory web, with all its fictitious movement and power, whether called ether, devil, or mortal mind, is doomed to disappear.

5   **Material "Thoughts" Lines of Force.**—"*No thought, no feeling, is ever manifested save as the result of a physical force. This principle will before long be a scientific commonplace*" (Herbert Spencer).

The next thing of importance found was that each of these lines of force was what has been called a "thought," and each "thought" a high-
10 tension electrical current vibrating at a different rate. So-called good "thoughts," have a high vibration, and bad "thoughts" a lower speed of vibration. Both are purely material, and even more outside the spectrum than the Marconi or Hertzian waves.

In *Method and Results*, Professor Huxley said: "I believe we shall arrive
15 at a mechanical equivalent of consciousness, just as we have arrived at a mechanical equivalent of heat." What has hitherto been misconceived of as "mind" is now proved to be this "mechanical equivalent of consciousness," the exact opposite of the Mind that is God.

These "thoughts," so-called good, bad, and indifferent, may be said to
20 sweep across the human "mind" of a man all mixed up together. They appear to pass at the rate of about twenty miles an hour.[2] So we find Professor Myers speaking of "The stream of consciousness in which we habitually live."

Each "thought" has a different effect upon the so-called "mind,"
25 which is merely a series of closed electrical circuits vibrating in unison with different "thoughts," as they pass over it, somewhat as the transmitter of a telephone vibrates on account of the passing current, so giving the impression of what are called sound waves.[3] These "thoughts" can be short-circuited[4] and destroyed, as each consists of a series of small oval-
30 shaped particles, a negative electrical charge at one end and a positive charge at the other. By slightly turning one particle they all short-circuit each other to an infinite distance on either side.

Human "Thoughts" Merely External Beliefs.—A mortal does not create "his thoughts." Every so-called thought that ever made a man
35 apparently think, say, or do anything, existed, as far as it could be said to exist, only as an illusive, "non-mental," contradictory opposite to true thoughts, ages (to use the human phraseology) before there was any material sign of human being, or even of what is called the material world. Because of false concepts of time and space, these false beliefs appear as

40   [1] "The ether is doubtless a mysterious agent which we have not yet learnt to isolate; no phenomenon can be explained without it" (*The Evolution of Forces*, Dr. Le Bon).
   [2] "Mortal thoughts chase one another like snowflakes, and drift to the ground" (*Science and Health*, p. 250, Mary Baker Eddy).
45   [3] "Mortal mind is the harp of many strings, discoursing either discord or harmony" *Ibid.*, p. 213).
   [4] To "short-circuit" a current or charge in any given spot is to create a path of comparatively low resistance whereby the current ceases beyond that spot or the charge there disappears.

though spread out over æons of time, cinematographic pictures [1] apparently passing in rapid review as mere mechanical automata. Professor Clifford truly said all unconscious action must be "mechanical and automatic." The human personality is a mere mechanical machine, void of any life or intelligence, and the so-called "mind" is merely a "harp of many strings."

When you really understand what the material world pretends to be, you will recognise that the only things that can harm you are these "thoughts," or false, "non-mental" impressions, which, until they are destroyed, come sweeping over the "stringed" instrument called the human "mind." When you understand this, fear is a thing of the past. How can you possibly be afraid of being harmed by these thoughts when you really understand that they are merely high-tension electrical currents, absolutely powerless when you know how to deal with them! All that a human being can do is to intensify them and to make them seem a little more powerful at the moment. He cannot thereby harm you if your mental work is properly done.

"Thoughts" Intensify Themselves.—When a person is said to be "thinking," [2] that which theoretically happens is, that thought is intensifying itself on the so-called "mind" of the person who is admitting the thought into his consciousness. When a hypnotist, for instance, is hypnotising a person, the thought hypnotises the one who is hypnotising just as much as the one hypnotised. The so-called "mind" of the hypnotiser being a series of closed electrical circuits, the thoughts, sweeping along, intensify themselves by means of this human electrical instrument, and so harm him as much as, or more than, the person who is being directly influenced.

Pain a Mental Effect.—Some years before my investigation of mental healing was commenced, I had to examine into a system for stopping pain electrically, and found that it could be instantly stopped by passing a high-tension electrical current through the nerve, if the current were made and broken with sufficient rapidity. Just over 450 makes and breaks per second were necessary. When the current was cut off the pain returned. Pain is recognised as entirely a mental effect. Marini, the Italian poet, was so engrossed once with his poetry that he was badly burnt before he became aware of it.

When you are in pain you are simply suffering from an individual and collective belief in one special form of evil. If you knew with sufficient certainty to give absolute conviction and confidence, that there is only one God, good, and that good can neither cause nor utilise pain, as it is a

[1] "We hardly do anything else than set going a kind of cinematograph inside us. We may therefore sum up what we have been saying, in the conclusion that the mechanism of our ordinary knowledge is of a cinematographical kind" (*Creative Evolution*, Henri Bergson).

[2] As already stated, "picturing" is a better expression. It was this malicious picturing of evil that Ezekiel referred to when he said: "Thou shalt see greater abominations. . . . Son of man, hast thou seen what the ancients of the house of Israel do in the dark, every man in the chambers of his imagery?" (Ezek. 8:6, 12). These ancients were the first to be destroyed by the "slaughter weapon," the evil thoughts in the latter days (Chap. 9, verse 2).

non-reality, and in reality all is joy, peace, and harmony, it would instantly cease. Instead, we have been educated to believe in the power of evil, and consequently experience the sad results such false belief inevitably brings. This is the punishment for disbelief in God, good, the penalty for breaking
5 the First Commandment. Pain being merely a mental effect, is permanently cured by right thinking. Temporary relief is obtained when wrong thinking is momentarily stopped by an anæsthetic.

The Human Mind.—"*It must be firmly maintained that it is the whole body that is the organ of mind*" [1] (Sir J. Crichton-Browne, M.D.).
10 Each individual so-called mind is merely matter, only of a finer texture than what is generally called matter,[2] and invisible to the normal human sight. It permeates the body as water does a sponge,[3] and is necessarily of the same shape as the denser mass called the body. This material, human "no-mind," a carnal, false mentality, mis-named mind, can
15 become separated from the body, and appear to pass without difficulty through ordinary matter, which is merely materialised false thought, or human belief.

"Thou art a little soul [human mind] bearing about a corpse" (Epictetus). No wonder St. Francis called his body "brother ass."
20 Huxley wrote: "If the hypothetical substance of mind is possessed of energy, I for my part am unable to see how it is to be discriminated from the hypothetical substance of matter."

"Inner experience entitles us to posit the existence of something which is not the brain,[4] nor in any absolute sense the correlate of the brain, but

25 [1] "The Hygienic Uses of Imagination." An Address on Psychology, delivered at the Annual Meeting of the British Medical Association, 1889.
[2] "His body is as material as his mind, and *vice versa*" (*Science and Health*, p. 290, Mary Baker Eddy). Namely, the so-called mind is no mind.
[3] "*Mortal mind* and body combine as one." "Divine Science shows it to be
30 impossible that a material body, though interwoven with matter's highest stratum, misnamed mind, should be man" (*Ibid.*, pp. 409 and 477). Pythagoras seems to be the first to have stated that what he called the soul resembled the body, which died when the soul withdrew. The so-called mind is mistakenly translated in the Bible and spoken of elsewhere as the "soul," which in its root meaning implies Deity,
35 while this false mind forms no part of the real man, being merely a false mentality. Where referring to the material man the word "soul" should be translated "human sense." In A.D. 1562 theology was confused over the apparent facts. Luther wrote: "I permit the Pope to make articles of faith for himself and his faithful—such as the soul is the substantial form of the human body, the soul is immortal,—with all
40 those monstrous opinions to be found in the Roman dunghill of decretals" (*Luther's Works*, Vol. II, fol. 107). The Bible speaks of body, soul, and spirit. The human body and soul are mortal, not part of the real man. God is Spirit, Soul. The manifestation of God, good, as man and universe, can only be spiritual and immortal. John Goodsir, Professor of Anatomy in the University of Edinburgh, who was
45 not only a naturalist, physiologist, and anatomist of European reputation, but also a philosophical psychologist of the first rank, taught that "Man in his constitution consists of three elements—a corporeal, a psychical, and a spiritual"; these he treated as of the Sarx, Psyche, and Pneuma; and that it was in the last of these, and not in his corporeal element, that his personality resided.
50 [4] Several cases have been recently reported by medical men, for instance, by Dr. Etienne Destot, Surgeon to the Tribunal of the Seine, showing that the brain is not indispensable. Dr. Bruch, of Algiers, reports a case where an Arab, after an accident, lived for two months with no brains left, yet showing no signs of brain trouble.

a distinct entity constituting the very self of each of us, the bearer of our conscious states, and the principle of their unity. Moreover, this self is not only a principle of unity in consciousness, but a centre of conscious activity, a something that can produce and experience effects" (The Rt. Hon. Gerald Balfour, late President of the Society for Psychical Research, 5 in the *Hibbert Journal*).

Many leaders in science have recognised that this so-called human mind and body cannot exist permanently.

A Mechanical Concept.—" *The real nature of the relation between mind and brain is unthinkable*" [1] (Sir J. Crichton-Browne, M.D.).   10

No wonder the well-known Thomas A. Edison, deep in the study of matter, is reported to have spoken as follows at a recent interview: "I cannot see any use of a future life. There is no more reason to suppose the human brain—what you call a soul—to be immortal than there is to think that one of my phonographic cylinders is immortal. The brain is a 15 recording office where records are made and stored. It is a mere machine." Mr. Edison, the reporter stated, explained the will-power which drives the brain, as possibly a form of electricity, and declared "whatever it is, it is material." This is perfectly correct with regard to the material man. The true man is God's consciousness, individualised intelligence. Man's 20 innate spirituality can and must be recognised and utilised by the human consciousness, to bring out immediate, harmonious environment and experiences.

A Chemical Concept.—At the recent International Physiological Congress, Reuter reports Professor Charles Richet, of Paris, as saying: 25 "Every person differed, not only mentally, but in chemical constitution from his neighbour. Every illness, every form of poisoning, produced in the blood definite substances, leaving traces which not even years would efface. Every living being was, perchance, a chemical mechanism and nothing more." This latter is true of the human.[2]   30

The Basic False "Mentality."—The individual "conscious mind" is like an island, an "isthmus lordling," in a deep ocean. It appears as separated from all other lands, but on going below the sea it widens and widens until ultimately you find it part of the entire globe, completely connected with every other island. So the so-called "mind" (both in its 35 upper and lower strata) is merely ethereal, materialised thought, and is connected with the "mind," or basic false individuality, of every human being, there being only one "subconscious mind," named for convenience "mortal mind," because it is purely a false, and therefore doomed, "mentality." Scientific men speak of the ether, theologians of the devil. 40 Ether, devil, and mortal "mind," all three are merely different names for the same false concept, and are wholly illusory, a basic false "mentality."

[1] "The Hygienic Uses of Imagination."

Professor Macdonald has recently said to a reporter of the *Daily Mail* (August 4, 1911): "Except for the mind the body would be a piece of mechanism." He 45 differentiates between soul, mind, and brain, and said: "There is at least a possibility that mind is an outside influence, only affecting the brain when the latter is in certain states."

Upon this visionary basis or belief, wrongly called the mind of man, all matter rests, and this "mind" does not respond to any really good thought, that is, thought of God, as it only vibrates with material thoughts, and even this vibration is purely illusory.

5   The "Subconscious Mind."—"*Mind still remains to us an impenetrable mystery*" [1] (Sir J. Crichton-Browne, M.D.).

Later, as demonstrated results disposed of false theories, it became evident that the so-called "subconscious mind," or basic false mentality of each individual, is divided into what, for convenience, may be called 10 "cells" [2] or vibrating diaphragms, and that each thought of sin and each thought of disease has its corresponding cell in the "subconscious mind," which cell, when caused to vibrate, is a temptation of sin, or of disease. Your "subconscious mind" is the part of the ether called "you." Now when your so-called "conscious mind" vibrates synchronously, or in 15 unison with the "subconscious mind," "you" are "conscious" of the vibration, that is, of the impression, whether this is in the form of what is usually called thought, and you think it, or in the form of materialised thought, that is, matter, and you see it; whether these are coming into "consciousness" in the future, called "about to happen," or whether 20 they have already come into "consciousness." When required for a beneficial purpose, this result can be brought about by the action of God through true prayer.

The action of so-called thoughts on the human consciousness is exactly like that of sound on a tuning-fork. If the anger cell is clean, and an angry 25 "thought" passes over a man, it will have no effect; just as the note A will have no effect upon a tuning-fork tuned to the note C. If there are, however, small ultimate particles on the anger cell, when the angry "thoughts" pass over the human mechanism, the cell will vibrate and the man be angry, as the electric particles damp down the cell and allow it to 30 vibrate with the angry thought, just as pitch put on the C tuning-fork will lower its note so that it vibrates with the lower note A. When the action of God, ever-active good, has obliged these particles, which are electrical, to short-circuit themselves, then the cell, being freed from them,[3] will only vibrate with higher thoughts—thoughts of love, etc., just as the tuning-35 fork, when the pitch is cleaned off, or some of the metal filed away, will vibrate with higher vibrations. When the "consciousness" is attuned rightly, low vibrations, such as so-called thoughts of disease or hate, will not act upon it and thereby show their effect upon the body. The material

---

[1] "The Hygienic Uses of Imagination."
40 [2] "So long as any hospitality is given to the unideal within, so long will the tempting voices without be given a hearing. When, however, through patient efforts the courts of consciousness are made inaccessible to every unholy thought, the seductions of objective evil will have lost their charm and the true freedom of right choice will have been obtained" ("Selective Living," by John Willis, in 45 *Christian Science Sentinel*, August 28, 1909).
[3] " . . . . mortals should so improve material belief by thought tending spiritually upward as to destroy materiality" (*Science and Health*, p. 545, Mary Baker Eddy). "The vibrations of the ether . . . represent the last stage of the dematerialisation of matter, the one preceding its final disappearance" (*The* 50 *Evolution of Matter*, Dr. Le Bon).

body, and indeed, as will soon be recognised, the whole environment, expresses the condition of the individual human "consciousness," and improves instantly that it is purified, or that the thoughts are changed for the better by the cessation or destruction of the wrong thoughts, leaving the better, or so-called good thoughts, the higher vibrations, to become 5 apparent.[1] These particles cannot get on the cells again.

The Material Body.—*"Materialism is simply a logical blunder"* (Sir J. Crichton-Browne, M.D.).

The material body is merely a massing together of electrons,[2] which take the shape of and have their apparent movement through the action of 10 "thoughts" on the so-called human "mind," and which a little time after death alter their grouping by decomposition.[3]

> "For of the soul [human consciousness] the body form doth take,
> For soul is form, and doth the body [more solid matter] make"
> (*Edmund Spenser*).   15

"Every right action and true thought sets the seal of its beauty on person and face, and every wrong action and foul thought its seal of distortion" (John Ruskin).

The Electron.—Later on I found that at some of the places where these lines of force, or electrical high-tension currents cross, the inter- 20 action of these lines, one upon the other, forms the electron, or, as chemists have called it, the ion, which is believed by scientific men to be the smallest particle of matter.[4] These electrons, which, as Mr. Arthur Balfour mentioned, when President of one of the British Association Meetings, are spoken of as a stress in the ether, are simply a twist in the two cross lines of 25 force caused by their mutual attraction. They are vibration in two dimensions instead of one, at the junction of the two lines of force. As the union of the male and female is apparently required in the animal, vegetable, and mineral kingdoms to produce so-called life, so it requires the junction of two lines of force and the interaction of positive and negative 30 polarity to produce the electron, the smallest particle of matter.

From this can be understood Lord Kelvin's belief in his "vortex-ring." In *Æther and Matter* Sir Joseph Larmor says: "The material molecule is entirely formed of ether, and of nothing else," and speaks of it as a small vortex, with an enormous speed of rotation.   35

That advanced thinker, Professor W. K. Clifford, in 1875 wrote: "There is great reason to believe that every material atom carries upon it a small electric current, if it does not wholly consist of this current."

[1] "Remove the leading error or governing fear of this lower so-called mind, and you remove the cause of all disease as well as the morbid or excited action of 40 any organ" (*Science and Health*, p. 377, Mary Baker Eddy).

[2] "Consciousness constructs a better body when faith in matter has been conquered" (*Ibid.*, p. 425).

[3] "It is likewise proved that the body of a dog and that of a man have the same composition" (*The Evolution of Matter*, Dr. Le Bon).   45

[4] The oval-shaped particles of which the lines of force are composed are smaller. They consist of a positive electrical charge at one end and a negative charge at the other.

Earlier still Sir Isaac Newton suggested the existence of a stress in the ether surrounding a particle of matter. Faraday did his best to eliminate the supposed difference between matter and energy.

Professor J. B. Bose has shown how the identity of response to stimula-
5 tion exhibited by matter, whether animal, vegetable, or mineral, demons-
trates the underlying unity of these three. He has also shown "that the most general and most delicate sign in life is the electric response," and has proved that this electric response, "considered generally as the effect of an unknown vital force," exists in matter. He has also shown the "fatigue"
10 of metals and their response to excitants, depressants, poisons, etc. M. Guillaume, in *La Nature*, contends that the mutability of solid matter constitutes "a kind of inferior life that has been unsuspected hitherto, but that can no longer be neglected by the attentive observer."

Professor J. J. Thomson, F.R.S., now Sir Joseph Thomson, a few years
15 ago gave a series of lectures, in which he explained the method by which he had measured what he called the corpuscle, also called the ion or the electron. He had proved its electrical character and measured its velocity—from 2,000 to 6,000 miles per second. These corpuscles were, as he expressed it, "the ultimate particles common to matter of all kinds."
20 Sir William Crookes, a good many years ago, it may be recollected, prophesied the discovery of the ultimate particle of matter, which, in 1886, he called "protyle," "formless mist," or "the foundation stones of which atoms are composed." [1]

Sir Humphry Davy, in a lecture before the Royal Institution, in 1809,
25 speaking of a possible substance common to all metals, said: "If such generalisations should be supported by facts, a new, a simple, and a grand philosophy would be the result." [2]

Matter.[3]—"*I would ask all educated people to keep their minds open, and not to close them, and think they already know about the Universe and*

30 [1] *Proc. Roy. Soc.*, 1880, No. 205, p. 469.
[2] *Works of Sir Humphry Davy*, Vol. VIII, p. 325.
[3] Since the foregoing was written the following report appeared in the *Daily Telegraph*, of December 6, 1910:—
"Members of the Authors' Club assembled at a dinner last night listened to a
35 most interesting address on 'New Elements in Chemistry,' by Professor Sir William Crookes, one of the greatest living authorities on the subject. He said the very idea of an element as something absolutely primary and ultimate, was growing less and less distinct, until to-day we admitted the possibility of resolving the chemical elements into simpler forms of matter, or even of refining them away
40 altogether.
Opinions differed as to the constitution of the electron. Some consider it to be an electrical charge on a material substratum, others saw no necessity for the material nucleus, and considered the electron to be pure disembodied electricity, thus approaching closely to the old idea of Buscovitch, accepted by Faraday, that
45 the atom was only a centre of force.
A bit of radium that would go into a thimble had almost suddenly shaken our belief in the conservation of substance, the stability of the chemical elements, the undulatory theory of light, and the nature of electricity; had revived the dream of alchemists and the preservation of perpetual youth, and had cast doubts
50 on the very existence of matter itself.
If we had disestablished the idea of the fixity of the old-fashioned elements,

the things in it, because as yet they have hardly begun. There are chapters and chapters to be opened" (Sir Oliver Lodge).

"Matter is theoretically the realm of fatality, while consciousness is essentially that of liberty" (Henri Bergson in *Life and Consciousness*). Matter is the "objective supposition of Spirit's opposite" (Mrs. Eddy), merely a manifestation of illusive thoughts. Hegel and many other philosophers have looked upon thought and thing, and even thought and being, as one. Matter can be correctly defined, in accordance with natural science, as electricity, simply a massing together of electrons, and can be caused to appear and disappear in two different ways: [1]—

(1) Either by the action of the so-called human mind, by strong determined thinking or will-power, when the electrical tension is merely released, or altered, or

(2) By turning to God in thought and denying the reality of the phenomena. The lines of force or thoughts themselves are then short-circuited,[2] and not only the matter, but the apparent cause of the matter, ceases its apparent existence in the material world or world of false consciousness.

The first method is that used by sorcerers, witches and hypnotists, and the latter is the way in which Jesus the Master-metaphysician worked. The former harms all concerned, the latter benefits the whole world, as it is the destruction of evil and is the only right method of treatment, that is, of prayer.

"Already our notions concerning the nature of matter have been revolutionised. . . . It now seems that they [the electrons] are electricity itself. . . . Whither this will lead us can only with the greatest caution be pre-imagined. In any case, the consequences of this discovery, philosophical as well as scientific, are stupefying in the possibilities they open up to the thinker, as well as to the man of practical science. At last science begins to join hands with philosophy. What will be the philosophy of a hundred years hence imagination pales before the effort of attempting to conceive" (*A Hundred Years Hence*, T. Baron Russell).

What is electricity? No one knows, and no one ever will know. Edison

we would say we still have matter to fall back on. But philosophers had not respected even the sacredness of matter itself. Physicists were now beginning to say that in all probability there was no such thing as matter; that when we had caught and tamed the elusive atom and split it into 700 little bits, these residual particles would turn out to be nothing more than superposed layers of positive and negative electricity. He refrained from speculating as to what would happen to us if some clever researcher of the future discovered a method of making these alternate layers of plus and minus cancel each other out!

Mr. Charles E. S. Phillips said it had become the habit to look to physicists and chemists to clear up mysteries that surrounded us, and those who worked in the borderland, like Sir William Crookes, had great responsibility thrown upon them, and were looked to by the whole world as leaders.

[1] Jesus was making a scientific statement of fact when he said: "Whosoever shall say unto this mountain, Be thou removed, and be thou cast into the sea; and shall not doubt in his heart, but shall believe that those things which he saith shall come to pass; he shall have whatsoever he saith" (Mark 9:23, and 11:23. See also Matt. 17:20, and 21:21, 22; Luke 17:6; Ex. 7:12. Also *Science and Health*, p. 86, lines 13, 30; p. 87, line 2; and p. 43, line 3).

[2] "Electricity is . . . the least material form of illusive consciousness, . . . which destroys itself" (*Science and Health*, p. 293).

says: "We are still ignorant of the true character of electricity; indeed, to me, after all the years I have spent in studying electricity, it is more a mystery now than ever." "We know nothing about the composition of any body whatever, as it is" (Huxley).

5   **Matter Merely Ethereal Phenomena.**[1]—It will therefore be seen that matter is not something real, but it is ethereal, or of the ether, a manifestation of false beliefs, and the miracles of Jesus illustrate the action of perfectly regular true mental laws. He could not possibly have worked in opposition to law. Anyone, therefore, can do these miracles if
10 he understands the laws and, as the result of applying them, lives a good enough life, that is, a life of sufficient unselfishness. If a person, however, thinks that he, the material man, works them, he will find that he will not progress. He has to know that God, good, alone acts.[2]

   Motion.—Before beginning my investigation for the *Daily Express*
15 I never understood how a piece of matter could possibly move, as either it was in its place, or it was not, and any movement from one of these conditions to the other was to me inconceivable. Now it is clear in the light of present-day knowledge, that matter never moves, and that any apparent movement is merely successive dematerialisation and materialisa-
20 tion, in other words, that which we see is merely a series of ethereal cine-matographic pictures, without any life or reality, which appear and dis-appear so rapidly that they give the impression of continuous movement. Even when matter is stationary, it is no less a series of vanishing, cine-matographic pictures. Professor Osborne Reynolds has proved this mathe-
25 matically, and says: "Such motion has all the character of a wave in the medium; and that is what the singular surfaces, which we call matter, are—waves. We are all waves." [3] Parmenides said this change is a transi-tion from that which is to that which a moment ago was not.

   Mr. Bertrand Russell, late Fellow of Trinity College, Cambridge,
30 in his valuable work, *The Principles of Mathematics*, writes: "There is no transition from place to place, and no physical existence of velocity and acceleration." This is true of so-called matter.

   Gravity.—"*You sometimes speak of gravity as essential and inherent to matter; pray do not ascribe that notion to me, for the cause of gravity is
35 what I do not pretend to know*" [4] (Sir Isaac Newton).
   What is called gravity, as my brother, Colonel H. E. Rawson, R.E., long ago pointed out, is merely an electro-magnetic force, the mutual

---

[1] "At best, matter is only a phenomenon of mortal mind, of which evil is the highest degree; but really there is no such thing as *mortal mind*" (*Unity of Good*,
40 p. 50, Mary Baker Eddy). "Matter and the ether are intimately connected, they are unceasingly interchanging energies, and are in no way two separate worlds" (*The Evolution of Forces*, Dr. Le Bon).
   [2] "Then answered Jesus and said unto them. Verily, verily, I say unto you, The Son can do nothing of himself, but what he seeth the Father do" (John 5:19).
45 "I can of mine own self do nothing" (John 5:30). "With God all things are possible" (Matt. 19:26).
   [3] "On an Inversion of Ideas as to the Structure of the Universe" (*Rede Lecture*, 1902).
   [4] *Letter to Bentley*, January 17, 1693.

attraction of the electric particles and due to synchronous vibration. This counterfeits the spiritual reality of omnipresent Love, which draws all men closely together, making of them one harmonious whole. "As the heavenly bodies attract—incline to one another and are held together by the eternal law of gravitation, so heavenly souls lean to and attract one 5 another, and are bound together by the eternal law of love" (Max Müller). Nothing proves more clearly the unreality of any material attraction, be it called gravity or love, than the obvious fact of its ultimate "separation" as matter; whereas real love, being spiritual attraction, is eternal in its manifestation of perfect at-one-ment.   10

Time.—"*Now is eternity, now I am in the midst of immortality*" (Richard Jefferies).

The apparent action of material thoughts at any given moment is merely due to our limited senses, which hitherto have prevented us from being conscious of any thought either before or after it comes into apparent 15 action. When you recognise that the material world has nothing to do with your real self, and is, at best, only a dream without a real dreamer, you will see that philosophers are right when they say there is no such thing as time.

> "Never the spirit was born, the spirit shall cease to be never;   20
> Never was time it was not; End and Beginning are dreams!"
> (*Sir Edwin Arnold*).

"What we perceive of the universe are only the impressions produced on our senses. The form we give to things is conditioned by the nature of our intelligence. Time and space are, then, subjective notions 25 imposed by our senses on the representation of things, and this is why Kant considered time and space as forms of sensibility. To a superior intelligence, capable of grasping at the same time the order of succession and that of the co-existence of phenomena, our notions of space and time would have no meaning. . . . Time is, for man, nothing but a relation between 30 events" (*The Evolution of Forces*, Dr. Le Bon). As Kant pointed out, space and time do not concern "things as they are in themselves," but only as they appear to our senses, being limitations imposed on the human mind by its very nature.

There is real time in the real world, and this is expressed in the suc- 35 cessive unfolding of ideas to the spiritual man. "Mind measures time according to the good that is unfolded" (*Science and Health*, p. 584, Mary Baker Eddy).

"We are here face to face with that final inexplicability at which, as Sir William Hamilton observes, we inevitably arrive when we reach 40 ultimate [material] facts; and, in general, one mode of stating it only appears more incomprehensible than another . . . that it [time] cannot be expressed in any terms which do not deny its truth. The real stumbling-block is perhaps not in any theory of the fact, but in the fact itself. The true incomprehensibility perhaps is, that something which has ceased, or 45 is not yet in existence, can still be, in a manner, present—that a series of feelings, the infinitely greater part of which is past or future, can be

4

gathered up, as it were, into a single present conception, accompanied by a belief in its reality" (John Stuart Mill).

The Scientific "Now."—"*To stop short in any research that bids fair to widen the gates of knowledge—to recoil from fear of difficulty, or adverse*
5 *criticism—is to bring reproach on Science. There is nothing for the investigator to do but to keep straight on, 'to explore up and down, inch by inch, with the taper of his reason'; to follow the light wherever it may lead, even should it at times resemble a will-o'-the-wisp*" (Sir William Crookes, F.R.S.).

All this is now easily explained, and it is possible to prove by direct
10 experiment that what we call time is merely limited human perception. Out of a total of at least five hundred cases, of all kinds, my first result proving this may be given as an instance.[1] Ages ago it was discovered and taught that there was no such thing as time. Everything, as far as it can be said to be happening, is happening at the same time, and the only reason
15 why one cannot see a thing at any given time, is because of this supposed human material limitation. Thinking over this, one sees that, if it is true, it ought to be provable by direct experiment. We ought to be able to pray now, and the effect of that prayer should have been as efficacious in the past as it has been generally admitted to be in the future.[2]
20 It is obvious that to the material senses we cannot alter what has (to those senses) already happened. We can at best only wipe out all recollection and all traces of it in the present and future. Again, if praying to produce an effect in the past, all we can do will be to prevent that past having been as bad as it would otherwise have been without the prayer.
25 Recognising that there is nothing impossible to God, a resolve was made to try the effect as soon as possible. The next day a letter was received from a sister-in-law written the day before, on a Monday, and asking for help through the recently discovered method of scientific prayer, the deep, systematic, right thinking which follows upon a right understanding of
30 God and man. On receipt of this letter on Tuesday morning, recognising that there is no such thing as time, and that, therefore, practically the letter had only just been written, and knowing that now and always man is a perfect spiritual being, made in God's image and likeness, I denied the reality of the physical trouble, and realised as clearly as possible the
35 perfect God and perfect man, thus praying in the way that Jesus told us. By the next post a letter came saying that a wonderful thing had happened, and how directly the letter had been written she was perfectly well. Thus were these logical deductions proved correct, as they have been many times since, by the best of all proofs, experimental tuition. Isaiah, speaking
40 of the last days, says: "And it shall come to pass, that before they call, I will answer" (Isa. 65:24). This time has now come; the thoughts on the subject that have always been there are now being recognised and understood.

[1] Since the first edition of *Life Understood* was published, students of it have
45 found that they have been able to obtain similar results by working in the way shown. Results are the only proof and the only value of a theory.
[2] "You may also ask how belief can effect a result which precedes the development of that belief. It can only be replied, that Christian Science reveals what 'eye hath not seen'" (*Science and Health*, p. 553).

The Metaphysical View of Time and Space.[1]—The fallacy of what is called time is easily seen on looking at it from a purely metaphysical standpoint. In Mind everything is available; in heaven you only have to think of anything to have it. There is no limit of time in eternity. All the vistas of the past and present are spread out to the mental vision at the   5 moment they are thought of. No gulf of time separates the thinker from his thoughts, hence no time limit enters into the purely mental realm, and there is no other.

The only gulf of any description that ever separates mankind from good, is the gulf of vacuity or ignorance of an ever-present God expressed in   10 infinite and perfect spiritual ideas filling all space, and always available to man.

We have now learnt that the so-called material accompaniments of any experience have no more reality than the sense entertained of them, and have also proved the practical effect produced on so-called material pheno-   15 mena by thought corrected in accordance with the ideal standard. We can therefore face intelligently a so-called past event with the same assurance that we can face a present difficulty, knowing that both are merely false impressions. Each must be reduced to the common denominator, absolute good, which is the requirement of God in accordance with Scripture, and   20 therefore in accordance with Principle. We in this state of consciousness can now prove by demonstration that "That which hath been is now; and that which is to be hath already been; and God requireth that which is past" (Eccles. 3:15).

"The past and the time to be are *one*,   25
And both are *now*" (*Whittier*).

It is of great value to recognise this power and to see that there is no loss of time between the moment when a patient turns to God, in the form of writing to a practitioner for help, and the time the consequent prayer, or treatment, is humanly said to commence. This knowledge is invaluable   30 in many different ways.

When, for instance, you have been in conversation with anyone and have forgotten to work for the mutual benefit—by realising heaven as you speak, knowing that in the perfect world man speaks truth and man knows Truth, as the only action is that of God, Truth—you can make up   35 for this by work done afterwards. You must not forget, however, that a golden opportunity has been lost, as you might have prayed at the time and afterwards as well, and so more completely cleared away wrong thoughts. Space [2] is merely an apparent limitation in human consciousness which fails to recognise the unity of the one Mind and its one conscious-   40 ness, the Christ. "The subjective states of evil, called mortal mind or matter, are negatives destitute of time and space; for there is none beside God or Spirit and the idea of Spirit" (*No and Yes*, p. 16, Mary Baker Eddy).

[1] "Every great advance in the sciences consists of a vast generalisation revealing deep and subtle analogies" (Jevons).   45
[2] "The notion of space is as little clear as that of time. Leibnitz defined it as the order of co-existence of phenomena, time being the order of their succession. Space and time are perhaps two forms of the same thing" (*The Evolution of Forces*, Dr. Le Bon).

The Ethereal Chart.—To use as an ethereal diagram or chart this theoretical aspect of thought, which is the only logical deduction from the facts accepted as such by the natural scientists of to-day, assists in indicating to human consciousness a sense of the indispensable footsteps, whereby 5 to free itself of itself. These footsteps are the denial of any power or even reality in evil, and the affirmation of eternal truth.

Let it be clearly understood that this explanation of the basic workings of so-called matter is not a presentation of facts, but their expression in physical terms, symbolic of the apparent internal workings of matter, just 10 as an algebraical formula is used by a mathematician to indicate a law and shorten a so-called mental process.

Were the internal workings of so-called matter as harmless as the algebraical formula, it would be of little importance; but the acceptance of the conditions of matter with all its attendant phenomena, false as 15 they are, and the individual and universal assent thereto, maintains and ensures its temporal manifestation, and allows of all the discordant conditions under which mankind is suffering. When a man grasps this, he will hasten not only to deny the existence of matter, and all material theories, but he will probe matter to its depths, uncover the false theory upon which 20 it is built, and find that its very foundations are utterly false, only so-called thoughts or lines of force—mere verbal expressions—which all admit can instantly fade away into the land of forgotten dreams. Thus will all fear of it be lost for ever. This wholly fearless, because intelligent, attitude is essential to gain dominion over evil.

25   THE NON-REALITY OF MATTER

"*When Bishop Berkeley said there was no matter and proved it, it was no matter what he meant*" (Byron).

Up to recent years the indestructibility of matter was regarded as a dogma, to cast a doubt on which would have been regarded as rank 30 heresy, while to advance the suspicion that there is, perhaps, no such thing as matter, but that all phenomena are merely due to force, as is accepted by the scientific world to-day, would have made the audacious innovator forfeit any right to be taken seriously. Now the throne of "force" or "energy" is being overturned. They "have returned to the nothingness of 35 things" (Dr Le Bon).

"To-day it is true, in all its fulness and strength, that the greatest and profoundest students of Psychology, and of the kindred sciences, most of these sciences new, and all of them reconstructed by fuller knowledge, are agreed, with practical unanimity, that the old past theories, or 40 rather hypotheses of materialism, of nihilism, of empiricism, have been proven untenable and altogether worthless, and that the so-called physical sciences have never been at all capable of taking sides in the controversy which is now about ended"[1] (J. W. Heysinger, M.D.).

Scientific Views.—"*It is only within the last thirty or forty years that* 45 *there has gradually dawned upon the minds of scientific men the conviction*

[1] *Spirit and Matter before the Bar of Modern Science.*

that there is something besides matter or stuff in the physical universe, something which has at least as much claim as matter to recognition as an objective reality, though, of course, far less directly obvious to our senses as such, and therefore much later in being detected" (Professors Stewart and Tait).

A remarkable change in views has taken place lately. In 1900 Dr. Heydweiler, a German, undertook to satisfy himself, by experimenting, as to whether two ounces of different elements uniting chemically really always give two ounces of compound; an undertaking which to most of his contemporaries appeared just as necessary as to prove that water really becomes ice at the freezing point. Heydweiler found that the result of two weighings never agreed, and the differences were larger than could be accounted for by unavoidable variations of the balances, etc. The experiments lasted for a long time and were repeated with the same results, and the final conclusion to which he, and those working with him, came, was that there is an actual loss of matter in every chemical change. This, when carried to its logical conclusion, means that matter is not a reality. If it is possible to make a certain weight of oxide of iron or other chemical disappear to the senses—as even the most elaborate balances are only aids to our senses—it cannot be held to be any longer impossible to make any other substance disappear, and given sufficient number of changes, the whole of matter must cease its apparent existence.

At the time it seemed quite impossible that these results could be correct, but they have been since confirmed by the experiments of Dr. Le Bon.[1]

It is only comparatively recently that scientific men have recognised that matter is electricity or force, and it was only in the year 1902 that Professor Osborne Reynolds, F.R.S., LL.D., M.I.C.E., Professor of Engineering at Owen's College, Manchester, one of the ablest mathematicians of the day, gave the world the result of twenty years' hard work, showing in the "Rede Lecture"[2] that he had proved mathematically that matter was a non-reality. I have never heard even a suggestion that he has made a mistake in his mathematical proof. Having theoretically proved the non-reality of matter, he postulated an impossible ether in his endeavour to prove what really existed, not recognising that the only reality was God, as perfect Mind and its manifestation. He says: "Matter represents the absence of mass," and again: "Matter is measured by the absence of mass." Professor Rouse Ball writes of this as matter being "a deficiency of the ether."

"Transcendentalism has been defined as a hole in a sand-bank after the sand-bank had been taken away. It is not transcendentalism, but matter, that modern physical science finds to be a theoretical hole in a theoretical medium"[3] (Arthur Chamberlain). It is merely "a great heap of nothing and nowhere to put it."

That leading scientific worker, Dr. Gustave Le Bon, in his latest book,

---

[1] "Contrary to the principle laid down as the basis of chemistry by Lavoisier, *we do not recover in a chemical combination the total weight of the substances employed to bring about this combination*" (*The Evolution of Matter*, Dr. Le Bon).
[2] *Rede Lecture*, 1902.
[3] "The Non-existence of Matter" in *The Christian Science Journal*, November, 1909.

The Evolution of Forces,[1] which is practically a text-book of material science, gives, in the calmest way, as if he was enunciating what ought to be known to every student, the fundamental principles of the material world as follows : (1) Matter, hitherto deemed indestructible, slowly vanishes by
5 the continuous dissociation of its component atoms; . . . (5) Force and matter are two different forms of one and the same thing; (6) . . . Matter therefore is continuously transformed into energy; . . . (8) Energy is no more indestructible than the matter from which it emanates.

The formulas of mechanics are disappearing. Dr. Le Bon writes:
10 "Professors who continue to teach the formulas of mechanics renounce more and more their beliefs in them. This fictitious universe, reduced to points to which forces are applied, seems to them very chimerical. 'There is not a single one of the principles of rational mechanics which is applicable to realities,' recently wrote to me one of the scholars who have
15 most deeply sounded the problems of mechanics, the eminent Professor Dwelshauwers Dery.

"Quite recently M. Sabatier, Dean of the Faculty of Sciences at Montpelier, propounded in an interesting inaugural lecture with the title, 'Is the Material Universe Eternal?' the question whether it was quite certain
20 that there was not a real and progressive loss of energy in the world, and more recently still, in a memoir on the degradation of energy, one of our most far-seeing physicists, M. Bernard Brunhes, expressed himself as follows: 'What is our warrant for the statement that the universe is a limited system? If it be not so, what signify these expressions: the total
25 energy of the universe, or, the utilisable energy of the universe? To say that the total energy is preserved, but that the utilisable energy diminishes, is this not formulating meaningless propositions?'"

In answer to a letter in which Dr. Le Bon set forth his ideas on this point, the same physicist wrote to him: "The 'nothing is lost' should
30 be deleted from the exposition of the laws of physics, for the science of to-day teaches us that something is lost. It is certainly in the direction of the leakage, of the wearing away of the worlds, and not in the direction of their greater stability, that the science of to-morrow will modify the reigning ideas."

35 Besides those already mentioned, many deep thinkers are trying hard to fit in the old false ideas with the new ones now coming to light. Sir Ray Lankester—and he is quoted by Geddes and Thomson—in *Evolution of Sex*, says: "The bodies of the higher animals which die, may from this point of view be regarded as something temporary and
40 non-essential, destined merely to carry for a time, to nurse, and to nourish

---

[1] This book is one of the International Scientific Series. The translation is edited by Mr. F. Legge, of the Royal Institution of Great Britain, and in it appear many paragraphs which show the radical change that has recently taken place in the scientific world. Dr. Le Bon is a member of the Royal Academy of Belgium, and a
45 very advanced worker, one of the ablest of modern scientific men. M. G. Bohn, in *Revue des Idées*, January 16, 1906, writes: "The beginning of Dr. Le Bon's work produces in the reader a deep impression; one feels in it the breath of a thought of genius. . . . Dr. Le Bon has been compared to Darwin. If one were bound to make a comparison, I would rather compare him to Lamarck. Lamarck was the
50 first to have a clear idea of the evolution of living beings."

the more important and deathless fission-products of the unicellular egg."
In *The Nature of Man*, Metchnikoff says: "Scientific proof exists, therefore, that our bodies contain immortal elements." The reverse of this
is true; man, however, is immortal.

The astronomer, Professor Larkin, has said: "Science now impera-
tively demands a Conscious Power within protoplasm—the only living
substance, and Science knows that this power is mental." It is not, however, the apparent power of the human mind, but the power of Mind.
Everything is in Mind. Mind is not *in* anything.

Lately, scientific men have recognised that matter is only something
falsely conceived of by the human consciousness. Professor Ostwald, of
Leipzig University, one of the leading men of the day, says: "Matter is
only a thing imagined, which we have constructed for ourselves very
imperfectly to represent the constant element in the changing series of
phenomena." Huxley writes: "After all, what do we know of this terrible
matter, except as a name for the unknown hypothetical cause of states of
our own consciousness."

"The charge of materialism could only be brought against such a man
by those abject materialists who have never had a glimpse of the pro-
founder fact that the universe, as known to us, consists wholly of mind,
and that matter is a doubtful and uncertain inference of the human
intelligence" (Grant Allen).

Sir William Crookes, speaking before the British Association in 1879,
said: "We have actually touched the borderland where matter and force
seem to merge into one another—the shadowy realm between the known
and unknown . . . here, it seems to me, lie ultimate realities, subtle,
far-reaching, wonderful."

The following short list of the more plausible hypotheses accounting
for the properties of matter, together with the remarks thereon of W. W.
Rouse Ball, may be of interest.

Descartes' Continuous Matter: "There seems to be no way of reconciling such a structure of matter either with the facts of chemical changes
or with the results of spectrum analysis."

Popular Atomic Theory: "The difficulties to which it leads appear to
be insuperable."

Boscovitch's Hypothesis: "It has been described, perhaps not unjustly,
as a mere mathematical fiction."

Elastic Solid Ether: "In spite of the difficulties to which this hypothesis
necessarily leads, and of its inherent improbability, it has been discussed."

Vortex Ring and Vortex Atom Hypotheses:[1] "The above theories are
now regarded as untenable."

Ether-Squirts Hypothesis "Rests on the assumption of the existence
of a world beyond our senses."

The Electron Hypothesis: "Seems very artificial."

---

[1] As a column of water rotating at a sufficient speed would oppose a blow with
a bar of iron as if it were a column of steel, so a vortex whirl of minute particles
would give every appearance to the senses of solid matter. The speed of radio-
active particles is supposed to be 100,000 times that of a bullet when leaving the
muzzle of a rifle.

The Bubble Hypothesis: This is the theory put forward by Professor Osborne Reynolds, and whilst it is not correct it is founded on what he had proved, namely, the non-reality of matter. Consequently we find Professor Rouse Ball writing of it as follows: "This theory is in itself
5 more plausible than the Electron Hypothesis, but its consequences have not yet been fully worked out."

Philosophic Views.—"*There are more things in heaven and earth . . than are dreamt of in your philosophy*" (Shakespeare).

For ages philosophers have recognised that the material world is not
10 all that we have thought it to be. Even a few quotations will show how gleams of scientific truth came to them, though none grasped its practical side, and how to apply it to human experience so as to replace discord with harmony. Aristotle, for instance, whose teachings have been followed by the civilised world for centuries, not only said that matter was negative,
15 but stated that the source of all motion only moves as an object of love. "It is pure mind with no object but itself: it is thought, with thought as its object—pure self-consciousness with nothing beyond. It is God." [1] Hume correctly threw doubt upon all the so-called sciences.

Herbert Spencer says that what is real is permanent, what is not real
20 is not permanent. Paul popularly defined the position over 1,800 years ago in the words: "For the things which are seen are temporal; but the things which are not seen are eternal" (II Cor. 4:18).

The great Immanuel Kant, admittedly a giant amongst philosophers, at the end of the eighteenth century wrote to the effect that against other
25 criticisms of the doctrine of immortality one may adduce the transcendental hypotheses; all life is essentially only intellectual, and not subject to time-changes, neither beginning with birth nor ending with death. He also said that this world's life is only an appearance, a sensuous image of the pure spiritual life, and the whole world of sense only a picture swimming
30 before our present knowing faculty like a dream, and *having no reality in itself*. For, he says, if we should see things and ourselves as they are, we should see ourselves in a world of spiritual natures with which our entire real relation neither begins at birth nor ends with the body's death.

John Fiske also, the well-known historian, Professor of Philosophy at
35 Harvard and St. Louis, who in his earlier days was an agnostic, but whose last work was written to prove that science led irresistibly to the doctrine of immortality, wrote: "The untrained thinker who believes that the group of phenomena constituting the table on which he is writing has an objective existence, independent of consciousness, will probably
40 find no difficulty in accepting this sort of materialism. If he is devoted to the study of nervous physiology, he will be very likely to adopt some such crude notion, and to proclaim it as zealously as if it were important truth, calculated to promote, in many ways, the welfare of mankind. The science of such a writer is very likely to be sound and valuable, and he will tell us
45 about Woorara poison and frogs' legs, and acute mania, and it will probably be worthy of serious attention. But with his philosophy it is quite otherwise. When he has proceeded as far in subjective analysis as he has in the

---

[1] *Harmsworth Encyclopædia.*

study of nerves, our materialist will find that it was demonstrated a century ago, that the group of phenomena constituting the table *has no real existence whatever* in the philosophic sense. For by 'reality' in philosophy is meant 'persistence, irrespective of particular conditions,' and the group of phenomena constituting a table persists only so far as it is held together 5 in cognition. Take away the cognising mind, and the colour, form, position, and hardness of the table—all the attributes, in short, that characterise it as matter—at once disappear. . . . Apart from consciousness, there are no such things as colour, form, position, or hardness, and there is no such thing as matter. This great truth, established by Berkeley, is the very 10 foundation of modern scientific philosophy; and, though it has been mis-apprehended by many, *no one has ever refuted it,* and it is not likely that anyone ever will." How useless has always been the intellectual grasp of a theory, however correct, without some definite method of putting it into practice. 15

Professor Max Müller has said: "To speak of matter and substance as something existing by itself and presented to the senses is mere mytho-logy. . . . And yet we are asked by materialists to believe that the per-ceiving subject, or the mind, is really the result of a long-continued development of the object, or of matter. This is a logical somersault which 20 it seems almost impossible to perform, and yet it has been performed again and again in the history of philosophy." [1] Grant Allen writes: "The universe, as known to us, consists wholly of mind, and matter is a doubtful and uncertain inference of the human intelligence." The poet-philosopher, Walt Whitman, writes: "Afar down I see the huge first 25 Nothing, I know I was there."

Hundreds of years ago the Indian philosophers looked upon the material world as Maya, or illusion, thinking, however, that when this illusion disappeared, they would find themselves merged in the one great Being whom we Westerners call God. They thought that we should lose our 30 individuality; not recognising, as Jesus told us, that "the kingdom of God is within" (Luke 17:21), within reach of our own individual consciousness at the present moment, and that therefore our individuality can never be lost. That old idea is changing. All men are getting nearer the truth. The following was the definition of our future given by Archdeacon Wilber- 35 force to a Brahmin in India, with which definition the Brahmin quite agreed: "Conscious identification with universal Life without the loss of my own sense of individuality." Principle is always individual in its intelligent self-expression.

This Suppositional Opposite World a Dream.—"*I felt with amaze-* 40 *ment we are all plunged into a languid dream. Our hearts fat, and our eyes heavy, and our ears closed, lest we should see with our eyes and understand with our hearts, and be healed*" (Ruskin).[2]

It was very difficult to understand how the material world, which seemed so very real, could be a non-reality, until I learned to look upon 45 it as a suppositional opposite world. For instance, if, as is happily quite

[1] *Three Introductory Lectures on The Simplicity of Thought.*
[2] See Isa. 6:10.

4*

impossible, someone in heaven should say, How fortunate that we are not in a world where there are sin, sickness, and trouble, he would be talking of a suppositional opposite world. Yet such is the world which we have ignorantly believed real, at best a dream from which we have to wake up.
5 There is not a single proof that can be advanced that this material so-called state of consciousness is not just as much a dream as the worst nightmare that anyone ever had. As Zophar said: "He shall fly away as a dream, and shall not be found" (Job. 20:8).

> "Health, peace, salvation universal,
10 Is it a dream?
> Nay, but the lack of it a dream,
> And failing it, life's love and wealth a dream,
> And all the world a dream" (*Walt Whitman*).

"We are such stuff as dreams are made on and our little life is rounded
15 with a sleep" (Shakespeare). "And surely it is not a melancholy conceit to think we are all asleep in this world, and that the conceits of this life are as mere dreams" (Sir Thomas Browne). "For we are born at all adventure: and we shall be hereafter as though we had never been" (Wisdom of Solomon 2:2). "Human life is a dream and a journey in a
20 strange land" (Marcus Aurelius).

Cause Must be Good.—God, being cause, must be good; for evil is negative, and cannot therefore be an original creator. If two causes, one good and the other evil, originally existed, one must have destroyed the other long ago. The very nature of evil is self-destructive.
25 One of the proofs of the non-reality of matter is the evil that appears to exist. If matter were real then the evil would be real, and God, good, must have made it, as God created everything. If God created it, good alone is responsible for the evil. This is impossible. Evil could not emerge from good. If it is an unreality, God cannot even know of it.
30 How is it possible that there should be a God who is Love itself, who could possibly fail to relieve the human race, if He were conscious of the trouble? God's consciousness, the Christ, is seen as spiritual perfect man, self-consciousness or understanding of good, which therefore cannot be conscious of evil. Even a human being cannot be conscious of evil whilst
35 he is conscious of even relative human "good."

THE SO-CALLED EVOLUTION OF THE MATERIAL WORLD

"*The law of evolution applicable to living beings is also applicable to simple bodies; chemical species are no more invariable than are living species*"
40 (Dr. Le Bon).

From what has been already said, you will see that the so-called material world is simply a world of false sense, apparently originating in material thoughts or lines of force, matter being a manifestation of these thoughts. Material man and all lesser phenomena are but the illegitimate offspring
45 originating in a false mentality.

Consequently, spiritual evolution, or the continual grouping together of the perfect ideas in heaven throughout eternity is the only true evolution, and what is now put before you is merely an accurate statement of the

false belief about the spiritual world, as it falsely appears in human consciousness. "The use of a lie is that it unwittingly confirms Truth, when
handled by Christian Science, which reverses false testimony and gains a
knowledge of God from opposite facts, or phenomena" (Mary Baker
Eddy).   5

Birth and Death.—Material evolution appears to take place through
a process of birth and death, which are now found to be merely temporary
successive changes, false views of the real and permanent men, animals,
plants, and mineral life, counterfeiting the glorious, spiritual heaven and
earth and men, which have been discovered to be always here at hand,   10
whatever we may have appeared to see, hear, or think to the contrary.
This will soon be almost universally acknowledged and the instantaneous
nature of the effect of this intelligent acceptance by the majority is now to
be put before you.

Lines of Force.—The starting of the material world, as far as one   15
can say that such a thing ever started, was simply the false non-mental
concept, appearing as lines of force or material thoughts,[1] and everything
that has what is called happened, or is going to happen materially has
always existed, as far as it can be said to exist at all, in the form of thoughts
of which we successively become conscious.[2] These material thoughts have 20
no existence, as they are at best but the false claim of a false sense of
existence.

Electrons.—As this so-called start of a material world is merely lines
of force, so-called material evolution continues, as it were, in a dream, and
the electrons appear, as already explained.   25

The production of the electron by the action of one line of force upon
another is the first example of the action of the male and female, the false
belief in, not only a material cause, but a divided cause, and as a consequence, an apparent lack of certain qualities in each individual consciousness.   30

Aqueous Vapour.—"*Particles gradually accreting out of the formless
mist*"[3] (Sir William Crookes).

These electrons mass together, and appear as aqueous vapour, of which
the whole of the illusive material universe at one stage consists. Then the
particles begin to revolve, and ultimately the whole of our solar system   35
appears as a mass of aqueous vapour revolving round a centre, that which
is known as one of countless suns. Since this knowledge came to me, one
of the leading atronomers in America has publicly stated, in a paper read
by him, that he has proved mathematically that the world evolved from
aqueous vapour, and not from fiery gases. Having to introduce Sir Robert 40
Ball, when he gave his lecture on "Comets," at the Queen's Hall, I had
an opportunity of a long talk with him on the origin of the comets and other

---

[1] "Sin existed as a false claim before the human concept of sin was formed"
(*Retrospection and Introspection*, p. 67, Mary Baker Eddy).
[2] "The belief of sin . . . is an unconscious error in the beginning,—an em- 45
bryonic thought without motive; but afterwards it governs the so-called man"
(*Science and Health*, p. 188, Mary Baker Eddy).
[3] Presidential Address to the Chemical Society, March 28, 1888.

moving bodies in the heavens, and he told me that he knew of nothing that would prevent the theory that I had put before him from being correct. Charles A. Young, Professor of Astronomy at Princeton, says in *Elements of Astronomy*: "It appears probable that the original nebula instead of being purely gaseous . . . was made up of finely divided particles of solid or liquid matter." Dr. Le Bon also has written: "Atomic elements . . . only seem to be nuclei of condensation in the ether. . . . What was to be one day the universe was then only constituted of shapeless clouds of ether."

The Constellations.—As time appears to pass, portions of this aqueous vapour become detached by centrifugal force, and themselves begin to revolve; and as these separate portions of aqueous vapour become compressed by the force of gravity, so the sun and different planets that revolve round it are formed.[1] Whoever connected the symbolic accounts of the Creation that we find in the first and second chapters of the Book of Genesis, was evidently inspired, because it may be recollected hat the second account or symbolic idea of how the material world started, begins in the sixth verse of the second chapter with the words, "But there went up a mist from the earth." Ever since its formation the earth has been getting steadily hotter owing to the compression due to gravity.[2] This the above-mentioned American astronomer also confirms.

So-called Solid Matter.—The action of gravity continues, and gradually, through countless changes,[3] solid matter is formed. First the mineral, then vegetable life appear, so like the mineral that there is hardly any line of demarcation.[4] Then so-called evolution goes slowly on and higher thoughts become apparent, and vegetable life is followed by the lowest animal life, which is indistinguishable from it. This material evolution continues through the different grades of animal life, the amœba, worm, reptile, mammal, and higher forms of animals up to the Catarrhine ape, and, finally, the material man, whose evolution steadily continues and will appear to continue until everything objectionable or even limited has disappeared, self-destroyed.

> "Move upward, working out the beast
> And let the ape and tiger die" (*Tennyson*).

The successive changes through which the child in the womb passes, before it is ultimately born as a human being, are among the many proofs

[1] Sir George Darwin, of Cambridge University, thinks that the earth and moon formed one body at least a million years ago.

[2] I have since read that Lord Kelvin is said to have held that gravity was amply sufficient to account for the underground heat of the earth, the heat of the sun, and that of all the stars (*Astronomy of To-day*, by C. G. Dolmaye).

[3] Sir Charles Lyal estimates the minimum of time necessary to produce the geological formations at 200 millions of years. Huxley estimated that 1,000 million years had elapsed since the beginning of the incrustation of the earth.

[4] Professor Schrön has shown how molecules of matter pass first through a granular phase, and then a fibrous phase before becoming finally homogeneous. Thus, the future crystal behaves like a living being. According to Ostwald, crystals can generate spontaneously, and also by affiliation. The former has been believed to be impossible to the living being.

not generally known of this sequence of evolution. During this evolution of each separate class of material phenomena everything becomes more like its spiritual reality as the material counterfeits advance towards self-destruction. For instance, the flowers of to-day are not only more gorgeous, but many are exquisite in their sweet simplicity and purity.   5

That everything becomes steadily less material is one of the proofs that matter is always advancing towards its final disappearance. This is equally true of every individual mortal of to-day, although it is not apparent owing to the increasing wrong thoughts attacking him.

Material Man.—The human conception of man appears at first hardly 10 more than a mere brute beast; then he begins to obtain a knowledge of good, his love towards his family being probably his earliest good. Then the knowledge of good gradually evolves until man recognises the existence of a being superior to himself, and begins to lift his thoughts in what is known as prayer. As with the other classes of matter, the local evolution 15 of races continues, constantly slowing down through men turning to many gods, instead of to the one God.

The Idea of God Evolving.—The idea of God gradually evolving, penetrates through the "mist" of human consciousness, as recorded in the Bible, until we learn how to pray rightly, and obtain a knowledge of what 20 God really is, namely, a living Principle, absolute good; Life itself, Love itself, Truth itself. We prove our knowledge of God by the effects which follow, and such demonstration of the Christ Truth is Immanuel, or God with us. (See Matt. 1:23.)

John Stuart Mill said: "Every question that has God in it passes 25 through three stages: ridicule, discussion, adoption." We are now in the third or final stage, and all over the world men are beginning to recognise that there is no such thing as matter, and that the only reality is God. In its fullest significance the term God includes manifestation—the spiritual kingdom.   30

The Inevitable End of Matter.—"*And God shall wipe away all tears from their eyes; and there shall be no more death, neither sorrow, nor crying, neither shall there be any more pain: for the former things are passed away*" (Rev. 21:4). "*They shall obtain gladness and joy; and sorrow and mourning shall flee away*" (Isa. 51:11).   35

When enough, not in numbers but in clearness and depth of thought, recognise the non-reality of matter, they act as one great open channel for the action of God, and every manifestation of evil, that is, all sin, sickness, worries, troubles, and limitations—all this material sense of things, with its self-destructive laws, its illogical sense of existence, its 40 remorseless tyranny, and suicidal ignorance, disappears, and all mankind are freed. We then find ourselves perfect and divine, expressing God, and in a perfect world, absolutely joyous, governed by Life, Truth, and Love. "And I saw a new heaven and a new earth: for the first heaven and the first earth were passed away; and there was no more sea" (Rev. 45 21:1). This is what is falsely called "the end of the world." It is really the end of all evil and limitation, the end of what Carlyle speaks of as the "ever-dying universe."

When the end of evil comes, thank God it comes for the whole of
humanity and for the whole of the material kingdom. "For it is written,
As I live, saith the Lord, every knee shall bow to me, and every tongue
shall confess to [openly acknowledge] God" (Rom. 14:11). (See Isaiah 45,
5 verse 23). "Nevertheless we, according to his promise, look for new
heavens and a new earth, wherein dwelleth righteousness" (II Peter 3:13).
"For, behold, I create new heavens and a new earth: and the former shall
not be remembered, nor come into mind. . . . and the voice of weeping
shall be no more heard" (Isa. 65:17, 19). "We now know that matter
10 vanishes slowly, and consequently is not destined to last for ever" (Dr.
Le Bon). Sir William Crookes in *Modern Views of Matter* says: "This fatal
quality of atomic dissociation appears to be universal. . . . The whole
range of human experience is all too short to afford a parallax whereby the
date of the extinction of matter can be calculated."

15   **Meaning of the End of the World.**—"The Lord said . . . as truly as
I live, all the earth shall be filled with the glory of the Lord" (Num. 14:20,
21). "For the earnest expectation of the creature waiteth for the manifestation of the sons of God" (Rom. 8:19).

There is a widespread disinclination to face that unpopular event
20 ignorantly called "the end of the world." This has arisen from an entirely
mistaken view of the event, and it is due to the ignorance of what is then
really about to take place, and of the real meaning of the second coming
of Christ, that so many incorrect prophecies of the date have been put
forward; so many, indeed, that the whole subject has come to be looked
25 upon by those who have not studied the question as more or less ridiculous,
and any serious consideration of it as unpractical.

Now that it is understood to mean solely the end of all troubles and
limitations, and that this end has been found to rest upon a scientific basis ·
that can, and indeed must, be understood and demonstrated, it will be
30 seen that no question of to-day demands more urgent and careful attention.
It is of vital importance to every individual on earth, and for this reason:
If the ushering in of that greatest event in human experience finds mankind
asleep and ignorant of how to face it, then it will be forced upon the
attention by a series of unparalleled disasters. On the other hand, should
35 it find the world awake and instructed how to meet it, there will be a
time of unspeakable joy and gladness with perfect health and normal
human enjoyment; complete immunity from all temptation to sin;
a progressive unfoldment of tangible beauties hitherto undreamed of ;
universal harmonious relations between individuals and nations, with
40 mental co-operation on an ever-widening scale. There are definite and
indispensable human footsteps, however, before this great end can be
reached and the gloom of night change to the glory of eternal day.

It has been truly said, "Until metaphysical science becomes popular,
the weak or vain will never advocate it." Proofs of the value of the true
45 science of mind can be obtained by anyone, and even its popularity is now
close upon us. Nothing is more astonishing to an intelligent thinker than
that, with all the illumination thrown upon human life by the law of good,
the utterances of prophets, earth's wisest scientific writers, and the

manifest effects of scientific demonstration (which anyone with a little trouble can verify for himself), even a single individual should for a moment delay to learn of Truth, until the inevitable moment arrives when he is forced by suffering to gain this knowledge.

The "end of the world" simply means the end of all false material 5 mentality, all sin, sickness, worries, troubles, and limitations, literally their final disappearance, even to remembrance, for ever. All matter is dematerialised, melts into nothing, "And the world passeth away, and the lust thereof: but he that doeth the will of God abideth for ever" (I John 2:17). "The grass withereth, the flower fadeth; but the word of our God 10 shall stand for ever" (Isa. 40:8). "The earth [the material sense of earth] is clean dissolved" (Isa. 24:19). "Flesh and blood cannot inherit the kingdom of God" (I Cor. 15:50). In other words, we all wake up from this self-maintained dream, to find ourselves in an absolutely glorious world, in which we, the real beings, have always been and always shall be. 15 "Behold, I shew you a mystery; We shall not all sleep, but we shall all be changed" (I Cor. 15:51).

As the result of the rapid spreading of truth that is now taking place all over the world,[1] the prophecy of Hosea in chapter 13, verse 14 will be fulfilled: "I will ransom them from the power of the grave; I will redeem 20 them from death," and the whole of humanity will find that they are in reality perfect, deathless beings, with perfect powers—for example, the power of going instantly from one place to another (that is, from one idea, or group of ideas, to another), the power of mentally speaking to or hearing any one, and of knowing instantly anything needed. In fact, all will find 25 themselves made in the image and likeness of God, that is to say, expressing the attributes of God. It is through the Christ, Truth, that this marvellous change takes place. Our salvation "is not of ourselves, it is the gift of God." Jesus said: "No man can come to me, except the Father which hath sent me draw him; and I will raise him up [the Christ will lift him up in con- 30 sciousness] at the last day" (John 6:44).

We shall then not only find that we see everything as it really is, but we shall understand and appreciate the wondrous fellow-beings around us. "He will destroy in this mountain the face of the covering cast over all people, and the vail that is spread over all nations. He will swallow up 35 death in victory; and the Lord God will wipe away tears from off all faces" (Isa. 25:7, 8).

The Power of Truth.—"Look unto me, and be ye saved, all the ends of the earth: for I am God, and there is none else" (Isa. 45:22).

Archimedes is reported to have said: "Give me a fulcrum on which to 40 rest, and I will move the earth." An earnest or logical thinker cannot fail to see the avalanche now let loose upon the world, and that the truth now plainly set forth, demonstrated as it has been by innumerable incontestable

[1] The growth of the knowledge that is going to bring about the end is increasing in geometrical progression; that is, the increase in each year is far greater than in the 45 previous year. Like a rolling snowball the knowledge grows. Dr. Le Bon, in The Evolution of Matter, points out the great effects that are thus produced by very small changes in a cause, not only physically, but socially. He states that "this observation will explain many historical events."

proofs, must either be blasphemy, so pernicious that it is practically inconceivable, or it inaugurates a final revolution, increasing the action of the only lever that can, and is, moving the whole world—the lever of right thinking resting on the fulcrum of Truth.

5   **Be of One Mind.**—*"Stand fast in one spirit, with one mind striving together for the faith of the gospel"* (Phil. 1:27).

The power of this unanimity of thought in even a small circle was shown on the day of Pentecost when "they were all with one accord [like-minded] in one place. . . . And they were all filled with the Holy
10 Ghost" (Acts 2:1, 4).

It must be clear to anyone that if thought is the basis of everything, the majority, not estimated by numbers, but by power, resulting from clearness of thought, must rule even a million-fold clouded minority. "Be perfectly joined together in the same mind and in the same judgment"
15 (I Cor. 1:10). As shown hereafter, judgment is the destruction of evil by the denial of evil. When those realising that there is no reality in matter, and that the only reality is spiritual, form a majority in weight of thought, the minority instantly recognise it, and, as this *general recognition* constitutes the only law that can possibly act, this false material sense must
20 cease, and can never again have even its illusory sense of existence. It is the denial, or Angel Michael, that brings this end.[1]

As all that is necessary is to change the general "thought," it will be easily recognised that individual work cannot be too highly estimated in these days of rapid circulation of knowledge. "Great floods have flown
25 from simple sources" (Shakespeare).

The End Unexpected.—*"There shall come in the last days scoffers, walking after their own lusts, And saying, Where is the promise of his coming? for since the fathers fell asleep, all things continue as they were from the beginning of the creation. . . . Nevertheless we, according to his promise,*
30 *look for new heavens and a new earth, wherein dwelleth righteousness"* (II Peter 3:3, 4, 13). "*For when they shall say, Peace and safety; then sudden destruction cometh upon them, as travail upon a woman with child; and they shall not escape*" (I Thess. 5:3).

"They were eating and drinking, marrying and giving in marriage,
35 . . . And knew not until the flood [2] came, and took them all away; so shall also the coming of the Son of man be. . . . Watch therefore: for ye know not what hour your Lord doth come. . . . For in such an hour as ye think not the Son of man cometh" (Matt. 24:38, 39, 42, 44). He "shall come in a day when he looketh not for him, and in an hour that he is not

---

40. [1] Daniel says: "And at the time of the end . . . shall Michael stand up, the great prince . . . . and there shall be a time of trouble, such as never was . . . and at that time thy people shall be delivered, every one . . . and they that turn many to righteousness [shall shine] as the stars for ever and ever" (Dan. 11:40, and 12:1, 3). Mrs. Eddy writes: "When God bids one uncover iniquity, in order to
45 exterminate it, one should lay it bare. . . . 'Nothing is hid that shall not be revealed.' It is only a question of time when God shall reveal His rod and show the plan of battle" (*Miscellaneous Writings*, p. 348).
    [2] The last flood will take a literary form, the outpouring of ideas of truth submerging all human hypotheses.

aware of" (Matt. 24:50). "Watch therefore, for ye know neither the day nor the hour wherein the Son of man cometh" (Matt. 25:13).

So rapid and efficient are the means of communicating with the mass of mankind to-day that there is no difficulty in impressing the majority of the thinking world at any given moment with any aspect of truth. Let the 5 thoughtful consider seriously the result of such collective change of thought on any previously accepted fundamental subjects, even upon the reality of evil, matter, and death.

Troubles at the End.—*"For then shall be great tribulation, such as was not since the beginning of the world to this time, no, nor ever shall be"* 10 (Matt. 24:21).

Right throughout the Bible we are told of the troubles for which we have now to prepare. The modern seers, foreseers of the cinematographic pictures called the material world, fully confirm those of the past.

Even if we put aside the whole Bible as a gigantic fable, we must, in the 15 light of present knowledge, admit the liability to danger from the forthcoming unparalleled disasters and troubles that accompany the end of this dissolving dream. Shall we meet them as masters or servants? "This know also, that in the last days perilous times shall come. For men shall be lovers of their own selves, . . . Having a form of godliness, but deny- 20 ing the power thereof" (II Tim. 3:1, 2, 5). Every prophecy dealing with this subject foretells the horrors which are now not the less near because only just beginning to be recognised by the "watchmen on Mount Ephraim." (See Hosea 9:8 and Jeremiah 31:6.) "Howl ye; for the day of the Lord is at hand; it shall come as a destruction from the 25 Almighty. . . . Behold, the day of the Lord cometh, cruel both with wrath and fierce anger, to lay the land desolate. . . . And I will punish the world for their evil, and the wicked for their iniquity; and I will cause the arrogancy of the proud to cease, and will lay low the haughtiness of the terrible" (Isa. 13:6, 9, 11).   30

It will be seen, by those who understand the apparent action of false mentality, that these troubles are no individual fancy of the prophets, but are inevitable, logical conclusions, resulting from the thought-intensifying action of human consciousness, until instructed in truth. The mad panics from fear of fire and the way that one patient becoming 35 hysterical in a hospital ward will cause other patients to follow suit, are instances of the way that evils will sweep over the world. To stem the tide of this "flood" of evil, solely the result of suicidal ignorance, is the greatest privilege and highest possible work of man and woman to-day.

The Power of United Right Thinking.—The practical omnipotence 40 that lies behind collective right thinking is signified by Isaiah in the chapter following that above quoted, where he says: "The Lord of hosts [collective] hath sworn, saying, Surely as I have thought, so shall it come to pass; and as I have purposed, so shall it stand: . . . this is the hand [spiritual power] that is stretched out upon all the nations. For the Lord 45 of hosts hath purposed, and who shall disannul it?" (Isa. 14:24, 26, 27).

The Darkest Hour.—*"There shall be famines, and pestilences, and earthquakes, in divers places. All these are the beginning of sorrows. . . .*

And because iniquity shall abound, the love of many shall wax cold" (Matt.
24:7, 8, 12).

Sin brings its own hourly punishment, though the sequence is not
always recognised at the time. This trouble increases and becomes
5 ultimately so terrible in its last stage that in despair a world turns to God
as the only hope of relief. "Satan produces all the maladies which afflict
mankind" (Martin Luther). The love of sin will be quenched through the
dread of suffering. It is only needful to learn and practise the method of
right thinking now set forth, to obtain complete immunity against every
10 form of evil. If sufficient know the truth they can protect a tortured
world.

All prophets have foretold terrible times of suffering when the end
comes. Not only do the thoughts exist in theory that will be manifested
as these troubles, but as the world more generally recognises that matter
15 is only a manifestation of "thought," so will it be much easier for anyone
to get results; consequently if a man thinks wrongly about himself, it
will have much more effect in a year's time than it has now, and it has far
more effect now than it had two years ago. Most people are frequently
picturing discordant conditions in connection with themselves through-
20 out the day, and such wrong thinking will be much more dangerous in the
near future than at the present time; as even when a man knows that such
false thoughts are harming him, either causing his trouble or rendering it
more likely to happen, he cannot cease this deleterious process unless he
knows, and indeed has practised, the true art of right thinking, which is an
25 essential necessity of life.

On the other hand, owing to the general mental awakening, right
thinking is even now far more effective for good than ever before, both
upon individuals and the masses. In fact, so effective is it, that what is
only the natural result of law and order is termed by the uninstructed
30 onlooker a miracle.

Any who do not know "the truth," and do not know how to pray
rightly, will have a terrible time in these last days. We have to gain as
great an understanding as possible from now onwards, so as to protect,
not only our best-loved ones and those nearest in touch with us, but also
35 as large a number as possible from the immediate effects of their ignorance
and consequent wrong picturing, or imaging forth of evil.

We must start at once to gain this knowledge of truth, for Jesus himself
has pointed out that "the night cometh, when no man can work" (John
9:4). Even now, if a worker is attacked by, for instance, severe pain, before
40 he is sufficiently advanced in the knowledge of God, he loses all power of
helping himself, and has to appeal to a fellow-worker for relief.

The Loosing of the Devil.—"*The great dragon was cast out, . . . into
the earth, and . . . persecuted the woman . . . and went to make war
with the remnant of her seed*" (Rev. 12:9, 13, 17). "*And I saw an angel
45 come down from heaven . . . And he laid hold on the dragon, that old
serpent, which is the Devil, and Satan, and bound him a thousand
years, And cast him into the bottomless pit, and shut him up, and set a seal
upon him, that he should deceive the nations no more, till the thousand*

years should be fulfilled: and after that he must be loosed a little season"
(Rev. 20:1-3).

There could not have been so many centuries of diabolical cruelties
had there not been some mistaken motives and some hidden evil at work.
It is only now that we know what this evil was, although Paracelsus 5
cleared up a good deal of the mystery. He showed, for instance, that the
clay figures used by witches, into which pins were stuck, were merely
used as mechanical aids to assist in the intensification of the so-called
"thoughts" of those unhappy channels of this diabolical black art.
Mohammed recognised this evil power sufficiently even to prohibit the use 10
of chessmen modelled in human form. It must not be thought for a moment
that this evil, this skeleton in the cupboard, has been finally disposed of by
any such periodic temporary imprisonments; for this "Devil, and Satan,"
has merely been "bound," and the Apocalyptic vision is now just about
to be finally fulfilled, when "The devil is come down unto you, having 15
great wrath, because he knoweth that he hath but a short time" (Rev.
12:12). Fortunately, Truth is first in the field.

In old days it was comparatively easy to locate the practiser of witchcraft, until fear became frenzy and discrimination disappeared in wholesale
slaughter. In the days now just upon us, when the door to this human 20
so-called power, devilish to both practiser and victim, has been unlocked,
it follows that every member of the community must be either a channel
for good, or else a practiser of witchcraft, knowingly or unknowingly;
actively engaged either on the side of God or "the devil"; dealing out life
and good or death and its attendant forerunners, sin, suffering, and sick- 25
ness. Horrors hitherto unconceived of will be experienced, except by those
who know enough of the truth not only to warn their fellow-creatures, but
to put plainly before them the remedy, whilst they themselves are steadily
and daily working in a haven of peace and safety. These will still the
tempest and stem the tide of the sea of iniquity that is about to flood the 30
material earth, and harm any unfortunate enough to be still resting on an
illusory, material basis.

It is a significant and most instructive fact that this diabolical mania
followed the last great liberation of thought. Again we stand on the threshold of a threatened repetition of the same conditions, only in a much more 35
aggravated form, and of a more extensive, nay, world-wide nature. The
last liberation of thought was a mere rushlight in comparison with the
general conflagration now liable to take place; hence we must learn how
to protect ourselves from these troubles, by rising into a higher plane of
conscious action. In this way, not only do we render ourselves immune 40
against any form of evil, but we free ourselves from the minor troubles to
which we have grown accustomed, and can destroy the dangerous thoughts
before they affect others.

Satan Loosed for Destruction.—"*That old serpent, which is the
Devil, and Satan . . . must be loosed a little season. . . . And shall go* 45
out to deceive the nations . . . and fire [purification] *came down from God
out of heaven, and devoured them*" (Rev. 20:2, 3, 8, 9).

Those not understanding the illusive nature of evil may ask, Why

let people know this if it is so harmful? The answer is, that ignorance is no safeguard. The world is ready, and it is time to uncover evil; [1] to let people see what they are doing; to state the truth, and so save the victims from the results of their own wrong thinking; to enable the victims to
5 protect themselves and those malpractising on them; to hasten the passing of legislation that will chain this growing evil; and, most important of all, to bring the evil up to the surface so that the true workers will see and destroy it, and so rapidly hasten its forthcoming end. The angel has thrust in his sickle, for the harvest of the earth (the scientific world) is ripe, and
10 will be reaped, although the vine of the earth is not yet ready for the sharp sickle (see Rev. 14:15). This latter moment was foreseen in the Apocalypse as this devil that deceives being "cast into the lake of fire [purification] . . . for ever and ever" (Rev. 20:10). "But when the fruit is brought forth, immediately he putteth in the sickle, because the harvest is come"
15 (Mark 4:29).

A pure consciousness, believed to be John the Evangelist, to whom we owe an eternal debt of gratitude for having pierced the veil of the future, holds up to us in vivid types exactly what is threatening. "The devil is come down unto you, having great wrath, because he knoweth that he hath
20 but a short time" (Rev. 12:12). The teachings of Jesus on the subject are equally clear. He said: "Except those days should be shortened, there should no flesh be saved: but for the elect's sake those days shall be shortened" (Matt. 24:22).

Now the remedy is at hand whereby, instead of meeting brute beast
25 with brute beast, we can protect these poor victims of infernal thoughts, both by destroying the thoughts as they commence to act, and also by forewarning the victims and showing them beforehand the way to think, so that they can get out of their difficulties. Fighting as beast against beast, never did help man permanently out of his difficulties; the only fight has
30 to be in our own consciousness, where the evil thoughts have to be denied and so destroyed.

We have to obey the words of Moses, "Thou shalt not suffer a witch to live" (Ex. 22:18), but we have to do this, not by putting a criminal behind a closed door, or by destroying the mechanical structure called a
35 body, and so leaving the evil free to continue its course, but by the destruction of the devilish thoughts and the purification of the minds of these victims, and this we must do by clearing our own thoughts upon the subject, and not by dwelling in thought upon the evil.

It should never be forgotten that these "thoughts," even when working
40 in their most deadly form, are absolutely powerless in the face of truth understood and applied, either by the victim who "thinks" them, or by anyone else working on his behalf.

Signs of the End.—"*And there shall be signs . . . and upon the earth distress of nations, . . . Men's hearts failing them for fear, ...*
45 *for the powers of heaven shall be shaken. And then shall they see the Son of*

[1] "It is a rule in Christian Science never to repeat error unless it becomes requisite to bring out Truth. Then lift the curtain, let in the light" (*Miscellaneous Writings*, p. 346, Mary Baker Eddy).

man coming in a cloud with power and great glory. And when these things begin to come to pass, then look up, and lift up your heads; for your redemption draweth nigh" (Luke 21:25–28). *"Then the eyes of the blind shall be opened, and the ears of the deaf shall be unstopped. Then shall the lame man leap as an hart, and the tongue of the dumb sing"* (Isa. 35:5, 6).   5

"Let no man deceive you by any means: for that day shall not come, except there come a falling away first, and that man of sin be revealed, the son of perdition; Who opposeth and exalteth himself above all that is called God, or that is worshipped; so that he as God sitteth in the temple of God, shewing himself that he is God" (II Thess. 2:3, 4). This is a 10 warning against the inflation of human personality that in some cases accompanies the recognition of man's mental powers. When this comes about, those with a knowledge of the letter, but lacking the spirit of Christianity, that is, sufficient love of their fellow-men, exercise their human will-power as a means of dominating their fellows. This will- 15 power is "non-mental," and pure hypnotism.

Fortunately the end of all evil is at hand. Through the mist of materiality gleams the brightness of Christ's coming, although "we . . . groan within ourselves, waiting for the adoption, to wit, the redemption of our body" (Rom. 8:23). We are losing our ignorance, and all over the world the 20 knowledge that man is a perfect spiritual being in heaven now, is breaking through, and coming to people of all denominations. "As the lightning cometh out of the east, and shineth even unto the west; so shall also the coming of the Son of man be" (Matt. 24:27). "And then shall that Wicked be revealed, whom the Lord shall consume with the spirit of his mouth, 25 and shall destroy with the brightness of his coming: Even him, whose coming is after the working of Satan with all power and signs and lying wonders" (II Thess. 2:8, 9).

Sin, sickness, troubles, limitations, and even matter, are a non-reality, merely false concepts, and capable of being easily and effectually destroyed, 30 bit by bit, through a knowledge of how to think rightly. All over the world troubles of every kind are being got rid of, and extraordinary results are being obtained by all classes; so extraordinary that people do not care to speak of them, except to those whom they find have had similar experiences. One of the best-known clergymen in England told me that he 35 dared not tell any of his congregation the things that had been happening to him. Another, equally well known, said that he had been "simply doing miracles." In both these cases they had been working in the way to be explained later. Another friend, a staid, elderly man of business, told me that he had not said a word to anyone of the powers that he had dis- 40 covered in himself, as he was afraid that his hearers would think he was going mad. Doctors and scientific men have told me things that they have not dared to tell others, as they did not want to be called either fools or liars. What does all this mean? It only means that thought is getting loosened, that the general belief that it is impossible to act mentally on so- 45 called matter is disappearing, and it is therefore much easier to obtain results. Jesus and the prophets pointed out that this would be the case, when the end came. Speaking of the true workers, he said: "He that believeth on me, the works that I do shall he do also; and greater works

than these shall he do; because I go unto my Father" (John 14:12). "For
the Father loveth the Son, and sheweth him all things that himself doeth:
and he will shew him greater works than these, that ye may marvel"
(John 5:20).

5   **Education.**—Too much attention cannot be paid to this vital question.
Education does not require to be done away with. The demand of progress is for higher and more scientific training. This must consist of an
elimination of false material foundations and the substitution of the
eternal facts of truth, whereby man can prove each step as he advances
10 towards the glorious reality that lies within—within reach of his own
consciousness.

The first lesson to be learned is the fallacy of the limitations that have
hitherto bound us down to mental groping in the dark. "There is no
dearth of learned formulas to conceal our ignorance" (Dr. Le Bon). On
15 account of this ignorance the majority have been condemned to spend
nearly all their time, day after day, in ceaseless material steps, and even
thus they merely eke out a precarious and unsatisfactory existence, to be
shared by those who have been hitherto ignorantly thought to be "dependent on them." These wearisome efforts are all made in the face of a
20 certainty of ultimate death and a constant possibility of endless troubles
and misery, even for those who are most loved, until they meet with what
is dreaded by nearly all, and yet is ignorantly called a "happy release."

The second lesson to be learned is that infinite possibilities of good lie
at our door, merely waiting the exercise of an unrecognised capacity
25 inherent in every individual. God-given powers are available for everyone.
Why delay to claim our rightful inheritance of unlimited good?

The question is: How is this rightful inheritance to be attained? There
is only one answer: by treatment. Treatment is the realisation of the
spiritual facts concerning God and man, the dwelling in uplifted thought
30 on an ever-present God who is All-in-all, and on His infinite manifestation. The practitioner "effacing the claim of material personality and sense
testimony, and fixing his thought steadfastly upon God and the Christ-
idea, rises to the realisation of God's omnipotence, omniscience, omnipresence, and omni-action, and through this aspiring sense, this clarified
35 vision, exalted desire, and genuine meekness, he finds his ascension 'unto
the Father,' he enters the 'holy of holies,' where sense is lost in sight,
'and beholds God's work finished and complete.' This conscious realisation reveals the immaculate concept, unsullied, uncontaminated, and
unconditioned by matter, as it was 'in the beginning.' The displacement
40 and effacement of false sense by the assimilation of the truth heals, and
there dawns the innate and supreme satisfaction which is born of the
understanding that God is All-in-all . . . Jesus demonstrated this God-
likeness of consciousness. This satisfied sense was his abiding state, and it
is thus seen that it is indigenous to all true individuality or spirituality"
45 (E. C. Romery, in the *Christian Science Sentinel*, September 30, 1911).

This conscious realisation of God flooding our consciousness, as we
blend all thoughts with our Maker and ascend into the regions of purest
thought, heals not only sickness, but sin; it removes from our hearts all

sense of human personality, all sense of material desires and difficulties, and gives an unspeakable knowledge of the constant presence and infinite protection of the triune God—Life, Truth, and Love—which uplifts and sustains us above all material troubles, giving an abiding sense of "the peace of God, which passeth all understanding" (Phil. 4:7). "In quietness 5 and in confidence shall be your strength" (Isa. 30:15). "Where the Spirit of the Lord is, there is liberty" (II Cor. 3:17).

HEAVEN

First let me summarise the position. Heaven is not a far-off distant state which we reach by death, but a perfect state of consciousness existing *now*. 10 Jesus said, "The kingdom of God is within you," and the alternative marginal translation is "The kingdom of God is among you" (Luke 17:21); that is to say, all the love, life, truth, joy, wisdom, knowledge, and beauty that we see around us is part of heaven, permanent and perfect. In front of the spiritual man may be said to flash a series of cine- 15 matograph pictures, which pass at the rate of about twenty miles an hour. All the sin, disease, troubles, and limitations are part of these cinematograph pictures, for man is not a material being liable to sin, disease, and death; he is, always was, and always will be, a perfect being, in a perfect world, governed by a perfect God. Of the material or cinematographic 20 picture man, Jesus said, "Ye are of your father the devil . . . there is no truth [reality] in him. When he speaketh a lie, he speaketh of his own, for he is a liar and the father of it" (John 8:44). The only apparent life, love, joy, etc., of the material man is the real life, love and joy, partially shining through the cinema pictures and giving the appearance of reality to 25 them.

All the good is part of heaven, made by God. All the evil, sin, disease, worries, troubles, and sufferings are in the cinema pictures, and men have been humbugged, fooled, and hypnotised to believe themselves to be material beings, liable to sin, disease, and suffering. There is not a word of 30 truth in it. Man always was, is now, and always will be a spiritual being, a perfect being, in a perfect world, governed by a perfect God. Philosophers have taught that there is no such thing as time, and this is now found to be correct. All these illusory cinema pictures existed millions of years ago just as much as they exist now. Predestination, therefore, is true, and these 35 pictures must, unless they are destroyed by the action of God, present their false appearance at their predetermined time. Fatalism, however, is not true, because when a cinematographic picture man turns in thought to God, he opens his human mind, and then the action of God by means of his spiritual self, through his material self, as through a channel, destroys 40 some of the evil, that is to say, thins the mist of matter, and he sees heaven more as it really is. He sees, for instance, a healthy man instead of one diseased; a happy man instead of a miserable being.

Heaven, mathematically, is a world of four dimensions, of which we see three. The fourth dimension is infinity. Man has existed for infinite time; 45 an infinite number of God's glorious ideas have come to him; he has grouped these ideas into an infinite number of perfect combinations of

what, in the material world, we call art, music, literature, etc. These
radiate out from him into infinite space, giving infinite joy and happiness to
an infinite number of perfect beings. He has known an infinite number
of these peerless spiritual beings, and has become conscious of the beauties
5 of an infinite number of spiritual worlds, because each of the infinite
material worlds around us is merely a material *mis*representation of a real
spiritual world, of a beauty which it is absolutely impossible to imagine,
much less to describe. With regard to the future, an infinite number of
new ideas will come to man; he will group these together into an infinite
10 number of sublime combinations; he will revel in the beauty of an infinite
number of new resplendent worlds, and will exchange ideas with an
infinite number of divine spiritual beings, whom he has never met before.
Man has infinite Love, infinite Life, infinite Truth, infinite wisdom,
infinite knowledge, infinite joy. In fact, man has no limitations whatsoever,
15 except that he can never know the whole of reality; for instance, he can
never know the infinite number of spiritual beings, he can never know all
the wonderful worlds, he can never know all the ideas and combinations
of ideas, for the unfolding of God's infinitude is eternal life. Each divine
being has, however, the Christ capacity, and can know instantly any idea
20 of God, can be with any spiritual being, and can be conscious of any of the
marvellous beauties of any spiritual world directly he so desires. The
spiritual man has, however, no personal volition, for he is governed by the
will of God, being God's consciousness. The awakening of a spiritual
desire is God's law in operation, and a natural precursor of the unfoldment
25 which satisfies that desire.

Now let me see if I can give you a slight idea of that wonderful world,
heaven: First of all, what gives us the greatest happiness in this world?
Unquestionably when we love somebody intensely and that love is
returned. Now, in heaven, the love that you have towards a spiritual being
30 whom you have just met, and the love he has towards you, is infinitely
greater than the love that can exist between any two material beings, as it
is the infinite love of God, seen unveiled.

To interchange ideas with those we love gives us the next greatest
amount of happiness. In heaven we are always interchanging ideas with
35 those we love with an infinite love, and these are not ordinary ideas such
as come to the material man. Take the most beautiful ideas that you have
ever had. For instance, the most perfect music that has ever delighted you,
the most perfect poem you have ever heard, the most perfect picture you
have ever seen. They are not to be compared with the perfect ideas that
40 are always being passed on to you by your fellow-man, because these are
God's ideas, created by God, and therefore absolutely perfect.

The third source of great happiness in heaven is creation, the grouping
together of the ideas. Firstly, you have the joy of creating the thing, as
you have in the material world, whether it is in writing a book or carving a
45 piece of wood. Secondly, you have the joy from seeing the happiness that
your creation gives to your fellow-man. In heaven your creations are
absolutely perfect; you are continually grouping together the beautiful
ideas of God that come to you, into wonderful and perfect combinations,
which radiate out from you into infinite space, giving joy and happiness.

Continually you are having people whom you love intensely, thanking you
for this wonderful creation, and giving you in exchange ideas that they have
grouped together. As each has all wisdom, intelligence, and knowledge,
you fully appreciate, and get a maximum amount of joy, infinite joy, from
interchanging, one with another, these combinations of ideas that you 5
launch into eternity.

The next source of great happiness is scenery. A man once told me that
his idea of heaven was beautiful scenery, a beautiful sunset, for instance.
In heaven we can wander with those we love amongst infinite worlds of
incalculable beauty. Each of the material planets and stars is really a 10
spiritual world of absolute perfection, seen by us wrongly, and you can
never get tired of visiting these worlds because they are infinite in number.
Each of these is a different world, and therefore gives you fresh pleasure as
you explore its beauties. In heaven, all being governed by the one Mind,
God, there are no conflicting interests, no jealousies, no mistakes. Life is 15
one continual existence of absolute perfection. You never can get tired of
this, because there are infinite ideas in Mind, in God, and therefore infinite
combinations. There are also infinite spiritual beings with whom to exchange ideas, and infinite worlds to be visited. You are continually meeting
new people, who show you infinite love, and going with those whom you 20
love to new worlds, and to wander thus is no troublesome task. There is no
calculation of ways and means, no preparations to be made or paraphernalia
to be taken, and no doubt as to whether there are dangers ahead.
It is a perfect mental world, the realm of infinite Mind, where man always
exists, always has existed, and always will exist, as part of God's conscious- 25
ness, in a perfect position from which he is never removed. All that can be
said to move are the ideas of God, which continually circulate in that vast
infinite Mind, idea after idea coming to you in the form of perfect combinations of ideas, which you pass on to your fellow-man, that he may
obtain joy therefrom. He, in exchange, passes you fresh combinations, and 30
you group and re-group these ideas, each one presenting new beauties.
There is no trouble about living, because God is your Life; there is no
trouble about wondering where the food is to come from the next day,
because your food is the ideas of God, and those ideas are infinite, continually unfolding to you, and always obtainable.   No sickness or disease 35
can harm you because you are made in the image and likeness of God, part
of God's consciousness, and where God is no evil can exist. Take the
hundred happiest days that you have ever had in your life, and group all
the happiest moments together, and the happiness is not to be compared
with the bliss that you will continually enjoy. "Eye hath not seen, nor ear 40
heard, neither have entered into the heart of man, the things which God
hath prepared for them that love him" (I Cor. 2:9).

This is the wonderful world in which you, a wonderful being, and
all those you now see materially around you, will shortly find yourselves
when the whole world appears to wake up and gain a knowledge of Truth, 45
a real absolute knowledge of God. "For now we see through a glass,
darkly" (I Cor. 13:12), but the day is fast approaching when "they all
shall know me, from the least to the greatest" (Heb. 8:11). This is the
perfect world in which we are all going to wake up to find ourselves.

Then you will see those loved ones whom you appear to have lost and will see them as they really are; all the good that you ever saw in them intensified a million-fold. Then you will never lose them again, but will be found to be closer to them than the material man has ever been; you
5 will mentally traverse with them the celestial realm, God-crowned because God-created.

SECTION THREE

THE HUMAN "MIND" THAT IS "NO-MIND"

"There are more things in heaven and earth, Horatio,
Than are dreamt of in your philosophy" (*Shakespeare*).

"Entirely ignorant as we are, we certainly cannot venture to set bounds 5
to the mind's power. . . . There are many more things in the reciprocal action
of mind and organic elements than are yet dreamt of in our philosophy"
(Henry Maudsley, M.D., LL.D., F.R.C.P.).

The human or material man appears to be a marvellous being when even
a few of his limitations are destroyed, and so extraordinary are his seeming 10
powers, counterfeiting the infinite capacities of the one Mind, that many
think the real spiritual being exists in the material person. This is because
they confuse the individualised subconscious "mind" [1] with the real
spiritual man who is made in the image and likeness of God, cognisant of
and reflecting good only.   15

"Had science turned its attention to these phenomena with even a
fraction of the energy and study which such transcendental facts demanded,
we should have advanced far beyond our present limits of knowledge; but
instead it has chosen to simply ignore the facts as inconvenient" [2] (J. W.
Heysinger, M.D.).   20

The Subconscious Mind or Basic False Mentality.—"*A formidable
range of phenomena must be scientifically sifted before we effectually grasp
a faculty so strange, so bewildering, and for ages so inscrutable as the direct
action of mind*" [3] (Sir William Crookes, F.R.S.).

All psychologists have recognised what has been called the subconscious 25
mind, although it can be more accurately designated the illusory, mortal,
subconscious, or basic false mentality. Dr. Schofield calls it the "unconscious mind," but if it were mind at all it would be conscious. Myers
calls it the "subliminal self," but the real self is spiritual. Schopenhauer
calls it "the better consciousness," but both conscious and subconscious 30
minds are equally bad. McCunn calls it "the soul," but this word in the
Bible, according to its context, nearly always means the human "no-mind."
The translation is wrong, through want of knowledge. It has also been
called the "principle of life," the "abdominal brain," the "communal
soul," and the "subliminal consciousness." The members of the Society 35
for Psychical Research generally speak of the "supraliminal" [conscious]
and the "subliminal" [subconscious] after the old psychologists. Some
speak of the "conscious" and "self-conscious" minds. T. J. Hudson, who
has given a good deal of time to the examination of the so-called "mind,"
writes in *Law of Mental Medicine*: "I prefer to assume that man is 40

---

[1] "Lower so-called mind" (*Science and Health*, p. 377, Mary Baker Eddy).
[2] *Spirit and Matter before the Bar of Modern Science.*
[3] Presidential Address, British Association, 1898.

endowed with two minds. As a working hypothesis, I am logically justified
in this assumption, for the reason that everything happens just as though
it were true. I have chosen to designate one of the two minds as the Objective Mind [conscious] and the other as the Subjective [subconscious]
5 Mind. It is entirely safe to say that not one fact has yet been brought to
light, by the psychological experts of this or any other age, that disproves,
or tends to disprove, the fundamental fact of a dual character of man's
mental organism."

This "sub-conscious mind" or "basic false mentality" is recognised
10 by theologians under the name "devil," by scientific men under the name
"ether," and by the leading mental sects under the name "mortal mind."
Professor Bergson, recognising some of the facts, says that consciousness
transcends the brain and that, though each man is distinct from his fellows,
the separation between individual consciousness may be much less radical
15 than we suppose.[1] It is ignorance of this lower false mentality and its workings that has resulted in such troubles and limitations in the past. Now
that we know how to think we can destroy evil thoughts, both in our conscious and subconscious minds.

Sense Impressions.—The sense impressions are absolutely wrong.
20 Astronomy, optics, acoustics, and hydraulics, all prove this fact. We are
now learning the significance of it. It was not so very long ago in the world's
history that the leading scientific men thought that the sun moved round a
flat earth. To come to later times, Dr. Pearson, when he first took up a
globule of potassium and was told it was metal, exclaimed, "Bless me ! how
25 heavy it is!" simply from expecting it to be so, whereas potassium is
excessively light. Professor Bennett tells us of a Scottish procurator-fiscal,
who, on having to exhume a body, declared when the coffin appeared that
he perceived a strong odour of decomposition, which made him so faint
he had to leave. On opening the coffin it was found to be empty. All have
30 at some time or other been entirely deceived by the senses.

HUMAN SO-CALLED "POWERS"

*"The statement to which I am prepared to attach my name is this: That
conjoined with the rubbish of much ignorance and some deplorable folly and
fraud, there is a body of well-established facts beyond denial and outside any
35 existing philosophical explanation, which facts promise to open a new world of
human inquiry and experience, are in the highest degree interesting, and tend
to elevate ideas of the continuity of life, and to reconcile, perhaps, the materialist and metaphysician"* (Sir Edwin Arnold).

"If there be truth in even one case of telepathy, it will follow that the
40 human soul is endowed with attributes not yet recognised by science"
(Andrew Lang). All the so-called powers that man appears to exert are
merely continually changing, false mental impressions, cinematographic
pictures, having no power of any kind. Receiving these impressions has
been vaguely called telepathy. "So much is certain—that in particular
45 cases we can put out the feelers of our soul beyond its bodily limits, and

[1] Presidential Address before the Psychical Research Society, May, 1913.

that a presentiment, nay, an actual insight into the immediate future, is accorded to it (Goethe in *Conversations with Eckermann*).

Memory is Mental.—"*And the Jews marvelled, saying, How knoweth this man letters, having never learned?*" (John 7:15).

So ignorant have we been that, until quite recently, it was thought necessary to wade laboriously through a mass of so-called facts, indeed, often to commit to memory burdensome details, to obtain needful knowledge. Here and there we find men who knew better. Some have thought that we pigeon-holed matters of which we became conscious, and, as in a systematically organised library, could bring up before us words, or whole columns of words, or groups of mental pictures, when required.

This is entirely wrong. The attempt to remember, looked at from the point of view of a natural scientist, is an attempt to get the so-called conscious mind to vibrate synchronously with the subconscious mind, or lower false mentality.[1] In heaven a man knows instantly everything he needs, being an individualised consciousness, governed by Mind. When this truth is sufficiently recognised by you, the action of God is made manifest in the material world, and this realisation is prayer in its true meaning. The disciples said of Jesus, "Now are we sure that thou knowest all things" (John 16:30). Through the realisation of God the mist of matter is thinned, and we see the real man more as he is, namely, knowing what he needs instead of being ignorant. From a natural science point of view the two portions of the mind vibrate synchronously and together, and the demonstration is said to be made. By praying in a scientific way the limitations of the human being can be overcome, and the so-called abnormal powers now to be referred to are found to be as natural and harmless as any other human procedure, when under proper control.

Thought Sequences Repeated.—Sometimes, under exceptional circumstances, an individual gets ethereally in touch with a series of cinematographic pictures that, existing as far as such things can be said to exist at the moment, have already happened. He can also get in touch with those about to happen in the future. The individual then appears to see again and to foresee the events. From the former the false idea of reincarnation has arisen. The sense of having before lived what we are now experiencing is known as "paramnesia," and is due to getting in touch with the cinematographic pictures beforehand. Sir Walter Scott, in *Guy Mannering*, says: "How often do we find ourselves in society which we have never before met, and yet feel impressed with a mysterious, ill-defined consciousness that neither the scene nor the subject is entirely new; nay, we feel as if we could anticipate that part of the conversation that has not yet taken place."

Charles Dickens writes, in *David Copperfield*, "of a feeling that comes over us occasionally of what we are saying and doing having been said and done before in a remote time—of our having been surrounded, dim ages ago, by the same faces, objects, and circumstances—of our knowing

[1] De Quincey, in *The Confessions of an Opium Eater*, writes: "Of this, at least, I feel assured, that there is no such thing as forgetting possible to the mind."

perfectly what will be said next, as if we suddenly remembered it !" Rossetti, in *Sudden Light*, writes :

> "I have been here before,
> But when or how I cannot tell."

5 Edward Dowden and Oliver Wendell Holmes also refer to this. Coleridge writes :

> "Oft o'er my brain does that strange fancy roll,
> Which makes the present, while the flash doth last,
> Seem a mere semblance of some unknown past."

10 Hardy writes, in *A Pair of Blue Eyes*, "Everybody is familiar with those strange sensations we sometimes have, that our life for the moment exists in duplicate, that we have lived through that moment before, or shall again." Tennyson writes, in *The Two Voices* :

> "Moreover, something is or seems,
15 > That touches me with mystic gleams,
> Like glimpses of forgotten dreams—
> Of something felt, like something here :
> Of something done, I know not where;
> Such as no language may declare."

20 And in the *Early Sonnets* he writes :

> " . . . . 'All this hath been before,
> All this hath been I know not when or where.'"

Sir James Crichton-Browne, in *The Cavendish Lecture on Dreamy Mental States*, besides quoting, amongst others, the above, says that sometimes 25 there passes through the mind in a few minutes, years of one's prior life. Sir Francis Beaufort, in a letter published in the autobiography of John Barrow, describing what happened when he was nearly drowned,[1] writes : "Every incident of his former life seemed to glance across his recollection [2] in a retrograde succession, not in mere outline, but the picture being filled 30 with every minute and collateral feature, each act of it accompanied by a sense of right and wrong." Sir James Crichton-Browne also writes : "And since Beaufort's time many persons rescued from drowning have given an account of their expiring thoughts, substantially the same, and in harmony with what we are sometimes told of panoramic reminiscences in dreamy 35 mental states. A domestic servant who consulted Dr. Hughlings Jackson, when communicating to him the warning of his epileptic seizures, said : 'It seems as if I went back to all that occurred in my childhood; as if I see everything so quick and so soon gone that I cannot describe it.'" One of the best-known thought-readers speaks of the thoughts flitting by like the 40 nearer external objects when in a railway train.

[1] See Dean Farrar in *Julian Home*, Chapter XXV, p. 306, "Memory, the book of God."
[2] This has just happened to a friend of mine. In his case he lived through his life again as he fell forward into his bathing machine, after his foot had been badly 45 torn by his having to wrench it out of the chain of the pier in which it had been caught.

These are some of the many proofs that the whole of our so-called human life has its apparent existence in the shape of "thoughts," ethereal vibrations, both in the past and in the future, until destroyed by the action of God.

Sight is Mental.—"*For nimble thought can jump both sea and land,* 5 *as soon as think the place where he would be*" (Shakespeare).

For centuries the many wonderful and hitherto inexplicable powers of human beings have been more or less recognised. For instance, it has been found that man has the power of seeing things in any part of the world. I was once asked to accompany a well-known medical man, pro- 10 bably the leading medical authority on the human "mind," to test another well-known doctor, who found that he had psychometric powers—that is to say, he could see things at a distance. Amongst many other wonderful things he described his sister, who had been lecturing about 200 miles away, giving many details of the room, the people, and so on. No one 15 present knew anything of the facts, but on making inquiries afterwards we found that there had been only two mistakes out of the many statements made.

"We can know the truth more accurately than the astronomer can read the stars or calculate an eclipse. This mind-reading is the opposite of 20 clairvoyance." (*Science and Health*, p. 84, Mary Baker Eddy). Jesus, amongst his many marvellous powers, exercised this capacity of seeing things at a distance. "Before that Philip called thee, when thou wast under the fig tree, I saw thee," were his words when Nathanael expressed surprise at Jesus's knowledge of his nationality and character. The accuracy 25 of this statement is evidenced by Nathanael's reply: "Rabbi, thou art the Son of God" (John 1:48, 49).

Clairvoyance.—In the Talmud is mentioned a "fourth Sight," by which means all that a person is doing, wherever he may be, can be seen by another. There are frequent references in occult literature to various ways 30 of gaining this power. The human consciousness is always inventing new methods of apparently overcoming its own limitations. Such methods are all mere limitations, disguised as apparent aids. Remember that the so-called mental is really "non-mental."

A well-authenticated instance is that of General Sir John MacNeill, v.c., 35 Equerry to Queen Victoria. On March 24, 1878, he was in the library at Windsor Castle, when he saw the *Eurydice* being lost off the Isle of Wight. So real was it that he exclaimed aloud, "She is foundering!" He mentioned the matter to several people at the time, afterwards finding out that the vessel foundered at that moment. Canon Warburton, when in Lincoln's 40 Inn, was wakened one night by *seeing* his brother in the West End "catching his foot in the stair and falling headlong" full length down the stairs, just when and as it occurred.

Seeing with the Nose and Ear.—The eye is not necessary for sight. Professor Lombroso, a most able and painstaking investigator, in his book, 45 *After Death—What?* gives the case of the fourteen-year-old daughter of one of the most active and intelligent men in Italy. "She had lost the power of vision with her eyes," but "as a compensation she saw with the same degree of acuteness at the point of the nose, and the lobe of the left ear. In this way she read a letter which had just come to me from the post-office, although I had blindfolded her eyes, and she was able to distinguish the figures on a dynamometer." Col. H. S. Olcott gives details of a child he knew who for two years could read anything held against the back of her head, and of a young Hindu woman who "was able to read books and distinguish colours when held to her finger tips, the little toe, and the elbow, and to hear at the umbilicus."

Professor Lombroso then gives other instances of the same kind. Eight cases are cited by Petetin, and another by Carmagnola, in which a girl "saw distinctly with the hand, selected ribbons, identified colours, and read, even in the dark." There are also other cases mentioned by Despine, Frank, and Dr. Augonva. Professor Lombroso concludes by saying: "The truth is that it is absolutely impossible for us to give a scientific interpreta-tion of these facts—facts which bring us to the vestibule of that world which is properly spoken of as being still occult because unexplained."

Dr. Heysinger writes: "In the case of Mollie Fancher, in Brooklyn, N.Y., who has been examined during many years by the most eminent neurologists, we have surely a living miracle. She has for many years been blind, paralysed, without apparent sensation, without food and almost without drink, without the performance of any of the ordinary bodily functions, and yet she is bright, clear, intelligent, and I have recently received a letter from her most beautifully and correctly written—and, as Dr. Hammond said of this case, 'She did not see—at least with her eyes.'"[1]

Physical sight is an ethereal effect, the thing seen vibrating along the lines of force of which the ether is composed, direct to the human mechanism or so-called mind (see, however, p. 63, line 24).

Paintings.—It is interesting and instructive to note that when you are looking, for instance, at a portrait, you have become ethereally in touch with the thoughts portrayed—one of the illusory cinematographic pictures that constitute the material person. You are in ethereal touch with the so-called man, with the pride and cruelty, the wisdom, nobility, and love that the thoughts represent. That is why a portrait painter has to have what Malcolm Bell calls "insight into the deeper mental recesses of his sitter." If you analyse this more closely you will see that in looking at a portrait your real spiritual self in heaven is in mental touch with the spiritual being who is seen falsely in the material world. In the material world the picture puts you in ethereal touch with the material thoughts constituting the material form. In the Appendix is a copy of a letter written to an artist friend a few years ago, which may be of use to those who wish to understand the position better. When discordant material thoughts are destroyed by right thinking, while the artist does his work, he obtains what is called a speaking likeness. When the thoughts of evil are destroyed, and the best side of the character is shown, he obtains a result which stamps him, not only as a genius, but as a benefactor to his fellow-men, for he gives us a grouping of ideas which indicates, although faintly, the true man.

---

[1] *Spirit and Matter before the Bar of Modern Science.*

Hearing is Mental.—*"Mind is eye and ear together, blind and deaf is all else besides"* (Plato).

Hearing also is entirely ethereal, and can be developed. The human "consciousness" can "hear" at any distance. What theoretically takes place, although such a thing cannot be said truly to happen at all, is that 5 the sound vibrates by means of the lines of the ether, "thoughts," impinging on the "consciousness," causing it to vibrate and receive a mechanical impression, called sound. "Mortal mind is the harp of many strings, discoursing either discord or harmony according as the hand, which sweeps over it, is human or divine" (*Science and Health*, p. 213, 10 Mary Baker Eddy).

It may be recalled that just after Elisha had made the axe head to swim he told the king of Israel at least three times where the king of Syria was pitching his camp. On Ben-hadad asking which was the traitor, "one of his servants said, None, my lord, O king, but Elisha, the prophet that is in 15 Israel, telleth the king of Israel the words that thou speakest in thy bed-chamber" (II Kings 6:12). Just afterwards, Elisha foretold that the king's messenger was coming for him, and predicted the raising of the siege of Samaria, and the death, on the following day, of the lord who scornfully denied the possibility of cheap food; all of which happened. 20

A well-attested instance is that of Sir John Drummond Hay, who, whilst Her Majesty's Minister in Morocco, was wakened from his sleep by hearing his daughter-in-law, who was at Mogador, three hundred miles away, say: "Oh! I wish papa only knew that Robert [her husband] was ill." On closing his eyes he again heard the same voice and words, when he 25 woke his wife, told her what he had heard, and noted it in his diary. Later, he found that Mrs. Robert Hay that night had used the precise words and had repeated them.[1]

In *A Hundred Years Hence*, T. Baron Russell writes: "Now that by suggestion alone we can with perfect precision cause a hypnotised person 30 (or even a person who has at some earlier period been hypnotised but has recovered his normal state) to hear—in his mind alone—sounds which have no objective existence, just as vividly and clearly as any sounds we can physically produce, does it seem extravagant to believe that the whole mechanism of sense, nay, the dark mind-gulf beyond mechanism, too, will 35 receive full illumination from the science of the coming time? Such a discovery would, of course, throw utterly into shadow anything we have yet learned of the nature of man. . . . Limited as we are by the knowledge of our own time, we cannot even conjecture whither such discoveries might lead us. All we can affirm is that the whole outlook of man, nay, the 40 nature of man himself, might very conceivably be changed by them, and the greatest problems of the thinker may be resolved."

Rapid Transmission of News.—I once asked one of the well-known explorers of Central Africa, who happens to be a friend of mine, how it was that news travelled with such rapidity in Central Africa. He told me 45 that when the natives wanted to know anything they merely took a little

---

[1] Attested details will be found in *Human Personality after Death"* by F. W. H. Myers, Vol. I, p. 396.

black boy, whom they first hypnotised and then questioned, when he was
able to see things at any distance, and reply correctly in every case. This
he had seen done half-a-dozen times. As a matter of fact, the boy, though
in a trance state, was partially de-hypnotised in this one respect, because
5 we are all more or less hypnotised into the belief that we have not this
power of sight—sight being purely mental. Being now aware of this, we
have to wake up and know the truth, namely, that man is never blinded,
but has perfect sight, perfect capacity to be conscious of any idea of God.
If the work is done in this way instead of by the wrong method, the other
10 faculties would not be paralysed, as in the case of the boy. All hypnotic
influence is wrong.

Many will recollect Sir Rider Haggard's psychic experience with his
dog, full details of which appeared publicly, and many confirmatory
instances might be given. Recently, in the *Spectator*, a letter from Sir Rider
15 Haggard was quoted, in which he says that "about twenty hours before
men, riding as fast as horses could carry them, brought the news of the
disaster at Isandhlwana to Pretoria, an old Hottentot informed me of what
had happened (here followed details of the fight). I was so impressed with
her manner that I went down to the Government Offices to repeat to my
20 superiors what she had said. . . . Sir Melmoth (then Mr.) Osborn
pointed out to me that it was impossible that such tidings could have
travelled 200 miles or so in about twelve hours. Nevertheless, it proved
perfectly correct."

The fact of news being transmitted in a wonderful way is now beyond
25 necessity for proof. The official reports made by the officers of the British
Army during the rebellion in India stated that the natives were able to
transmit news in a totally inexplicable way. Well-known writers on India,
such as Sir Henry Shakespeare and Dr. William Carr, confirm this,
and testify as to the fact of mental telepathy by Brahmin and Buddhist
30 priests.

As a young man I had everything that anyone could desire, but if I had
been told that I could have one wish, but only one wish, gratified, I should
have at once answered that I would prefer to cease to exist, because I knew
that I was no better than any other person; it was simply a question that I
35 did not have sufficient temptation, and I thought that at any time temptations might come that were too much for me. At one time I had arranged
to give up everything in England and go to India, hoping to find some
religion more useful than those available in the West. Fortunately, I met
Laurence Oliphant, who told me what a mistake his doing the same thing
40 had been. I now know that a man has to remain in the busiest centres,
where there are the greatest evils to destroy. The friend, with whom I had
been going to India, went, and told me afterwards that he had been for
about a year at one of the silent monasteries, the principal hall of which
was cut out of stone, underground. The day before he left he was sitting
45 quietly with his mentor, who suddenly said to him, "I should not do that."
Turning to him, my friend said, "How did you know what I was thinking
of doing?" The reply was simply a smile, and looking round at the thirty
or forty silent priests, who were sitting on the stone benches around, he
saw that they were all smiling. Then did the fact flash across his mind,

which he afterwards verified, that they were not really silent, as they communicated mentally with each other.

The relief of Mafeking was known the next day in Zululand, and also
700 miles away in the interior. Although Cairo is some 800 miles from
Khartoum, the fall of Khartoum and Gordon's death were known in the 5
bazaars of Cairo on the day it happened, and long before any information
reached Europe.

During the war in Somaliland quite a sensation was created in the
House of Commons when Mr. Harcourt stated that he had received a
satisfactory account of the situation, but that he did not propose reading the 10
telegram or sending it to the Press on account of "the exceeding rapidity
with which statements made in the House were conveyed to the utmost
corners of Somaliland."

Speech is Mental.—When one spiritual, immortal man in heaven
speaks to another, he is passing on or re-presenting the ideas that the action 15
of God has caused a fellow-being previously to pass on to him. That is to
say, God speaks to us by means of our fellow-men. In the material world
the human being has a false sense of these thoughts of God which
apparently give an impression of hearing sounds.

When in this material world, or false sense of the real world, the 20
thought is sufficiently uplifted, we get a far clearer sense of these thoughts
of God; so clear, it may even be, that they sound like a person speaking,
though none be visible, and some mistakenly believe that it is a finite God
speaking. This uplifted thought is the reason for the sounds heard by
Moses, Samuel, Paul, and by some living to-day who are personally known 25
to me, and who are following in the Master's footsteps. At the same time,
it must be recollected that whenever anyone speaks to you, the sounds are
God's thoughts, perceived materially and therefore falsely, as everything
in the material so-called world is simply a counterfeit of the real.

A few years ago, a man came to me for advice as to whether he should 30
allow his wife to continue daily "speaking mentally" to her sister in
America. He had constantly been able to verify the information given. I
advised him to discourage it as being too dangerous, and told him that it
was rather like experimenting with high-tension electrical currents in days
when we knew very little about them. Several times in the early days of 35
electricity, in the ordinary course of my professional duties, I have paid
the penalty of ignorance of high-tension electrical effects and burnt and
temporarily blinded myself. In the false, "non-mental" work the danger
is that in endeavouring to get better results, the worker forces the human
"consciousness," causing troubles of different kinds to arise, leading often 40
to insanity.

There is only one way of awakening dormant powers safely and properly,
and that is, in the way in which our Lord worked, namely, by knowing the
truth, turning in thought to God, and realising the truth; for instance, that
God being Soul, and man being made in the image and likeness of God, has 45
all understanding. Soul is the synonym that expresses God as the giver of
all wisdom and knowledge.

The first step is to open the door. Everything in the material world being

"pseudo-mental," we could practically prevent any given result by realising strongly enough that such result was impossible. This is the wrong way of working, as the human consciousness cannot judge of what is best. In our endeavours to gain truth, we must not outline human events, but must keep
5 an absolutely open mind, ready to receive more spiritual ideas. Then we shall be governed by God. "Prove all things; hold fast that which is good" (I Thess. 5:21).

Smell is Mental.—Speaking of the young girl already mentioned, Professor Lombroso says: "Her sense of smell was also transposed; for
10 ammonia or asafœtida, when thrust under her nose, did not excite the slightest reaction, while, on the other hand, a substance possessing the merest trace of odour, if held under the chin, made a vivid impression on it, and excited a quite special simulation (mimica). . . . Later, the sense of smell became transferred to the back of the foot."

15 **Reading the Past and Future.**—He continues: "Next appeared phenomena of prediction and clairvoyance, for she foresaw with what I would call mathematical exactness. . . . She later predicted things that were to happen to her father and brother, and two years afterwards they were verified. She clairvoyantly saw from her sick bed her brother in the
20 coulisses of a theatre (as in fact he was), distant by more than half a mile from the house." [1]

Sir David Brewster investigated the matter and testified to the power that man has of seeing the past. He wrote: "Not a leaf waves, not an insect crawls, not a ripple moves, but each motion is recorded by a thousand
25 faithful scribes in infallible and indelible scripture—only waiting for a suitable application to reveal themselves to the inquiring gaze."

It is recorded in the Bible that it was not necessary for people to tell our Lord of events. For instance, he knew the past of the woman at the well. There are several cases recorded of his knowing what was going to
30 happen, and often it is stated that he knew people's thoughts (Matt. 12:25; Luke 5:22; 6:8; 9:47; 11:17).

Agassiz, the famous naturalist, three times dreamed that he saw a fish, the characteristics even of which he had failed to recognise from its fossil imprint. The third time, upon awakening, he sketched and described the
35 fish, and later found that his dream was correct. [2]

Scientific Explanation.—"*Thoughts and images may be transferred from one mind to another without the agency of the recognised organs of sense*" [3] (Sir William Crookes).

Directly a person thinks of anything in the material world, even in the

40   [1] The reason why any results of this description are so difficult to obtain under test conditions, is that the thought of anyone that the results cannot be obtained, as a rule is sufficient to interfere with the vibrations, so delicate is the mechanism at work.
    [2] The book called *An Adventure*, recently published, to the good faith of the
45 authors of which Messrs. Macmillan & Co. testify, is simply a record of two people with special powers of sight, who were enabled to see the thoughts under present day form representative of what was happening in 1789.
    [3] Presidential Address, British Association, 1898.

past or future, he is immediately in faint touch along the lines of the ether with the thoughts or lines of force that constitute the thing thought of. The ordinary man is not conscious of these thoughts, as his human consciousness, through a belief in limitation, works so badly. Some people have not this false belief of limitation, and the "conscious mind" vibrates 5 in unison or synchronously with the "subconscious mind," or universal false belief, when the person knows the thing immediately. This is because the subconscious "mind" is the cinematographic pictures which constitute the past, present, and future of the material world. Sometimes he sees the thing happening, and sometimes he merely knows it intellectually. 10 This development is a curse or a blessing in proportion as a man knows how to destroy evil forseen or foreknown, and to realise the eternal reality of good.

Men are finding out that knowledge is not something to be gained only by study; they are learning that inspiration is scientific, and that they 15 ought to know anything in the material world that they rightly desire. The greater the number that grasp this fact, the easier it becomes for individuals to bring about this result. The only thing that prevents us all knowing anything that we need is the almost universal belief that this is impossible. 20

Inventions.—When a man tries to invent, he is merely trying to read thoughts. We ought to be able to see an invention ethereally—miscalled mentally—before it is manifested materially. Soon many will be able to do this, especially those who know how to work scientifically by true prayer, in order to bring out improved results. Inventions then will increase with 25 great rapidity right up to the end of all human limitations. The work now done by human mechanism will be largely superseded; accurate views of human theories will be generally held; and the time now wasted in going from place to place, and carrying out many mechanical duties, will be utilised in more advanced and interesting work. 30

In *The Evolution of Matter*, Dr. Le Bon says: " I have more than once in my researches come across problems, the solutions of which would modify the march of civilisation more profoundly than all the changes of constitutions and reforms. It is only in the progress of science that great social transformation can be looked for." Dr. Le Bon also says: "Science 35 [material science] has not yet any glimpse of the time when it may discover the true First Cause of things, nor even arrive at the real causes of a single phenomenon. It must therefore leave to religions and to philosophies the care of imagining systems capable of satisfying our longing to know. All these systems represent the synthesis of our ignorance and of our hopes, 40 and are, consequently, only pure illusions."

"Scientific statements change. What is true in one age, becoming antiquated in another, is replaced by further developments. . . . There are things even now being dreamed of in philosophy which were once outside its pale altogether. Philosophy is becoming a far more comprehensive 45 thing than it used to be" (Sir Oliver Lodge, F.R.S.).

The above are perfectly accurate statements, and the great social transformation, due to religion and philosophy, corrected by science, is now shortly about to take place, when man finds himself the image and likeness of God, the consciousness and expression of Mind, in a perfect world of reality, resplendent with glorious mental conceptions, the result of the perfect work of the one Mind, God.

The Divining Rod.[1]—This is a useful form of thought-reading,
5 whereby the thought-reader is able to tell when he is standing over water, and to indicate it by unconscious action in various ways, such as the turning or twisting of a rod in his hands. The use of a rod is a mere limitation, and unnecessary.[2]

I remember a few years ago, when in conversation with a well-known
10 scientific man, saying that before very long we should find such results as a man knowing whether he was standing over gold-bearing rock by his hair standing on end, or by some such inconsequent sign. A day or two afterwards I read an account of a man in America who, when he stood over oil in quantity, knowingly or otherwise, was at once seized with severe
15 illness.[3]

Evil Effects when Reading.—"*Passing through the brain of a Walter Scott or a Dickens such knowledge* ["of the tragic events and turpitude of life"] *becomes purified and protective, and has nothing but a wholesome effect when sown broadcast, but passing through the brain of an Aphra Behn or a*
20 *Zola, it grows infective and deadly and disseminates a moral plague around. And thus ideas, like microbes, may by cultivation be attenuated and rendered harmless, or raised to a higher malignancy*"[4] (Sir J. Crichton-Browne).

It is a mistake to read books by people who are not of a satisfactory character. Directly you read them you are in ethereal touch with the
25 individuality of the person who wrote the book, and if he is not the right class of man, wrong thoughts are more likely to affect you, unless you are protecting yourself in the right way. If a man is protecting himself thoroughly, I do not think that he would find himself reading such books.

Scientific Method of Working.—"*Jesus . . . needed not that any*
30 *should testify of man: for he knew what was in man*" (John 2:24, 25).

In order to gain knowledge in the right way, we must turn to heaven and realise the truth, for instance, that God is Soul, the Principle of all knowledge, and that, therefore, man, the spiritual man, instantly knows everything necessary. The action of God as Truth then destroys the
35 particles on the cells of the human mechanism that give the trouble, with the result that the two portions of the machine work better together, and in this way requisite and legitimate knowledge of the past, present, or

---

[1] Professor Barrett has made an interesting report to the Psychical Research Society on his investigations, showing that results have been obtained that cannot
40 be explained by any generally recognised theories.

[2] I have recently been consulted with reference to an electro-mechanical apparatus for bringing about the same result, which is said to act perfectly. Since this was written it has been taken up and successfully used by W. Mansfield & Co., of Brunswick Street, Liverpool.

45 [3] Recently, a "water-diviner" from Bolton stated that he has been able to locate beds of iron ore near Barrow by using a steel rod instead of the usual hazel twig. Details are given in the *Western Mail* of August 17, 1911.

[4] "The Hygienic Uses of Imagination."

future is conveyed.[1] It is interesting to note, however, that working thus the knowledge does not always come to your consciousness in the way above mentioned. Sometimes somebody will give you the information, or you will see it in a paper or book.

Thought-Reading.—*"Were I now introducing for the first time these inquiries* [the results of his researches into so-called spiritualistic phenomena] *to the world of science I should choose a starting point different from that of old. It would be well to begin with telepathy,[2] with the fundamental law, as I believe it to be"* (Sir William Crookes).

The power of thought-reading is nowadays very common. Mark Twain prided himself on his powers, and said that he often knew what people far distant were thinking, or made them know what he was thinking. He called it "mental" telegraphy. Well-known recent instances are those of Mr. Zanzig and Mr. Zomah intensifying material thoughts so that their wives could perceive them. Such intensification is not only a wrong and dangerous method of working, but very tiring, and therefore those working professionally in this way do not use this ethereal method of communication unless absolutely necessary, relying, as far as possible, upon codes and other means. What has been called brain work has always been regarded as most tiring, and truly so, not being mental in any degree, but purely physical. Mental work is spiritual and natural, and nothing is so resting. It is thinking of God and His world.

The power of reading human thoughts can be applied before they come into seeming action, whilst in action, or after they have acted.[3] Many instances beyond all question could be given, among them the experiences of Emanuel Swedenborg. His scientific position and the publicity of the results obtained make his experiences worth referring to. He was able to give to a company assembled at dinner at Gothenburg all the details of a fire that was then taking place at Stockholm, over two hundred miles distant. I remember well how puzzled I was as a boy to understand why people did not try to find out the reason for this. There has recently been a similar incident, where the Rev. Dr. Sanders, a distinguished Presbyterian clergyman, of the United States, who has these psychometric powers developed, vividly described a serious fire taking place two hundred miles away, the details of which turned out to be accurate.

[1] "When mortal man blends his thoughts of existence with the spiritual and works only as God works, he will no longer grope in the dark" (*Science and Health*, p. 263, Mary Baker Eddy).
[2] M. Bergson has said: "I consider that those experiments [those published by the Society of Psychical Research] have brought out so much evidence for telepathy as to render it so highly probable as to be practically certain. I myself have read through all the forty volumes of cases collected by the Society, and I do not think anyone could do so without feeling as convinced as I do. . . . There is a considerable amount of evidence to show that the medium is—in part at least—material . . . apparently no distance presents any difficulty to telepathic communication" (interview published in *Morning Post*, June 16, 1914).
[3] "It is the prerogative of the ever-present, divine Mind, and of thought which is in rapport with this Mind, to know the past, the present, and the future" *Science and Health*, p. 84. Mary Baker Eddy).

Lack of Knowledge Results in Trouble.—A lady, a friend of mine, experienced great unhappiness until she was able to cut off thoughts. She knew what ideas were coming to the people to whom she spoke, and the difference between what was said and the false thoughts that came con-
5 tinually distressed her, as she was of a sensitive nature. Had the truth been known to her she would not only have prevented the thoughts affecting her, but would have destroyed them, and so prevented them harming those who were intensifying them.

Early Experiences.—Anyone who is interested in the early history of
10 thought-reading will find a paper by my brother in volume eleven of *Proceedings of the Psychical Research Society*. This was reproduced in the *Daily Mail* some few years ago with a few experiences of mine in so-called thought-reading, made about twelve years previously, the only time I ever tried anything of the kind. These results merely prove that which every-
15 one must have more or less experienced, namely, that sometimes people think the same thoughts at the same time.[1] This means that they are in ethereal touch with the same ideas along the lines of the ether, and these false thoughts cause a similar vibration in the human consciousness.[2] In the reality both are fully conscious of the same ideas of God, but in their
20 full spiritual perfection.

Work Mentally Only by Thinking of God and Heaven.—An absolute rule, never to be broken, should be made, namely, *Never attempt to work mentally except by turning in thought to God and heaven.* This is the essence of the whole of what is now put before you. With the exception of
25 a few boyish experiments at the age of fourteen, I have never taken any part in either spiritualistic or hypnotic experiments. It was only in the light of the knowledge of truth that the recognition came to me of the divine protection which steers one safely past such mistaken and useless attempts to gain knowledge of truth, and I am thankful for all the seeming circum-
30 stances in the past that have led up to this.

Foretelling the Future.—There are hundreds of well-authenticated instances of this. It is merely reading thought before it comes into apparent action, and therefore, instead of being called "second sight," should rather be called first sight.
35 Professor Lombroso, after exhaustive experiments, declared his belief in the power of accurately foretelling the future. Professor Hulin, of the University of Ghent, gives instances of his own knowledge of prediction, and I have records filed away of between fifty and one hundred cases.

The Confederate General, John B. Gordon, whom Dr. Heysinger cites
40 as a most capable man, both in military and civic life, devotes a whole

---

[1] Doubt has recently been thrown on the possibility of thought-reading. This is because it is very difficult to obtain such results in front of a strong thinking critic. It is like trying to pick up electric signals when a strong alternating current machine is at work overpowering the weaker vibrations. When one knows how to think
45 rightly such interfering vibrations can be destroyed by the action of God, and the limitless powers of man demonstrated.

[2] In the *Daily News* of August 31, 1911, appears an account of tests made by Professor Balfour Stuart, Mr. Edward Ward, and others, confirming the thought-reading powers of Lillian Bibby, aged eleven.

chapter in his *Reminiscences of the Civil War*, to various premonitions of
death among soldiers, one of which was that of his own brother, who
foretold the circumstances of his own death at the battle of Chancellors-
ville. This occurred as foreseen. Abraham Lincoln was depressed on the
morning of his assassination, as he had just had the same dream as had   5
come to him before the horrors of Bull Run and before another terrible
disaster to the Northern armies.

Mr. Andrew Lang, in his introductory chapter to *The Prophecies of the
Brahan Seer*, gives, amongst others, the following instance of this power:
"On June 15, 1908, a lady, well known to me, and in various fields of   10
literature, told me that, calling on another lady the day before, she had
seen a vision of a man previously unknown to her, who thrust a knife into
her friend's left side. I offered to bet £100 against fulfilment. In the autumn
my friend, again calling at the same house, met the man of her vision on
the doorstep. Entering, she found her friend dying, as her constitution did   15
not rally after an operation on her left side, performed by the man of the
vision, who was a surgeon."

One of the best-known cases related is the following, which is called the
"Seaforth Prophecy." It dates from the time of Charles II, and was said
to have been uttered by Coinneach Odhar Fiosaiche, a famous Brahan seer   20
(Alexander MacKenzie—*The Prophecies of the Brahan Seer*).[1] He was said
to have given the prophecy before being burnt alive by the wife of the third
Earl for clairvoyantly seeing and telling her that the Earl was unfaithful
to her in Paris:—

"I see a chief, the last of his house, both deaf and dumb. He will be the   25
father of four fair sons, all of whom he will follow to the tomb. He will
. . . . die mourning, knowing that the honours of his line are to be
extinguished for ever . . . the remnant of his possessions shall be
inherited by a white-coifed lassie from the East, and she is to kill her sister.
And as a sign by which it may be known that these things are coming to   30
pass, there shall be four great lairds in the days of the last deaf-and-dumb
Seaforth: Gairloch, Chisholm, Grant, and Rassay—of whom one shall be
buck-toothed, another hare-lipped, another half-witted, and the fourth a
stammerer."

This prophecy was fulfilled to the letter, the chief being Lord Sea-   35
forth, F.R.S., the last of his house, who, through an attack of scarlet fever,
became deaf and for a time dumb, and, after the death of his four sons,
died heartbroken in 1815, paralysed in mind and body. His eldest daughter,
Mary, who inherited, came from India, and her sister died from injuries
received in an accident when the elder daughter was driving. Even the   40
four lairds with the peculiarities mentioned were in existence when Lord
Seaforth died. In an article called "Prophecy and Coincidence," in *The
Nation*, of July 3, 1909, giving particulars of this case, the writer says,
"The inquirer who pronounced the prophecy and its fulfilment to be a case
of mere coincidence would, in all probability, declare St. Paul's Cathedral   45
and Westminster Abbey to be purely natural formations."

Robert Nixon, known as the Cheshire prophet, foretold so many events

---

[1] Lockhart, in *Life of Scott*.

5*

that James I commanded his attendance at Court. Nixon, who was a
stubborn, drivelling fool, refused, on the ground that he would be starved
to death there. Being made to go, his greediness made him so troublesome
to the cooks that they locked him up, and, being forgotten, he was, as he
5 had foretold, starved to death.

Swedenborg and many others foretold the exact time of their deaths as
well as those of other people.

One of the most remarkable dreams in English history was that related
by the well-known writer, the Rev. S. Baring-Gould. A detailed account
10 appeared in the London *Times*, of August 28, 1828. On the evening of
May 11, 1812, John Williams, a wealthy Cornish miner, had a dream which
was repeated three times, in which he saw a tall man dressed in a brown
coat with yellow buttons, draw a pistol from under his coat and fire at a
small man dressed in a blue coat and white waistcoat. He heard the report
15 of the pistol, and saw the bloodstain on the waistcoat, saw the man fall, and
the colour of the face change, as in death. In his dream he asked who the
man was who had been shot, and was told that it was the "Chancellor."
During the day Mr. Williams went to Falmouth, where he related the
details of the dream to everyone he met. One of his hearers said that the
20 description of the man shot was not that of the "Lord Chancellor," but of
Mr. Perceval, the Chancellor of the Exchequer and Prime Minister. The
following day the news of Mr. Perceval's assassination arrived. A few
weeks afterwards Mr. Williams went to London and pointed out the spot
where Mr. Perceval was shot by Bellingham, and it was found that the
25 description of the dress of each of the men was exact in every detail.

The murderer is now unsafe.[1] One of the signs of the times is the
description in the *Daily Mail* of March 30, 1911, of the trial of a farmer
named Strong, for murder. Miss Pauline Gerard, a clairvoyante, called as
chief witness, gave evidence that on seeing the scene and describing the
30 details to him, "He interrupted my description, crying, 'That is I! It is
terrible!'" As two detectives had been hidden in the room, the accused
tried to excuse his confession, which gave all the details, by saying that the
psychometrist had "paralysed him with fright," and that he "seemed to be
under her spell, and told her whatever she willed."[2]

35   **Genius.**—So-called genius is simply the synchronous vibration of
the so-called conscious human "mind" with the subconscious "no-
mind," or basic false mentality—that is, the vibrations take place uni-
formly together—both being, as it were, different strata of the ether, so

---

[1] In *Cassell's Saturday Journal* of September 9, 1911, an article, entitled "The
40 Trial of the Wrongdoer," gives some half-dozen instances of murderers that have
been detected through thought-reading of various kinds. Amongst them is the case
of Sir Astley Cooper, the famous physician, who, when called in by the police,
to his amazement detected a murderer through apparently seeing a dog sniffing at
a bloodstain which had escaped detection. This was after he had finished his
45 examination. Yet there was no dog discoverable in the cell. The man was hanged,
but the mystery of the dog was never solved.
[2] The reason why hitherto it has always been difficult to obtain such a result in
the case of well-known murders, etc., is that there is too much thought on the subject which interferes with the ethereal vibrations. When working properly such
50 interfering thoughts can be destroyed by the action of God.

that a person becomes conscious of the material thoughts apparently causing the subconscious, lower "no-mind" to vibrate. Professor Lombroso
looked upon genius as a form of insanity. Myers calls it "a subliminal
uprush." True genius is the genius of Christianity, "works more than
words." This genius shines with a selfless humility. Professor Bateson, at   5
the British Association Meeting (1914), stated that he believed that the
artistic gift of mankind would prove to be due to the absence of some
factors which in the normal person prevent the development of these
gifts. The instrument was there, but it was "stopped down." This is quite
accurate.   10

Calculating Boys.—There have been some half-dozen so-called calculating boys, such as the astonishing Tamil boy, and George Bidder, who
became President of the Institution of Civil Engineers. When between
twelve and fourteen, the latter could give an answer instantly to practically
any mathematical question that was asked. His grand-daughter told me   15
that he never made any calculations, but as a rule seemed to see the figures
in front of him, and simply read them out. One of my engineers had the
same faculty partially developed. Zerah Colborn, who could not on paper
do simple multiplication or division, could give instantly the square or
cube or square root or cube root of practically any number. All this is   20
ordinary thought-reading.

Trance Speaking.—Not only do people in a trance condition often say
what would be considered absolutely impossible, considering their past,
but they will sometimes speak in a language with which they have never
been acquainted. The head of one of the religious sects in England once   25
asked advice with reference to a man who had been his stenographer a few
weeks before, and who was then speaking and writing Chinese fluently,
having never known a word of that language. He wanted to know whether
it was of God or of the devil, as this would make a considerable difference
to his future policy. After answering a few questions, he told me that the   30
stenographer at these times went into an ecstatic condition and was
tongue-tied. By this he meant that he was unable to answer questions
whilst speaking or writing Chinese. It was then easy to show him that it
had nothing to do with God and equally nothing to do with any devil, but
was simply an abnormal state of human consciousness, a state, however,   35
now fairly common. Whenever a person obtains abnormal results, he is
bringing them about in the wrong way if he at the same time loses any of
his ordinary powers even for a moment or two. There have been many
instances of this nature. Professor Richet, for instance, describes a French
lady, who wrote whole pages in Greek, although not even knowing the   40
Greek alphabet. Every day results of this kind are becoming more frequent. Gibbon writes: "The knowledge of foreign languages was frequently communicated to the contemporaries of Irenæus. . . . The
divine inspiration . . . is described as a favour very liberally bestowed
on all ranks of the faithful."[1] M. Ribot, the great French psychologist,   45
says: "It is the unconscious which produces what is commonly called
inspiration." It is by true prayer that a man is really inspired.

---

[1] *The Decline and Fall of the Roman Empire.*

Somnambulism.—Some people frequently, whilst in an apparently unconscious state, do most wonderful things, using, however, at these times a power which all men possess. There are many instances, one of the best known being that of a man in Edinburgh, who in his sleep climbed a
5 rock that it was impossible to mount in the ordinary state. These powers are usually exerted at times of great excitement. I remember hearing of an old lady who rushed into her burning house and got out her piano unaided. We all know that at times we are capable of exerting phenomenal strength and phenomenal powers. A man who is hypnotised frequently does this.
10 It must be recollected that in all cases of abnormal excitement, the man is simply hypnotised, not by any human being, but by the thoughts influencing him, and he so acts on account of the intensity of the thoughts passing over him. This is harmful. We must learn to exercise unusual powers, when required, without the slightest excitement or abnormal condition,
15 and this can only be done by turning in thought to God and heaven, relying upon a spiritual, perfect, and ever-active unalterable law, the law of divine Mind.

Ghosts and Visions.[1]—The material man has still greater apparent powers. The material "no-mind," mistranslated in the Bible the soul, fits
20 into the material body like a hand into a glove, or rather throughout the body like water in a sponge.[2] It is exactly the shape of the body, which grows as this "no-mind" gradually increases in size, or as some would say, it is conformed to an idea of maturity. This is the reason for what are called visions of departed spirits at the moment of death. The more ethereal
25 form then easily leaves the more tangible body, and although the passage from place to place cannot be instantaneous, it appears to be almost so. The human "mind" is material, bearing somewhat the same relation to ordinary matter that vapour does to water, and can be seen only by those who are what is called psychic.[3] This is the reason for the theosophist's
30 belief in an astral body, which is really the individual human "mind." Under their system this so-called human mind is called the "etheric body."

Professor W. F. Barrett, lecturing at the City Temple, gave details of a little girl, known to him, whose mother was horror-struck on finding

35   [1] There have been many so-called spirit appearances that hitherto have not been cleared up. That of "Jeffrey," the ghost that troubled the Wesley family in 1716, was evidenced by sight, sound, and touch. Samuel, the elder brother of John Wesley, the famous divine, a man of shrewd sense, was completely puzzled.

[2] "Matter and mortal mind are but different strata of human belief. The grosser
40 substratum is named matter or body; the more ethereal is called mind. This so-called mind and body is the illusion called a mortal, a mind in matter. In reality and in Science, both strata, mortal mind and mortal body, are false representatives of man" (*Science and Health*, p. 293. Mary Baker Eddy).

[3] The American Society for Psychical Research, in its Journal of June, 1907,
45 has given details of experiments showing that there is an unaccountable loss of weight just after death. Dr. Duncan MacDougall made most careful experiments, and found a loss of weight of from $\frac{3}{8}$ to $1\frac{1}{2}$ oz. 50 gr. at the moment of apparent death. He writes: "A loss of substance occurs at death not accounted for by known channels of loss. Is it the 'soul substance'? It would seem to me to be so."
50 He shows that it is probably much lighter than air, which weighs about $1\frac{1}{4}$ oz. per cubic foot.

that the child knew all about the suicide of her uncle, who, she said, had appeared before his death was known, and asked her to pray for him. It is a sign of the times to find at such a place a Professor of the Royal College of Science for Ireland lecturing as he did on occult phenomena. This is not a solitary instance, for, a little time before, I had been asked to 5 repeat at the same place a lecture in which had been given the scientific reasons for the so-called miracles of Jesus and other hitherto unexplained phenomena. Professor Barrett stated that the living influence which projected the telepathic impact from one mind to another, often created the phantasm or image of the person, and this living impulsive power remained 10 operative after death. This is not so, it is merely due to the thoughts intensifying themselves on the human consciousness, and there is nothing living about it except the spiritual reality that is at the back of it all, which is not under any circumstances visible to the human senses. The case given by him of Lord Combermere having been photographed as a legless 15 man sitting in his chair in the otherwise empty library, after his death from an accident which necessitated the amputation of his legs, comes into a different class of phenomena. Had the portrait been that of the human consciousness of Lord Combermere, the legs would have shown. A psychic person can always apparently see the limbs which appear to have been 20 amputated, as he sees that portion of the "consciousness," which is in no way lessened by the more material amputation. "Thoughts are matter of a finer grade, and thought-forms are clearly visible by many who have made a speciality of this higher sense of sight" (Stenson Hooker, M.D.).

In 1889 an inquiry was undertaken by the Society for Psychical Research, 25 when about 17,000 answers were received. The coincidences of death, when one in a normal state of health had a "death warning," was 1 in 43, whereas, if chance alone had operated the proportion mathematically was 1 in 19,000. The committee held it to be proved that "between death and apparitions of the dying person a connection exists which is not due to 30 chance alone." Sir Oliver Lodge says: "The fact of their existence has been thoroughly established."

The Apparent Power of the "No-Mind" to Move Instantly.— The human so-called mind has apparently the power of almost instantaneous movement.   35

Professor Lombroso gives a number of instances of doubles, that is to say, of what seems to be a living person appearing at a distance. This is merely the human consciousness, or in some cases even the material "mind" and body, being seen by another person. They may also be merely ethereal, materialised forms, material thoughts made visible, which have 40 nothing to do with the so-called living person, as shown by Dr. Reid's investigation in America.

The case of Mrs. Butler, given by Augustus Hare in his *Story of My Life*, is well known. For many nights this lady dreamt that she visited a beautiful house. About a year later she found herself in the house of her 45 dream, and was able to give details of it, and bought the house very cheaply owing to its reputation of being haunted. The ghost in this case was merely the "consciousness" of Mrs. Butler, temporarily freed from a belief of

being bound in a solid body.[1] Madame Meurier twice saw at the foot of her
bed her dead brother after the Chinese rebels had murdered him. This,
similarly, was his human "mind," before it passed into the next state of
consciousness. In fact, instances of things of this sort are so numerous that
5 it is hardly worth while giving details of them.

There have been many similar results in the past. One of the best
instances is recorded by Lapponi, who, as Professor Lombroso writes,
being physician to the Pope, would not be likely, except under strong
conviction, to put on record matters so opposed to the Roman Catholic
10 beliefs. He gives the case of Alfred Pansini, who at the age of seven
spoke as a born orator, frequently in languages of which he had no knowledge, and recited whole cantos of the *Divine Comedy*. At the age of ten
so marvellous were the results obtained by Alfred and his brother Paul,
aged eight, that it is worth while giving Professor Lombroso's account:
15 "At the age of ten, with his brother Paul, aged eight, without knowing how
or why, he was himself transported in half an hour from Ruvo to Molfetta.
Another day the two children found themselves, in a scant half-hour from
Ruvo, seated in a boat at sea near Barletta. Another time, in ten minutes
they were at a distance from Ruvo, and in front of the house door of an
20 uncle of theirs, before whom Alfred made the prediction that they would
not be able to depart next day, not until fifteen days had elapsed. In fact,
the next day the uncle's horse was taken ill. Then the aunt hired a carriage
to take back her nephews to Ruvo. But no sooner had they been recon-
signed to their parents than they disappeared again, and again found them-
25 selves at Trani. Being sent back to Ruvo, they disappeared once more and
found themselves at Bisceglie. Then, convinced that they were struggling
in vain against superior powers, they betook themselves to Trani, to await
the expiration of the fifteen days." [2]

Remember that this is not an impossibility at all, but a thing that before
30 long, owing to the rapid general disappearance of man's limitations, will
be recognised as a natural proceeding. Jesus not only went instantly from
the centre of the Sea of Galilee, but after "walking on the sea," "about
five and twenty or thirty furlongs" from the land, in boisterous weather,
"immediately the ship [and all the disciples] was at the land whither they
35 went" (John 6:21). No wonder the people said: "Rabbi, when camest thou
hither?" (verse 25).

---

[1] "In sleep, memory and consciousness are lost from the body, and they
wander whither they will apparently with their own separate embodiment"
(*Science and Health*, p 491. Mary Baker Eddy).
40 One of the best accounts of a psychic person seeing the human mind leave
the body is given in full detail by Andrew Jackson Davis in *Great Harmonia*,
Vol. I, p. 157. Another, given by a medical man, is mentioned by Mr. Myers, and
is reported in the *Proceedings of the Society for Psychical Research*, Vol. VIII,
pp. 180–193. Dr. Baraduc has published some interesting photographs taken
45 shortly after the death of his wife. In these a kind of mist is visible. Cases of those
who are psychic seeing this mist are reported. Louisa Alcott, the well-known
author of *Little Women*, relates how, at the moment of death, she saw, as it were, a
thin smoke arise from her sister Bertha and vanish. The doctor told her this was not
an hallucination but the life departing visibly. Dr. Patrick O'Donnell says that he
50 has photographed this at the Mercy Hospital, Chicago.
[2] *Ipnotismo Spiritismo, Roma*, 1906.

Dr. Shepley Park states that the negroes on the Gold Coast had mental means of communication at a distance which were "the monopoly of a kind of secret society." Their results were obtained very simply, and by means of continual practice. It was claimed that a few of them could materialise the entire body at a distance. The records of travellers teem 5 with similar instances of occult phenomena, and Professor Lombroso gives numerous instances in his book *After Death—What?* Nor are these results confined to modern times. History records many cases. It is said that Epimenides of Crete had power to send his soul (human conscious- ness) out of his body and recall it at pleasure. During its absence his body 10 was as dead, being cold and inanimate. Of Hermatimus, a prophet of Clazomanae, it is recorded that his soul left his material body and wandered into every part of the world. So much was his wonderful gift of divination prized by the people that they erected a temple to him and paid him "divine honours." 15

In *Invisible Helpers*, its author gives many instances of aid given by the human consciousness, apart from the body, in attempts to help those at a distance. This method of working is, however, unsatisfactory, and highly dangerous to both parties, interfering with the individuality of those influenced. This is the reason why such great precautions are taken and 20 grades of probationary periods are considered necessary for those endeavouring to help their fellows in this mistaken way. When these would-be helpers learn how to think rightly, real and lasting aid can be safely and efficiently given by almost all of them, after a few days', indeed, after a few minutes' practice, instead of only by a few persons, and that 25 after years of study.

Amongst many others, Mrs. Besant has referred to this practice. She says : "I know of more than one person in England who can slip out of the body, remain conscious while out of it, and return into the body"[1] ("Theosophy" in *Questions and Answers*). 30

All the above are instances of the wrong way of working, and bear clearly their fallacy on the face of them.

DANGER AHEAD

Dangerous and Useless Experiments.—One business client of mine, who for two years had been practising regularly every night in this 35 wrong way, told me that he had given it up on account of its danger, as, although conscious, he was over two hours one day before managing to get back again into his body. The body, when left, through ignorance of

---

[1] A number of attested cases are given in *Phantasms of the Living*, some of them having been investigated by the London Society for Psychical Research. Col. 40 Olcott refers to various historic cases of living beings leaving their bodies and working at a distance, and writes : "As to living witnesses, I am one myself, for I have seen the doubles of several men acting intelligently at great distances from their bodies, and in this pamphlet that I hold in my hand [*Hints on Esoteric Theosophy*] will be found the certificates of no less than nine reputable persons—five Hindus 45 and four Europeans—that they have seen such appearances on various occasions within the past two years. . . . And now is this double—which is nothing but what is commonly called the 'soul'—immortal? No, it is not" (Lecture delivered at Madras, April 26, 1882).

how to take it along with the "consciousness," has every appearance of
death, and the man is in many cases spoken of as in a trance. Irving
Bishop, the well-known thought-reader, frequently fell into these death-
like trances. Finally, while in America, he was taken to a hospital, where,
5 without waiting to see if he was really dead, they took out his brain in an
attempt to discover to what his abnormal powers were due. This I was told
by a friend of his, who was boiling over with fierce indignation at what he
spoke of as "his murder."

Harmful Results.—Any endeavour to obtain in this way results
10 of this sort, thought-reading, clairvoyance,[1] leaving the body, etc., is a
mistake and dangerous. All so-called miraculous results must only come
naturally, and through turning in thought to God, in the way science
demands, and without previously picturing what is about to appear. Let
"good" work. If you are doing true mental work, false, unrecognised
15 "thoughts" will be destroyed before they take form in so-called conscious
thought each day, without your worrying about the future. Then so-called
good thoughts, better beliefs, will act. "Sufficient unto the day is the evil
thereof," the Master said (Matt. 6:34). Each day, bringing its work,
brings also the power to accomplish that work.
20 It is sometimes rather difficult to tell to a certainty when wrong thoughts
have been destroyed. When all fear is entirely gone it will almost always be
found that the wrong thoughts are destroyed. Very often before this point
has been quite reached, you have done sufficient work to prevent them
doing appreciable harm, and it is well to consider that if you go on working,
25 you may waste much valuable time through leaving more important calls
unheeded. If you simply work when you are conscious of the wrong
thought, you will lose no time.
Occult workers will tell you of the great dangers run in (their idea of)
mental working, and theosophy teaches you not to interfere with another
30 man's "Karma," namely, the experiences it is believed he must pass
through in this "state of incarnation" on account of his life in the past.
The reason for this is that they merely accentuate material thoughts,
rendering them still more dangerous to all concerned, instead of mentally
working, and so destroying such false thoughts. It is a good thing that in
35 the practice of occultism and theosophy people are warned against
"mental" working, because any use of the material "no-mind" in the
way taught by them is fraught with increasing danger. These systems do
not teach the right, and therefore the scientific, method of prayer, although
they are rapidly changing. Praying in the way that is now pointed out, by
40 turning in thought to God, and never picturing the material man, nor even
the spiritual reality of any individual, you cannot possibly harm anyone,
and must do good to yourself and to those you are endeavouring to help.
Dr. Franz Hartmann, the well-known philosopher and authority on
occultism, writing in the *Theosophist* of October, 1909, with reference to

45   [1] "If you are under a very great nervous strain, if you have overworked yourself
so that you are nervously weak, if your temperature goes up beyond 102 or 103
degrees, then you will tend to become clairvoyant or clairaudient" (Annie Besant in
Man's Life in This and Other Worlds).

an article about "True and False Yoga," written by Marie Russak in the *Adyar Bulletin* of August, 1908, says: "This article has again forcibly called my attention to the disastrous results arising from meddling with occult practices without understanding their real nature. I have before my eyes a long list of friends and personal acquaintances, who, within the 5 last few years, have become victims of their 'psychic researches,' for which they were not ripe, and in which they persisted in spite of all warning. Some of them became insane, some incurably diseased, others obsessed and morally depraved, and not a few of them ended by suicide. They were not unintelligent and uneducated people; on the contrary, one of them was 10 a great and well-known scientist and inventor, noble-minded and generous; several were writers and poets of some distinction, and a few even public lecturers on theosophical subjects and on spiritualism—things, however, of which they had very little personal experience, and of which they knew only from reading." 15

How entirely different is this to the manifest results that accrue from practice of the right method of working, now known to us. Available to all seekers for truth, this is now brought to your special notice. An absolute beginner, correctly taught, can, with a proper motive, often at once, and always with absolute safety to himself and all others, get results of great 20 variety and seemingly of the most miraculous nature,[1] while daily becoming more conscious of an increasing sense of peace and joy and harmony, both within and around. These results are obtained by the realisation of God.

THE SAFE WAY TO WORK 25

The Appearance of Jesus when the Doors were Shut.[2]—The miracles of Jesus were not contrary to law nor the workings of the human mechanism. He utilised a power that is available to all, the power of divine Mind, which enables humanity to cast off its limitations. When the human consciousness has left the body, it then when seen, looks like the body, and 30 can pass without difficulty through matter. This is not the right method of working, and is dangerous. The body should be dematerialised, or at all events, taken along with the "consciousness." The best-known instances of this are the sudden appearances of Jesus to the disciples, although the doors were shut. He had scientifically dematerialised the grosser sub- 35 stratum of human belief, named matter, or carnal body, in the grave, and the more ethereal matter, or "consciousness," could then move instantly from place to place. In other words, he reappeared to his disciples in a less material form. Sooner or later it will be found that many men will develop their so-called powers, and, like Jesus, will apparently go ethereally from 40 place to place without the "consciousness" leaving the body.[3] It is

---

[1] . . . and you will have touched the hem of the garment of Jesus's idea of matter. Christ was the 'way'; since Life and Truth were the way that gave us, through a human person, a spiritual revelation of man's possible earthly development" (*Miscellaneous Writings*, p. 75. Mary Baker Eddy). 45

[2] See John 20, verse 19.

[3] "Divest yourself of the thought that there can be substance in matter, and the movements and transitions now possible for mortal mind will be found to be equally possible for the body" (*Science and Health*, p. 90).

extremely dangerous to attempt anything of this nature unless a man
clearly understand the spiritual science that governs this class of phenomena, and knows how to apply the rules of life, as taught by our Lord and
referred to hereafter, subordinating the human limitation to the divine
5 requirement.

Since the above was written, a most interesting article by T. S. Baldwin,
inventor of the United States dirigible airship, has appeared in one of the
magazines. In the beginning, he deals with the so-called mental co-
efficient in flying,[1] and ends his article as follows: "First we shall fly a step
10 in a crude machine; we have begun to do that; then in time we shall sail
the air in great ships, and in some remote day man will pass through the
air in his own body solely. No one who has keenly felt the joy and triumphs
of flight in his own person can fail to believe in this last prediction." This
prediction, soberly given in the public press by a practical man like Mr.
15 Baldwin, says much for the advanced knowledge of the reading public
on the subject of the development of mental power. Mankind cannot too
quickly rise beyond this limited and dangerous sense of a false, illusory
mental basis, and gain the knowledge of the only true mental power, that
of Mind, God, which alone gives man perfect safety and his God-given
20 dominion over the whole earth.

DIVINE POWERS

A Scientific Remedy.—*"Were it fully understood that the emotions
are the masters, and the intellect the servant, it would be seen that little could
be done by improving the servant while the master remains unimproved.*
25 *Improving the servant does not give the masters more power of achieving their
ends"* [2] (Herbert Spencer).

As a rule the so-called conscious mind is only a clog on the action of
the "subconscious mind," owing to our inherited belief in limitation.
When, by what is called hypnotism, the "conscious mind" is quieted,
30 abnormal powers are manifested. By right thinking, the "conscious mind"
can be prevented from exercising this harmful power. Fortunately, the
miracles of Jesus are absolutely scientific. Anyone can do a miracle if he
has sufficient knowledge and leads a good enough life; that is, one
sufficiently unselfish. Jesus himself said: "He that believeth on me, the
35 works that I do shall he do also; and greater works than these shall he
do; because I go unto my Father" (John 14:12).

How are we to know whether what we believe is true or not? Jesus
answered this question when he said: "These signs shall follow them that
believe: In my name [nature] shall they cast out devils . . . " (Mk. 16:17).
40 By far the most important thing that mankind individually can do is to
turn in thought to God in the scientific way that Jesus taught. No words
can emphasise too strongly the importance of what is about to be put before
you, namely, the practical method of destroying evil of every kind and of

---

[1] In the *Times* of June 3, 1911, appears the following remark: "It is fairly obvious
45 that in long-distance races the temperament of the airman counts more than anything else."
[2] *Feeling versus Intellect.*

purifying the human consciousness. If you understand and put it into practice you will be well repaid. All science worthy of the name is divine.

Thought, from a natural science point of view, theoretically exists as a high-tension electrical current external to man, and thought after thought sweeps across the "consciousness." If you see an angry man and think he 5 is angry you increase the vibration of the thoughts making him angry, and momentarily he is worse. This, although it is only temporarily harming him, is naturally an absolutely wrong thing to do.

The Denial or "Michael."—"*For the grace of God that bringeth salvation hath appeared to all men, Teaching us that, denying ungodliness* 10 *and worldly lusts, we should live soberly, righteously, and godly, in this present world*" (Titus 2:11, 12).

When you see an angry man, if you turn in thought to heaven and realise—that is, make real to yourself—as clearly as you can, that there is no anger in heaven, the action of God destroys the angry thoughts, which 15 for the moment are the cause of his anger, and instantly the man ceases to be angry. This is the denial, or emptying of the human consciousness that cannot be filled with truth if already full of evil thoughts—false beliefs. Disease, sin, and death are not in God, and by knowing the unreality of evil, we demonstrate the allness of God, good. You have, however, done 20 neither the man nor yourself any permanent good although you have helped the world, because we are just so many thoughts nearer the end of the material world; that is, of all troubles, including sin, sickness, death, and other forms of so-called materiality. It is the denial of matter (there is nothing but God) which brings all evil to its end, as shown in Daniel 12, 25 verse 1. This denial of evil is in the Bible called the Angel Michael (Hebrew, "like unto God," Prince of Israel), which destroys "Satan" and "Satan's angels," namely, the wrong thoughts that attack us (Rev. 12:7), giving the sublime courage that enables us to face unflinchingly odds that seem overwhelming. In II Timothy 2, verse 15, we read, "Study to shew 30 thyself approved unto God, a workman that needeth not to be ashamed, rightly dividing the word of truth." Ferrar Fenton translates these last six words as follows: "Arranging in order the reason of the truth."

The Affirmation or "Gabriel."—"*Who shall stand in his holy place? . . . He shall receive the blessing from the Lord, and righteousness* 35 *from the God of his salvation*" (Ps. 24:3, 5).

The above-mentioned blessing is the blessing of Christianity—health, holiness, and immortality. These come into manifestation as we learn better how to realise God.

To help an angry man permanently, you have to use this other edge of 40 the sword of Truth and dwell upon the exact opposite, namely, the truth; thinking, for instance, of God as Love, and man, being in heaven, as absolutely loving. This is the affirmation.[1] "Piety is the daily reviewing of the ideal, the steadying of our inner being" (Amiel). "Wherefore my

---

[1] "Self-conscious communion with God" (*Science and Health*, p. 29. Mary 45 Baker Eddy). "Reach up to my Eternity, otherwise you will not be able to protect the mind against the assaults of evil" (Jivanmukta).

counsel is that we hold fast to the heavenly way" (Plato). This is not only our duty but our privilege.

The action of God then takes place (through you), purifying the false consciousness of both, cleansing the anger cells in the subconscious or
5 lower stratum,[1] and both of you are permanently more loving, less susceptible in the future to the deleterious action of an angry thought, and ultimately the stage is reached when "the prince of this world cometh, and hath nothing in me" (John 14:30). "Stand in his holy place" and "receive the blessing from the Lord, and righteousness from the God of his salva-
10 tion" (Ps. 24:3, 5). "Be ye transformed by the renewing of your mind, that ye may prove what is that good, and acceptable, and perfect, will of God" (Rom. 12:2). God's will is always the bringing about of good. "Mentally practise divine self-realisation, become conscious that the Logos, which is the mystic Christ, the image and nature of the Mother-
15 God, is within you 'unborn.' Be receptive to its promptings, acknowledge it, recognise it, realise it" (*Mystic Immanence*, Archdeacon Wilberforce). When once the "consciousness" is thoroughly purified, the wrong thoughts coming subjectively, in moments of quiet meditation, for instance, will not bring about any response; they will only be apparent when coming
20 objectively, namely, when we see or hear wrong things, and these we destroy by reversing them.

"The mind is the man; if that be kept pure a man signifies somewhat; if not, I would very fain see what difference there is between him and a brute" (Oliver Cromwell). Paul says: "Finally, brethren, whatsoever
25 things are true, . . . just, . . . pure, . . . lovely, ... think on these things . . . and the God of peace shall be with you" (Phil. 4:8, 9).

The affirmation of good is the sweet Gabriel thought, clear and peaceful. "Thou wilt keep him in perfect peace, whose mind is *stayed* on thee" (Isa. 26:3). "The peace of God, which passeth all understanding"
30 (Phil. 4:7). "I am Gabriel, that stand in the presence of God; and am sent to speak unto thee, and to shew thee these glad things" (Luke 1:19). "The Holy Ghost shall come upon thee, and the power of the Highest shall overshadow thee" (Luke 1:35). "I send an Angel before thee, to keep thee in the way, and to bring thee into the place
35 which I have prepared" (Ex. 23:20). "He will guide you into all truth" (John 16:13)

Constant Conscious Communion with God.—"*Bring God down into your heart. Embalm your soul in him now, make within you a temple of the Holy Spirit*" (Amiel). "*Draw nigh to God, and he will draw nigh to
40 you*" (James 4:8).

Having reversed the wrong thought, recognise that the perfection of that wonderful world of reality is due to the eternal action of God, and rest in God; dwell in thought in the reality, realise the perfect world as long as you possibly can; our thought should not dwell elsewhere. He that "shall
45 abide in thy tabernacle, who shall dwell in thy holy hill [the secret place of the most High] . . . walketh uprightly, and worketh righteousness,

---

[1] "If mortals would keep proper ward over mortal mind, the brood of evils which infest it would be cleared out" (*Science and Health*, p. 234).

and speaketh the truth in his heart" (Ps. 15:1, 2). "There is an inward
sight, which hath power to perceive the one true Good" (*Theologia
Germanica*"). This being "on the mountain" is "prayer without ceasing,"
and is absolute protection against every form of evil. "Because thou hast
made the Lord, which is my refuge, even the most High, thy habitation; 5
There shall no evil befall thee, neither shall any plague come nigh thy
dwelling. For he shall give his angels charge over thee, to keep thee in all
thy ways" (Ps. 91:9–11).

> "In conflict with unholy powers
> We grasp the weapons He has given—   10
> The light and truth and love of heaven" (*Whittier*).

"Abide in him [realise the Christ]; that, when he shall appear [in the
last days of evil], we may have confidence" (I John 2:28), having so purified human consciousness that evil thoughts can have no effect upon it.
"So then with the mind I myself serve the law of God" (Rom. 7:25). 15
"Let it be your business to keep your mind in the presence of the Lord:
if it sometimes wander, and withdraw itself from him, do not much disquiet yourself for that; trouble and disquiet serve rather to distract the
mind than to recollect [re-collect] it" (Brother Lawrence, Eighth Letter).
The effect of constant right thinking in the way pointed out, this pray- 20
ing without ceasing, deep, systematic thinking, is the highway of holiness,
and is beautifully illustrated in the life of our Master. Even in his early
days he evidently lived constantly in conscious communion with God.
This spiritual communion is our Eucharist. Jesus started from a point to
which we are advancing. The pure Virgin birth resulted in purity. Pro- 25
fessor Huxley has said that "the Virgin birth presented no difficulty to
him, as virgin conception was a fact of nature." Medical men have found
that this is possible.[1] We know now that the expectant thinking of millions
over a series of years as to the time of the Messiah must have had a great
effect.   30

Reverse Every Wrong Thought Instantly.[2]—"*For our light
affliction, which is but for a moment, worketh for us a far more exceeding
and eternal weight of glory; While we look not at the things which are seen,
but at the things which are not seen: for the things which are seen are temporal;
but the things which are not seen are eternal*" (II Cor. 4:17, 18). 35
Our thoughts must be spiritualised to apprehend Spirit. "Walk in the
Spirit, and ye shall not fulfil the lust of the flesh" (Gal. 5:16). Now our
progress depends *solely* upon the number of seconds in which during the
twenty-four hours we are thinking of God and heaven, and we have by
reversal to use every wrong thought as a sign-post to turn us to God.[3] 40

---

[1] See *Facts and Fallacies regarding the Bible*, by Dr. W. Woods Smythe, F.M.SOC.
LOND., p. 167.
[2] "Evil let alone grows more real, aggressive, and enlarges its claims; but, met
with Science, it can and will be mastered by Science" (*Miscellaneous Writings*,
p. 284. Mary Baker Eddy).   45
[3] Balzac said that seeing the things of the material world as those of the spiritual
world in their rational and consequential ramification "opens to man his true career
and the infinite dawns upon him, and he gets a glimpse of his destiny."

In this way, also, error tends to its own destruction, for, like Moses, by handling the serpent, first recognising and then reversing the wrong thought, we turn it into a staff, something to help us in our journey from false sense to Soul. Every step must be towards spirituality. With intel-
5 lectual wrestlings we must destroy the false concept of materiality.

The constant reversal of the wrong thoughts in this way as they come to you throughout the day explains the meaning of the words "watch and pray." "Moral truth is divine, and whoever breathes its air and walks by its light has found the lost Paradise" (Horace Mann), that is, has gained
10 the millennium and the perception of infinite possibilities. "For our con-versation is in heaven; from whence also we look for the Saviour, the Lord Jesus Christ" (Phil. 3:20). Esdras was inspired with this scientific truth, as recorded in the words: "The evil is sown, but the destruction thereof is not yet come. If therefore that which is sown be not turned upside down,
15 and if the place where the evil is sown pass not away, then cannot it come that is sown with good" (II Esdras 4:28, 29).

One denial to about twenty affirmations is enough, as the denial is the destruction of the thoughts, and once destroyed another denial is useless; whereas you can never realise the truth too much. To take two or three
20 denials one after the other without their following affirmations in between is not scientific.

Wrong Thoughts.—"*The wicked . . . will not seek after God: God is not in all his thoughts*" (Ps. 10:4).

A wrong thought is any thought that, carried into effect, would harm
25 anyone; even a thought of disharmony is a wrong thought, and harms someone, although only temporarily. "Behold, I will bring evil upon this people, even the fruit of their thoughts, because they have not hearkened unto my words, nor to my law" (Jer. 6:19)—the law of good. Fortunately, this law of good is demonstrated directly we think rightly, because the
30 action of ever-present divine Principle then takes place.

Any thought but one of perfection is a wrong thought. Jesus himself said, "Why callest thou me good? there is none good but one, that is, God" (Mark 10:18). If you think "There's an angry man!" unless you destroy the wrong thought by reversal you are sinning, because you are
35 helping to make the man more angry, and diminishing your own resistance to anger. You destroy the wrong thought and thereby stop the man being angry by the denial, and you lessen his liability to respond to angry thoughts, and your own liability as well, by the affirmation. This affirma-tion should be, if possible, the exact opposite of the evil, the existence of
40 which has just been denied. If you can sufficiently clearly reverse the thought in your own consciousness, by realising that there is no anger in heaven, all is love, peace, joy, harmony, bliss, and so on, you will never be angry again.

If you think, "I cannot understand," you are making it more difficult
45 to understand, clogging your powers of perception. You have to deny this wrong thought, and realise, for instance, that, as God is the Principle of wisdom and intelligence, man, the real, spiritual man, reflects that wisdom and intelligence, and therefore has all necessary knowledge. "The higher

the ideal of yourself, the more rapid your spiritual growth; see yourself
ideally as Divine, and you will become it" (Archdeacon Wilberforce).
The thought, "I shall never finish this work to-night," tends to prevent
your finishing it; and after denying this, by realising that in the true,
mental realm, the kingdom of heaven, man's work never fails to be finished 5
in time, and the realisation that all God's ideas are finished, complete, and
perfect in heaven—remember that it is here, round you—in the reality,
will bring about the demonstration, and the work will be duly done. If
you think, "What a bad day, how miserable the holiday-makers will be,"
you are not only helping to make the day worse, but are making them more 10
miserable. The realisation of the gloriousness of heaven and the joy therein
—in His "presence is fulness of joy" (Ps. 16:11), "the sons of God shouted
for joy" (Job. 38:7)—will alter this, and they will receive "beauty for
ashes, the oil of joy for mourning, the garment of praise for the spirit of
heaviness" (Isa. 61:3). 15
We have to uncover every root of evil and probe the trouble to the
bottom in order to find out the erroneous belief, the apparent cause of the
trouble; then deny this false claim and let the action of God bring about
the completion of our work, instead of relying on the broken reed of human
intelligence and trying to do it ourselves. This purification of all error is 20
our baptism.

The Two-edged Sword of Truth.—*"He placed at the east of the
garden of Eden Cherubims, and a flaming sword which turned every way, to
keep the way of the tree of life"* (Gen. 3:24).
You have to overcome evil with good, to help throughout the day, 25
instead of harm, by using the two-edged sword of Truth. This sharp
sword, with two edges, which the saints "joyful in glory" use, is the
denial of the evil, or unreal, and the affirmation of the good, by means of
which the human "consciousness" is purified. "I saw . . . one like unto
the Son of man, . . . and out of his mouth went a sharp two-edged 30
sword" (Rev. 1:12, 13, 16). "For the word of God is quick, and powerful,
. . . . piercing even to the dividing [as you deny the evil and affirm the
good] asunder of soul [false consciousness] and spirit" (Heb. 4:12).
"Who maketh his angels spirits; his ministers a flaming fire" (Ps. 104:4).
You have to "look not at the things which are seen, but at the things which 35
are not seen: . . . the things . . . eternal" (II Cor. 4:18).
"He who the sword of heaven will bear, Should be as holy as severe"
(Shakespeare). The holiness comes from the constant use of the sword,
the constant praying, and we cannot be too severe on the error or too loving
to the individual, forgiving "seventy times seven." "God forgive us all" 40
(*Macbeth*).
Jesus, the great Exemplar, said: "Let him deny himself, and take up
his cross daily and follow me" (Luke 9:23). This grand statement shows
the method of dealing with every wrong thought that comes to us. We have
even to deny the existence of any human, mortal self. When the thought 45
of the trouble comes before one, supposing, for instance, you have a
headache, you have even to deny yourself; that is to say, deny that the
material thing called you is you at all. "Take up thy cross daily," that is

to say, do not simply try to forget it, but deal with it scientifically, daily
handle the evil by denying its existence, and realise the opposite. In the
case of headache, for instance, turn in thought to heaven and realise that
there is no headache (in heaven), and then think of the bliss and the peace
5 and the joy in that wonderful world, which is here at hand, if we only
realise it. This latter is the affirmation. From this may be seen the height
to which we have to follow Jesus; we have to follow him in thought to God.
"I, even I, am the Lord; and beside me there is no saviour" (Isa. 43:11).
One of the sayings attributed to Jesus runs as follows: "If any man will
10 come after me, let him deny himself and take up his cross daily, rejoicing,
and follow me" (Macarius, Hom. V, 6).

The two-edged sword or reversal of error, "with which Truth decapi-
tates error" (Mrs. Eddy) is not only referred to in different places, but under
different types in the Bible. Not only is it the Angel Michael and the Angel
15 Gabriel, "for he shall give his angels charge over thee, to keep thee in all
thy ways" (Ps. 91:11), but the "greater light to rule the day" is the
affirmation, "and the lesser light to rule the night" (Gen. 1:16) is the
denial, which rules the night of ignorance and materiality, the "darkness
[which] was upon the face of the deep" (Gen. 1:2), rules it out of existence
20 and finally destroys it. The "greater light" and the "lesser light," it may
be recollected, were "to give light upon the earth, . . . to divide the light
from the darkness" (Gen. 1:17, 18), and this is what the two-edged sword
of Truth does. Again, it is the "rod" and the "staff" [1] spoken of so constantly throughout the Bible. "Thy rod and thy staff they comfort me"
25 (Ps. 23:4). The root meaning of the word "staff" is "to make firm, to be
unmoved," hence it is the affirmation. The word "rod" means "to switch
or sway or bend," and signifies "to rule over." Hence it is the speaking
with authority, and the "rod", or denial, has to be firm and vigorous.[2]
Its characteristic is spiritual strength, it is "God's thunderbolt" that
30 ultimately brings the material world, the false sense of sin, sickness, and
suffering to an end. Daniel saw this when he said: "And at the time of the
end . . . shall Michael stand up, the great prince . . . and there shall
be a time of trouble, such as never was . . . and at that time thy people
shall be delivered, every one . . ." and he adds "they that turn many to
35 righteousness [shall shine] as the stars for ever and ever" (Dan. 11:40, and
12:1, 3).

Paul, speaking of the end of the world, writes: "For the Lord himself
shall descend from heaven with a shout, with the voice of the archangel,
and with the trump of God" (I Thess. 4:16). In the only other place where
40 the word archangel occurs we are told who the archangel is, "Michael the
archangel, . . . contending with the devil [evil]" (Jude, ver. 9).

Jesus pointed out, in Matthew 13, verse 39, that the angels were "the

[1] According to Cruden, the rod and staff were "the ensigns of power and
government." Harris translates Psalm 110, verse 2, as follows: "He gave me the
45 rod of his power: that I might subdue the imaginations of the peoples." Job,
speaking of the wicked, said: "Neither is the rod of God upon them" (21:9). See
Isaiah 10, verse 24.
[2] "Insist vehemently on the great fact which covers the whole ground, that
God, Spirit, is all, and that there is none beside Him. There is *no disease*" (*Science
50 and Health*, p. 421. Mary Baker Eddy).

reapers" that destroyed the tares at "the end of the world." The tares
are the evil "thoughts," or, as John calls them, "Satan's angels," which
Michael destroys. Paul speaks of his "thorn in the flesh" as "the messenger of Satan" (II Cor. 12:7). "The tares are the children of the wicked
one [mortal mind, or false mentality, alias the devil, alias the ether]; The 5
enemy that sowed them is the devil; the harvest is the end of the world;
and the reapers are the angels" (Matt. 13:38, 39), messengers of Truth,
Michael and Gabriel.

Another reference to the denial and affirmation is in Rev. 3:19, "As
many as I love, I rebuke and chasten." The word rebuke comes from 10
re, back: *bouque* (Fr. *bouche*), the mouth, suggesting the idea of turning
out through the mouth, i.e., denying the evil. Chasten means to purify.
The affirmation is the purification of the human mind.

"We have to work out our own salvation with fear [reverence] and
trembling". It is error that has to tremble before you. "For it is God which 15
worketh in you" (Phil. 2:12, 13). "For the windows from on high [spiritual
perception] are open, and the foundations of the earth [the basic false
mentality] do shake . . . the earth [the false concept of it—the real earth
is spiritual] is clean dissolved" (Isa. 24:18, 19).

Man the Male and Female of God's Creation.—"*He made two* 20
cherubim of gold, beaten out of one piece made he them " (Ex. 37:7).

The cherubim typify the denial and affirmation, or "fulness of knowledge," male and female, from between which the Word of God comes.
Knowing that God destroyed evil by means of our spiritual selves—we, not
the mortals, but the real spiritual beings, individualise the power and 25
activity of God—I could not understand how it was that He healed by
means of the angels Michael and Gabriel, until I recognised that the angel
Michael indicated the male element, and the angel Gabriel the female element in each real man. "So God created man in his own image, . . . male
and female created he them" (Gen. 1:27). That is to say, He did not create 30
separate males and females, but He created you, the spiritual being, with
the mental characteristics of the male, namely, strength, courage, wisdom,
and frankness, and the female complements of these, love, virtue, intuition,
and refinement. "There is neither male nor female: for ye are all one in
Christ Jesus" (Gal. 3:28). There is no male and female as separated kinds 35
of beings. Each and all reflect the complete capacity of Mind as its manifested reflection male and female, one complete.

Antony, speaking of Brutus, says :—

> "His life was gentle, and the elements
> So mix'd in him, that Nature might stand up, 40
> And say to all the world, 'This was a man!'" (*Shakespeare*).

This shows the real strength, the invincible might of Spirit, that we
all have to recognise as our own. We have to show ourselves true men, male
and female complete.

Striving a Joyous Realisation.—"*The man is praying who doth* 45
press with might out of his darkness into God's own light" (R. C. Trench).

Do not be satisfied with merely turning to the reality in a comfortable
sort of way and denying and affirming, but reverse every wrong thought as

carefully as you can. "So then with the mind I myself serve the law of God" (Rom. 7:25). Do the work exactly as if a person were on the point of dying and you had about a minute of time in which to destroy the death thoughts, alias belief in death, that would apparently snatch him away. By
5 working in this way, soon, at least 50 per cent. of your reversals will lead to an instantaneous demonstration, either complete cure or perceptible improvement. In addition, when you really have to help a person at the point of death, you will rise to an equal extent above your usual clearness of realisation and obtain a proportionately better result. It is this striving
10 that does the work, the trying one's very best to think of the reality, the perfect world, heaven. An advanced scientific worker—he with ten talents [1] —has to get a much clearer realisation of God than a beginner—he with one talent—to obtain the same result. Each, in ordinary cases, will get an instantaneous demonstration, if he does his very best, and has not the
15 slightest fear that the demonstration will not be made. Fear is the thing that would stop us. Fear that one is not good enough, fear that one does not know enough, or fear that one has not got a clear enough realisation. In fact, we have a hundred reasons why God should not be God and Truth should fail. "Do that which is assigned to you, and you cannot hope too
20 much, or dare too much" (Emerson).

Whilst the beginner, who has just learnt how to think rightly, and so to apply the remedy which science offers to all of us, will get in ordinary matters just as good a result as a more advanced worker, if he will only rely on God, the latter will be of much more use to the world in cases where
25 the evil is hidden and the beginner cannot discern the cause of the trouble. Here the true and more advanced worker will at once discern the cause, and being uncovered (discovered) the belief in evil is easily overcome.

Then at last we obtain justice. "Divine Mind is the immortal law of justice as well as of mercy" (Mary Baker Eddy), and in exact proportion as
30 we serve God by turning to Him in thought, so do our troubles and the troubles of those for whom we are working, disappear. The realisation of the absolute justice, love, and truth in divine Mind has resulted in the dismissal of a blackmailing action in twenty minutes, which counsel had advised the defendant, a banker, could not possibly be won by him.

35 **Scientific Working Restful.**—"*To be spiritually minded is life and peace*" (Rom. 8:6).

There is nothing troublesome about this striving, for being truly scientific, it is a joyous realisation, a glorious plunge into substantial existence, a rest in action of divine Love, strengthening one for the daily
40 duties, however great the demand. Active right thinking is man's natural element and occupation. "Rejoice in the Lord alway" (Phil 4:4).

Man Cannot Retrograde.—"*I know that, whatsoever God doeth, it shall be for ever*" (Eccles. 3:14).

The action of God is perfect, that is to say, when a wrong thought is
45 destroyed by the denial of its existence, that destruction is permanent, and we are one thought nearer the end of the so-called material world.

[1] See Matthew 25, verses 14–30.

When the human mind is purified by the realisation of Truth, the affirmation of the real, this purification, so far as it goes, is also fortunately permanent. "I know that, whatsoever God doeth, it shall be for ever" (Ecc. 3:14). "Perfection . . . requires the hand of time" (Voltaire). Every time that you turn in thought to God you are nearer to the good. God's work cannot be reversed, man never retrogrades. "Ye know that your labour is not in vain in the Lord" (I Cor. 15:58).

Treatment.—"*We have this treasure in earthen vessels, that the excellency of the power may be of God, and not of us*" (II Cor. 4:7).

The term "treat" is defined by Webster as "to subject to the action of," and "treatment," he states, is "good or bad behaviour toward." Webster defines "prayer" as "the act of earnestly asking for a favour, supplication, entreaty." Right throughout this book it has been shown that so apparently potent is thought that it is not possible for thoughts of a person to come to you without the person being directly influenced. The same applies equally to animals and inanimate objects. Hence, with an accurate knowledge of the action of the so-called "mind," and true knowledge of God as Mind, the old method of "prayer" naturally becomes more accurately defined as treatment of the person or thing prayed for.

It is also shown how everyone, when thinking at all, must be "treating," followed by either good or evil. True "treatment" gives direct help through prayer. The false "treatment" of the charlatan, or so-called scientist, is directly harmful to the persons.

If the thoughts are good, the effect is good. If they are thoughts (so-called) of evil, that is, false thoughts—for all real thoughts are God's thoughts, and true—the evil is intensified. "For whatsoever a man soweth, that shall he also reap" (Gal. 6:7). We have to bring "into captivity every thought to the obedience of Christ" (II Cor. 10:5).

It is a fact in Science that if a man is ill, or in any trouble, and another seeing him should realise sufficiently either God or the perfection of the real spiritual man, the trouble vanishes instantly.

Perhaps the most essential reason for the study and practice of the Science of Mind is for self-protection against the ignorant, the unintentional, and the malicious attempts of evil in these its last days. This is not selfishness, because it is only thus that the mortal can avoid prematurely passing into another state of consciousness, and so prove the Principle of Life "through living as well as healing and teaching" (*Science and Health*). Thus do we help all mankind, and especially those united in true spiritual affection, to remain in even happier companionship and on the same stage of existence, to the end of evil. There can be no greater cause for lament than the decease of an advanced scientific worker through the attacks of the majority of human beliefs or of what is known as animal magnetism. Fortunately, Love is omnipotent, and all that is necessary for absolute peace is sufficient understanding of and practical obedience to the First Commandment, which leads to a magnificent and essential, individual and universal fulfilment of the Golden Rule of Life.

This fulfilment is the constant reversal of any wrong thoughts concerning other persons that come into the human consciousness. To carry out this reversal there must be no human thought of the material person or

even of his actual spiritual reality; any error that has been suggested as attached to the person must be denied with all the mental power with which you are equipped through your relationship with God. What a change from the old verbal and "non-mental" method of bespattering our
5 fellow-workers with the mud in which our human mentality wallowed. The more deadly the belief in the existence of the evil, the greater the need for the energetic denial and instantaneous affirmation. "And let none of you imagine evil in your hearts against his neighbour; . . . these are things that I hate, saith the Lord" (Zech. 8:17).
10   The affirmation of truth, the opposite of the evil threatening, must follow like lightning, replacing every picture of the material, and carrying you high into the realm of celestial harmony and beauty, so that you consciously dwell with God, experiencing a restful peace of mind impossible to express in mere words, "that true eternal peace which is God
15 Himself, as far as it is possible to a creature" (*Theologia Germanica*).
      In this way, taking up, one by one, each and every difficulty, moral, intellectual, physical (so-called), or financial, with which our loved ones are troubled (and all the world are loved), we turn the light of Truth upon them, and lo ! we find there is nothing to treat except our own wrong view
20 of the trouble, and so, blessing and blessed, we go on our way rejoicing, glad witnesses to the Truth.
      This is the only true treatment in the specific sense of the term, and the only right and radical treatment of evil. For ages the aspiration toward good, viewed only from a religious point of view, and divorced from its
25 scientific basis, has been named "prayer." To this unnatural separation is due the attenuated results of the earnest prayers of multitudes of religious people. Religion and science are now viewed correctly, as eternally one, and their truth is proved in the only perfect way, namely, by practical results.

30   **Personal Treatment.**—When praying (treating) for a person, without his having asked you to do so, you have no right to think of him, not even to realise his spiritual reality. This is personal treatment, i.e., thinking of a person, and is wrong. When thinking of the spiritual reality of a patient there is, as a rule, a sense of his human individuality; this is
35 absent when thinking of the ideal man, the Christ, the consciousness of God, of which each man is an individualisation, and yet the action of God takes place just as much on the person that you are trying to help. The work is done when you have reversed the existence of the wrong thoughts that make him appear to you to be in trouble.
40   When you treat personally, unless you are an advanced worker, and I would even say, have always worked only in the highest way, namely, by the realisation of God and heaven, you cannot help thinking a little of the material person—at all events to begin with.
      When a beginner is treating, this sense of a person's mentality may
45 develop into an actual mechanical action upon the human consciousness of the individual thought of. This happens when the beginner, as healer, thinks of the human patient, instead of God and the ideal spiritual man, and thinks so vividly that a picture is formed of the material face, or even

of a material body. This may be called "picturing," a term that more accurately expresses what is called "thinking." For this reason, personal treatment or mentally realising the spiritual reality of the patient is wrong, unless he has asked for help. To form any picture of the material or attempted outline of the spiritual, even in one's clearest realisations, is 5 wrong; hence the symbolic teaching of things spiritual. If an individual asks for help it is a sign that his human consciousness is not very bad; that is, that the counterfeit "mind" is not easily affected by the thoughts of sin or disease, as the case may be. The mechanical action referred to above will then have no appreciable effect. If his mechanism is in a bad state, and 10 easily affected by the wrong class of thought, against which he has asked for your help, then the mechanical vibration that takes place if a picture of the human person be formed by the would-be healer, will sometimes upset him, and cause an aggravation of the symptoms, and this even if you are trying to think of his spiritual self. This is sometimes wrongly 15 called "chemicalisation," [1] by those who do not understand the position. The one who is most harmed by such mistaken working is always the would-be healer.

When you treat, it should be clearly understood that you are the person for whom, in the first instance, the error has to be destroyed. When the 20 false belief in the disease or trouble that appears to be connected with the patient is thoroughly destroyed in your own "consciousness," and the truth realised of the perfection of man as God's image and likeness, then it is that the so-called patient is freed. You become a channel through which Truth works. It may be compared to a burning-glass, concentrating 25 the rays of the sun on to rubbish that has to be burnt up. You merely have to hold the burning-glass in place.

Thinking of the spiritual reality of the patient is not the highest treatment. It is not possible to outline humanly Mind's spiritual idea, and there is a danger of a faint picture of a man's human individuality dimming 30 the clear realisation of God's perfect idea. The whole work of treatment is to impersonalise the error and realise God's perfect idea as His image and likeness. If the work is done simply by the realisation of God, it is best of all. Lose every thought in the inspiring consciousness of the presence of God.   35

The work should be done entirely in one's own consciousness, by turning out one's own false concept of a seemingly sick or sinful person and knowing the truth about God's man. Reversing evil in this way we catch glimpses of the Saviour, Christ.

I quite admit that some of the best mental workers do not confine 40 themselves to this method of working, but "Time makes ancient good uncouth; they must upward still, and onward, who would keep abreast of truth" (Lowell).

Impersonal Treatment.—We have nothing to do with anything except our own thoughts of things. If, when we think wrongly of our 45 fellow-man or his troubles, we clearly enough correct our human ideas by

[1] For definition of "chemicalisation" see *Science and Health*, p. 168, line 32 (Mary Baker Eddy).

turning in thought to the reality, denying the existence of such troubles in heaven and affirming the truth, the evil, of which we have been humanly conscious, disappears, not only to ourselves, but to all others. The action of God has taken place on the person we are trying to help. The reason for
5 this is that there is only one basic false mentality, only one suppositional opposite of God and the Christ. For this reason, when the counterfeit thoughts are destroyed in what is miscalled your "mind," they are destroyed in the one universal, material consciousness, the basic false mentality called mortal "mind," and thus are destroyed for the whole of
10 humanity.

The difference in the patient is seen by all onlookers, he being a part of the one mortal "mind," their false consciousness. The fight is one solely with the thoughts as they enter our human consciousness. If we can keep them out by turning in thought to God, as shown, they cannot act, as they
15 are destroyed, and the so-called miracle is done. The only power an evil thought has, and that is only apparent, is when we give it a temporary but false sense of life or power, by letting it enter our so-called consciousness. All that there is of a patient is our false concept of God's man.

One is often asked, Why does not impersonal treatment then help the
20 whole world? Naturally it will, if that be the intention. On the other hand, when you think, "Now I am going to help So-and-so," you have, as it were, switched on to the particular person, and are in ethereal touch only with him. You must not then think of him again. Think only of the ideal world. Then the action of God takes place through you chiefly upon that portion
25 of his mind that is the cause of the trouble. It is just as if you turned a polished mirror so that the reflected rays of the sun would fall on a dark spot and light it up. We have to keep this mirror, our "consciousness," pure and holy, so that it reflects all the light possible, and each one's work is individual or collective, as occasion demands.[1]
30 Working in this way, there is no mental clashing, and we can utilise to the full the statement of our Master, "Where two or three are gathered together in my name, there am I in the midst of them" (Matt. 18:20).

The Rod of Iron.—When you have realised what it is to hold clearly in thought to the divine spiritual reality of what humanly appears, for
35 instance, as a raving madman, and to have the feeling of defying hell to do its worst, driving out of your human consciousness all suggestion even of the seeming existence of evil, with the denial of its power and the denial of its reality, wringing lying thoughts out of the human false consciousness, like the last drops of water out of a sponge; and when you then see the
40 "legion of devils" disappear, and the sweet child thought change the demoniacal countenance before you, then you will understand what Daniel meant when he said: "At that time shall Michael stand up, . . . and at that time thy people shall be delivered" (Dan. 12:1). You will then also

---

[1] The foregoing are merely indications of the scientific method of working
45 and are in no sense a formula for "treatment." The full understanding of the rules and practice of Mind healing is only to be gained by deep and unprejudiced study of Mrs. Eddy's writings, and more especially of *Science and Health with Key to the Scriptures*, the systematic reading of which is necessary to any student intending to become proficient in the Science of Life.

know what it is to "rule . . . with a rod of iron ['tend as a shepherd with irresistible power' [1]]; as the vessels of a potter shall they [false thoughts] be broken to shivers: even as I received of my Father" (Rev. 2:27). "The Son of man shall send forth his angels" (Matt. 13:41). "Thou madest him to have dominion over the works of thy hands; thou hast put all things under his feet" (Ps. 8:6). "The Son of man hath power on earth to forgive sins, . . . the multitudes . . . glorified God, which had given such power unto men" (Matt. 9:6, 8). "He that believeth on me the works that I do shall he do also; and greater works than these shall he do" (John 14:12).

The Practitioner.—It is not difficult to see how such scientific destruction of sin, disease, and death must always benefit the one working. It is this constant denial of all reality or power in evil and realisation of Life, Truth, and Love, for the benefit of patients that gives such a wonderful sense of refreshment, peace, and rest to the true physician. How widely different from the exhaustion following all attempts to heal with what is wrongly called the human "mind," or through other physical efforts attending material methods.

Dematerialisation.—After Enoch, Melchisedec, Elijah, and Jesus understood paradise, in other words, had succeeded in habitually obtaining a glorious sense of the reality, they dematerialised, that is, rose above the sense of matter, and so disappeared from the view of those still under the belief of material laws. At the last moment, before this happened, they must have seen what is spoken of in the Book of Revelation as the new heaven and the new earth, and as the last error of their material consciousness disappeared, and the vista opened up, the glorious world appeared, and they seemed to find themselves in heaven, where they really always had been.

It may be recollected that the purified human consciousness of Stephen "being full of the Holy Ghost, looked up steadfastly into heaven, and saw the glory of God, . . . And said, Behold, I see the heavens opened" (Acts 7:55, 56).

Possibly many, of whom we have no record, dematerialised. How was it that "the Lord . . . buried him [Moses] . . . but no man knoweth of his sepulchre," and yet "his eye was not dim, nor his natural force abated" (Deut. 34:5-7). Why did that wonderful philosopher, Lao-Tze, leave his home where he was venerated, and go up to the mountain, and then (about 500 B.C.) entirely disappear? Why is it said that the same thing happened to Buddha after he gave up his kingdom? Why is nothing known of the death of John, the beloved disciple, whose writings show such a knowledge of the fact that there is no death? It is recorded that he was immersed in boiling oil by the Emperor Domitian without being killed. Jesus, the third time that he appeared to his disciples, after his so-called death, speaking to Peter of the "loved" disciple, said: "If I will that he tarry till I come, what is that to thee? follow thou me. Then went this saying abroad among the brethren, that that disciple should not die"

---

[1] Grant's *Translation of the Bible.*

(John 21:22, 23). All these men knew the truth. They knew what Jesus, the Messiah, endeavoured to teach to the world, but they did not sacrifice themselves to the same extent. None of them was pure enough to be the Saviour of mankind. To Jesus, the Christ, was reserved this honour. Him
5 must we love and reverence. I have had far more love and reverence for the Master since the right understanding of his life and mission came to me, than I ever had when I tried to look upon his material self as the only Son of God.

In these last days the age seems too material and too much under the
10 control of false laws to allow of an individual ascension above material limitations until the tide of false mental activity rises and works in an opposite direction. To change the hearts of mankind to this essential, right mental activity, and so stem the great tide of mortality that has so far appeared to devastate the kingdom of heaven that is within the reach of
15 all, is the noblest, because the God-appointed task of the scientist of to-day. Jesus, foretelling the events attending the "end of the evil world of matter," said: "Therefore every scribe which is instructed unto the kingdom of heaven is like unto a man that is an householder, which bringeth forth out of his treasure things new and old." [1] And the Bible record of those times
20 adds, in simple but strangely significant sequence, these words: "When Jesus had finished these parables, he departed thence" (Matt. 13:52, 53). Alas! that even to this hour, nearly two thousand years after the departure of the great Prophet, the symbolism of even the latter-day scribes has not been properly understood, and because this is so, the same gospel of
25 Matthew records the prophecy of these "scribes'" reception by those who do not understand (see Dan. 12:10): "Behold, I send unto you prophets, and wise men, and scribes: and some of them ye shall kill and crucify; and some of them shall ye scourge in your synagogues, and persecute them from city to city: That upon you [at the end of the world] may come all the
30 righteous blood shed upon the earth, from the blood of righteous Abel unto the blood of Zacharias son of Barachias, whom ye slew between the temple and the altar" (Matt. 23:34, 35). Throughout the world's history, the greatest evil is found in the highest spiritual centres (Eph. 6:12), which, of all other places, should be the surest haven of refuge for mankind. The
35 record continues: "Verily I say unto you, All these things shall come upon this generation. O Jerusalem, Jerusalem, thou that killest the prophets, and stonest them which are sent unto thee, how often would I have gathered thy children together, even as a hen gathereth her chickens under her wings, and ye would not! Behold, your house is left unto you
40 desolate"[2] (Matt. 23:36-38).

[1] "Let them bring them forth, and shew us what shall happen: let them shew the former things, what they be, then we may consider them, and know the latter end of them; or declare us things for to come" (Isa. 41:22).
[2] Since the above was written the world's greatest latter-day prophetess has
45 passed from our sight. A messenger of the Spirit of Truth, a scribe of God's appointing to this last age, of her writings Daniel's prophetic utterance may well be re-echoed: "None of the wicked shall understand; but the wise shall understand" (Dan. 12:10), but this great messenger's written statement of Truth, which is demonstrable by all, will continue to be poured into the ears of the waiting world
50 in "translated messages" by those who do "understand" in response to her

The immense importance of the prophecy of Jesus concerning the latter-day scribes, about to be fulfilled, can be fully appreciated now that the scientific fact has been established that the whole world has to be reached and the thought changed. "Go ye therefore, and teach all nations" (Matt. 28:19).   5

"Our life in the midst of the world," St. Francis of Assisi said, "ought to be such that, on hearing and seeing us, everyone shall feel constrained to praise our Heavenly Father." Yet his latter days were darkened. At the end he rose above the mist, and it was with a glad heart and outstretched arms that instead of overcoming, he welcomed "Sister Death."   10

> "Life is the test of love, and love, of life;
> Godlike endeavour is the way of God. . . .
> The only sin is not to try, the only good,
> To live courageously, for life supreme
> Is love, and going is the goal" (*Albert D. Watson*).   15

irresistible appeal to mankind for the manifestation of the Love that is its God, its Life, the Life of the world. "I long, and live, to see this love demonstrated. I am seeking and praying for it to inhabit my own heart and to be made manifest in my life. Who will unite with me in this pure purpose, and faithfully struggle till it be accomplished? Let this be our Christian endeavour society, which Christ organises 20 and blesses" (*Pulpit and Press*, Mary Baker Eddy). The night that Mrs. Eddy passed on, and on the following night, I was discussing with a fellow student what the trouble could be which was foreshown, both in the Bible and Great Pyramid, as taking place in A.D. 1910, in the religious centres of the latter days. It was clear that none of the troubles that had taken place was of sufficient importance, 25 and it was hoped that as so little time was left, some mistake had been made. On the next day the sad news of her death, on December 3, 1910, was received.

6

SECTION FOUR

PHILOSOPHIC APPROACH TO TRUTH

According to Plato, a philosopher is one who apprehends the essence or reality of things in contradistinction to the man who dwells in appearances and the "shows" of sense. He speaks of him as a man who grasps the eternal and immutable and insists upon seeing things together, viewing them as a whole, setting his affections upon that which really exists.

The views of philosophers have been greatly misunderstood through ignorance on the part of those referring to them. Some people have so material an outlook that they fail for a time either to take in or lay to heart even the teaching of this advancing great school of thought, which for years has been endeavouring to get at the truth, and melt frozen dogma with moonbeams.

Take Hume's philosophy, for instance. In Huxley's *Life of Hume* he says: "It is hardly necessary to point out that the doctrine just laid down is what is commonly called materialism. But it is nevertheless true that the doctrine contains nothing inconsistent with the purest idealism." So in the present day the highest teachings are largely misunderstood, and even when partially understood are not often carried out in life practice. It is indeed this partial misunderstanding of truth that makes life practice difficult; while a clear understanding makes life natural, simple, and joyous.

The office of philosophy, which has been called the handmaid of religion, is the same as that of natural science, namely, to correct mistakes. Every man is a scientist, if in disguise, and every scientist a philosopher, although he may be a poor one, and the two must be combined to elicit truth. Divine philosophy is saving the world. It is, to use Plato's words, the apprehension of the reality of things; in other words, a knowledge of God, knowledge of good, that is saving us and all mankind.

"Yet I doubt not through the ages one increasing purpose runs,
And the thoughts of men are widen'd with the process of the suns" (*Tennyson*).

That eminent scholar, Dr. Westcott, who was Bishop of Durham, and who prepared the text which was the basis of the revision of the King James version of the Bible, writing of the Gospel of St. John, shows that by the use of the definite article the absolute is distinguished from the relative. The knowledge of absolute Truth is what we require, not the relative truth that Pilate demanded in the words, "What is truth?" This absolute Truth is scientific. It is the truth about God, "with whom is no variableness, neither shadow of turning" (James 1:17). Chambers's Dictionary defines "truth" as "agreement with reality," and "relative" as "not absolute."

Evil is of No Value.—If God is Mind and this Mind knows of evil, then all in that Mind cannot be good. How can Truth know a lie? Many people, seeing the logical difficulty, that if evil is real, God knows of it, and allows it, if He did not even create it, try to get out of the difficulty by saying that evil is of value and therefore good, as it turns man to God. This does not make evil good, as it would be far better if man turned to God, good, infinite Mind, to destroy the evil concepts and false sense of 5 limitation, without the incentive of trouble, whether in a lesser or in a worse form. If people would only do this in the first instance, before the wrong thoughts came, they could not be affected by them. Evil cannot be the medium for good. The only outcome of evil is sin, which annihilates itself. 10

That evil, sooner or later, compels man to turn in thought to God, is one of the many proofs of its non-reality; as this very turning in thought to God leads to the destruction of the evil, and therefore its disappearance. We can only overcome evil with good, intelligent good, God.[1] Anything that is real must have always existed and must always continue to exist, 15 and evil could never have always existed, because of its self-destructive nature.

A false view arises out of a false concept of God as a person altogether apart from man, instead of the true God, whose manifestation is the true man. Then it is seen that God and man are not two, but eternally co- 20 existent as Principle and its idea.

So long as a lie is kept quiet, or safeguarded by public opinion, it has a chance of being believed, but directly it is brought out into the open, the daylight of Truth is brought to bear upon it, when it is seen to be a lie, and loses its power because no one believes it; known to be a lie, it fades 25 away into its native nothingness. Evil in the form of sin destroys itself, because it is continually bringing such punishment upon man, in the form of disease, etc., that ultimately he cannot stand it and gives it up, when the punishment ceases. If knowing how to pray scientifically, he sets to work at once to free himself, freedom is easily gained. Similarly, with sickness, a 30 man will try all sorts of methods of getting well before he turns to God. Ultimately, when every other help fails, he turns to Principle as a last resort, thinking it cannot do much harm and may possibly do a little good. Then he finds out the truth of being, and is amazed to see how blind he has been, and how illogical his previous ideas were; "how great man is, and 35 how good God is."

Jesus hardly ever mentions sin, except in connection with repentance and forgiveness. As Dr. Inge says : "Our Lord's teaching is very severe and exacting, but fundamentally happy and joyous. . . . No war is declared against the ordinary sources of human happiness."[2] 40

The less we think of ourselves the happier we are. To overcome pride and its twin sister, self-consciousness, we have to deny their existence, and to realise that in heaven man never thinks of himself, but thinks only of God and God's ideas. The spiritual man is never self-conscious. God only is self-conscious. "To make an end of selfishness is happiness. This is the 45 greatest happiness, to subdue the selfish thought of 'I'" (Buddha).

---

[1] See Rom. 12, verse 21.
[2] *The Paddock Lectures*, for 1906.

We have to gain every bit of good, every bit of happiness out of life that
we can, and if we have sufficient knowledge of Truth, continual joy will
come to us without harming others or ourselves. This is our birthright.
We are entitled to be happy, and if we are not continually happy then some-
5 thing is wrong; we cannot be praying properly or sufficiently.

Process of Self-Destruction of Evil.—"*For our light affliction, which
is but for a moment, worketh for us a far more exceeding and eternal weight of
glory.   While we look not at the things which are seen, but at the things which
are not seen*" (II Cor. 4:17, 18).

10 Evil, although it does no good, appears to do good, for it is caused to
destroy itself; as when we see something that is wrong, it reminds us to
turn to God and reverse the thought, when the evil, whatever it is,
instantly disappears. So any seeming evil can always be reversed, and in
this way turned to good account by those who know the necessity for right
15 thinking, and how to pray scientifically. If there were no suffering or
trouble in the world, people would not take any trouble to learn how to
pray rightly. They would go on dreaming out their lives, and enjoying what
they called good, continuing apparently to die, and be born. They would
never work mentally in order to steadily improve upon the so-called good;
20 that is, to get rid of limitations, and to obtain a higher sense of unlimited
spiritual perfection. We have to do this before we can find ourselves in
heaven, with nothing left but absolute good, God. Evil crieth out : "Let
us alone; what have we to do with thee . . . art thou come to destroy
us?" (Mark 1:24). We must not therefore fear when we see troubles
25 gathering round us, cinematographic pictures posing as dangerous realities.
It is only a sign that the end is near, and an incentive to work and rejoice
at the approaching end of the sin and ignorance that are the only cause of
these false troubles. "Ignorance is the only real evil" (Annie Besant).

A Present Devil and a Future God!—According to old, indeed
30 many present, theories, the devil, if not more powerful, is at least on a par
with God. The first sends us good to do us harm; the second sends us evil
to do us good. The inconsistency of these ideas is illustrated by the remark
of the child as it killed the fly, "Go to God, little fly."

All sin and subsequent suffering are the result of ignorance, which
35 Shakespeare speaks of as "the curse of God." All evils are destroyed by a
knowledge of truth. " . . . And ye shall know the truth,[1] and the truth
shall make you free" (John 8:32). "Truth . . . liveth and conquereth for
evermore . . . she is the strength, kingdom, power, and majesty, of all
ages. Blessed be the God of truth" (I Esdras 4:38, 40).

40   "And from the lips of Truth one mighty breath
           Shall, like a whirlwind, scatter in its breeze
           That whole dark pile of human mockeries;
           Then shall the reign of Mind commence on earth,
           And starting fresh, as from a second birth,
45   Man, in the sunshine of the world's new spring,
           Shall walk transparent, like some holy thing" (*Thomas Moore*).

[1] The Greek words are *he aletheia*, meaning "the absolute truth," as opposed to
aletheia, used elsewhere and meaning merely "a relative sense of truth," namely,
what is correct in the material world.

What is Truth?—*"Truth is a mighty instrument, whatsoever hand may wield it"* (Rev. J. Caird).

"O, love Truth, prize it beyond all fame and power and happiness! It is the day-star from on high that shines to us in this gloomy wilderness of existence; there is still hope of him who knows and venerates its light, and dare determine to hold fast by it to the death" (Carlyle). 5

Since Truth is God, one of the three following statements must be true: (1) that all is matter. This is most logically put forward by Haeckel, if his premises are granted; (2) that everything is partly spiritual and partly material, as so illogically held by many people; (3) that all is Spirit, as we are told in the Bible. 10

With regard to the first, if matter is real or permanent (the two mean practically the same thing), Haeckel and the first proposition must be correct. None of the Churches or religious bodies agree with this view.

If God created evil, then the second is true, but not otherwise. 15

If the third is true, then we have a glorious religion, absolutely practical and scientific, available to all, at this moment and always. It is the religion of absolute and universal good, and divinely true.

The Truth of Being.—The following shortly indicates the ultimate conclusion which regenerated philosophy has brought to light, now that all 20 human philosophy is overshadowed and is dropping its mere speculative theories under the correction of Truth. God is cause, Spirit, the Principle of all good. There can be only one cause and that cause must be good. A bad cause as the essence of everything is unthinkable, for the one fundamental basis of all evil is that it is self-destructive. Cause cannot exist 25 without its manifestation. Therefore cause, God, and His manifestation, the spiritual beings,[1] and spiritual ideas, must exist, and must always have existed, absolutely perfect, making an absolutely perfect world, which is called heaven. This is the truth of being.

God is infinite Mind, and whatever Mind knows is the manifestation 30 of Truth, namely, the spiritual universe, including the individual intelligent idea, man, the image and likeness of good.

Two Horns of a Dilemma.—You have two horns of a dilemma now before you, (a) to believe in a God that even if he be not evil himself, not only made evil and the awful horrors in this material world, but made 35 human beings so badly that they could not help doing evil, and suffered punishment because they did it, or, (b) to believe in a God that, knowing our troubles, is either unwilling or unable to remove them.

The Only Alternative.—The only alternative is to believe in and prove the existence of a God who is All-in-all, who is absolute good, who created 40 the universe, including man, spiritual and perfect, a divine universe, which always was and is now (though hidden to mortals by material illusion) perfect and complete, governed by the Principle of good; and that the whole of this material world, with all its sin, sickness, and suffering, is an absolute delusion with no reality of any kind or description, it never 45 was created, and is not even a dream.

---

[1] "The universe of Spirit is peopled with spiritual beings" (*Science and Health*, p. 264. Mary Baker Eddy).

Man's Better Understanding of God.—Sin, sickness, death, and all evils of every sort are neither Truth, nor manifestations of Truth, and therefore cannot possibly be true. Being untrue, they are lies, and necessarily unreal. It may be stated that you can find to-day thousands, probably
5 millions, of human beings who are rapidly getting rid of sin, sickness, or suffering by merely knowing that it is a lie, that all in reality is God, Mind,[1] and its manifestation, spiritual, perfect, and All. With this additional evidence, can there be the slightest doubt which of the foregoing statements is true, or which you are going to believe from to-day?

10 **Two Impossibilities.**—Scholastic theology correctly teaches us that God is Spirit and God is infinite, and yet it even still states that evil is real. If the latter were true, then there would be either evil in God or else evil exists outside what is infinite. Both are evident impossibilities. Habbakuk recognised this when he wrote, "O mighty God . . . Thou art of
15 purer eyes than to behold evil, and canst not look upon iniquity" (1:12, 13). There is only one logical solution, however difficult it is for poor material, ill-taught, illogical humanity to understand properly, namely, that evil is not real. I challenge anyone to produce any other either logical or demonstrable explanation of the difficulty.
20 God is Truth. It follows that evil cannot be Truth, and must therefore be untrue. What is untrue must be unreal. Therefore, to believe evil real must be a mistake of ignorance, and obviously sin, a failure to obey the First Commandment to have only one God. To prevent this sin we must "Watch and pray" and guard our consciousness, the city of the Holy
25 Ghost, as we would guard our children against all evil. Man is not a material thing liable to sin. Man is divine, spiritual and perfect. Evil can have no authority from God, good. Exercise man's divine right and exorcise evil by knowing its unreality. Deprived of its prestige and divested of its self-imposed, false authority, it collapses of its own nature, and man is free.
30 Glorious freedom, infinite possibilities, continual happiness, eternal, perfect existence, belong to each of us.

God Finite if not Omnipotent.—All great logical thinkers have felt the difficulty arising out of the supposed reality of sin and matter.
John Stuart Mill said that God could not be omnipotent. Professor
35 James, in *A Pluralistic Universe*, says: "I believe that the only God worthy of the name must be finite." Benjamin Jowett, in *Predestination and Freewill*, wrote: "God is greater by being finite than being infinite." Warschauer tries to prove that God is not All-in-all. He says, in *Problems of Immanence*: "If God is all, *then what are we?* Granted the basal axiom of
40 this type of immanentism, it follows with irresistible cogency that our separate existence, consciousness, volitions, and so forth, are merely illusions." That is so, for there is no "separate existence" from God. It is the material belief of evil as real and necessary, that alone is responsible

---

[1] "For those who have eyes to see and minds accustomed to reflect, . . .
45 throughout the stellar universe—our own little universe, as one may call it—there is intelligent and conscious direction; in a word, there is Mind" (Professor Alfred Russel Wallace, O.M., F.R.S.).

for any supposed separation between God and man or man and his fellow-man. "There is no real Divine Immanence which does not imply the allness of God"[1] (R. J. Campbell, D.D.), and, it may be added, the goodness of man as image and likeness of and co-existent with omni-present good. 5

Is God Unwilling or Unable to Abolish Evil?—W. R. Inge, M.A., D.D., an exponent of the latest views of theology, in *The Paddock Lectures* for 1906, delivered at the General Seminary, New York, referring to the religious problem of evil, spoke as follows : "That problem has been stated once for all in the words of Augustine : 'Either God is unwilling to 10 abolish evil, or He is unable; if He is not willing, He is not good; if He is unable, He is not omnipotent !' No Christian can consent to impale himself on either horn of this dilemma. If God is not perfectly good and also perfectly powerful, He is not God. . . . The only other alternative, if we refuse St. Augustine's dilemma, is to deny, to some degree, the absolute 15 existence of evil, regarding it as an appearance incidental to the actualisation of moral purpose as vital activity. And in spite of the powerful objections which have been brought against this view, in spite of the real risk of seem-ing to attenuate, in theory, the malignant potency of sin, I believe that this is the theory which presents the fewest difficulties." 20

Now the difficulty is solved. Light is pouring in upon the world. We retain our perfect God, infinite and omnipotent, and hurl all sin and trouble for ever from its self-erected pedestal into its native nothingness, the dust of materiality from which the false belief in it arose. "The Lord God formed man of the dust of the ground" (Gen. 2:7). What a parody upon 25 man created in the "image" and "likeness," of God "in his own image" (Gen. 1:27).

> "Then came that voice as soundless as the light. . . .
> I saw no phantom shape, no sound I heard,
> But life unveiled itself in vivid thought, 30
> Distinct, imperative, and luminous. . . .
> For now mine eyes had seen Eternity,
> The source, the truth, the work and urge of all;
> The soul of things, the light ineffable
> That all the wide star-spaces floods with life; 35
> This, *this* was God, and there was none beside" (*Albert D. Watson*).

The Evolution of Philosophy.—A rough summary of the con-clusions arrived at by the leaders of the different schools of thought in the past may be of interest, showing how, although some have been quite close to the truth, they have failed to grasp it, or to give us any reasonable 40 explanation of the universe, or practical method of how to get out of our difficulties. (See Appendix.)

It is not of importance that we should recognise the gradual evolution of philosophy until it agreed with religion and science, but it is of interest to see how this evolution was gradually brought about, and it is of value to 45 understand it when talking with those who have studied philosophy and look at life from this point of view, so as to be able to help them.

---

[1] *Divine Immanence and Pantheism.*

The New Theology.—This movement, the theologian's latest attempt
to amalgamate religion and philosophy on a semi-metaphysical basis, is
a sign of the awakening of the world to the glorious news, the second
coming of Christ, namely, the knowledge that we are all spiritual beings
5 in heaven now, each an individualisation of the Christ, God's consciousness. Some of those who partially see the truth are trying to fit it in with
their old ideas. This is impossible. New wine cannot be put into old bottles.
Consequently they are continually finding themselves in an absolutely
illogical position.

10   Many, for instance, believe that God made the material world for some
good reason, and that the spiritual man, the perfect, divine likeness of
God, which always has existed and always will exist perfect, is, in some
way impossible to explain, improved by the troubles to which the material
man, whom they do not recognise as merely a counterfeit, is being sub-
15 jected. Others doubt the miracles of Jesus, failing to perceive that matter
being a false concept of "thought," appears and disappears in accordance
with the thought held. The New Theology is simply an attempt on the
part of the more spiritual workers to break through the chains of old
theology that have hitherto fettered them, and they are getting closer and
20 closer every day to Truth, lifting the human thought heavenwards.

    "If Christianity is anything at all, it is the teaching of absolute Truth;
and if absolute Truth is not scientific, then there is no science in the
world" (Frederick Dixon).

HOW TO UNDERSTAND ADVANCED WRITINGS

25   A difficulty that has, unfortunately, prevented many able thinkers in
the past from trying to understand the Bible is that they have not apprehended the real meaning of inspiration, which is due to the normal action
of God on a human being, that causes him to exceed his usual capacity,
and enables him in a scientific way to obtain otherwise hidden knowledge,
30 by thinking of God. "We are, indeed, more than we know, and occasionally
hear ourselves utter things we know not" (Emerson).

    Misinterpretations of Truth.—It has been often said that you can
prove anything to be true from the Bible, and that all sorts of meanings
can be "read into it," attributing to writers statements of facts that never
35 entered into their calculations. The same accusations have been levelled
by some against correct interpretations of spiritually scientific writings.

    There is only one permanent scientific basis of all truth, and upon this
foundation all true statements must rest. This being so, they do not admit
of any possible final mistranslation, because truth understood can always
40 be demonstrated in visible proof of its right reading. Every true statement
thus proves itself consistent all through the degrees of our understanding
of its meaning up to infinity.

    The correct reading of any statement will always be demonstrable if
true, and will also be found consistent with progress in all its degrees
45 upwards. These degrees are absolutely independent of any direct intention
on the part of the writer, who can never change the original root meaning,

and therefore infinite significance of the words used to express even the simplest statement of truth. All discoverers of truth will tell of the continual unfoldment of their own early written expressions, as they rise to the higher understanding of Truth.

Nothing is so dangerous as to judge any interpretations of scientific 5 writings not as yet tested by those judging. Misjudgment by such critics would place them under a serious disadvantage until the right interpretation is proved by demonstration.

Definition of "The Scriptures" or "Canonical Writings."—*"The charter of our inheritance and the security of our standing"* (Charnock).   10

That "the scripture cannot be broken" (John 10:35) is a scientific fact of deepest moment, but to apprehend it fully, necessitates a clear understanding of the real meaning of the word "scripture." There has been attached to the term a specific significance as applying to the written record of the Bible or Canon of Scripture. This, while allowable, should 15 not be wrongly supposed to narrow in the very least its fuller meaning, which can only be discerned in the light of absolute Science. A knowledge of Science is required in order that "the thirty thousand different readings in the Old Testament, and the three hundred thousand in the New" should not confuse one.   20

The dictionary defines "scripture" as "primarily a writing," while it defines "writing" as "the act of forming letters with a pen; any written composition." "Letter" is defined as "a mark or character." What a vast flood of light is thus thrown upon the word "scripture," now that absolute Science has revealed to us the truth that the whole spiritual universe and 25 man in reality is the graphic expression of Mind, a perfect image and likeness of God, and from its minutest details to its infinite All, "unbreakable," and eternal, because mental, spiritual. The very fact of the "breakableness" of all material phenomena proves their illusive nature as being wholly foundationless.   30

The word "scripture" is absolutely consistent throughout the entire human grades or shades and degrees of its meaning. It is applied by the infant thought to the Bible as the truest writings, and the law of God as there set forth is final and unalterable. Thought outlined by God is eternal. None can interfere to prevent the action of this law of God. Any and all 35 thoughts *not* outlined by Life, Truth, and Love, as God, are illusions, breakable, and eventually bound to disappear. The Bible itself contains its own proof, because it answers to this standard of demonstrable truth. The original, actual, and eternal canonical writings are in the original sense of those words, the living realities, the *spiritual manifest effects of God's law.*   40

Fear of Criticism Betrays Doubt of Truth.—Truth does not shirk cr fear the strongest light that may be thrown upon it. Indeed, the intelligent criticism of honest inquirers leads to the elucidation of partially understood facts when based upon Truth, and such inquiry is welcomed by every scientific and therefore true religionist. The difference between the 45 truly wholesome agitation of honest inquiry and a mute, stolid, unquestioning acceptance is as great as that between a keenly active circulation in the human organism and the torpidity which ultimates in atrophy and death.

6*

Harnack describes the critical science of the present day as "a dance of
death," and the higher critics as "men who live for a time on the smell of an
empty bottle." This is because they take away what they think is poisonous
mental food, without giving us anything in exchange.

5   The spirit of modern criticism, which many have feared was under-
mining the authority of the Bible, is merely a sign of the dawning intelligence of the age. Although it may appear to some Churches to shake the
very foundation upon which they thought religion to be built, it should be
wisely welcomed by them, as it is merely the removal of the false ideas
10 which hitherto have, in places, hidden the real value of the precious stone
that is within. This removal of encrusted theories enables it now to be cut
and polished, so that the whole world may view and understand its beauties,
when, like the diamond, it will be found that each facet but reflects new light.

This is equally true, both of the Old Testament and of the New.
15 Romanes, one of the leading scientific men of the age, has stated that there
is not one of the doctrines and teachings of Jesus, "whether in natural
science, ethics, political economy, or elsewhere, which the subsequent
growth of human knowledge has had to discount."

The Bible the Book of Books.—"*The regulator of the rights and
20 duties of all; a universal charter*" (Lacordaire).

Our Bible is a wonderful and indeed priceless treasury and collection
of writings, by far the finest and most valuable that have ever been
gathered together.[1] It is always an interesting book; and when understood,
its deeper meanings become awe-inspiring. It is difficult to imagine ever
25 getting tired of studying it. D. L. Moody has said: "I believe the Bible to
be an inspired book because it inspires me." A mine of wealth, it contains
jewels of every kind and pearls of great price, which can be found directly
you have the "Key"[2] that opens up the spiritual and scientific interpretation, in which lies its real value. Not only is the history of the world
30 given in detail, but although "of that day and that hour knoweth no man,"
the approximate time of the end of all evil, the way in which that end is
coming about, and the important accompanying details, are given. All the
important particulars of future international relations, for instance, can be
found therein. It may be added, however, that in view of facts thus brought
35 to light it is obvious that any time spent in such research for material details
would be better employed in mitigating impending evil by scientifically
destroying the wrong thoughts which are laid open in the Bible for the
benefit of the world.

Difficulties in Understanding the Bible.—"*Now we have received,
40 not the spirit of the world, but the spirit which is of God; that we might know
the things that are freely given to us of God*" (I Cor. 2:12).

---

[1] "The Bible is the learned man's masterpiece, the ignorant man's dictionary,
the wise man's directory" (*Miscellaneous Writings*, p. 364, Mary Baker Eddy). At
45 the same time "The Sermon on the Mount, read each Sunday without comment
and obeyed throughout the week, would be enough for Christian practice. The
Word of God is a powerful preacher, and it is not too spiritual to be practical, nor
too transcendental to be heard and understood" (*Message for* 1901, Mary Baker
Eddy).

[2] *Science and Health with Key to the Scriptures* (Mary Baker Eddy).

The surface reading of the Bible is historical and full of inspirational types. Until you have the "Key," you will continue to find it difficult to understand, as our knowledge and interpretation of it have hitherto been so very limited. A portion of it is inspirational in the highest possible sense, such as Revelation, Genesis, Isaiah, Jeremiah, Daniel, and that wonder- 5 ful but little-studied book of Esdras. Even the grouping of the books, chapters, and verses has unquestionably been governed by the same Principle; a knowledge of the meaning of numbers shows this clearly. Possibly there have been mistakes made in compiling it, and naturally there are many mistranslations, now, in the light of Truth, easily dis- 10 cernible, and so no longer misleading.

Taken as a whole, when even partially understood, it is an unfailing guide to man. It is being found of practical use in every department of life; for confirming one's work, and for enabling one to understand what is happening and is going to happen, and so seeing what should be done to 15 minimise the troubles coming upon the world. In fact, it contains almost everything that one wants to know, and proofs of this are being received daily. This is now being recognised in differing degrees by a rapidly increasing number of earnest students, who have recognised the "little book" of the Apocalypse (Rev. 10:9). When understood in its true mean- 20 ing, the Bible will be found to be a safe and scientific guide to Truth. The basic facts of God and creation, as there set forth, educate the student to wisely discern between good and evil.

Professor Sir J. R. Seeley has said that "The greatest work of individual literary genius shows by the side of the Bible like some building of human 25 hands beside the Peak of Teneriffe." As one advances it will be found the most fascinating book possible; indeed, it is most difficult at times to tear oneself away from it. The world is now finding this out.

In 1895 it was estimated that during the preceding three years there had been more Bibles sold than in all the previous years. This increase 30 must have continued steadily since. In 1909 there were over 13,000,000 copies issued by the Bible Societies alone, of which over 3,000,000 went to China. When it is realised that since its foundation in 1804, the British and Foreign Bible Society has issued over 300,000,000 copies of the Scriptures, one-third of this total in English, and that the Bible is trans- 35 lated into over 500 languages, some idea of the numbers now studying this book of books can be obtained.

One difficulty in understanding the Bible is that each passage has a threefold significance, and needs to be interpreted from the three points of view from which human consciousness has viewed existence, before 40 its fullest meaning can be gained. Of these three points of view—the material, the intellectual, and the spiritual—the latter alone is of deepest import.[1] It is partly owing to this that there is such a difference of opinion

---

[1] Since writing the above I have found that in the fourth book of *De Principiis*, Origen, one of the ablest of men, and well versed in occult matters, explains at 45 length his views on the interpretation of the Bible. It has (he says) a "body," which is the common and historical sense; a "soul," a figurative meaning to be discovered by the exercise of the intellect; and a "spirit," an inner and divine sense, to be known only by those who have "the mind of Christ" (Phil. 2:5).

with regard to the Bible. One man will take the spiritual interpretation, another the material. The third will sometimes take the spiritual and sometimes the intellectual, and often two men will lose their tempers over differing interpretations of a certain passage, and part with the reverse of
5 Christian feelings towards each other, instead of being absolutely loving, and helping each other to a better understanding, by calmly and intelligently submitting their different points of view, as would be the case if they knew how to think scientifically and therefore rightly. When endeavouring to gain or to express the spiritual meaning, if you continu-
10 ously try to think of God as Truth, and man as knowing and speaking truth, as clearly as you can, you will find it to be of the highest possible value. Perhaps no command has been so little understood as that the Sabbath day should be "kept holy." Primarily it was a resting from the exercise of creative power. No man is keeping the Sabbath holy who is
15 maintaining the reign of false mental law, which is productive through the human being of all the sin, disease, and death of to-day. There is only one law to obey, and that is to love God and love our neighbours as ourselves.

The real difficulty and real value of the Bible lies in its spiritual interpretation. Dr. Rudolf Steiner, a German scholar of repute, writes: "No
20 man can rightly understand the historical truths of such documents as the Gospels, unless he has first experienced within himself the mystical meaning which they contain." This understanding can be obtained when the meaning of the words "The kingdom of God is within" is grasped.

To study the Bible properly, not only such books as Cruden's *Con-*
25 *cordance*, Smith's *Dictionary of the Bible*, and various translations are useful for reference, but also a dictionary such as Webster's, so altered has the meaning of Biblical words become through the endeavour to make their significance suit our late theological ideas. Young's *Analytical Concordance* is useful, as it gives the original Hebrew and Greek words used,
30 with their literal meanings.

We cannot pretend to have a real knowledge of the Bible until we know far more than presents itself on the surface. We cannot even know how to study it properly until we gain the understanding of the principle of its numerical structure through unfoldment of the meaning of its numbers and
35 names. As an instance of this, see I Samuel 23, verse 28, and Revelation 13, verse 18.

Professor Huxley has written as follows: "It appears to me that if there is anybody more objectionable than the orthodox Bibliolater, it is the heterodox Philistine, who can discover in a literature, which in some respects
40 has no superior, nothing but a subject for scoffing, and an occasion for the display of his conceited ignorance of the debt he owes to former generations.

"Twenty-two years ago I pleaded for the use of the Bible as an instrument of popular education; and I venture to repeat what I then said: 'Consider the great historical fact that for three centuries this book has
45 been woven into the life of all that is best and noblest in English history, and that it has become the national epic of Britain; that it is written in the noblest and purest English, and abounds in exquisite beauties of mere literary form; and, finally, that it forbids the veriest hind, who never left his village, to be ignorant of the existence of other countries, and other

civilisations, and of a great past, stretching back to the furthest limits of the oldest nations in the world. By the study of what other book could children be so much humanised, and made to feel that each figure in that vast historical procession fills, like themselves, but a momentary space in the interval between the eternities!' The Bible has been the Magna Charta of the poor and of the oppressed. Down to modern times no State has had a Constitution in which the interests of the people are so largely taken into account; in which the duties, so much more than the privileges, of rulers are insisted upon, as that drawn up for Israel in Deuteronomy and Leviticus. Nowhere is the fundamental truth that the welfare of the State in the long run depends upon the righteousness of the citizen so strongly laid down."

Numbers and Names.—There is an immense gain in even a slight knowledge of the deep significance attached to every number and to their groupings. All matter is vibration, and can be reduced to its numerical value. No one can pretend to have a scientific knowledge until he understands the principle underlying the science of numbers. Lord Kelvin writes: "I often say that if you can measure that of which you speak, and can express it by a number, you know something of your subject; but if you cannot measure it your knowledge is meagre and unsatisfactory."

This significance naturally attaches to names. These are only groupings of numerical vibrations to convey certain definite meanings. Important historical events are constantly recorded in a mere name, and handed down to all generations. So universal was this method that if you look up the meanings of names in Cruden's *Concordance*, and follow each as it appears in the Bible record, a mere novice studying the Bible will rapidly arrive at an excellent bird's-eye view of the material history and its spiritual interpretation. In fact, a beginner, paying also due attention to the meaning of numbers, would speedily outdistance the most experienced Bible scholar who has failed to explore this mine of wealth.

Anglo-Israelites.—We need also to understand the references to the Anglo-Israelitish race,[1] opening up as they do the accuracy of the prophecies with the details of the history of these latter days and the necessary steps to be taken to bring about the end of materiality. This subject is well worth investigation, and discloses facts which have an important bearing on the great changes shortly about to take place.

Bible Symbolism.—With the ancient writers in the Bible, symbolism is largely used throughout, partly for the purpose of brevity, in order to save the large amount of writing that otherwise would have been requisite. "I have multiplied visions, and used similitudes, by the ministry of the prophets" (Hos. 12:10). In *The Treatise of the Tilling of the Earth*, by Philo Judæus, he points out that Moses through his great knowledge "was

---

[1] Professor C. A. L. Totten, of Yale University, says: "I cannot state too strongly that the man who has not seen that Israel of the Scripture is totally different from the Jewish people, is yet in the very infancy, the mere alphabet, of Biblical study, and that to this day the meaning of seven-eighths of the Bible is shut to his understanding." Remember that this is seven-eighths of the material meaning.

accustomed to fix the most felicitous and most expressive appellations" to all things. In referring to the portions of the Bible said to have been written by Moses, he says: "In the allegorical explanations of these statements, all that bears a fabulous appearance is got rid of in a moment and the truth is
5 discovered in a most evident manner."

I may mention a few of these symbols. In the story of Adam and Eve the serpent symbolises "human allurements." This is not always the meaning of a serpent, as the serpent referred to in speaking of Dan symbolises "sound judgment," and a brazen serpent typifies "endurance."
10 Words are used, not casually, but with an underlying definite meaning. For instance, take the word "horse"; this is used as symbolising "appetites and passions." A "rider" consequently is used as a man who, having no skill, is carried away, thrown off, and comes to grief. A "horseman," on the contrary, is the skilful rider who holds under control the "appetites and
15 passions." Again, a flock of sheep refers to everything in a man's consciousness. A "shepherd" leads the flock away from folly, injustice, etc., whereas the "keeper of sheep" allows them to surfeit themselves on anything that comes to hand, and consequently they suffer. The effect of the symbolism is lost to the Western mind owing to the differing conditions. We cannot
20 appreciate the symbolism of water as the essence of life, any more than that of the shepherd, until we understand the conditions in the past.[1] The Chaldees made a special study of this symbolism, and Abraham and Moses were evidently well acquainted with the knowledge gained therefrom.

Symbols.—It is also necessary to appreciate the usual meanings
25 attached in the East to the symbols so freely used by the writers. Before the end of evil, it is essential that all these meanings must be openly declared to the world by those who understand them, so helping to make clearer the vital and scientific teaching of the Bible. Not a moment need be wasted in studying these subjects apart from the Bible record, as all knowledge of
30 necessary references, etc., comes naturally to those who pray in the right way, and rely upon prayer to obtain such knowledge. Valuable time may be saved, and far deeper meanings discovered, by utilising the power of gaining knowledge through inspiration. "God . . . giveth wisdom . . . and knowledge. . . . He revealeth the deep and secret things" (Dan. 2:20, 21,
35 22). Paul said: "When it pleased God . . . to reveal his Son in me, . . . immediately I conferred not with flesh and blood . . . but I went into Arabia. . . . Then after three years I went up to Jerusalem" (Gal. 1:15-18).

INSPIRATION

40 " *What else have science and religion ever had to fight about, save on the basis of this common hypothesis, and hence as to whether the causation of such or such a phenomenon has been 'natural' or 'supernatural'? For even the disputes as to science contradicting scripture, ultimately turn on the assumption of inspiration (supposing it genuine) being 'supernatural' as to its causation.*
45 *Once grant that it is 'natural' and all possible ground of dispute is removed*" (Romanes).

[1] See *The Song of our Syrian Guest*, by W. A. Knight.

Inspiration has been much misunderstood. You can always do any-thing better than usual by utilising the power of God, of good. Inspiration is natural and scientific and you can obtain any knowledge desired for a good purpose. In the past we have based our views of God and His power, the Christ, not upon inspiration and revelation, our God-given powers, but 5 upon "the sand of human reason."

The question is, how is this action to be brought about when required? It is by the realisation of God, of the Christ, through the practical under-standing "of the mystery of God, and of the Father, and of Christ; In whom are hid all the treasures of wisdom and knowledge" (Col. 2:2, 3). 10 "There is a spirit in man: and the inspiration of the Almighty giveth them understanding" (Job. 32:8). Plato noted that poets "utter great and wise things that they do not themselves understand." Great writers nearly all believe in inspiration, but they have believed it necessary to wait until the inspired moment comes. Many, such as Horace, Ibsen, George Eliot, 15 and George Sand, have written of it.

George Eliot, for instance, said that in all her best writing there was a "not herself" which took possession of her, and that she felt her own personality to be merely the instrument through which this spirit, as she expressed it, was acting. Hawthorn recognised this action, and once thought 20 of making it the subject of a story. Thackeray told his children that the story of *The Newcomes*, probably his masterpiece, had been revealed to him somehow as in a dream.

Coleridge says the same of his *Kubla Khan*. Wordsworth has described his inspired state in his "Prelude." This "lamp of genius," as Schiller 25 calls it, died away gradually in his early life. George Sand said she wrote continuously and without plan, and literally without knowing whither she was going—even without being aware of the social problem she was elaborating. Robert Louis Stevenson, in his Essay, *A Chapter on Dreams*, confesses that portions of his most original novels were composed in the 30 dreaming state, and speaks of the talent of the "little people who manage man's internal theatre."

Mozart, who at the age of four could play minuets and understood the theory of music, began to compose at the age of five. He not only had a taste for melody but his productions broke none of the complicated laws 35 of harmony that take an ordinary mortal years of patient study to master. He said: "If you think how you are to write [music] you will never write anything worth hearing. I write because I cannot help it!" He heard his music in a dream before he wrote it out. Schubert, who composed the *Erl King* when only eighteen, was another genius. One of his masters said: 40 "I cannot teach Franz Schubert anything; he must have learned music directly from heaven." Directly he read Shakespeare's verses "Who is Sylvia?" and "Hark, hark, the lark," the melodious tunes to which he put them flashed into his mind. Beethoven said: "Inspiration is for me that mysterious state in which the entire world seems to form a vast harmony, 45 when every sentiment, every thought, re-echoes within me, when my whole body shivers and my hair stands on end."

Jacob Boehme (A.D. 1574–1624), the great mystic, and father of German philosophy, who was only a working shoemaker, but whose whole time

was spent in deep and original thought, expressed in some of his writings
a wonderful knowledge of the truth. He wrote, "Blessed art thou therefore
if thou canst stand still from self-thinking and self-willing, and canst stop
the wheel of thy imagination and senses; forasmuch as hereby thou mayest
5 arrive at length to see the great salvation of God, being made capable of all
manner of divine sensations and heavenly communications. Since it is
nought indeed but thine own hearing and willing that do hinder thee, so
that thou dost not see and hear God. . . . This thy willing moreover stops
thy hearing. . . . And having brought thee hither, it overshadows thee
10 with that which thou willest; it binds thee with thine own chains, and it
keeps thee in thine own dark prison which thou makest for thyself; so that
thou canst not go out thence, or come to that state which is supernatural
and supersensual" (*Of The Supersensual Life*). Had such a man only been
shown the practical method of working—praying—what a change would
15 have taken place in the world.

Professor Lombroso speaks of "numerous men of genius who at some
period of their lives were subject to hallucinations," and exclaims, "How
many great thinkers have shown themselves all their lives subject to mono-
mania or hallucinations!" Many of the contemporaries of Swedenborg
20 believed him to be, if not insane, at least a monomaniac, and Professor
Lombroso, who was a great specialist on such matters, concurs in this
opinion, and amongst others, places Loyola, George Fox, Savonarola, and
Luther in the same category. Socrates thought he was guided through life
by an inner voice. I believe Lord Beaconsfield drew attention to the narrow
25 dividing line there is between what is called genius and what is called madness. "Great wits are sure to madness near allied" (Dryden). Gladstone
was an example of this. At the same time, as Lord Salisbury said: "He was
a great Christian," to use his own words, he was constantly "dwelling in
the inner court of the sanctuary, whereof the walls are not built with hands."
30 What splendid results would have followed if these individuals had
understood the scientific method of working.

Madness.—According to Dr. Forbes Winslow, insanity is rapidly
increasing, the ratio now being 1 in 277, and the average annual increase
during the last decade being 2,394. He also says that there are at present
35 149,000 mentally defective persons at large, uncertified, unprotected, and
uncontrolled.[1] All this trouble is simply caused by wrong thinking, not
only on the part of those afflicted, but on the part of those responsible for
them. Thousands have become insane through those who love them constantly thinking wrongly of them instead of rightly.

40 **Inspiration Scientific.**—"*Incredulity is based wholly upon supposed
personal experience, and will believe nothing else. Hence, it cannot be reasoned
with, as it is always scornful in its reliance on this often most fallacious testimony*"[2] (Professor William H. Hudson).

For the last thirty years I have been responsible for numberless experi-
45 ments and investigations of every kind, electrical, mechanical, and

---

[1] Lecture at Caxton Hall, February 27, 1911.
[2] *Materialism and Modern Physiology of the Nervous System.*

chemical. Trained as an electrician in my earlier days, I spent many evenings in the local hospital whilst serving my time as an engineer. Since then I have often been required to investigate and advise on new medical discoveries, and acted, during its existence, as electrical expert to the Institute of Medical Electricity, founded under the auspices of the chief 5 scientific men of the day. This institute, which was almost entirely due to the work of Colonel Wallace, was, practically without remuneration, doing most valuable advanced experimental work under Mr. Carpenter, years before X-rays and Finsen rays were even thought of by the ordinary medical profession. Suddenly, I think in 1888, a circular was received by 10 all medical men, including those on the Council and connected with it, some of whom were of European reputation, saying that, if retaining any connection with it, their names would be struck off the rolls of the leading medical institution. The institute was immediately closed.

My work during seventeen years of my life was the professional elucida- 15 tion of difficult business problems, the examination and reporting upon new inventions and discoveries of every kind, and, to a lesser extent, advising upon and assisting in their early development. Whilst there has therefore been but little difficulty in understanding the details of the material world, it would have been absolutely impossible to account for the 20 apparent action and interaction of matter had I not learned: (1) that inspiration is scientific, and (2) that the secret of obtaining requisite knowledge is the recognition and realisation of God, of the one Mind, and the spiritual or real man's unity with God, and his consequent possession of any knowledge directly it is needed. "If any of you lack wisdom, let him 25 ask of God, that giveth to all men liberally . . . and it shall be given" (James 1:5). "For God speaketh once, yea twice, yet man perceiveth it not" (Job. 33:14).

The basic false mentality—that has been called the "subconscious mind," "mortal mind," and the "ether"—includes everything in the 30 material world, past, present, and future. If, when a mortal is dwelling on an idea, his human sense, miscalled conscious mind, vibrates synchronously with this basic false mentality, he is then brought into touch with any details that he requires to know. True prayer destroys the mist of matter that prevents this desired action of material mechanism. "If 35 there be a prophet among you, I the Lord will make myself known unto him" (Num. 12:6).

Proofs of Its Truth.—"*They that seek the Lord understand all things*" (Prov. 28:5).

Out of the hundreds of cases where knowledge has been gained in this 40 way by the realisation of God and His manifestation, not once, as far as I am aware, has it turned out to be wrong. "There is a God in heaven that revealeth secrets" (Dan. 2:28). "Wherefore, brethren, covet [desire eagerly] to prophesy" (I Cor. 14:39). Knowledge can be in this way gained by anyone, and what has been stated cannot be true unless each can prove 45 it. "For ye may all prophesy" (I Cor. 14:31). Jesus was the greatest example. "And the Jews marvelled, saying, How knoweth this man letters, having never learned?" (John 7:15). The disciples said to him: "Now are

we sure that thou knowest all things" (John 16:30). "God . . . hath
determined the times before appointed" (Acts 17:24, 26).

It may be said: How can you obtain a greater knowledge of that which
does not exist? You cannot. All that you gain is a further and better (less
5 bad) knowledge of God and God's ideas, the reality, which is hidden by the
mist of matter.

"He hath given me certain knowledge of the things that are, namely, to
know how the world was made, and the operation of the elements: The
beginning, ending, and midst of the times: . . . And all such things as are
10 either secret or manifest, them I know. For wisdom, which is the worker
of all things, taught me: for in her is an understanding spirit, holy, one
only, manifold, subtil, lively, clear, undefiled, plain, not subject to hurt,
. . . She is the breath of the power of God, and a pure influence flowing
from the glory of the Almighty: . . . I perceived that I could not other-
15 wise obtain her,[1] except God gave her me; and that was a point of wisdom
also to know whose gift she was; I prayed unto the Lord, and besought
him" (Wisdom of Solomon 7:17, 18, 21, 22, 25, and 8:21).

PRACTICAL DEMONSTRATIONS

The Ether and Matter.—"*Knowledge may enter the human mind
20 without being communicated in any hitherto known or recognised ways*"[2]
(Sir William Crookes). "*Of a truth it is, that your God is a God of gods,
and a Lord of kings, and a revealer of secrets*" (Dan. 2:47).

It has already been stated that material knowledge not only sometimes
flashes into one's consciousness, but comes in all sorts of ways, and a few
25 instances may be given. "Let the specimen suffice to those who have ears.
For it is not required to unfold the mystery, but only to indicate what is
sufficient" (St. Clement of Alexandria).

I had been satisfied that matter is electricity and a non-reality, and that
the ether—only another name for material or universal consciousness,[3] or
30 mortal "mind," the basic false mentality—consists of lines of force, high-
tension electrical currents at right angles to each other, and that matter can
be caused to appear and disappear instantly in two ways, scientifically
different. In one of these the electrical tension in the ether is increased or
released, in the other the lines of force are short-circuited and so destroyed,
35 leaving better thoughts to be manifested.[4] The "riddle of the ether" and

---

[1] "Howbeit when he, the Spirit of truth, is come, he will guide you into all
truth: for he shall not speak of himself; but whatsoever he shall hear, that shall he
speak: and he will shew you things to come. . . . All things that the Father hath
are mine: therefore said I, that he shall take of mine, and shall shew it unto you"
40 (John 16:13, 15).

[2] Presidential Address, British Association, 1898.

[3] "Electricity is not a vital fluid, but the least material form of illusive consciousness" (*Science and Health*, p. 293, Mary Baker Eddy). Illusive consciousness,
the ether, devil, mortal mind, cosmic consciousness, unconscious mind, sub-
45 conscious mind, subjective mind, subliminal self, better consciousness, communal
soul and basic false mentality, are all different names for the same thing.

[4] "This so-called mind is self-destroyed. The manifestations of evil . . . show
the self-destruction of error or matter and point to matter's opposite, the strength
and permanency of Spirit" (*Ibid.*, p. 293).

the relationship between the ether and matter had still to be solved. I accordingly one day prayed, realising that in the real world, God, being the Principle of all true knowledge, man, the divine man, is instantly conscious of what he needs to know. Immediately afterwards a scientific man came for advice on an interesting point. He said that, amongst the ultra rays of 5 light, there were some which, thrown upon an object, would cause it to disappear from sight, although it was still in its position, and asked how he could best localise the rays.

Disappearance of Matter.—In the course of conversation he told me of an important experiment. He had taken 1 lb. of oxygen and 1 lb of potas- 10 sium, and placed them in an exhausted glass tube, which was then hermetically sealed. On passing a high-tension current through the tube, $1\frac{3}{4}$ lb. of the contents instantly disappeared, the chemical balance upon which the apparatus stood registering the loss of weight as the current was turned on. He then told me that he had proved mathematically (200 pages of 15 equations were required) that the electron was created by the action at right angles of two lines of force of definite length upon each other, and he thought that the action of the high-tension current had resolved the electrons into the original lines of force, which then passed easily through the glass and disappeared. As a matter of fact, these lines of force are not 20 finite in length, but, as beliefs, extend indefinitely in false space. It took two years before Dr. Romocki, then the chemist on my staff, was able to confirm the mathematical proof.

A few days afterwards, a friend of mine, one of the leading chemical authorities in England, confidentially gave me details of somewhat similar 25 chemical experiments which had just been carried out under test conditions before a selected body of leading scientific men, and had been pronounced by them as wholly inconsistent with any conceivable theory of matter. These experiments were shown to them, to establish priority of date for the discoverer, who did not care to publish them until he had 30 found the reason for the results.

"The Earth Helped the Woman."—It was then that I recognised that we were on the eve of the great intellectual revolution that must attend the scientific recognition of the non-reality of matter, and I understood the meaning of the words in Revelation 12, verse 16,[1] "And the earth [the 35 leading scientific thought of the day] helped the woman, and the earth opened her mouth [by stating the truth], and swallowed up the flood which the dragon cast out of his mouth" [the wrong use of this newly gained mental freedom].

Crookes's Berlin Lecture.—The following finale in Sir William 40 Crookes's Berlin lecture, which was shortly afterwards delivered, then showed me that already the leaven was at work: "This fatal quality of atomic dissociation appears to be universal . . . the whole range of human experience is all too short to afford a parallax whereby the date of the

[1] Rotherham's translation of verse 15 is significant. It is as follows: "And the 45 serpent cast out of his mouth, *behind* the woman, water as a river, that he might cause her to be river-borne" (see *Miscellaneous Writings*, p. 373, Mary Baker Eddy).

extinction of matter can be calculated."[1] This knowledge is now available.
"For we know in part, and we prophesy in part" (I Cor. 13:9).

"We are living in an extraordinary age . . . it is a time for the open
mind and the open vision in all departments of thought" (Sir Oliver
5 Lodge).

"The whole history of science shows us that, whenever the educated
and scientific men of any age have denied the facts of other investigators on
a priori grounds of absurdity or impossibility, the deniers have always
been wrong"[2] (Professor Alfred Russel Wallace).

10   **Non-Reality of Matter.**—Another case of knowledge gained inspirationally in a seemingly indirect manner may be given. I tried for some time
by ordinary means, during the first eighteen months of my examination
into "mental" phenomena for the *Daily Express*, to obtain mathematical
proof of the non-reality of electricity, but without success. Although in the
15 application of the method of scientific and true prayer I had as yet
experienced practically no failure of any importance, doubt seized hold of
me in this matter of obtaining knowledge that apparently must include
abstruse mathematical calculations. I shrank from possible failure, but
gained some courage through remembering that it was equally scientific for
20 the information to reach me through the channel of my head engineer or
chemist, both of whom were first-class mathematicians. Recognising that
hesitation was not reliance on Principle, and that fear had the upper hand,
I prayed five times during two days for the required knowledge so requisite
for the clearing up of the mystery of evil. The following morning I
25 received from Mr. Wake-Cook a copy of the Rede Lecture given by
Professor Osborne Reynolds, referring to his mathematical proof of the
non-reality of matter already mentioned. "And herein is that saying true,
One soweth, and another reapeth. I sent you to reap that whereon ye
bestowed no labour: other men laboured, and ye are entered into their
30 labours" (John 4:37, 38). Mr. Wake-Cook wrote: "Here he has proved
mathematically what you have been telling us for some time". In this way
the twenty years' life-work of one of the most advanced mathematicians of
the day, until then entirely unknown to me, was rendered available by a
few minutes' prayer.

35   This instance also illustrates the necessity of keeping an open mind as to
the channel through which information may reach you. To look for help
through any special channel is more or less to close the door to all others.
We must leave Principle to decide what is best. God's way is always perfect,
the way of good (see Ps. 18:30).

40   A third example may be given. Having found that the ether consists of
lines of force, high-tension electrical currents, I had the same difficulty as
other investigators in not being able to find out what was believed to exist,[3]
namely, the positive electron, although the negative electron was easily

---

[1] "Modern Views of Matter." An Address delivered before the Congress of
45 Applied Chemistry at Berlin, June 5, 1903.
[2] Speech at the Grand Hotel, Birmingham, June 25, 1910.
[3] "In the chemical theory of electricity, over and above the known elements
there should be two others—the positive and negative electrons" (Dr. Nernst,
Professor of Chemistry, Göttingen University).

discoverable. Neither was it clear how these lines of force or material thoughts were destroyed by the action of God. I therefore prayed for knowledge two or three times in two days. The next day a well-known inventor called upon me for advice with regard to a system of wireless telephony. In the course of conversation a remark of his led me to put my 5 difficulty before him. He at once gave me two solutions, one of which I knew must be accurate because it fitted in with all the other basic theories of the material universe already found to be correct.

"Correct" and "Accurate."—The words "correct" and "accurate" do not mean "true" when applied to the theories of matter now advanced. 10 They merely denote accordance with the final beliefs of material so-called science. The only true statement that can be made with reference to matter is that it has no reality. Reality means permanence.

Short-circuiting.—The inventor then explained that each seeming line of force or so-called thought consisted of innumerable adjacent small 15 particles, oval or egg-shaped, not touching each other, and lying with the longer axis at right angles to the general trend of the line of force. The greatest diameter is just equal to the distance apart of their centres. One of their ends is positive and the other negative. Now, when a man denies the reality of sin or sickness in heaven the action of God causes the seeming 20 sin or sickness to disappear. What then takes place, from a theoretical point of view, is that one of these particles, or thought-germs, is slightly turned. The positive ends of adjacent particles then repel each other, and the dissimilar ends attract each other until each adjacent particle is slightly turned. The positive end of each particle having thus come nearer the 25 negative end of the adjacent particle, the turning action is increased by these portions attracting each other until each particle has been turned at right angles. Being oval, the positive end of each particle then touches the negative end of the adjacent particle, and the whole line of force is short-circuited and finally ceases to have even its temporal or material sense of 30 existence, and there is in its place what even material scientists admit to be NOTHING [1]—nothing cognisable under any circumstances by the

[1] "The only power of evil is to destroy itself" (*Science and Health*, p. 186, Mary Baker Eddy).

As in the case of the healing of sin and disease, results are not always obtained 35 immediately, especially when trying to find out details in connection with the spiritual world. For instance, Mrs. Eddy says: "Few persons comprehend what Christian Science means by the word *reflection*" (*Ibid.*, p. 301). Seeing that here was some important knowledge to be gained, I set to work to find the real meaning. To do this took me two-and-a-half years, and I had to pray specifically over 20,000 40 times for it, more than twenty times a day, before I found it out. The information was well worth obtaining. It opened up to me through reversal a knowledge of the spiritual world that was wonderful, indicating that which is happening in heaven, and showing how to work out logically the details indicative of what is there taking place. These logical deductions have been demonstrated by thousands of results in 45 the so-called material world, and can be proved by anyone with sufficient under-standing and enough humility to subordinate material so-called knowledge.

I once lost a pair of gloves, and in order to find out whether I had properly understood the Principle that underlay the action of good in the materialisation of what is called matter, I treated every day for over a year before they were found, 50 and the right understanding of Truth demonstrated. In one important case I

material senses with any aid whatever, and nothing that can even be logically made apparent to the so-called intellect. God's real and perfect world,
is, however, present everywhere and always discernible by the true senses.

PROPHESYING,[1] PREDESTINATION, FATALISM

5   *"And every course of self-discipline thus steadily and honestly pursued
tends, not merely to clear the mental vision of the individual, but to enable the
race, by developing that power of immediate insight which, in man's highest
phase of existence, will not only supersede the laborious operations of his
intellect, but will reveal to him truths and glories of the unseen, which the*
10 *intellect alone can see but as through a glass darkly"* (Dr. W. B. Carpenter).
One of the facts that have made it a little difficult to understand the
prophecies in the Bible is that each recorded stage of human experience,
in obedience to the action of material thought, imitating the reality, fore-
shadows what is to appear in subsequent ages. This continues until the
15 material counterfeit is destroyed by the action of Truth. Consequently
each prophecy may foretell a series of events liable to happen in their predetermined order at different periods throughout the Bible history, each
series of events being simply a repetition of what has happened before, but
conforming in details to the improved normal conditions of each period.
20 Further, a prophecy often refers to entirely different events, such as the
history of a certain period, and events in the life of an individual. The
importance of scientific and therefore accurate interpretation of prophecy
is that we can begin sooner to destroy the groups of thoughts that might
later give trouble if left to be dealt with at any given moment. So we purify
25 and lift up the remaining human experience, and ensure painless instead
of painful progress.

Value of Historical Evidence.—What we call history is merely an
apparently periodical repetition of events happening all at the same time,

treated every day for three-and-a-half years before succeeding in my demonstration,
30 and destroying aggressive evil that was a menace to humanity. Treatment is the
name given to true prayer, in order to differentiate it from the old limited method
of prayer by asking. Mrs. Eddy says: "Self-denial, sincerity, Christianity, and persistence alone win the prize" (*Ibid.*, p. 462).
In working for material knowledge I realise that God being the Principle of all
35 knowledge, man—the spiritual man—knows instantly anything he needs. When
trying to obtain a better knowledge of God and the spiritual world, I found that my
most efficient method was simply to try and realise God as Truth to the best of my
ability. It seemed then to be easier to lose the false sense of self in the realisation of
God. You must remember, however, that you can build up in your own conscious-
40 ness mistaken ideas as to the best method of working, which then become so-called
laws, as far as you are concerned. No difficulties on this point can possibly happen,
however, to the consistent worker who obtains his knowledge from the right source,
as all true knowledge is demonstrable here and now.
      [1] It must not be forgotten that prophesying is only reading thought. Although
45 those in the past who lived in thought close to God, and did not limit their powers
by wrong thinking, were able often to prophesy accurately, in most cases they were
liable to make mistakes and only partially to read the thoughts that later were about
to act. It is through want of knowledge of the material world that lovers of God and
the Bible have claimed too much, and so alienated scientific men, who should have
50 been, and now will be, their strongest supporters.

and which individually are only counterfeits, or taken as a whole are re-counterfesances of actual facts in the real world, called heaven. These periodical repetitions enable us to check our readings of the prophecies, and so accurately foresee future troubles. Taken in time, the evil thoughts can then be easily destroyed.

Spiritual Significance.—Let it be well understood, as has been pointed out before, that the spiritual interpretation of the Bible is the important one to understand. Without the guiding star of Truth—"The Key to the Scriptures"—all human researches, whether geological, geographical, geometrical, or historical, end in smoke. Like a will-o'-the-wisp, they lead nowhere. It is not until the great searchlight of Truth is turned into the empty chambers of ethereal imagery,[1] the dark recesses of mortal false theories, where material sense distorts and misrepresents spiritual facts, that the grand verities of existence can be discovered by reversing the lie.

Likewise, it is not until scientific truth has interpreted the purely symbolic character of all material records that historical events can be scientifically handled with any particular benefit. They then take their rightful place. "Now all these things happened unto them for ensamples: and they are written for our admonition, upon whom the ends of the world are come" (I Cor. 10:11).

That "knowledge is power" is a truism, and more especially does this apply to foreknowledge. How many times has the expression, "If I had only known" been used! It is evident that if we knew exactly what evil lies before us it would be far easier, now that we know how to destroy the false thoughts which cause all the trouble, to destroy them before they are mani-fested, and so finally to expunge their mortal record. Prevention of repetitions of evil is better than cure, and best of all when it is final.

Recognising this, it will be seen that the final fight now taking place with evil is merely a repetition, in a little different form, of what has taken place in the past; and the exposure of the mistakes that have been allowed in the past enables us to prevent their recurrence in the present and in the future. Foresight has never been so essential as at present, when matter is hastening to its self-inflicted doom, and human history is appearing in its most intricate and dangerous form.

The Value of Prophecy.—Again, when one recognises that so much of the material universe, called past, present, and future, is invisible to imperfect human sight, the immense value of the prophecies is seen. How can one be afraid of the future when we are in possession of the power of dominion over all evil, and it is seen mapped out in detail, like one of Cook's tours, giving even the time of arrival and the menu for the day. Fear, then, has no hold on one, and it is possible all the time to work, helping and protecting others, instead of working directly to protect oneself. Remember that in prophesying, reading thought, one always, if working properly, detects the worst thoughts. These can then be destroyed by scientific prayer, when better thoughts alone remain and appear.

The paramount importance of the sayings of our Master lies in their spiritual significance. Nevertheless, helpful sidelights may be thrown on

[1] See Ezekiel 8, verse 12.

them by an intelligent knowledge of the human incidents which called
them forth.

The prophecies of the Bible not only relate to what has been happening
in the past, but also foretell what is now happening, and about to happen.
5 Indeed, the only object of correctly reading past history is to enable us
better to understand the future, and so enable us to protect those whose
admitted want of definite knowledge of the enemy's method of attack can
only be spoken of as pride in ignorance, and those whom a Pharisaical
belief in the extent of their spiritual awakeness, coupled with a superficial
10 knowledge of the letter of spiritual teaching, renders easy victims to the
unforeseen dangers that line the way of those who have not yet found out
that Love alone leads safely.

Vibration the Cause of the Apparent Unity.—Now we know that
a material thought is only apparent vibration, that every planet, every star,
15 every human being has its definite numerical value, in terms of whole
small numbers. Consequently the whole of the material universe is theoretically a system of vibrations, every combination bearing its exact
mathematical relationship to all the other parts. This is the material
representation, or rather counterfeit presentment or misrepresentation, of
20 the absolute law, order, and system that exist in the spiritual universe
where all is governed by God as Principle, and reflects God. Every single
thing, therefore, must have its exact and perfect position and bearing in
relationship to all the other spiritual realities, hence the typical significance of each detail.
25   The sun and its planets, arranged in the scale of their space relationship to each other, exactly reproduce the musical spacing of a fundamental
note and its harmonies. Most probably it will be found before long that the
human body, with its heart, represents the sun, and that the arrangement
of the electrons exactly repeats the arrangements of the planets. Theore-
30 tically it should be so, as the spacing is based upon relationships corresponding to the radius of the whole small numbers. It will be found that
everything in the material world is governed by this relationship of the
whole small numbers, which power a modern writer incorrectly calls
"the Voice of God."

35   **Astrology.**[1]—*"Thus saith the Lord, Learn not the way of the heathen,
and be not dismayed at the signs of heaven; for the heathen are dismayed at
them"* (Jer. 10:2).

One of the most important symbolisms in the material world is found
in the sidereal system. We need not, like the heathen, be dismayed when
40 we find that there are signs of impending disasters in the future, as by true
prayer we can destroy all such evil thoughts. In the sidereal system is
symbolised, not only the spiritual reality of the sun, planets, and stars,
but the history of the world and the history of every human being. At first
sight it seems very difficult to see how this can be so. On investigation it
45 will be found to be very simple. It merely is because the whole of the

---

[1] "Astrology is well in its place, but this place is secondary" (*Miscellaneous
Writings*, p. 334, Mary Baker Eddy).

material world, past, present, and future, appears, as far as anything in the material world can be said to be apparent, at the present moment in the form of thoughts, material and therefore false thoughts.

Abraham undoubtedly studied the stars. Goethe and Bacon gave details of their horoscopes to account for certain characteristics, whilst nearly every physician and man of science in medieval Europe was an astrologer. It was looked upon as a difficult but real science. Chaucer, Dryden, Scott, Bulwer-Lytton, Sir Richard Burton, Kepler, and Napier the mathematician, all gave a considerable amount of attention to the subject, and Richelieu and Napoleon firmly believed in it. It is not advisable, however, to give time to it in the present day, as information worth having can be much better obtained in other ways. All needful knowledge is close at hand in a readily available form, and directly we know how to pray scientifically we can gain it.

Astrological results are due, not to any effect that the constellations have, but to the fact that every four minutes a different main vibration acts upon the earth. Each planet also appears to come into so-called action upon any particular portion of the earth every four minutes, and has its vibratory number, which can be reduced to its digit or fundamental value. From this series of vibrations can be mathematically calculated, not only a man's material future,[1] but the thought that comes to him at any given moment, as every thought, like every sound, has its vibratory value.[2]

It is a great waste of time to try and find out either the past, the present, or the future in this way, as this only prolongs illusions which have to be destroyed before dominion can be gained by man and perfect happiness thus eventually reached. We have enough to do to learn how to work in the proper way. When a man learns how to think rightly he can destroy any so-called bad influence when its preordained time comes, and thoroughly protect himself and all those around him.

Numerical Value of Names.—The same sound in every language has the same vibratory number. If you add up the numbers of the different sounds in your name and obtain its fundamental value, you will find that it is the same number as the fundamental value of the vibration that theoretically must act at the moment of your birth; and as astrologers will say, of the number of the planet under which you were born. Every letter, or rather sound, has its recognised value in numbers.

Until this remote, but none the less positive action is seen and recognised as illusory, this planetary action does apparently take place, and people and things continue like a picture gallery, showing forth the apparent results of such illusory action. Truly an ignominious position for beings who have in reality absolute dominion over the whole earth.

It has been said that "an undevout astronomer is mad." The laws of mathematics are just as true in heaven as they are in this so-called material world. We have, therefore, to gain a better sense, a spiritual sense, of these laws, and their relation to heavenly realities.

[1] Many well-known men, such as the noted political leader, Parnell, have had a rooted belief in the ill luck of certain numbers and days.

[2] "The Chaldean Wisemen read in the stars the fate of empires and the fortunes of men" (*Science and Health*, p. 121, Mary Baker Eddy).

Predestination Correct.[1]—"*Whom he did predestinate, them he also called: and whom he called, ... them he also glorified*" (Rom. 8:30). "*Having predestinated us . . . being predestinated according to the purpose of him who worketh all things after the counsel of his own will*" (Eph. 1:5, 11).

5 Predestination is correct as far as anything can be said to be so in the material world, that is to say, it is a fundamental false belief. It is not long ago that the predestination of a few human beings to be saved was taught by the Church. "No man can come to me, except the Father which hath sent me draw him" (John 6:44).

10 Dr. Inge writes in *Personal Idealism and Mysticism*, "The motive power is not in ourselves. We cannot even will to please God without the help of His will. The experiences of the saints, as recorded by themselves, offer no support to a voluntaristic psychology of religion."

"Blessed is the man whom thou choosest, and causest to approach unto 15 thee, that he may dwell in thy courts" (Ps. 65:4). "God; Who hath saved us, and called us with an holy calling, not according to our works, but according to his own purpose and grace, which was given us in Christ Jesus before the world began" (II Tim. 1:8, 9). "For by grace are ye saved . . . . it is the gift of God" (Eph. 2:8). Grace is the action of God on you 20 that makes you treat, or pray in the right way. This action of God is known as the Holy Ghost or Holy Spirit.

Dr. G. Thompson, in his *System of Psychology*, says: "I have had a feeling of the uselessness of all voluntary effort, and also that the matter was working itself clear in my mind. It has many times seemed to me that 25 I was really a passive instrument in the hands of a person not myself."

"When I watch that flowing river which, out of regions I see not, pours for a season its stream into me, I see that I am not . . . a cause, but a surprised spectator of this ethereal water" (Emerson).

Dr. Franz Hartmann, in his *Life of Paracelsus*, says: "Men do not think 30 what they choose, but that which comes into their mind. If they could control the action of their minds, they would be able to control their own nature and the nature by which their forms are surrounded." This can now be and is being done, but by God.

"There's a divinity that shapes our ends,
35   Rough-hew them how we will" (*Shakespeare*).

Solomon, with his great human knowledge, showed his recognition of the fact that everything happening in the material world has its appointed time: "To every thing there is a season, and a time to every purpose under the heaven: A time to be born, and a time to die . . ." (Eccles. 3:1, 2).[2]

40 [1] Henri Bergson, in *Creative Evolution*, says that the doctrine of teleology, set out by Leibnitz, "implies that things and beings merely realise a programme previously arranged."

[2] There are many references in the Bible to matters being preordained. See Job 7, verse 1, and 14, verse 5; Daniel 8, verses 13, 14, 19; 10, verse 1; 11, verses 27, 45 35; and 12, verse 11; Habakkuk 2, verse 3; Acts 17, verses 26, 31; Galatians 4, verse 4; 2 Esdras 4, verses 33–37; Revelation 1, verse 3; Psalms 39, verse 4; I Peter 1, verse 20; Romans 8, verse 29; 11, verse 20. Augustine (A.D. 354–430), the great Christian philosopher, taught that salvation or damnation were predetermined by God, and that man could alter nothing, the whole history of the world being 50 definitely settled beforehand.

"Appointments" not to be Kept.—In this enlightened age, having found out how to pray, it is our privilege to break such time-honoured but disastrous "appointments," the result of human ignorance, binding each succeeding generation by preconceived links of iron fate. We have been slaves to the false thoughts that, as chains welded by false teachings and false theories, are bound about us by false fears. We now can gain the dominion that is our birthright.

Every material thought, unless destroyed by true prayer, comes into seeming action at its predetermined time. "The thing that hath been, it is that which shall be; . . . Is there any thing whereof it may be said, See, this is new? it hath been already of old time, which was before us" (Eccles. 1:9, 10). It is even possible to calculate out mathematically a thought that will come to a mortal at any given time. This is done by calculations based upon the vibrations acting upon the world and upon the individual at the moment of birth and at the moment when he appears to be brought into contact with certain vibrations or ethereal things, wrongly called "thoughts."[1] You can, however, destroy any unsatisfactory "thought" by true prayer, either beforehand or at the moment that it commences to act. Other "thoughts" that were equally predestined will then be manifested. Man has therefore no free-will whatsoever until he learns how to think rightly,[2] and even then it is due to the action of God, and he cannot tell the form in which the improved condition, the better belief, is going to be manifested. The difficulty of Socrates is thus solved.

The Cartesian doctrine that animals are walking automata is not only true as far as the material animals are concerned, but is equally true as regards mortals, which are only the highest material animals. Every so-called mental quality that man possesses is found in animals in differing degrees. Even with the smallest animals one sees this. Sir William Dawson says: "An amœba shows volition, appetite, and passion." Professor Schmidt states that unconscious mind is in plants, consciousness in animals, and self-consciousness in man.

Sir Oliver Lodge writes: "Many great and universally recognised thinkers: Plato, Virgil, Kant, I think, and Wordsworth, all had room for an idea more or less of the kind; . . . Whatever it is that controls our physiological mechanism, it is certainly not our consciousness; nor is it any part of our recognised and obvious personality."

Descartes looked upon animals as merely machines, and many others consider all vital phenomena below what has been generally recognised as consciousness, as being merely mechanical. Darwin called this "instinct," and said that, begun "in chance," it acts favourably to the perpetuation of species. Animals, and therefore human beings, certainly do not require their brain to actuate their limbs in apparently an orderly and conscious manner. There are many experiments that prove this. For instance, Pflüger touched the thigh of a decapitated frog with acetic acid, which it

[1] An Arab Sheik once showed me how this could be done, and proved to me, conclusively, that it was not mere thought-reading.

[2] "The motion of the arm is no more dependent upon the direction of mortal mind, than are the organic action and secretion of the viscera" (*Science and Health*, p. 160, Mary Baker Eddy).

wiped off with the foot of the same side. He then cut off the foot and re-applied the acid. The headless frog tried to wipe it off with the stump but failed. After some fruitless efforts it ceased, but seemed unquiet, and at last made use of the foot of the other leg and wiped off the acid. These results
5 have been confirmed by many.

"As a medical man I know something of human suffering, but never have I seen depicted on the face of man or woman the horror and pain of suffering which I have seen presented in the limited power of expression possessed by the lower animals " [1] (Dr. W. Woods Smythe, F.M.SOC. LOND.).
10 Although, in the case of these experiments, it is claimed that no pain could have been experienced, what cold-blooded cruelties have been carried out in the name of science! Inability to help humanity out of its troubles drives man to cause fresh trouble in a vain attempt to gain a knowledge of how to palliate them.

15   **The Hopeless Injustice of the Material World.**—How can man help doing evil until he knows how to pray? Sin is simply moral madness. A human being never made his own "consciousness," and he never made the thoughts that attack him. According to the famous declaration of the American Republic, "Man is born free," whereas human birth is obviously
20 an entrance into the most abject slavery, wherein, compelled to do wrongly by an inexorable, temporary, so-called law, we are punished for every wrong thought and its consequent wrong word and wrong deed. What shameful injustice! Surely no further proof of this material world being hell is required. From this state of imagined slavery we only start to free
25 ourselves when we learn how to think rightly.

Professor Lombroso, a specialist on criminology, came to the conclusion, from the examination of numerous criminals, that their actions were caused by degeneracy, not by volition. He consequently was an opponent of our punitive system. It has been said that fear of punishment
30 has never really made man honest. The only way is through purification of the human consciousness. This is certain and permanent.

Mr. Arthur Balfour, former Prime Minister of Great Britain, and a deep thinker, writes of man : "Whether it be proper to call him free or not, he at least lacks freedom in the sense in which freedom is necessary in order
35 to establish responsibility. It is impossible to say of him that he 'ought,' and therefore he 'can,' for at any given moment of his life his next action is by hypothesis strictly determined." [2]

This is true in the case of all labouring under a mistaken belief of God's law and government. But it is not the case when a man knows how to
40 think scientifically. This theory only becomes an apparent law when it is given its temporary seeming power through either the consent of an individual, or even an apathetic assent thereto. It then enchains man. *Universal assent to fallacious hypotheses results in the present chaotic condition of the material world.*

45   **Fatalism Untrue.**—Fatalism is not true, as there are two things that a man can do to protect himself : (1) he can destroy an inharmonious

---

[1] *Facts and Fallacies regarding the Bible.*
[2] *Mind*, October, 1893.

thought by the denial of its reality or existence as spiritual fact; (2) he can purify his human consciousness through the affirmation of the truth until no wrong thought can have any effect upon him.

Years ago, as just stated, the whole of the material thoughts or beliefs that were going to be manifested in the material world were fixed in relation   5 to each other, one may call it "in position," in this material false consciousness, and were bound to appear at the predetermined time, unless destroyed scientifically by true prayer. We have been merely seeing them piecemeal owing to our limited sense. Philosophers are right when they say that, in fact, there is no such thing as time, and equally right when they say that   10 there is no such thing as space. There is, however, true time and space in heaven.

The easiest way of looking at the material world is as a series of cinematographic pictures, fixed in position, and hiding heaven from us. When you treat, you destroy the evil in the pictures; that is, you thin the mist of   15 matter, when we see heaven a little more like what it really is. The film, representing these pictures, can be looked upon as cut into lengths and placed one behind the other; each one, as they recede from you, being of a shorter length. Then, the one next you being gradually lifted, as time goes on, you see heaven more clearly, until the last disappears, and you appear   20 to gain a knowledge of heaven as it really is.

The Prophecies of Moses.—*"We have also a more sure word of prophecy; whereunto ye do well that ye take heed, as unto a light that shineth in a dark place, until the day dawn, and the day star arise in your hearts"* (II Peter 1:19).   25

There are many wonderful prophecies in the Bible, marvellous examples of thought-reading. Amongst the most important are those of the great prophet and leader, Moses, in Deuteronomy, where is given the covenant with the children of Israel. In chapters 28–30 Moses foretells the future of the Israelites. He proclaims the laws which these children of Israel had to   30 obey, and follows with the blessings that would come on them if they should "hearken unto the voice of the Lord" (28:2), and all the curses that "shall come upon" them if they did not hearken (28:15). He gives in detail that which would happen, and in verse 15 shows the punishment that would befall them on account of the sins that they would commit, which   35 sins are clearly set out in II Kings 17, verses 7–23. This punishment is "the curse" referred to in Daniel 9, verse 11. In that wonderful thirtieth chapter, where he lays down distinctly the covenant and the principle upon which it is based, the law of good, Moses says: "It shall come to pass, when all these things are come upon thee, the blessing and the curse, . . . That   40 then the Lord thy God will turn thy captivity, and have compassion . . . And thou shalt return and obey the voice of the Lord, and do all his commandments . . . The Lord will again rejoice over thee for good" (Deut. 30:1, 3, 8, 9). This good is now being enjoyed by the descendants of the children of Israel. Moses pointed out that "This commandment   45 . . . is not hidden from thee, neither is it far off. It is not in heaven, . . . Neither is it beyond the sea, . . . But the word is very nigh unto thee, in thy mouth, and in thy heart" (30:11–14), showing that what should happen would be the result of right thinking, with its resultant right speaking and right acting.

This has already been materially fulfilled in the experiences of the Israelites. It has still to be fulfilled intellectually, and the curse threatens
5 to "come upon" them who do "not hearken" (Deut. 28:15) to the truth now set forth.

The Covenant.—The above prophecies deal with the history of the Israelites from that time up to the present, when the final blessings are being fulfilled; but they have been partially fulfilled, in period after period,
10 by the children of Israel leaving the worship of the one God, good, and being forced back with the necessarily resulting trouble and disappointments, until finally they see the truth, and the truth sets them free. "The secret of the Lord is with them that fear him; and he will shew them his covenant" (Ps. 25:14). This covenant is referred to over and over again
15 throughout the Bible, and cannot be broken, because it is the everlasting covenant between God, the Principle of good, a living, all-inclusive, ever-active Principle, and man, His manifestation. This covenant involves the invariable manifestation of good in response to right thinking. *If you think of perfection, good must ensue.* If you think evil, this evil will be manifested
20 more or less. "My covenant will I not break, nor alter the thing that is gone out of my lips" (Ps. 89:34). The spiritual meaning of these prophecies has an individual significance to those who are striving to order their lives by the inner teachings of the Bible, and so catch its higher meanings.

The importance of this covenant is shown by the fact that the word
25 translated "testament" should be translated "covenant." The Old Testament is "the book of the covenant," from which Moses "read in the audience of the people" (Ex. 24:7). The "ark of his testament," to be "seen in his temple" in the latter days (Rev. 11:19), should be translated "ark of his covenant."

30 "And now I stand and am judged for the hope of the promise made of God unto our fathers: Unto which promise our twelve tribes, instantly serving God day and night, hope to come" (Acts 26:6, 7).

The Book of Revelation.—*The Revelation of Jesus Christ, which God gave unto him, to shew unto his servants things which must shortly come
35 to pass*" (Rev. 1:1).

Even the sceptical John Stuart Mill conceded that revelation is ordinary, normal, and to be expected if the existence of God could be proved. The existence of God can now be demonstrated.

The best instance of consecutive prophecy, or thought-reading, is pro-
40 bably the Book of Revelation.

Jesus speaking of the Comforter, said: "He will shew you things to come" (John 16:13), and in II Peter 1, verse 19, we are told that there is "A more sure word of prophecy; whereunto ye do well that ye take heed, as unto a light that shineth in a dark place." It is foretold that at the end of
45 the world we shall be able to prophesy, "Your sons and your daughters shall prophesy" (Joel 2:28). Jesus also pointed out that responsibilities were incurred by the disciples knowing things not yet fulfilled, and we have to act so as to make the fullest use of the knowledge so gained, for the benefit

of the world. In view of the undeviating law of justice, it is useless, when
the knowledge is gained, to shirk responsibility, unless you are prepared to
take the punishment that such a throwing over of your fellow-men
entails.

The Apocalypse is believed by many to have been written about A.D. 97   5
by John, when about ninety-six years of age. In addition to its deeper
significance, it is a political and religious history of the countries then
forming the Roman Empire—the determining factor in the world's history
—from the time in which it was written, up to what is wrongly called "the
end of the world." It is given in detail, but in symbolic language, and many   10
men, even such as Luther, thinking chiefly on a material level, objected to
its use.

Although, as pointed out (Rev. 1:3), the time of which he was prophesying was just about to begin, "keep those things which are written therein:
for the time is at hand," this book has been difficult to understand partly   15
because the same period of time is dealt with from differing points of view
in successive portions of the book. In the same way historians deal in
successive chapters with the same period from the point of view of politics,
art, science, etc.

Value of the Book of Revelation.—"*Quench not the Spirit. Despise*   20
not prophesyings. Prove all things" (I Thess. 5:19–21).

The object of the elucidation of its historical meaning is that it proves
incontestably the use of the Bible as a help in foretelling what is about to
take place, and, by inference, the absolute necessity of working scientifically as the only method of escape from the horrors that are coming upon   25
material false workers amongst mankind in the latter days, which, as all
prophecy shows, are now right upon us. The Apocalyptic fore-vision, by
inference, proves the value of the Bible, as giving us the scientific understanding of God that alone points us to the way of escape that has been
provided, as shown throughout this lecture. This will be readily acknow-   30
ledged by all students who can demonstrably prove the scientific basis upon
which this revelation rests. Forewarned is forearmed; and when the method
and result of the enemy's attack are known, as they are when the Book
of Revelation is understood, all danger is over for the individuals who
through open-minded search after truth become seers. The whole of their   35
energies can then be devoted to watching and working to save their fellow-
men by destroying the wrong thoughts before they come into seeming
action. This is our work.

The Book of Revelation in one important significance describes the
history of the persecution of mankind by thoughts of pride, tyranny,   40
Pharisaism, and criticism; the attempted control of the one over the many,
and the ultimate triumph of good. These thoughts are now attacking mankind, but in a more subtle, and therefore more dangerous form than in any
former period.

In the past, the history of religion has openly shown the deplorable   45
results of this ignorant though, in most cases, well-intentioned control of
the strong over the weak, both in the case of individuals and communities.
We have now learned that no individual has any power over another. The

apparent control is due to the seeming action of "thoughts," which equally
attack the strong and the weak, the controller and the controlled, the seeming hypnotist and the seeming victim, harming all until they know how
to protect themselves, individually and collectively, and so find that they
5 are in reality contrôlled only by God, good.

FELLOW-SOLDIERS

We have to recognise these unfortunate individuals as people fighting
on our side in the same battle and against the common foe, and our duty
and privilege is to protect them. We have to "love all Christian churches
10 for the gospel's sake; and be exceedingly glad that the churches are united
in purpose, if not in method. . . ." (*Christian Science versus Pantheism*
p. 13. Mary Baker Eddy). There is far worse trouble coming upon the
world through those who to-day personalise the thoughts of criticism,
jealousy, cruelty, and Pharisaism, imagining that they are exponents of
15 the highest truth, than ever came from those whom these thoughts
attacked in the past. We must not allow ourselves to think of them,
not even to think of their spiritual reality. The work must be entirely
impersonal, as far as others are concerned. We must clear our human consciousness from the guilt of believing in the lie about our fellow-men and
20 so adding to their burdens. Thus we help them. Until a thought of a person
calls forth a feeling of love towards him the work is not properly done.

It is our own human consciousness that requires purification, so that,
when the lying thoughts come to tempt us to believe in the existence of
evil, our realisation of Truth is so clear that the particular evil ceases to
25 exist, not only in our own "consciousness," but in that of every other
human being, namely, in the universal, basic, false mentality, called the
subconscious mind. "For we wrestle not against flesh and blood, but
against principalities, against powers, against the rulers of the darkness of
this world, against spiritual wickedness in high places" (Eph. 6:12).

30 **Impersonality of Evil.**—As we grow in the understanding of God,
and man and his relations with his fellow-man, so obvious does the
impersonality of evil, even in its most dangerous forms, become, that we
can measure our growth in the understanding of God by our ability to
really love those who may seem to be the most violent in attacking us. Our
35 safety lies in the love that wells from our hearts, resulting from our realisation of God as Love. Then Love surrounding us, forms an absolutely
impervious citadel, a sure refuge into which not one poisoned arrow can
find its way.

To those not really understanding the position, it is well to repeat that,
40 as a rule, those through whom these thoughts attack, are trying their
hardest to be of use in the world. They are acting under a mistaken sense
of duty, not knowing how to protect themselves, and it is they who are
harmed by such wrong thinking, not those whom they attack. There should
be no contests with individuals, the contest is with ethereal thoughts,
45 grouped together under the name of false systems, human, and illusive.

We have therefore to be as loving as we possibly can towards those who attack us, and to take every opportunity of helping them indirectly by clearing our human mechanism or "consciousness" of the wrong thoughts, the wrong concept of the true thoughts. It is that which requires altera-tion. 5

One way in which the impersonality of evil is clearly shown all through the Bible will be found in the meanings of the names attached to its individuals, cities, and places.[1] These all express differing conditions reached in the stages of the human consciousness in its progress towards the mortal's final sense of God. These conditions are represented in every 10 succeeding generation, and serve as valuable waymarks, in truly intelligent efforts to help our fellow-men.

In considering the best battle-ground in which to destroy error in the final fight now started, we have to follow in the steps of our great leader, Jesus the Christ. The essential difference between his method of warfare 15 with evil and those of other advanced spiritual workers, such as Gautama Buddha and Lao-Tze, was that, after he had once attained the necessary wisdom, he went actively into the thick of the fight, only going away for as short periods as possible, to gain the necessary clearness of thought and peace of mind, solely obtainable by dwelling in deep, conscious com- 20 munion with God.

Jesus never relied upon material steps, never threatened force, never gave instructions to his followers to use material means, but depended solely on his realisation of God and the force of his superhuman example. Let us follow this example with all humility and with such holiness as is 25 vouchsafed to us, relying upon the purification of our own so-called "mind" and the casting out of evil ideas about our fellow-men, to raise the standard of Christ so that the glorious protection of Mind is utilised by our fellow-men. Jesus easily, in fact, with far greater ease, could, like those teachers above mentioned, have contented himself with announcing great 30 truths, supporting them with irresistible logic, until he rose above material consciousness; but a more scientific and more unselfish love for his fellow-men led him to continue in the fight to the extreme limits of his human powers, leaving instruction to his disciples in all ages in the following: "I pray not that thou shouldest take them out of the world, but that thou 35 shouldest keep them from the evil. . . . As thou hast sent me into the world, even so have I also sent them into the world" (John 17:15, 18).

We likewise should not choose the position where we can most peace-fully do our mental work, whilst the so-called world seethes and boils with inhuman, so-called mental strife, which throws the scum to the surface, 40 enabling it to be cast away. We should be actively at work, safeguarded, in our allotted posts, above all material strife, helping writhing humanity, holding the citadel of God, allowing no thought of evil into our "con-sciousness," lifting all mortals who come in touch with us, radiating out divine love. With our knowledge of God, we should offer to others the 45 shield of faith in God, good; and when, through unfortunate past bringing-

[1] "The substitution of the spiritual for the material definition of a Scriptural word often elucidates the meaning of the inspired writer" (*Science and Health*, p. 579, Mary Baker Eddy).

7

up, it is not taken, we should hold it over those attacking us until they
themselves have escaped the toils of venomous evil, and are able to grasp
their weapons of offence and defence, man's God-given power over evil,
and come with radiating joy into the noble band of workers, sons of God,
5 the saviours of mankind.

Let every man who claims the title "man," claim also his right of
permanent and perfect existence, and fall into the ranks in this final
fight, the ranks of right thinking, and its consequent right doing. This
will ensure the rapid attainment of that permanent universal peace which
10 always must follow right thinking.

Our work is clear. It is to be prepared and to obtain such a knowledge
of true prayer that we can do our share in reducing the troubles. From the
summit of ceaseless true prayer, uplifting conscious communion with God,
so often referred to in Scripture as the mountain of the Lord, the heavenly
15 pictures, hitherto revealed only in glimpses, may be seen expanding into
the limitless horizon of infinite Spirit, the teeming universe of unfathom-
able Mind. Here, infinite as God, his creator, stands God's perfect man,
the male and female of God's creating, perpetual witness to the continual
unfoldment of inexhaustible good.

20 In the undimmed sunlight of Truth, all the grandeur and minutiæ of
spiritual creation stand revealed as they ever have been, are, and ever will
be in the sight of God, perfect, uncontaminable, eternal.

This promised land is here for all, now and always. The crossing of the
Jordan, the river of judgment—in other words, the attainment of the point
25 of discrimination between the true and the false—is soon to become
apparent and to be apprehended by one and all. Then, indeed, will consciousness rise to the Life which is eternal and the mortal concept will fade
away in the dazzling realisation of the stupendous nature of our God, in
Whom is found—

"All we have willed or hoped or dreamed of good.
30   Not its semblance but itself" (*Robert Browning*).

SECTION FIVE

SO-CALLED MENTAL EFFECT

"Chisel in hand stood a sculptor-boy,
    With his marble block before him;
And his face lit up with a smile of joy   5
    As an angel-dream passed o'er him.

"He carved the dream on that shapeless stone
    With many a sharp incision,
With Heaven's own light the sculptor shone—
    He had caught the angel-vision.   10

"Sculptors of life are we as we stand,
    With our lives uncarved before us,
Waiting the hour when at God's command,
    Our life-dream passes o'er us.

"If we carve it then on the yielding stone   15
    With many a sharp incision,
Its heavenly beauty shall be our own—
    Our lives that angel-vision" (*G. Washington Doane*).

Medical Needs.—"*What we need and want in medicine, is something corresponding to those splendid flashes of imagination which yielded the* 20 *heliocentric theory of the planetary system, the theory of gravitation, the undulatory theory of light, the theory of evolution, and the germ theory of infectious disease—some fundamental and far-reaching generalisations in pathology and physiology which would vivify and vitalise some part at least of the mass of dead material facts which have been accumulated*" (Sir J. 25 Crichton-Browne, M.D., LL.D., F.R.S.).

The Effect of So-called Thought.—All great thinkers have recognised to some extent the effect of "thoughts," while few have discovered that these are ethereal vibrations, and that we do not create them, but that they come to us, the condition of the "no-mind" determining those to 30 which we respond. None of these early searchers after truth reached the height from which was made in our own day the discovery that there is no real mind or consciousness, except that which is a reflection of the one Mind, which is God, good, All-in-all.

A good instance of the effect of thought, well-verified, is given in a 35 careful, detailed report on the subject made by Professor Langley. In the Philippine Islands he saw the priests walk barefoot over a bed of stones, heated red-hot by fire. When an acolyte was able to pass over the stones he qualified and became a priest. Those who have seen the novices attempt the test say that it is quite easy to tell from the look on their faces whether 40 there was sufficient belief to pass unharmed.

In the Fiji Islands the same rite is carried out, and it is stated that one of the Government meteorologists held a thermometer 6 ft. above the heated stones, when it registered 282 degrees. It took about half a minute to walk across the stones, and no signs of burning or blistering were seen on the men's feet. Professor Bickerton tells me that in New Zealand he exposed a "show" of this kind, where it was done by trickery.

Not only are we affected by our so-called thoughts, but everyone upon whom our thoughts rest is likewise affected, either for good or for evil. Carlyle in *The French Revolution* wrote: "Man is what we call a miraculous creature, with miraculous power over man." We must learn how to think so that this power is the power of good, and not human will-power which is devilish.

Listening to the still small voice, we hear the voice of God. The power is not the blind force we see in the material universe. Elijah recognised that God, good, was not in the great and strong wind that rent the mountains, and broke in pieces the rocks in front of him, nor was "good" in the earthquake or the fire (I Kings 19:11, 12). Real power is the expression or manifestation of God, good, "the Son of God," that is, the true nature of each of us. Paul speaks of the Christ as the wisdom and power of God. Understanding the power of Mind over matter, the spiritual power divinely directed gives us absolute dominion over all matter and every possible form of evil. This dominion can be utilised by each one of us, here and now. "Now is come salvation, and strength, and the kingdom of our God, and the power of his Christ" (Rev. 12:10).

Until forty years ago, no one of modern times ever showed us how to think rightly in a scientific manner, and how with unfailing certainty to stop ourselves thinking wrong and harmful "thoughts," nor even made clear that ideals of a mortal become manifested, whether heavenly or devilish, if the intensification be sufficient to manifest them. "How few think justly of the thinking few. How many never think who think they do" (Schopenhauer).

The following will be of value to those who have not recognised that the essence of right doing is right thinking.

"As he thinketh in his heart, so is he" (Prov. 23:7).

"Behold, I will bring evil upon this people, even the fruit of their thoughts" (Jer. 6:19).

"What a man thinks, that he is; this is the old secret" (The Maitrâzana Upanishad).

"There is nothing either good or bad, but thinking makes it so" (Shakespeare).

"Think well! Do well will follow thought" (Tennyson).

"It is the thought of man; the true thaumaturgic virtue, by which man works all things whatsoever. All that he does, and brings to pass is the vesture of a thought" (Carlyle).

"All that we are is the result of what we have thought; it is founded on our thoughts, it is made up of our thoughts" (Dammapala).

"What a man thinks, that he becomes" (Hindu Upanishad).

"What a man thinks, that he is" (King Solomon).

"The happiness of your life depends upon the quality of your thoughts; therefore guard accordingly" (Marcus Aurelius).

"My mind is myself. To take care of myself is to take care of my mind" (Plato).

"A thought that has taken root is like a living plant, and plant-like will grow" (Clifford Harrison).

"Ainsi toute notre dignité consiste dans la pensée. . . . Travaillons donc à bien penser; voilà le principe de la morale" [1] (Pascal).

"La pensée humaine, comme Dieu, fait le monde à son image" [2] (Lamartine).

"On earth there is nothing great but man. In man there is nothing great but mind" (Sir William Hamilton).

"Life . . . is the product and presence of mind" (Professor Bascorn).

"Do not think that what your thoughts dwell upon is of no matter. Your thoughts are making you" (Bishop Steere).

"The power of the will and the intention of the soul is the main point in magic as in medicine. A man who wishes everybody well will produce good effects. One who grudges everybody all that is good, and who hates himself, may experience on his own person the effects of his poisonous thoughts" (Paracelsus).

> "'Thy bonds and thy beliefs are one in kind,
> And of thy fears thine irons wrought,
> Having weights upon thee, fashioned
> Out of thine own thought" (*Swinburne*).

"Disease of the body is so much influenced by the mind that in each case we have to understand the patient quite as much as the malady" (*British Medical Journal*, January 18, 1896).

"Faith and hope . . . are but two of the many mental medicines which a judicious physician may use" (*Lancet*, January, 1883).

"Faith is as powerful an influence for good or evil now, as it has ever been" (*Lancet*, February 28, 1888).

"It [the secular imagination] is one of the most effectual of those psychical agencies by which we may modify the conditions of health and disease" (Sir J. Crichton-Browne, M.D., LL.D., F.R.S.).

"It is impossible for us to deal knowingly and wisely with various disorders of the body without distinctly recognising the agency of states and conditions of minds, often in producing and always in modifying them" (Sir Andrew Clark).

"The mental cortex has to be reckoned with, more or less, as a factor for good or evil in all diseases of every organ, in all operations, and in all injuries" (Dr. Clouston, Inaugural Address to the Royal Medical Society, 1896).

"Most people recognise that there are rare and striking effects of mind on body—few fully recognise its every-day effects. I trust I have established that the mental factor is present in some way or other in all diseases" (A. T. Schofield, M.D., F.R.C.S.).

"Means acting directly on the mind . . . are fully as powerful and effective in disease of a purely bodily character as in mental disease" (Sir John Forbes).

[1] "Thus all our worth exists in thought. . . . Endeavour, therefore, to think well; herein lies the principle of goodness".

[2] "Human thought, like God, makes the world in its image".

"It never rains but it pours," and "Troubles never come singly," are amongst the many evidences of the harmful effects of wrong thoughts.

Confidence.—"*Strive thou to win, but win with the help of God*" (Sophocles).

5   We have all experienced the effect of confidence and want of confidence, but only a few have recognised that this is only a question of right thinking or wrong so-called "thinking." Still fewer have consciously tried to correct such wrong working, and hardly any systematically do this in a scientific way. T. S. Baldwin, the well-known American, writes: "After 10 years of practice as gymnast, I was never able to turn a double somersault without definitely willing the act and drawing in my mind a clear picture of the revolutions of my body in the air before rising from the leaping-board. Every difficult gymnastic feat requires mental deliberation in advance, for the mind cannot suddenly and radically divert its course of action on a 15 plane where it has, because of the force of gravity, not learned to feel at home. This mental handicap has, until very recently, blocked the path to the discovery of the law of flight." Now that we understand the laws of Mind such miscalled mental deliberation is not required. One right thought at any given instant is sufficient, if our understanding of God is 20 adequate.

I once accepted an offer of one hundred pounds from one of the leading papers to write eight articles on "How to Learn Golf," and in these articles pointed out the great gain through what may be wrongly called "mentally" playing the shot before actually moving the limbs.[1] Attention was also 25 drawn to many other points, such as the undesirability of straining the eyes by reading a newspaper before playing any important match. Just as these articles were finished, I found that the whole effect was "non-mental," and the articles were based upon an entirely wrong foundation. Even where I had found out the so-called "mental" effect, I had failed to grasp the 30 difference between the true mental action of the Mind that is divine Principle, and the counterfeit human mechanism. I therefore rightly estimated my articles as valueless, not being based upon true Science, and they were never published.

The following year, having learnt the scientific method of thinking, I was 35 never beaten at golf, although not playing very often. On the last day of the year, to prevent defeat I had to do the last three holes of a well-known London course in 2, 2, and 3; bogey being 3, 4, and 5. The subsequent remark of the winner of that year's Open Golf Championship to me was: "I should think it is an absolute record!"

40   On another occasion, after judging in the kite and parachute competitions at the Alexandra Palace, I entered for a gold medal which was being competed for by a number of experienced shots, volunteers, regulars, and others, although I had not touched a gun for ten years, and was inexperienced in the use of a rifle, having never even fired a rifle in a competi- 45 tion. The shooting was arranged to be of a most difficult character, and up to my last shot I had obtained nothing better than an "inner," as I was

---

[1] Randegger in his primer on singing, directs the pupil to "mentally aim at the pitch of the sound before singing it."

combining material means (taking aim) with the treatment. At my last shot, knowing that I had done all I could when combining matter and Mind, and that I had to get a bull to win, I resolved to rely solely on Principle. Having to stand erect and fire from the shoulder, I looked right away from the target, and directly I had realised God to the very highest of 5 my ability, pulled the trigger, with the result that I obtained a bull, and won. A friend of mine, who similarly knew nothing of rifle shooting, but who had learnt the power of the one Mind, was bracketed second, having failed to rely solely on his realisation of Truth, but having aimed as well as having treated at the same time, so combining material means. Another 10 friend, a well-known Naval man, when firing in his Admiralty test, obtained a bull's-eye every shot. This was believed to be a record. In his case, even at the 1,000 yards distance, directly he treated, the target seemed to him only to be a few feet away, and he merely had to fire at a bull's-eye apparently the size of a hat. 15

The above two examples are given, out of a personal experience of some hundreds of the kind, as showing that the unfailing reliance on God at all times will enable you to do so-called miracles. The constant working in this way for small things not only enables the greater works to be done, but has been of value to many who have been convinced by the uniformity of the 20 results obtained. As we advance in our knowledge of God and divine law, we also rise naturally to higher planes of action. "Think often on God, by day, by night, in your business and even in your diversions. He is always near you and with you; leave Him not alone" (Brother Lawrence, Tenth Letter). 25

Psychotherapy.—Ever since we have had historical records, so-called healing with the human "no-mind" has been practised under different forms, sometimes intentionally, often unconsciously, and always more or less ignorantly, and with more or less harm. In olden times the magicians were the medical men. Sophocles said: "For it is not the way of a wise 30 surgeon to waste tears and enchantments on a disease that needs the knife."[1]

"It would appear that in all ages hypnotism has been known, though not under that name, as a means of curing diseases. It is also known that amongst the Greeks and Romans, and in many Oriental nations in olden times, priests performed cures by throwing people into deep sleep; and 35 that in England in the seventeenth century several individuals claimed to have power of healing the sick by stroking with their hands. Such influences were pretty generally held to be supernatural and connected with religion"[2] (Sir Henry Morris, Bart, M.D., F.R.C.S.).

In the middle of the seventeenth century a man called Kelmont said 40 that there was a kind of magnetic attraction and repulsion connected with an ethereal element which penetrated all bodies, and kept them in motion Through it he stated that men, by means of their imagination, could work on each other. Their will could also be asserted on drugs, which obtained through it a special therapeutic power.[3] 45

[1] *Ajax*, line 582.
[2] "Suggestion in the Treatment of Disease" (*British Medical Journal*, June 18, 1910).
[3] *Psychotherapy* (Hugo Münsterberg).

Maxwell, a Scottish physician (1581–1640) said that disease was a reduction of this ether in a man, and as it was possible to influence this ether in another man, cures at a distance could be thus produced. Mesmer, who thought it was due to a magnetic fluid, and Braid, who thought that
5 the action was mental, were amongst the first in modern times to bring into prominence direct conscious healing with the human "mind," and they, fortunately for mankind, were discredited by regular physicians, who have hitherto objected to any encroachments upon what they considered their domain.
10 In 1851 Dr. Gregory (Professor of Chemistry in Edinburgh) and Dr. Hughes Bennett described the phenomena as due to suggestion.
A third revival took place in 1866 with the publication of Liébeault's book, when Bernheim, Dumont, and Beaunis joined the movement, thinking mistakenly that it was of use. Liébeault, who was a man of high
15 character, advocated suggestion, as Sir Francis Cruise, the well-known Dublin doctor, has stated, "when the personality of the subject is partially or almost completely extinguished" by hypnosis. This, Sir Francis who is an authority on hypnotism states, "is the essence of modern hypnotism" [1] and is only another form of making a person do what you want him to do,
20 and which you may or may not think is good for him. As a matter of fact, suggestion is wrong with or without hypnosis.
Later Charcot, Richet, and Janet followed. In other countries Forel, Moll and Vogt, Wetterstrand, Dubois, Bechterew, Beard, Hammond, Osgood, Prince, Peterson, Putnam, Sidis, Kraepelin, Zeihen, Sommer,
25 van Reuterghem, von Schrenk-Notzing, Ladame, van Eeden, Tokarsky, Hamilton, Creed, Brauch, and in England, Bramwell, Carpenter, Cruise, Hack Tuke, Lloyd Tuckey, Wingfield, and Woods, gave serious attention to the matter.
Through Charcot's great name and fame, the Nancy doctors employed
30 hypnotism in every class of disease, but Charcot abandoned it because, as he said, it did more harm than good, and added to the disorder of already disordered systems.[2]
More recently Freud, Breuer, and Münsterberg have developed the ordinary method of hypnotising by giving human suggestions with the
35 object of removing so-called "mental" causes, invisible because ethereal, and in England we have a few well-known men, some most unselfish and pure minded, working more or less in the same mistaken way.
"Though hypnotism has from time to time been revived, and there have been periods when it excited great interest on account of its constant
40 effects, it has invariably fallen back again into disfavour, owing to the uncertainty of its action, and its failure on a large scale as a therapeutical agent. Moreover, it has been found too dangerous for general use in medical practice" (Sir Henry Morris, *The Law of Mental Medicine*).
From the earliest times, and with all nationalities, we have evidences of

45 [1] Introductory chapter to *Treatment by Hypnotism and Suggestion*.
  [2] A doctor writing in *The Times* of January 8, 1914, on hypnotism, says: "Charcot gave up the practice in his wards, as he told me himself, because he found that it was liable to increase the disorder of disordered nerves and do more harm than good."

different forms of non-mental, ethereal working which, with the object of retaining individual power, have been kept more or less secret. Amongst the savages in Africa we have special castes; in Australia we have the Koonkie; in Siberia we have the Shamon, who are supposed to mediate between man and the gods; in the Antilles the Bohuti heal diseases, which 5 are regarded as punishment from the gods; the Indians have their Piachas, who live in lonely spots for years whilst they learn from the priests the necessary ceremonies; in China the priests of one school of medicine frighten away diseases by mystical writings pasted upon the walls of the sick room, while believers in another school drink water into which the 10 freshly written sacred writing has been dipped; the Mohammedan swallows pieces of paper containing texts from the Koran; in Japan monks remove diseases which are supposed to have magical origin or to be induced by the devil; in India they have many grades; in Assyria and Babylonia medicine was exclusively in the hands of priests; among the old Egyptians Isis was 15 supposed to reveal to worshippers in her temples the right remedies, through the medium of dreams; in the same way the Greeks attached medical influence to temples,[1] sacred springs, rivers, and tombs. It is no wonder many people have thought that the miracles of Jesus the Christ were in some way merely a modification of these many different forms of 20 so-called healing, failing to see the essential difference, namely, that Jesus worked by the realisation of Truth, God, the others by different forms of hypnotism, namely, thinking of material people and things.

St. Patrick, the Irish Apostle, healed the blind by laying his hands upon them. St. Bernard is said to have healed eleven blind and eighteen lame 25 people in one day at Constance. At Cologne, it is stated, he healed twelve lame, three dumb, and ten deaf people.

Bede, the great historian, tells us of cures performed by St. John of Beverley during the eighth century. Many biographers testified as to the healing done by Bernard of Clairvaux at the beginning of the eleventh 30 century. J. C. Morison [2] says that thirty-six miraculous cures in one day seemed to have been the maximum.

Martin Luther, the leader of the Reformation, and St. Francis Xavier, the leader of the Counter-Reformation, in the sixteenth century, were both said to be healers; Luther, whose cure of Melanchthon by prayer is well 35 known, wrote: "Therefore there must exist a higher medicine, namely, the religious belief and the prayer through which the spiritual medicine can be found in the word of God."

In the seventeenth century the Irishman, Valentine Greatrakes, felt himself to be the bearer of a divine mission and healed numerous sick. At 40 first he cured king's evil by laying on of hands; later, fever, wounds, tumours, gout, and finally all diseases.

Cagliostro, in the eighteenth century (about 1780), owed part of his fame to his healing powers. Farmer-General Laborde states that Cagliostro attended over 15,000 sick people during the three years he was at Strasburg, 45

---

[1] "Strange healings do take place under religious influences; and this is true. And at no time in history were such miraculous cures more frequent and wonderful than in the temples of Æsculapius or of Serapis" (Sir Clifford Allbutt).

[2] *Life and Times of St. Bernard.*

7*

and that only three of them died. Many circumstantial details have been testified to, such as the instantaneous healing of the Prince de Soubise, after having been given up by the doctors. It is stated that crowds used to besiege his house, leaving numerous sticks and crutches as "marks of
5 gratitude." His demoniacal power is referred to on page 257, line 12. About the same date John Wesley healed the sick by prayer.[1] George Fox the Greater, also healed.[2]

In the nineteenth century Prince Hohenlohe-Waldenburg-Schillens- fürst, Canon of Grosswardein, was a healer of world renown. In one year,
10 1848-9, over 18,000 came from all over the world for treatment. The ex- king of Bavaria wrote to Count von Sinsheim, testifying to his cure by the Prince, and Professor Onymus, of Wurzburg, reported a number of cases that he had seen cured. Richter, an innkeeper, at Royen, in Silesia, apparently cured, in the years 1817-18, many thousands of sick persons in
15 the open fields, by touching them with his hands. Thousands also flocked to Pastor Grassner in Germany for healing, as thousands now make a pilgrimage to Lourdes, and have gone to Treves, with its Holy Coat, St. Winifred's Well in Flintshire, the tombs of St. Louis, Francis of Assisi, Catherine of Siena, and to any place that sufficiently appealed to the
20 imagination.

As I write, particulars are received of a petition to the Belgian Govern- ment, signed by nearly 200,000 persons, for permission to erect churches for a creed called "Antoinisme." Antoin is a coalminer, who heals, it is claimed, by "mere spiritual means." He "has become so immensely
25 popular that he is now considered as being gifted with divine power." Results of this sort are continually being obtained by different people. They are a nine days' wonder, and sooner or later the so-called power is lost, leaving the individual intellectually and physically deteriorated, and in some cases a mere wreck of humanity.[3]

30 Father Ignatius not only cured,[4] but gave diseases to people, and claimed to have raised from the dead. I know the man who was sent by one of the leading daily papers to investigate into one instance of the latter. He gave me details of his investigation, and was satisfied that it was a correct claim.

35 The stories related of the healing done by Francis Schlatter, Dupuis, and others in modern times have hardly been even referred to by the Euro- pean daily newspapers, the results being so wonderful as to make editors fear to state them lest they should be thought to be drawing too much upon the credulity of their readers. I once offered to go abroad for one of the
40 leading daily newspapers, for which I was doing some investigation work at the time, and to supply for publication details of the healing that was then being done publicly. Several hundred people a day were being healed. In thanking me for the offer, the editor said that the general public were so ignorant that even if it were inserted as a definite fact many would think
45 that it was only "another newspaper lie."

[1] John Wesley's *Journal.*
[2] *Annals of the Early Friends*, by Jane Budge.
[3] Antoin died a few years after this was written.
[4] *Life of Father Ignatius*, by Baroness de Bertouch.

T. J. Hudson, PH.D., LL.D., gives many cases of mental healing in *The Law of Mental Medicine*.

The King's Touch.—Pyrrhus, King of Epirus, had the apparent power of assuaging colic and affections of the spleen by laying the patients on their backs and passing his great toe over them. The Emperor Vespasian cured nervous affections, lameness, and blindness, solely by the laying on of hands (Suelin, Vita, Vespas.). According to Coeilus Spartianus, Hadrian cured those afflicted with dropsy by touching them with the points of his fingers, and himself recovered from a violent fever by similar treatment. King Olaf healed Egill on the spot by merely laying his hands upon him and singing proverbs (*Edda*, p. 216). The formula used on such occasions was, "Le roi te touche, allez et guerrissez,"[1] so that the word was connected with the act of touching—physical contact. In England a disease cured by the kings was called the king's evil; and in France the power of so-called healing was retained by the kings until within the memory of men now living. Amongst the German princes this curative power was ascribed to the Counts of Hapsburg, and they were also said to cure stammering by a kiss.

Lecky, the historian, says that the efficacy of the king's touch "was asserted by the Privy Council, by bishops of two religions, by the general voice of the clergy in the palmiest days of the English Church, by the University of Oxford, and by the enthusiastic assent of the people."

Many miracles were attributed to Edward the Confessor, and, since his time, the healing by king's touch was a recognised method of cure. Dr. Samuel Johnson as an infant was one of the last to be touched, when, in 1712, he and about 200 others were touched by Queen Anne. Dr. Tooker, the Queen's Chaplain, and William Cowles, the Queen's Surgeon, both testified to the healing done by Queen Elizabeth, who, however, stated, "God alone can cure your diseases." There are many records of cures by King Charles I and King Charles II. The latter in one month touched 260 at Breda. In 1669 he touched 2,983 people, and in 1682, 8,500. According to Macaulay's *History of England*, the total number touched in his reign was 92,107. In 1684 the throng was so great that six or seven of the sick were trampled to death.

CONTEMPORARY VIEWS ON MENTAL EFFECT

Thoughts in action admittedly appear to control the muscles, as in the playing of music, the forming of a letter with a pen, the strokes of an artist's brush upon his canvas. If the human consciousness has apparently complete control over muscular action, why does it not equally control all other functions of the body? It has this apparent control, and this is now being taught by scientific men.

Lord Kelvin in *The Fortnightly Review*, March, 1892, says: "The influence of animal or vegetable life on matter is infinitely beyond the range of any scientific inquiry hitherto entered on."

Martin Crane, in *Right and Wrong Thinking*, deals very fully with "mental" effect.

---

[1] "The king touches you, go and recover."

President Hall, of Clark University, is reported as saying, before a
session of the American Medico-Psychological Society in Boston, that
"the relations between the body and the emotions are of the closest" and
"there can be no change of thought without a change of muscle." He also
5 suggests the possibility that the right course in thinking might develop the
muscle as well as the right course of exercise.

Professor C. A. Strong, of Columbia University, says, "Recent psychologists tell us that all mental states are followed by bodily changes. . . .
This is true of desires, of emotions, of pleasures and pains, and even of
10 such seemingly non-impulsive states as sensations and ideas. It is true, in a
word, of the entire range of our mental life. The bodily effects in question
are, of course, not limited to the voluntary muscles, but consist in large
part, of less patent changes in the action of heart, lungs, stomach, and other
viscera."

15   Professor James, of Harvard University, has said: "All mental states
 . . . . lead to inconspicuous changes in breathing, circulation, general
muscular tension, and glandular or other visceral activity, even if they do
not lead to conspicuous movements of the muscles of voluntary life . . .
all states of mind, even mere thoughts and feelings, are motor in their
20 consequences."

Professor Ladd, of Yale, says: "Even the most purely vegetative of the
bodily processes are dependent for their character upon antecedent states
of mind."

Professor Münsterberg, of Harvard, said, in his Lowell Institute lectures,
25 that the slightest thought influences the whole body, and, further: "There
is never a particle of an idea in our mind which is not the starting-point for
external discharge," or in less technical language, the starting-point for
some bodily action. In illustration, he said that thinking increases the
activity of the minute perspiration glands of the skin. This has been
30 measured so accurately by the proper apparatus that it is possible to determine the activity or intensity of a person's thinking by its effects upon these
glands.

Dr. W. G. Anderson, of the Yale Gymnasium, has made similar
observations upon the athletes of that University, with like results. A man
35 perfectly balanced on a table would find his feet sinking if he went through
mental leg gymnastics, thinking about moving his legs without making the
movements. This shows that it is thought which sends the blood to the legs
even when they are entirely at rest. Dr. Anderson says, "Pleasurable
thoughts send blood to the brain; disagreeable ones drive it away."

40   How important the above statements are in the light of our present
demonstrable knowledge that all the phenomena of human life are ethereal
illusions, the body equally with the so-called "mind."

Professor Barrett, Professor of Physics of the Royal College of Science,
Dublin, says: "A red scar or a painful burn, or even a figure of a definite
45 shape such as a cross, or an initial, can be caused to appear on the body of
the entranced subject, solely through suggesting the idea." [1] A friend of
mine once saw, to her astonishment, what appeared to be a great red scar

---

[1] *The Humanitarian*, 1895.

right across the face of her brother, who was asleep. On waking up he told her that he had dreamt that he had been fighting, and had had a sabre-cut, exactly where the scar appeared. The appearance passed off in a short time.

St. Francis of Assisi furnishes an early historical case of this kind. His contemplation of the wounds of Jesus was of such an intense character and so long continued, that his own body finally presented appearances similar to the vivid picture which he had so long entertained. Not only were there similar wounds in his hands, in his feet, and side, but the appearance of nails in the wounds was so realistic that after his death an attempt was made to draw them out, supposing them to be really nails. There have been something like ninety or a hundred well-authenticated cases of a similar character since the time of St. Francis.

Professor Elmer Gates, of the Laboratory of Psychology and Psychurgy, Washington, D.C., plunged his arm into a jar filled with water up to the point of overflow. Keeping his position without moving, he directed his "thinking" to the arm, with the result that the blood entered the arm in such quantities as to enlarge it and cause the water in the jar to overflow. The Professor went even further than this. By directing the "thoughts" to his arm for a certain length of time each day, for many days, he permanently increased both its size and strength, and he instructed others so that they could produce the same effect on various organs of the body, thus demonstrating the accuracy of the suggestion of President Hall, of Clark University, that muscle can be developed by thinking (so-called), as well as by exercise. Sandow, the teacher of physical culture, has found the same thing.

Changed Mental Conditions Create Chemical Changes.—Professor Gates has dealt fully with the results of thinking in a long series of most comprehensive and convincing experiments. He found that change of the mental state changed the chemical character of the perspiration. When treated with the same chemical reagent, the perspiration of an angry man showed one colour, that of a man in grief another, and so on through the long list of emotions, each mental state persistently exhibiting its own peculiar result every time the experiment was repeated. These experiments show clearly, as indicated by Professor James's statements, that each kind of thinking is followed by changes in glandular or visceral activity, and the production of different chemical substances which were being thrown out of the system by the perspiration.

Professor Gates's conclusions are very definite: "Every mental activity creates a definite chemical change and a definite anatomical change in the animal which exercises the mental activity." And again, he says: "The mind of the human organism can, by an effort of will, properly directed, produce measurable changes of the chemistry of the secretions and excretions." He also says: "If mind activities create chemical and anatomical changes in the cells and tissues of the animal body, it follows that all physiological processes of health or disease are psychological processes, and that the only way to inhibit, accelerate, or change these processes, is to resort to methods, properly altering the psychologic or mental processes."

That is, he has clearly shown and states that the most effective and best way to change these physical processes is to change the thinking. And again, he says: "All there is of health and disease is mind activity." And once more: "If we can know how to regulate mind processes, then we can cure diseases—all disease." In another place he says: "Mind activity creates organic structure, and organisms are mind embodiments."

He gives his conclusions with definiteness and precision: "Every emotion of a false and disagreeable nature produces a poison in the blood and cell tissues." He sums up his results in the statement, "My experiments show that irascible, malevolent, and depressing emotions generate in the system injurious compounds, some of which are extremely poisonous; also that agreeable, happy emotions generate chemical compounds of nutritious value, which stimulate the cells to manufacture energy."

His results go to swell the weight of demonstrable proof of the entirely ethereal character of what is called material organisation.

As to the effects of erroneous thoughts on the body, we have the authoritative utterances of acknowledged scientific observers.

Professor Hall says: "The hair and beard grow slower, it has been proved by experiment, when a business man has been subjected to several months of anxiety. To be happy is essential. To be alive, and well, and contented is the end of life, the highest science and the purest religion." As a matter of fact, these four states are a manifestation of the condition of the "consciousness," and neither causes nor even conditions to be aimed for.

T. J. Hudson, PH.D., LL.D., says of disease induced by erroneous suggestion, that it is safe to say nine-tenths of all the ailments of the human race may be traced to this source. He also writes: "For untold ages suggestion was the only therapeutic agency available to man. Medicine, if we date its advent from Hippocrates, 'the father of medicine,' who flourished about 400 B.C., is a modern institution when compared with this long line of healers who wrought their therapeutic wonders by the aid of suggestion in its myriad forms."

"The North American Indian believes that evil spirits are responsible for all his diseases; and his medicine man tells him that he can frighten away such evil spirits by making hideous noises, supplemented by a diabolical make-up. He prepares himself accordingly, and seating himself before the wigwam door, in full view of the patient, proceeds to make things unpleasant for all concerned, and positively unendurable for the evil spirits. The latter generally flee in the course of a day or two, leaving the patient to recover. I have authentic information from educated Indians, who assure me that for 'the poor Indian, whose untutored mind sees God in clouds or hears him in the wind,' this method of healing is generally more effective than are the material remedies of the educated physician." [1]

Again, he writes: "Dr. Hack Tuke's great work [2] contains a voluminous record of the observations of cases of medical men, of both ancient and modern times, demonstrating the control of the mind over the body in health and disease."

[1] *The Law of Mental Medicine.*
[2] *Illustrations of the Influence of the Mind on the Body.*

Albert Moll, a well-known scientific authority on this topic, who cannot be accused of exaggeration, says in his work on hypnotism: "There are few people who are not injured when they are assured on all sides that they look ill, and I think many have been as much injured by this cumulative process as if they had been poisoned."

Dr. Still, an American osteopath, writing of osteopathy (cure by manipulation to restore the normal condition of nerve control), says: "With this thought in view I began to ask myself, What is fever? Is it an effect, or is it a cause, as commonly described by medical authors? I concluded it was only an effect, and on that line I have experimented and proven the position I then took to be the truth, wonderfully sustained by nature responding every time in the affirmative. I have concluded, after twenty-five years of close observation and experiment, that there is no such disease as fever, flux, diphtheria, typhus, typhoid, lung-fever, or any other fever classed under the common head of fever, or rheumatism, sciatica, gout, colic, liver-disease, nettle-rash, or croup. On to the end of the list, they do not exist as diseases. All these, separate and combined, are only effects. The cause can be found and does exist in the limited or excited action of the nerves which control the fluids of part or the whole of the body. It appears perfectly reasonable to any person . . . who has familiarised himself with anatomy and its working with the machinery of life, that all diseases are mere effects, the cause being a partial or complete failure of the nerves to properly conduct the fluids of life." Mercifully we are rapidly awakening from this form of insanity.

Professor Münsterberg, speaking of the remedy for modern diseases, says: "We need more training in self-discipline, in continuous effort, in voluntary attention, and in thoroughness . . . the fault is in ourselves, in our prejudices, in our training, in our habits, and in our fanciful fear of nervousness." Perhaps one of the most striking instances of the change of thought on the subject of mental healing is the discussion that took place recently in the Reichstag, on a Bill to suppress medical quackery in Germany. One member spoke of "innumerable instances of animals being cured in this way," and so many members testified of their own knowledge of mental healing, that a daily paper the following day commented as follows: "The debate proves once more what extraordinary progress occultism has made in this country of recent years." [1]

The above is quite sufficient to show how necessary it is to turn out every wrong thought that comes into one's mind. It has been shown also that there is only one right, because scientific, method of doing this, which is certain in its results and beneficial to all concerned.

A Purely Metaphysical Basis Requisite.—The quotations herein given clearly show how the advanced workers in the scientific world are recognising the fact that all is mental. It only remains for them to advance from their semi-metaphysical reasoning to a purely metaphysical basis and find that all is Mind and its manifestation. They will then begin to think in a scientific way, if only for the purpose of self-protection, as they recognise the enormous power let loose in the world. This so-called power, although

---

[1] "Curious Reichstag Debate" (*Daily Telegraph*, March 10, 1911).

illusory and not permanent, must appear in a series of unparalleled disasters
in these latter days, unless the belief in material power disappears, being
destroyed through a right understanding of its false claims. "The devil is
come down unto you, having great wrath, because he knoweth that he hath
5 but a short time" (Rev. 12:12). "Of all the dangerous mental habits that
which schoolboys call 'cocksureness' is probably the most perilous; and
the inestimable value of metaphysical discipline is that it furnishes an
effectual counterpoise to this evil proclivity" (Huxley).

Medical Recognition.—Sir Andrew Clark says: "It is impossible for
10 us to deal knowingly and wisely with various disorders of the body without
distinctly recognising the agency of states and conditions of minds, often
in producing and always in modifying them." [1]

Dr. Clouston, in his inaugural address to the Royal Medical Society in
1896, says: "I could have related remarkable cases to you from my own
15 experience, and out of books, of functional disease being brought on, and
being cured, by mental impressions only, of functions being suspended
and altered from the same cause—nay, of actual organic lesions being
directly caused and cured by mental impressions. "Warts have been
'charmed' away; scurvy among sailors has been cured by the prospect of a
20 naval fight; gouty swellings have disappeared when 'Mad dog' or 'Fire'
was cried out suddenly to the sufferers. All these things have happened,
but they occur only really while some influence or other for good or evil is
taking place. This, however, must be sufficiently powerful to usurp the
supreme post of government." [2]

25 Dr. J. H. Sealy writes: "I shall now consider the mind as a source of
cure, and as an agent equally potent, and as frequently used for the removal
of corporeal malady, as I have shown it to be active in its production." [3]

Sir John Forbes writes: "Means acting directly on the mind, and
influencing other parts of the body through it, form an important class of
30 remedies, and occupy a much larger space in actual therapeutics than is
commonly believed, and deserve to occupy a still larger. Their occupation
is fully as powerful and effective in disease of a purely bodily character as in
mental disease." [4]

Sir Clifford Allbutt, K.C.B., M.D., F.R.S., Regius Professor of Physic,
35 University of Cambridge, writes: "In many a severe functional malady, to
arouse latent reserves by a rekindling of hope and courage may compass a
marvellous cure, and a lively rally even in some by nature incurable . . .
in many instances the new position is maintained permanently. The annals
of our own times, the annals of our churches and religious 'Armies,' are
40 rich in such witness." [5]

The Lancet records a case of Dr. Barkas, of a woman of twenty-eight
years of age, who, with supposed disease of every organ and pains everywhere, was cured by doses of pure distilled water.[6] Dr. Schofield, referring

---

45
[1] *Lancet*, 1855, II, p. 315.
[2] *British Medical Journal*, January 18, 1896.
[3] *Medical Essays*, II, p. 76.
[4] *Nature and Art in Disease*.
[5] *British Medical Journal*, June 18, 1910.
[6] *The Lancet*, 1894, II.

to the case, says: "This is a valuable experiment as excluding every material remedy whatever, and proving that it is the mental factor alone that cures, however it may be generally associated with material remedies."[1] Burnt sugar was a common prescription of Sir William Gull.

Dr. Hack Tuke says that mental therapeutics without hypnotism can cure toothache, sciatica, painful joints, rheumatism, gout, pleurodynia, colic, epilepsy, whooping cough, contracted limbs, paralyses, headaches, neuralgias, constipation, asthma, warts, scurvy, dropsy, intermittent fever, alcoholism, and typhoid fever: and avert impending death.

Dr. Schofield says: "Does any practical medical man, after all, really doubt these mental powers? If, then, this power is so well known, why in the name of common-sense should it be pooh-poohed and ignored as it is? For although these drugs are still administered, but few medical men now believe that they are the entire cause of the cure; for very gradually it is beginning to dawn upon us that most nervous diseases at any rate are easily and naturally treated by mental therapeutics, and that the still persistent efforts to cure them by the stomach are neither reliable nor rational."

Sir Frederick Treves, the well-known surgeon, writes: "I look forward to the time when people will leave off the extraordinary habit of taking medicine when they are sick, and when it will be as anomalous for persons to die of scarlet fever, typhoid, cholera, and diphtheria, as it would be for a man to die of a wolf's bite in England."

About the much-misunderstood question of functional and organic disease, Dr. Schofield says: "We have seen that the powers of the conscious mind over the body are well-nigh immeasurable; and knowing, as we now do, that our old division into functional and organic diseases is merely the expression of our ignorance, and that all diseases, even hysterical, involve organic disturbance somewhere, we are prepared to believe that faith and other unorthodox cures, putting into operation such a powerful agent as the unconscious mind, or, if you prefer the formula, 'the forces of nature,' are not necessarily limited to so-called functional diseases at all."

Dr. Buzzard's Presidential Address to the Neurological Society, 1891, shows how fine are the differences between functional and organic diseases of the nervous system. As a matter of fact, there is no definite line of demarcation. At the end of a long list of medical opinions, quoted by him on this subject, Dr. Schofield says: "I trust I have succeeded by the mouths of many witnesses in fully establishing my thesis that there is, after all, a large and weighty body of testimony to the presence and importance of the 'vis medicatrix naturæ' and to the general power of mind over disease."

As is the case with many other leading thinkers and practical workers, Dr. Schofield has been unable to write all he thinks, or even to put forward all he knows, on account of the general ignorance, and therefore scornful scepticism, on the subject.

[1] *The Force of Mind.*

Admitted Ignorance.—"*An unlimited scepticism is the part of a contracted mind, which reasons upon imperfect data, or makes its own knowledge and extent of observation the standard and test of probability. In receiving upon testimony statements which are rejected by the vulgar as totally*
5 *incredible, a man of cultivated mind is influenced by the recollection that many things at one time appeared to him marvellous, which he now knows to be true, and he thence concludes that there may still be in nature many phenomena and many principles with which he is entirely unacquainted. In other words, he has learned from experience not to make his own knowledge his test of probability*" [1]
10 (Abercrombie).

De Fleury, observing that the medical treatment of mind is yet a science in its infancy, says: "There can be no doubt that the fields of psycho-physiology, psycho-pathology, and psycho-therapeutics are as yet almost untouched."
15 Dr. Schofield says: "The point to be decided is whether the force of mind in disease is a real and important subject for study—whether it is one of practical value to medical men. I think I have said enough, and quoted enough, to show that the opinion of a large number in the profession, who are worthy of our highest respect, agree that it is. It is a subject
20 alluded to everywhere, and taught nowhere; and no single day passes in a medical man's life but he and his patients must suffer consciously from it. Is it, then, a subject that could be taught with advantage in our schools? Emphatically, yes; and one, too, which, if properly taught, would be found of absorbing interest." [2]
25 In 1872 the *Medical Times* in one of its editorials said: "The question how mental influences may be practically applied, controlled, and directed for therapeutical purposes is certainly one well worth the pursuit of the scientific physician."

Why is it that medical men have not sooner recognised the mental factor
30 in disease and codified the laws relating thereto? Dr. Schofield suggests "The limitation of the human mind, which, when it has spent a term of years in the steady study of one class of phenomena presented in medicine, finds it both painful and difficult to consider another." [3]

The *British Medical Journal* of April 12, 1890, suggests as another
35 reason, the inherent difficulty of the subject itself: "The influence of the mind on the body is a subject whose study involves so many of the fundamental and difficult problems in Nature, that it would be strange if it were popular amongst men whose first aim is to be practical. Yet another authority suggests that the ignorance of the medical man of the period as
40 to the mental factors in medicine is due to four reasons: want of instruction on the subject in medical schools; the difficulty of the study without teachers or text-books; the uncertainty of the utility of the knowledge when acquired; the dread of being thought singular or old-fashioned." [4] Dr. Schofield says, "I would add a fifth, namely, Prejudice."
45 Pereira's *Materia Medica* devotes only three pages out of 2,360 to "psychic therapeutics."

---

[1] *Intellectual Powers.*
[2] *The Force of Mind.*   [3] *Ibid.*   [4] *Ibid.*

Dr. Shoemaker, of Philadelphia, in the *System of Medicine*, spares one page out of about 1,200; but most of the other authorities, including far larger works, devote none, and it is only during the last few years that men like Dr. Schofield are beginning to write openly on the subject and give us the benefit of their experience. "That which is ignored in physiology is 5 not likely to be admitted in pathology; what is never taught in the clinique is not often practised in the sick-room."

Dr. S. Weir Mitchell writes in *The Physician*:—

"There are among us those who haply please
To think our business is to treat disease,   10
And all unknowing lack this lesson still,
'Tis not the body, but the man is ill."

Hitherto many important statements as to so-called mental action have not been appreciated, because, having no practical result, they led to nothing. Now, in the light of the vital discovery that "all is Mind and its 15 infinite manifestation," we find them invested with new importance and value, as they show the necessity of each man learning the scientific method of thinking, whereby he can protect himself and others against the troubles to which attention has hitherto uselessly, and indeed dangerously, been drawn.   20

Practical Experience.—"*We are so far from knowing all the agents of nature, and their various modes of action, that it would not be philosophical to deny any phenomena merely because in the actual state of our knowledge they are inexplicable. This only we ought to do: in proportion to the difficulty there seems to be in admitting them should be the scrupulous attention we bestow on 25 their examination*" [1] (Laplace).

It has been said that a grain of proof is worth a pound of argument, and before I knew anything of mental healing, the so-called mental results obtained by people who had come to me for advice on other matters had often greatly puzzled me, showing me that our existing theories were 30 insufficient to account for the results obtainable.

So-called Mental Effect on Muscles.—Mr. Eugen Sandow, for instance, when consulting me once, asked why it was that he could influence a muscle never consciously used, and cause it to grow.[2] He said that a short time before, for five minutes every day for a fortnight, he 35 steadily thought that a muscle in the middle of his back was growing, and at the end of the fortnight it stood out as big as his fist, although never used. He attributes the success of his treatment largely to the fact of mental concentration upon the area and particular organs exercised, and tells me he has found that concentration has a dual effect, as the mind is 40 developing in an almost corresponding degree to the muscles. This development is ethereal and not truly mental.

The leading trainer of women's muscles, chiefly the internal ones, consulting me about her business some little time ago, asked me how she could teach her teachers to "teach in the same way as she taught," because she 45

---

[1] *Analytic Theory of Probabilities.*
[2] See *Science and Health*, p. 198, l. 29.

could get results in a week that they could not get in a month. I did not
then know that it was simply the direct and indirect action of her human
mind upon the internal muscles of the pupils, and although I looked carefully into the matter, I could not be of any use.

5   Professor Arthur Keith, Hunterian Professor, Royal College of Surgeons, speaking of the growth of human beings, says: "This problem of
growth is most marvellous, and things which we hardly deem credible are
coming to light." [1]

On Animals.—Major Wood, again, wanted me to show him how to
10 teach his son to break horses as successfully as he could. His method was
simply to pull them over on to his knee by muscular force, and quietly let
them down to the ground. He then turned them on to their backs helpless
with their legs up in the air, when in a minute or two they were perfectly
broken, however savage they had been before. I could not help him at all,
15 not having then learned that the results obtained were solely due to the
action of the human "mind." It is now clear why Rarey's secret of training
horses died with him—namely, because he never knew it himself.

The difference in the success of one fancier and another in producing
new varieties, either of animal or of vegetable so-called life, is largely a
20 question of the way in which they think.

On Human Beings.—"*For none of us liveth to himself*" (Rom. 14:7).
Professor Alex, who could paralyse or blind a man instantly, and as
instantly release him, as you will see if you look up the account of various
tests of his powers in the *Daily News* about six years ago, came to me twice
25 for advice. This was after my examination into mental healing had commenced, and, being a thoroughly well-intentioned man, he was delighted
when it was pointed out that the cause of the many personal difficulties he
had had in the past had been this wrong use of his human "mind." He said
that he had long thought that the results must be due to the action of his
30 human "mind" on the subconscious "mind" of the person acted upon, and
he would never so use it again. Even when a person tries to do good in this
way he can neither do any real good to others, nor can he have a happy life
himself. Professor Alex recognised the reason for this.

On Inert Matter—I was asked by the *Daily Mail* to look into the results
35 of Mr. Hart, who claimed to be able to move matter with his mind. Details
of his experiments were published in the *Review of Reviews*. It did not take
very long to discover that all his results were purely physical, the motion
of air being the cause of the movement, which had nothing to do with the
action of the mind, and it was possible to reproduce them by ordinary
40 physical means. Without telling him this, I asked him why he did not get
the same results when the article he moved was entirely covered by glass;
and he said that it seemed to insulate his thought, which he recognised
was an electrical current. I then told him to what his results were really
due. A few days afterwards, under test conditions, he moved in any
45 required direction an aluminium needle, entirely closed in by a glass shade.
At the end of a quarter of an hour perspiration was streaming down his
face, he was dead tired, and could no longer cause the slightest movement.

[1] Lecture at the Royal Institution, March 16, 1911.

This convinced him of the truth of what had been explained. On seeing the results, he quite recognised that one could not work in this way at all without harming himself, and admitted that the right method was by turning in thought to God and heaven, so avoiding the evil that resulted from moving matter in the way he had done. 5

Being consulted once with reference to a novel and interesting discovery in aerial flight, the inventor, an experienced business man, told me that he had been experimenting with friends for some time, and they had been able to cause a match-box to rise several feet from a table by the use of their "minds" alone. He told me that it was extremely tiring, and was 10 delighted to understand the reasons, and the proper way of working, as they so entirely agreed with his own experiences and ideas.

On Watches.—There are many instances of how the hypothetical, ethereal forces called the human mind apparently affect matter, visible and invisible, without such direct action being recognised. For example, a 15 common experience is that a watch will go well on one person and badly on another. With some people, no watch will keep regular time at all. A new watch, with a Kew certificate, went perfectly on a friend of mine, but always gained when worn by his sister-in-law. A relation of mine has had the same experience, although all the conditions, as far as could be told, 20 were the same.

On Vegetable Life.—"*He that would grow roses in his garden must first have roses in his heart*" (Dean Hole). It is well known that some people can wear cut flowers on their person for a long time; on others they die in a few hours. This is solely an ethereal or miscalled mental effect, and varies 25 according to the subconscious belief on the point, and the effect thereof on the individual and those around who may be acted upon. Plant life is very susceptible to "thought," and all trees and plants can be hypnotised. For a long time we have known that plants and animals get on better under one who loves them, and is therefore constantly dwelling upon their good 30 qualities, and, until recently, the main reason for this had not been discovered.

Dr. Ward, the paleobotanist of the United States Geological Survey, in his Memorial Address on Charles Darwin, says: "Darwin looked upon plants as living things. He did not study their forms so much as their 35 actions. He interrogated them to learn what they were doing. The central truth, towards which his botanical investigations constantly tended, was that of the universal activity of the vegetable kingdom—that all plants move and act." Professor Francis Darwin pointed out, in his opening address at the British Association meeting in 1908, that plants appear to have 40 memory, and that "in plants there exists a faint copy of what we know as consciousness in ourselves." Henri Bergson, in *Life and Consciousness*, says, "The faculty of moving, and probably, therefore, also of consciousness, may occasionally re-awaken in vegetable life. Consciousness might exist in nature wherever there is living matter. At least it is not impossible." 45

> "I hold you here, root and all, in my hand,
> Little flower—but if I could understand
> What you are, root and all, and all in all,
> I should know what God and man is" (*Tennyson*).

Platform Displays.—It will be a surprise to many when they awake to the fact that intentionally to become a witness to platform displays of the abnormal action of human thoughts is to participate in that action and to share in the inevitable evil results therefrom, unless one is steadily
5 working to protect oneself. Only one motive renders such a course allowable—namely, to attend with the express purpose of destroying the wrong thoughts in connection with the display. The world's stage provides us with ample work in getting rid of evil without adding to our dangers and difficulties by going out of our way to meet them.

10   **A Warning.**—I cannot too emphatically repeat that any method of producing results through the effect of human thoughts, is absolutely wrong and harmful to the worker and all parties concerned.

MENTAL HEALING

The Bible Testimony.—"*If ye abide in me, and my words abide in*
15 *you, ye shall ask what ye will, and it shall be done unto you. Herein is my*
Father glorified, that ye bear much fruit; so shall ye be my disciples" (John
15:7, 8). "*Heal the sick, cleanse the lepers, raise the dead, cast out devils*"
(Matt. 10:8).

The Bible, from beginning to end, is full of references to spiritual
20 healing, which, far from being an exception, is, though sadly unusual, a perfectly natural fulfilment of divine law. The following quotations are some of the definite allusions by the most advanced workers of ancient times, as interestingly recorded in the Bible:—

"If thou wilt diligently hearken to the voice of the Lord thy God, . . .
25 and keep all his statutes [always think rightly], I will put none of these diseases upon thee, . . . for I am the Lord that healeth thee" (Ex. 15:26).

"Ye shall serve the Lord your God, . . . and I will take sickness away from the midst of thee" (Ex. 23:25).

"If there be a messenger with him, an interpreter, one among a thousand,
30 to shew unto man his uprightness: Then he is gracious unto him, and saith, Deliver him from going down to the pit: I have found a ransom" (Job. 33:23, 24).

"I cried unto thee, and thou hast healed me" (Ps. 30:2).

"That thy way may be known upon earth, thy saving health among all
35 nations" (Ps. 67:2).

"Bless the Lord, O my soul, and forget not all his benefits: Who forgiveth all thine iniquities; who healeth all thy diseases" (Ps. 103:2, 3).

"He sent his word, and healed them" (Ps. 107:20).

"For it was neither herb, nor mollifying plaister, that restored them to
40 health: but thy word, O Lord, which healeth all things" (Wisdom of Solomon 16:12).

"I have seen his ways, and will heal him: . . . Peace, peace to him that is far off, and to him that is near, . . . and I will heal him" (Isa. 57:18, 19).

45   "Heal me, O Lord, and I shall be healed" (Jer. 17:14).

"I will restore health unto thee, and I will heal thee of thy wounds" (Jer. 30:17).

"Behold, I will bring it health . . . and I will cure them" (Jer. 33:6).

"But unto you that fear [deep reverence, *Chambers's Dictionary*] my name [nature] shall the Sun of righteousness arise with healing in his wings" (Mal. 4:2).

The references in the New Testament are too well known to need quota- 5
tion.

Dr. Joseph Parker, the late well-known preacher of the City Temple, has put the case concisely from a religious point of view: "If we believe the New Testament, we believe that men were once 'made whole' without medicine or doctor. If this was a fact in New Testament times, why may 10
it not become a fact in the present day? If it be a fact, it is the most bene- ficent fact in history, and being such, it ought, if possible, to be recalled and re-established. To grasp the question wisely, and thoroughly, we must go back to Christ's own time and think of him.

"Did Christ heal men? Yes, he did.   15

"Did Christ's apostles heal men? Yes, they did.

"Was this healing mechanical, surgical, medicinal? No, it was not.

"Was the healing spiritual, sympathetic, mental? Yes, it was.

"Is Christ the same, yesterday, to-day, and for ever? Yes, he is.

"Does Christ still work and reign? Yes, he does.   20

"That settles it."

If the full scientific import of the previous Scriptural statements be con- sidered, it will be seen that they point straight to the truth as now put forth.

Our Present Duty.—"*Pray one for another, that ye may be healed*" (James 5:16).   25

Jesus definitely told us of our healing power. He said: "And these signs shall follow them [not only 'you'] that believe; In my name [nature] shall they cast out devils; . . . they shall lay hands [spiritual power] on the sick, and they shall recover" (Mark 16:17, 18).

In the Orthodox English Church service to be read to the sick, the fol- 30
lowing remarkable passage occurs: "Wherefore, whatsoever your sick- ness is, know you certainly, that it is God's visitation"! If this were true any remedial measures of any kind or description whatsoever would be in direct opposition to God, and the worse you are the better. No wonder that whereas in the early days of Christianity healing was done within the 35
Church and to go to a doctor was heresy, in later times the Church has failed to heal, except in a small percentage of cases. The commandments of Jesus on this point were definite, and in direct opposition: "Heal the sick, cleanse the lepers, raise the dead, cast out devils" (Matt. 10:8). Proof of our understanding of what the Master taught is required to-day, not pro- 40
fession only. Demonstration is the only proof.

Moses not only should have been able to heal through his knowledge of God, but we are definitely shown that he did. Speaking to the Israelites he said: "Ye shall serve the Lord your God, and he shall bless thy bread, and thy water; and I will take sickness away from the midst of thee" 45
(Ex. 23:25). At one time this "I" seemed to refer to God, as apart from his instrument, man, in this case Moses.

The Apostle James said: "The prayer of faith shall save the sick, and

the Lord shall raise him up; and [most important of all] if he have committed sins, they shall be forgiven him" (James 5:15). "Rely upon no
other Physician, for, according to my apprehension, He reserves your case
to Himself. Put, then, all your trust in Him, and you will soon find the
5 effects of it in your recovery, which we often retard by putting greater confidence in physic than in God. . . . Continue, then, always with God"
(Brother Lawrence, Eleventh Letter).

We have to be about our "Father's" business, and we are not doing our
bounden duty unless we are daily healing sin and sickness. "What a
10 beautiful thing it is to work, and to live, and be happy" (R. L. Stevenson).

Raising of the Dead.—*"Heal the sick, cleanse the lepers, raise the
dead, cast out devils"* (Matt. 10:8).

There are seven cases of the intentional raising of the dead, details of
which are recorded in the Bible; three by Jesus (Luke 7:14, and 8 :54;
15 John 11:43), each apparently more difficult; one each by Elijah (I Kings
17:22), Elisha (II Kings 4:34), Peter (Acts 9:40), and Paul (Acts 20:9).
These are exclusive of the man who was unexpectedly resuscitated by
touching the bones of Elisha (II Kings 13:21), and of the supreme demonstration of the power of God by Jesus, when he passed unvanquished from
20 the tomb.

Jesus must have worked in accordance with regular laws. His words,
quoted above, must have been for all time. God, as the Principle of all law
and order, could not act against law and order, as expressed in God's man,
the image and likeness of good, for God and the good man co-exist, as
25 Principle and idea. Why should we die? [1] "For God made not death:
neither hath he pleasure in the destruction of the living . . . for righteousness is immortal" (Wisdom of Solomon 1:13, 15). There are many other
instances related of the raising of the dead. Paul said: "Why should it be
thought a thing incredible with you, that God should raise the dead?"
30 (Acts 26:8). Five hundred years before Jesus demonstrated the law of life,
the great thinker, Lao-Tze, wrote: "May not a man take a dead thing and
make it alive?"

Is it possible that this power could have been almost permanently lost
to humanity about A.D. 300? Gibbon, the historian, says: [2] "But the
35 miraculous cure of diseases of the most inveterate or even preternatural
kind, can no longer occasion any surprise, when we recollect, that in the
days of Irenæus, about the end of the second century, the resurrection of
the dead was very far from being esteemed an uncommon event; that the
miracle was frequently performed on necessary occasions, by great fasting
40 and the joint supplication of the church of the place, and that the persons
thus restored by their prayers, had lived afterwards among them many
years." [3] This power was lost sight of when Christianity was made a State
belief, and the priests were so sunk that they actually claimed the healing
as their prerogative. In the fourth century the Council of Laodicea forbade

45 [1] See Ezekiel 18, verse 31.
  [2] *The Decline and Fall of the Roman Empire.*
  [3] Mr. Dodwell concludes that the second century was still more fertile in miracles
than the first.

anyone, except those duly authorised by the Bishop, to exorcise devils. Christianity at that time became but a name, not a living flame, and the teachings of Jesus became to the Church mere words, and so lost their practical significance. "But they mocked the messengers of God, and despised his words, and misused his prophets, until the wrath of the Lord 5 arose against his people, till there was no remedy (II Chron. 36:16). "For if the dead rise not, then is not Christ raised : . . . For he must reign, till he hath put all enemies under his feet : . . ." (I Cor. 15:16, 25). "Christianity has been tried for 1,900 years. Perhaps it is now time to try the religion of Jesus" (Dean Milman). 10

After the procession at the Eucharistic Congress, which took place at Vienna, in 1912, seventy-three people were so ill that they had to go to the hospitals, and three were seized with religious mania. What a parody on religion.

"O death, where is thy sting? O grave, where is thy victory? The sting of 15 death is sin [belief in a power other than that of God]; and the strength of sin is the [false] law [of universal consent]. But thanks be to God, which giveth us the victory through our Lord Jesus Christ" (I Cor. 15:55–57). "In the way of righteousness [from Anglo-Saxon *rihtwis*, alias right knowing, wise as to what is right—Skeat's *Etymological Dictionary*] is life; and 20 in the pathway thereof there is no death" (Prov. 12:28).

ACTION OF THOUGHT

"*Success in mental healing by scientific methods is best promoted by first acquiring a clear understanding of the law under which the healing is effected. In other words, scientific methods require scientific knowledge for their success-* 25 *ful application*" [1] (T. J. Hudson).

Now, curiously enough, the ordinary metaphysician objects to "thoughts" being spoken of as "lines of force," whereas the one name is just as much a misnomer as the other; for the only true and therefore permanent thoughts are God's thoughts, which are spiritual and eternal, 30 the real things in the real world. These conceived of materially and therefore falsely, are what have been called theoretically "lines of force" or "thoughts," and as "ethereal lines of force" they have to be intelligently seen to be powerless, just as certainly as that matter, the more solid form of material thoughts, has to be known to be substanceless. In fact, if 35 anything, "lines of force" is the more useful term, because it cannot possibly be applied to God's thoughts. A still better, because less material term, is "false beliefs."

Homœopathy.—It is now easy to understand why Hahnemann, the founder of Homœopathy, said that it was not the drug, but what he 40 would call, for the want of a better name, "the spirit of the drug," that did the work. He declared that the world would never solve its problems until it entered the mental realm.

Nobody until recently has ever been able quite satisfactorily to explain how it is possible that a small dose of poison can have exactly the opposite 45

[1] *The Law of Mental Medicine.*

result of a large dose; but all opposition, in Hahnemann's case, was con-
founded, if not silenced, by the wonderful success which attended the
application of the supposed law in actual practice. At the same time,
Hahnemann had to flee on account of his failure in the case of one of his
5 patients, whilst some homœopathic doctors were imprisoned. "The fact
remains that Hahnemann was eminently successful in curing diseases,
and his following has assumed colossal proportions, in spite of the ridicule
heaped upon him on account of the infinitesimal doses prescribed" [1]
(T. J. Hudson).

10   **The Cause of Disease.**—From what has been said it will be seen
that the cause of disease is the same as that of sin; namely, it is the action
of "lines of force," vibrating at certain definite rates of vibration, which
cause certain parts of the mechanism of the human "mind," which for
purposes of explanation are called cells, to vibrate at a similar rate of
15 vibration, so giving the effect of the disease or sin, as the case may be. The
explanation of these so-called cells renders clear the mystery of the cells of
the material scientist, and shows up their elusive character.

Whilst the whole effect can be spoken of as "mental," so it can also be
expressed as "material," and still better as "ethereal," for, as has been
20 pointed out, these are merely different names for the same thing. All are
purely illusory, and have no real existence and no reality, for they are not
of God.

Poison.—If a negro in Central Africa eats a small quantity of, say,
strychnine, it acts as a tonic. If he eats a large amount it will kill him; if he
25 takes an overdose of some poisons he may merely be sick. The mental
workers say it is the general belief in the deadly effect of the poison that
kills the man. Medical men scoff and say that it is the drug. Which is
correct?

The fact, looked at from a natural science point of view, is that the
30 material drug consists of millions of electrons massed together, each the
material manifestation of "two lines of force" vibrating at a definite rate,
and crossing at right angles. All the lines of force vibrating at that particular
rate are "a universal belief," an ethereal force that, alone, can kill its own
materially conceived person.

35   It is not the inert drug that kills the person. That which kills is the
excessive vibration of these "lines of force" acting upon the human
"mind," and, so to speak, tearing it to pieces. A few merely stimulate
action. Hahnemann's mysterious "spirit of the drug" can now be understood as a purely ethereal, mistaken belief.[2]

40   You will also now see the action of so-called will-power in such cases.
Human will-power simply alters the vibration of the line of force or
thought, so changing its usual action, and producing another equally
disastrous result.

[1] *The Law of Mental Medicine.*
45 [2] According to Mr. Stephen Paget, Dr. A. M. Kelles states that the figures for
Hahnemann's dilutions are as follows: Fifth dilution, 1 part in 132,500; tenth
dilution, 1 in 97,656,250,000; thirtieth dilution, 1 in 931,322,574,615,478,515,625,
million, billion, billion, and that "Hahnemann preferred the thirtieth dilution"
(*The Faith and Works of Christian Science*).

One of my staff left me to go to the West Coast of Africa to try to find out how to prevent the scourge of fever that was doing so much harm at the time. When he came back he was full of the fact that he had discovered an absolute remedy. This, he said, was that the homœopathic dose, as given in footnote on previous page, was much too strong, and that, if the 5 dose was diluted to a hundredth or a thousandth of the strength, I forget which, it was effective. This was simply due to the fact that he was a very strong thinker, and was dead certain this would be so, and impressed his patients with the belief.

All Action in the Material Seeming World only Apparent.— 10 Those who have sufficient knowledge of the human miscalled "mind" to understand without difficulty what has been here stated, will see that this method of verbally presenting what takes place is necessary, to enable inquirers more quickly to grasp the fact that matter has no power to act. Some students find it difficult at once to accept the more radical and final 15 statement already made, namely, that the whole of this action is only apparent, as really all material phenomena are, as shown, merely false beliefs in the existence of a series of cinematograph pictures, each picture coming along slightly different, all without an iota even of substance or reality. Endeavouring to alter conditions by material means is like trying 20 to wash out a magic-lantern picture on a screen. If you change the slide the picture changes, namely, if you change the thought the manifestation alters.

Cancer and Humanity.—Mr. Arthur Balfour, presiding, in July, 1909, at the annual meeting of the General Council of the Imperial 25 Cancer Research Fund, which was held at the Royal College of Surgeons, warned the public not to expect the immediate discovery of some accurate and active remedy of the disease.

"Such expectations did not take sufficient account of the fact that these great problems could only be attacked by dealing with them as part of a 30 great biological whole. All our discoveries were due to a broad scientific outlook, which had produced unexpected results and conclusions. For example, investigation of the action of microscopic organisms had discovered the same kind of common cause producing such utterly different things as alcohol, pearls, and whooping cough. 35

"One result of the investigations carried on under the Fund had been to show that bacteriology would give but little assistance in dealing with cancer. But some important conclusions had been reached. The staff had decided that heredity was almost negligible as a cause of cancer."

"Some Ray of Hope."—Sir Alfred Pearce Gould, K.C.V.O., Senior 40 Surgeon to the Middlesex Hospital, in the Bradshaw Lecture, delivered before the Royal College of Surgeons, said that "cancer was the result of a breach or failure of fundamental cell law, a law so majestic that obedience to it resulted in perfect development, perfect health, the full measure of days, and disobedience to it might slowly spell out all the inscrutable woes 45 of cancer. . . . It was quite a frequent occurrence for a grafted cancerous growth, after attaining some size, to slowly shrink and disappear, and in

some series of experiments a large proportion of the grafts that had 'taken'
had, after a period of growth, spontaneously vanished. . . . His present
purpose was not to vaunt a remedy, but to state a fact—that cancer, even
when advanced in degree and of long duration, might get better, and might
5 even get well. There is," he continued, " cure of cancer apart from operative removal. All therapeutic cures are obtainable only by the working of
physiological forces, and the first hope of therapeutic success comes from
observation of the efficiency of unaided Nature to accomplish cure. In the
darkness of night it is everything to know that there is a sun towards which
10 the earth is revolving, and that if we fix our eyes on the east we shall soon
see the grey promise of dawn, and then the many-coloured heralds of the
golden sun itself. And, as the victims of cancer call to us in the dark night
of despair, 'Watchman, what of the night?' it is much to know that for
cancer-stricken man there is also a sun of healing. *When the biologist shall*
15 *know the laws that govern cell-growth, with a knowledge akin in its sweep and*
accuracy to that of the astronomer, he will have power—the power to prevent,
to control, and to cure cancer." [1]

Hope Fulfilled.—Now we actually know the laws that govern, not only
"cell growth," but cell purification, and ultimate dematerialisation, which
20 is far more important.

Appearance and Disappearance of Matter.—*"Strictly speaking, I*
am unaware of anything that has the right to the title of an 'impossibility,'
except a contradiction in terms. There are impossibilities logical, but none
natural. A 'round square,' a 'present past,' 'two parallel lines that intersect,'
25 *are impossibilities, because the ideas denoted by the predicates, round, present,*
intersect, are contrary to the ideas denoted by the subjects, square, past,
parallel. But walking on water, or turning water into wine, or procreation
without male intervention, or raising the dead, are plainly not impossibilities
in this sense" (Professor Huxley).
30   The value of the results obtained in my investigation of mental healing
is not to prove that all disease is mental, so called, because all open-
minded, thorough investigators have found this to be the case; neither is
it to prove that matter can be caused to appear and disappear, as this can
be done, and in two different ways, scientifically different. The value is to
35 show that there are two different methods of working, the right and permanent, and the wrong and temporary way. We have to prove the latter
logically, and demonstrate the former beyond all question, by instantaneous, practical results of an extraordinary and epoch-making character,[2]
which are not miraculous, but divinely natural to the enlightened spiritual
40 understanding.
    In earlier days, knowing that Jesus could not possibly create matter, it
was difficult to see how he performed his miracle of the loaves and fishes.
We know now that what he did was to destroy the thoughts that would have

---

[1] Extract from *Daily Telegraph*, December 8, 1910. The italics are not in the
45 original.
    [2] "The epoch approaches when the understanding of the truth of being will be
the basis of true religion. At present, mortals progress slowly for fear of being
thought ridiculous" (*Science and Health*, p. 67, Mary Baker Eddy).

prevented those persons present from being conscious of the ideas of God, which were seen by them as material loaves and fishes. This miracle could not have been done unless the material thoughts that were manifested as material loaves and fishes had been there; and they could not have been seen unless the real spiritual loaves and fishes, which were counterfeited 5 humanly or materially, had existed in the real world, heaven, heaven being here right at hand.

Some honest workers, using right methods, but not yet having perceived the fundamentally illusive nature of matter, have criticised these statements, saying that working in the right way matter cannot be made to appear and 10 disappear. I have had probably over one hundred cases which have been brought about solely by the realisation of God and His manifestation, and many other students, working in the right way, are obtaining like results. Probably the greatest of the miracles of Jesus was the demonstration over sense limitations which resulted in the disappearance of the ship, his dis- 15 ciples, and himself in the middle of the lake of Gennesaret, and their appearance at the shore. "Immediately the ship was at the land whither they went" (John 6:21). I have only had one undoubted case of this nature, and one doubtful one. These were of no importance, except as illustrating the action of a great Principle at work. In both instances only the body was 20 moved, and it was protected from danger. The thought that came was, "There is nothing but God." This thought came instantly and spontan-eously, without any preliminary recognition that treatment was necessary.

"There is Nothing but God."—This truth, which naturally includes the statement, "and His manifestation," is the quickest, simplest, and 25 greatest of all denials and affirmations, and its effect on matter is in pro-portion to one's knowledge of the greatness of the statement.

It is this realisation that, when thought by sufficient people, brings about the so-called end of the world, namely, the end of all matter.

Two Methods of Working.—"I am not without hope that a truly 30 scientific system of psycho-therapeutics may eventually be evolved, which will harmonise all the facts of human experience that pertain to the subject-matter" (T. J. Hudson).

Early in my investigation the accuracy of the statement that growths such as cancer could be caused to disappear instantly by two absolutely 35 different methods became evident.

There are probably fifty or sixty different sects of what have been called "mental" workers, who claim to be able to heal and do what are called miracles of various kinds. They are divided into two broad classes. Not more than five, at the outside, work in the way that the Master-meta- 40 physician taught us, as shown in the Bible, namely, by turning in thought to God and heaven. The rest picture out what they consider is best for themselves, or for the person for whom they are working, and then dwell persistently on it to bring about the visible manifestation. This is absolutely wrong. It is practically impossible to tell what is best or even what is really 45 good for ourselves or for others. All the sects say, "Stop wrong thinking." Where they differ is in the thoughts they entertain after they have turned from the wrong thought; as naturally, if the outlook be not filled with some

good thought, wrong thoughts will appear—"seven other spirits more
wicked" (Luke 11:26)—whereas if only you stop picturing falsely and
think in the way now shown, the difficulty will always disappear, and what
is commonly called a miracle take place.

5 .   The basis on which the fifty-five sects work is what may be called knowing a lie; and if a man is a strong enough "picturer," or, to put it in other
words, if he is enough of a hypnotist, he can cause the cancer to disappear instantly by knowing a lie, namely, forcing himself into picturing
that there is no cancer in the place where materially it appears to be. This
10 is working solely with matter, and cannot be the right method. Jesus said:
". . . And ye shall know the truth, and the truth shall make you free"
(John 8:32). And, again, "God is Spirit [R.V. marginal]: and they that
worship him must worship him in spirit and in truth" (John 4:24). It has
been demonstrably proved that those who work by turning in thought to
15 God can also cause a cancer to disappear instantly, by knowing the truth,
namely, that there is no cancer in God, or on the real man, the four-
dimensional, spiritual man, the individualisation of the Christ, who dwells
not in flesh. "To-day the healing power of Truth is widely demonstrated
as an immanent, eternal Science, instead of a phenomenal exhibition"
20 (Mary Baker Eddy in *Science and Health*, p. 150).

Alteration of Electrical Tension.—This puzzled me for some
time until it became clear that, working in the wrong way above explained,
the tension of the lines of force was merely altered and they were not
destroyed by this material working; consequently, although the millions
25 of electrons which were massed up together in the form of cancer disappeared, the (apparent) lines of force remained. These lines of force in
about three months' time are manifested again in some form of trouble,
and the reason why this has not been recognised before is because sometimes they take form as the same disease, sometimes another form of
30 disease, and in some cases even a form of sin. In every case inquired into,
where the apparent action had been directly hypnotic, the new trouble was
found to be worse than the old.

We have to recognise that there are many examples in the Bible of the
wrong method of prayer; for instance, the tearing of the forty-two children
35 by she-bears when Elisha [1] was mocked (II Kings 2:23, 24).

In most of the few sects who work by turning in thought to God, such
turning in thought goes no deeper than a mere faith, which, while resulting
in temporary palliation, must deepen into understanding before invariably
good results can be obtained and the many varied forms of evil be unfail-
40 ingly destroyed.

[1] There was a great lack of spirituality in Elisha; for instance, he only asked for
a double portion of the spirit of Elijah (verse 9). It is not surprising therefore that
he smote the river Jordan with the mantle of Elijah, and said: "Where is the Lord
God of Elijah?" (verse 14), and that the sons of the prophets said: "The spirit of
45 Elijah [not the spirit of the Lord] doth rest on Elisha" (verse 15). It is a very great
question whether he did not raise the son of the great woman of Shunem with the
human mind, after lying upon him and warming him with his own body (2 Kings
4:34) after he had failed to raise him from a distance (verse 31). In the Bible we see
that many who afterwards obtained great power of prayer by the realisation of God
50 commenced by using the human mind. A notable instance is that of Moses.

The reason for the disappearance of, say, a cancer, and the development of something else when the apparent healing is done the wrong way, can be more easily understood when the fifth fundamental principle of the material world, given by the advanced scientific worker, Dr. Le Bon, already referred to, is recognised, namely: "5. Force and matter are two different forms of one and the same thing." His eighth fundamental principle shows why it is possible to heal in a scientific way so that there is no return. It is as follows: "8. Energy is no more indestructible than the matter from which it emanates." The lines of force or so-called energy being destroyed, no trouble can arise therefrom in the future.

Short-Circuiting Particles.—Working in the right way, as explained, the seeming "lines of force" or thoughts of which the ether is composed are short-circuited, alias reduced to nothing (that is, what even a natural scientist would call nothing) by the action of God, Truth. They destroy themselves by the negative and positive portion of each thought-germ acting upon the positive and negative portion of the adjacent thought-germs, of which the line of force is composed, so that these particles being self-destroyed, there are no longer any lines of force to roll up into any discordant form, or to cause trouble by any different vibration, a negative form of good having been replaced by a better belief.

Reappearance of the Disease.—Another thing that puzzled me, however, was that sometimes even when a person had been healed in the scientific way by turning in thought to God, the trouble seemed to return. The longest interval known to me was twelve years. The purification of the "mind" is necessary for permanent healing.

In the subconcious "mind" of the material man every sin and every disease has, what, *for purpose of simplicity, may be called its cell*. If the cells are clean, nothing can cause them to vibrate; for instance, supposing the anger cell to be quite clean, no angry thought can possibly make that man angry, and even if a million people try to hypnotise him into being angry, the intensification of the thoughts that takes place cannot have the slightest effect, as the anger cell is incapable of vibrating with the vibration which apparently produces anger.

Hypnotists have discovered this, and claim that by hypnotism a man cannot be made to do a thing that he would not do under ordinary circumstances. This is incorrect. If a man's "consciousness" is fairly right, no ordinary thought will have any appreciable effect, and he will not sin in that particular way. When he is hypnotised, however, unless the particular cell in question is perfectly clean, the wrong thoughts may be so intensified that, entirely against his inclination and will, he may commit the sin referred to. This is only one of the many dangers of hypnotism.

When the cells are all clean the mortal merely suffers from a sense of limitation, and may be called a "sinless, though limited, human consciousness."

The ether or sum total of material consciousness consists of so-called lines of force, apparently infinite in number and in terms of so-called space, at right angles to each other, each of these lines of force or thoughts assisting to produce a different effect. One, for instance, that of anger,

another smallpox, a third fever, a fourth depression, and so on. This, as
has already been pointed out, is only because, being like Marconi waves,
they have different vibrations. If, therefore, any particular cell in the subconscious or lower "no-mind" is not clean, and an apparent thought or line
5 of force, powerful enough to cause it to vibrate, should sweep over it, the
cell will vibrate, and the man will have the temptation to sin or be ill,
miserable, or wearied, as the case may be. The thought may not be intense
enough to cause the cell to vibrate synchronously, but may be accentuated
by the wrong "thinking" of others, or by the person's own "thinking"
10 of evil. If you continue dwelling upon the thought, the trouble becomes
intensified: "Behold, I will bring evil upon this people, even the fruit of
their thoughts, because they have not hearkened unto my words, nor to my
law" (Jer. 6:19)—the law of good.

What are called bad thoughts are low vibrations, and what are called
15 good thoughts, high vibrations. All material thought is, however, more or
less bad. Nothing in the material world is perfect. Only God's ideas are
perfect. Good is absolute, evil is relative and in all its degrees illusive.

Synchronous Vibration.—The reason why with some people the
anger cell, for instance, will respond and vibrate in unison with the angry
20 thought, is that it is tuned synchronously, owing to the condition of the
"consciousness" at birth, the result of false mortal beliefs. If ever a human
being is unfortunate enough to be born with sufficient small ultimate
particles on the surface of the typhoid "cell," or "vibrating diaphragm,"
every time a typhoid thought appears to touch him, the cell will vibrate in
25 unison with it, and he will have typhoid. If the typhoid cell is clean it will
have no effect. If he "thinks" that he is, or others are, going to have
typhoid, he is intensifying the typhoid vibrations, making them more likely
to appear real to him or them. When you know how to think rightly,
the action of God, as you realise the truth (the affirmation), purifies the
30 human individual, that is, cleanses the cells by causing the particles, which
are electrical, to short-circuit each other. In this way we can get rid of every
so-called hereditary or other evil.

The Beam in the Eye.—The would-be metaphysician may wonder
at this way of presenting the so-called facts. He must remember that the
35 materialist requires to be led along a path that he understands. He must
also recollect that his view of matter is just as untrue as that of the scientific
man, for there is no material consciousness, no human thoughts, no sin nor
sickness, nothing but God and God's ideas.

Startling Home Truths.—Every time a man states anything false
40 to be a fact, it becomes more apparently tangible to the five senses. If
someone, hearing the fallacious statement, agrees, it becomes far more
tangible, and if a number of persons hearing, also accept the statement as
true, the mischief done to each and all is incalculable. Now, if a man says
in a public place: "Sin is an unavoidable inheritance, and no man can
45 attain to sinlessness," the result is devilish; he is leading each one straight
into the committal of his besetting sin. If he says: "All must die," he is
practically preparing a future coffin for each of his hearers. If some have
symptoms of illness causing them anxiety, such a statement is quite enough

to cause fatal developments. If he advocates intelligent preparation for a
future death, he is conducting his assenting hearers as on the wings of the
wind towards that death. A sermon preached on such lines is more deadly
in its effects upon the attentive and devout listener than any newspaper
article ever written. Well may the prophet scientist of centuries ago cry 5
aloud to a hypnotised nation: "Turn ye, turn ye from your evil ways; for
why will ye die?" (Ezek. 33:11). "Awake thou that sleepest" (Eph. 5:14);
words re-echoed by the world's greatest prophetess, Mary Baker Eddy,
who adds: "and awaken the world." Never has there been such need of this
warning as to-day, when the power of mental and so-called mental action 10
is becoming understood by an awakening world, the latter bringing proportionately more alarming results.

Sin and Its Punishment.—"*Success or failure in a practitioner often
depends as much on his expertness in moral treatment as on his skill in simples*"
(Sir J. Crichton-Browne).   15
It has always been well understood that glaring forms of sin inevitably
lead to disease if persisted in. It has only recently, however, been discovered that there is a far more intimate relationship between sin of every
kind and disease than has ever been dreamed of by mankind. When, as
Professor Elmer Gates has shown us, even an angry thought creates harm- 20
ful poison in the system, it is not surprising to find that every wrong
thought of every kind creates physical trouble. Sooner or later, "Be sure
your sin will find you out" (Num. 32:23). It is only the mystery underlying
disease that has prevented its disappearance long ago. If one hour of hatred
can produce sufficient poison to kill eighty men, as Professor Gates has 25
shown experimentally, just think for one moment of the appalling result
to poor humanity of an international war. We recoil from this picture of
needless suffering.
"Medical science has never grasped—never perhaps set itself to grasp—
the intimate connection between moral fault and disease. . . . The 30
bringer of light and happiness, the calmer and pacifier, or investigator and
stimulator, is one of the chiefest of doctors. Such a doctor was Jesus"
(Matthew Arnold in *Literature and Dogma*).

The Freeing from Sin.—"*As a rule, ignorance is the mother of wickedness, and wisdom the mother of goodness*" [1] (H. Weinstock).   35
It is fortunate that in most cases of sin, at least seventy-five per cent. of
the trouble is over when a man has seen that the sin in the past has not
been his fault, but his misfortune. The other twenty-five per cent. goes
when he sees that wrong thought brings sin, and sin must bring unhappiness. Understanding that he is a perfect spiritual being, he then ceases 40
his wrong "picturing," and thinks rightly. He is then free from further
punishment for the past sin. "You must rouse in men a consciousness of
their own prudence and strength if you wish to raise their character"
(Vauvenargues). "Philo taught that where the Logos had not stirred in a
man there was no moral responsibility" [2] (Archdeacon Wilberforce). 45

---

[1] Sermon on *The Jewish Idea of God*, preached in the Jewish Synagogue in
Sacramento, 1902.
[2] *Mystic Immanence*.

8

"We will not sin, knowing that we are counted thine" (Wisdom of
Solomon, 15:2).

The punishment for sin is removed only as the sin is discontinued. The
human is never punished after sin is removed. The punishment can only
5 affect you through false "picturing." When you know the sin has no power,
as it has no existence, the sin and its punishment are removed for ever.
This is the only forgiveness of sin.

If a sinner can only reverse every thought of his sin as it comes into his
so-called mind, he *must*, sooner or later, get rid of his sin, as the action
10 of God is continually purifying his mind. "For the law of the Spirit of life
in Christ Jesus hath made me free from the law of sin and death" (Rom.
8:2). The less he dwells on his sin the better it is for him. Remember, it
is not his fault. He never made his so-called mind. He never made the
thoughts that attack him. It is not his fault, it is his misfortune. It is he
15 that suffers, not you, therefore do not add to his difficulties by speaking
of them or even thinking of them. "When thou art beginning to correct
an evil habit, though thou shouldest transgress thy law a first, a second, a
third, nay, a twentieth time, do not despair, but rise up again, and resume
the same diligence, and thou shalt surely prevail" (St. Chrysostom).
20 "Our greatest glory is, not in never falling, but in rising every time we
fall" (Confucius).

The Way of Escape.—

> "*Endeavour to be good, and better still, and best;*
> *Success is nought—endeavour's all*" (Robert Browning).

25   The human being will be saved when reason, "the most active human
faculty," awakens man's sense of moral obligation, and shows him that
sinning brings no happiness, but merely trouble. "Success in sin is down-
right defeat" (Mary Baker Eddy). Further, that the only way of escaping
punishment is to stop sinning, and the only way to stop sinning is to stop
30 wrong "thinking." Then the glories of heaven grow clearer and the
millennium dawns.

Now that fallacious hypotheses, to which an apathetic general consent
has for ages been given, have been discovered to be mistakes, it is obvious
that the time has arrived, which has been foretold by the greatest of the
35 world's metaphysicians of modern times, Mary Baker Eddy, in the following words of wisdom: "When needed tell the truth concerning the lie."
In these words rests the inspiration of what is being stated.

I am inclined to think that the only absolute proof to a sceptic of the
truth of what is now put before you is this power of getting rid of sin. As
40 far as I am aware, I have never had a case of a person coming for help over
a besetting sin, where the result has not been instantaneous, and the victim
has gone on his way rejoicing.[1] In some cases this result has taken place
when the sinner was miles away. In others he was personally unknown,

---

[1] Since this was written I have had one failure. In this case the applicant did not
45 tell me what the sin was, and was shot two or three days after he applied, before I
discovered (what I think was the case) that he was being hypnotically forced into
the sin by other people. In a case of this sort one has chiefly to destroy the hypnotic
thoughts attacking the other people, and free the victim.

but his trouble was spoken of. As far as I know, the healing has been permanent. In one, perhaps two, cases there has been a slight relapse, but that merely temporary. In no case has the individual asked for help more than three times in all. Where the sickness has been due to sin, or the patient has not asked for the removal of the sin, sometimes the fight has been pro- 5 tracted. But the sin must go if the work is continued, as the result is due to the action of God. When the sin goes it will be found that the sickness has gone. "Whosesoever sins ye remit, they are remitted unto them" (John 20:23). "For this purpose the Son of God was manifested, that he might destroy the works of the devil" (I John 3:8). 10

"Greater Works."[1]—To change the thoughts of the mass of mankind from dwelling upon evil, and even from a fatal contemplation of a material world, with its false laws of imagined necessities, to the true thoughts of the allness of good as the law of all cause and effect, the living Principle of existence, is the greatest of all work to be done to-day. 15

THE EVOLUTION OF PRAYER

" Prayer is the soul's sincere desire,
Uttered or unexpressed;
The motion of a hidden fire
That trembles in the breast" (James Montgomery). 20

As with everything else in this self-destructive material world, there has, fortunately, been a steady continual evolution in prayer. Archdeacon Wilberforce, in *There is no Death*, quotes the following :—

"God is God from the creation,
Truth alone is man's salvation, 25
But the God that now you worship,
Soon shall be your God no more;
For the soul in its unfolding,
Ever more its thought remoulding,
Learns more truly in its progress 30
How to love and to adore."

The attenuated answers to prayer have been as a rule merely the result of human "picturing," and there are many statements in the Bible showing the result of this so-called thinking. Jesus made this perfectly clear, and his enunciation of the so-called law is repeated at least five times: Luke 35 17, verse 6; Matthew 17, verse 20; Matthew 21, verses 21, 22; Mark 9, verse 23; and 11, verse 23.

Material Gods.—In olden times man worshipped a multiplicity of gods—constellations, fire, earth, air, or water, animals, even so-called inanimate objects, such as trees and plants, which ultimately evolved into 40 the worship of relics, pictures, etc. These ancient gods had usually the ordinary characteristics of the human race, and were both so-called good and evil. The same gods are still believed to have power over man, as is testified to, every time anyone says, "The fire burns me," "the earth can bury out of sight," "the air stifles," "water drowns," "the trees crush," 45

[1] See John 14, verse 12.

"the plant poisons," "the relics heal," "the pictures delight me." Whether man's prayers were answered, simply depended upon the belief of the suppliant in the result of his prayer. This is still the case with mistaken prayers.

5 This worship was classified under three heads: (1) mere adoration or prostration in token of submission; (2) asking, sometimes as a favour, sometimes as a right; (3) definite action, sometimes involving gifts, sometimes merely sacrifice of time or position with the object of currying favour. The material forms of bowing down to these false gods can now be finally,
10 because scientifically, destroyed.

Semi-human Gods.—Semi-human gods were merely a kind of human being with supposed divine powers, for instance Jehovah, a jealous god of hate and of love, who revenged himself on his enemies; the heathen gods of mythology, such as Moloch, Jupiter, and their counterparts in
15 Eastern countries.

Their worship was usually in two forms: (1) asking as a favour or in return for some act of homage; (2) acts which usually took the form of sacrifice, sometimes of human beings, sometimes of animals, and sometimes merely the laying of gifts on the altar with the object of propitiating
20 the deity and preventing it harming the suppliant. These gifts were usually taken for the priests' use.

When official Christianity took the place of paganism, the so-called Christians worshipped saints and other human beings, some dead, some alive. They even went back to their inanimate gods, and worshipped bones,
25 relics, pictures, etc. The belief in such gods led to the tyranny, intolerance, and bloodshed that disgraced the Christian religion in the Middle Ages.

Anthropomorphic God.—This, the god of the nineteenth century, had not lost the human qualities which tainted the ideas of the early barbarians, and was very little better than the idea of the god that
30 appreciated the prayers ground out in a praying-machine in the East. According to our forefathers, God was a revengeful god, and not only slew Saul and many others, but required a human sacrifice in the shape of His "dearly beloved Son, Christ Jesus." In addition, He did not always hear the suppliants, and used evil as a method of making people good, even if
35 He did not use it as a means of punishing the beings He was believed to have so inefficiently created that they were capable of, and in fact could not help, sinning. He is even said to have foretold that people were going to sin, and then eternally punished them for what they could not help doing. Many, indeed, believed that He created evil, taking literally Isaiah's words
40 in chapter 45, verse 7, "I . . . create evil," not discerning its spiritual or scientific interpretation. They failed to see that when the action of God leads to an understanding of what constitutes sin, often that which seemed good to the unenlightened thought, is recognised as evil and thus becomes wilful sin.

45 So, in the period of systematic destruction of the material misconception, the human ideal, always rising and continually reaching out to this higher standard, eventually ultimates in total elimination, not only of sin, but of every false belief, and, finally, of every belief in limitation.

The One God.—"*The effectual fervent prayer of a righteous man availeth much*" (James 5:16).

The worship of the one God, although closely allied to the anthropomorphic god, is of a higher order :—

(1) Asking, the prayer being answered if the human belief in the response was sufficient. This form of prayer is dangerous, and to my personal knowledge has led to many serious troubles, physical, so-called "mental," and moral, due to the suppliant forming his own concept of the material results to ensue. Without irreverence, we may call this teaching God His business. "We know not what we should pray for as we ought" (Rom. 8:26). "For who knoweth what is good for man in this life?" (Eccles. 6:12). "Your Father knoweth what things ye have need of, before ye ask him" (Matt. 6:8).

When a man says : "Please God take away my headache," if he thinks of God his headache is very slightly diminished. When he says, "take away my headache," it is made worse by his thinking that he has a headache, and so intensifying the thought. When, however, he thought of God, he was permanently a little less liable to headaches, whereas the intensification was only temporary and did no permanent harm. If he thinks strongly enough that the headache is going, there is a hypnotic effect reducing the headache. This is of no permanent value.

A well-known leader in the religious world told me that numerous men of the highest possible moral character, having given up their lives to religious teaching, had absolutely "gone to the devil" through the belief that they were being led by God in response to their prayers, by which they had ignorantly brought about their own personal desires. How can a method of prayer that leads to such results possibly be right? It was easy to explain the essential difference of realising that the real or spiritual man is always led by God, and that the material counterfeit man cannot be, as it is always "of the devil," however good it may appear to be.

(2) Asking and believing that the prayer would only be answered if it were good for the individual or institution prayed for. This, the way in which a great many orthodox Christians of the earnest thinking type pray, is a great step in advance, and if a man could eliminate the preliminary recognition of the evil it would be a safe though limited method. It, however, "brings the seeker into closer proximity with divine Love," [1] and is one of the foundation stones upon which our loved English Church has been built, and by means of which it has weathered the storms with which evil has endeavoured to wreck it. The steadily advancing tide of enlightened thought is now leading the Church out of its early stages into the infinite unfoldment of an ever-present God.

(3) Contemplation of God. This contemplation of higher ideals marked again a great step and has led to many beautiful results. "The Spirit itself maketh intercession for us" (Rom. 8:26). Many evidences of the value of

---

[1] Mary Baker Eddy.

this form of prayer are found in the lives of the mystics and such men as
Brother Lawrence and St. Francis of Assisi. "Let all our employment be
to know God. . . . He is with us; seek Him not elsewhere" (Brother
Lawrence, Fifteenth Letter).

5   "*When a man turns toward God* the thick cloud of error which deprived
him of vision is quickly withdrawn from before him . . . truth uses the
word as a goad, and smites the slumberers and awakens them, and when
they are awake they look at the truth and also understand it; they hear and
distinguish *that which is, from that which is not* . . . let not that which is
10   only made be put in by thee in the place of him who is not made, but let
him, the everliving God, *be constantly present to thy mind* . . . why the
body exists, and why it falls to decay, and why it continues, thou canst not
know until thou hast raised thy head from this sleep in which thou hast
sunk, and hast opened thine eyes and seen that God is one. . . . Therefore
15   (it is that) thou dost wallow on the ground before demons *and shadows*,
and asketh vain petitions from that which has not anything to give"
(Melito to Antonius Cæsar, about A.D. 150). The italics are not in the
original.

The One True God.—"*As soon as we are with God in faith and love,*
20   *we are in prayer*" (Fénélon).

Lastly we come to the worship of the one true God, the God of whom
to think is a revelation of celestial bliss, when we begin to understand Him.
Even here we must differentiate our prayers, because at the present time
there are three different degrees of this method of prayer, all good and
25   effective, but differing very appreciably in results.

(1) Meditation on God. We have learnt that contemplation, "looking
attentively," is not sufficient; we have to meditate or "consider
thoroughly" and let our understanding of God lead to the knowledge of
God that is eternal life. "This is life eternal, that they might know thee
30   the only true God" (John 17:3). Millions of earnest men and women of
differing religious beliefs are now striving daily to obtain the highest knowledge of God that they know is necessary, and thereby daily obtaining
answers to their prayers.

(2) Affirmation of truth. Hundreds of thousands of these have advanced
35   beyond meditation to affirmation; that is, knowing that they are spiritual
beings in heaven now, and claiming their God-given birthright, their
freedom from sin, sickness, worries, and troubles of every kind, their
spiritual at-one-ment or unity with God that Jesus persistently taught.
This, whilst benefiting the individual, is a comparatively selfish form of
40   prayer, and the evolution of sufficient purity was necessary to fit man to
receive the revelation that came to the world forty-four years ago. Jesus
said, nearly two thousand years ago: "I have yet many things to say unto
you, but ye cannot bear them now" (John 16:12).

(3) The denial and affirmation. Man now wields the two-edged sword
45   of Truth, and so becomes a clearer channel through which God acts instantly
a channel for—the denial, symbolised in the Bible as the Angel Michael,

which is the destruction of evil, and the affirmation or realisation, as the
Angel Gabriel, which results in the purification of the human consciousness, whereby it becomes a still clearer channel for the denial of evil, or
action of God in bringing the so-called material world to an end.

When we know how thus to pray, we have to "watch and pray," and 5
"pray without ceasing." That is, the thoughts have to be watched with the
alertness of a faithful watch-dog guarding a house. Every wrong thought
has to be pounced upon and reversed. Every time we do this it becomes
easier. "And many strokes, though with a little axe, Hew down and fell
the hardest-timbered oak" (Shakespeare). 10

We must not do this from a material standpoint. We have to live in
the presence of God, to be continually thinking of the perfect world that
is here around us. Continually think of the perfect God and His perfect
action; dwell with reverential thought on God as Mind and all things as
being good and spiritual. Lose all sense of material self in the realisation 15
of the spiritual selfhood of God, and thus become a channel through which
God works. Our progress depends upon the number of seconds during the
twenty-four hours in which we are so realising Truth, and in this way, and
this way only, by deep, holy, systematic thinking, do we reach an ever-
fuller realisation of the kingdom of heaven. 20

"Ye are not yet out of gunshot, . . . set your faces like a flint, for
you have all powers in heaven and on earth on your side" (John Bunyan).
An ecclesiastical leader, in a letter to me, writes: "The night of
materialism is far spent, and the dawn of the new heaven and the new
earth is breaking; but we may hasten the coming of the day of God, if, 25
amid the delusions of the present, we live in, and affirm, the eternal and
divine." "He that believeth on me [the Christ], the works that I do shall
he do also; and greater works than these shall he do; because I go unto my
Father" (John 14:12), and yet as Mr. Edward Kimball has said: "Our
race appears to be one long monotone of petition to God and everything 30
else, in order that it may be delivered." Can it be pretended that in the
past we have understood the teachings of Jesus the Christ?

FAITH-HEALING

"*Paracelsus made a broader discovery than that* [of mental effect] *three
hundred years before Braid was born; for he distinctly intimated that a false* 35
*belief, however induced, is just as efficacious for therapeutic purposes as a true
one—'Faith' being the sole condition precedent; and Pomponazzi, in the
sixteenth century, gave utterance to an expression of identical import*" [1]
(T. J. Hudson).

Sir Clifford Allbutt, K.C.B., M.D., F.R.S., Regius Professor of Physic, 40
University of Cambridge, writes: "It is true, no doubt, that the solitary
and disconsolate heart, closed to common circumstance, may be more
susceptible to other appeals, may offer less resistance; so that, as we have

[1] *The Law of Mental Medicine.*

seen, unknown wells of energy may be tapped and fading and vacillating forces replenished. Then it is that the influence of a clerical minister, of a gentle friend or Bible-woman—brief angels' visits lifting up human hope and love into Divine love—may be twice blessed, blessed materially and 5 spiritually. But even then the physician can take no active part in hypnotising the smitten sufferer with promises of corporeal repair. Indeed, in the more formal spiritual ministrations his part can never be direct; they are not obviously his business, and even a religious patient resents the divided mind. Notwithstanding, the sick man does feel dimly that diagnosis limited 10 to material phenomena is imperfect; that its insight ought to penetrate to mental and spiritual, as well as to bodily conditions; and he would say, did he know how, Do you understand *me*, or am I only a case? This seems to be our modest part in faith-healing; and with it these reflections must end. How tentative and inconclusive they are no one is more painfully 15 aware than the writer himself." [1]

Faith-healing, in its attenuated and merely temporary postponements or interchange of evil, is very far from the healing done by the action of God, when a man has learned to think rightly. Faith without knowledge has to be greatly increased and deepened through understanding of divine 20 working, and the nature of infinite Life.

A consulting physician of Harley Street, probably the leading medical authority on the so-called human "mind," a man of deep religious conviction, invited me to go to his house one afternoon, to meet about a dozen of the leading faith-healers, or, as he called them, spiritual healers, with a 25 view to helping them.

He commenced by saying he had found that faith-healing was done all over the world, by faith in God,[2] drugs, doctors, massage, mental suggestion, hypnotism, hydropathy, electricity, electric light, X-rays, radium, coloured light, relics, holy wells, amulets, and even incantations to devils. 30 As far as he could tell there was no difference between the healing done by these different faiths, and, in fact, at one end of Lake Zürich there was an establishment where they healed by incantations to devils and at the other end they healed by prayer to God, and he thought that the healing done at the devil end of the lake was, if anything, the better of the two. The records 35 were certainly better kept.

He then said: "Does this mean that all this healing is due to the action of God?" No one answered him, and he turned to me asking if any difference could be pointed out.

My reply was that if anyone was ill, and if either the patient or another 40 person stopped wrong "thinking," and "pictured" a lie strongly enough, namely, forced himself into sufficiently outlining the material patient as well, the sufferer would appear to be well instantly, and he could precede that knowing by asking God or by incantations to devils. Neither had anything to do with the apparent healing, as the action was solely due to the 45 human thoughts of a material man as being well, and was therefore purely hypnotic, and of no permanent value. Nearly all supplicatory prayer is of

---

[1] "Reflections on Faith Healing" (*British Medical Journal*, June 18, 1910).
[2] This doctor has stated that there were in England over a hundred centres for healing by faith in God.

this character, and often harms the individual, so certain is the one praying of the existence of the trouble prayed against, and so persistently does he dwell upon it. "Then shall his mind change, and he shall pass over, and offend, imputing this his power unto his god" (Hab. 1:11).

Return of Trouble.—The above is not true healing. Although the person may appear to be well, in about three months some other trouble arises. The reason why this was not previously known is because sometimes the same disease comes back, sometimes another, and sometimes even a form of sin.

I then told how a well-known doctor, who had been for some time trying to heal by prayer, had come to me for advice in a case of cancer. Before he told me anything of the case, I gave him the results of my investigation into the method of healing in the way that he was working, that is, by asking God to remove the cancer. This was to give him confidence, as an accurate statement of so-called facts must necessarily invariably be found consistent with so-called human experience. I told him that, working in the way he did, he could get rid of cancer, but that about three months later trouble would come; either cancer would reappear, or the patient would suffer from another form of disease, such as boils, or even a form of sin, such as anger. He then said: "Why, that is extraordinary, I will tell you what has happened. I got rid of the cancer, and three months afterwards it came back. I got rid of it again, just three months ago. Now read the letter just received from the husband of my patient." This letter was to the effect that the cancer had not come back, but that the wife had developed fits of anger so bad that they practically amounted to mania. He said that he could not keep her in the house, and asked what was to be done.

Saint Teresa regarded the "ecstasies" in which the apparent healing so often took place, as one of the chief perils of conventual life, when as Sir Clifford Allbutt says, "the domination of a stronger will—a 'magnetic personality'—often prevails." Quite correctly she said: "Suspect everything which weakens the use of our reason, for by such a way we shall never attain to the liberty of the spirit."

The Harley Street physician I have referred to admitted that every disease could be imitated by the action of the nerves—an action called "nerve mimicry." The real fact is that all diseases are ethereal, what may be called "non-mental," and are sensibly manifested in numberless grades of beliefs and combinations of symptoms, which depend upon the persistency with which the idea of them is regarded (1) by the individual, (2) by the general thought. Those believed to be the result of mimetic action are more faintly outlined, and consequently very slight mental action will cause them to disappear. Ordinary diseases are deeper seated and require more work. Soon, however, even the worst cases will respond instantaneously. Unfortunately, at the same time evil thoughts will have more apparent reality. This is when the general view of the subject has somewhat changed, and the power of thought is recognised. Then instead of the evil being chained round mortals by the universal belief, the wonder will be if it should not at once disappear when they turn in thought to God.

No Real Healing with the Human So-called "Mind."—Jesus
8*

made it clear that there is no real healing by means of false mentality. In
the 11th chapter of Luke, he points out that he could not cast out devils
through Beelzebub, because "if Satan also be divided against himself, how
shall his kingdom stand?" [1] but "when a strong man armed keepeth his
palace, his goods are in peace." That is to say, a determined thinker will
temporarily protect himself, "But when a stronger than he shall come upon
him," meaning that when a strong "thinker" has evil "thoughts" about
him, "he taketh from him all his armour wherein he trusted," or, more
literally, he seems to have lost his power of thinking good thoughts. "When
the unclean spirit is gone out of a man"—that is to say, when by hypnotic
action a man appears to be well—the unclean spirit "taketh to him seven
other spirits more wicked than himself; and they enter in, and dwell there:
and the last state of that man is worse than the first" (Luke 11:18, 21, 22,
24, 26). This, as has just been pointed out, is what actually takes place, and
this is the danger that is now coming upon the world.

It is only when a man has learnt how to pray scientifically, and lives his
scientific religion, that it becomes possible, and indeed quite easy, to protect himself against any hypnotic attack.

Supplicatory Prayer.—"*Whosoever shall say unto this mountain,
Be thou removed, and be thou cast into the sea; and shall not doubt in his
heart, but shall believe that those things which he saith shall come to pass; he
shall have whatsoever he saith*" (Mark 11:23).

The only result obtained by supplicatory prayer, when no realisation
of God takes place, is produced by strongly "thinking" during or after
the prayer is finished, that the thing desired has or must shortly come to
pass. The former is simply picturing lies, the latter is an attempt to teach
God, the Principle of all good, what is good. Any result is solely due to
the action of material thoughts, and can only be produced by persons with a
false mentality of a certain class, the kind that can easily bring about direct
hypnotic results. This is not only useless, but does harm to a man. "Faith
produces miracles, and whether it be true or false faith, it will always produce the same wonders" (Paracelsus).

For this reason, were it not for the fact that some religious people
fortunately pray by fervent realisation of a spiritual existence—the
Quakers in olden days, for instance—the prayers for the sick in church
would, even more often than at present, be the death-knell of the patient.
The habit of intense realisation of God is one of the reasons why there
have been many wonderful answers to prayer in the past.

If we merely ask of God, this asking must imply more or less a doubt
as to whether our prayer is likely to be answered. In fact, the highest
form of supplicatory prayer is to ask God to grant our petition "if it be
good for us." This must imply either a want of knowledge on our part of
what "good" is, or a doubt as to God's intention to help us. In any case,
it is presuming to suggest to a personal God what is the best thing to be
done; suggesting to absolute good, a living, omnipresent Principle, what
good is; from the standpoint of imperfection defining perfection.

---

[1] When Satan is divided against himself, namely, when the human consciousness
recognises the fallacy of its own supposed law, the law no longer acts.

Now that the truth is known, it seems strange indeed, on looking back, that, considering the marvellous purity and ability of many thinkers in the past, mankind has hitherto failed to grasp the fact that all we have to do is to know that we have absolute good around us, and that this good is spiritual and heavenly. The inevitable conclusion that all is Mind, and mental, and anything else that may appear to exist is material illusion, must have followed directly men began habitually to get the results which must have inevitably followed from this correct method of prayer—the soul's communion with God. " God, Thou art Mind !" (Robert Browning).

Individual results are now being obtained, indeed, to an extent little believed. But when the general change of "consciousness" that is close at hand brings in, as it must, accumulative results, all will be forced to acknowledge truth and find that true science and health are coincident and eternal.

Suggestion.—Apparent healing can be done also by human suggestion, of which there are three kinds—audible suggestion, "mental" suggestion, and auto-suggestion, all unscientific and of no permanent value. You must differentiate these cases where the trouble arises from the constant conscious picturing by a person that he has a certain disease. Should he stop this wrong picturing, but neglect to realise the affirmation of truth, the disease, in the cases where the beliefs causing it are not very vivid, will disappear, or diminish, in proportion as he stops intensifying them; but this is not true healing, as the trouble is liable at any time to return, when thoughts of the same kind, and apparently vivid enough to affect the person, attack him.

Sir Francis Cruise, M.D., has given the following saying of a great Irish physician : " Remember that to inspire a patient with hope and confidence is as valuable a stimulus towards recovery as half the drugs in the Pharmacopæia," and adds, " Now that I am old, I understand how right and wise he was. This was treatment by *suggestion*." [1] This class of suggestion is harmless, as it is merely getting the patient to cease intensifying the cause of the disease. Cures by suggestion are admitted by medical authorities not to be of a permanent character.[2]

Dr. Frederick Van Eeden, in *World's Work* of September, 1909, gives a good many particulars of apparent cure by suggestion, amongst others, that effected by Professor Hirt, the nerve specialist, of Breslau, in 1890, on the son of Professor Dr. Klopsch. Professor Hirt used the method of suggestion advocated by Dr. Liebeault, and one treatment was sufficient to produce a seeming cure, although every method of medical treatment had previously been tried in vain.

Dr. Liebeault used suggestion a great deal, and when he retired, in 1891, physicians came from all parts of Europe to the dinner given in his honour. The way in which Dr. Liebeault was first treated by his academical colleagues is described by Dr. Hilger in the following way : " Though Liebeault never indulged in complaint or bitterness on account of the neglect he suffered from his academical fellow-workers, and only quietly insisted

[1] Introductory chapter to *Treatment by Hypnotism and Suggestion*.
[2] *Treatment by Hypnotism and Suggestion*, by Dr. Lloyd Tuckey.

that his results should be investigated thoroughly and without prejudice,
they had nothing for him but a contemptuous shrug of the shoulders and
shake of the head. For fourteen years the patient doctor worked on, under
neglect, contempt, and derision, until, in 1880, an old college friend of his,
5 Dr. Lorrain, visited him, and fixed the attention of Professor Bernheim on
his remarkable cures. Bernheim, who was at first as sceptical as the others,
and could hardly suppress a pitying smile at his first visit, became soon
deeply interested in what he saw, and then felt the greatest admiration for
the good and simple man who had endured for so many years the foolish
10 misjudgment of his colleagues without one word of bitterness."

The reason for this treatment by the medical profession is because they
have found by experience that this method of healing is neither scientific
nor permanent, and no more satisfactory than the so-called healing by
drugs, whilst it is extremely dangerous both to patient and practitioner.
15 At the same time a clear distinction must be drawn between mere mental
suggestion and direct hypnotic effects, the latter being much more
dangerous.

Dr. von Schrenk-Notzing has shown that some people under the
influence of hashish are as susceptible to verbal suggestion as if they were
20 under hypnotic influence.

Dr. Van Eeden, in his article, says: "As a matter of fact the doctor
never cures a disease; he enables the body to cure itself by assisting it in
the struggle against hostile influences or disturbances. Even the surgeon
does no more than remove obstacles; the cells of the body do the really
25 curative work. And in this work they are directed and assisted by what
we call the Psyche, that part of the body which is not directly perceptible
by the senses." He also writes as follows: "When I lectured in a city of the
Middle West, before an audience of university students, and reminded
them of the errors of official science, and the danger in entirely denying ·
30 the cures of quacks, instead of investigating them, a doctor stood up, white
with indignation, and said in a tremulous voice: 'Sir, you are trying to
make quacks of them all.'"

Binet, about eleven years ago, published his standard work on suggestibility. He found that, when using an impressive way of questioning, he was
35 able completely to falsify the memory of children. Of one hundred and
forty-three only two had enough independence of judgment to reply
accurately. Dr. Van Eeden, remarking upon this, writes as follows: "You
are in your turn invited to reflect on what is happening daily in courts and
in police headquarters, when some of those whose suggestibility co-
40 efficient is high—some of the ninety-eight per cent. non-resistants—are
submitted to the 'mild suggestions' of a questioning police officer, a
coroner, a judge, or a lawyer. I remember quite well that when I was a boy
of ten I was questioned into a guilt, being entirely innocent. And though it
may be true that suggestibility lessens in riper years, we may be quite sure
45 that at least fifty per cent. of the average of men retain enough of it to be
entirely unreliable as witnesses under the suggestive pressure of a head-
strong policeman, a pompous judge, or a shrewd lawyer."

He also writes as follows: "The soul of a child, and in lesser degree, of
the grown-up man, can be shaped by suggestive influence in any form; it

can be bent, crooked, twisted, adulterated—morally and mentally—to an extent depending on its degree of plasticity, its inborn original force of resistance, and the power of suggestive forces at work." The definition of suggestibility, as given by Bernheim, is "the aptitude of the mind to receive an idea, and the tendency to transform it into action."   5

The above will show how absolutely necessary it is to understand what is taking place, and to gain sufficient knowledge of the truth to be able, not only to discern between the true and the false methods of working, but to protect oneself and others against the evil effects of material thoughts unknowingly intensified by ignorant workers. I know of cases where 10 "mental" suggestion has caused innocent beginners in mental working to falsely make terrible accusations against true workers. They were practically hypnotised into believing it and incriminated themselves.

"Mental" Suggestion.[1]—The term "mental" suggestion, which is often wrongly attached to mental work of the right kind, requires a word 15 of explanation. Any putting forward of future material results, with the object of inducing these outlined results, is purely hypnotic suggestion, material means, and wholly wrong. Statements of truth, which are based on scientific fact, such as "You are absolutely well," should be put forward only when the patient has sufficient knowledge to understand thoroughly 20 the point of view from which you are speaking—namely, absolute truth. Such a statement as "You will be well to-morrow," is wrong; it also is based upon a lie—namely, that the man is ill, whereas all men are in reality spiritual and perfect. "I believe that you will be well to-morrow" is a legitimate statement when it is true. If you do not believe it you are sinning. 25 It is often unwise, as it is of the greatest importance to give the patient complete confidence, and such a prophecy unfulfilled weakens such confidence.

The only true suggestion is the holy suggestion of God's thoughts coming to man in the real world, and however clouded these may be by the human channel through which they reach mankind, they can never 30 rank as mere repetition of material thoughts, intensified by so-called human beings, to further results in a predetermined direction. These holy thoughts are "the true Light, which lighteth every man that cometh into the world" (John 1:9). "He that followeth me shall not walk in darkness" (John 8:12). "Thy word is a lamp unto my feet, and a light unto my path" (Ps. 119:105) 35 which always leads Godwards.

Most of the faith-healers reject with indignation the idea that they heal with the material "no-mind," and say the work is only done by the Christ whom they invoke, while admitting that they cannot teach others to heal, and holding it a special gift; whereas all can heal when they pray in 40 the right and scientific way. "If we were well accustomed to the exercise of the presence of God, all bodily diseases would be much alleviated thereby." "Ye should leave off human remedies . . . comfort yourself with Him, who is the only Physician of all our maladies" (Brother Lawrence, Twelfth and Thirteenth Letters).   45

[1] There can be no doubt that cures of certain kinds of diseases have been effected by . . . faith-healing cults, all of which cures come under the head of healing by suggestion" (Sydney Holland).

One test of whether a man is working with the human mind or by the power of God is whether he is tired or invigorated by his work.[1]

The Real Test.—The real test of true working is whether, as the result of the work done, sin disappears instantaneously, continually, and
5 not occasionally, from those we are helping, and without any recurrence, even of temptation. If so, you may rest assured that the change is brought about in the right and permanent way—namely, by turning in thought to God, for it can be done in no other way. "Without me ye can do nothing" (John 15:5).

10   DIVINE HEALING

"Call unto me, and I will answer thee, and shew thee great and mighty things, which thou knowest not . . . Behold, I will bring it health and cure, and I will cure them, and will reveal unto them the abundance of peace and truth" (Jer. 33:3, 6).
15   Professor Harnack has shown that the healing of sin and sickness was the vital element that underlay primitive Christianity, and was the cause of its rapid growth in its early days. Again, we have come to a stage when the exercise of the same God-given power is bringing about an extension of Christianity, inspiring and far-reaching in its results, as it ultimately
20 affects every individual member of the human race, alive or so-called dead.

The effect of healing done in the way that Jesus taught is entirely different from the results following so-called faith-healing or any form of hypnotic influence. The former is "the effect of God *understood*."[2] We cannot heal habitually in this way until we obtain a scientific knowledge of
25 God and the universe. In Wyclif's Bible the passage, "to give knowledge of salvation unto his people by the remission of their sins" (Luke 1:77), is rendered, "to give science and health to his people unto the remission of their sins."

The certainty of scientific healing constitutes its utility. Based upon a
30 demonstrable Principle, it never fails when properly practised. Although some unenlightened people sneer at divine healing, the antagonism is nothing like what it was against homœopathy about fifty years ago. Those practising it are usually honoured and respected, though sometimes laughed at and often criticised. This criticism and the abuse that now and
35 then divine healing meets are of actual advantage as an advertisement. A clergyman once came to me for information and treatment because of the marked difference in the spirit of the replies of the two classes of witnesses

---

[1] In the *Daily Telegraph* of November 7, 1913, appeared an account of the cures of a Bishop who believes that he heals by the power of God. In the first case
40 mentioned, that of Mrs. Manny, who had long suffered from abscesses on the eyes, "the Bishop put his hands on her head and prayed in silence, slowly passing his hands over her eyes. Her groans continued for a time. Then they ceased gradually, a smile flickered over her face, and grew. At last she was radiant, and sank back from the *apparently exhausted* prelate. Her face was expressive of relief." The newspaper
45 report continues: "After six 'cures' other people pressed forward; but Bishop — said it was *exhausting work*, and he felt too tired for more 'cures' that day. Incidentally, he denounced some other faith-healers as seekers of notoriety and impostors."

[2] *Christian Science versus Pantheism* (Mary Baker Eddy).

in a legal inquiry where, owing to insufficient realisation of Truth, the patient had died. The results he has since obtained by true prayer are wonderful.

The Key to the Miracles of Jesus.—Jesus, the Master-meta-physician, told us how to pray. He said: "All things whatsoever ye pray 5 and ask for, believe that ye have received them, and ye shall have them" (Mark 11:24, R.V.). "Ye ask, and receive not, because ye ask amiss" (James 4:3).

Although this first passage is the key to the so-called miracles of our Lord, no logical thinker has ever made sense of it unless he knew what is 10 now put before you. For this reason, it was mistranslated in the Authorised Version, which reads: "Believe that ye receive them." Many other passages similarly have been incorrectly translated, in order to "make sense," or rather, make them agree with preconceived ideas. What the words really signify is: believe the truth—namely, that you are now a spiritual 15 being in heaven, a son of God, and that you—being spiritual—"have received" everything you can possibly need (realise this, make it real to yourself); then you, the material being (the counterfeit), "shall have" it, namely, you will be out of your human difficulty, for your Father "hath blessed us with all spiritual blessings in heavenly places [1] in Christ" 20 (Eph. 1:3). "It is your Father's good pleasure to give you the kingdom" (Luke 12:32), for "Behold, the kingdom of God is within you" (Luke 17:21). You never know the form of good that you will receive, but you can be certain that the want will disappear.

Amongst many proofs of the above statement, it may be mentioned that 25 one of the foremost clergymen of the day said in my presence to another friend of mine, also a theological leader: "There is no question about it, this truth has given me the knowledge of how to pray in the way that Jesus did, and I have been obtaining results that can only be spoken of as miracles."

The Bishop of Durham writes: "We could not limit the virtues of the 30 hidden life, the indwelling Christ, to our spiritual experience only. The humblest caution befits us when we discuss the relation of the spiritual to the physical, and particularly of faith to healing. It is most credible that in untold instances the maladies and the fatigues of this tabernacle are mysteriously affected for relief by the remembrance that Christ is our life." 35

"If Christ be not raised" in our consciousness "your faith is vain; ye are yet in your sins" (I Cor. 15:17). Mere faith is not sufficient; an understanding of Christ is necessary. What is the proof of our knowledge of the Christ? Paul answered, with no uncertain voice: "For if the dead rise not, then is not Christ raised" (verse 16), "and we are found false witnesses of 40 God" (verse 15). Let us raise the dead, so called, and thus prove our knowledge of God and His Christ.

The healing of sickness has aptly been called the "bugle call." It brings people to be relieved of their troubles, and this ends in their being freed of their sins. I would like to say at once that the healing of sickness is not 45 sufficient proof of the truth of what is now being put before you. The only absolute proof is the constant instantaneous healing of sin. This cannot be

---

[1] Marginal translation, "things."

done with the material "no-mind." In any case, the disappearance of
sickness, except where the cases are continuous, instantaneous, and permanent, is no proof that a man is working in the proper way. H. T.
Butlin, F.R.C.S., D.C.L., LL.D., writes : "Every medical man of large and long
5 experience must have seen patients recover who, according to our laws and
theories, ought not to have recovered, and he often finds it quite impossible
to explain, even to himself, the reason." [1]

I once gave a lecture on new inventions and discoveries [2] at the request
of a clergyman, whose wife had been healed of internal ulceration and a
10 fibroid tumour in three weeks by true prayer, when given up by the medical
faculty as hopelessly incurable. A week after the lecture, at the request of
this clergyman, I had a talk with some of his congregation, and indicated
to them the true method of prayer. telling them how and where to find the
full explanation. Within a fortnight there were eighteen cases of so-called
15 miracles, performed by those who had been present, many of whom
obtained and studied the text-book to which I had referred them.[3] Most
of these were cases of healing. The clergyman himself instantaneously
healed one of his parishioners, who had been suffering for some time from
a painful form of paralysis.

20 **God Destroying Matter.**—*"The Son of God was manifested, that
he might destroy the works of the devil"* (I John 3:8).

Truth always dispels illusion, therefore the action of God upon the
illusory material world is always destructive,[4] destroying evil and
inharmonious thoughts, and purifying the human "consciousness" by
25 causing the destruction of apparent particles on the cells of the subconscious or lower "no-mind."

Results of True Prayer.—*"Come unto me, all ye that labour and
are heavy laden, and I will give you rest"* (Matt. 11:28).

The healing of physical sickness is only the gateway to higher thought
30 and action. "Sickness is the schoolmaster," [5] pointing the way to the
understanding of God and man. The healing of sin is the real purpose of all
knowledge.

The first result of knowing how to think scientifically is that one obtains
an easy, scientific method of getting rid of sin out of oneself, or rather out
35 of this false sense of oneself, for we all seemingly have something from
which we would gladly be freed. Every time that you reverse a wrong
thought the result of the affirmation is, that the action of God permanently
purifies your human "consciousness" somewhat, and you are a better
man morally, intellectually, and so-called physically. "And the Lord shall
40 deliver me from every evil work" (II Tim. 4:18). This improvement never
can be annulled. "For myself, I wish no other prayer but that which

---

[1] "Spiritual Healing" (*British Medical Journal*, June 18, 1910).
[2] See p. 316.
[3] *Science and Health with Key to the Scriptures* (Mary Baker Eddy). This book
45 can be obtained on loan free of charge from all Christian Science Churches and
Reading Rooms. A copy is also available in most public libraries.
[4] "Divine Life destroys death, Truth destroys error, and Love destroys hate"
(*Science and Health*, p. 339).
[5] Mary Baker Eddy in *Rudimental Divine Science*, p. 11.

improves me in virtue. I would fain live more nearly as I pray" (Santa
Teresa). "He who rises from his prayer a better man, his prayer is
answered" (George Meredith).

The second result is that you can heal not only sickness but sin,
instantaneously.   5

Thirdly, you can get your fellow-man out of any sort of trouble what-
sover. There is no limit of any kind.

Fourthly, you can obtain perfect peace of mind and happiness—no
worries, no troubles. "Peace I leave with you, my peace I give unto you"
(John 14:27). "To be spiritually minded is life and peace" (Rom. 8:6). 10
"The peace of God, which passeth all understanding" (Phil. 4:7). "Thou
hast made us for Thyself, O Lord; and our heart is restless till it rests in
Thee" (St. Augustine).

Finally, all limitations disappear. No human being can desire much more.

My own experience is that feelings of anger ceased to trouble me in   15
about eight months. Two months later, irritability became a thing of the
past, and it is now about six years since I was annoyed. The peace and
happiness that constantly surround one are only a question of degree.
We know that we have the panacea for every evil. "Come unto me, all ye
that labour and are heavy laden, and I will give you rest" (Matt. 11:28). 20
"If in this life we would enjoy the peace of paradise, we must . . . hinder
our spirits wandering from Him on any occasion; we must make our heart
a spiritual temple, wherein to adore Him incessantly" (Brother Lawrence,
Fourteenth Letter).

The knowledge of the infinite ideas that are instantly available to the 25
spiritual man in heaven, and the realisation that he has instantly any idea
that he needs, will overcome any limitation from which a human being
may be suffering, financial or otherwise, if he will only stop "thinking"
that it is hopeless, and that he will still be in want. "I will never leave thee,
nor forsake thee" (Heb. 13:5). "The thoughts of his heart, these are the 30
wealth of a man" (Burmese saying).

Results According to Law.—The healing done in the present day by
true prayer is now being recognised by the medical faculty. Only to-day,
I have heard of four cases of healing in an English hospital, just brought
about through a friend, all having been given up by the senior surgeon.   35
He had no objection to the use of prayer, and in every case the result was
successful, the worst case being entirely healed in eleven days.

Every week, at least 5,000 testimonies are publicly given of divine
healing, and testimonies are given probably in every city of any importance in the world.[1] In England alone I estimate that at least 1,000 people 40

[1] For over ten years I have attended these testimony meetings practically every
Wednesday evening, rarely missing one. For the first three years I took careful
notes of the results given. These I examined into where possible and checked the
statements made by cross-examination at the time, and again later in many cases.
Edward Kimball writes: "Men are told that they must believe to be saved. Which 45
of the many creeds must we believe? [There are said to be about 140 different
Christian sects.] We cannot believe them all. What must we do to be saved?
Christian Science promises more by way of deliverance and benefit than all else
known to humanity. The real question, therefore, is this: Does Christian Science
fulfil its promises or not?"   50

per week on an average are healed, many having been given up as hopeless by the medical faculty. A veritable army of workers is spreading the truth throughout the world, and demonstrating their knowledge of God in a way that is beyond question, namely, by habitually healing sin and sick-
5 ness. Every now and then, however, one comes across a person who alleges wrong diagnosis or coincidence [1] as the only reason for the apparently wonderful cures. As a complete answer to such arguments, the following experience one autumn may be given. Help had been asked for in a case where continued pain for two years had culminated in suffering which
10 kept others in the house awake at night, and which even heavy injections of the latest known drugs would not allay. Work began at 8 p.m., and for ten and a half hours the truth was realised as clearly as possible, and every time the moaning commenced, through the realisation that there was no pain in heaven, nothing but absolute bliss, peace, harmony, joy, etc., the
15 action of God stopped the pain. The rest of the time, the affirmation alone was used, to so purify the human consciousness that the pain thoughts, false beliefs, could not cause it to vibrate synchronously. After 4 a.m. there was no sound, and by 6.30 a.m. all severe pain had left, and the patient never even moaned again.
20 Going back to the City in the morning, the recognition that every time a wrong thought is reversed, it should be done with all the care and thoroughness with which love for a fellow-man had caused such reversals throughout the previous night, brought also the determination to try to do this in the future. The additional gain of so working, is that when the
25 time of trial comes, and again Goliath has to be met in single combat, one rises just as much in the face of the greater need as the experience of the previous night had stimulated one to rise above the former level.

At that time I was practically certain that in the course of my experience of this right method of praying, in over fifty per cent. of the cases
30 instantaneous effects followed. Not that the healing was completed in half the cases, but that a favourable change was at once noticeable. I had thought that seventy-five per cent. were instantaneous, but when questioned on this point, reduced my estimate to over fifty per cent. to be on the safe side. On the way to my office I began to wonder whether this
35 estimate could be excessive, and thought it would be wise for three months to see what the percentage of instantaneous results was, when the thoughts were reversed. During that period, out of the many cases, incidental or otherwise, where the counterfeit thoughts had been reversed (by the denial and affirmation) only one occurred, as far as I am aware, when there was
40 not an instantaneous benefit; in the case of disease either complete healing or noticeable improvement. The one exception was a bad case of sclerosis of the spinal cord in a visitor at a friend's house. Even in this instance, the nurse and daughter both said they thought the patient was better. During these three months there were numerous cases of trouble of many different
45 kinds, apart from disease, where there were only two possibilities, either entire elimination of the trouble, or no result at all. Some of these difficulties were merely mentioned casually, but all yielded with one

---

[1] This word is here used in its popular sense.

reversal, in demonstration of the working of divine Principle.[1] "More things are wrought by prayer than this world dreams of" (*Morte D'Arthur*, Tennyson). "I can of mine own self do nothing" (John 5:30). "With God all things are possible" (Matt. 19:26). "I can do all things through Christ which strengtheneth me" (Phil. 4:13). In the majority of these cases, the 5 work was done impersonally, in so far as the patient was concerned, namely, by thinking only of God and His manifestation when an account of the trouble was being given. It is wrong to think of the spiritual reality of any person unless you have been asked for help, and even then it is better to do the work impersonally by destroying in one's own "con- 10 sciousness" all false sense of the error seemingly apparent to oneself. When this is accomplished, the patient is freed.

To obtain really good results it is necessary to get right away in thought from the material world, and lose the physical sense of material things in the realisation of God and His ideas. This dawning sense of the spiritual, 15 this sixth sense, is hallowed in its self-consecration to God. The realisation of man's unity with good lifts us into a new world; it teaches the facts with regard to supernal realities; it cleanses us from all thoughts unlike God; and when mortal thought would draw us to earth again, the very earth and mortals around us seem blessed by the breath of God, in which we have 20 for a time seemed to live.

> "I knew I felt . . . what God is, what we are,
> What life is—how God tastes an infinite joy
> In infinite ways—one everlasting bliss,
> From Whom all being emanates, all power   25
> Proceeds: in whom is life for evermore" (*Robert Browning*).

Early Instantaneous Results.—"*Unto you that fear* [*reverence*] *my name* [*nature*] *shall the Sun of righteousness arise with healing in his wings.*" (Mal. 4:2).

If even a beginner will pray in this way, keeping an absolutely open 30 mind, and not thinking that God will possibly not act, that is, that God will not be God, the demonstration will be made. I think that one-third to one-half of beginners who work on these lines obtain instantaneous results within a fortnight, depending upon how closely they watch the thoughts that come to them, and instantly reverse the wrong ones by denial and 35 affirmation. There is very little to learn, but a great deal to unlearn; we must learn to unlearn what we have learnt amiss.

> "Ah, God, for an open mind!
> Ready to lose and to find;
> Teachable, quick to discern,   40
> And as brave to unlearn as to learn."

The Holy Ghost.[2]—True prayer is solely due to the action of God.

---

[1] "God has made man capable of this, and nothing can vitiate the ability and power divinely bestowed on man" (*Science and Health*, p. 393, Mary Baker Eddy).

[2] Writing of the Constantinopolitan Creed, Adolf von Harnack, Professor 45 of Theology at Berlin University, writes: "It looks therefore as though the writer of the Creed did not conceive the Holy Ghost as a person, but as a power and gift. This is indeed literally the case. No proof can be shown that about the middle of

This action is the Holy Ghost, "Divine Science; the development of eternal Life, Truth, and Love " (M. B. Eddy). It is the action of God on the real man that makes man what he is, namely, the knowledge or consciousness of God, or in other words, God's power of thinking of His own ideas.

5 When the human is thinking of God, the Holy Ghost being the action of God that makes man the consciousness of God in the reality, so it is the same action of the Holy Ghost that is recognisable in the present material world as making the human being think of God. True, or scientific prayer is the incoming of the Holy Ghost, or Holy Spirit, which "reveals and 10 sustains" God's universe. It is the kingdom of God, which, I believe, only comes once in its seeming fulness to man, until he can heal practically everything instantaneously, but which, when it comes, leaves him with the knowledge of what John meant when he wrote: "I was in the Spirit on the Lord's day" (Rev. 1:10), "And I saw a new heaven and a new earth" 15 (Rev. 21:1) "that great city, the holy Jerusalem, descending out of heaven from God, Having the glory of God" (Rev. 21:10, 11).

Dr. Inge writes: "This last idea, that the Holy Ghost is the copula, who 'in perfect love dost join the Father and the Son,' is not, as is usually supposed, an original speculation of Augustine's, but is found in Victorinus, 20 to whom he owes so much." [1] "Our Lord imposed no rigorous ceremonies on his disciples. He taught them to enter into the closet; to retire within the heart, to speak but few words; to open their hearts to receive the descent of the Holy Spirit" (Madame Guyon).

All Can Heal.—All will find that they are able to heal, as this is 25 done entirely through the action of God, God being the Principle of good and not a being requiring supplication. This action is the Holy Ghost or Comforter,[2] the "Spirit of truth" of which the prophecy of Jesus is recorded in John 14, verse 17. It is the mental realisation of the truth that enables us to heal, and the Holy Ghost is the spirit or holiness of this 30 truth, that abides "with you for ever" (John 14:16), and heals and "shall teach you all things" (John 14:26). All that is necessary to be able to heal continually is to learn how to pray scientifically and how to demonstrate the Christ-life, and so to remain a consecrated channel for spiritual good to mankind.

35 If a man, when praying, will not think of the material world or the patient, but will form his very best concept of God and heaven, and will strive to realise this concept to his utmost, and will not think that God will not act, then he will get an instantaneous result.

Those whose duty has hitherto led them to dive most deeply into false

40 the second century [the time our Apostles' Creed was compiled] the Holy Ghost was believed in as a person. This conception, on the contrary, is one of much later date, which was still unknown to most Christians in the middle of the fourth century. . . . In the Creed the Holy Ghost is conceived of as a gift." Dr. Swete's *The Apostles' Creed* deals fully with the evolution of the early Christian view of the 45 Holy Ghost.
    [1] "The Paddock Lectures" for 1906.
    [2] Eustace Miles points out that the Greek word "parakletos," translated "Comforter," means "one who urges you forward and inspires you." This was the meaning attached to the word "parakalo" in the speeches of Demosthenes to the 50 Athenians.

knowledge, spoken of as scientific, will be the first to appreciate the
enormous import of the complete exposure of its theories, and to advance
most rapidly in the apprehension of the real facts and the understanding
of spiritual, and therefore natural mental science. Consequently such work
will be the most potent factor in the bringing about of universal salvation. 5
"And the earth [the scientific thought] opened her mouth [gave out the
knowledge of truth to the world], and swallowed up the flood which the
dragon cast out of his mouth" [false "non-mental" working] (Rev. 12:16).

The Medical World.—The medical world stands at the parting of the
ways. The discovery of the fact that not a part but all reality is Mind and 10
mental renders the medical knowledge, that before was helpful, actually
the reverse. The universal advance in knowledge demands advanced
practice, to avoid a greater present danger to both practitioner and patient
alike. There is no standing still with safety on the revolving wheel of
progress. In the mental era now entered upon by the world, the possession 15
of this medical knowledge must become through its intelligent reversal
the most potent instrument for good, whereas unreversed, such retain-
ment of false pictures becomes just as surely the most deadly danger to its
possessor.

No one will understand better than the educated medical worker how 20
a knowledge of evil which necessitates the constant picturing of it in its
various manifestations of disease, must necessarily intensify such wrong
picturing and recoil on the head of every practitioner who does not know
how scientifically to protect himself by the understanding of God, dwelling
on universal good. 25

It is generally admitted that the majority rules, and it is now clear that
this majority is not calculated by the number of persons, but by the depth
of thought. In every case of sin or disease there is not only the individual
belief or faith in evil to measure and outweigh, but the general consent to
accepted pictorial prognostications. These, it is now proved, constitute 30
the only so-called law affecting material conditions. The medical man
stands in the very responsible position of being the chief agent of adminis-
tration of these laws of general belief. When a doctor even tolerates the truly
scientific mental treatment of his patient, the case generally progresses
more rapidly; when he acknowledges possible good through such treat- 35
ment, recovery is a foregone conclusion; but when the doctor, accepting
this wonderful truth of the non-reality of evil and the allness of Mind,
good, as the greatest discovery in the world of medicine, subordinates all
surgical and other material aid, then it will be found that such changed
attitude and modified practice subserves the interests of the medical 40
faculty whilst leading the way to a higher knowledge and truer practice.
Healing will be found, under such circumstances, practically always
instantaneous. All material methods are merely a needful "suffer it to be
so now" in moments of immediate necessity, until the principle of right
thinking is sufficiently established to *prevent* any further developments of 45
disease.

It is now obviously self-evident as a scientific fact that glorious developments in the healing of sickness lie waiting at the door of every medical

man to-day. When it is seen that knowledge of Truth, instead of taking
away his life's work, is merely pointing him to "greater works" than have
ever before been even attempted by the medical faculty, he will not delay
a moment longer to utilise this power in the interests of humanity. While
5 the scientific medical practitioner of to-day stands in the forefront of the
battle, fighting against the last stage of the physical self-imposed suffering
of a self-deceived, cruelly treated world, true science is teaching the truth
that will *prevent* sin and recurring disease, and finally destroy all evil, by
turning universal thought in the direction only of Life, Truth, and Love
10 as God. Magnificently equipped for God's work, invested as he already is
with an authority conferred by the temporary democratic law of human
belief, that holds sway over king and beggar alike, the medical man has
complete dominion over every form of disease, whether called functional
or organic. Let him offer this temporal authority on God's altar, consecrate
15 it anew to divine Mind and its infinite manifestation, absorb the grand
truths of uninterrupted, all-harmonious scientific being, and open his door
to the waiting and suffering multitudes. Let him who has borne the burden
and heat of the day be the wearer of a crown of rejoicing, the gift of an
emancipated grateful world. Casting his "net on the right side" (John
20 21:6) he gains an abundance of work with a superabundant reward. The
millennium of universal health will quickly bring to such workers new and
more joyful occupations not yet come to light, because of the veil that sin,
disease, and death have spread over human intelligence.

The coming flood of literature now about to be brought forth, is, with
25 a few exceptions, the most important by far of any yet produced.[1] Written
from a new standpoint, based upon spiritual science, it will consist for the
main in contradiction of mistaken hypotheses, and the reinstatement of
man in his natural mental element.[2]

A rapidly increasing fungus growth of spurious mind culture is now
30 springing up, claiming to instruct mankind as to how to obtain whatever
seems to be desirable. It must inevitably lead to dire suffering. It is essential
that the flood-tide of pure literature should sweep away this final attempt
of evil.

The Man in Authority.—"*Speak the word only, and my servant*
35 *shall be healed. For I am a man under authority, having soldiers under me:*
and I say . . . to my servant, Do this, and he doeth it. . . . And Jesus
said unto the centurion, Go thy way; and as thou hast believed, so be it done
unto thee. And his servant was healed in the selfsame hour" (Matt. 8:8, 9, 13).

While all can heal, the man invested with authority is the man most
40 capable of enforcing law. The medical man has been humanly invested

---

[1] "We err in thinking the object of vital Christianity is only the bequeathing
of itself to the coming centuries. The successive utterances of reformers are essential
to its propagation. The magnitude of its meaning forbids headlong haste, and the
consciousness which is most embued struggles to articulate itself (*Message for*
45 *1901*, p. 30, Mary Baker Eddy).
[2] "This movement of thought must push on the ages: it must start the wheels of
reason aright, educate the affections to higher resources, and leave Christianity
unbiased by the superstitions of a senior period" (*Miscellaneous Writings*, p. 235,
Mary Baker Eddy).

with the authority of giving the verdict of life or death, although no one need submit to the latter. At the present moment the world will meekly accept his verdict. Let this be the verdict of life and perpetual health, and so let him bring blessings for the whole human family.

Main Points in Instantaneous Healing.—The question of whether 5 the work can be done instantaneously or not can be answered at once in the affirmative. Whether any specific evil will be overcome instantly depends upon four main points.

(1) Upon the condition of the so-called cells in the subconscious or lower so-called "mind" of the patient; in other words, his condition of 10 "no-mind."

(2) The imagined strength or intensity of the thoughts attacking, namely, the tenacity of the error.

(3) What people around are picturing. In a hospital, for instance, where the doctors and nurses view the patient as passing through the successive 15 stages of the disease, they may intensify the faint outlinings until they are as dangerous as the worst ones.

(4) On the condition of the so-called "mind" of the healer. This, in its turn, depends upon—

(a) His spirituality and knowledge of God. 20
(b) His technical knowledge, or ability to deal with the conditions of the case. For instance, his power of reading thought and of discerning the condition of the patient's so-called "mind."
(c) The life he leads. To do really good work, that is, to get instantaneous and permanent results in a large percentage of cases, one 25 must strive to live a life of true unselfishness, always thinking of what is best for a fellow-man and the human race, and acting up to one's highest sense of right.
(d) His love towards all humanity. It is this that makes him strive his very best to realise God, with the view of being of use to the 30 world.

We cannot heal instantaneously case after case completely unless we live habitually as in the presence of God. That is, as far as possible, every moment of the day we must be actively conscious of God and His manifestation. We must never let anything but the highest possible thoughts 35 dwell in our "consciousness." "Prayer is nothing but the application of the heart to God, and the internal exercise of love; so that we ought to pray without ceasing, and live by prayer" (Madame Guyon).

> "He prayeth best who loveth best
> All things, both great and small" (*S. T. Coleridge*). 40

The above applies literally in its fullest significance to the scientific leaders of all classes. The enormous responsibility attaching to such workers in this final crisis of the human consciousness cannot be too highly estimated. While the doctor, responsive to the faith of his patients, hastens to heal the body, the scientific leaders hasten to teach mankind the truth, 45 whereby they can heal diseased imagination and mental affliction, and, in fact, the insanity of sin in all its forms. The field of operations for both these great classes of mankind to-day is of world-wide dimensions.

Love.[1]—"*A new commandment I give unto you, That ye love one another; as I have loved you, that ye also love one another*" (John 13:34). "*For God is love*" (I John 4:8).

What hidden wealth lies in the true meaning of this word of words, "heaven's signet"! Its scientific explanation can only be fully reached when approached with a sense of profoundest awe and solemnity. Where is the human standard of measurement, comparison with which can indicate even a fraction of it? As close as the centre of one's being, it extends beyond human conception of the farthest star! Gentler than the softest whisper, it can quell the strident discord of a material world! Softer than the fall of a snowflake, yet the dynamic force that holds the universe for ever in its grasp! Omnipresent, it admits no even imaginary rival! It claims all that really is, for its essence and necessity are universal at-one-ment.

Standing where I do, as its humble student, and having caught some first faint gleams of its wondrous glory, I would add but few words under this heading, for guidance in obtaining its priceless gift, and for this sufficient reason—the import of the whole of this message is directed to that one end. It shows how to wield this divine, irresistible power, and how to protect oneself against the serpent,[2] material sense, which purports to bite the heel of the woman and struggles to destroy the spiritual idea of Love. A right understanding of what is now gladly set forth, in response to the call of humanity, cannot fail to bring to the seeker the reward of Love, of obedience to whose demand this book itself is the outcome, and to whose all-pervading influence its wording is with confidence submitted.

Love is supreme cause, the distributor of all the perfection indicated in the conception of the reality—heaven—as defined previously. Love and knowledge are halves of one unsevered whole. "He who foolishly believes is foolish; without knowledge there can be no faith. God does not desire that we should remain in darkness and ignorance. We should all be recipients of the divine wisdom. We can learn to know God only by becoming wise. To become like God we must become attracted to God, and the power that attracts us is Love. Love to God will be kindled in our hearts by an ardent love for humanity, and a love for humanity will be caused by a love to God" (*De Fundamente Sapientiæ*). Love includes "the whole duty of man" (see Eccl. 12:13). This means true love.

God, omnipotent, omnipresent good, the origin of all wisdom, and the divine Principle of all intelligence, does not allow of any remaining in ignorance of Truth. We are wise in hastening to acquire all essential knowledge of Life as a practical, spiritual, and eternal existence, and so save time wasted in useless preliminary suffering through lack of Truth. For

[1] "The vital part, the heart and soul of Christian Science, is Love. Without this, the letter is but the dead body of Science, pulseless, cold, inanimate" (*Science and Health*, p. 113, Mary Baker Eddy).

[2] See Amos 5, verse 19; 9, verse 3, and Revelation 12, verse 9.

whether by slow or rapid footsteps, suffering or joyous experience, the end arrived at must inevitably be the same, eternal Truth.

The struggles of paganism against Christianity, which, unfortunately, have continued, in one form or another, during the last two thousand years, have been the struggles of man for his personal benefit as against the demands of the universal law of love taught by Jesus.

Love is the Principle of Christianity, and love the outcome of its divine rules.[1] "When it is asked whether anyone be a good man, it is not asked what he believes or what he hopes, but what he loves. Little love is little righteousness, great love is great righteousness, perfect love is perfect righteousness" (St. Augustine). "To love abundantly is to live abundantly, and to love for ever is to live for ever." "Love someone, in God's name, love someone, for this is the bread of the inner life, without which a part of you will starve and die" (Max Ehrmann). "In this case to give is to receive" (Westcott).

Love necessitates the welling out of the utmost tenderness, the outcome of a compassion, which is induced by the intense desire to be of service (see Acts 20:35). This desire makes man ever on the watch to utilise this power of love, unknown to the recipient or otherwise, and so to be a channel for the love of God which passeth all understanding, for it is the spiritual real man, man being the love, life, and truth of God. We have to love others, as Shakespeare says, "with a respect more tender, more holy and profound than mine own life." "To love one's neighbour is after all to love in others that which is Divine and eternal" (A. T. Schofield, M.D.). "Whosoever hateth his brother is a murderer" (I John 3:15). Hate is the absence of love when we are thinking of our fellow-men. We must either love or hate. Work continually to be more loving. "Charity shall cover the multitude of sins" (I Peter 4:8). This love is the essence of Christianity. Gautama, the founder of Buddhism, who mistakenly looked upon all so-called material life as "suffering," yet taught that the scientific principle which ultimately led to release and happiness was universal, inclusive love. This love is unselfish, impartial, because it is Love, God. "He that loveth not knoweth not God" (I John 4:8). More love is what the world needs. We must, as soon as possible, raise up our love for the man in the street until it is always equal to that for our nearest and dearest, and free from all personality other than is necessary in order to have an object of this love. "Love one another" (John 15:17). "Abound in love . . . toward all men" (I Thess. 3:12). We must get entirely free from all material sense impressions. True prayer alone will do this. The wrong method of prayer creates difficulties. "He who, being a man, remains a woman, will become a universal channel. As a universal channel the eternal virtue will never forsake him. He will re-become a child"[2] (Lao-Tze).

---

[1] Almost all my early instantaneous results were obtained by realising God as Love and the absolute love in heaven. When, in testing the statement that God was Principle, I first obtained an instantaneous result from that realisation, my love for God seemed to disappear, and it took me some months before I regained a more comprehensive idea of God. Then my love for God returned far stronger than it had ever been. Many others have lost their feeble idea of God and found it enhanced a thousand fold. (See p. 371 l. 36.)

[2] *Tao-Têh*, or *The Simple Way*.

"As a mother loves, who, even at the risk of her life, protects her only son, such love let there be towards all beings" (Metta Sutta). "Beloved, let us love one another: for love is of God" (I John 4:7).

The Power of Love.—"*See that ye love one another with a pure heart*
5 *fervently*" (I Peter 1:22).

Whenever even a bad case comes to our knowledge, arousing the intense desire to help, which true love gives, and this help is given, there follows a feeling of glorious spiritual uplifting, and immense spiritual power over evil, with a sense of triumph and unity with God, a joy quite inexpressible.
10 The healing is then, as far as I am aware, instantaneous. "I will heal their backsliding, I will love them freely" (Hos. 14:4). "Faith . . . worketh by love" (Gal. 5:6). "Love is the everlasting worker of miracles. . . . Love is the saviour, love is the perpetual wonder of life"[1] (E. H. Griggs).

"So it is not the speech which tells, but the impulse which goes with the saying,
15　And it is not the words of the prayer, but the yearning back of the praying"
(*Ella Wheeler Wilcox*).

The Protective Power of Love.—This may be easily proved if you find yourself with a so-called dangerous animal. All that is necessary is to lose all sense of the fierce seeming animal and realise God as Love, or
20 realise the absolute protection of God as omnipresent Love around you, and no harm can ensue. Now we have the secret of Daniel's control over the lions in their den, and of the angel that "shut the lions' mouths" (Dan. 6:22). The same remarks apply to the human beast, man, who is much more dangerous, and not so easy to help. This only means, however,
25 that you must more completely get away from picturing the material man, and more clearly realise divine Love. "Love [divinely] as many persons and as many creatures as you possibly can" (Blackie).

"Love being the highest principle, is the virtue of all virtues; from whence they flow forth. Love being the greatest majesty, is the power of all
30 powers, and whence they severally operate: And it is the . . . power from whence all the wonders of God have been wrought by the hands of His elect servants, in all their generations successively. Whosoever finds it, finds nothing and all things"[2] (Jacob Boehme).

Three Phases of Love.—"*Speech, Prophecy, Science, Faith, aglow*
35 *with Love, are lamps that cheer our eyes and guide us through the darkness of the world*" (Edgar Daplyn).

There are three different phases of love, the material—we may call it the human—the intellectual and the spiritual.[3] The lowest is the material love, the highest type of which is the love of the mother towards the child, which

40　[1] *Christian Science Sentinel*, August 10, 1910.
　　[2] *Of the Supersensual Life.*
　　[3] A marked illustration of these three phases may be traced in the married life of Mrs. Eddy, and are symbolically referred to in her letter to the First Church of Christ Scientist, Boston (*Miscellaneous Writings*, p. 139). This letter also contains a
45 call to love and a lesson of how to love our fellow-man, as well as the early history of this teaching in the Christian Science field, typified in the story of the building of the First Church.

includes purity and constancy. This is the love that gives you happiness by merely being with the loved one.

> "She never found fault with you, never implied
> Your wrong by her right: and yet men at her side
> Grew nobler, girls purer . . .   5
> None knelt at her feet, confessed lovers in thrall;
> They knelt more to God than they used—that was all"
> *(Elizabeth Barrett Browning)*

The happiness that is felt in the presence of true workers is because they are always at work destroying the false pictures that would otherwise 10 now and then result in discomfort to their companions.

We need to manifest towards the so-called other sex, as the result of treatment, the qualities that, as humanly seen, are so often apparently lacking; towards the woman, strength of character, courage, wisdom, and frankness; towards the man, the complements of love, virtue, intuition, and 15 refinement. Most important of all, we need to pray by realising in the spiritual man the qualities that we are tempted to believe lacking in those with whom we come in contact; with a woman, strength, wisdom, etc.; with a man, love, refinement, etc. These qualities lying dormant in either sex require to be recognised to demonstrate the completeness of each one, 20 as "the one" which on God's side is a majority.[1] This realisation or recognition of the spiritual, perfectly balanced male and female qualities of each, results in the alteration of each "consciousness" by the action of God, and thus proves each individual reflection of Mind to be male and female. "Let the 'male and female' of God's creating appear" (Mary 25 Baker Eddy). This spontaneous levelment of the individual consciousness can come only to those who are consistent in their habitual practice of right thinking and consequent right doing.[2]

This realisation of the male and female of God's creating is bringing to light on earth to-day men and women gloriously equipped to deal with their 30 fellows in the spirit of Christly capacity and true gentleness that can conquer all seeming opposition to Truth and Love, and lead to higher joys. Such men and women will save the world in the times of dire trouble that are now liable to be manifested. "Sympathy . . . may prove . . . a treasure in itself to its possessor." "To be patient, sympathetic, tender 35 . . . to love always—this is duty" (Amiel).

"Perhaps the truth is, that there has scarcely been a town in any Christian country since the time of Christ where a century has passed without exhibiting a character of such elevation that his [or her] mere presence has shamed the bad, and made the good better, and has been 40

---

[1] "Union of the masculine and feminine qualities constitutes completeness. The masculine mind reaches a higher tone through certain elements of the feminine, while the feminine mind gains courage and strength through masculine qualities. These different elements conjoin naturally with each other, and their true harmony is in spiritual oneness" (*Science and Health*, p. 57, Mary Baker Eddy).   45

[2] "For the Lord himself, being asked by a certain person when his kingdom should come? answered, When two shall be one, and that which is without as that which is within; and the male with the female, neither male nor female" (II Clement 5:1). Clement was a disciple of Peter and afterwards Bishop of Rome. Eusebius speaks of this epistle as "the wonderful Epistle of St. Clement."

felt at times like the presence of God himself" (*Ecce Homo*, Seeley). Of Charles Kingsley, his wife wrote: "Who lived in the presence of God here."

The greatest intellectual love is the giving to your hearers the utmost
5 that they can take in. "Feed my lambs. . . . Feed my sheep" (John 21:15, 16). If the truth is so expressed as to interest them the whole time,[1] they willingly take in the spiritual food of which you give them as much as they are prepared to receive at the time. "There is nothing so good to the human heart as well-agreed conversation, . . . for love is agreement
10 of thought" (Richard Jefferies).

Purity.—"*The life that by prayer and purity of heart keeps in touch with the very source of life itself . . . is the only life worth while*" (M. E. Duckler). "We only know our relations to God through our relations to each other. . . . The Garden of Eden surely exists still on earth, for those who
15 have faith and purity enough" (Charles Kingsley).

The influence of the highest spiritual love is felt when men and women are better and more determined to live their religion, after you have spoken with them.[2] When you love truly you will understand "the hidden manna" (the constant happiness that comes from truly loving and being
20 truly loved, the food for constant joy), the "white stone" (the necessary antecedent purity, "the corner stone of all spiritual building") and the "new name [nature] written" (Rev. 2:17) therein, which is the indescribable internal peace and joy and realisation of God that true love brings. "The joy of heaven is the joy of love, the key to it is in Christ" (James Hinton).
25 "Love propagates anew the higher joys of Spirit" (Mary Baker Eddy).

May all accepting these words, from this moment consecrate themselves afresh to God; God that is Love itself, infinite, pure, Spirit. All nations, all denominations, all sects, whatever their knowledge of God, can so pray that God works through them, thus forwarding the universal brotherhood
30 that is so rapidly coming, and gaining for themselves and others purity of thought, and therefore purity of life, by which we obtain joys unspeakable and "the peace of God, which passeth all understanding" (Phil. 4:7).

---

[1] The late W. T. Stead, at a public dinner at which I spoke, said that he had once asked me to come to tea one afternoon. He had asked as mixed an audience
35 as possible, about twenty-five people in number, a doctor, a surgeon, different classes of clergymen, various mental workers, atheists, agnostics, etc., etc., and he and his family stood for spiritualism. He said that I arrived punctually at 4.30 and started talking, and, he went on, "I assure you, gentlemen, Mr. Rawson talked without stopping even right through dinner-time until a quarter to twelve, when
40 he had to leave. Not a single man had left, and when he had gone they all expressed the same thought, namely, that they were sorry he could not keep on speaking for several hours more. I do not know a single man who could have held a mixed audience all that time in the way he did." The reason for this was that when he asked me, I saw, from the twinkle in his eye, that he had some joke on. Consequently
45 I treated every day beforehand, realising that man speaks Truth and man knows Truth. If you had asked one of those present why he was so interested, I am sure that he would have said that I kept on clearing up points about which he wanted to know. This is the true manifestation of intellectual love.

[2] "I long, and live, to see this love demonstrated. I am seeking and praying for
50 it to inhabit my own heart and to be made manifest in my life. Who will unite with me in this pure purpose, and faithfully struggle till it be accomplished?" (*Pulpit and Press*, p. 21, Mary Baker Eddy).

THE FALSE DIVISION OF THE SEXES

In the endeavour towards the attainment of a perfectly balanced male and female consciousness, complete in each one, and thus alone capable of adequately dealing with all problems that may arise, let it be clearly understood that the position to be aimed at is entirely spiritual. It is a levelment of purely mental qualities, the right adjustment of conditions that generations of mistaken hypotheses have rendered scientifically abnormal. The so-called woman has been ground down and belittled through lack of the male qualities, whilst the male has been brutalised through want of those usually called feminine.

The Union of Mental Qualities.—"*And to Salome enquiring 'how long death shall have power' the Lord said, so long as ye women bear children. For I came to destroy the works of womankind. And Salome said to him, I have done well then in not bearing children. But the Lord answered saying, Eat every herb, but that which hath bitterness do not eat. And Salome enquired when should be known the things about which He was asked [i.e., when the kingdom of God shall come]; the Lord said, When ye shall have trodden down the garment of shame, and when the two shall be one, and the male with the female neither male nor female*" [1] (St. Clement).

Granted that we are in the last days, and that with the disappearance of death there is no need for birth, it is evident that the main motive of the marriage relation no longer exists, and any other motive is essentially a mistake, leading materially downwards instead of spiritually upwards. The right adjustment in the individual human consciousness of both male and female begins scientifically for the first time on the intellectual plane, when the man and woman can meet, and calmly, patiently, and courageously face the mighty "intellectual wrestlings" that must precede the complete recognition and subsequent exposure of the false laws of matter and their fatal results, and the attainment for themselves and all mankind of a perfectly balanced understanding of God, man, and the universe, and the laws relating thereto.

Platonic Friendship.—The intellectual grasp and complete exposure of false theories must precede the intelligent denial of all material laws and consequent effacement of human footsteps in wrong directions, and lead to a truly scientific and unbroken friendship entirely opposed to so-called Platonic friendship, which, because of its failure, has rightly become a by-word. This is because the intellectual intercourse of the latter, instead of solving existing world problems, has but brought forward fresh ones, and in so many cases led into hopeless individual difficulties. Such unhappy experiences of mentalities struggling to emerge from the slough of materialistic beliefs have been due to the want of the recognition of the allness of the one Mind and its mental manifestation. There has been no guiding Principle at the back of the desire for spiritual at-one-ment. "Grant me grace never to love anything but through thy love and for thy love" (Avrillon).

[1] Clem. Alex. exc. Theod. 67.

234 SECTION FIVE

Dangerous Whirlpools.—Many of the world's best workers could tell how even a kindly act towards beginners, reaching out for human sympathy in time of need, has led to slanderous misrepresentation. Such, indeed, possibly inspired Pope's words: "For fools [the uninstructed]
5 rush in where angels fear to tread." It is sadly needful to be more than a little wise in dealing with the inflammable nature of the present abnormally divided male and female consciousness, to avoid the risk of possible subjection to the unjust criticism of grosser natures, which brings us face to face with a general impurity undreamed of.
10 It is essentially true that "Unto the pure all things are pure," and equally true that one of the cruel aspects of ignorant human consciousness is unjust criticism of imaginary conditions by lower mentalities. Individuals, often not recognising their own tendency to respond to evil thoughts, never perhaps having been really tested, are quite unable to gauge a pure
15 and fearless nature, struggling to work out hitherto unsolved human problems for the universal good. "For the Scripture saith, The untested man is unworthy." [1]

God's Protection.—So complete is the infinite protection of divine Principle, forever surrounding those who "walk the untrodden in the
20 hitherto unexplored fields of Science," [2] and find themselves in the face of possible danger when trying to help their fellow-men, that any misjudgment of them or harsh injustice will be overruled, and the honest intent of fearless workers made clear. The lurid glare, though it be as a lightning flash, which ill-natured criticism is apt to throw upon the path
25 of those bravely pressing forward, serves but to show any dark, lurking, hidden dangers that otherwise, by ensnaring the feet of ignorant but well-meant endeavour, might have retarded the progress of a world.
Pure-minded, earnest students of Truth can never be injured by the reckless arrows of false imputations. A thousand such shafts may "fall at
30 thy side, and ten thousand at thy right hand," but they can never touch the true servants of God, nor harm any but the archers. Science makes it clear that a wrong thought dwelt on inevitably harms ignorant as well as vicious thinkers.

A Warning.—A few words of special warning may be added should
35 any earnest students feel inclined to follow their own individual human methods in the attainment of this ideal, rather than take the advice and warnings of those who, reaching out for the truth with needful guidance, have already explored the way, solved great problems, successfully fought the fight, and gained invaluable experience.

40 **The Marriage Tie.**—Fearless intercourse on the highest intellectual plane is compatible with the highest morality, but on the lowest material plane it is neither truly Christian nor scientific.
There is only one condition in which free intercourse on the lowest human plane of action is allowable, and compatible with morality and

45 [1] *Didascalia*, 11, 8, and *Constitutions*, 11, 8.
[2] *Miscellaneous Writings*, p. xi (Mary Baker Eddy).

scientific progress, and that is loyal companionship under the legal institution of marriage. This condition has been the basis of the highest present civilisation, and will continue to support progress until the intellectual and spiritual plane is alone found attractive, as the levelment of individual male and female consciousness brings nearer universal dematerialisation of   5 all evil.

Unity With Spiritual Advancement.—Consistent advancement in higher understanding of truth will never separate husband and wife, nor any true companionship, but will bring all into a far closer at-one-ment on that higher plane where, if the demand for courtesy, patience, gentleness,   10 and love is greater, closer bonds of spiritual unity are being rapidly welded, and will prove to be the only bonds that can never be broken. Thus only do we prove that we are linked in a conscious eternal unity which admits no taint of material earthly sense.

The greater demand for demonstration of heavenly qualities is not sur-   15 prising when we recognise that in the endeavour to attain to a perfectly balanced individual male and female consciousness, complete in each one, multitudinous and diametrically opposite views must be brought together and closely analysed without clash of arms. This is essential to progress. No material union on the lower plane has hitherto ever proved equal to   20 this strain in the historical record of human experiences. Indeed, the reverse picture faces us on many sides. How often a happy and seemingly united pair, who are entirely at one in the ordinary round of married life, are seen to betray a painful incompatibility of temperament on the first attempt to ascend into the mental plane of free interchange and discussion   25 of new thoughts regarding the fundamentals of existence. It has unfortunately often come to the point of a loving (!) husband forbidding a beloved wife to think, speak of, or look into a religion which she feels to be unquestionably true. "I came not to send peace, but a sword. For I am come to set a man at variance against his father, and the daughter against   30 her mother, and the daughter in law against her mother in law. And a man's foes shall be they of his own household" (Matt. 10:34-36).

Spiritual Consecration Necessary.—If this has been the case in the past, what must be the demand of to-day for these higher qualities, standing as we do, facing an entire mental revolution of old laws resting   35 on misconceptions and fatal to all in their results? It is obvious that the progress of the world demands every working moment from such students as are able to demonstrate harmonious, intellectual, and spiritual companionship, for the purpose of working out higher problems of the essential rules of life for the benefit of humanity. This work necessitates the exer-   40 cise to the fullest possible extent of both male and female qualities; by the man, intuition, gentleness, refinement, patience, thoughtfulness for others, in fact, all that love implies; by the woman, wisdom, courage, frankness, energy, and unfailing application.

When the ideal unity aimed at for all is declared, and the paths leading   45 thereto are understood, much becomes clear that might otherwise seem obscure, and much generous help will be afforded the world's workers by all truly pure and loving natures, in place of any old opposition that may have arisen through misconception. "That is true love which is always the same, whether you give everything or deny everything to it" (Goethe).

Intellectual blending of male and female qualities of thought in individual human consciousness is essential for the final complete denials 5 and consequent effacement of these antiquated but deadly laws. Spiritual at-one-ment or true unity is the eternal outcome of the omnipotent action of the eternal law of good.

> "So links more subtle and more fine
>   Bind every other soul to thine
> 10   In one great brotherhood divine" (*Adelaide A. Procter*).

Need for Fulfilment of the World's Highest Standard.[1]—In rendering to Cæsar that which is his just due, it is impossible to be too conscientious in the payment to the uttermost farthing of this debt, not only in the absolutely honest and faithful relation between husband and 15 wife, but in all intercourse with the other sex. As we advance it becomes more and more evident that neither by word nor deed can we run counter to the human requirements demanded by the popular conscience in the endeavour to safeguard its feeble human standard of right. Any deviation from the above course can only lead to needless suffering for all con- 20 cerned.

Other loving companionships on the material human plane compatible with morality and Christianity are those that exist between intimate members in the families growing out of and resulting from the above legal contract. "Simplicity ought to be in our affections, purity in our intentions. 25 Purity doth apprehend and taste of God: Simplicity doth tend towards Him"[2] (Thomas à Kempis). "Self-restraint and purity, the knowledge of noble truths, . . . this is the greatest blessing" (Teachings of Buddha).

Practical Results the only Proof.—To judge accurately of the rightness of human intercourse between men and women it is necessary 30 to discern the motive which brings them together, whether it be a person they go to see or a Principle they meet to discuss and further apprehend. Only the latter motive justifies the wisdom or utility of the meeting.[3] What can prove the motives of those who meet? The works that result in their lives will place them beyond all possible misconception on this 35 point.

The Mighty Purpose to be Accomplished.—So far in human history the highest realisation of happiest earthly experience has been rudely interrupted by the cold enshrouding mist of death. Having been investigated and exposed, this needless interruption of a false material law leading 40 to death and further immature counterfeits of God's man, is now doomed to disappear. In the light of scientific truth, even the present generation

---

[1] See Matthew 22, verse 21 and 5, verse 26.
[2] *Imitation of Christ*, Book II.
[3] Foreseeing these untrodden human footsteps, the greatest spiritual seer of 45 our own times has expressed it in these words: "'What went ye out for to see?' A person, or a Principle? Whichever it be, determines the right or the wrong of this following." *Miscellany*, p. 117 (Mary Baker Eddy).

will be re-established on a sound basis of health and joyous existence, opening up glorious vistas of spiritual at-one-ment and eternally unfolding perfect ideas. There is a mighty purpose to be accomplished. Individual advancement will always be the result of self-forgetful co-operation for others' good.   5

Joy.—"*Joy is the grace we say to God*" (Jean Ingelow).
"There are wit, humour, and enduring vivacity amongst God's people" (Talmage). "Joy is a duty" (Van Dyke). It is a health-giving duty (see Prov. 15:13, 15 and 17:22). "Wondrous is the strength of cheerfulness" (Carlyle). "A laugh is worth a hundred groans in any market" (Lamb). 10 Always laugh when you can; it is cheap medicine" (Byron). "Talk happiness, the world is sad enough without your woe. No path is wholly rough" (Ella Wheeler Wilcox).
A leader of the New Theology writes: "Love is essentially self-giving. It is the living of the individual life in terms of the whole. In a finite world 15 this cannot but mean pain, but it is also self-fulfilment." True love certainly does not mean pain, but the contrary. In the past it has meant pain simply because we did not know how to pray or how to love. Now Love always brings with it joy, an indescribable joy, because Love when sufficiently realised, destroys sin, sickness, and every kind of trouble.   20
As Aristotle points out, the distinctive mark of true happiness is the full realisation of the activity peculiar to each individual. It is only by a joyous and useful life that we can show our gratitude for what we have been taught. "Sorrow is the mere rust of the soul. Activity will cleanse and brighten it" (Dr. Johnson). "The fruit of the Spirit is love, joy, peace 25 . . ." (Gal. 5:22). "Your joy no man taketh from you" (John 16:22). Love means happiness, Love means life, Love means every single thing that is worth having. When love is lived, it is no mere theory, it is practical religion, the religion of God, for Love is God, and love to be real must be spiritual. "Feeling is everything. A name is sound and smoke clouding 30 Heaven's glow" (Goethe).
This must be the experience of thousands besides myself. Where are the cares and troubles of ten years ago? Gone, never to return. Where is the increasing despair at the horrors enacted all around us? Drowned in the joy of alleviating the misery of others. ",We will rejoice in thy salvation" 35 (Ps. 20:5). There is no time to be unhappy, there is no time for anything but work—work that brings a heavenly inestimable joy. Sin, suffering, and sickness disappear from right and left directly they present themselves to the one keeping watch in prayer, and we find ourselves in "the midst of the paradise of God," of good (see II Cor. 12:4, and Revelation 2:7). 40 For "in thy presence is fulness of joy" (Ps. 16:11). This fulness of joy comes through treatment, and through treatment alone. Even in the present improved human experiences of mortals there is great joy. As Spinoza has said, joy is the "transition from less to greater perfection." Freedom from fear is the gateway of happiness, and this freedom can be 45 obtained when we know how to think so that the action of God destroys the thoughts that cause the fear. Then the evil thoughts that you have felt cannot act. "Joys want eternity" (Nietzsche).

9

Grief is comparatively easily destroyed. "What's gone and what's past help should be past grief" (Shakespeare). " Better is one smile for the living than fountains of tears for the dead" (Anon.).

Beauty.—"*Goodness and love mould the form into their own image, and cause the joy and beauty of love to shine forth from every part of the face*" (Swedenborg).

It is interesting to note, and it has been observed by many, that "imagination and beauty have a truth of their own which can be felt, not stated." The art, poetry, and drama of the ancients "we cannot excel. Those in their beauty represented truth, which is eternal. Beauty is the apotheosis of truth" [1] (Sir Oliver Lodge). "Beauty is God's handwriting; a wayside sacrament. Welcome it in every fair face, every fair sky, every fair flower, and thank for it Him, the fountain of all loveliness" (Charles Kingsley). "Beauty has an expression beyond and far above the one woman's soul that it clothes . . . it is more than a woman's love that moves us in a woman's eyes. . . . The noblest nature sees the most of this impersonal expression in beauty" (George Eliot).

"Beauty," Professor Alfred Russel Wallace says, "is a spiritual mystery. Even Huxley was puzzled by the beauty of his environment. What is the origin of beauty? Evolution cannot explain. Nevertheless, of course, evolution is a sound hypothesis." [2] Here you get the ultimate outcome in a nutshell. Spiritual reality on the one hand, material theories on the other; and one of the world's greatest thinkers, after many years spent in the investigation of its mysteries, standing seemingly as puzzled as a little child, while we know that, in fact, man is always standing perfectly poised, reflecting a living Principle, with its heavenly manifested realities of beauty and goodness ever available in abundant profusion around. Thank God for this beauty.

Directly a man really grasps the significance of the momentous facts now set forth, his expression changes, the principal difference being in the expression of the eyes. These have been called "the windows of the soul." When a person becomes a would-be mental worker whilst still resting on a material basis, amidst ethereal intricacies which purport to be "mental," because invisible to normal human sight, it can be known by the alteration in his expression. His eyes become hard and steely. The palm of the hand also shows the condition of the "consciousness" or "no-mind." This is the mark of the beast referred to as follows : " If any man worship the beast and his image, and receive his mark in his forehead, or in his hand, The same shall drink of the wine of the wrath of God, . . . and they have no rest day nor night" (Rev. 14:9–11). Now they can protect themselves, finding peace in God.

This is the sign of those who keep the covenant between God and man, referred to by Moses, "Love the Lord thy God," namely, think good and you will receive good. "And thou shalt bind them [these words] for a sign upon thine hand, and they shall be as frontlets between thine eyes" (Deut. 6:5, 8). When a person's ideas grow nearer to truth, the eyes

---

[1] Birmingham Lecture, October 25, 1910.
[2] Interview by Harold Begbie (*Daily Chronicle*, November 4, 1910).

brighten and yet become softer, and a beautiful look gradually grows upon
the countenance.[1] Sometimes, as people have spoken to me of God, God's
love has shone through the seeming endless mist of matter, and I have
seen them look like angel beings. This marvellous beauty is the sign
referred to in Revelation 7, verse 3, "Hurt not the earth . . . till we have   5
sealed the servants of our God in their foreheads," and in Ephesians 1,
verse 13, "Ye were sealed with that holy Spirit of promise" (see also
Ezek. 9:4, Revelation 14:1 and 22:4). I have a letter from the brother of a
well-known clergyman who, when very ill, had asked for treatment to enable
him to preach a sermon. He writes that of all the sermons he had ever heard   10
his brother preach, this one had been the most inspired, although no one
thought that he could at the time possibly face his audience. He said that
the vast congregation were profoundly moved, and that the expression on
his brother's face had been just like "the face of an angel." This was the
third time that this friend had been similarly helped, and, alluding to the   15
first occasion, he characterised it as "his miraculous sermon." Such is
the power of God. According to Maeterlinck, Plotinus had the most divine
intellect of any man who ever lived. In his moments of inspiration it is
said his face shone with a light not of earth. Mr. F. Taylor writes: "The
transcendent, spiritual reality within the earthly image shone through the   20
mask of flesh. By sheer intellectual and spiritual energy he attained into
union with God; became one with that undefinable reality, which is the
flame in the prophet's heart, the love and purity which comes from goodness of character, the light and life of every man that cometh into the
world, and the one undying self in which we all live and move and have   25
our being." "The true aim of education is to develop a real love of beauty"
(Plato), for "All beauty and goodness are in and of Mind."

> "Beauty is truth, truth beauty—that is all
> Ye know on earth, and all ye need to know" (*Keats*).

If you are always watching for opportunities to be kind, and making   30
use of such opportunities, you will find, not only inestimable joy in this
demonstration of love, but the beauty that love gives will shine through
your face in ever-increasing variety of expression, and you will receive in
return "such sweet smiles and hearty thanks." This is the true beauty,
which is spiritual, and shines through and beautifies the plainest features.   35
It has been said that no old person has any right to be ugly, as he has
had all his life in which to grow beautiful. Now we know the secret of how
to become beautiful, we must continually pray, think rightly, "Till we all
come in the unity of the faith, and of the knowledge of the Son of God, unto
a perfect man, unto the measure of the stature of the fulness of Christ"   40
(Eph. 4:13). "The essence of all beauty I call love" (Elizabeth Browning).
"And he who loveth wisely, well, and much, the secret holds of the true
master touch" (Ella Wheeler Wilcox).

---

[1] This change in the eyes that comes when a man treats is no doubt the origin of
the frequent reference in the Acts to what Sir William Smith calls Paul's "peculiar   45
habit of looking steadily when about to speak" (see Acts 7 :55). This "steadfastly
beholding" is also noted when he was about to heal (Acts 14:9).

SECTION SIX

ETHEREAL "NO-MIND"

"*The carnal mind is enmity against God*" (Rom. 8:7).
Notwithstanding the phenomenal results apparent, instances of which
5 have been pointed out, the human so-called "mind" can cognise nothing
absolutely, can do nothing good, nor provide anything either real or permanent. Its very best seeming effects are nothing more than counterfeits of
reality. "They that are in the flesh cannot please God" (Rom. 8:8). "As
it is written, There is none righteous, no, not one" (Rom. 3:10). Jesus
10 showed that even the purest human (being material or carnal mind and
body) could not be really good, as he said: "Why callest thou me good?
there is none good but one, that is, God" (Matt. 19:17).

Good is Absolute, Evil Relative.—What we call good is only
more or less bad, and you can always suggest an improvement upon
15 everything except the spiritual realities of heaven. The principle of mathematics is, however, true, and therefore cannot be improved. God, good, is
absolute; that is, nothing can be better, because nothing is less than perfect
in heaven. Evil is relative; that is, everything can be either better or worse
in the seeming material world, this world of evil. Jesus said: "Ye [the
20 material so-called you] are of your father the devil, . . . He . . . abode
not in the truth because there is no truth [reality] in him. . . he is a liar,
and the father of it" (John 8:44). We are also told: "Yet hath he seen no
good: do not all go to one place?" (Eccles. 6:6). "If we say that we have no
sin, we deceive ourselves" (I John 1:8). "All that is in the world, . . . is
25 not of the Father, but is of the world. And the world passeth away"
(I John 2:16, 17). "He that committeth sin is of the devil; for the devil
sinneth from the beginning." John then refers to the apparent duality of
man, and continues: "For this purpose the Son of God was manifested,
that he might destroy the works of the devil. Whosoever is born of God
30 . . . . cannot sin, because he is born of God" (I John 3:8, 9). "The carnal
mind [the human mind, called also the soul] is enmity against God: for it
is not subject to the law of God, neither indeed can be. So then they that
are in the flesh cannot please God" (Rom. 8:7, 8).

"We know that we are of God, and the whole world lieth in wicked-
35 ness" (I John 5:19) is another reference to the apparent duality of the
world. Paul knew that the material counterfeit cannot be the man here
spoken of, for in Romans 9, verse 8 he said: "They which are the children
of the flesh, these are not the children of God." We all agree with what
Paul says, "In me . . . dwelleth no good thing: . . . how to perform
40 that which is good I find not. [Remember that this "I" is the mortal
counterfeit.] For the good that I would I do not: but the evil which I
would not, that I do. . . . It is no more I that do it, but sin that dwelleth
in me." Then he continues, with a burst of exultation, "For I delight in
the law of God after the inward man" (Rom. 7:18–20, 22).

Conscience.—What we have humanly called good depends upon our conscience, and that has depended upon the way in which we have been brought up. Knowledge of truth has now lifted man above any hereditary limitations or arbitrary educational influences. I was once told that a tribe in Central Africa considered it an absolute necessity to their welfare in after life to kill and eat their parents when they got to a certain age. It certainly was better for the parents to be fattened up for a year, as they used to be, and then painlessly killed, when asleep, and eaten, than to be left in the jungle to starve, the fate of the aged of the neighbouring tribes. The Chukches stone their aged, and some of the Indian tribes give them over to tigers. "Sin is not imputed when there is no law" (Rom. 5:13). Darwin, in his journal of the voyage of H.M.S. *Beagle* round the world, gives the reply of the Tierra Del Fuegan boy to the question why they ate their old women when hungry, instead of their dogs : "Doggies catch otters, old women no."

Sin.—"*All unrighteousness* ['*a way that is not right*'] *is sin*" (I John 5:17).

One night, when at work for patients, listening for about a minute-and-a-half to a train at a distance trying to mount a hill, I suddenly recognised that this was wasting time, and, on consideration, saw that it could only be looked upon as sinning. This was because I had two patients then habitually in pain, and a minute-and-a-half's prayer for one of them would certainly have given relief more or less, possibly permanently. "To him that knoweth to do good, and doeth it not, to him it is sin" (James 4:17). "The problem remains to seek evil rather in self than in Satan, Satan only showing the limits of our self-knowledge" (Schleiermacher). Now when we find this evil in our so-called consciousness we can destroy it instead of moaning over it as we used to do in the past.

" . . . sin is a lie from the beginning,—an illusion, nothing, and an assumption that nothing is something."[1] It is the outcome of evil or the devil, "a liar and the father of it" (John 8:44). It is purely illusory. If you either love or fear sin, you are making something of it, and in either case you are punished for belief in a power other than that of God; a disobeying of the grand First Commandment: "Thou shalt have none other gods before me" (Deut. 5:7). That which you mentally admit and dwell upon as possible will appear at some time and in some form as manifest evil. Destroy the idea of sin as something real, and you destroy the love or fear of it, as the case may be, and sin disappears. Fear unconquered becomes the conqueror. The belief in sin, "the miasma of earth" (Mary Baker Eddy), is due to the action of wrong thoughts—thoughts unlike God—upon a human so-called "mind" not sufficiently purified. If you destroy the sense of sin the sin disappears. We must, however, condemn evil in every disguise, and enlist to lessen sin, disease, and death, through Christ, Truth. It is a fight for immortality, with all its glorious happiness, and shared with those we now love. The punishment of sin is only removed as the sin is removed by being destroyed. The belief that at the last moment a man may be pushed into heaven by the prayers of another, or by a few tears on his

---

[1] *Message for* 1901, p. 13 (Mary Baker Eddy).

part, is responsible for a large amount of the sin prevalent. Men would not sin if they knew that they always had an adequate punishment. They would soon learn how to stop sin if they recognised that they were punished at once. Sin is never punished after its removal. The only punishment a man
5 receives is from material so-called thoughts. They cause all the trouble resulting from sin. Sin is a form of madness. When you know and prove by demonstration that sin has no power, the sin and its punishment are removed for ever.

Sin, sickness, and trouble, unfortunately, appear fearfully real to us in
10 this material dream-world, but they are not real in an absolute or philosophical sense; that is to say, the only reality is God and heaven. The realisation that the sin, etc., does not exist in heaven, where all is spiritual and perfect, will cure the sin and its consequences quicker than anything else, and enable a man to fight against it with ease instead of with difficulty.

15   **Persecution.**—Hitherto we have never had a standard by which to work. All so-called good in the material world has been relative. Hence the terrible crimes in the past, committed by good (?) men, the persecutions of Christians by would-be Christians. This persecution is by no means obsolete, and so distorted is the human standard of good that the perse-
20 cuted are often, on their emergence from trouble, the first to turn round and become the persecutors.

THE ABSOLUTE STANDARD OF GOOD

At last we have an accurate standard by which to gauge every thought, and each thought that will not stand the test cannot be too quickly cast
25 out from our "consciousness." This standard is the standard of absolute good, God, and to think in accordance with, and therefore live by this standard, is to find here and now the kingdom of God that is within (see (Luke 17:21).

The Unfailing Action of the Principle of Good.—So certain is the
30 action of God, the divine Principle of all good, that if anyone reading these words will only turn away in thought from the material to the true mental standpoint, deny the reality of his trouble, and, dwelling on God, good, lose all sense of a material world, by realising with sufficient clearness the omnipotence of His perfect action in the perfect world, heaven, he will be
35 healed instantaneously. No one can doubt this when the Principle at work is really understood. Cease all doubts and prove it for yourself at once. The eternal Truth heals now just as certainly as it did when the Saviour of the world, Christ Jesus, proved man's divine origin and the invincible power of the Christ.
40   Again, so certain and continuous is this ever-acting Principle, that, although some may not understand fully the statements and arguments now being presented, yet, if they accept them with an open mind and an earnest desire to know more of God, from that moment their troubles begin to disappear. This truth has been proved, and is being proved in thousands
45 of cases daily.

Apparent Two Worlds.—We have to keep quite clearly before us the difference between these seemingly two universes, the real and the unreal; always denying the reality of the unreal, or three-dimensional world, the material hell; and endeavouring to realise the perfection of the real and spiritual, or four-dimensional world,[1] heaven and our real consciousness, 5 now every hour growing clearer to the dawning spiritual senses, until the final disappearance of all illusion and the apprehension of the spiritual. "While we look not at the things which are seen, but at the things which are not seen: for the things which are seen are temporal; but the things which are not seen are eternal" (II Cor. 4:18). Many mix up the two, and this is 10 one of the chief difficulties with most of the principal so-called "mental" schools, which, accurately speaking, should be called "ethereal" schools. They believe that matter is a manifestation of Spirit. Whereas "That which is born of the flesh is flesh; and that which is born of the Spirit is spirit" (John 3:6). It is impossible to get such a result as the instantaneous 15 healing of cancer, and other false growths, in the proper way, which is a permanent cure, namely, by the purification of the patient's so-called "mind" or human consciousness, while this wrong idea of the world, and therefore of matter, is even tacitly accepted by the healer through ignorance. 20

COLLECTIVE FORCE OF FOOLISH BELIEFS

"What is the matter with this race? Everybody is afraid. They are taught as babies to be afraid. 'Don't eat that ice cream, my dear little thing.' 'Why not, mamma?' 'Oh, because you will have about fifty or sixty kinds of stomach-ache if you do'" (Edward Kimball). 25

From what has been said it will be recognised that any form of belief held by enough people in a community becomes a so-called law to that community, apparently active and seemingly affecting more or less every individual member. When this form of belief produces so-called good effects, apparently no harm worth mentioning is done; but when the belief 30 is a belief in evil, the members of the community, whose minds are receptive, and who do not know how to protect themselves, suffer in proportion to the condition of their so-called "minds" and the general intensity of the belief; it looks as if such suffering often wakens man to vital facts.

The effect of these general beliefs, at first merely ethereal thoughts, and 35 later intensified into materially visible trouble, is very noticeable in the case of disease. In countries where ignorance prevails amongst the lower classes, it is quite enough to strongly impress a native that he has fallen a victim to a prevalent disease, such as the plague, for him to show signs of it. On the appearance of these symptoms he gives up all hope and shortly disappears, 40 another victim to the curse of ignorance. Even in the forefront of civilisation the same results are just as prevalent. For instance, fifty years ago water-melons were considered rank poison to the majority. Dr. Tanner, at the end of his forty-days' fast, surprised everyone by gorging himself with this deadly fruit. With much astonishment the world woke up to the fact 45

[1] See Revelation 21, verse 16.

that sugar and water could not possibly hurt anyone when known to be harmless, and there was one bugbear less to the infant gourmet, another light, wholesome, and palatable food added to the list. Fruit pie, again, fell under the ban of general belief. At one time, in America, it was pie at
5 breakfast, pie between meals, pie at lunch, dinner, tea, and whenever Tommy could get into the larder. Then fear came pointing its finger, colic followed in its train, and before long, not only did Tommy suffer from his forbidden repast, but Tommy's father drenched himself with noxious draughts in the hope of vanquishing the enemy that was raging within.
10 Now fruit pie smiles serenely on nearly all its votaries, and Tommy sleeps quietly at night, the punishment for his raid on the family larder being confined to his father's slipper.

The Action of Food.—Not only has man learned that he need not be afraid of any kind of food, but he is learning that the apparent action
15 of food is purely owing to mistaken human beliefs, and that food is not necessary to sustain life. One friend of mine has recently fasted for forty days and for sixty days, while one frequently hears of men fasting from ten to twenty days with good effects, as far as health goes. Two friends of mine have for years never had more than a few pieces of bread-and-butter
20 daily, with either a little milk or some tea, and yet enjoy robust health. A client of mine, a well-known authority on food, told me that an acquaintance of his had, for over a year, only taken one mouthful per day, which he masticated until it disappeared, and yet was perfectly nourished. Of course, food at present is necessary, but a little later, when we know more, we shall
25 find that right thinking will be more effective than any food.

Be a Law of God, Good, unto Yourself.—Dr. Theodor Siebert, a German authority on diet, after fifteen years' observation of the diet of famous athletes and wrestlers, states: "The general result of my observations is this: Every person is a law unto himself." What better testimony
30 can we want than this to the fact that the result of food is solely a question of a person's "mentality," and the thoughts that come to him, and this can be judged of by what he thinks.[1] "They that wait upon the Lord shall renew their strength . . . they shall run, and not be weary; and they shall walk, and not faint" (Isa. 40:31).
35 Bacteria are affected by human thought just as much as any other animals, and the mental call by the patient to battle or to carousal is just as effective as the audible call with any other freebooter.

Belief in sickness is in many cases a mere foolish belief. Some parade their troubles in the hope of attracting attention; others commit suicide,
40 by attempting to win what one may almost call fame by their continual

---

[1] In the *Daily Mirror* of August 9, 1911, appeared an article on "A Serious Address Delivered by a Prominent Physician to a Gathering of Medical Men," in which this physician stated "Dangers lurk in every present form of food," saying also "It appears to me that it is really dangerous to be 'alive.'" The *Daily Mirror*
45 submitted the quotation to a food expert, who gave them twenty instances of the poisonous nature of well-known foods, and the dangers that are attached to ordinary things like the constant washing of the skin. This shows how the whole thing is not merely a question of what one does and what one leaves undone but what one thinks and what other people think.

ailments. Many are almost offended at the idea of possible health, and all are more or less flattered by any attentions to supposed bodily weaknesses. Many live a prey to constant fears, while the one hopelessly infectious disease called death everyone unanimously accepts as eventually his final and fatal ailment.   5

Sleep a Waste of Time.—Similarly, sleep seems at present necessary, but very little is required. A friend of mine for several years has not averaged more than three hours, and constantly has worked by my side the whole night through without the slightest ill effect. It is quite easy to work night after night for a patient, doing one's ordinary business through   10
the day, without the slighest feeling of either tiredness or sleepiness, and with no ill effects. Naturally, it is necessary to know the truth in order to obtain such results. Active thinking is the basis of all true existence. All that is necessary is to realise that man (the real man) never sleeps, for God is Mind, ever active, and man reflects that Mind and never sleeps (in the   15
reality), therefore no want of sleep can harm man as he is spiritual. Curiously, the realisation of the same truth will help a person suffering from insomnia, as, when fear has gone, and he recognises that sleeplessness will not harm him, the worry disappears, and the realisation that man is governed by the peace of God which passeth all understanding, soon gives   20
him the desired sleep. As man becomes less material, he always tries to remain awake as long as he possibly can, so as to be of more use to others. This motive leads to the habit of thought which brings best results to himself. It is now being more generally recognised that sleep is not necessary. An American doctor advises his patients not to sleep, saying that the mind   25
rests more when a man is quietly lying down than when he is unconscious. I have recently heard of a man in Philadelphia who has not slept for over ten years, and yet is in perfect health.

There are many other foolish beliefs binding man to matter, and no doubt each will readily recognise his own special seeming limitations, and   30
commence to get rid of them, with much advantage to himself and those around. The sooner he starts the better for him, and the sooner he will, with perfect confidence, be able to control the important things of life. An ounce of practice is worth many pounds of theory. Sir John Goss, the musician, used to put it thus, "An ounce of practice to a hundredweight of   35
theory."

DANGEROUS FALSE BELIEFS

A few of the more dangerous beliefs that have been founded on false premises may now be dealt with.

Hypnotism.—"*There are few powers at present available to man*   40
more dangerous than that which is displayed by the hypnotiser . . . this is a
power that no good man has a right to exercise" [1] (Annie Besant).
Hypnotism is a belief in the apparent control of one human being over another, leading, as Mrs. Eddy says, "to moral and to physical death." It is a mistakenly imagined fight in which the stronger overpowers the   45

---

[1] Lecture delivered at St. James's Hall, September 9, 1891.

9*

weaker. This false "mental," really higher physical, force is always more or less harmful, and in its varying forms of animal magnetism, "spiritual wickedness in high places," so-called "mental" malpractice, etc., is the greatest enemy of the human race that ever has had an apparent sense of 5 reality, or ever will have between the present time and its final total destruction, now, thank God, nearing with tremendous rapidity.

I was once asked by the Lord Chief Justice to draft a Bill for the stopping of mental malpractice. My reply was that the remedy would be worse than the disease, as it would draw people's attention to the harmful effects 10 obtainable. The time is now almost ripe for legislation on the subject. Undoubtedly hypnotic exhibitions at public entertainments should be prohibited by law, as in Switzerland, Holland, and other countries. I also think that its use should be limited to certified practitioners, until it can be stopped altogether.

15 As showing the dangerous power of hypnotism, Sir Henry Morris, Bart, M.B., F.R.C.S., writes: "Esdaile, it is said, on one occasion hypnotised a man in open court behind his back and without his knowledge." [1] Sir Francis R. Cruise, M.D., an authority on the subject, writes, and puts it in italics: "*as we use it, it will be for good or evil.*" [2]

20 There are five different forms of hypnotism, all of them wrong, and all of them merely altering human phenomena. With the exception of auto-suggestion, which again may be subdivided under two heads, all are the theoretical, ethereal action of one human consciousness over another. There is also the hypnotic action of thoughts upon a human being with-25 out such thoughts intensifying themselves on a second unfortunate individual.

Hypnotic Prayer.—Take, for example, one of the least obnoxious forms, namely, when a man prays for anything and then is certain that a per-conceived result is going to be brought about by the action of God. We 30 can never choose what is best for a man, and outlining desired results in this way can in any case only bring about what the person praying thinks is best, and both human beings are necessarily harmed to a certain degree, and are possibly harmed to a very serious extent. When praying for any-one in the right way, only good can come to both, and both so-called minds 35 are improved. "No good is certain, but the steadfast mind, the undivided will to seek the good" (George Eliot).

There are many forms of false "mental" science whose followers, choosing the results they desire, claim to be able to work miracles. All these methods are more or less bad. Even in the best cases the results can 40 never do any permanent good, and as certainly do some harm.

Hugo Münsterberg, an authority on hypnotism, writes: "For instance, I have steadily refused requests of students and others to use hypnotism for the purpose of overcoming merely bad habits, such as the habit of biting the nails. A child who finds some difficulty in sticking seriously to 45 his tasks might learn now this, and now that, under the influence of hypnotic

---

[1] "Suggestion in the Treatment of Disease" (*British Medical Journal*, June 18, 1910).
[2] Introductory chapter to *Treatment by Hypnotism and Suggestion*.

suggestions, but he would remain *entirely untrained for mastering the next lesson.* [The italics are mine.] In the same way some naughty traits might be artificially removed, but the child would not gain anything towards the much more important power of suppressing an ugly tendency of his own effort." Charcot, Richet, Brabinski, and many others have declared that for curative purposes hypnotism is very rarely useful, generally entirely useless, and often injurious.[1]

Dr. Schofield writes : "Faith cures exist of many varieties. There is the prayer and faith cure at Lourdes; which is based upon faith in God and the Virgin, perhaps mostly on the latter. Relic cures of all sorts; where the basis is faith in the holy emblems, seen or touched. Evangelical faith cures; based upon external Divine power. Mind cures; effected by the realisation of the power of mind over matter, or by the conscious effect of the mind of the healer on the patient. Christian Science cures; based on the unreality of disease, and the direction of the mind to the Divine. Spiritualistic cures; effected by a supposed fluid or magnetic influence passing from healer to patient. Direct faith-healing; effected by faith-healers, in whom the patient has confidence, and who heal on the spot".[2]

As already explained, if a man heals by thinking of God and the spiritual world, this is the true and scientific method. If he temporarily removes trouble by thinking of the material world, it is wrong and harmful to all concerned.

Unfortunate Workers.—If a man tries to use his so-called mind in the wrong way, it causes him, if anything, more trouble than the person whom he is influencing.[3] When I have asked a man who does this whether he is happy, whether he is healthy, and whether he is successful, his answer has been invariably, "No." Working in this way is like using a silk pocket-handkerchief to clean a door-step. The human "no-mind," or ethereal mechanical counterfeit of consciousness, is dangerous to itself, and if people use it improperly it inevitably leads from bad to worse. May God help such unfortunate workers, and that speedily.

Napoleon.—Once when lecturing before the Royal Engineers at Chatham, and referring to the different sources of so-called power likely to become available, I mentioned that the human so-called "mind" was at present the most available agent for utilising the latent power of the ether, or rather, that with which idolatry credits it. The following morning, at breakfast, mentioning that Napoleon was one of the strongest false

[1] *The Force of Mind* (A.T. Schofield, M.D.)
[2] *Ibid.*
[3] Recently, in one of the well-known London magazines, a signed article appeared entitled "Menti-Culture," in which is shown how one person can affect another, and compel the other to do what he wants. One paragraph runs as follows : "You may find that the other man will begin to feel that you are gaining some sort of influence over him, and he may in self-defence endeavour to terminate the interview. This you must not permit, for you have gained an influence, and you must follow it up. *Do not leave him until you get what you came for.*" The italics are those of the writer of the article. This shows how the wrong use of the human mind is gaining ground, and how essential it is to learn how to protect oneself and the hypnotiser against such a devilish system of working which otherwise damages both concerned.

"mental" workers of modern days, the General in command read me the
following words of Napoleon : "I have inspired multitudes to die for me.
God forbid that I should form any comparison between the enthusiasm
of my soldiers and Christian charity. They are as different as their causes.
5 And then my presence was required; the electricity of my look, my voice,
a word from me, then the sacred fire was kindled in all hearts. I certainly
possess the secret of that magic power which carries away other people's
minds : yet I could never communicate it to others. Not one of my generals
ever received it from me, or guessed at it; neither have I the power to
10 eternalise my name and my love in the heart. Now that I am at St. Helena,
now that I am alone, nailed to this rock, who fights and conquers empires
for me? What courtiers have I in my misfortune? Does any one think of
me? Does any one in Europe move for me? Who has remained faithful?
Where are my friends?" Ultimately, like all such workers, he broke down
15 altogether, and showed "painful signs of degeneration."[1]

This is the record more or less of all those possessing, or, more strictly
speaking, being possessed by, this so-called power. The greater the
development of the human "mind power" (so called), the greater the
unhappiness. Emerson, mistaking for a real power this hypnotic control
20 over the hypnotiser and hypnotised, wrote : "A river of command runs
down from the eyes of some men, and the reason why we feel one man's
presence and not another's is as simple as gravity; and this natural
force is no more to be withstood than any other natural force." Lord
Wolseley recognised this so-called power and wrote : "This is the influence
25 which men, with what I may term great electrical power in their nature,
have exercised in war. Cæsar, Marlborough, Napoleon, and many others I
could name possessed it largely. The current passed from them into all
around, creating great enthusiasm in all ranks far and near, and often
making heroes of men whose mothers and fathers even had never regarded
30 them in that light. This feeling is an addition of at least fifty per cent. of
strength and energy to the army where it exists." Such false stimulant only
leads to increased sense of weakness when removed, and the apparent
power must sooner or later die out.[2]

False Christs.—The reference in the New Testament to false Christs
35 and false prophets working miracles, is a reference to results obtained by
this hypnotic action. "And many false prophets shall rise, and shall deceive
many" (Matt. 24:11). "For false Christs and false prophets shall rise, and

---

[1] This lecture was given about ten years ago, and I stated that within ten years
the battles of the world would be decided in the air. Several of the papers scoffed
40 at my remarks the following morning. Recently one of the daily newspapers stated
that aerial supremacy would decide this war [1914-1918].

[2] One of the reasons for some of the extraordinary results that have been obtained
in the war now over, is that the Germans, both consciously and unconsciously, produced a hypnotic effect both upon their own side and the Allies. Elsewhere I have
45 pointed out that for this reason, once the Germans were cornered, the war would
rapidly end, as this hypnotic effect would act prejudicially against themselves. In
Rasputin's correspondence, which has been given in the *Sunday Herald*, it will be
seen that the late Empress, the Czarina, boasted that they had been able to hypnotise
the English statesmen. The realisation that there is no hypnotism, as God is the only
50 power and the only ruler, will stop anything of this kind.

shall shew signs and wonders, to seduce, if it were possible, even the elect"
(Mark 13:22). "Beloved, believe not every spirit, but try the spirits
whether they are of God: because many false prophets are gone out into
the world" (I John 4:1). The test of the true prophet is whether he turns
in thought to God or not. A very fair sign of this is whether he is always 5
loving and never blames or criticises others.

Occultism.—"*Occult—Hidden, secret, unknown*" (Chambers's *Etymological Dictionary*).

In the light of present scientific knowledge this term becomes obsolete.
All the mysterious phenomena that have hitherto been such a puzzle to 10
the world in general are now uncovered, and no longer veiled in the
mystery of a past age. There are still some who may use the term simply
because not sufficiently advanced in the right understanding of God and
the material universe to be able to account for what to them appears
mysterious, and is put aside as unsafe to be dealt with. Universal spread of 15
real knowledge enlightens this blind condition. There is no longer any
such thing as occult phenomena, as even the miracles of Jesus are now
easily understood, whilst the whole of the phenomena classed under the
terms hypnotism, spiritualism, etc., are no more occult than the simplest
acts of every-day life. It has been the mystery attached by ignorance to the 20
so-called miraculous events with which the Bible teems, that has throughout the centuries led to the complete failure to grasp its accurate scientific
significance, and so gain by reversal its true spiritual import. There is now
not a single incident in the Bible that can be called occult, or in any sense
mysterious. 25

Spiritualism.[1]—"*And when they shall say unto you, Seek unto them
that have familiar spirits, and unto wizards that peep, and that mutter:
should not a people seek unto their God?*" (Isa. 8:19).

The results obtained by spiritualists, so called, are simply due to the
intensification of human concepts by the so-called "mind" of the medium, 30
and in some cases by the "minds" of those present at the séance. "Spiritualism" is an entire misnomer, as its phenomena are entirely material.
"etherealism," or even "materialism," is a more accurate name.

There is no question as to the phenomena of "spiritualism"; Crookes,
Wallace, Hyslop, James, Richet, Lodge, and Cesare Lombroso[2] have all 35
testified to the results, but the theory based upon such phenomena is
absolutely wrong. I asked Sir William Crookes, who has vouched for the
existence of various forms of these phenomena, to what he thought they
were due. He said: "I have not the slightest idea, but I do not think that
they have anything to do with departed spirits." He has said: "I have 40
nothing to retract. I adhere to my already published statements. Indeed, I
might add much thereto. I regret only a certain crudity in those early
expositions which, no doubt justly, militated against their acceptance by

[1] "When the Science of Mind is understood, spiritualism will be found mainly
erroneous" (*Science and Health*, p. 71, Mary Baker Eddy). 45
[2] Lombroso, that great scientific leader and pioneer in the new fields of exact
learning, after most careful investigation, wrote that the phenomena of spiritualism "form such a compact web of proof as wholly to baffle the scalpel of doubt."

the scientific world. My own knowledge at the time scarcely extended beyond the fact that certain phenomena new to science had assuredly occurred, and were attested by my own sober senses, and, better still, by automatic record, . . . I think I see a little farther now. I have glimpses
5 of something like coherence among the strange elusive phenomena; of something like continuity between those unexplained forces and laws already known."

I should like here to pay a tribute to the courage with which Sir William gave to an ignorant world the results of his examination, not minding
10 whether he improved or injured his scientific position, but desirous only of contributing to our knowledge. A lesser man might have allowed the fear of ridicule from sceptical ignorance to deter him. Would that all had this moral courage. "An Englishman fears contempt more than death" (Goldsmith).

15 A tribute should also be paid to Sir Oliver Lodge, who, although wrong in his deductions from the facts in connection with spiritualistic phenomena with which he is acquainted, has, in the most courageous way, given his results to the public. He, fortunately, has at the same time drawn attention to the danger in the practice of spiritualism and the investigation
20 of its phenomena.

Professor Lombroso writes in *After Death—What?*: "In psychical matters we are very far from having attained scientific certainty. But the spiritualistic hypothesis seems to me like a continent, incompletely submerged by the ocean in which are visible in the distance broad islands
25 raised above the general level, and which only in the vision of the scientist are seen to coalesce in one immense and compact body of land, while the shallow mob laughs at the seemingly audacious hypothesis of the geographer."

J. W. Heysinger, M.D., writes: "Granting that an efflorescence, let us
30 say, from the medium, another from the bodies of those present, and a third from the atmosphere, perhaps, might be tangibly available as a framework, it is not at all incredible that bound ether, under strain, might be attracted to, and agglomerate with, and, acting under intelligent power, might possibly produce all the phenomena of materialisation, and those of
35 poltergeists, and other like manifestation. Such an interpretation might also serve to account for the almost universal employment of such terms as 'magnetism,' 'electricity,' 'animal magnetism,' 'etherealisation,' 'materialism,' and the like, applied in spiritualistic nomenclature simply because they seem appropriate, while no other terms are; but, as the most
40 careful tests show, the phenomena do not respond to electroscopes, magnetoscopes, galvanoscopes, or other similar instruments. . . . Phenomena of this character have been too common everywhere, in all parts of the world and during all past times, as well as at present for us, as scientific students, to ignore them. It may not be possible, at present, to explain
45 these phenomena, at least to fully explain them, but their substantial identity is so remarkable in all the narratives, that they must have some valid basis. . . . They involve telepathy and thought transference, and very often prevision, almost always clairvoyance; the physical manifestations clearly extend far beyond phenomena of these types alone. In fact

the physical and the non-physical seem to blend in these cases in such a
manner as to suggest a revision of all our conceptions of crude matter as
formerly held, and this is what science to-day, in the light of its recent
advances, stands ready to accept on proof." [1]

In *Reincarnation*, Mrs. Besant writes: "This Thought Force is, in the
Esoteric Philosophy, the one source of form; it is spoken of by H. P.
Blavatsky as 'The mysterious power of thought which enables it to produce external, perceptible, phenomenal results by its own inherent
energy.'"

So-called Proofs.—The following are claimed to be the proofs of the
truth of spiritualism :—

(1) You may see a figure seemingly indentical with a person who has
died or who is at the time alive; you can speak to him, touch him, weigh
him, photograph him, etc.; that is, the figure is just as material as an
ordinary human being.

(2) This so-called person will tell you things that you think only you
can possibly know, and tell you or enable you to see things that are happening at a distance, that have happened in the past, or are about to happen
in the future.

(3) He will tell you things that the dead (or living) person whom he
resembles did, and that no one else could possibly have known, except a
thought-reader, and which can be afterwards verified as correct. Sometimes information is given by automatic writing in a closed receptacle.
Sometimes the person is invisible, sometimes visible.

(4) The medium himself will sometimes give the above information,
and sometimes a voice will sound exactly as a person speaks or used to
speak, of whom he consciously knows nothing. The voice sometimes seems
to come from the medium and sometimes from someone else.

(5) The figure will appear to move from place to place, alter in size, or
weight, or shape; limbs, for instance, lengthening or appearing close to the
medium or at a distance.

(6) Material things of all kinds will be made to appear and disappear,
will be moved from place to place, or brought from a distance, and will
apparently alter in weight.

(7) Apparent healing will take place, and fire, etc., have no effect.

(8) Sounds of all kinds are heard; luminous appearances, phantom forms
and faces are seen.

(9) Miscellaneous occurrences of a complex and often diabolical
character will take place.

Stages in the Formation of Matter.—Close your eyes and imagine, say,
a rose. You are in ethereal touch with the rose. Do this when only partially
conscious of other things; it comes clearer. Mr. Carpenter stated that he
knew a man who every afternoon went into his study with drawn blinds,
and for an hour entrancing experiences would come to him, of travels
abroad, etc. If the rose is thought of when in a light trance, the rose can be
photographed and seen by those sufficiently psychic. If the same experience
takes place when the operator is in the ordinary spiritualistic trance, the

[1] *Spirit and Matter before the Bar of Modern Science.*

rose can be seen by all those present, although their hands, or any other form of matter, would pass right through it. Now should this occur when the sorcerer or witch, or to use more modern terms, the so-called medium —or, shall we say, the victim—is in a deep trance, the rose can be both seen
5 and touched, and if the thought of those present is sufficient, it can be kept for a day or two, until the general thought of death prevents those looking at it seeing God's perfect idea in any other way than a mass of decaying matter. "Sic transit gloria mundi." Remember that this cannot always be done when wanted. The phenomena are apparent only when thoughts are
10 there intensifying themselves on the so-called mind of the operator.[1]

The Explanation of Its Seeming Mystery.—The scientific reason for these wonderful results, most of which have been confirmed by many reliable people is that the "subconcious mind" or basic false "mentality" of the material man is always in ethereal touch with every thought in the
15 material world, past, present, and future, and a mixed medley of ethereal thoughts of every kind and description, with and without any logical sequence or benefit to mankind, are intensified on the so-called "mind" of the medium until they are manifested more materially in the form of what are called the spirits or the flowers, or other things that these spirits are
20 supposed to bring or produce. Thoughts are also similarly intensified so that you may hear what sounds like the voice of a human being, or see visions of the past or future.

Objections and Dangers.—On the other hand, it is admitted by all spiritualists with whom I have discussed this matter that the following
25 statements are correct:—

(1) By far the greater part, probably ninety-five to ninety-nine per cent., of the information gained at séances is absolutely wrong.

(2) Even when correct information is given, it cannot be depended upon, as nearly always there is more or less inaccuracy.

30 (3) In many cases investigation into "spiritualism" has done much harm, both to the human consciousness and physically. It often leads to mania.

(4) Serious bodily injury is sometimes inflicted on those present, and often property is damaged.

35 (5) It is almost always tiring, and sometimes excessively so.

(6) The so-called spirits constantly contradict themselves and other spirits on all points.

(7) Last but not least, it deteriorates the moral character.

This last point is only admitted by spiritualists to be the case in some
40 instances.

I remember laying before the President of the leading spiritualistic association scientific evidence of what spiritualism really is, i.e., merely

---

[1] Since the above was written, the following has appeared in the public press: "Major Darget . . . first fixed his eyes on his walking stick, and then concentrated
45 all his thoughts on a photographic plate in a developing bath. In a quarter of an hour the walking-stick was reproduced on the plate, and a similar experiment with a bottle was quite as successful. Each photograph was obtained in the presence of half a dozen witnesses."

false pictures, entirely void of any real, spiritual, mental substance, deceiving mankind, chiefly on account of the earnest and self-sacrificing endeavours of many Christian seekers after truth to pierce the veil of mystery that enshrouds the so-called hereafter, and so be of assistance to humanity. I explained to him the so-called origin of matter, and the two methods of causing it to appear and disappear, saying how in many cases when the things the spirits were supposed to bring were materialised in the room they would be dematerialised elsewhere, and that therefore they would be practically stolen. Whilst this explanation was proceeding his face had been getting longer and longer, and on hearing the last statement, he admitted that it was true, as often, when spirits had brought flowers, he had been able to find out in the neighbourhood the plant from which the flowers had been torn.

It will be found that the realisation of the non-reality of matter and the allness of God is sufficient to prevent the manifestation of any occult phenomena of this description.

Terrible Results.—In spiritualism, not only foolish, but horrible and dangerous results are obtained, as well as those which appear to be good, for the phenomena depend upon the individual condition of the medium and of those present. If a critic be there who is a disbeliever and strong thinker, no result will be produced, as his so-called "mind" will produce too powerful a negative result, and so prevent it. This is the reason why all occult phenomena are more or less disbelieved by strong thinkers in the West who start with a biassed view.

"Mediumship has supplied American asylums with thousands of lunatics." [1] Sir J. Risdon Bennett,[2] and others, have given similar testimony. "Five of my friends," writes a medium of eight years' standing, "destroyed themselves, and I attempted it, by direct spiritual influence." [3]

The method by which spiritualistic results are obtained is absolutely wrong, being the exact opposite of true mental spiritual working. Take one point alone: you are told to keep your "mind" as free from thought as possible,[4] whereas to fulfil, and therefore demonstrate, the law of life, exactly the opposite is necessary, namely, you should always be actively thinking and using your "consciousness," but as far as you can in the proper way, not by thinking of the material world, but by always thinking of the reality, heaven.

Deterioration of Moral Character.—In every case I have known, with the exception of the better-class Yogis in India, the human being has morally deteriorated sooner or later after commencing to materialise matter. This

---

[1] *The Edinburgh Review*, July, 1868.
[2] See *Diseases of the Bible*, p. 80.
[3] *Spiritualism Unveiled* (Miles Grant).
[4] A friend of mine, well informed on such subjects, has lately written to me as follows : " If in a room anyone thinks a medium is a cheat, she receives the idea that she must cheat. No one has a right to think a positive thought at a séance. The medium has to be in a negative condition, and any strong thinker on a downward line is very responsible." This is one of the many proofs of the danger of this system, and is also a reminder of the necessity of always actively thinking thoughts of Life, Truth, or Love, and so being non-receptive to any mental suggestions of evil under all circumstances.

is the explanation of the extraordinarily divergent views held with regard to materialising mediums, and such-like materialising occult workers. Obliged to earn a living by displaying their powers, there comes a day when, not being quite up to the mark, they resort to a little falsification, 5 and this lessening their own faith in their results, they lose the so-called power, and ultimately descend to absolute trickery, and indeed worse. Sooner or later the trickery is discovered, and then people say that all their results were equally fraudulent.

For instance, Professor Lombroso gives accounts of the tricks played by 10 a well-known medium, both when in the state of trance and when out of it, showing that the moral character was debased. There is little doubt about her original results. Mr. Hereward Carrington has written a book called *The Sorceress*, in which he gives particulars of this medium's "occult results." The importance of the book is that, while Mr. Carrington is 15 known for his exposure of spiritualistic tricks and started as a sceptic, he now admits the phenomena, although uncertain of the cause.[1] This medium was what is called "exposed" at Cambridge, and once told Professor Lombroso that at Genoa she was conscious of someone secretly ordering her to cheat, and felt compelled to obey. This shows how she 20 was hypnotised into evil, and illustrates the injustice and sin of judging harshly any who have been unfortunate enough to have fallen under the dangerous influence of so-called "spirits." [2] Professor Sidgwick, not knowing exactly what was taking place, was naturally disgusted with the trickery his investigations brought to light, and declared that he would "ignore 25 her performances in the future as those of other persons in the same mischievous trade were to be ignored." These were only due to the wrong thoughts which acted upon a medium that was receptive to such false thoughts. Such are the results of spiritualistic experiments upon mediums who otherwise might be living holy, and therefore happy lives, helping all 30 round them. When they understand what is taking place, and the danger of their position, they will make use of their knowledge to free themselves from this fatal outside control. These workers, on awakening to the truth, will be astonished to find the power that all possess of helping those who previously have been only mystified and further misled by their work.

35 "For a long time, writes Dr. B. F. Hatch, I was swallowed up in its whirlpool of excitement, and comparatively paid but little attention to its evils, believing that much good might result from the openings up of the avenues of spiritual intercourse. But during the past eight months I have devoted my attention to a critical investigation of its moral, social, and 40 religious bearings, and I stand appalled before the revelations of its awful and damning realities, and would flee from its influence as I would from the miasma, which would destroy both soul and body." [3]

---

[1] In *The Problems of Psychical Research*, Mr. Carrington gives details of the formation of an apparent being, *Little Stasia*, by Mlle. Stanislaw Tomczyk, a girl 45 of eighteen, under test conditions. This so-called being was photographed.

[2] Professor Huge Münsterberg, of Harvard University, has written an excellent account of two so-called séances. He thinks that her case is one of irresponsible double personality.

[3] *Spiritualism Unveiled* (Miles Grant).

The same results as in "spiritualism" are obtained more or less by other sects, who present an entirely different theory from such results, equally undemonstrable.

After Death—What? by Professor Lombroso, published since the above was written, bears out what has been said. He was an extremely able man, an eminent Italian criminologist and psychologist, whose honour and good faith have never been questioned.[1] His own testimony is corroborated in many respects by that of other distinguished men. The accuracy of his statements need not be questioned, only his interpretation of them. His book may be of use to the materialist, as it will show him that he has still something more to learn, and that he has entirely to remodel his old assumptions. It is not of much use to others.

To be fair to "spiritualists," it should be said that many live splendid lives and are examples to humanity. Many also have been turned from so-called atheism, agnosticism, and doubt to a study of the Bible by the phenomena they have witnessed, for instance, the late C. H. Hall. These, however, are the awakening thinkers, who have been usually living their religion, that is, doing the best, up to their understanding, for their fellow-men. This right purpose must eventually bring all earnest seekers to the true knowledge of God in any case.

There are also, every now and then, cases where mediums have been of use, but the belief that departed spirits are necessary for such a result is simply a limitation, and mediums do very different work as they learn to think in the right way, and give up the broken reed leaned upon in the past.

Planchette.—Planchette is merely a belief in limitation, those using it imagining that it is necessary to enable them to obtain so-called messages from the dead. As a matter of fact the results obtained are merely due to ethereal "thoughts" passing over the "consciousness" of the person using it, and over the instrument. Similar devices have been known for centuries, for instance, in China.

In Matla and Van Zelst's book, *The Mystery of Death*, particulars are given of an electro-mechanical instrument called the Dynamistograph. This is said to be a kind of telegraphic apparatus which will take the place of the medium, so that departed spirits can communicate with those still alive. Its action, again, is merely due to "thoughts" being intensified enough by the "mind" of the medium to cause the apparatus to act.

Such methods of communication were punishable with death in the time of Moses. "A man also or woman that hath a familiar spirit, or that is a wizard, shall surely be put to death" (Lev. 20:27). "So Saul died . . . for asking counsel of one that had a familiar spirit to enquire of it; And enquired not of the Lord: therefore he slew him" (I Chron. 10:13, 14). This death resulted from his mistaken appeal to the human consciousness, which was able to read the death thoughts that were about to attack him

[1] In consequence of a critical article that appeared in a newspaper on the work of Mazolo, that great philologist invited Lombroso, the writer of the article, to visit him. When a boy of fourteen appeared he thought that a practical joke was being played on him.

on the following day.[1] Saul, instead of destroying these thoughts, as he could have done if he had known how to pray rightly, allowed his fear to intensify them, and accordingly paid the penalty of ignorant disobedience to the messages of truth that had been presented to him by the prophet
5 while alive.

Grief for a " Departed " Friend.—Some obtain relief from their feelings of sadness, after losing a dear one, by attending séances, and thinking that they are in touch with their beloved for a time. It has been frequently proved that a gleam of spiritual understanding, bringing even a momentary
10 recognition of the fact that they are always with their dear one in the real world, both being spiritual and perfect, gives far greater relief. Often it has been instantaneous, and the late sufferer has left full of joy, determined to start a new life of helping others, looking forward to the rapidly approaching end of the mesmeric belief in separation. These thoughts enter the
15 "mournful man's darkened room" like beauteous angels guarding him from all false beliefs which would engulf him in a sea of misery. The fact that the mourners commence instantly to help their fellow-men through knowing how to pray, turns them from the selfishness of grief to their real and only duty and source of happiness, the helping of those around them.
20 Dr. Schofield writes : "Not a single sorrow exists that can touch us save through our own thoughts. These form, as it were, an atmosphere through which every external event must pass, and which determines its character and effect on us. The same event to one man is an evil he deplores, and to another a blessing in which he rejoices, solely on account of the different
25 minds through which it passes. A mind can thus be formed to which 'all things work together for good' (Rom. 8:28). Steadiness of purpose is always well marked under great pain or pressure." "To keep head against a rapid stream is different from paddling in a pond." "Thoughts are real things. From whence all joy, from whence all sorrow springs" (T. Tra-
30 herne).

Theory Unsound.—From what has been put before you, it must be acknowledged that there has been presented a consistent scientific theory of the working and of the effect of the so-called "mind," which fully accounts for all the ethereal (miscalled mental) and material phenomena of
35 spiritualism. It is exactly the reverse with the fragmentary theory propounded by spiritualists. This proves itself to be false, not only by its inconsistency with many other known material so-called facts, and its failure to bring to light any knowledge that enables mankind with certainty to destroy all forms of surrounding evil, but by its actual intensification, in
40 many cases, of such evil.

The absolute consistency of the theory now presented to you is proved, because (1) it perfectly explains all phenomena of the material world, however seemingly mysterious; (2) it enables each and all, in denying the reality of all material phenomena and affirming the reality of good, as Mind,
45 to demonstrate, in a practical manner, the allness and reality of God, good, and the ever-available power of God to overcome all evil.

In no way do all the other known theories more clearly prove their own false basis than through their utter inability to offer any permanent remedy

---

[1] See I Samuel 28.

for the evil around us, or even any correct explanation of the constantly changing phenomena of material evidence.

Magicians and Wizards.—Professor Lombroso writes that so-called magicians, wizards, and prophets, "are all true mediums, having an influence in the political and religious constitution of the community, individuals who act in our realm of space as if they were living in a space of the fourth dimension, upsetting our laws of time, space, and gravity; prophets and saints who predict the future and transport themselves through the air." Remember that this is the matured opinion of a scientific man of unquestionable position, after investigation into the subject.

Now we have the secret of the power that certain men like Cagliostro possessed. Figuier says : "The whole assembly felt a sort of terror when he appeared." Madame d'Oberkirch, who was very unwilling to believe in him, says that he predicted the death of the Empress Marie Theresa, and even foretold the hour at which she would expire. She writes : "His glance was so penetrating that one might be almost tempted to call it supernatural. I could not describe the expression of his eyes—it was, so to speak, a mixture of flame and ice. It attracted and repelled at the same time, and inspired, whilst it terrified, an insurmountable curiosity. I cannot deny that Cagliostro possessed an almost demoniacal power, and it was with difficulty that I tore myself from a fascination I could not comprehend, but whose influence I could not deny." His end was similar to that of all who have had this fatal power. After having been driven out of most towns, he lost his power, when he sank into an abject state of poverty, and at last, arrested by the Holy See, and "examined" by the Apostolic Court, he was condemned to perpetual imprisonment in a dungeon, where his only communication with mankind was when his jailers raised the trap to let food down to him. One day there was no sound, and that was the end of Cagliostro.

This general belief in witches and all classes of occult phenomena was simply due to the fact that the world in general thought that such results were possible. Consequently those with a peculiar class of mind were able easily to bring about alterations in the counterfeit aspect of spiritual realities, called matter, which until lately was difficult, because believed to be impossible, but which now is daily becoming more common as people see that it is possible

Divination.—There are many sects in the world whose followers can read thought, giving different reasons for it. There are many psychometrists who, on taking anything in their hand, will answer almost any question about its history that you choose to ask, and some of them can read future thought. There are numerous clairvoyants who have similarly developed this capacity. All these have various limitations of belief, and the work is very tiring.

The "spiritualists" think that it is a departed "spirit" who is the actor, not recognising that it is merely the mechanical working of the so-called "mind" of the medium. In Central Africa some of the witch doctors do the same thing, others obtain these results by hypnotising boys. The same result is obtained by members of a tribe in Abyssinia.[1] In other cases . people mix up this practice with palmistry, crystal-gazing, and the telling of events by the use of cards and various so-called magic spells and black arts, a large portion of their results being just ordinary thought-reading. 5 The use of cards, crystals, etc., is quite unnecessary to obtain these results, were they not believed to be necessary.[2]

Another limited method of thought-reading is by means of colours. The different colours are simply different vibrations, and therefore, from the sequence of varying colours, which are caused to alter their position 10 by the vibration of ethereal thoughts of differing numerical value, can be calculated out mathematically the vibrations that are about to act at any given time in the future.

It may well upset one's old scientific theories to see on one's own table pieces of cardboard covered with differently coloured silks jumping up in 15 the air one after the other with mathematical accuracy, and from no apparent cause known to the scientific world.

Except in a few cases, the results obtained by various forms of divination are so very uncertain that they cannot be relied upon. The only way in which absolute certainty can be obtained (and ultimately beneficial 20 results must invariably ensue), is by working with an absolutely pure motive and in the truly scientific way in which our Lord, the Master-metaphysician, worked, namely, with spiritually awakened consciousness. In this way only can we be sure of the real value of any result obtained, and are certain never to be harmed (See Ezek. 13:23).

25 **Extraordinary Powers of Animals.**—There are many cases of the possession of extraordinary powers by animals. One instance probably will suffice. T. J. Hudson in *The Law of Mental Medicine*, commenting on communication between ants, writes: "I shall avail myself largely of Romanes' so-called 'complete résumé of all the more important facts of 30 animal intelligence,' known to science at the time he wrote. From this we learn, first, that the sense of sight in ants is extremely limited; secondly, that they are destitute of the sense of hearing; and, thirdly, that they have some very complete and perfect means of communicating intelligence to . each other.[3] The one observable fact that gives colour to this supposition 35 is that they bring themselves into physical contact with each other by means of their antennæ whenever an emergency arises requiring a con-

---

[1] I was once retained to make a report of the prospects of the commercial development of Central Abyssinia. I saw all the travellers in that country that I could, and my staff read up all the literature obtainable. The instances of the 40 exercise of so-called·"mental" power in that country, in all sorts of ways that were credibly stated, were extraordinary.

[2] The present methods of such thought-readers who foretell trouble at certain dates, either correct or imaginary, and then as the time approaches, pester and in some cases terrorise the victim with letters requesting payment to enable them to 45 further investigate and so guard the individual against the evil, should be legally stopped. Such action intensifies any forthcoming threatening trouble, the thought causing which by their methods cannot possibly be destroyed.

[3] "Bees also are capable of receiving impressions from their fellows which excite in them emotions they are able to communicate to their companions" 50 (*Evolution and Function of Living Purposive Matter*, W. C. Macnamara, F.R.C.S.).

sultation, or necessitating the assurance of a command. But the question at once arises : Is the sense of touch, per se, equal to an explanation of all the facts relating to the conveyance of the intelligence required to organise and administer the complicated system of governmental polity, to adjust social relations, to maintain discipline in war and enforce a division of 5 labour in peace, to organise and maintain an army of defence, to discipline its forces and command it in action, to build bridges and construct pontoons and ferries for the passage of vast armies over streams otherwise impassable, to invade successfully the domains of foreign tribes and capture and enslave their inhabitants, and, finally, to inaugurate and main- 10 tain a system of slave labour vastly more successful, and, let us hope, more humane, than any that has ever prevailed in the history of mankind?" (See also p. 365.)

DISASTROUS SELF-MADE LAWS

Tiredness.—*"They that wait upon the Lord shall renew their strength;* 15 *. . . shall run, and not be weary; and they shall walk, and not faint"* (Isa. 40:31).

The wrong method of working with the human so-called "mind," in the endeavour to act upon matter, is extremely tiring, and I know of no one who has worked at a stretch for more than a few hours without being 20 fatigued. This is because the whole process is purely physical, moving matter. Working in the right way a man can continue for many consecutive hours, not only without getting tired, but feeling refreshed at the end, "mentally" and physically better, and truly more awake. Six or seven hours' consecutive work at night is quite a common occurrence with those 25 working scientifically, and when need be they work all night for several nights consecutively, following their usual duties in the daytime, without showing or feeling the slightest signs of fatigue.

Disease.—Already the medical profession admits the mental cause of disease in many cases. Dr. Clifford Allbut says: " It is an undoubted 30 clinical fact that granular kidney is often produced by prolonged mental anxiety." Sir B. W. Richardson writes: " Diabetes from sudden mental shock [ethereal intensification] is a true, pure type of a physical malady of mental origin." Sir James Paget tells of a young man who on his birthday had hæmoptysis and for nine years afterwards on each birthday, being 35 quite free in the intervals. Sir George Paget says : " In many cases I have seen reasons for believing that cancer has had its origin in prolonged anxiety." Dr. Murchison says : " I have been surprised how often patients with primary cancer of the liver have traced the cause of this ill-health to protracted grief or anxiety. The cases have been far too numerous to be 40 accounted for as mere coincidences." Dr. Snow (*Lancet*, 1880) asserts his conviction that the vast majority of cases of cancer, especially in certain parts, are due to mental anxiety. Dr. E. V. Hartmann writes : " The surest way to be attacked with an infectious disease is to be afraid of it, whilst the physician under like circumstances is very rarely attacked. Lively fear 45 and the thought of sickness is of itself sufficient to cause the same." Not that there is any cause or power in fear, but merely that fear occasions

continuous and vivid ethereal impressions to take seemingly a more
material form. Dr. Stokes says: "The first sight of cholera patients gives
rise to symptoms of cholera afterwards." Dr. Lloyd Tuckey writes:
"There is no more effectual depressant, no surer harbinger of disease,
5 than fear." [1]

   Fear.—"*Fear not: for I am with thee*" (Isa. 43 : 5). "*For that which
troubled thee, whatsoever it was, was not without anywhere, but within, in
thine own opinions, from whence it must be cast out before thou canst truly
and constantly be at ease*" [2] (Marcus Aurelius).
10   When a man is afraid, he is *physically* in touch with certain ethereal
thoughts that are attacking him, or are about to attack him in the future.
Fear has been very much misunderstood. Like many other things in the
material world, it is, under present conditions, temporarily useful if you
only use it properly; and when fear of any particular thing is felt, set to
15 work mentally and vigorously to destroy the thoughts that are attacking or
about to attack, and are therefore making you afraid. Vague or indefinite
fear has to be destroyed by the denial of the reality of fear and the realisation of the absolute fearlessness and trust in God that exist in the reality,
in heaven, the true, all-harmonious consciousness that is always good.
20 "Worry is the oldest child of fear," one of the devil's brood, and if you go
on picturing that you are having trouble, or are going to have it, you are
intensifying those ethereal forms of trouble, and so doing your best to
bring about their material appearance as soon as possible. "For the thing
which I greatly feared is come upon me" (Job. 3:25). "Depression and low
25 spirits," Matthew Arnold says, "when yielded to, become a species of
death." "Fear is a habit of mind," as Victor Longheed says in his *Vehicles
of the Air*, and to continue being afraid is a very bad habit, a shocking habit.
"For fear is nothing else but a betraying of the succours which reason
offereth" (Wisdom of Solomon 17:12). An Oriental proverb says: "The
30 plague killed 5,000 people. 50,000 died of fear." Unseen ethereal vibrations, such as what may be termed "disease thoughts," are, on account of
being unrecognised by the multitude, much more far-reaching in their
effects. When recognised, however, they are much more easily destroyed,
because they are, fortunately, not acted upon by powerful workers with
35 the human "mind," who seldom have the delicate mechanism needful to
feel faint ethereal vibrations.
   If an individual human consciousness be highly strung or highly
trained, it will feel the thoughts when they vibrate very slightly. This is
the case with what are called highly nervous people. If they go on fearing,
40 "picturing" strongly that they have the trouble, or are about to have it,
they may intensify these ethereal thoughts so much that the thing feared
will visibly come about. Whereas, if they work in the way pointed out, the
thought or thoughts will be destroyed, and either the trouble will not
arise, or they will be permanently free from it, as the case may be. In this
45 way an awakened individual gains some advantage from being sensitive,
as this brings him more easily in conscious touch with discordant vibra-

----

[1] *Treatment by Hypnotism and Suggestion.*
[2] *Meditations.*

tions, so enabling him more readily to utilise his knowledge of Truth, that they may be destroyed.

Sometimes, feeling that there was work to be done for myself, but not understanding clearly enough what it was, and having work of importance to do for others, instead of entirely destroying—as it is always safer to do 5 —the discordant faint vibrations of which I was dimly aware, I have left them alone, feeling confident that any trouble would be overcome when necessary. Sometimes this has taken place in such a way as to be a practical lesson to one present; as the difficulty thus foreshadowed has come into manifestation, and then being dealt with scientifically has consequently 10 been seen to disappear. "For God hath not given us the spirit of fear; but of power, and of love, and of a sound mind" (II Tim. 1:7).

Will-Power.—Some people seem to imagine that human will-power is a different form of evil from that which appears as simple individual wrong "thinking." This is not so. Will-power is simply due to ethereal 15 thoughts of a definite intent, intensifying themselves on a so-called human mind, and differs merely in degree from ordinary so-called human thoughts. Again, some seem to think that there is a supposed intelligence in the human "no-mind," the twists and turns of which have to be guarded against. There is nothing of the sort. Thought after thought comes 20 along in doleful, predestined procession, their want of order and sequence only matched by their baseless pretensions to power.

"Mental" Malpractice.—*"True nobility is exempt from fear"* (Shakespeare).

When other people are said to be thinking and talking wrongly of you, 25 malpractising, as it is called, they cannot possibly harm you if you know how to protect yourself and pray in the right way. They only harm themselves, and it is our duty, indeed our privilege, to destroy the false thoughts that are seemingly attacking and causing them to malpractise, or otherwise they will be punished. This is done by destroying the false thoughts 30 attacking your own mind and making you picture them as thinking and talking wrongly of you. When you have done this they stop malpractising, for there are no vibrations there to make them do it.

We have no right, however, to influence others in any human direction; indeed, we should not even let our thoughts rest upon them. Leave each 35 man free to work out his own salvation. We have enough to do in keeping our own outlook pure and wholesome.

"As silent night foretells the dawn and din of morn," so prophetic foresight warns us that the false peace of ignorance precedes the final battle and victory that come with the universal dawn of Truth, and compass the 40 destruction of a counterfeit world.

When you really understand human theories, and the battle of true spiritualisation versus etherealisation, and obtain the understanding that finally subordinates all so-called human laws, how can you possibly be frightened by what have been shown to be merely high-tension electrical 45 currents, mere human thoughts that, unless destroyed, pass over you at their predetermined time? These have no more power to harm than the cobwebs through which you unconsciously pass in early dawn. The only seeming control that they have had is the hypnotic power that you have hitherto allowed them, by accepting the general belief about them. These vibrations cannot possibly evade your mental work, and their destruction is only a question of your praying, that is, doing your mental work, 5 steadily and properly. "Who art thou, that thou shouldest be afraid of a man . . . which shall be made as grass; And forgettest the Lord thy maker?" (Isa. 51:12, 13).

Fortunately, not all thoughts are strong enough to act or are intensified sufficiently to act, as shown by the remark to his children of the old 10 man who was dying: "I have had a long life full of trouble, most of which never happened." In any case, wrong picturing by others, even when specifically directed with a view to harm you, cannot permanently damage your human consciousness, as it can only intensify the wrong thoughts. If you are working rightly you reverse the evil, and the malpractice merely 15 results in your being lifted up and helped.

"Drawing Fire."—Such is the nature of evil; not only to destroy itself, but to lead to its own destruction. You will find that the persons most malpractised on, if working rightly, have always the broadest backs. They not only are capable of standing, but draw off the fire from those who 20 are perhaps less able to protect themselves through lack of the knowledge of God, and consequent power of realising Truth and protecting themselves.

Malicious "Mental" Malpractice.—Intentional miscalled "mental" malpractice is but little understood. In the present rapidly approaching end of all sin and limitation, the milder forms of sorcery, witchcraft, 25 hypnotism, and animal magnetism, have developed into this "sin of sins." Unfortunately, those practising it know almost as little about it as those malpractised upon. If all who ever exercise this murderous (miscalled) power understood it, they would know that it harms most of all themselves, and would flee with horror from the living hell they are bringing down 30 upon their own heads. At the time they may seem to be more or less having their own way, but if their feelings were analysed it would be admitted by them that there was no happiness. Success is merely the spur to more devilish work, which at the bottom of their hearts they hate. This loathing of the means increases the bitterness that shuts off the love from others 35 which is in reality their due, and the love toward others that increases our awakening happiness, in fact, is the source of all life's happiness. "Envy is the atmosphere of hell," love that of heaven. The agony to which no verbal description of hell can do justice, and the ultimate protracted, fearful death that must befall the pitiable victim of such actively evil thoughts 40 as cause a man to malpractise, do not help him. Cursed to the last moment by himself and others, he gains nothing by such a course, but loses all. "Wide is the gate, and broad is the way, that leadeth to destruction" (Matt. 7:13). Nothing will save him from the full measure of punishment except the ceasing to practise this devilish work. Up till now, its mystery 45 has protected it. Ignorance of the subject, however, is disappearing. The worst form of this is the unforgivable sin which "shall not be forgiven him, neither in this world, neither in the world to come" (Matt. 12:32), not until the end of all evil.

Preventive Legislation.—When I was asked by Lord Alverstone, then Lord Chief Justice, a few years ago, to prepare a Bill to check this terrible scourge, more terrible to the practitioners than those practised on, I pointed out that the remedy would merely intensify the disease, until the world knew enough to be able to protect itself, and that if the Bill were put 5 forward it would do more harm than good, attracting the attention of those who were vicious and ignorant; the only real cure was to awake, and through steady mental work in the right way, to break down this false power by knowing its nothingness, and realising that the only power is that of God, good. 10

During the last five years a great change has come about, and all over the world this false power is being more or less recognised and practised. Soon it will be found that laws will be passed to deal with the matter and civil justice "will pass sentence on the darkest and deepest of human crimes" (see *Message for* 1901, p. 20, by Mary Baker Eddy). 15

Undoubtedly an Act should immediately be passed prohibiting all advertisements descriptive of disease of any kind, and the sooner it is considered "bad form" to talk of disease or human troubles in drawing-rooms or home circles the sooner will poor, ignorant, suffering humanity be freed from its bondage. 20

The fatal mistake of drawing the attention of a nation to any one disease is shown by the prophecies in the Bible with regard to the fatal ravages of one particular form. The eyes of the public cannot too soon be opened to the great mistake now being made and the necessity for its being dealt with in a scientific way, so making full use of the prophetic warnings in the 25 Bible on this point.

Matter Refined up to Dematerialisation.—Fortunately, the human consciousness never gets worse. It is always steadily being purified and refined, until it is dematerialised and no longer appears, any false sense of existence having ceased altogether. You may say: "Oh, I knew a young 30 man who was perfect—in later life he was a devil." The reason is that his mind was always bad, but the particular class of devilish thoughts never attacked him when he was young. The human consciousness always improves as the human being gets older, because of the self-dematerialisation, owing to the continuous action of God. When we turn in thought to 35 God in the right way, then this action takes place rapidly.

Death.—"*For God made not death : neither hath he pleasure in the destruction of the living. For he created all things, that they might have their being: and the generations of the world* [heaven] *were healthful; and there is no poison of destruction in them, nor the kingdom of death upon the* 40 *earth* [the spiritual earth]: (*For righteousness is immortal*)" (Wisdom of Solomon 1:13–15).[1]

The false belief that Soul and the real man are in the body has deluded us into the idea that death is a friend, a stepping-stone into heaven. This is a lie, for death is an enemy, the result of deadly ignorance which has to 45 be met and vanquished through understanding of Truth. "The man that wandereth out of the way of understanding shall remain in the congregation

[1] See also Ezekiel 18, verse 32, and 33, verse 11.

of the dead" (Prov. 21:16). "For the law of the Spirit of life in Christ Jesus hath made me free from the law of sin and death" (Rom. 8:2). Ignorance and fear kill over fifty million people a year, more than one-and-a-half every second.

5   The fact is that there is no real death. The phenomenon is merely a false belief due to a false assumption, the general consent to which has constituted a false ethereal law, or, as might be expressed in other words, has led to the disastrous result of a universal mistaken belief in death as a necessary human experience, with its consequent doleful manifestation.

10 "For I have no pleasure in the death of him that dieth, said the Lord God: wherefore turn yourselves, and live ye" (Ezek. 18:32). Man simply hypnotises himself or is hypnotised into dying. Andrew Lang states that in Australia, "whenever a native dies, no matter how evident it may be that death has been the result of natural causes, it is at once set down that the 15 defunct was bewitched." We have much to learn from nature's children.

Many sinners, even criminals, live to a green old age because they have a stronger belief in life than in death. But when the grim expected enemy overtakes them they have no knowledge of truth wherewith to ward off his attack. Even those living a life approaching a human idea of perfection 20 succumb when death appears on the scene, as mere human goodness is no protection; the innocent child, the saintly character, the intellectual giant, the vicious criminal, all fare alike if equally ignorant. Understanding of God is the only safety. Knowledge that God is Life, and that there is nothing else, no sin, no disease, no death, as God is All-in-all, is the spiritual 25 armour through which no dart can pierce, no evil slay. "To know thy [God's] power is the root of immortality" (Wisdom of Solomon 15:3).

We have traced in this work the fatal result of even one wrong thought. What must be the daily, even hourly, result to humanity of the common consent to one false assumption? We have also traced the irresistible 30 power of one good thought; the one with God that must always be a majority. What must be the result to mankind of the common consent to this one scientific fact, but the swift and total destruction of the last enemy? What a glorious awakening is now taking place through the dawn of truth. Now that the so-called power in the material, ether-world is 35 proved to be merely false belief, it is easily seen how a false assumption of the reality of death, and therefore of birth, with all the false string of beliefs in sin, sickness, and trouble that bind one to the other in successive dream pictures, slays a man; "For to be carnally minded is death" (Rom. 8:6); whereas the belief in the unreality of it all lifts him from hell to 40 heaven. "Turn ye, turn ye from your evil ways; for why will ye die, O house of Israel" (Ezek. 33:11). "My people are destroyed for lack of knowledge" (Hosea 4:6).

Continuity, as Professor Drummond says, is the "Law of Laws." "If a man keep my saying [and realises his immortality], he shall never see 45 death" (John 8:51). "The last enemy that shall be destroyed is death" (I Cor. 15:26). Science opens wide the portals into Life. "In the way of righteousness [wise as to what is right [1]] is life; and in the pathway thereof

---

[1] Skeats' *Etymological Dictionary*.

there is no death" (Prov. 12:28). "For all the boundless universe is Life. There are no dead" (Lord Lytton).

Death Unnecessary.[1]—"*The man of the future is man triumphant over dying nature, exulting in the freedom and privilege of spiritual life*" (Professor Dana). "*Whosoever liveth and believeth in me shall never die*" 5
(John 11:26).

Death is merely a passing from one state of experience to another material phase of the dream of life upon a mechanically evolved ethereal earth called matter, and an entirely needless experience. It will for ever cease when man changes his false, mistaken views of life as material, and, 10 understanding the law of Life and its manifestation as wholly good and eternal, stands aghast at the bald imposition that for so long has devastated the home circles. When the mortal appears to die, and no signs of life are visible, it only means that his human consciousness is not being sufficiently acted upon by the thoughts passing over it to make the body move. "In 15 the present uncertainty as to the presence or absence of life in doubtful cases, it is impossible to argue the matter intelligently until science can present some simple and certain test of death, which it has not yet been able to do"[2] (J. W. Heysinger, M.D.).

Dr. Stenson Hooker, Honorary Secretary of the Association for the 20 Prevention of Premature Burial, writes me: "There is only one test, and one only sure one, viz., decomposition of the tissues."[3] At the public meeting of this society, when I had to second the resolution on this subject, over four hundred cases of premature burial were given. Precautions should always be taken to prevent premature burial. Professor Michael 25 Foster says: "The difference between a dead human body and a living one is still, to a large extent, estimated by drawing inferences rather than actually observed."[4]

After death, the hair on bodies exhumed is often found to have continued to grow. Short and scanty when buried, it is found to be long and 30 massed up. The skin of a serpent, properly dried, retains its bright colours for many years. At intervals it sheds its scales, as if the animal were alive.

---

[1] Bergson speaks of being "able to beat down resistance and clear the most formidable obstacles, perhaps even death."
[2] *Spirit and Matter before the Bar of Modern Science.* 35
[3] Some interesting experiments have recently been carried out by Professor Raoul Pictet, of Geneva. He froze goldfish to minus 20 deg. C. for three months, and brought them to life, and many other animals were frozen for considerable periods without apparent harm.
[4] The Marquis d'Ourches offered two prizes, amounting to 25,000 francs, for 40 some simple, certain sign of death, but without success, although the money was distributed among those sending the best suggestions. A case has just been reported in the papers (March, 1914) where Don Francisco Cabrero, conductor of the orchestra at the Novedades Theatre, at Barcelona, was just about to be buried when he was seen in the coffin to move his right arm. There were, it is said, no 45 signs of decomposition. Dr. Spiro Tashiro, professor of physiology at Chicago University, has discovered a test which he thinks shows with a certainty whether a person is dead or not. The test is made by crushing a piece of muscle, when if the person is alive, the crushed muscle gives out more carbonic acid gas than the uncrushed piece. Medical men are now of opinion that there is life in the tissues for 50 some time after death.

There have been well authenticated cases of vivi-sepulture, that is, suspended animation whilst a man is buried. Colonel Townshend, according to Dr. Cheyne, could, under test conditions, "die or expire when he pleased, and yet, by an effort or somehow, he could come to life again."

5   **Raising from the Dead.**—"*The wages of sin is death ; but the gift of God is eternal life*" (Rom. 6:23).

Actual death, not that such a thing as the unfortunate temporary belief called death can be scientifically called actual, does not take place until post-mortem decomposition sets in. This is shown by the blackening under
10 the armpit and abdomen. Until then the material form can be what is called raised from the dead, as this is really only a revivifying of the human mind, until again it appears to act upon the body and move it.[1] This is why there have been so many records of people in the past being able to raise from the dead. Apollonius of Tyana, for instance, is said to have
15 raised a young woman, and St. Dominic, born in A.D. 1170, was claimed to have this power. Whenever a man was a strong enough "picturer," and was certain that he could raise the corpse, he succeeded, if the so-called mind had not become permanently separated from the body and awakened to a new phase of experience. I know of two such cases in late years. This
20 is quite different, however, from the way in which Jesus the Master worked.

Until the man wakens from the dream of death to find himself in a separate state of consciousness—this dream of another phase of material existence—a psychic person, one who has developed a power of seeing
25 things that the ordinary person does not recognise, can see the human consciousness, which sometimes remains in the more solid body and sometimes wanders about. Under such conditions it appears to have a connection with the body by means of what has been described to me in various ways by those who have sufficiently good sight to see it. The best
30 description is, I think, "a thin cord of light." This may be "the silver cord" that is spoken of in the beautiful passage in Ecclesiastes 12, verse 6, as being broken. When the cord is no longer visible, the general opinion is that the person cannot be "brought round again." In any case, when post-mortem decomposition sets in, the material form goes to ruin, having
35 been forsaken by the so-called mind, that has hitherto held the particles together and caused their apparent action. When this false consciousness has passed into another state of consciousness or phase of the dream,[2] it is of no use trying any further to raise "it" from the dead, although the old

[1] It may be recollected that Jesus pointed out, both in the case of Lazarus and
40 the daughter of Jairus, that what was thought to be death was practically a state of coma, or only a form of sleep. Jesus said: "Our friend Lazarus sleepeth; but I go, that I may awake him out of sleep" (John 11:11). He also said: "Why make ye this ado, and weep? the damsel is not dead, but sleepeth. And they laughed him to scorn" (Mark 5:39, 40). How typical of the modern reception of new truths.
45 [2] According to the Talmud, this takes place twelve months after death, and until then the dead can be brought up by necromancy. It also says in the Sabbat, that the soul (the soul is the human mind) of a man watches over his corpse for seven days. In the Zend-Avesta, the Bible of the Parsees, it is written: "When the man is dead, on the third night, when the dawn appears, the soul enters the way
50 made by Time and open both to the wicked and to the righteous."

illusive ethereal form, equally with any other material forms, alive or dead, may be seen at any time, if the disbelief in the possibility is not too strong.

At the so-called end of the world all the material beings wake up to find themselves in heaven, whether they are in this state of consciousness or in the next state of consciousness.

No Spiritual Advancement or other Gain by Death.—Although

death has apparently released a mortal, his human consciousness is still, however, in exactly the same condition as previously. If the man has suffered from anger, he is still liable to be angry in the next phase; if he has suffered from headaches, he will still suffer from headaches, until he has gained sufficient knowledge of Truth to free himself. There is an important difference, however, in the case of a man dying, say, from consumption, for when he wakes up he has ceased to suffer from consumption; that is, he knows that he has never died from it, and consequently the fear of it has to a great extent gone. This, put into the language of a natural scientist, is that the lines of force, the vibration of which appears as what is called consumption, are not then attacking him. If, however, later on, these consumptive thoughts again attack him, before his human consciousness is purified, he will be down with consumption again, and may have a second fight, or even pass into another state of consciousness and have a third fight with the same disease. This is because the consumption cell in the basic false mentality has not been sufficiently cleaned or purified. The only way of doing this is by the affirmation, that is to say, by turning in thought to God and dwelling on God, and the perfection of the infinite unseen realities, the manifestation of God.

"When the belief in the power of disease is destroyed, disease cannot return" (*Miscellaneous Writings*, p. 58, Mary Baker Eddy). But belief in the powerlessness of disease will never be obtained by submitting to its decree. This belief is only destroyed when the mind is purified in this respect. Death is not purification. Purification is obtained by systematic treatment against the troubles, including disease, that have still the power of harming man. This power is evidenced by man's fear of them. When the fear has gone for ever it means that the mind is purified in respect of that trouble of which the fear has gone, and no longer can it kill him or even harm him. A mere intellectual knowledge that a disease has not killed him has not taken away the fear that again that disease may cause him to pass into another stage of consciousness. On the contrary, it has already shown him that it has this apparent power over the human being. Sufficient knowledge of God would have protected him, and would protect him in the next stage of consciousness, but this knowledge must be obtained, and is not gained by death. If death was a release from any particular form of evil, then it would be a simple way out of a difficulty to accept the verdict of death and be thankful for the release, looking forward to this easy method of shirking the next battle. "If mortals are not progressive, past failures will be repeated, until all wrong work is effaced or rectified" (*Science and Health*, p. 240, Mary Baker Eddy). Those whose minds are completely purified "shall not be hurt of the second death" (Rev. 2:11) in any form. Their human minds have then reached the stage of purification to which Jesus had attained just before his ascension.

There is one respect in which a man is better off after death, namely, that having awakened to find he has not died, he gains a certain amount 5 of disbelief in death, and as a consequence, the fear of annihilation in most cases disappears. Naturally, all these changes do not in any shape or way affect the real spiritual man, who is always in heaven, perfect.

Suicide No Release.—*"Death is the greatest of earth's illusions; there is no death, but only changes in life conditions"* [1] (Annie Besant). 10 *"I am come that they might have life"* (John 10:10).

There is, however, no need for any such experience as that disappearance called death, which is merely a result of widespread ignorance. It will be seen from the complete exposure of the seeming mystery called death, that there is not the slightest gain in committing suicide. The "conscious-15 ness" of the suicide not having been changed, he will still have exactly the same liability to trouble after death, that is, in a new phase of the dream. If he is "hard up" here, he will be "hard up" there; if jealous here, he will be jealous there; miserable here, miserable thoughts still attack him. Now and here, he has presented to him the right and only solution of how to 20 get out of all his difficulties, the unfailing, ever-ready Principle, upon which he can absolutely rely, and he will never gain the reward of perfect happiness by eluding the straight path thereto.

To disappear in so-called death is not by any means to drop the illusion of birth or death. When the illusion of a fleshly man, with its limitations of 25 birth and death, beginnings and endings, has been destroyed by being scientifically overcome and not submitted to, then, and then only, will take place what seems to us to be the finding of the true likeness and reflection everywhere. "Behold, I shew you a mystery; We shall not all sleep, but we shall all be changed, In a moment, in the twinkling of an eye, 30 at the last trump: for the trumpet shall sound, and the dead shall be raised incorruptible, and we shall be changed" (I Cor. 15:51, 52).

Human wearisome experience continues just as apparently real beyond the grave as on this side of it. There is no more pitiful illusion of a tired mortal than that anything in the shape of relief or rest from the ceaseless 35 troubles of this world that the ordinary man has, awaits him in a "beyond the grave." How can this be so when "the wages of sin is death"? (Rom. 6:23).

Victory Over Death.—*"So when . . . this mortal shall have put on immortality, then shall be brought to pass the saying that is written, Death 40 is swallowed up in victory"* (I Cor. 15:54).[2]

Death has to be overcome by the purification of the human conscious-ness, and entire freedom, not only from disease, but from sin has to be obtained. "The last enemy that shall be destroyed is death" (I Cor. 15:26). Jesus proved Life to be deathless. His teachings live in our hearts. 45 We must prove our understanding of them by demonstration of the truth we may voice.

---

[1] *The Ancient Wisdom.*
[2] See also Isaiah 25, verse 8, and Hebrews 2, verses 14, 15.

The "great high priest" Jesus was "tempted like as we are, yet without sin" (Heb. 4:14, 15). When the human mind is sufficiently purified by dematerialisation of the particles of matter, then takes place the second coming of Christ. This is first individual and then collective, and means the recognition of the fact that we are spiritual beings in heaven now. This includes the corollary that the material man is not the real man and has nothing to do with us. We prove this by destroying the false images of ourselves, called mortals. Then "Unto them that look for him shall he [Christ] appear the second time without sin unto salvation" (Heb. 9:28). This recognition of what we are—sons of God, spiritual and perfect—is an absolute shield, "the shield of faith," which protects the so-called mortal man against every evil to which he is thought to be heir. "Even so must the Son of man be lifted up [lifted in thought to God]: That whosoever believeth in him [the Christ-man] should not perish, but have eternal life" (John 3:14, 15). "Why will ye die, O house of Israel?" (Ezek. 18:31). "If a man keep my saying [knows the truth], he shall never taste of death" (John 8:52). "I will ransom them from the power of the grave; I will redeem them from death" (Hos. 13:14).

What Happens at Death.[1]—"*There is no death! What seems so is transition*" (Longfellow).

The question is often asked, Where is the next world, the next phase of consciousness? It is here around us. That is to say, when a man sails away into the land of the unknown, whose frontier posts are query marks, he does not go away to some distant place, but those around merely fail to see the same false picture or inverted image of the real, spiritual man, that we previously were hypnotised into seeing as the false material pictures pass by. This does not mean that, as the theosophists think, he is in the astral state. He is merely cut off from us by the false universal and individual belief in separation, but his human mind is still conscious of a body, another material body, neither more nor less real than his former one, and only another material counterfeit or false sense of his spiritual body. When he wakes up from the nightmare of death he cannot possibly see those whom he is certain he has left in another world; but he still sees the same heaven, materially; that is, has the same false material sense of the same spiritual universe that he saw before he appeared to die, only he sees it, so to speak, from another point of view. Any advanced mathematician, sufficiently desirous of demonstrating this mathematically, could, of course, do so, as all so-called material facts are capable of mathematical statement. Professor Cayley, the famous mathematician, declared his belief that every mathematical truth has an objective correlative in this world. We now see how accurate is this statement.

---

[1] It must not be forgotten that, as Dr. Le Bon says, "Nature knows no rest." The whole of what is called "a dead body" is a mass of so-called life—molecules vibrating with terrific rapidity. It is worth mentioning that the so-called "death agony" has been shown by Sir William Osler and others to be a fiction, except in certain cases of poisoning and heart attacks, the pain from which can be reduced by amyl nitrite if proper mental treatment cannot be obtained.

BIRTH, ITS MYSTERY SOLVED

"It is very possible that many general statements now current, about birth and generation, will be changed with the progress of information" (Agassiz).

5   Ruskin, unconscious probably of the truth he was giving out, has said, in the *Eagle's Nest*: "Among the new knowledges which the modern sirens tempt you to pursue, the basest and darkest is the endeavour to trace the origin of life, otherwise than in Love." This Love is God, and man is the love of Love, the love of God.

10   If this is heaven counterfeited, as seen materially, do we not lose sight of a portion of it when a man is removed by death to what is called another world? No, and for these reasons: (1) There is only one world and that is the spiritual universe, heaven, the kingdom of God that is within reach, here now. The so-called next world is merely another phase of the dream
15 in which the real world, heaven, is seen again as a material world, with material people on it, perceived seemingly as another world. (2) No one, in reality, ever leaves the earth, through death or otherwise. Man being spiritual and having life eternal, and the real earth also being spiritual, this illusory separation between man and the earth can be proved by demonstra-
20 tion to be false and needless; but this demonstration cannot be made until the lying evidence is so far self-destroyed that we recognise its possibility. Only that consciousness which is prepared and ready to receive truth can so far understand it as to bring out such higher possibilities of phenomena.

25   We can prove now that there is no separation if, when desiring to meet a friend, who is alive but absent, we realise clearly that there can be no separation in the one Mind. Then instantly the friend appears, or in some other way the sense of separation is destroyed.

    Phenomena, if real, must be spiritual and eternal, but as in the case of
30 the transfiguration of Jesus, spiritual truth shines through the manifestations of what are called normal conditions in every age. Omnipresence must be proved individually and collectively to be true, and this by demonstration, in direct opposition to all supposed limitations of imaginary laws. Thus upon the mount of uplifted consciousness, the spiritual meeting-
35 place on the shore of time, the "verge of heaven," will be again enacted scenes of the transfiguration of mortals; and men, no longer enshrouded by clouds of seeming mystery, will shine as beacon lights upon the world, heralds of spiritual bliss, glorious resplendent beings. "Love makes people believe in immortality, because there seems not to be room enough in life
40 for so great a tenderness" (R. L. Stevenson).

    In proportion as individual understanding of law and order pierces the misty veil of false consciousness, so scientifically this demonstration will rise to its highest possibility in the consciousness that is purified from everything but its limited sense, till soon again, in the light of the true
45 knowledge that is now being diffused abroad, will be demonstrated that there is no separation, but only a delusion called death, the temporary result of ignorance, and soon to be universally destroyed.

Counterfesance.[1]—*"The act of forging; forgery"* (Webster).

Then, if man is never separated from the earth, he being spiritual, here now if we could only see him, why is there not another visible material counterfeit of the spiritual reality of a person who is seemingly removed by death to another world, that is, another state of dreamland? There is[2]—but there can be no inter-communication between individuals in such differing false states of belief as those who imagine they have died and left their friends, and those who believe that they have been left behind owing to their friends having died and passed into another world.

God being individually reflected by the one who has seemingly disappeared, is certainly continually reflected, and His reflection must therefore be again counterfeited in the human concept, the material misrepresentation of the earth and its inhabitants, from whatever plane of false consciousness it may be viewed. When one individual departs, there appears in his place a new-born child, maintaining the number in this so-called world, but as this is only another picture, a meaningless form, it does not appear in any way as expressing the individual who has apparently departed. This child presents another false human aspect of the same spiritual individuality as before, but in the human consciousness it is pictured as a new "person" altogether, because of the abnormal interruption called death. If these new human beings were never conceived of there would be no birth, and if there were no birth there could be no death. Similarly, if there is no death there cannot possibly be any birth.

The man who has apparently died, turns round in his sleep, as it were, to find himself in what he conceives of as another material world. He sees, however, the same portion of heaven, only he sees it materially in another series of dream pictures. As even the human mind does not retrograde, he seems to exist as an adult and not as a little child in the new state of consciousness in which he finds himself. This man, though finding himself alive, can no more communicate with those who are in another state of consciousness, apparently left behind, than can a person who is awake enter into the conscious human experience of one who is asleep and dreaming. As a matter of fact they are and have been always together in the same world, heaven. Until the individual has passed into and therefore become again a slave in another state of false consciousness there can be nothing but the majority of wrong beliefs concerning that state that can prevent him being what is called raised from the dead. These states of false consciousness, of which there may be a hundred or more, interpenetrate each other here and now. The best illustration is that of two looking-glasses inclined at the top towards each other, and a man standing in the middle. He sees an untold number of reflections of himself. When the end of the world comes it is like tilting the top of these looking-glasses away from each other. All the reflections disappear and there is only the one man left.

---

[1] See also Appendix p. 349.

[2] "Whatever seems to be a new creation, is but the discovery of some distant idea of Truth; else it is a new multiplication or self-division of mortal thought, as when some finite sense peers from its cloister with amazement and attempts to pattern the infinite" (*Science and Health*, p. 263, Mary Baker Eddy).

Fleeting Dream Pictures.—In other words, the pageant of this so-called material world is only a succession of fleeting dream pictures,[1] false views of the real world seen as what are called successive periods of history. This may be called a periodic law of repetition, although it is no
5 law, but simply habit. Fortunately, it will soon be universally discovered that we have never been subjected to any loss or separation, but merely have temporarily lost sight of the false sense of each other, and the so-called dead have simply accepted another false view of the real spiritual inhabitants and real universe. It will be seen that there is no such thing as
10 "extinct species," but merely change of visible form.

This is why we find in the Bible one man after another seen as successive dream pictures, types of someone else to follow. Abel, Abraham, Joseph,[2] Joshua, Jeremiah,[3] and others, have been pointed out by the commentators as earlier types of the spiritual man that was later materially seen as Jesus
15 of Nazareth, the highest human conception of a spiritual being possible in that age; but not having the key, they were unable to follow the idea to its logical conclusion. Looking back, we find that the characters and groupings of events that stand out in the past successive ages of history, prefigure in an extraordinary way the characters and groupings of the
20 succeeding ages. In other words, history repeats itself.

An interesting case of this repetition is the passage of the Israelites out of Egypt, with the crossing of the Red Sea, and the passage of the Israelites out of Media, when "the most High then shewed signs for them, and held still the flood, till they were passed over" (II Esdras 13:44). This was
25 referred to by Zechariah as follows : "All the deeps of the river shall dry up : and the pride of Assyria shall be brought down" (Zech. 10:11). Again in the present days will this be repeated, and the waters of death will be dried up until advancing man awakens to find himself already in the holy land—God's world, "for the first heaven and the first earth were passed
30 away; and there was no more sea" (Rev. 21:1).

Another interesting case is the two destructions of the city of Jerusalem. Captain Weldon, writing in *The Evolution of Israel* of the description by Jeremiah of the current events round the Jerusalem of his day, says : "The whole of the passages just quoted fit in so exactly and so appropriately
35 into the story of the destruction of Jerusalem by the Romans that it is difficult to believe it possible that the events of two sieges, even of the same city, could be so exactly paralleled."

It is not possible to change the universal so-called "mental" miasma of mortals, until individual understanding and demonstrations prove its

---

40 [1] "In short, the world the mathematician deals with is a world that dies and is reborn at every instant—the world which Descartes was thinking of when he spoke of continued creation." "We merely do nothing else than set going a kind of cinematograph inside us. We may, therefore, sum up what we have been saying, in conclusion, that the mechanism of our ordinary knowledge is of a cinematograph
45 kind" (*Creative Evolution*, Henri Bergson). Professor Richet has said "Every living being was, perchance, a chemical mechanism and nothing more."

[2] Luther says : "As it was with Joseph and his brethren, so it was with Christ and the Jews."

[3] St. Jerome and others have stated that Jeremiah prefigured the Christ, and have
50 given detailed accounts of the parallel.

unreality, and thereby publish the good tidings abroad; this rapidly awakens the universal thought, sweeping away dustheaps from the ethereal workshop of earthly picturing. The ordinary man requires practical proof of everything. He is tired of barren, illogical theories. In this age, fortunately, this universal change of methods can be and is being rapidly 5 brought about; and as man bends his stiffening, crystallising theories in humble but scientific, and therefore all-potent, prayer to God, the great universal, democratic command will be given by God through man collectively—Let us make man in God's image and likeness. The carrying out of this command will be accomplished by knowing and loving only God, and 10 man as His image and likeness, the eternal manifestation of Life, Truth, and Love, through consistent fulfilment of Life's Golden Rule of right thinking and the consequent right acting. Then will the corresponding phenomena instantly and universally appear in obedience to divine law, and it will be seen that all is good, and good is All-in-all and eternally present to be 15 worshipped and loved. Then in the glad light of the seventh day of spiritual understanding material phenomena fade and disappear, together with the false mentality that conceives and makes them visible, and man recognises spiritual truth as tangible reality.

Nicodemus.—This scientific revelation throws light upon some of 20 the mystical sayings of our Master to Nicodemus in the third chapter of St. John's Gospel, which, until lately, I for one had only considered from one point of view, whereas every passage in the Bible has its material, intellectual, and spiritual significance.

Jesus said: "Except a man be born again, he cannot see the kingdom of 25 God" (verse 3). Nicodemus must have been not only eager to learn, as his midnight visit showed, but an able man, for he was "a ruler of the Jews" and also "a teacher of Israel." [1] He evidently imagined that Jesus alluded in some sense to a material birth, for he said: "How can a man be born when he is old? can he enter the second time into his mother's womb, and 30 be born?" (verse 4). Jesus then made it clear that there were two apparently diametrically opposed concepts of man, one the true spiritual being in heaven; the other only a mere mechanical apparatus, the counterfeit called the fleshly man, simply a false sense of the real man, as he said: "That which is born of the flesh is flesh; and that which is born of the Spirit is 35 spirit" (verse 6). He also showed that the false sense of the material man had to be got rid of by purification, and that he could only reach heaven (or rather the mortal get rid of the material sense), because the real spiritual man is already in heaven. Jesus said: "And no man hath ascended up to heaven, but he that came down from heaven, even the Son of man 40 which is in heaven" (verse 13). He could not have been speaking of himself, because he said later to Mary: "I am not yet ascended to my Father" (John 20:17). He also said : "Except a man be born of water and of the Spirit, he cannot enter into the kingdom of God" (John 3:5). Later, he said: "Marvel not that I said unto thee, Ye must be born again" (verse 7), 45 and went on to show how little his hearer understood either of the material negative or of the real spiritual world. Nicodemus evidently could not see

[1] Revised Version.

how a new material counterfeit of him—his real self—could appear to others as a little child, for he said: "How can these things be?" (verse 9). Jesus's reply was: "We speak that we do know, . . . and ye receive not our witness" (verse 11), and then, after illustrating man's ignorance of any
5 accurate knowledge of the material world, by his inability to trace the movements of the winds, he evidently said that it was no use trying to explain to a materially encrusted man more advanced science, saying: "If I have told you earthly things, and ye believe not, how shall ye believe, if I tell you of heavenly things?" (verse 12).

10 **Unprejudiced Hearing Necessary to Gain Truth.**—These words of Jesus hold good to-day. The man who, whilst trying to gain a better knowledge of the spiritual world, will listen and take in the hitherto hidden explanation of the material so-called laws, which apparently bind and limit him, is the man who, by reversal of the false ideas that come to him, finds
15 himself regarding life from a new standpoint, and most quickly gains a clear sense of the details of the real spiritual facts, and so finds heaven, now and here. A knowledge of these spiritual details, sooner or later, is essential. There must be no excuses for ignorance.[1] We dare not dream away our time in a false state of security, relying upon the letter alone, but must be
20 actively at work, consciously inspired, gaining a better knowledge of God by the reversal of the constant succession of false, lying beliefs that we have been taught to believe true, and in which we should no longer show our belief by daily acts.

"History Repeats Itself "—History repeats itself, and in a more intri-
25 cate form. Whilst all the material features of these successive dream pictures are more or less different, you will find that they coincide each with the other, a steady alteration for the better continually taking place. As in printing, one impression after the other is put upon the paper until we see a complete whole built up from separate plates, so, by comparing these
30 impressions, we are enabled better to understand the details of the whole false mechanical world process. At the present time we have in front of us a series of past pictures, called successive historical records. Let us look upon them as portions cut off a long cinematographic film, each placed one behind the other, and all hiding heaven, which is behind the last one. Mrs.
35 Besant speaks of the "recurrent cycles in history," for which she states reincarnation "affords the only sufficient explanation." Now we have the true explanation. Examining the latter end of each series of these successive dream pictures, with the help of the Bible prophecies, we can, in the light of the new knowledge that has dawned upon the world, "turn backward
40 the telescope" of to-day "with its lenses of more spiritual mentality," [2] upon this human history. We can then predict with fair certainty the future that lies before us, in this latter end of the series that now in the next few years is about to come into view. Let us hasten to learn how to destroy the evil foreseen, and so purify these pictures that, instead of confusion and
45 misery, we may find ourselves surrounded by the peace and happiness that accompany all true understanding. In this way only can we make intelli-

---

[1] "Ignorantia legis neminem excusat" (Ignorance of the law is no excuse).
[2] See Preface to *Pulpit and Press* (Mary Baker Eddy).

gent use of past history, "Declaring the end from the beginning, and from ancient times the things that are not yet done" (Isa. 46: 10).

Remember that all these kaleidoscopic pictures are but varying counterfeit views of the one perfect spiritual reality, viewed either individually or collectively, and all appear seemingly at different periods, but to speak 5 more accurately, at the same moment, being merely different false views of the reality. Our work is to awake to this fact, and hasten the glad time when the material man dematerialises, that is, appears to awake and see again those loved ones who have disappeared from sight, and to see his fellowmen as they really are, spiritual beings in the real world, heaven. What a 10 glorious time awaits us. Does not our "heart burn within us" (Luke 24: 32) even at the human forecast. "Beloved, now are we the sons of God, and it doth not yet appear what we shall be : but we know that, when he shall appear, we shall be like him; for we shall see him as he is" (I John 3: 2). 15

Not only are correlative types of individuals to be found, but you will see exactly the same coincidences, not only throughout nature, but in everything; for instance, in the writings of the prophets, the writing of an individual being duplicated by the building of a temple, the history of a nation, and otherwise. So exactly is this the case that Haeckel's "gastraea 20 theory"—based upon his "fundamental biogenetic law," that ostogeny or development of the individual is a recapitulation of the phylogeny or development of the race—applies equally to man as to lower so-called forms of life. I have tried to refrain as much as possible from speaking in too advanced, technical language, except where the terms used were com- 25 ing into general use, and it was therefore of educational value, but it is sometimes instructively amusing to see what can be done in this way. The use of highly technical terms is, as Sir Hiram Maxim once said, a mere cloak for ignorance. This statement you can carry further probably than Sir Hiram intended, as you can always, if you know enough, use 30 "the language of the people," and with telling effect.

A Mechanical World.—The mechanical material world has been compared to a clock. The accepted theories concerning human life, with their regularly recurring birth, sin, disease, and death, are the works, wound up and set going, the dial-plate acting as a tell-tale of how regularly 35 or irregularly they are being acted upon by the mechanical pressure. The earth, with its inhabitants and entire material phenomena, is like one large clock. Each day it is wound up by its owners. Each individual who at sundown admits that it is essential its material procedure shall be repeated during the next twenty-four hours, is winding up his clock-work earth; 40 and, so long as this mechanical imitation of the real earth and man is kept going, mankind is simply maintaining its own limitations, and content to centre its whole interest in a nursery-toy imitation of its real kingdom, the true and living spiritual earth and heaven and man. The true man acts entirely independently of any preconceived material line of procedure or 45 so-called law of necessity.

The whole world of the reality is all bound up together and maintained by the underlying, everlasting, living Principle, but in this suppositional

world all the real ideas are counterfeited in a series of seemingly material things, also seemingly held together and governed by cruel, imaginary laws. These have an apparent power until men awaken to the unreality of mere fleeting shadows. This accounts for many seemingly mysterious coin-
5 cidences, such as the history of individuals and nations being read in the stars, and the marvellous apparent working of the law of numbers. The Principle of the science of numbers is as true in the material universe as in heaven, only we get a false sense of it here, when applying it to material phenomena, which prevents us from seeing its accurate and harmonious
10 working. There is no retrograde step, and each of these false series of pictures continues in appearance, gradually being refined until its end comes, when finally the last material record of the last mortal fault fades away, and is what is called dematerialised by the greater weight of right thinking. In this so-called end of the material world of evil all the succes-
15 sive series of fleeting dream pictures will completely disappear at the same time, and immortal man and the lesser ideas will be clearly seen every-where as spiritual and perfect.[1]

Scientific Confirmation.—The German geologist, Edward Suess, in *Das Antlitz der Erde*, speaks of "a great and yet unknown rhythm in the
20 evolution of living beings—a rhythm dependent on periodic changes in the inorganic environment." He was on the verge of a great discovery here—a glimmer of truth had been caught by the inquiring "mind."

A leading article, "Is it Possible to be Original?" in the *Daily Mail* of January 7, 1911, says: "Ideas march along in extended order. They are
25 not isolated discoveries made by specially brilliant individuals. Their influence is in the air. It is felt by numbers of thinkers at a time." And another instance "is offered us by M. Lichtenberger in his admirably lucid study of Nietzsche. One of the famous German philosopher's most famous theories, the one that he thought must paralyse the world, was the
30 theory of the eternal return. . . . Briefly, it is that everything which hap-pens must have happened in exactly the same way any number of times before, and will go on happening at intervals for ever."[2] The unreality of material phenomena had not yet dawned on him.

Maunder's *Scientific and Literary Treasury*, under the article "Life,"
35 gives the following interesting facts: "The proportion of births to the actual stationary population of any place, expresses, or is relative to, the

---

[1] Although this succession of dream pictures is not elaborated by Mrs. Eddy, it is the only logical deduction from her writings, and, moreover, the knowledge was obtained by treatment, by the realisation of God. As it was realised that "man
40 knows Truth," thoughts came flashing into the human mind, fitting in with the spoken words of a conversation close by. So the truth became clear to human com-prehension. Since then additional proofs of its correctness have accumulated. Amongst other passages confirming this view the following may be quoted: "My beloved Edward A. Kimball, whose clear, correct teaching of Christian Science
45 has been and is an inspiration to the whole Field, is here now as veritably as when he visited me a year ago. If we awaken to this recognition, we should see him here and realise that he never died; thus demonstrating the fundamental truth of Christian Science" (*Miscellany*, p. 297, Mary Baker Eddy. See also *Science and Health*, p. 548, line 18 onwards).
50 [2] This theory will be found at the end of *The Will to Power*. The same idea has recently been put forward by two others working quite independently.

average duration of life in that population." "The mortality of a place always appears to be proportionate to its fecundity; as the number of births increases, so does the number of deaths at the same time." "For example, suppose the proportion of births to be in the ratio of 1 to 28, the average life of the inhabitants of the place will be twenty-eight years." It will be 5 seen from this that the number of individuals on this earth does not vary. Obviously the numbers in any given locality vary.[1]

Sadler enunciated the following law: "The prolificness of human beings, otherwise similarly circumstanced, varies inversely as their numbers," and he says that statistics prove that the number of conceptions is always 10 greatest in the most "mortal" years and *vice versa*.

Population, dynamically considered, is the result of two pairs of opposing forces; (1) the numerical relation between the births and deaths of a given period; and (2) immigration and emigration. The intensity of these opposing forces operating on population depends upon a variety of causes. 15 Any statement as to the total population of the world must be to a large extent an estimate, as the difficulties of obtaining any accurate basis for calculations have hitherto proved insurmountable.

My father, Sir Rawson W. Rawson, who was President of the Royal Statistical Society, and one of the two English delegates to the International 20 Statistical Society, of which he was President until his death, gave a good deal of time to this question, but with little result, and, although at first sight one may seem to find many estimates and seemingly authoritative statements upon this subject, it will be found that the following quotation from the article on "Population" in the *Encyclopædia Britannica* (9th 25 edition) is a fair promise of all that can be hoped for, upon looking deeper into the assumptions upon which such calculations have been based: "So great, indeed, is the uncertainty in which all such calculations are involved that an eminent French statistician, M. Block, abandoned all attempt to deal with the problem, dismissing the subject in the following 30 note: 'Nous nous abstenons de donner le chiffre de l'ensemble de la population de la terre; personne ne connaît ce chiffre.'[2] With this view of the matter we entirely agree. . . . We venture to say that any person of fair intelligence and ordinary education would, even without any statistical training, come to the conclusion that there was nothing 35 certain to be known on the subject, which these figures profess to illustrate."

Many theosophists are gradually coming to the conclusion that the number of individuals is fixed. Mrs. Besant writes: "If the number of egos in the world be a fixed number how do you account for the increase 40 in population? It is a doubtful matter to begin with whether there is or is not an increase of the population of the globe, however great may be the

---

[1] The Press have drawn attention to the large increase in the proportion of boy babies, not only in Great Britain but in the other militant countries, during the war that is now in progress [1914-1918]. This has been the case in the other great wars. 45 Authorities are not agreed on this point. The number of boy babies is always larger, I believe, than the number of girl babies, but a greater percentage die at an early stage.

[2] "We abstain from giving the figure of the entire population of the earth; no one knows this figure." 50

10*

increase on any particular area. No census of the total population has ever been taken, no statistics are available for our guidance." [1]

It is interesting that Pythagoras (569–470 B.C.), one of the most wonderful men of ancient times, is said to have taught that the same events recur 5 again and again, in regular cycles. Pythagoras, who had travelled much, founded a brotherhood, in which study and personal purity were the rules of life. He was a wonderful mathematician, and the first to show that number—vibration—was the basis of material phenomena. He asserted the unity and eternity of God as against the varied beliefs of mythology, 10 and appears to have been the first to discern that the arrangement of the heavenly bodies presented intervals synchronous with musical rhythm; and that the earth and planets revolved round a central point. In many other directions he exercised the powers that have been shown are available to all men. For instance, he is said to have tamed wild beasts instantly, to 15 have foretold the future, and to have been able to move instantly from one place to another. The great solution of all his problems would have speedily followed had he discerned the practical method of permanently destroying evil in a scientific way. His memory was ardently cherished by his disciples, who had the greatest faith in his teachings. Considering the terrible results 20 that must have followed the general publication of his knowledge to a world uninstructed in true science, no wonder that in that age they were unwritten and kept secret, nothing being published about them until fifty years after his death. The little that was published is said to have had a great influence upon Plato, who lived about fifty years later than Pytha-25 goras.[2]

The Darwinian Theory of Evolution.—The "mental" age pictured in the opening of the sixth seal of the Apocalyptic vision of things to come is now well established. Old things are rapidly passing away, new "things," as thoughts, are obtaining and maintaining their rightful place in man's 30 views of existence. Material theories and hypothetical speculations have for individuals been already swallowed up in demonstrable facts, and to-day are on the eve of so being for the mass.

The difficulties so bravely faced by Darwin, of accounting for "a single centre of creation"—a single birthplace of the race; the descent of indivi-35 duals from a single pair or hermaphrodite; the various means of dispersal, etc., all disappear in the greater light of the mental era that has dawned. Mankind rubs its eyes in astonishment, to inquire where are any possible material limitations of time or space, whether there can be any, when there is no longer obstructive substance in matter? The centre of creation is 40 Mind's perfect poise. The complete manifestation is the reflected image and likeness of perfection everywhere, which can be seen from every point of view to lead back to its divine source. The graduations of human misconceptions are found to disappear, giving place to "diviner conceptions,"

[1] *Reincarnation.*
45 [2] I have since found that Pythagoras was acquainted with Daniel, and I am satisfied that his results were obtained by true prayer and not through his knowledge of vibration, as many have thought. It also explains why after his death there were two schools of his disciples, differing as to his teachings. Like Jesus and Gautama Buddha, he left no record in writing of what he believed.

until, rising above all sense of material illusion, the origin and ultimate of species and universe are discovered to be in Mind, and eternally spiritual and perfect.

Now this general awakening to the knowledge of Truth is leading to a vast reorganisation of ideas in every direction, and soon the following 5 Darwinian puzzles will be understood by all.

"Cause of Variability." All the intricate, elaborate theory of material evolution will be recognised as merely the externalisation of "thoughts," and the material structures of the world as only "buildings," each layer of "bricks" resting on its predecessor, smoke rings in the towers of Babel, 10 mere human inventions. The ethereal architect is found to be builder, mason, carpenter, furnisher, and indeed, house itself. The "professor" of medicine to-day is foreshown to be the "educated" invalid of to-morrow.

"The Survival of the Fittest" merely records the disappearance of error and the *appearance* of a better belief. 15

"Species Once Lost Do Not Reappear." Mistakes found to have been mistakes are not again made, and therefore obviously species, false forms of reality, once "lost sight of," do not reappear.

"Absence of Intermediate Varieties at the Present Day." All mystery surrounding the absence to-day of intermediate varieties of species dis- 20 appears in an instant.

"Mutual Affinities of Organic Beings." The law of gravity, as illustrated in its highest expression as the "mutual affinity of organised beings," disappears before the explanation of gravity as nothing more than the electro-magnetic attraction of illusory particles, now to be dealt with by the higher 25 law of Mind.

"Geographical Distribution," being but distribution of thoughts, is easily understood, and the puzzle of how it has come about that "forms of life change almost simultaneously throughout the world" is solved.

Not only can all the multitudinous forms included within each of the 30 great kingdoms of this world be "traced back to a pair" of progenitors, but all the four kingdoms themselves, although seen from many individual standpoints, merge into one, all-inclusive manifestation of one false mentality, one miscalled mind, universally repeated in countless ethereal forms of mortal individualities. 35

Material evolution, in which St. Augustine, St. Bede the Great, St. Gregory of Nyssa, St. Thomas Aquinas, all believed, might be more accurately expressed as being a gradual but temporary apparent appearance of material counterfeits, imitations of mental tangible realities. St. Augustine understood material beliefs better than most theologians, as he 40 wrote that the animals were created "by a process of growth, whose numbers *the after-time unfolded* from imperfect to perfect forms." Gesenius pointed out that this unfoldment was "evolution, not conversion." These mental tangible realities dawn upon the human consciousness, being rapidly "brought to light by the evolution of advancing thought" as 45 man turns to God, to the one Mind that is all-good, and proves, through demonstration of the unfailing power of Principle to heal disease and sin, that its manifestation is essentially life, truth, and love, and therefore of necessity eternal, real, and universal.

Spiritual evolution in its reality is the continual redistribution of perfect ideas in new combinations of infinite variety and beauty.

Unnatural Science.—*"If nothing is to be called science but that which is exactly true from beginning to end, I am afraid there is very little*
5 *science in the world outside mathematics. Among the physical sciences I do not know that any could claim more than that each is true within certain limits, so narrow that, for the present at any rate, they may be neglected"* (Huxley).

The truth to which attention has been directed makes it abundantly
10 clear that what has hitherto ranked as natural science is entirely unnatural, and must be henceforth relegated into the category of old wives' fables. Natural science has served its day, indeed, it has been a good and faithful servant, but like the old family coachman, its day is past, and the modern chauffeur whirls this bundle of misconceptions with greater and greater
15 rapidity to its destined end. Both the old tried servant and the new mechanically trained assistant are merely temporary aids to a desired end. In other words, the theoretical explanation in its details, as put before you, is only a temporary, though necessary, stepping-stone to enable the mortal more easily to throw off the false ideas that have until lately enwrapped him
20 in a material dream. The material mortal is only a belief in a kingdom divided against itself (see Matt. 12:25). The final belief that loses itself, as the dream disappears, is that all this constantly changing series of phenomena is only heaven around us, hidden by a series of cinematographic pictures, each following with lightning rapidity. Hence there are
25 no lines of force that destroy themselves, no vibrating ether, no gathering electrons, no electrical self-intensification of thoughts, no changing conscious or subconscious mind, no material body that is dematerialised, no motion of matter, no material gravity, no limited time. This whole so-called scientific explanation is merely the complete instead of the frag-
30 mentary, will-o'-the-wisp theory of material phenomena. Temporarily useful? Yes. Accurate? Yes. True? No; for there is nothing but God and His manifestation. An intimate knowledge of this glorious and tangible but hitherto undiscerned reality can only come to the human consciousness when, casting off its old ideas, it advances gladly along the path of true
35 Science, and man proves his scientific knowledge by habitual, instantaneous demonstration, the destruction of sin, sickness, and every form of evil, blessing the day that he gained even a grain of truth, and being daily blessed by those with whom he comes in contact.

Unnatural Religion.—*"For God hath not given us the spirit of fear;*
40 *but of power, and of love, and of a sound mind"* (II Tim. 1:7).
In a book called *Non-Churchgoing: Its Reasons and Remedies*, numerous authors, including Sir Oliver Lodge, Mr. J. R. Macdonald, and some half-dozen ministers and various persons of position and experience, explain the reason why people do not go to church. The *Daily News*,[1] writing about
45 this book, says: "There is considerable agreement among the authors. All assume that church-going is on the wane. 'The world is deserting the

[1] March 31, 1911.

church; that is the fact!' This is the general opinion. Next, most allow that unbelief is not increasing. 'The nation is growing temperate; its manners are improving; the amenities of life are more desired.' 'War is denounced as an evil'; 'civic morality is strengthening.' Towards the weak and suffering there is shown a tenderness and an effective sympathy never before 5 observed."

This being the case, there must be something wrong in the Churches. What is it? It is that they are not up to date. The difficulty is due to the material basis upon which the whole of the Churches' concept of God, man, and heaven rests. Men want something better. They want a religion 10 that is of practical value to them every moment of the day; something that will make them live a more holy, more unselfish life. The only religion that can do this must be based upon Spirit. Pure religion is wholly spiritual, and is the outcome of man's growing understanding of his right relationship to God and his fellow-man. The Churches, instead of moving with 15 the times, taking advantage of the evolution in religion and general enlightenment that has been, and is now rapidly spreading, have been bound down, hypnotised by ancient, crystallised, dogmatic views, blinded by the mist of materiality, so that they cannot yet hear the bugle call of the second coming of the Christ, but wrangle about material trivialities within 20 themselves, instead of spreading news of the glorious world that is here around us waiting to be realised. Fortunately, the mist is thinning, and this band, containing many splendid workers, is beginning to see that one and all have to drop every taint of materiality and think of spiritual things alone —of God and God's world. Until recently the Churches have hardly even 25 called forth anything beyond a superficial faith in facts from which man's highest reasoning powers recoil. "Were I a preacher, I should above all things preach the practice of the presence of God, . . . so necessary do I think it and so easy, too" (Brother Lawrence, Fifth Letter).

The following, which appeared a short time ago in one of the leading 30 papers, is a very just criticism. "Some years ago the Japanese sent a deputation to the West with instructions to report whether Christianity was a religion which could be adopted as the State religion of Japan. The deputation returned disappointed, and reported that they found such discrepancy between the practice and profession of Christianity, that they 35 were unable to recommend it. That the Japanese nation are not satisfied with the Christian religion was clearly shown at the Church Congress at Liverpool yesterday, by the Rev. Herbert Moore, who said there was a tendency in Japan to create a new religion upon the foundations both of Christianity and Buddhism." 40

There has been a great change recently in the Church. Many are now teaching that true prayer is the realisation of God, conscious communion with God.

Geoffrey Rhodes in *Medicine and the Church*, says: "At the recent conference the Bishops at Lambeth admitted with regret that 'sickness has 45 too often exclusively been regarded as a cross to be borne with passive resignation, whereas it should have been regarded rather as a weakness to be overcome by the power of the spirit.' That there exist potentialities of healing apart from physic to-day no one can refute, but it is to be feared the Church and the medical profession have much lost ground to recover."

The following extracts from a letter written by Dr. Gore, Bishop of Birmingham, to Stephen Paget, F.R.C.S., and published by the latter in
5 *Medicine and the Church*, show how anxious the true workers are to obey literally the teachings of Jesus the Master: "I should wish to make a little more of your admissions as to Mental Therapeutics. Thus, if, as you admit, there are so many functional disorders, and they are curable by mental influences—and religion is a great mental influence, and this influence
10 ('Quietism') is much needed in such and other cases—I should demand of the Church that it should recognise, far more explicitly, this field of legitimate curative power, and control it, and claim it by showing the power to use it. . . . My own experience in the case of well-to-do people when sick or dying is that the medical profession is very much inclined to
15 exclude religion in any form from sick-beds till it cannot be of any use. I do most seriously want to reform (1) the Church, (2) the medical profession, in the light of what you admit."

Dr. Gore wants no better evidence to prove to him that the medical profession have not to learn how to cure by mental influence, but by
20 obtaining a spiritual knowledge of God, than the article by H. G. G. Mackenzie, M.B., on "Medical Aspects of Mental Healing" in *Medicine and the Church*. In this article details are given of a meeting of the Harveian Society held a little time ago at Oxford, when a paper of great and permanent value was read by Dr. Claye Shaw on the "Influence of Mind as a
25 Therapeutic Agent." A number of well-known medical men, authorities on mental healing by suggestion, hypnotism, etc., were present, and took part in the discussion, giving details of their experience, and the author sums up the result of the paper and the discussion as follows: "Here we have grouped together the expression of the opinions of trained minds of
30 responsible medical men. The differences are comparatively slight. The agreement is remarkable. Not one of them (though in one case as many as 4,000 records are in his hands) claims to have cured what are usually called organic conditions. The whole question is as to the best way in which suggestion can be brought to bear on patients whose lives are in many cases
35 rendered miserable by persistent, but none the less 'functional,' ailments."

It has been clearly pointed out throughout this work that there is no limit to the power of God, and therefore to the class of ailment, mental or physical, that can be healed by true prayer. It has also been pointed out that mental suggestion, with the object of inducing improved material
40 results, is purely hypnotic suggestion and wholly wrong.

The reason why the medical man has not looked kindly upon the presence of the clergyman in the sick-room has been that he has found by experience that such presence is not beneficial. There are two causes for this. If the clergyman dwells upon the hereafter, and the necessity for
45 preparation for a rapidly approaching end, the patient at once outlines in thought the death picture, and prepares for the worst. In the second case, the visitor often, instead of calming the patient, excites him, and leaves him full of anxious thoughts, instead of leaving him happy and hopeful.

When the Churches and all true workers wake up and teach truth, instead of what is practically pantheism, the millennium will be understood, and then it will soon be here for humanity; and very shortly after its recognition all suffering and limitations will be things of the past—a forgotten nightmare and therefore no-thing (see Rev. 7:17 and 21:4). "No one can fight against God, and win" (Mary Baker Eddy).

"Though the mills of God grind slowly,
    Yet they grind exceeding small;
Though with patience He stands waiting,
    With exactness grinds He all." [1]

World's Preparatory School.—It has been suggested that there must be something wrong with true mental workers when those around them are critical and not living a high enough life. The reason for this trouble is clear to those understanding the action of evil.

When man and woman are living their highest and carrying their knowledge of science and religion into their daily life-practice, they sometimes become objects of criticism and even of dislike or jealousy to those who do not properly understand their motives and actions.

This results, not only in wrong thoughts of such true workers (from which, however, they can protect themselves by persistent mental work), but it results in wrong thoughts about those associated with them in their work. Remarks of these associates, such as "He can never get on as long as he is there," "He is becoming a hypnotist," "He is becoming prejudicially affected," naturally do harm if such associates who are thus hypnotically acted upon do not protect themselves by frequently turning to God in thought and knowing the truth, namely, that no evil can touch them because they are spiritual, etc.

It is a curious thing that if these co-workers have a slight knowledge of truth and are themselves endeavouring to use their highest mental powers, such malpractice affects them more than it does those ignorant of mental effects, who merely blunder on as best they can. The result is that whilst the beginners in mental work benefit themselves personally by such work, and the effects are seen in their improving circumstances and greater freedom from worries and troubles, they are liable to become more critical of those around them. These, in turn, expect a higher standard of life from them, and consequently malpractise on such beginners, and increase the difficulty.

The only way out of this is constant, steady, daily, mental work, treating especially for love, so that the students prove in every way to those around them the value of their advancing knowledge of truth, not only by being more thoughtful for others, but by not speaking evil of their fellow-men.

Were the position fully recognised, it would be seen that to be at work in such a centre of attack is a privilege, and if taken advantage of, is of incalculable value, for it will result in a free passport through the far more perilous conditions to which the world is hastening.

---

[1] Longfellow, *Retribution*, from the German of F. von Logau.

Such troubled groups of advanced workers are but the senior pupils in the world's preparatory school, and if they persevere they will be the ones to earn the golden scholarship of permanent peace and happiness which can only be won through experimental tuition. God will bless them (see
5 Matt. 10:22).

"With blessings beyond hope or thought,
With blessings which no word can find" (*Tennyson*).

SECTION SEVEN

OUR DUTY

"*Fear* [reverence] *God, and keep his commandments: for this is the whole duty of man*" (Eccles. 12:13). "*But what is thy duty? The demand of the hour*" (Goethe).   5

"Prove to me only that the least
Command of God's is God's indeed,
And what injunction shall I need
To pay obedience?" (*Browning*).

We have to recognise our duty at the present time. As has been said, 10 "The continual sharpening of the knife is tiresome, if, after all, we have nothing to cut with it." "It is our duty to seek success—the success of the other man" (W. H. Parmenter). We have to "abound in Love and Truth" and to heal sin and sickness. We have to practise diligently and lovingly Christ's Sermon on the Mount, which now, with our new know- 15 ledge, we find can be lived instead of only pondered over. Jesus pointed out that there were only two commandments—to love God, and love our neighbour. The law of Life demands the fulfilment of these. Obedience to them is essential, and the only thing that can give us present and per- manent happiness is loyalty to God, and its result, which is the helping 20 of our fellow-man. To do this, we have to get rid of the results of our falsely educated habit of wrong thinking, and to learn how to think rightly. "He who would have full power must strive to get power over his own mind" (*Boethius*, King Alfred). This is the only way in which we can relieve others from their present troubles, and also from the waves of 25 trouble that prophets and readers of thought have continually foretold as inevitably coming in the latter days. These troubles are beginning, and by learning how to think rightly we can protect a certain number of those we love, that number depending upon our knowledge of truth, and the life that we lead. "Sanctify them through thy truth: thy word is truth . . . and for 30 their sakes I sanctify myself, that they also might be sanctified through the truth" (John 17:17, 19). "Faith without works is dead" (James 2:20, 26). We have huge tasks before us. Let us fit ourselves so as both to ward off and destroy the unseen foe, which must be recognised, and destroyed as soon as recognised. "For then shall be great tribulation, such as was not since 35 the beginning of the world to this time, no, nor ever shall be" (Matt. 24:21). Remember that such a passage refers to different successive material dream pictures, and consequently refers, not only to the flight of the descendants of Benjamin from Jerusalem in A.D. 70, but also to the latter days, which are now upon us, in which like incidents occur in new 40 dress and are even now being recognised as happening in our midst by those who have learned how to discern the signs of the times.

Man's Dominion.—*"For this purpose the Son of God was manifested, that he might destroy the works of the devil"* (I John 3:8). *" On the first page of the Bible is the declaration that God gave man dominion over all the earth. If this is true, we ought to have dominion over our body, our business, our*
5 *household, our affairs, our environments, our circumstances, our condition"* (Edward Kimball).

Fortunately we have absolute dominion over all evil, over every sense of want, moral, mental, and physical. We have to acquaint ourselves with the nature of the false claims of error, and, with spiritual alertness, to lay the
10 axe at the root of all evil. Recognise the everlasting grandeur and immortality of the power of this God-given authority. "Live greatly, so shalt thou acquire unknown capacities of joy" (Coventry Patmore). Life has now to be more than a sense of existence; it must be "a sense of might and ability to subdue material conditions" [1] of every kind. "Wait patiently on
15 illimitable Love, the lord and giver of Life. *Reflect this Life,* and with it cometh the full power of being." [2] Again and again, right throughout the Bible, we are told of this sovereign power. "And God said, . . . let them have dominion . . . over all the earth" (Gen. 1:26). "The upright shall have dominion over them in the morning" (Ps. 49:14). Now the morning
20 is breaking as the new light is spreading all over the world. "Dominion . . . shall be given to the people of the saints of the most High" (Dan. 7:27). How is it that all have not this dominion? We all have power to overcome and we shall overcome every so-called law of matter. Nothing can dispossess you of your power to think and therefore act rightly, for you are
25 the son of God. This is "the gift of the grace of God" (Eph. 3:7). "For the kingdom of God is not in word, but in power" (I Cor. 4:20). "The seeds of God-like power are in us still" (Matthew Arnold). "The power of the Divine Image within man gave him immediate command of Nature" (Plato). "Self-reverence, self-knowledge, self-control. These three alone
30 lead life to sovereign power" (Tennyson). The only fatal mistake is the mistake of giving in.

We must obey Christ's loving demand, "Be ye perfect." If this demand was valid when he spoke it, it is as valid to-day, and therefore possible to fulfil. We gain this dominion by knowing, feeling, and proving that Love,
35 God, alone governs man. Might and majesty attend every advancing stage of this understanding. "Great, not like Cæsar, stained with blood, but only great as I am good." Exercise this dominion and destroy sin, sickness, and suffering all around you, "For it is God which worketh in you" (Phil. 2:13). The exercise of this dominion is only a call to higher duties,
40 not a release from cares and responsibilities. If you can maintain this dominion, nothing can cause you to sin or suffer. "You have simply to preserve a scientific, positive sense of unity with your divine source, and daily demonstrate this (Mary Baker Eddy). "But if thou dost receive nothing into thy desire, then thou art free from all things, and rulest over
45 all things at once, as a prince of God. For thou hast received nothing from thine own, and art nothing to all things; and all things are as nothing to thee" (Jacob Boehme).

---

[1] *Unity of Good,* p. 42 (Mary Baker Eddy).
[2] *Pulpit and Press,* p. 4 (Mary Baker Eddy).

Humility.—*"What doth the Lord require of thee, but . . . to walk humbly with thy God?"* (Micah 6:8).

We find that "humility is perpetual quietness of heart. It is to have no troubles. It is never to be fretted or vexed, irritable or sore. To wonder at nothing that is done to me, to feel nothing done against me. It is to be at rest when nobody praises me, and when I am blamed or despised, it is to have a blessed home in myself where I can go in and shut the door and kneel to my Father in secret, and be at peace, as in a deep sea of calmness, when all around and above is trouble." The material man can do nothing, and we may well say with Robert Browning:—

" . . . Looking within and around me, I ever renew,
With that stoop of the soul, which in bending, upraises it too,
The submission of man's nothing-perfect, to God's all-complete,
As by each new obeisance of spirit, I climb to his feet."

Humility of this description is the laying down of a sham power, and the taking up of omnipotence; it is true genius. "To think first of others is the secret of gentleness" (Elizabeth Gibson). The spiritual man never thinks of himself. He thinks only of God and God's ideas. "We desire now to lose the thinking of ourselves in thinking for others. . . . There is the Ideal! We are to be saviours of men, lovers of men, inspirers of men in self-forgetfulness" (Stopford Brooke).

Glorify God.—*"Let your light so shine before men, that they may see your good works, and glorify your Father which is in heaven"* (Matt. 5:16).

We have to keep these "embodiments," that we have hitherto called "ourselves," free from sin, sickness, worries, and troubles, and make them glorify God, so that people will think, "How unselfish and thoughtful for others they are, how well and happy they always are, how quickly difficulties disappear; what is the reason for it all?" And when they hear to what it is due, they say, "That is what we want; we must endeavour to understand it!" In this way evil is made to glorify God. "The wrath of man shall praise thee" (Ps. 76:10). "Unto us a child is born: . . . his name shall be called Wonderful" (Isa. 9:6). "Let yourself and not your words preach for you" (Amiel), and yet all desires must disappear, "desire for personal gain, personal loves, personal attainments, and, last and subtlest of all, desire for personal perfection, for the personal self must be lost in the one self, that is, the self of all that lives" (Annie Besant). This does not mean that man finding himself loses his individuality. Each scintillates with infinite variety.

Progress Necessary.—*"The world is advancing, advance with it"* (Mazzini).

When we learn to think rightly, that is, scientifically, we must not be satisfied with being what in the olden days we called good, otherwise we become self-righteous, and cover the rotten foundations with a coat of plaster. "They must upward still and onward, who would keep abreast of truth" (J. R. Lowell). "He who ceases to become better, ceases to become good" (Oliver Cromwell). God affords us fresh opportunities as we use

those we have had. We must continually go up higher. As we understand
that we are spiritual beings here, so do we learn our capabilities for good,
and find that still greater sacrifices, not of joys, but of self-consciousness
and sloth, are necessary. This is the pathway to the true glory of im-
5 mortality. Our ability to do so-called miracles depends on how we are
advancing, not upon how good we are. "The great man is he who knows
that the spiritual will conquer" (Emerson). It must conquer and destroy
all evil.

> "So with every error conquered draw nearer to thy peace,
10   And in Life's great song triumphant hear the discords falter—cease"
>   (Violet M. Firth).

Be Selfless.—"*The truth is that the cause of all sins in every person
and every instance is excessive self-love*" (Plato). "*We must get rid of all
thought of self before we can gain peace or happiness*" (Emerson). "*Success
15 and happiness are only to be had in giving up our own will*" (General
Gordon).[1]

We have to learn to do right, merely because it is right, without the
slightest regard for results. This doing right because it is right is called by
Buddhists "Parikamma." We then grow to love to do right because we love
20 good. This is the love of God, and the results to mankind of this love are
in proportion to the understanding of what God is. Let all human desires
merge into the desire for others' good. Then shall we understand the words
of Job: "Yet in my flesh shall I see God" (Job 19:26). "All good thinkers,
so far as they are good, are characterised by indifference to results"
25 (James Hinton). "Duty never yet did want his meed" (Shakespeare).

This, however, is not sufficient. "Put off thine own will, and there will
be no more hell" (*Theologia Germanica*). "Desire is personal and therefore
selfish" (Annie Besant). We have to lose self in love, to become absolutely
selfless, having no will of our own (called in Buddhism "Virāga"), so that
30 we allow the action of God to cause us always to do what is right. Looking
away from self, the kingdom of God within, always present, will bear us
upward, heavenward, until we find within it home, the City of Zion, Love
itself. "There is but one virtue—to forget oneself as a person: one vice,
to remember oneself" (Fichte). We know more now, namely, that the
35 thing to be forgotten is the seeming material world and material man. The
thing to be remembered is the real spiritual world and the real spiritual
man. Then the action of God is seen. Lao-Tze, the great Chinese philosopher, who, like his contemporary, Gautama Buddha, must have been

---

[1] The Hindu and Buddhist scriptures are full of the necessity for renunciation
40 of all personal desires. In the *Bhagavad Gîtâ* we read: "He whose Buddhi is everywhere unattached, the self subdued, dead to desires, he goeth by renunciation to
the supreme perfection of freedom from Karma" (Discourse XVIII, 49). In the
Udânavarga we read: "The steadfast, who care not for the happiness of desires,
cast them off, and do soon depart [to Nirvana]." The *Dhammapada* says: "I have
45 conquered all, I know all, . . . I left all, and through the destruction of thirst I am
free." When Gautama attains Buddhahood, it says: "The mind, approaching the
Eternal, has attained to the extinction of all desires." At the same time, as Annie
Besant points out in *Reincarnation* "action is not to be stopped because the disciple
no longer seeks the fruit of action as reward. 'Inaction in a deed of mercy becomes
50 an action in a deadly sin.' (*Voice of the Silence*)."

individually very close indeed to the truth, said: "The pure men of old acted as they were moved, without calculation, not seeking to secure results. They laid no plans. Therefore, failing, they had no cause for regret; succeeding, no cause for congratulation."

He also said: "He acts by non-action, and by this he governs all," and again: "By non-action there is nothing that may not be done. One might undertake the government of the world without ever taking any trouble— and as for all those who take trouble, they are not competent to the government of the world." (It will be found that the word "trouble" means "material steps.") Lao-Tze knew well that right mental action (the realisa- tion of God), was the only action of any value to man, and that the fewer the material steps, and the greater the reliance on the Principle of good, the better the results. In *Tao Têh* he writes: "Therefore the wise man knows without travelling, names things without seeing them, and accomplishes everything without action." 15

"Meekness, selflessness, and love are the paths of His testimony, and the footsteps of His flock" (Mary Baker Eddy). "Closeness to Christ necessitates separation from self" (A. R. Wells). "Love of God's will . . . is a higher degree of love, inasmuch as it requires us to renounce our own will" (St. Francis of Sales). Plato insisted that the true art of living is an act of dying to mere sense, in order more fully to exist in intimate union with goodness and beauty (see also I Cor. 15:31 and Phil. 1:21). He further insisted that the proper aim of man is not pleasure, but truth, beauty, and right, which are to be sought for their own worth. "It hath been said: 'The more of self and me, the more of sin and wickedness.' So likewise it hath been said: 'The more the self, the I, the me, the mine, that is, self-seeking and selfishness, abate in a man, the more doth God's I, that is, God Himself, increase in him'" (*Theologia Germanica*). We must exterminate self and thus find God's man, made in His image and likeness. "He who gains a victory over other men is strong, but he who gains a victory over himself is all-powerful" (Lao-Tze). "You can have neither a greater nor a less dominion than that over yourself" (Leonardo da Vinci). "Cast away personality, sacrifice it; what is left is the essence of life— Love" (Tolstoy).

Pride.—"*The wicked, through the pride of his countenance, will not seek after God: God is not in all his thoughts*" (Ps. 10:4).

"Pride is certainly the most naked form of sin, for pride is self-deification. It may be madness of disease, it may be rebellion, but inasmuch as it claims to be a law to itself, it is the very principle of sin come to self-consciousness. Augustine and Thomas Aquinas both say that pride is the beginning of sin, though not its root. We might equally well say that it is the end of sin, its completed development in self-chosen independence of God" [1] (W. R. Inge).

"Search thine own heart, what paineth thee
In others, in thyself may be; 45
All dust is frail, all flesh is weak;
Be thou the true man thou dost seek" (*Whittier*).

[1] "The Paddock Lectures" for 1906.

Criticism.—"*Love is kind and suffers long; Love is meek and thinks no wrong*" (Bishop Wordsworth).

Impersonal criticism brings out facts, with the object of comparing them with prior knowledge, and so elucidating truth and helping the world.
5 True criticism is open-minded and constructive; false criticism is prejudiced and destructive. The highest criticism is scientific judgment. This separates not evil persons, but evil thoughts from the good, separating them in order to destroy them. In this way the false conclusions are reduced, and so the only support of evil is weakened and its final destruction in
10 every form hastened.[1]

Never under any circumstances indulge in the false luxury of personal criticism, the antithesis of love. Love "beareth all things, believeth all things" (I Cor. 13:7). "Hypocrite, first cast out the beam out of thine own eye" (Matt. 7:5). If you thoroughly cast the beam out of your own
15 eye, or consciousness, there will be nothing to criticise, as the wrong thought that you are conscious of will be destroyed, and the victims freed. "For the accuser of our brethren is cast down. . . . Therefore rejoice" (Rev. 12:10, 12).

"Scepticism is deliberate, distrustful of appearances, grave, and candid.
20 Incredulity needs no thought, but is peremptory and scornful, and, not being reasonable, it cannot be reasoned with. The one is a high strong mental virtue . . . the other is a sign of mental debility"[2] (W. H. Thompson).

A man as a rule criticises in people the fault from which he himself
25 suffers most. Recognise yourself as the chosen instrument of God, His dear son, and look upon all men as His and your dearly beloved. "Thou shalt love thy neighbour as thyself" (Matt. 19:19). Not only avoid all forms of personal criticism, but all forms of wrong thinking, or indeed any thinking of others, except for the purpose of helping them. "The wise
30 man knows no distinctions; he beholds all men as things made for holy uses" (Lao-Tze).

Talking of Others.—"*Let none of you imagine evil in your hearts against his neighbour*" (Zech. 8:17). "*Let every man sweep the snow before his own door, and not trouble himself about the frost on his neighbour's tiles*"
35 (Chinese).

Talking of others is one of the most insidious forms of evil. Few are altogether free from this dangerous habit. Let others be sacred to you. We should only talk of others in order to help them, and even then we should be very, very certain of our ground. With your mind stayed on Truth,
40 aflame with divine Love, this holy region can be approached. "Unselfish thoughts are the very portals of Heaven, and to dwell day by day in thoughts of peace toward every creature will bring abounding peace to their possessor" (James Allen). "Not only speak charitably, but feel so" (Elizabeth Fry).

45 [1] "Christian Science is the higher criticism because it criticizes evil, disease, and death—all that is unlike God, good—on a Scriptural basis, and approves or disapproves according to the word of God" (*Miscellany*, p. 240, Mary Baker Eddy).
[2] *As to Ourselves.*

When, in your hearing, a fellow human being ventures upon this
dangerous ground of voicing evil of another, then hasten firmly, even if
silently, to deny any reality to evil. Consistently reverse every material
statement, and translate every false picture, however bad, back into its
true meaning, and so gain its original spiritual truth. "Watch ye and pray, 5
lest ye enter into temptation" (Mark 14:38). "Charity suffereth long, and
is kind" (I Cor. 13:4). "Sweet mercy is nobility's true badge" (Shakespeare). "Love your enemies, bless them that curse you, do good to them
that hate you, and pray for them which despitefully use you, and persecute
you" (Matt. 5:44). Love must be enthroned in consciousness. Love God 10
with an intense love, and love your neighbour far more than yourself.
Proof, not profession, is essential. Practical love is the divine way to heaven.
"Shall we ever all learn this? . . . When we do the wide world will indeed
be a beautiful place" (Edgar Daplyn). Let us hasten to learn and practise
this Godlike quality.   15

Friends.—*"Blessed is the man who has the gift of making friends, for
it is one of God's best gifts. It involves many things, but above all, the power
of going out of one's self, and seeing and appreciating whatever is noble and
loving in another man"* (Thomas Hughes).
  "A faithful friend is a strong defence: and he that hath found such an 20
one hath found a treasure." A true friend is one who, remembering to deny
all apparent error, never forgets that his friend is really perfect, being the
spiritual image and likeness of God, and in heaven. The greatest advantage
of a friend is to have someone to love, someone to help. One mistake that I
made as a young man was never to allow anyone to help me without doing 25
an equal amount for him in return. Another mistake was thinking that to
live my thanks without verbally stating them was sufficient. All men should
be our friends, our loved ones. Then comes true happiness, perpetual
happiness. All are then lovers, united in the enduring bonds of the true
spiritual friendship, which constitutes the basis of all happiness. "Fellow- 30
ship is heaven, and lack of fellowship is hell" (William Morris). As Bacon
says, friendship doubles our joys and halves our sorrows. To a true
friend we can be ourselves and tell everything. Then we know that there
is nothing that can make him think worse of us. The definition of a friend
by Pythagoras was "Another I." "He's true to God who's true to man" 35
(J. R. Lowell).
  It is wise never to rely absolutely upon human so-called friendship,
which is material. Rely solely upon God. "Thou wilt keep him in perfect
peace, whose mind is stayed on thee" (Isa. 26:3). A friend always wants
to help you, but sometimes his idea of help is different from yours. Again, 40
mortals are subject to fits of aberration until they know how to think rightly
and carry right thinking into practice, and will do things that you would
have thought impossible. Some of those who I know desired to help me,
have had what have been practically fits of insanity, in which they have
incriminated themselves, with no other apparent object than that of pre- 45
judicing me. "Judge before friendship, then confide till death." Remember
that should a friend turn upon you it is not his fault, but his misfortune.
It is your business then to protect him by thinking rightly yourself. Do

not think of him. Turn to your one and only true friend—God, and the
trouble will then have been of use. The worst of all friends is the flatterer.
It has been truly said, "flattery is a disease of friendship."

Be Unselfish.—"*By being the most unselfish he is the most secure*"
5 (Lao-Tze).
The Stoics used to say that a selfish man is a cancer in the universe, and
Philo finds the root of sin in selfishness. The first step downwards of the
prodigal son was: "Give me the portion of goods that falleth to me"
(Luke 15:12). As Bacon said, like bees we kill ourselves in stinging
10 others.
Selfishness comes from thinking that you want something and that you
may lose what you have. Such thoughts breed unhappiness. "So long as
you persist in selfishly seeking for your own personal happiness, so long
will happiness elude you, and you will be sowing the seeds of wretched-
15 ness. In so far as you succeed in losing yourself in the service of others, in
that measure will happiness come to you, and you will reap a harvest of
bliss" (James Allen in *From Poverty to Power*).
Unselfishness in the old mistaken methods of so-called living, as a rule,
meant self-sacrifice, suffering, and giving way to others. Now we find that
20 unselfishness is happiness, joy, continuing bliss, everything that is good.
Further, viewed in the light of the knowledge of truth, and therefore
understood scientifically, it is an unseen power, lifting a man out of a
very prison to put him upon a throne. Jesus expressed this in the misunderstood saying: "He that loseth his life . . . shall find it" (Matt.
25 10:39). In other words, in proportion as the material self is lost sight of,
forgotten, dissociated from man's real self, so does he gain power over that
material self and all its seeming troubles. Thus he wields that spiritual
government which alone gives him, when fully apprehended, dominion
over all matter.
30 We have to lead a life of true unselfishness, always mentally working
in the way already pointed out, so as to help each one with whom we come
in contact. "One can create a heaven for many lives" (Elizabeth Gibson).
We must not do this by thinking of them, of the material individual. This
is wrong and absolutely hypnotic. Never, if you can help it, let your
35 thought rest on the material concept of those you love. Be "willing
rather to be absent from the body, and to be present with the Lord"
(II Cor. 5:8). Turn in thought at once to God and realise Him and the
true spiritual consciousness and you cannot fail to help, and are less likely
to be separated from those you love on earth, in exact proportion to the
40 depth of your realisation of man's unity with God, Spirit, in heaven.[1]
"Sin is selfishness; Godliness is unselfishness" (Chevalier). "Where the
love of self is banished, there dwelleth the love of God" (Jacob Boehme).
"Pity is the touch of God in human hearts" (W. O. Smith, D.D., LL.D.).

[1] See 1 John 3, verse 17, and 4, verse 12.

OUR RESPONSIBILITY

" *That system is most divine which is most effective and which is most in accord with the spirit of Christ*" (Canon Plumtre).

As there is nothing but God, there is in reality only good. There is, therefore, only one false representation of God, one material, universal 5 consciousness, called by scientific men the ether, by others the devil and mortal mind, and if we scientifically destroy the evil thought as it first presents itself to our own individual so-called consciousness, it is destroyed for all. In thus fulfilling our responsibility we are, fortunately, one step nearer the end of the so-called material world. 10

Judgment-Day.—"*For the ear trieth words, as the mouth tasteth meat. Let us choose to us judgment: let us know among ourselves what is good*" (Job 34:3, 4).

This destruction of evil is what is spoken of throughout the Bible as judgment. "All nations shall come and worship before thee; for thy 15 judgments are made manifest" (Rev. 15:4). "But he that is spiritual judgeth all things" (I Cor. 2:15). The meaning of "to judge" is "to point out or declare what is just"; the meaning of "judgment" is "the comparing of ideas to elicit truth" (*Chambers's Dictionary*). When, passing along the street, we see the evil and compare ideas, and declare what is just, 20 judgment takes place and the evil is destroyed. "Judge not according to the appearance, but judge righteous judgment" (John 7:24). "To do justice and judgment is more acceptable to the Lord than sacrifice" (Prov. 21:3). "For the Father judgeth no man, but hath committed all judgment unto the Son: . . . And hath given him authority to execute 25 judgment also, because he is the Son of man" (John 5:22, 27). "Do ye not know that the saints shall judge the world?" (I Cor. 6:2). "I can of mine own self do nothing; as I hear, I judge: and my judgment is just" (John 5:30). It is absolute justice, that if you think rightly by turning to God, the evil should be destroyed, as all is mental, and God the Principle of good. 30 The material man never made his "consciousness," and never made the ethereal "thoughts" that attack him. Why should he allow himself to be punished by believing the lie? "The Lord is known by the judgment which he executeth" (Ps. 9:16).

Judgment takes place daily, however, every time one reverses a wrong 35 thought. It is this constant judgment that leads to righteousness, by the purification of the so-called mind. "For when thy judgments are in the earth, the inhabitants of the world will learn righteousness" (Isa. 26:9). "When we are judged, we are chastened [made pure] of the Lord, that we should not be condemned with the world" (I Cor. 11:32). "Judgment-day 40 as used in the Scriptures, signifies the final destruction of all evil, all sin, sickness, worry, and every limitation, which takes place at the end, by the action and reaction of right thinking. "The word that I have spoken, the same shall judge him in the last day" (John 12:48). This results in consentaneous conscious, mental action of the whole body of 45 right thinkers. "Because he hath appointed a day, in the which he will judge the world in righteousness by that man whom he hath ordained"

(Acts 17:31). "It is he which was ordained of God to be the Judge of quick and dead. To him give all the prophets witness" (Acts 10:42, 43). "My righteousness is near; my salvation is gone forth, and mine arms shall judge the people; the isles shall wait upon me,[1] and on mine arm shall they
5 trust" (Isa. 51:5). "Which executeth judgment for the oppressed" (Ps. 146:7). "Zion shall be redeemed with judgment, and her converts with righteousness" (Isa. 1:27).

> "So let it be. In God's own might
> We gird us for the coming fight.
10 And strong in Him Whose cause is ours,
> In conflict with unholy powers,
> We grasp the weapons He has given—
> The light, and truth, and love of heaven" (*Whittier*).

"And the most High shall appear upon the seat of judgment, and misery
15 shall pass away, and the long suffering shall have an end: But judgment only shall remain, truth shall stand, and faith shall wax strong: And the work shall follow, and the reward shall be shewed, and the good deeds shall be of force, and wicked deeds shall bear no rule" (II Esdras 7:33–35).

This gives each of us an enormous responsibility. Not only every
20 wrong thought that comes into our consciousness should be "judged," but every single thing that we do should be prayed for—"judged." "If the world shall be judged by you, are ye unworthy to judge the smallest matters?" (I Cor. 6:2). We must be always either harming or helping ourselves and others. Which are we going to do?

25 "Upon every side we hear the prophecy of a great religious revival which is to sweep over all Christendom. Scarcely a day goes by in which this prophecy is not repeated in some religious paper, or by some minister whose sermon is reported in the daily press . . . referred to as forerunners of an extensive or universal revival which shall awaken the people
30 of all Christian lands" (Archibald McLellan).

Let us not delay and so put off the time of deliverance that awaits us. "It is your duty to yourself to make each day a success." "We are making to-morrow's character to-day. . . . Faithfulness to-day is the only way to ensure success in some distant to-morrow" (*Great Thoughts*).

35 "**Choose You This Day.**"—*Behold, now is the accepted time; behold, now is the day of salvation*" (II Cor. 6:2). "*Jesus saith, except ye fast to the world [2] ye shall in nowise find the kingdom of God; and except ye make the sabbath a real sabbath,[3] ye shall not see the Father*" (*New Sayings of Jesus*, from the Oxyrhynchus Papyri).

40 There has now been set forth the fundamental law that governs all existence, and rests upon demonstrated proofs. Each individual can test and prove for himself the truths of this law of ever-present Life, omnipotent Mind, ever-present good, God, and accept or reject it. The question here presents itself as to how far one has any power of choice as to the
45 acceptance, or otherwise, of the ruling of unalterable law, and how such choice could affect our life experience.

---

[1] "Be still, and know that I am God" (Ps. 46:10).
[2] *Think not of the material things.*
[3] *Sabbath* means *rest*.

Moses, probably the greatest natural statesman, or, to speak more accurately, the greatest natural lawgiver the world has ever seen, after setting before a great race the law of life and its contradictory opposite of death, says: "Choose life" (Deut. 30:19), the Life that is God, the law of Soul; and later in history the great leader, his successor Joshua, reminding 5 them again of this law, said: "Choose you this day whom ye will serve" (Josh. 24:15). Anyone reading this book will at once see that a deep significance attaches to these words as to choice, and there is now no shadow of doubt as to their meaning. It goes without saying that life is governed by law, and equally that to oppose fundamental law is impossible. 10 So the power of choice lies merely in whether we willingly accept and obey the law of God, good, by right thinking, or live in seeming opposition to it, dwelling upon the opposite thoughts of evil, with all the attendant worries and troubles that must then result. The word "seeming" is used advisedly, for the startling fact remains, that the inevitable end 15 reached will be the same—eternal good.

The Apparent Law of Evil.—"*There is no peace, saith the Lord, unto the wicked*" (Isa. 48:22).

Then comes the question, In what lies the importance of any individual or collective choice or action? Simply this: the difference it makes to us 20 *now.* A period of opposition or contradiction to the ruling of the law of good can only be at best a series of attempts and failures, increasing limitations, hopes disappointed, scant happiness, mixed with worry and, more or less, discord; a life that proves, by its own failure to succeed in living, the fallacy of its imaginary laws of existence. But during such period, 25 the fundamental law does not suspend action, and a man choosing evil is merely being self-conducted through a path of needless suffering towards his inevitable, conscious acceptance of the law of Life, the ever-active Principle of good, God, Spirit. We can only accept or reject a lie when it presents itself. 30

The Law of Good.—"*Who shall stand in his holy place? He shall receive the blessing from the Lord, and righteousness from the God of his salvation*" (Ps. 24:3, 5).

From the point of willing obedience to and acceptance of the ruling of good, a life experience becomes one of increasingly harmonious con- 35 ditions. Hope is fulfilled, joy exceeds anticipation. If disease at first appears, it is met and mastered, while there comes a growing sense of restful confidence in a never-failing law of good, ordering our affairs. Progress in all directions replaces limitations, proving every step of the way that progress is, must be, included in a *law* of infinite good. 40

Each one's responsibility to his fellow-man is to speak the truth as he knows it, and to continue in living up to an ever-advancing understanding of the great law of "infinite Mind and its infinite manifestation." It remains only for each and all to have for himself and themselves a period of (1) ignorance and sin, with their inevitable attendant suffering and 45 discord, or (2) science and peace, with triumphant progress in infinite eternal good and joy unspeakable. Too much stress cannot be laid upon the time of the choice given by the great leader Joshua—"choose you *this* day" (Josh. 24:15). Evidently the day on which the statement was made was the time recommended for choice, testing, and demonstration. This choice fortunately is free to all, being due to the action of God.

> "For a cap and bells our lives we pay,
> 5   Bubbles we buy with a whole soul's tasking:
> 'Tis heaven alone that is given away,
> 'Tis only God may be had for the asking" (*J. R. Lowell*).

Why, indeed, should you suffer another needless pang when the solution of all problems lies opened up before us, within reach of all? This
10 solution is the covenant referred to throughout the Bible, the covenant between God and man, namely, that if man thinks good, has but one God, good, he will receive only good. It was on account of this covenant that Paul was able to say: "By the grace of God I am what I am" (I Cor. 15:10). "And we know that all things work together for good to them that love
15 God, to them who are the called according to his purpose" (Rom. 8:28). "Call upon me in the day of trouble: I will deliver thee, and thou shalt glorify me" (Ps. 50:15).

LEARN TO PRAY RIGHTLY [1]

"I may say to my critics, Try the experiments; investigate with care and
20 *patience as I have done. If, having examined, you discover imposture or delusion, proclaim it and say how it was done. But, if you find it to be a fact, avow it fearlessly, as 'by the everlasting law of honour you are bound to do'"* (Sir William Crookes, F.R.S.).

The whole of the facts laid before you show that the only intelligent
25 way of living is always to think rightly,[2] and this can only be done on a scientific basis. Progress demands greater scientific knowledge. We must plant our standard of thought on the rock of Christ,[3] the spiritual idea, the true idea of God and His manifestation. Maintain it in place with truth, water it with activity, prune it with wisdom, guard it will love, and it will
30 become the tree of life, spreading in every direction, whose leaves are for the healing of nations, whose fruit—love, joy, peace, gentleness, meekness, etc.—enriches mankind; an immortal plant, whose seed is the seed of Truth, the seed that "is in itself" (Gen. 1:11), whose intelligence and substance are God. "In the midst of the street of it, and on either side of
35 the river [the channel of pure thought], was there the tree of life, which bare twelve manner of fruits, and yielded her fruit every month: and the leaves of the tree were for the healing of the nations. And there shall be no more curse" (Rev. 22:2, 3).

---

[1] "My prayer, some daily good to do
40   To Thine, for Thee;
        An offering pure of Love, whereto
          God leadeth me" (*Mary Baker Eddy*).
     [2] "To keep my mental home a sacred place" ("My Prayer," *Christian Science Sentinel*).
45   [3] I Corinthians 10, verse 4.

The Habit of Reversal.—"*Useless thoughts spoil all; that the mischief began there; but that we ought to reject them, as soon as we perceived their impertinence to the matter in hand, or our salvation; and return to our communion with God*" (Brother Lawrence, Conversation 2). "*I looked beyond the world for truth and beauty: Sought, found, and did my duty*" (Elizabeth 5 Browning).

Fortunately the rule of life is absolutely simple. Whenever any wrong thought, a thought unlike God, good, comes into our consciousness, we have:

(1) At once to turn our inward gaze to God and heaven;

(2) Deny there the existence of the wrong thing of which we have been 10 thinking;

(3) Realise, as clearly as we possibly can, the existence of the opposite of the wrong thing thought of; and

(4) Dwell upon the perfection of that opposite as long as possible.

"Therefore turn thou to thy God: keep mercy and judgment, and wait 15 on thy God continually" (Hos. 12:6), "and be renewed in the spirit of your mind" (Eph. 4:23). Think deeply of the glorious reality, the kingdom of God that is within

> "And wake a white-winged angel throng
> Of thoughts, illumed . . .   20
> And o'er earth's troubled, angry sea
> I see Christ walk,
> And come to me, and tenderly,
> Divinely talk" (*Mary Baker Eddy*).

"How can we be with Him but in thinking of Him often? And how can we 25 often think of Him, but by a holy habit which we should form of it? You will tell me that I am always saying the same thing: it is true, for this is the best and easiest method I know; and as I use no other, I advise all the world to use it. We must know before we can love. In order to know God, we must often think of Him" (Brother Lawrence, Ninth Letter).   30

Think Rightly.—"*Charity . . . thinketh no evil*" (I Cor. 13 : 4, 5). "*Whatsoever things are true . . . honest . . . just . . . pure . . . lovely . . . of good report . . . think on these things*" (Phil. 4:8).

"Watch and pray, that ye enter not into temptation" (Matt. 26:41). Station love, "justice and gratitude as sentinels along the lines of thought." 35 Refuse to allow evil in your consciousness, let the least thought of it turn you at once to Truth, so that you enter your heritage of freedom "where the Spirit of the Lord is" and turn in thought instantly, "turn ye" to "that great city, the holy Jerusalem, descending out of heaven from God" (Rev. 21:10), the kingdom of God that is within. On recognising error, let the 40 two-edged sword of Truth,[1] the universal panacea, flash, and the denial, the battle-axe of divine Science, will sweep away the phantoms of mortal illusion and show "Satan as lightning fall from heaven" (Luke 10:18), leaving the view of the Holy City, the new Jerusalem, clearer to your vision, giving you a foretaste of "infinite, boundless bliss." With this 45 practical method of utilising the divine power of good, we can now be, as Stopford Brooke writes of Browning's *Euthycles*, "so spiritual that we can soar out of our most overwhelming sorrow into the stormless world

---

[1] See Hebrews 4, verse 12.

[heaven] where the gods [spiritual beings] breathe pure thought and for ever love; and, abiding in its peace, use the griefs of earth [by reversal] for the ennoblement of the life of man."

Man One with God.—"*I have turned your attention to this sublimely affecting subject of our vital connection with God, not for the purpose of awakening temporary fervour, but that we may feel the urgent duty of cherishing these convictions. If this duty becomes a reality to us, we shall be conscious of having received a new Principle of Life*" (Channing).

Realise continually the fact that you are one with God, an individualisation of the Christ. Never allow any wrong thoughts of self, and never even think of yourself as a material man. Such mistakes are malpractising upon yourself, thinking lies, and therefore intensifying the difficulties to which your material self is subject. "He that believeth not the Son . . . the wrath of God abideth on him" (John 3:36). "It pleased God, . . . To reveal his Son in me" (Gal. 1:15, 16). "At that day ye shall know that I am in my Father, and ye in me, and I in you" (John 14:20). Lose all sense of self and the material world in this clinging to God. "Set your affection on things above, not on things on the earth" (Col. 3:2). "Draw nigh to God, and he will draw nigh to you" (James 4:8). "Whosoever loves God thus, will devote his whole soul and strength to God, preferring His grace [1] to the whole world" (St. Francis of Sales). As we go on dwelling in thought on good in this way, so does our view of heaven get clearer and clearer. "My hopes in heaven do dwell" (Shakespeare). Would that we could always dwell thus. This living in the presence of God is absolute protection. "We are confident, I say, and willing rather to be absent from the body, and to be present with the Lord" (II Cor. 5:8). "Pray without ceasing" (I Thess. 5:17). "Prayer is the spiritual balm, the precious cordial which restores to us peace and courage" (Amiel). In *Of the Supersensual Life*, Jacob Boehme writes: "Disciple: How shall I be now able to subsist in this anxiety and tribulation arising from the world, so as not to lose the eternal peace, or not enter into this rest? Master: If thou dost once every hour throw thyself by faith beyond all creatures, beyond and above all sensual perception and apprehension . . . and yieldest thyself fully, and absolutely thereinto; then thou shalt receive power from above to rule over death, and the devil, and to subdue hell and the world under thee: And then thou mayest subsist in all temptations, and be the brighter for them" St. Ambrose says: "Prayer is the wing wherewith the soul flies to heaven, and meditation the eye wherewith we see God." This flying to heaven is merely the endeavour to rise in consciousness to the true sense of heaven, now and here.

> "Some men live near to God, as my right arm
> Is near to me; and thus they walk about
> Mailed in full proof of faith, and bear a charm
> That mocks at fear, and bars the door on doubt,
> And dares the impossible"[2] (Prof. *J. S. Blackie*).

[1] The action of the Holy Ghost or Holy Spirit—the action of God on man— when, after the second coming of Christ to him, he understands God better, and prays rightly. "The prophets . . . prophesied of the grace that should come unto you: . . . at the revelation of Jesus Christ" (I Peter 1:10 and 13).

[2] *Sonnet on Chinese Gordon.*

In this way doing our work, minute by minute throughout the day, we "watch and pray," and "pray without ceasing." We have ever to dwell in the presence of God, and so we shall discern the rhythm of Spirit, and "catch glorious glimpses of the Messiah or Christ." Upton truly says at the beginning of his Hibbert lectures, that "All wholly satisfying and 5 effective religious belief arises out of the immediate feeling of God's self-revealing presence in our consciousness."

Sign-posts on the Way.—"*I say that man must travel in the way of God. Day and night . . . his turning to God must be greater; the fire of his love must flame more brightly. Then day by day, he will make progress*" (Baha' Ullah). 10
Our progress depends chiefly upon the length of time during the twenty-four hours that we are realising God and heaven, and we have, by constant reversal, to use every evil thought, every trouble, every twinge of pain, every sad thought, as a sign-post, directing us to God. "For our light affliction, which is but for a moment, worketh for us a far more exceeding 15 and eternal weight of glory; while we look not at the things which are seen, but at the things which are not seen: for the things which are seen are temporal; but the things which are not seen are eternal" (II Cor. 4:17, 18). "It makes no difference whether a person stares stupidly at the sky, or down upon the ground. So long as his attention is directed to 20 objects of sense, his soul is looking downwards, not upwards" (Plato's *Republic*). "For our conversation is in heaven; from whence also we look for the Saviour" (Phil. 3:20). In this way error tends to its own destruction, for, like Moses, by handling the serpent we turn it into a rod, something of use; namely, by the denial, the action of God, working through us as a 25 channel, destroys the wrong thoughts; and by the affirmation, God purifies our human consciousness, and that of those for whom we are working.

Demonstration the only Proof.—"*Faith without works is dead*" (James 2:17).
Through this constant thinking of the reality, God and heaven, we 30 obtain the necessary knowledge of God. The phrase translated in the Bible "knowledge" of God (epignosis), should be translated "full or exact knowledge," and that necessarily is "scientific" knowledge of God, and therefore scientific knowledge of the truth. This is what the whole world is striving for. This is the truth that sets us free, and the only proof is 35 demonstration, the instantaneous and continuous healing of sin, sickness, troubles, and limitations. This is the truth that Jesus, "the most scientific man that ever trod the globe," [1] taught. "Heaven and earth shall pass away,[2] but my words shall not pass away" (Matt. 24:35). This is because such words of Jesus were statements of truth, and many of his statements 40 heal, when understood and dwelt on, in other words, realised. Such statements are immortal, and such demonstrations are Immanuel, or God with us. (See Isa. 7:14 and Matt. 1:23.)

Give Tithes to God.—When we are not sufficiently advanced to do things entirely by treatment instead of materially, we must not fail at all 45

---

[1] *Science and Health*, p. 313, Mary Baker Eddy.
[2] Dematerialise.

events to pay our tithes. That is, if the work is likely to take thirty minutes,
pray at least during three minutes of that time; if it will take sixty minutes,
then give six to prayer. If you do this you will find that the work is not only
much better, but more quickly done, and not only will you actually have
5 saved more time than the ten per cent. that you have thus devoted to the
realisation of God,[1] but you are permanently better fitted to do your
material work well in the future, as your human consciousness is purified.

This denial and affirmation, this realisation of Truth, is the only right
treatment of evil. For ages, viewed only from a religious point of view, and
10 divorced from its scientific basis, it has been named "prayer." To this
unnatural separation are due the attenuated results of the earnest prayers
of multitudes of religious people.

"Pray Without Ceasing."—*"Pray without ceasing. In every thing
give thanks"* (I Thess. 5:17, 18).
15 Unfortunately, partly through ignorance, and partly through lethargy,
up to the present we have been apt only to turn to God when we want to
overcome difficulties, instead of praying without ceasing, and so preventing
the mischief beforehand, thus hastening our own and all mankind's
deliverance from evil by its total destruction. We must be "willing rather
20 to be absent from the body, and to be present with the Lord" (II Cor.
5:8). "We and God have business with each other" (Professor William
James). Our business is to love God, to love good, and this includes the
love of our neighbour.

Here Lies Safety.—
25   *"More things are wrought by prayer than this world dreams of.
Wherefore let thy voice rise like a fountain for me night and day"* (Tennyson).

"When thou prayest, enter into thy closet, and when thou hast shut
thy door, pray to thy Father which is in secret; and thy Father which
seeth in secret shall reward thee openly" (Matt. 6:6). This means that we
30 have to enter into "the sanctuary of Spirit," and shut the door of human
consciousness to every thought of matter, every thought unlike God. We
"have right to the tree of life, and may enter in through the gates [spiritual
understanding] into the city [spiritual consciousness]" (Rev. 22:14).
"He that dwelleth in the secret place of the most High shall abide under
35 the shadow of the Almighty" (Ps. 91:1), and be protected from the heat
and burden of the day.

Do Not Waste a Second.—
     *"Redeem thy mis-spent time that's past,
And live this day as if thy last"* (Bishop Ken of Bath and Wells).

40 Never fail to pray, you can never regain the lost opportunity. Continually turn to God in thought. Any evil lightly passed over must be met
sooner or later, and perhaps under more strenuous circumstances. When
you have only a moment in which to treat, keep a running accompaniment
of thoughts such as the realisation of God as Truth, as Love, or as Life.

45   [1] See Isaiah 6, verse 13, and Genesis 28, verse 22.

Which of these you choose, should depend upon the individual conditions. If you are always well it is not so urgent to realise God as Life; which of the other two you chiefly realise should depend upon whether your love for others or your knowledge of truth is most above the average. This helps one to become evenly balanced, morally, intellectually, and 5 physically, until Mind alone rules supreme.

Throughout religious services I try to keep my thoughts fixed in the reality, denying every statement of evil in what is read, and realising as clearly as possible every statement of truth. This is like the soap and scrubbing-brush in the mental bath that we take during scientifically 10 religious services. We must strive to think equally rightly during the surging rush of daily business life. "Come, and let us join ourselves to the Lord in a perpetual covenant" (Jer. 50:5), the covenant of thinking only of good.

After understanding true prayer I tried to pray for the congregation 15 generally whenever a moment was available. About ten years ago, when it became clearer that during services patients should be healed, the work was done for those present who came specifically to the services with that object ; later, for the one whose need was greatest, and a few years ago I recognised that the one to be prayed for was that one whose healing at the 20 service, either of sin or of sickness, would be of the most benefit to humanity. Results are in accordance with our thoughts, and this equally applies to the object of our prayers. We cannot tell whom it is best to help. The instantaneous healing of a beggar from sin, sickness, or want, may revolutionise a nation.[1] 25

Consecration of Self.—*"No man has come to true greatness who has not felt in some degree that his life belongs to his race, and that what God gives him He gives him for mankind"* (Phillips Brooks).

> *" Thou art not here for ease and pain,*
> *But manhood's glorious crown to gain."* 30

So used have we been in the past to hear others talking of sin, sickness, and suffering, as if they were normal and unavoidable, that, unfortunately, we have fallen into the same habit of evil thought, and constantly put ourselves into direct touch with conditions that, were we wider awake, we should carefully avoid. A crowd of people will rush to obtain a newspaper 35 full of appalling horrors, innocently unaware that in so doing they bring into their homes a devastating army of ethereal, wrongly called "mental," bacteria. A sensibility to the suffering of others, without a knowledge of how to help them that has led many gentle natures to the verge of insanity, is now merely the call to wield the "rod of iron," [2] the invincible power 40 Mind confers upon man. This destroys with unfailing certainty the rampant evil, and rescues its innocent victims from the throttling grasp of false law.

[1] Since this was written I have recognised that each denial of error or statement of truth, as I mentally make it, should help the member of the congregation for whom 45 this help is of most benefit to humanity; for one a realisation of love, for another the denial of pain, for a third the realisation that man knows and loves Truth.

[2] See Psalms 2, verse 9, and Revelation 2, verse 27.

We have to offer a firm resistance to the old false habit of talking gossip, or even talking uselessly of material things of the world. We have to endeavour as quickly as possible to view life from its truer mental standpoint. We should never think, say, nor do anything, except with the 5 object of helping another in some way, or becoming ourselves better men. This may make a person somewhat silent at first, but he will soon have plenty to say that is worth hearing. "The Lord is in his holy temple: let all the earth keep silence before him" (Hab. 2:20). "Jesus saith, Except ye fast to the world, ye shall in no wise find the kingdom of God; and except 10 ye make the sabbath a real sabbath ye shall not see the Father" (*New Sayings of Jesus*, from the Oxyrhynchus Papyri).

Being silent with people will not surprise them, if you pray. Most people prefer hearing themselves speak, and you will find that if you silently deny any error that may come up, and realise the truth, they will 15 enjoy themselves and think you a most sympathetic listener. Under some circumstances, "To say nothing is, like honesty, generally the best policy" (C. Evans Jones). At the same time, "a word fitly spoken is like apples of gold in pictures of silver" (Prov. 25:11). "Make yourselves nests of thoughts which care cannot disturb, nor pain make gloomy, nor poverty 20 take from us" (Ruskin).

Better Beliefs.—"*Seek ye the kingdom of God; and all these things shall be added unto you*" (Luke 12:31).

Do not limit good by thinking that your demonstrations must be made in the way that you expect. Do not try to teach God His business. "It is 25 the Lord; let him do what seemeth him good" (I Sam. 3:18). When you pray to dispel evil or limitation, you cannot know what form of good will appear in its place, as this depends upon the material so-called thoughts that are latent, and which then come into action. These are humanly bound to pass over you at that particular time. Whenever wrong thoughts are 30 destroyed, so-called good thoughts then take their place. These, again, can be destroyed by scientific prayer, and still better ones be manifested. These, again, can be destroyed until the last moment, when your material consciousness is finally and completely dematerialised by the action of God as you realise Truth and Love. So-called good human thoughts are 35 never really good; they are only good in comparison with other material thoughts, and if you are certain that a particular kind of good will come you may intensify these thoughts until they act, and very likely so prevent thoughts that are ever so much better from appearing. Rely not on human intelligence. "The carnal mind is enmity against God" (Rom. 8:7).

40 **Trust in God.**—"*Thou wilt keep him in perfect peace, whose mind is stayed on thee: because he trusteth in thee*" (Isa. 26:3).

When men know how to pray rightly, "None can trust too much in God; and no one has ever been forsaken by Him who has turned to Him with his whole heart and leant upon Him with loving confidence" 45 (German Mystics). If, when you are doubtful how to act, you pray scientifically, and do then what first comes into your consciousness, you will find that you have done what is right. By following this principle you obtain perfect trust in God, trust in good, and are always doing what is best.

Before, however, you can thus get rid of all responsibility, you must have demonstrated your knowledge of how to pray scientifically, and this you do by the habitual instantaneous healing of sin and sickness. Self must be eliminated as well as belief in human personality, belief in a person who is capable of choosing that which is best. "Be what you ought to be; the rest 5 is God's affair" (Amiel). "Trust in the Lord with all thine heart; and lean not unto thine own understanding. In all thy ways acknowledge him, and he shall direct thy paths" (Prov. 3:5, 6). Leave self for God; abandon as fast as possible all reliance on material means. "Nothing venture, nothing have." "One on God's side is a majority" (Wendell Phillips). "Not failure, 10 but low aim is crime" (J. R. Lowell).

At the same time, as Dr. Inge says: "Illumination is not granted to the mere thinker, but to him who acts while he thinks, and thinks while he acts. . . . No one can try to purify himself, even as God is pure, without knowing the meaning . . . of sin." [1] 15

Even when with others, always leave human arrangements, as far as possible, to them, and rely upon your prayers to bring about the manifestation of the action of God through them. "It is not in man that walketh to direct his steps" (Jer. 10:23). "Rest in the Lord, and wait patiently for him" (Ps. 37:7). Never push forward your own ideas. "Wait on thy God 20 continually" (Hosea 12:6). We have to practise simplicity, the ultimate of wisdom, and we must give up that "mythological material intelligence called *energy*" (Mary Baker Eddy), and in its stead present to all the idea of divine humility, divine wisdom, and the consequent divine power. "Be strong and of a good courage; be not afraid, neither be thou dismayed; for 25 the Lord thy God is with thee whithersoever thou goest" (Josh. 1:9).

Do Not Limit God.—"*If God be for us, who can be against us?*" (Rom. 8:31).

Do not limit "the Holy One of Israel" (Ps. 78:41). "He hath done marvellous things" (Ps. 98:1). "In thee, O Lord, do I put my trust" 30 (Ps. 71:1). Each time that you try to do things by prayer alone it becomes easier. "I can do all things through Christ" (Phil. 4:13). "Do that which is assigned you, and you cannot hope too much or dare too much" (Emerson). "Stand fast therefore in the liberty wherewith Christ hath made us free" (Gal. 5:1). Never rely upon the broken reed of human 35 assistance. Jesus, in the Garden of Gethsemane, said to the sleeping students: "Could ye not watch with me one hour?" and then, receiving no response, finally turned away from any human aid, to find, in consequence, the unfailing, living support of God, Spirit, as All-in-all.

Pray until Fear is Destroyed.—"*Fear ye not, neither be afraid:* 40 *have not I told thee from that time, and have declared it? ye are even my witnesses. Is there a God beside me? Yea, there is no God; I know not any*" (Isa. 44:8).

Fear is man's recognition of the evil thoughts that are attacking or are about to attack. Destroy the fear and the trouble cannot happen. The sign 45 by which one can tell when the work has been done well enough to rely solely upon prayer to overcome a difficulty, is whether, after having

[1] *Personal Idealism and Mysticism.*

prayed, all fear that the evil may not be destroyed has disappeared. "Seest thou how faith wrought with his works, and by works was faith made perfect?" (James 2:22). If, morning and evening, man turns to God in true prayer, and works against the different forms of false thought, it will be
5 found that his work throughout the day is much reduced.

Nothing too Difficult.—

"Arouse thy courage ere it fails and faints;
God props no Gospel up with sinking saints" (Langbridge).

Let nothing appear to you to be too difficult of accomplishment.
10 "Difficulties are the things that show what men are" (Epictetus). Like Chatham, never accept the verdict "impossible." Nothing is impossible to God. Try to do everything by prayer, and although you may fail sometimes, the fact that you try difficult things not only makes the difficult things ultimately become easy, but it makes your demonstrations over easy things
15 a certainty. Whenever you get an opportunity, even where possible failure appears likely to do a little seeming harm, and always when it would only affect yourself, take no material means, but turn to God in thought and pray. Rely then solely upon the prayer to bring about the required result through the action of divine Principle, that unerringly guides and protects
20 men, instead of trying to force your way through the miasma of earth by doing it materially. If you treat thus and can get rid entirely of the thought that your prayer will not be heard the demonstration will be made, and the difficulty will disappear. "Ye shall go and pray unto me, and I will hearken unto you" (Jer. 29:12). Jesus said: "He that believeth on me, the works
25 that I do shall he do also; and greater works than these shall he do; because I go unto my Father" (John 14:12). These greater things have not yet been done, and we have to recognise that we have to do them. "If thou trust in the Lord, strength will be given thee from heaven, and the world and the flesh will be made subject to thy sway" (Thomas à Kempis).

30 ## OUR WORK

"The Spirit of the Lord God is upon me; because the Lord hath anointed me to preach good tidings unto the meek; he hath sent me to bind up the broken hearted, to proclaim liberty to the captives, and the opening of the prison to them that are bound; To proclaim the acceptable year of the Lord. . . . But
35 *ye shall be named the Priests of the Lord: men shall call you the Ministers of our God"* (Isa. 61:1, 2, 6).

Our aim must be the greatest good for the greatest number. "To render less the sum of human wretchedness" (Whittier). We have to wake up from this hideous dream of life in matter and stand shoulder to shoulder
40 with those of other religious views, fighting against evil in the final so-called mental fight, the battle of Armageddon—the anti-christ, versus the Christ.[1] (See Revelation 16, verse 16.)

"We have hard work to do and loads to lift,
Shun not the struggle—face it—'tis God's gift" (*Goethe*).

45   [1] No one ought to attempt any "mental" working except on true scientific lines. The best way of gaining the necessary knowledge for this is from a systematic

Many of these comrades have neither weapons nor any defensive armour. Some have the armour, namely, the intellectual knowledge of the truth, the knowledge of the letter, but are not using it. We have indirectly to shield and protect both these classes by the application of our knowledge of the truth, demonstrating over the evil that is endeavouring to attack us 5 through them. This we have to do, however much in their writhing from the torture of an unseen and even unrecognised enemy, they try to injure "him . . . that bringeth good tidings of good, that publisheth salvation; that saith unto Zion, Thy God reigneth !" (Isa. 52:7). "By loving whatever is lovable in those around us, love will flow back from them to us, and life 10 will become a pleasure and not a pain" (A. P. Stanley).

At the same time we cannot do the work of everyone else, and we must be careful not to attempt to "steady other people's altars." We must weed our garden instead of pulling up what we regard as weeds in that of our neighbour's, and often pulling up in our endeavours some of the plants 15 that, left alone, would have borne lovely flowers if not beautiful fruit. "There is an idea abroad among moral people that they should make their neighbours good. One person I have to make good—myself. But my duty to my neighbour is much more nearly expressed by saying that I have to make him happy" (R. L. Stevenson). 20

reading of *Science and Health with Key to the Scriptures*, by Mary Baker Eddy. Directly I saw that there must be a great truth underlying the statements made, I determined that for twelve months I would read no books but the Bible, *Science and Health*, and works by the same author; this does not include mere reference to technical literature for business purposes. I also determined that I would never read 25 less than ten pages of *Science and Health* any day, and as much more as was possible. These resolutions I kept to, and I cannot be too thankful, as it enabled me to get a good idea of the facts without being disturbed by any other form of so-called "mental" science. At the end of these twelve months I thought I knew something. At the end of another six months I found that I was only on the borderland of know- 30 ledge, and it was not for two-and-a-half years after having started that I was absolutely certain that Christian Science presented the highest truth. And yet within a week of being retained to examine into it—and I had never heard of it until a few days previously—Truth had healed instantaneously through me.

Since this time I have never studied any other writings, though I have referred 35 to many, not for the old purpose of learning truth, but simply to acquaint myself with the various beliefs of the human mind for the sole purpose of knowing better how to expose their fallacies, and so enable them more easily to be destroyed by the denial of their truth and reality. It will, by this time, be clear to those who have intelligently followed the statements made, that such false beliefs merely bind one 40 down to a submission to false, evil power until denied and so destroyed.

Never mind if you cannot understand *Science and Health* at the first reading, and there appear inconsistencies. They will all clear away as the false ideas, upon which previous conclusions have been based, disappear through the true knowledge gained, until you find that you can heal instantaneously, not only sickness and sin, 45 but help a fellow-being out of any trouble under the sun. This power of demonstration gained therefrom is the proof of its scientific accuracy, and until a man can get these results he has no right to criticise. His failure is an absolute proof that he has not understood the teaching. "By their fruits ye shall know them" (Matt. 7:20). You will not find it a difficult thing to do, even at the beginning, and it increases 50 in ease and simplicity in proportion as we progress in our understanding of God, until it is found that all we have to do is to live in the presence of God, to allow no false thought to enter our consciousness, and to banish instantaneously any recognition of evil by the denial of its reality, turning instantly in thought to the real world, heaven, that glorious world, the kingdom of God that is within reach of all. 55

Each man has to work out his own salvation. We only help our fellow-men by treatment—other than our patients—as the thought of them comes into our consciousness, destroying the evil thought that is attacking us and freeing both. We can, however, explain the truth to them and so
5 point out the way of salvation. "If any man hear my words, and believe not, I judge him not: for I came not to judge the world, but to save the world" (John 12:47). "Whatever enlarges man's facilities for knowing and doing good, and subjugates matter, has a fight with the flesh. Utilising the capacities of the human mind uncovers new ideas, unfolds spiritual forces,
10 the divine energies, and their power over matter, molecule, space, time, mortality; and mortals cry out, 'Art thou come hither to torment us before the time?'" (*Message for 1902*, p. 10, Mary Baker Eddy).

Have No Doubt.—"*Neither be ye of doubtful mind*" (Luke 12 : 29). "*I have never found God failing when I trusted in Him*" (Oliver Cromwell).
15 If, when doubtful how to act, or what to say, you pray, realising that God is the Principle of all knowledge, and that therefore man knows instantly everything he needs, you will find that the Angel Gabriel has come to you, and that you will be shown unmistakably what is the right thing to do. "Gabriel, make this man to understand," "I am now come
20 forth to give thee skill and understanding" (Dan. 8:16, and 9:22).
When we are consistently living our religion and do not care one iota what we think, say, or do, so long as it is what is right, and we do not care one iota about the human consequences of saying or doing what is right, then the right thing to do will always prove to be the thing most desirable
25 at the moment, and it must be so if you have but one desire, and that to do only what is right. In addition, true Christianity is perfect ease and perfect simplicity. "My yoke is easy, and my burden is light" (Matt. 11:30). Our sheet-anchor is hope in God. (See Psalms 42, verses 5, 11.)

Let God Lead You.—"*What we need is a profound faith in God's
30 ruling of all things*" (General Gordon).
When you are further on, however, you will find, with a good motive, you can do any one of, say, five different things, and all that you have to do is pray clearly enough, when you will find that the one you do will appear humanly to have been the best thing for you to have done. "In quietness
35 and in confidence shall be your strength" (Isa. 30:15). (This does not mean that it is right to do evil that good should come of it. It is never right to do evil, when recognised as such, under any circumstances.) This makes life absolute simplicity, as all that you have to do is the first thing that appears to you to be right. "Have faith in God" (Mark 11:22), in good. Then, if
40 you are working rightly, divine Principle will always lead and protect you, and nothing will come to you but what is good, or what you are capable of turning into good by reversing it. We have to give up nothing but our belief in a power other than that of God, our belief in evil. "God is our refuge and strength, a very present help in trouble. Therefore will not we
45 fear" (Ps. 46:1, 2). "For this God is our God for ever and ever: he will be our guide even unto death" (Ps. 48:14). "Be still, and know that I am God" (Ps. 46:10).

A Cup of Cold Water.—*"I hope that you and I will never lose enthusiasm"* (Benjamin Jowett).

Whilst not casting your pearls before swine, so as to prevent the recurrence of the words of Festus: "Much learning doth make thee mad" (Acts 26:24), never compromise conscience. "Look on the fields; for they 5 are white already to harvest" (John 4:35). There is a famine for the word of God. Be ever aflame with divine Love, and if you realise clearly enough that man, the spiritual man, speaks truth, because when man speaks, God, Truth, speaks, you will say just what is right and give "living water" (John 4:10) to all that are thirsty.   10

In voicing truth to a willing listener whom you are helping, always make your statements of truth positively, and show at once that you have not the slightest doubt as to the facts. "If any man speak, let him speak as the oracles of God" (I Peter 4:11). When you are talking, however, with a person who does not agree with you, it is often wise to preface your 15 statements with "I believe so and so," or "I think so and so." In this way you will avoid antagonising him. Never argue if you can possibly avoid it; in fact, never argue with people. "To explain is better than to argue" (Lord Morley). "If they speak not according to this word, it is because there is no light in them" (Isa. 8:20). "Let your speech be alway with 20 grace, . . . that ye may know how ye ought to answer every man" (Col. 4:6).

> "To have done whatever had to be done . . .
> To have turned the face of your soul to the sun . . .
> To have made life better and brighter for one,   25
> This is to have lived" (*Clifford Harrison*).

Give Thanks.—*"Pray without ceasing. In every thing give thanks"* (I Thess. 5:17, 18).

Never allow yourself to be afraid of mentioning with gratitude the blessings you have received from knowing how to pray aright. "Arise, 30 shine; for thy light is come" (Isa. 60:1), " . . . as many as ye shall find, bid to the marriage" (Matt. 22:9), and never think that it is waste of time to be continually giving thanks for your blessings. The most practical form of gratitude is helping others. When an antagonistic man has heard for the third or fourth time, each time from different people, the advantages that 35 they have received from true prayer, he begins to think that there must be something in it. "He that winneth souls is wise" (Prov. 11:30).

"Thank God each day, each hour, thank God for all !
And He shall judge what things are great, what small !" (*Rose Henniker Heaton*).

Payment.—*"If we have sown unto you spiritual things, is it a great 40 thing if we shall reap your carnal things?"* (I Cor. 9:11).

Sometimes a man, being helped mentally, and becoming a permanent recipient of priceless treasure, is unwilling to make a return of which he is capable. This is proof that to work for such a one would be to spend time which it were better for humanity should be given to others, who, receiving 45 the truth, in their turn spread it abroad, and themselves become centres for the spread of truth and the healing of sin and disease. The primary

object in life is to bring as many people as possible to the knowledge of
Truth, so that they can relieve themselves and others of suffering.

The only thing that is worth doing in this material world, and the only
thing that will bring us any permanent happiness, is to help our neighbour,
5 and the action of the eternal law of good results of necessity in good to the
helper. The only way in which we can help ourselves and others is by
obtaining a better knowledge of God, and so learning to be better men ourselves. This, therefore, is the keynote of all right endeavour, which God
never fails to reward.

10   **A Call to Every Man.**—"*Then saith he unto his disciples, The harvest
truly is plenteous, but the labourers are few ; Pray ye therefore the Lord of
the harvest, that he will send forth labourers into his harvest*" (Matt.
9:37, 38). "*The harvest is the end of the world*" (Matt. 13:39).

This call is our highest work to-day, and gives us the greatest happiness.
15 "A man does his best thing easiest" (Emerson). "The harvest truly is
plenteous" (Matt. 9:37). "Arise, shine; for thy light is come, and the glory
of the Lord is risen upon thee, . . . and his glory shall be seen upon thee."
(Isa. 60:1, 2). "By the obedience of one shall many be made righteous"
(Rom. 5:19). "Ye are the light of the world. A city that is set on an hill
20 cannot be hid" (Matt. 5:14). "It pleased God, . . . To reveal his Son in
me" (Gal. 1:15, 16). Be "kings and priests unto God" (Rev. 1:6). "Let
your light so shine before men, that they may see your good works, and
glorify your Father" (Matt. 5:16). "To open their eyes, and to turn them
from darkness to light, and from the power of Satan unto God" (Acts
25 26:18). "Truth shall spring out of the earth" (Ps. 85:11).

Truth Attracts Those Ready.—"*Hope sees a possible fountain. Faith
draws the water. Love distributes the water to others*" (J. H. Jowett).

Pray daily that those who are ready for truth come to you, and then
those who are not ready will not appear and so delay the spread of know-
30 ledge. Realise that error cannot send those not ready, for in reality all are
ready for Truth, as there is nothing but Truth, for Truth is God. Dwell
on the affirmation that man knows Truth, loves Truth, and is led by
Truth. "How beautiful upon the mountains are the feet of him that
bringeth good tidings, . . . that publisheth salvation" (Isa. 52:7). "The
35 Gentiles shall come to thy light, . . . they shall call thee, The city of the
Lord, The Zion of the Holy One of Israel" (Isa. 60:3, 14).

Truth the Lamp of Understanding.—"*For when the vain imagination and ignorance are turned into an understanding and knowledge of the
truth, the claiming anything for our own will cease of itself*" (*Theologia
40 Germanica*).

"He that hath my word, let him speak my word faithfully" (Jer. 23:28).
"I say unto you every good word which men shall not speak, they shall
give account thereof in the day of judgment." [1] You must not try to think
out what is best for you to say to your hearers. This is relying upon a
45 broken reed. When explaining your grasp of religion, realise God as Truth,

[1] (From the Palestinian Syriac Lectionary of the Gospels, Codex C, edited by
Agnes Smith Lewis and Margaret Dunlop Gibson.)

a living Principle around you. Keep actively thinking that "man reflects Truth, man knows Truth," then your words will be inspired, "Make me to understand the way of thy precepts: so shall I talk of thy wondrous works" (Ps. 119:27). This will lead you to speak the truth, whatever truth may happen to be. It will help also your hearer, and he, on account of your realisation, will become hungry and thirsty, and drink in what you say, understanding it. "If any man will do his will, he shall know of the doctrine" (John 7:17). You also will learn more from that which you speak, as this is one of the ways in which God teaches us. "The entrance of thy words giveth light" (Ps. 119:130).

> "To know
> Rather consists in opening out a way
> Whence the imprisoned splendour may escape,
> Than in effecting entry for a light
> Supposed to be without" (*Robert Browning*).

If you forget at any time to pray, you can pray afterwards equally efficiently, provided that, just before commencing, you realise that your prayer is affecting the seemingly past events. As already mentioned, this is possible, as there is no such thing as time. All that you have to do is, before you pray, to recognise that the so-called past is now, and that therefore your prayer is affecting the past, and then the apparent difference in time makes no difference in the efficacy of your prayer.

The Morning Star.—"*How soon a smile of God can change the world!*" (Robert Browning).

When you see the far-away look coming on the face of the so-called atheist, the believer in a great First Cause, or on that of the wholesome agnostic whose logical reasoning has kept him previously from the blessings of so-called Christianity, and when you see the eyes soften and brighten— "the seal of God in their foreheads" (Rev. 9:4)—then will "the day star arise in your hearts" (II Peter 1:19), and you will understand the meaning of the words, "I will give him the morning star" (Rev. 2:28), and also of Paul's words, "I thank my God upon every remembrance of you" (Phil. 1:3). "He that hath an ear, let him hear what the Spirit saith unto the churches" (Rev. 2:29).

Demonstrable Truth.—One of the many proofs of the truth of what has been now put before you is that about one-fourth to one-third of those to whom it is clearly presented get an instantaneous result of some sort or other within a fortnight. It is only prejudice that keeps so many from trying, and scepticism or fear that prevents them from getting results. If the reader will study the true method of working, and persist in living his best and honestly trying for a fortnight to reverse the wrong thoughts, I am sure that he will obtain at least one noticeable result. If he continues so working, this will only be a forerunner of many others, sign-posts on the pathway towards Truth.

The Heralds of the Day.—"*God uses us to help others—so lending our lives out*" (Robert Browning).

Such students "bear witness of the Light" (John 1:7). They are the
11*

early morning beams, the world's true light, the heralds of the coming
day, that touch and tint the mountain peaks with roseate hues, and ever
brightening, bathe the granite rocks with God's redemptive glory, till they
too become a "light of the world," reflecting God's command, "Let there
5 be light" (Gen. 1:3). Then does this wondrous "light so shine" in every
nook and cranny of dead matter, and blazon out to distant worlds, unknown
to earthbound man, where one, maybe, on summer's peaceful night, feeling the love of nature round, says: "Watch yon wondrous star, perhaps
God's men are there." And on this light swells into day till only sinless
10 humanhood remains, mute witness of the final end and portal of eternal
day.

> "Love glorifies the common air,
> It clothes with light the mountain bare,
> And shows the heavens all shining there" (*Alfred Austin*).

NOTA BENE

15

The following are some of the main points dealt with in this work :—

REALITY

    i. Nothing exists but God and His manifestation. God, good, is
All-in-all.

20   ii. Therefore your existence and that of the real world—which is
now, always has been, and always must be, perfect—is solely
due to God.

    iii. God is Mind, and God, good, is infinite; hence "all is infinite
Mind and its infinite manifestation." [1]

25   iv. God, being the Principle of all good, could never know, and much
less have made, anything bad. The love, life, truth, wisdom,
intelligence, joy, beauty, etc., all being in the reality good, are
the outcome of God, only we do not cognise them properly.
They shine through the matter of this material world, which
30   hides their full perfection from us. For this reason we only
have a material or false sense of them, limited both as to
quantity and quality, so that they appear as poor imitations of
the real.

MAN IS SPIRITUAL

35   v. Consequently, as the offspring or manifestation of God, called
the son of God, you are not a material being. You are, were,
and always will be, in reality, a glorious being, spiritual and
perfect, governed by a perfect God, and existing in heaven, a
perfect state of universal harmony. The recognition of this
40   spiritual truth is the second coming of the Christ to the human
limited consciousness. This comes to each individual when he
is sufficiently receptive.

---

[1] *Science and Health*, p. 468, Mary Baker Eddy.

UNREALITY

vi. There is no reality, that is, no truth, no permanence, in the material world. It is a mere illusion, exactly similar to the illusion that the earth was flat or that the sun went round the earth.

vii. Therefore God never made the material world. It is a non-reality, always more or less bad, merely a false sense of the real, the suppositional opposite of good.

viii. All matter is not only unreal, but is, by its very nature, self-destructive. It merely hides heaven from us, and its false conception of itself, which is all that there is of it, will ultimately be self-destroyed on account of the action of God, Truth.

MATERIAL SO-CALLED " THOUGHTS "

ix. Everything we see is only materialised "thought," resting upon an ethereal basis or false mentality, which claims to be a creator, but is unreal and illusive.

x. All these thoughts, past, present, and future, as far as they can be said to exist at all, exist now, as hypothetical material thoughts, in a fixed position relative to all other material thoughts; and groups of them, owing to the human, limited sense, apparently come separately into action one after the other, unless they are in the meantime destroyed.

xi. Every material thing that we appear to see is, however, only a portion of an apparent series of cinematographic pictures, flashing past and, so to speak, hiding the real things, giving a false sense of continuous and progressive movement. The limited human capacity to see or cognise any of these pictures except at a predetermined time, gives the false sense of time.

xii. All the evil of the material world, although appearing so real, is imaginary, and only due to the seeming action of wrong thoughts. There is no material thinker. The thinker and these thoughts are one.

xiii. These wrong thoughts are not created by man, but—to use a material term—existed as false ethereal concepts, before they became manifested; that is, before the material world apparently started in its ghostly and ghastly series of lying illusions.

PREDESTINATION AND FATALISM

xiv. All these false thoughts are predestined; that is to say, each of these ethereal thoughts, unless destroyed, must come to man at a predetermined time.

xv. The material man, until he prays rightly, is a puppet, acted upon by these wrong thoughts, and obliged to dance in accordance

with the so-called thoughts that come to him, and the condition of his human consciousness. But—

xvi. Fatalism is not true; because man has the power of turning in
thought to God and reversing wrong thoughts, when—(a) by
the denial of error, evil thoughts are destroyed; and (b) by
the affirmation of truth the human consciousness is purified
so that bad thoughts will not act upon it.

xvii. When bad thoughts are destroyed, less bad thoughts appear to
act; if these are destroyed, so-called better ones are manifested, and these again give place to still better thoughts,
although we do not know beforehand the form in which this
improved appearance will be seen.

xviii. So-called thoughts in the material world appear in their relative
seeming positions, merely as opposite "non-mental" impressions of real facts, and the action of God is, not to cause them
to alter their position, but to destroy the illusion as to their
reality. The evil then disappears.

DEATH

xix. A mortal does not die for some little time after he seems dead.
He therefore can be what is called "raised from the dead."
Even when the mortal "passes away" he merely disappears
from sight. Death is the result of ignorance, and quite unnecessary.

xx. Those who think that they have passed on cannot communicate
with those who believe that they remain behind.

xxi. The so-called dead merely continue to pass from one stage of
material consciousness to another, apparently dying and
appearing in material world after world. They, fortunately,
are continually improving, owing to the action of God upon
the human or carnal "mind," until the human consciousness is
sufficiently purified to be entirely dematerialised.

xxii. On a mortal disappearing from sight, through so-called death,
there appears amongst us, shortly after, yet another false
sense, or material conception of the spiritual being, of which
the departed mortal has been a misrepresentation; only this
time the etherealised, illusive view of the real man becomes
visible as a newly-born human being, in consistent fulfilment
of human theories universally assented to, and so constituting
for the time a false law.

EVOLUTION

xxiii. So-called evolution is merely the successive appearance and
disappearance of groups of cinematographic pictures, illusive
ethereal impressions, forming successive periods in human
history.

xxiv. These successive periods are each merely a series of these false pictures, misrepresenting the same real facts, only each series having less materiality, and extending over a gradually shortening period of time.

xxv. By comparing these false ethereal impressions, or periodic 5 historical occurrences, one with the other, we are able to check the accuracy of our interpretation of the prophetic utterances with regard to the few last series now facing us, and still hiding heaven from us.

DEMONSTRABLE TRUTH 10

xxvi. There are, in fact, no lines of force, no vibrating ether, no gathering electrons, no self-intensification of thoughts, no changing conscious or subconscious minds, no material bodies, motion of matter, nor gravity, no time limitations, no sin, sickness, nor death. 15

xxvii. There is no necessity to believe what has been said. Each man can prove it all for himself. It is demonstrable truth, based upon absolute, unalterable science.

THE END OF EVIL

xxviii. When a governing majority, not in numbers, but in clearness 20 of thought, recognises the allness of God, infinite Mind, and realises that there is neither a primary cunning evil nor its secondary manifestation, called material men and things, for good is All-in-all, away must go this false concept of the perfect world, this false sense of sin, sickness, trouble, and limita- 25 tions, and so every discordant note in the universe is silenced, as the whole series of dream pictures, including the illusion called death, fades into its native nothingness, for THERE IS NOTHING BUT GOD AND THE MANIFESTATION OF GOOD. 30

Eminent Desirability of the End.—Let it be clearly understood that Life and its phenomena, the real man and universe, constitute a perfect, eternal, spiritual, and mental realm, an ideal state for which humanity has long yearned. Were the real universe formed of matter, were there no spiritual realities, then dematerialisation, through short- 35 circuiting of the particles, would mean annihilation for all concerned; but just because all is, in reality, Mind and mental, the destruction of the falsities which we have been taught to regard as "facts" and "things," and which we have, through false education, invested with all sorts of terrible shortcomings, including sin, discord, sickness, and death, is essentially 40 necessary to bring more clearly into evidence the permanent phenomena of the one glorious Mind. This Mind is reflected by the real man, so every man in his right Mind is a perfect thinker and can see and think only perfect things. It is to hasten the appearance of the perfection in all things, including that of our real, perfect selves, that we need to affirm perfection whenever we deny imperfection.

Always Follow a Denial of Error with Affirmations of Truth.— "Always distrust negations. . . . Always try for a positive form of any comprehensive denial" [1] (Sir Oliver Lodge). Even after such a denial as "there is no anger," it is essential, in obedience to the law of right thinking, at once, like lightning, to fill in with a thought of reality such as "all is Love, and man reflects that Love," or after "there is no decay," "all is Life and eternal," dwelling on this perfection. In this way, by obedience to the law of Mind and its manifestation, we are bringing out more clearly the existence of the higher phenomena of the one perfect Mind and its realities, which are mental, spiritual, and eternal.

No Loss of Pleasure.— There is no loss of pleasure when matter disappears, because matter gives no pleasure, but merely hides perfection from us and reduces the pleasure to which we have the right. All the beauty, the joy, the peace, in fact, everything that gives you any pleasure, is real and eternal. Matter is the mist which merely hides the real and results in suffering should you disobey the law of good, and allow yourself to think of the evil, whether it is your liability to sickness or your liability to be punished for sinful indulgences. As the matter disappears, so does our limited sense of pleasure increase, until it rises into the intense happiness and unspeakable joy of heaven, where bliss is Love in action.

So it follows that to short-circuit the whole of the false material universe only spreads out the perfect "facts" and "things" of heaven, and the perfect image and likeness of God, seen everywhere as perfect man, bringing a happiness that cannot even be imagined by the material man. The "vail," [2] as it were, of material errors is lifted for ever. A loved one that this "vail" has perhaps entirely hidden from the human view for many years is met in the glorious light of the new day; parted in sorrow, is met in a wave of welcoming joy; parted in weakness, is met in glorious beauty and strength; parted in fear, is met in the happy self-confidence of a reigning monarch. Man having dominion over all, there never can be any thought of fear again, and such a meeting is a mutual recognition of heavenly companionship amidst eternal realities, where all is known and acknowledged to be permanently of God. Man beholds all as "very good" (Gen. 1:31).

Truth is Essentially Demonstrable.— You need not believe one word of what has been said in this book. If you work in the way now brought to your notice, you will eventually prove everything for yourself. Pascal recommended doubters to behave as though they believed that which they did not understand, in which case they might come to believe it. Whilst pointing out the absolute fallacy of this, let us say, in the words of Paul, "Despise not prophesyings. Prove all things; hold fast that which is good" (I Thess. 5:20, 21).

[1] "Christian Revelation from a Scientific Point of View." Address before the National Free Church Council, at Portsmouth, March 9, 1911.
[2] II Corinthians 3, verses 14, 16.

CHRISTIAN SCIENCE OR SCIENTIFIC CHRISTIANITY

"*My doctrine is not mine, but his that sent me. If any man will do his will, he shall know of the doctrine, whether it be of God, or whether I speak of myself*" (John 7:16, 17).

There is only one scientific and demonstrable basis of the right way, and this can only be found by the intelligent study of Christian Science, the law of God, demonstrating its divine Principle, immortal Mind, God, supreme good. Intelligent study does not mean the mere acquisition of the letter and the repetition of truisms, but the daily logical deduction, from facts gained, of a higher platform of truth, from which one proves such deductions by the demonstration of the truth that underlies them. The mere demonstration of the cure of disease is not sufficient to prove intelligent and therefore correct study. Not even an instantaneous healing of sin, which is the only absolute proof of one's knowledge of the non-reality of evil and the allness of God, is sufficient. We have to prove our knowledge of God by the continual demonstration over every variety of false evidence in all its myriad forms.

When first asked by the Rev. J. Bruce Wallace to lecture upon Christian Science to the Alpha Union, at the Garden City, Letchworth, I did not see my way to do it, as, although there is no by-law against it in the Christian Science Church Manual, which contains rules of guidance for Christian Scientists, the custom in the Christian Science organisation is, that none but their trained lecturers give lectures on Christian Science. There have been many wise reasons for this, evidencing the wisdom with which the affairs of that body have been guided.

Not being nominally a member of the Christian Science Church, I referred Mr. Wallace to the member of the Christian Science Board of Lectureship resident in London, who did not, however, feel able to comply with the request. Upon this I received a second invitation to lecture, and felt that it was not to be refused, and gave Mr. Wallace a choice of subjects, recognising that any lecture I might give upon any subject would of necessity bear on the face of it the impress of the knowledge gained through my study and demonstration of the truth of Christian Science, for the leaven of this scientific religion now at work in the universe must touch all questions.

Such benefits have been received from my investigation of Christian Science and from the study of Mrs. Eddy's inspired writing (which enable us to understand the inner meaning of the Bible), and so much help has been received from fellow-workers in Christian Science, that it appeared wisest not to go against their custom. While trying to live Christian Science consistently, I have proved it to be not only wise, but essential, to follow all the rules of conduct that the founder, Mary Baker Eddy, points out, as I recognise that they are logically based upon the fundamental law of good. The enforcement of such rules of conduct, where the individul objects to the necessary obedience, so far from limiting right action, always results in forcing evil into self-betrayal. Such obedience will always be found, when fully understood, to rest upon an essential obedience to God, which must always precede any other demand. The material presentation of these rules of conduct must always be advancing in proportion with the student's understanding of their true significance.

Truth in Literal and Physical Terms.—In accepting the second
5 request, I was led to frame a lecture to meet the needs of all classes, upon the broadest lines, from the beginner to the deepest and most earnest thinkers, who have found hitherto hopeless difficulties in reconciling the inconsistencies between what has been popularly called natural science and religion. In the present work I have given fully and unreservedly—
10 with the exception of the meaning of certain Scriptural prophecies—what I have found to be true, explained from a natural science point of view, and expressed in literal or physical terms.

As a rule, I lecture extemporarily. In that case what was said had been written out. I once gave a lecture on new inventions and discoveries, and,
15 after speaking for an hour-and-a-half, concluded by saying: "The greatest discovery of modern days was that made by Mrs. Eddy of the way in which Jesus did his miracles, and Christian Scientists heal sin and sickness in the same way." This was the only reference to Christian Science; yet the lecture, being misunderstood, was misrepresented as having been a lecture
20 on Christian Science, although I had taken great pains to keep quite clear of the subject. The only misunderstanding that seems possible to have arisen here was that the action of good thoughts and bad thoughts was spoken of as being electrical. Some of those present may not have recognised sufficiently clearly that the so-called good thoughts that come
25 to the material man are not of God. They are purely material, only some are not so bad as so-called bad thoughts. Both are a false sense of God's thoughts, or God's thoughts materially cognised, and should never be confused with spiritual facts. God's thoughts are cognised only by the spiritual senses of the real man. Throughout this present work language
30 has been as carefully chosen as seemed possible, with the special intent to avoid such possible misconceptions. Many problems which Christian Science completely solves have been opened up in the present technical statement. The primary object of this work and of the original lecture has been to expose the fallacies of material hypotheses, and to the extent
35 necessary to attain this end the assimilated teachings set out in Mrs. Eddy's writings have been utilised. I have not, however, explained what is generally understood to be exclusively the letter of Christian Science, nor in any way differentiated between such teachings and knowledge gained of the material universe through the study of Christian Science. Except
40 when referring to the source from which to obtain true knowledge and how to apply it, the name of Christian Science has not been mentioned in the body of this book; nor has the wonderful work done by Mrs. Eddy been referred to, although expression has necessarily been given to the knowledge gained therefrom. Consequently, both somewhat resemble the
45 playbill of which Sir Walter Scott wrote as having "announced the tragedy of Hamlet, the character of the Prince of Denmark being left out." [1]

[1] During the time spent in revising this work for publication, my views with regard to the advisability of speaking openly of Christian Science from the plat-

An Exact Science.—*"When a faithful thinker, resolute to detach every object from personal relations, and see it in the light of thought, shall at the same time kindle science with the fire of the holiest affection, then will God go forth anew with creation"* (Emerson).

In speaking to inquirers, when presenting such an inversion of our old ideas, it is necessary to use crude illustrations to assist in conveying a correct meaning. It should be readily seen that in an exact science the official seal can only be attached to its textual statement by a master metaphysician. Such a statement will be found in *Science and Health with Key to the Scriptures*, by Mary Baker Eddy.[1]

Mrs. Eddy has pointed out to us the underlying Principle, which governs the fundamental facts of being, clearing up our ignorance and opening the pathway to the true knowledge of God, which destroys sin, and with unvarying certainty, based upon unalterable law, relieves mankind from every ill "that flesh is heir to." She writes :—

> "'Twas the Truth that made us free,
> And was found by you and me,
> In the life and the love of our Lord"[2]

She, however, distinctly reminds her readers that she had not undertaken "to embellish, elaborate, or treat in full detail so infinite a theme" (*Science and Health*, Preface, p. x). The wider application of the infinite Principle unfolded with scientific completeness in her writings has been left to students who understand sufficiently her advanced teachings. God's unfailing direction was too clearly realised by the rediscoverer of Christian Science for her to doubt the eventual preparation by the action of Principle of such students for this task all the world over. Mrs. Eddy's views on this subject are clearly expressed to the discerning reader of her works.

An Exposure of Fallacies.—*"The time approaches when mortal mind will forsake its corporeal, structural, and material basis, when immortal Mind and its formations will be apprehended in Science, and material beliefs will not interfere with spiritual facts"*[3] (Mary Baker Eddy).

I would therefore reiterate that this discourse is obviously not a lecture upon, nor does it pretend to be an elucidation of, Christian Science,[4]

form or otherwise, as occasion demands, have considerably broadened, although I do not lecture on Christian Science, leaving that to the authorised lecturers. I recognise that the time has come when the explanation of correct human hypotheses called material science, in the light of Christian Science, should be put forward so that full advantage of the latter may be spread abroad, for the benefit and salvation of mankind in dispelling its illusive theories. Christian Science is not the dogma of a sect. It is what we all want; Science, or true exact knowledge, of God and His Christ.

[1] This work, as a rule, requires reading over several times before one gathers the meaning of many of the passages. Our old ideas are so wrong that we are liable to attach the wrong meanings to passages in order that they should agree with our preconceived notions. As Mrs. S. A. Orne writes, "The lamp of intellect requires occasional snuffing, to throw the clear light of penetration on the page."

[2] Communion Hymn.

[3] *Science and Health*, p. 402.

[4] "The simplest problem in Christian Science is healing the sick" (*Miscellaneous Writings*, p. 55. Mary Baker Eddy).

but is primarily an exposure of the innumerable fallacies of human theories past and present, made evident through the study of Christian Science, and exposed with the object of their elimination and replacement by divine conceptions of reality. No work could, however, lay claim to
5 present a solution of the mysteries of this world without giving prominence to that discovery which solves the problem of existence, and heralds the final scene in material evolution, namely, the total disappearance of all sin, disease, and limitations.

Spiritual Accuracy.—At the same time, let it be clearly understood
10 that there is not a single statement in this book that is not in complete accord with the teachings of Mrs. Eddy. If any, through lack of a real understanding of her teachings, should endeavour to refute this statement, these, by unprejudiced study of this work, will find their objections disappear as they endeavour, through conscientious comparison with Mrs.
15 Eddy's writings, to find passages in contradiction of any statements made by her. Others, prompted by less worthy motives, without this warning, might have been led into open condemnation without any logical or other proof of their statement. The true Christian Scientist does not contradict what he does not amply prove to be wrong, and is always the first to rejoice
20 in any additional light. Mrs. Eddy lamented the inability of students to reply to the fundamental inquiries of the age. Few of her students ever attempt to explain in detail any advanced branch of her symbolic teaching, wisely referring the inquirers to her writings, until they have attained to a clearer understanding of the science that is the basis of her statements.

25 **False Brethren.**—"*In Christian Science mere opinion is valueless. Proof is essential to a due estimate of this subject*" [1] (Mary Baker Eddy). Any accusation of hypnotism levelled against students obtaining constant results of every description, by turning in thought to God, is malpractice of the worst description, and when persisted in is recognisable as
30 the sin against the Holy Ghost. (See Matthew 12:31.)

A Needful Warning.—In answer to the question, "*Do all who at present claim to be teaching Christian Science, teach it correctly?*" Mrs. Eddy has replied: "By no means: Christian Science is not sufficiently understood for that. . . . Time is required thoroughly to qualify students
35 for the great ordeal of this century" (*Miscellaneous Writings*, p. 43). Recognising the right of humanity to demand correct teaching of this all-inclusive Science, she repeatedly warns inquirers against the merely so-called Christian Scientist. Such a one, if not sufficiently advanced himself to be able to meet the inquiry of the highest intellect to-day,
40 shields himself behind vehement, dogmatic assertions, aimed against the true scientific interpretations, which he is unable from his limited outlook to comprehend, although accompanied by demonstration and sound logic. Many have not really advanced beyond the elementary class teaching which Mrs. Eddy instituted as a branch of her earliest church organisa-
45 tion. Such teaching is not supposed to give a complete knowledge of the fundamental truths of Christian Science, but merely to fit the student for

[1] *Science and Health*, p. 341.

deeper individual research on correct lines. We must seek "to discern the rhythm of Spirit," the reward of holiness.

In the most advanced class the teaching in the past has had to be largely elementary. In reply to an address from members of the May, 1905, class of her Metaphysical College, Mrs. Eddy writes as follows: "I am glad you enjoy the dawn of Christian Science; you must reach its meridian." [1]

Under the heading "Take Heed!" she writes: "We regret to be obliged to say that all are not metaphysicians, or Christian Scientists, who call themselves so. Charlatanism, fraud, and malice are getting into the ranks of the good and pure, sending forth a poison more deadly than the upas tree in the eastern archipelago. This evil obtains in the present false teaching and false practice of the Science of treating disease through Mind. . . . But while the best, perverted, on the mortal plane may become the worst, let us not forget that the Lord reigns, and that this earth shall sometime rejoice in His supreme rule,—that the tired watchmen on the walls of Zion, and the true Christian Scientist at the foot of the mount of revelation, shall look up with shouts and thanksgiving,—that God's law, as in divine Science, shall be finally understood" (*Miscellaneous Writings*, p. 368).

True Christian Science.—If you ask for an explanation of what true Christian Science is, I can refer you to the Bible, that mine of countless priceless treasures, where, amongst many other instructive passages, we are told, "Let the wicked forsake his way, and the unrighteous man his *thoughts*: [2] and let him return unto the Lord, and he will have mercy upon him; and to our God, for he will abundantly pardon. For my thoughts are not your thoughts, . . . saith the Lord" (Isa. 55:7, 8). For the scientific interpretation of this advice, reiterated throughout the Bible, but so long misunderstood, I would refer you to the writings of Mrs. Eddy, by far the greatest metaphysician of modern times, where the explanation of and the remedy for all the difficulties here dealt with can be found.[3] To these writings and to the consequent more intelligent study of the Bible, I owe the benefit of all the knowledge I have that is worth having; how to obtain inspirational knowledge, how to lead a better life, and how to help one's fellow-man. This priceless understanding results in an intense happiness, with a sublime realisation of "the peace of God, which passeth all understanding" [4] (Phil. 4:7).

"Sweet sign and substance
Of God's presence here" (*Mary Baker Eddy*).

[1] *Miscellany p.* 254.
[2] "The wicked, through the pride of his countenance, will not seek after God: God is not in all his thoughts" (Ps. 10:4).
[3] "The following words of a friend well voice the feelings of a great multitude: 'To me,' said this gentleman, 'one of the mysteries of our time is the success of Science and Health'" (B. O. Flower, in the *Twentieth Century Magazine*).
[4] "He could only say that he had rarely met with such capacity to enter some of the deeper aspects of truth, and he had seen the lives of Christian Scientists, tranquil, bright, cheerful. . . . They [his own church] ought to have had all along the elixir of life to give to their people. Had they lost it? Why was it that they so seldom met in the ranks of their own people any one of whom a visitor from Mars would say, 'What is the secret of that man's or that woman's life?' that radiant sense of the supernatural, that brightness and reality of spirit?" (Archbishop of York).

Mary Baker Eddy.—"*It is commonly said that, if he would be heard, none should write in advance of his times. That I do not believe, only it does not matter how few listen. I believe that we are close upon a great and deep spiritual change. I believe a new redemption is even now conceived, of the*
5 *Divine Spirit in the human heart, that is itself as a woman, broken in dreams and yet sustained in faith, patient, long-suffering, looking towards home. I believe that though the Reign of Peace may be yet a long way off, it is drawing near: and that who shall come to save us anew shall come divinely as a woman, to save as Christ saved, but not as He did, to bring with her a sword*"
10 (William Sharp in *The Isle of Dreams*).

It would not be natural to end without saying a few words about Mrs. Eddy, whom I revere as a leader, and love as a fellow-worker, and of whose writings I gratefully acknowledge myself a student, diligently searching daily in the inexhaustible mine of wealth that now is open to every earnest
15 worker.[1]

Of her physical condition in her 87th year, I cannot do better than quote "Dr. Allan McLane Hamilton, the expert alienist, who has devoted the last month to an exhaustive investigation of the mental condition of the Founder of Christian Science," a "medical expert who has figured in so
20 many famous cases during the last thirty-five years," and who was chosen by the Court to report on her mental condition, "having no sympathy with her religious teachings." In the *New York Times* of September, 1907, from which the above is taken, he says: "She is absolutely normal, and possessed of a remarkably clear intellect. . . . For a woman of her age,
25 I do not hesitate to say that she is physically and mentally phenomenal." He also speaks of "Mrs. Eddy's great vitality, and the absence of any of the usual tokens of mental breakdown natural to one of her great age."

> "God sends His teachers unto every age,
> To every clime, and every race of men,
30 > With revelations fitted to their growth
> And shape of mind, nor gives the realm of Truth
> Into the selfish rule of one sole race" (*J. R. Lowell*).

Descended from a long line of religious ancestry of our oldest and best English and Scottish families, imbued from her earliest days with deep
35 religious feeling, with great natural intellectual ability and spiritual fervour, even as a girl, a student of Natural Philosophy, Logic, and Moral Science, familiar with Hebrew, Greek, and Latin, and trained specially in rhetoric by Professor Sanborn, she was eminently fitted from the outset to receive the inspiration of Truth, which enabled her, not only to unveil the science
40 of God by rediscovering the true scientific meaning of the teaching and works of Jesus the Christ, but to place on record, founded on the Rock, a definite and accurate statement of absolute truth, for the guidance of man throughout all time. "For then will I turn to the people a pure language,

---

[1] Arthur Stanley, who was Dean of Westminster at the time that I was at school
45 there, and who was one of the most devout and spiritual men that I ever met, presented to the library a copy of Mrs. Eddy's principal work, *Science and Health with Key to the Scriptures*. This is her commentary of the Bible. The title page, which showed by his own handwriting his high opinion of the book, and its spirituality, has been mercilessly torn out by some dogmatic fanatic.

that they may all call upon the name of the Lord, to serve him with one consent. From beyond the rivers of Ethiopia my suppliants, even the daughter of my dispersed, shall bring mine offering" (Zeph. 3:9, 10).

This pure consciousness, fit channel for Truth, has taught the world how, sitting at the feet of our Master and Way-shower, the Galilean 5 Prophet, man, gaining a spiritual sense, loses a belief in a material self-hood, to find himself divine, the son of God. In demonstrating the truth of her words, "humility . . . is the genius of Christian Science," this great leader has told of early searchings after truth; of timidity, self-distrust, and sleepless nights; of utter friendlessness, desertion, wearying toil in the 10 wilderness of shattered hopes; of misrepresentations, bitter envy, ceaseless mockery, malicious falsehood, relentless persecution, agonies, and, thank God, of victories gained, uplifted by the sustaining power of what the world calls miraculous visions. Ablest to expose, "bravest to endure, firmest to suffer, soonest to renounce," and noblest to forgive, with self- 15 forgetfulness, purity, and love, with secret yearnings to be better understood, she demonstrated step by step along the rugged way the truth of the great revelation.

Then with a cry of "Follow your Leader only so far as she follows Christ," [1] she put her discovery into practice, though at times with 20 bleeding footsteps through self-sacrificing love for others. "Scourged and condemned at every advancing footstep," but sustained by the marvellous development of male and female qualities, splendid moral courage and unfailing love, she hurled "the thunderbolt of truth," while binding up the broken-hearted. Reasoning with the storm, Truth stilled the "tempest of 25 error," [2] and thus this messenger of God has been the means of bringing moral and physical salvation to hundreds of thousands of suffering men and women, who now bless her name. "A woman that feareth the Lord, she shall be praised. Give her of the fruit of her hands; and let her own works praise her in the gates" (Prov. 31:30, 31).   30

As the outcome of a life devoted to scientific research and demonstration, there has been founded a religion based upon changeless Principle, whose true followers, demonstrating wholeness of mind and therefore of body, are understanding and consequently proving the scientific basis of the so-called miracles recorded in the Bible, and rejoicing in their freedom. 35 They now, in their turn, are daily healing sin and sickness by putting into practice her motto of "Work—work—work—watch and pray," the song of Christian Science, and consequently are increasing in number with a rapidity unparalleled in the history of the world. This religion, based on absolute, unalterable Science, is about to revolutionise the entire universe, 40 and must bring us to its final result, for which all true lovers of humanity have for centuries devoutly prayed—namely, the end of all sin, sickness, suffering, and limitations of every description, even the seeming disappearance called death. Ignorance, or human consciousness, then no longer has its self-imposed, imaginary existence, and all apparently wake up out of this 45 hell of perpetual seeming troubles and limitations, to find themselves

[1] *Message*, 1901, p. 34.
[2] *Christian Healing*, p. 2 (Mary Baker Eddy).

Godlike beings, in a state of inexpressible constant happiness, in a world of wondrous glory, God's world. This is the only "end of the world." (See Matthew 24:3.)

"For as the lightning cometh out of the east, and shineth even unto the 5 west; so shall also the coming of the Son of man be" (Matt. 24:27).

"And what I say unto you I say unto all, Watch" (Mark 13:37). Watch your thoughts!

APPENDIX

SUMMARY OF INTELLECTUAL DEVELOPMENT

In the time of Socrates intellect or intelligence was the supreme principle around which all thought centred. With the Hindus it was just the opposite. Here the vital Principle was Life, the supreme Principle into which every- 5 thing ultimately merged, the intellect being a mere detail. One great school of ancient philosophy recognised nothing but passing sensations (Protagoras); another postulated a permanent "Ego," a "God," and a reason founded on their existence (Zeno); while Plato and Aristotle tried hard to adjust both of those into one system. In the modern schools, like 10 that of Herbert Spencer, the more physical powers hold the supremacy. We now find that Mind is the Lord of all, and that true philosophy is true religion and true science.[1]

From what has been said, you will recognise the real position, and will see that right through the history of philosophy there have been two main 15 lines of thought, both wrong, trying to harmonise themselves, but absolutely failing in the attempt. One school taught that there was a great Reality, imperfectly seen; and that, as time passed, we were obtaining a better knowledge of this Reality which we should ultimately reach. The other taught that the only Reality was the material world perceived by the 20 senses, and that the evolution in this material world steadily went on.

As already explained, the world of intellect is divided into three types of thinkers—the religious, the philosophical, and the scientific. The former refers the change in phenomena to the agency of a personal will, whether of gods or demons. The scientific refers phenomena to physical 25 antecedents; while the so-called philosophical or metaphysical (really only semi-metaphysical) varies between one and the other, and has endeavoured to refer phenomena to the Cause, Essence, or Spirit that they admit is at the back of the change in phenomena.

In the following sketch I have used capitals wherever Cause is referred 30 to, so as to make the meaning a little clearer.

Let us here again review the position. God created you and the real, tangible, mental, spiritual world, which exist now, always have existed, and always will exist, perfect. A material counterfeit world God never made, and is not conscious of, as it is a non-reality, more or less bad, a 35 false sense of the real, an illusion, the suppositional opposite of good. Matter or evil, by its very nature, produces self-elimination, and will ultimately lose even its false sense, by bringing about total disappearance, this final disappearance being brought about through the action of God, thanks to the nature of Truth. 40

[1] "Human philosophy has ninety-nine parts of error to the one-hundredth part of Truth, an unsafe decoction for the race. The Science that Jesus demonstrated, whose views of Truth Confucius and Plato but dimly discerned, Science and Health interprets" *No and Yes*, p. 21. Mary Baker Eddy).

The truths which are being placed before you have been recognised, more or less, by all the great thinkers.

Parmenides said that there was one changeless Being, the only Reality, and looked at the material, which he called "the changing many of becoming," as so much illusion. His philosophical opponent, Heracleitus, being, according to some critics, a materialist, took the opposite view, and said that the only Reality was the perpetual changing of the material.

It will presently be shown that Plato divided existence into four principles, Good, the Ideas, Number, and material basis of ends or material atoms. The Eleatic School believed that Principle consisted of only two elements—mental and material. Empedocles later divided the mental into love and hate, the material into fire, air, earth, and water. Anaxagoras believed in an indefinite number of atoms and, therefore, elements.

Plato, with his wonderfully logical mind, not only grasped the main facts, but pointed out clearly the difficulties there were in harmonising what appeared to be, with what logically must be true. He saw that the Reality consisted of Ideas, invisible, incorporeal Entities, existing, not in space, but in the realm of thought, eternal, self-subsistent, unchangeable and numerically plural and distinct, without being successive in time, as are the thoughts that daily come to the material man. He also saw the fallacy of the ordinary philosophical position. He assumed knowledge to be possible, implying something persistent, diverse, and plural, in contradistinction to the Heracleitic School, who denied persistence, and to the Eleatic, who looked at all existence as an unchangeable Unity. Plato insisted on the existence and apprehension of unity and variety. Where he failed was in seeing that his unchangeable Unity was God, and that the relative and unstable of the Heracleitic school, which we call the material world, was absolutely distinct and a non-reality. None of the philosophers until the nineteenth century have seen this solution of the whole difficulty.

In giving the following synopsis of Philosophy, I do not attempt more than to arrange some of the philosophers in their right order, and to give some of their chief tenets. Nor do I pretend to absolute accuracy, as when making definite scientific statements, but I give it as a matter of passing interest, teaching man to turn to something better.

The ancient philosophers were not only deep thinkers, but many of them held a very high political and commercial position. They are usually all described as physicists. The early theory, in what ought really to be called modern times, as the world has existed for immense periods, was that the universe existed on account of the conflicting wills of various gods.

Thales, 636–543 B.C., was the first to depart from this theory, by stating that matter, in the form of water, was the Cause of all things. If he had said, the basis of all material things, he would have been nearly correct, for, as shown in this work, all matter was originally aqueous vapour.

Lao-Tze, 604–500 B.C.—Although rather out of place amongst the Grecian philosophers, no history of philosophy could fail to mention this wonderful man, the founder of the highest known Chinese philosophy. Antedating Jesus the Christ by centuries, many of his sayings were identical with those of the Way-Shower. Like those of the Master, his teachings were all towards the purification of the individual consciousness, and the elimination of the material self. Being the keeper of the records, he under- 5 stood the doctrine of the Tao, the faith of the ancients, and the famous book of the Lo River, which contained much knowledge, now lost to the world, in its written expression, was probably well known to him. Many quotations from the principal collection of his sayings are given throughout this work.   10

Confucius, 550–479 B.C.—Having the benefit of personal intercourse, in 517 B.C., with Lao-Tze, then eighty-seven years of age, the teachings of this philosopher, although chiefly ethical, have left their traces on the minds of the Eastern world. He is said not to have believed in a personal God.   15

Zoroaster, who some say lived several thousand years before Christ, but who probably lived about 700–600 B.C., founded the Parsee religion, and is said to have taught the knowledge of Ormuzt, the supreme good principle, to the Magi, whom he spoke of as the possessors of spiritual power. Later on, certainly the Magi were workers with the human mind; 20 hence the words magic and magicians. The real history and teachings of Zoroaster have been lost.

Gautama Buddha, about 560–483 B.C.—As in the case of the teachings of Jesus Christ, so it has been difficult to find out exactly what the teachings of Gautama Buddha were. Undoubtedly he taught the 25 illusory character of matter, and that man would ultimately find himself part of God, but whether as retaining his individuality or losing himself has been doubtful. The general opinion in the past has been that he taught that man became merged in God. Colonel H. S. Olcott, in his lecture on "The Life of Buddha"—or to give him his full title, Gautama Buddha 30 Sakya Muni—at the Kandy Town Hall, Ceylon, June 11, 1880, said: "A most careful comparison of authorities and analysis of evidence establishes, I think, the following data: . . . He taught . . . everything in the world of matter is unreal; the only reality is the world of spirit . . . strive to attain the latter. . . . The only dispute between Buddhist authorities is whether 35 this Nirvanic existence is attended with individual consciousness, or whether the individual is merged into the whole, as the extinguished flame is lost in the ocean of air." Professor Huxley, in his lecture on "Evolution and Ethics," said: "The earlier forms of Indian philosophy agree with those prevalent in our own times in supposing the existence of a per- 40 manent reality, or 'substance' beneath the shifting series of phenomena, whether of matter or of mind. The substance of the Cosmos was 'Brahma,' that of the individual man 'Atman'; the latter was separated from the former only, if I may so speak, by its phenomenal envelope, by the casing of sensations, thoughts and desires, pleasures and pains, which make up 45 the illusive phantasmagoria of life. Thus the ignorant take for reality their 'Atman,' therefore remain eternally imprisoned in delusions, bound by the

fetters of desire, and scourged by the whip of misery. If the Karma is modifiable by self-discipline, if its coarser desires, one after another, can be extinguished, the ultimate fundamental desire of self-assertion or the desire to be, may also be destroyed. Then the bubble of illusion will
5 burst, and the freed individual 'Ātman' will lose itself in the universal 'Brahma.'"

This interpretation is gradually altering. Mrs. Besant writes: "Nirvana lies open before him, the fulness of spiritual knowledge, the Beatific Vision of which Christians have whispered, the peace which passeth
10 understanding."

If Buddha meant that Nirvana was the state which the material man attained when he was sufficiently purified and had lost all sense of material individuality, by gaining the knowledge that there was nothing but God, then his teaching on this point would agree with the view put forward in
15 *Life Understood*. The material so-called self is not real, and, as shown herein, at best only a series of cinematographic pictures.

St. Hilaire said that Gautama Buddha was "the perfect model of all the virtues he preaches; his life has not a stain upon it." Professor Max Müller says that his moral code was "one of the most perfect which the
20 world has ever known." Edwin Arnold speaks of him as "the highest, gentlest, holiest, and most beneficent in the history of thought."

Anaximander, 610–547 B.C., who set up the first sun-dial in Greece, and made the first map, went further than Thales, and stated that there were an infinite number of worlds, and that there was an infinite, indefinite
25 Substratum (apeiron) that underlay water, air, and fire, and which was the Cause of all, subject neither to old age, nor decay, and that "all things must resolve into that which owns their origin."

Anaximenes, 570–480 B.C., his pupil, differed from Thales, and stated, like Diogenes, that air was the essential Cause (arche), all substances, even
30 the soul, being formed by compression and expansion.

Pythagoras, 569–470 B.C., said to be the first to call himself by the name of "Philosophos," or lover of wisdom, had a wonderful knowledge of the material world, besides being a moral reformer. He is said to have studied in India, and to have given "the knowledge of things that are" only to his
35 pledged disciples. In the brotherhood he founded, study and personal purity were the rules of life. Intense fraternal affection was a marked feature of the school, and Pythagoras, being asked what a friend was, said, "Another I." He taught that man is immortal, and that the highest aim and blessedness of man is likeness to the Deity. He added earth and fire
40 to air and water, and stated that all things were mere modifications of Number, which was the Principle of all. Philolaus, his student, wrote: "Number is great and perfect and omnipotent, and the principle and guide of divine and human life." His pupils said that Number was the material of which the world was made. In this he got closer to the truth
45 as to the illusive character of the material world, for material phenomena, being, as has been shown, merely due to vibration in the ether, it follows that numerical rhythm alone is the so-called cause of the material world

and the adjustment of its phenomena. Without Number, the material world, as he said, would be chaos.

Pythagoras seems to have been the first to discover that the arrangement of the heavenly bodies depended upon intervals synchronous with musical rhythm, and stated that the earth and the planets revolved round a central 5 point. It is said that he heard "the ordered music of the marching orbs," a harmonic sound produced by the motion of the planets from which he calculated, by numbers, the ratio of distance and size of the Sun, Moon, Venus, and Mercury. He gave the name "Mathemata," learning *par excellence*, to the study of numbers and magnitudes, and showed 10 practically that he had a really good knowledge of the result of vibration in the material world. His knowledge of music [1] was such, it is said, that "he could use it for the controlling of men's wildest passions, and the illuminating of their minds." He is said to have tamed wild beasts instantly, to have foretold the future, and to have been able to move instantly from one place 15 to another. No wonder that his teachings were kept secret. He well knew the danger in those days of putting such knowledge into the hands of a then selfish and ignorant world. Even later, in the time of Jesus, when the world was further advanced, it was still not ready for the uncovering, and therefore purifying, of the hidden sinks of iniquity. The world is now 20 ready and waiting for truth and love.

Evidently Pythagoras had a good knowledge of much of the material information which now has been put before you, the futility of which was illustrated by the fact that it did not prevent him from starving himself to death. He is said to have believed in transmigration of souls, and said that 25 knowledge was merely recollection, and that, as Wordsworth later put it, "our birth is but a sleep and a forgetting," but as he also stated that the same events occur again and again in regular cycles, it looks as if he really knew something of what material death and birth actually are, and that his so-called transmigration of souls was only his presentation of the fact that what is 30 called evolution is merely successive false misrepresentations of the real spiritual world. Like many great teachers of olden times, he left no writings.

Zeno, born 490 B.C., his pupil, called by Aristotle "the Father of Logic," proved his logical gifts by maintaining that, not only the substance and movement of things, but the movement and change had no real existence 35 of their own, as motion was merely an illusion of the senses. Being so logical, he believed in the teaching of the Eleatic School, that "All is one," and "Ex nihilo nihil fit," or, "It is impossible that anything should be made out of nothing." It is wonderful how, through pure logic, he made a number of statements which hitherto had seemed impossibilities, 40 but now we find are correct, as far as the material world goes. His logical mind enabled him to confound his opponents by reducing their arguments to absurdity. For instance, he said that a multiple can be divided until we reach the indivisible units; but then an aggregation of indivisible units must be indivisible itself. Again, a flying arrow is at every moment of its 45 flight stationary in one particular spot. Further, if time and space are

---

[1] We understand but little of music. The greatest masterpiece is but a signpost to that infinite realm of harmony, in which music is forever included, and to the joy which awaits in its eternal unfoldment.

infinitely divisible, then motion is an illusion of the senses. Therefore, time and space are not infinitely divisible, but are one and continuous, and multiplicity is a mere illusion of the senses.

Ages of wrong thinking, until late in the last century, had encrusted
5 us with a blindness which prevented our seeing how illogical are the positions that thinkers are obliged to take up; or, even if we do see it, we throw it on one side, as taking too much trouble to clear up.

Heracleitus, 576–480 B.C., was known as "the weeping philosopher," as he was always grieving over the follies of mankind. His contemporaries
10 nicknamed him "The Obscure." His sayings were probably far beyond their grasp. Dr. Inge says his "scanty fragments contain flashes of the most penetrating brilliance," and he seems to have been the first to propound the Logos idea. Some of his sayings are almost identical with those in the Gospel of St. John. Yet many, misunderstanding his use of the
15 word "fire" as a material emblem, said that he went right back to matter, and imagined Being as a fiery Ether. He taught the transitoriness of everything individual, and that a fundamental law governed all nature, which he spoke of as Zeus, or the mind or law of Nature. His students, as did those of Hegel, split into two camps after his death, disagreeing absolutely
20 as to the meanings of his sayings.

Zenophanes, 576–480 B.C., the founder of the Eleatic School, put forward a vital Principle of pure Being, pervading and animating men and animals, and spoke of God as the One or the Eternal Unity, the First Cause and animating Principle of all things, asserting the unity and eternity
25 of God, as against the vile tales of mythology.

Parmenides, 488 B.C., his follower, added to this an important truth. As Dr. Beattie Crozier puts it in his *History of Intellectual Development*: "The material world . . . was degraded to a mere succession of fleeting ephemeral existences, coming into being and passing away as in a dream,
30 or, like the images in a mirror, shadowy and illusory appearances, without reality or independent existence of their own." You will see that he had found the truth about the material world, but did not understand the real world, heaven. He, however, believed in an eternal unchanging Being —namely, God, and denied the possibility of basing any arguments on
35 sensations, on the ground that they are deceptive and lead men into self-contradiction. How extraordinary that such an advanced thinker never found out and taught to others the scientific method of true prayer! What countless horrors would have been averted, which we now have to face and destroy!

40 **Anaxagoras,** 500–428 B.C., started a new era by announcing that Intelligence, an infinite Spirit, was the first Cause, and looked upon the material world as consisting of an infinite number of invisible atoms of different kinds, of the same size, mixed up together (originally all in confusion). He also got very close to the truth, as far as the material world is
45 concerned, in saying that mind,[1] in the character of "Principle of Motion,'

[1] This, of course, is the basic false mentality called the subconscious mind and the ether.

caused all this extended universe of atoms to revolve, when the like parts, by their own affinity, separated and formed the various masses of flesh, wood, iron, etc., this mind bringing the proper particles together to form the different portions of the material world. He was banished from Athens for supposed atheism.   5

Empedocles, 444–384 B.C., speaking of God, said: "He is all pure mind, holy and infinite, darting with swift thought through the universe from end to end." He pronounced the four elements gods, as he mixed the spiritual and the material together, and looked upon evil as a something attacking the good.   10

The Sophists, 460–380 B.C.—After the physicists came the Sophists, who were rightly attacked both by Plato and Socrates. Amongst them were Protagoras, Hippias, Polus, Corigas, Theodorus, and Hippocrates. The main subjects of their teaching were mathematics, astronomy, and rhetoric. As time went on, and their intellectual power increased, their ethics 15 became gradually debased, and they introduced an ostentatious disregard for truthfulness, etc. Fortunately, Socrates intervened, and changed the whole character of philosophy.

Democritus, 460–357 B.C., known as "the laughing philosopher," as, in contrast with Heracleitus, he found the follies of mankind amusing, 20 again got close upon the so-called facts of the material world. He looked at the material side and represented the world as made up of an infinite number of atoms in perpetual motion, of the same quality, but differing in size, shape, weight, etc. These he separated by an interspace of vacuum, in which they were free to move. He said that countless atoms are for ever 25 falling in a vast continuous stream, setting up vortices, in which the atoms get attached to one another, producing the natural bodies; differences of hardness, weight, etc., being due to the mode of combination. It will be seen that, whilst not quite anticipating the modern atomic theory of elements, he was very close to the material facts, as although the molecules 30 of matter are not vortices they can almost be spoken of each as a static vortex, produced, where two lines of force cross, by their action one upon the other. He stated that the gods had no influence, but that the atoms, by the necessity of their constitution, united and separated in different forms. He saw that the apparent diversity of phenomena, seen as a material 35 world, was due to our senses, and therefore could not be real. He was the last of the philosopher physicists.

Socrates, 469–399 B.C.—Next comes the great Socrates, a mystic, and almost the founder of moral science; in fact, Fouillée looked upon him as the creator of spiritual metaphysics, and speaks of his science as the science 40 of good in itself. He taught a great truth. He conceived of a supreme Power that not only arranged matters, but was a free creative and constructive Intelligence, a supreme Principle, Universal Cause,[1] around which all thoughts centred. This again marked a new era, inasmuch as he made this Intelligence a Power that worked for moral ends. Teaching that the soul 45

[1] *Phaedo*, Chapters 45 and 46.

of man partook of the divine, he had at critical times a consciousness of divine guidance, and maintained the doctrine of man's immortality as an article of faith, not of knowledge, although immediately before he drank his cup of hemlock he developed the grounds of his immovable conviction
5 of the immortality of the soul. At the same time, he recognised that good and evil in actions were the outcome of adequacy and inadequacy of knowledge. "Virtue is knowledge," was one of his platforms. Hence his untiring search for moral truth. Yet he did not believe in free-will.

Like all philosophers, he was swayed about from time to time. Xenophon
10 mentions his perplexity, and reports that while he said that men were not to inquire into the form of God, he maintained that the sense is God and the soul God; first that there is but one God, and afterwards that there are many. He taught quite truly that "virtue is knowledge" and "vice ignorance." "No man," said Socrates, "willingly does harm to himself,
15 and no man would do bad acts if he could foresee their consequences." It was this doctrine which chiefly influenced the Cynics, and, through them, the Stoics and Epicureans. On another point he was very far-seeing, because he looked upon the truth of that of which we are materially conscious as the "counterpart in nature of the moral ends which existed in the
20 mind of the Creator creating them," thus giving Plato a foundation for his counterparts of the Ideas. He stated that from the investigation of the former, or the material, we could indirectly, but with certainty, know the latter; that is, the spiritual realities of the material things.

You will have seen that it is now proved that this knowledge can only
25 be gained by reversing the material thoughts, and to expose the falsity of the material and to facilitate such necessary reversal is the only sane motive for investigation of any material phenomena.

One of the many practical things that Socrates taught was that, as the gods knew what was best, we should not pray for any opportunity of good,
30 but only for that which is good. It will be seen that this was an important step in the evolution of prayer. He also made another great discovery. This was, that when once the truth of things and their normal ends were discovered and applied, it would be impossible for man to go in contradiction to them. Hence his great and only watchword was "Knowledge."
35 This should be our watchword to-day: Know God, good. He recognised, in a way we do not, the importance of understanding the precise meaning of words.

This deep thinker was ultimately put to death on a charge of impiety, chiefly founded on the fact that he claimed to possess a "divine sign," by
40 which he was led. It probably was due, however, to his stubborn political opinions, and the fact that, by means of his superior knowledge, he constantly humiliated those he met, whom he considered conceited. Like many other thinkers, he left nothing in writing, and the testimonies of Xenophon, Plato and Aristotle differ as to his teachings.

45   **Antisthenes,** 444 B.C.; a pupil of Socrates, founded the Cynics, the most celebrated of whom was Diogenes, the well-known man of the tub. Their idea was to live according to Nature (so called), and to abandon all the common ambitions of mankind. If they had worked mentally in the

right way, as well as doing this, they would have revolutionised the world.

Aristippus, 435–356 B.C., another pupil of Socrates, founded the Cyrenaics. They believed in doing what was productive of pleasure, whilst avoiding any excess. Happiness, they thought, consisted in a multitude of 5 petty pleasures, rather than in a few great ones. By right thinking we obtain the great pleasures, as well as all lesser ones.

Plato, 428–348 B.C.—Then came Plato and the Academic School. Plato is said to have been his nickname, meaning broad-shouldered. He was a follower of Socrates until the death of the latter. Dr. Inge, in his 10 *Paddock Lectures for 1906* says: "Even to this day, I doubt whether any-one can be an orthodox theologian without being a Platonist." Prior to his day, as shown, almost every idea had been promulgated but the correct one—namely, that there is a real world, perfect, and that the material world is entirely separate and distinct, being merely a false sense of the 15 real world, with no reality or permanence about it.

Plato recognised a real or spiritual world, and classified it under two of his principles, Good and Ideas. He also believed in the material world and material atoms, and designated as Number what we now find to be vibration. In some places he speaks of the heavens, stars, earth, and our 20 souls as gods. He recognised man's apparent dual character, and said: "I am trying to find out whether I am more complicated and wicked than the serpent Typhon, or if I am of a simple nature, participating in divinity." [1]

This philosophy of Plato contained no principle of evolution, as he considered that his four principles had existed independently from all 25 eternity, and that the Supreme Good brought them together to form the world. He says: "Real being is always unchangeable, the same, and varia-tion is always limited to the phenomenal." In his *Timæus* he says that the Father of the world cannot be named; in his *Laws*, that men are not to inquire into His being.   30

Plato distinguishes between the phenomenal, which he calls visible, and the Ideal, which he calls cogitable. The visible he divides into two, optical phenomena and the material things; the cogitable, the real world, heaven, he also divides into two, mathematical and dialectical, or the field of Ideas.   35

He adopted the truths of his predecessors and fitted them into his School of Philosophy, failing to add, however, the cornerstone. He adopted the principle of change in the material world and the atoms of his predecessors, and recognised that by Number (which, as stated, apart from its mathematical significance, is vibration), they were formed into fire, 40 earth, air, and water. He evolved a system of Ideas which corresponded to the "inner nature and soul of things, as distinct from their outward visible forms," and gave them an actual independent existence of their own.[2]

---

[1] *Phædras*.
[2] Philo Judæus, born c. 20–10 B.C., taught that these Ideas were thoughts of 45 God existing before the creation of the material world of which they are the types. The totality of these Ideas was, he said, the Reason of God as Creator. Matter, according to him, was not even indirectly referable to God, its essence being a mere negation of all true being.

He was much closer to the truth than most people have thought. He wrote: "Of these celestial forms, few only can retain an adequate remembrance; and they, when they behold any image of that other world, are rapt in amazement; but they are ignorant of what this rapture means, because they do not clearly perceive. For there is no light in the earthly copies of justice or temperance, or any of the higher qualities which are precious to souls; they are seen through a glass dimly; and they are few who, going to the images, behold in them the realities, and they only with difficulty." [1] Another important truth he taught was, that the supreme Good did not "create," but disposed and arranged. His Ideas always had existed in Mind, and therefore did not require to be created in the strict sense of the word. The supreme God he looked upon as always at work for the higher ends of the Just, the Beautiful, and the True.

We now find that the only "creation" is the grouping together of new combinations of existing ideas and combinations of ideas, all God's ideas having always existed.

"Plato long ago prophesied that if a perfect man appeared, the world would crucify him, and Plato was right" [2] (Archdeacon Wilberforce). Justin Martyr, a professor of Pagan philosophy, who was greatly esteemed, wrote, after he had become a Christian, that he was sure that the Platonists were inspired by the word of Truth. Plato certainly, as Aristotle pointed out, proved, by his life and his teachings, how a good man is also a happy man.

Plato's Ideal Theory.—The School of Philosophy founded by Plato was called the Academy. Its main teachings were as follows:—

(1) The first step to knowledge is the correct definition of general terms.

(2) The things apprehended by the senses are, as Heracleitus taught, fleeting and changeable, but the characteristics or definitions of the different classes are permanent. (This is true: the characteristic of a lion is courage, which is permanent; the characteristic of a chair is support, which is also permanent.)

(3) This type or idea of the class, being permanent, exists outside the sphere of the senses.

(4) That we were able to recognise the types or ideas because our souls existed among them before we (the material beings) were born.

(5) There are superior and inferior ideas; the highest of all, the Creator, is the idea of the good, to know which, and to partake of which, is the hope and aim of the wise man. He did not pretend to give a reason for the origin of evil.

(6) In the *Republic*, Plato asserted that there is an idea corresponding to every material thing. Plato laid stress on the actual existence of Ideas apart from the objects of sense in which we perceive them. The Reverend James Gow writes: "This dogma was wholly mysterious to Plato himself, and he can only explain it in figurative language, but he had not the heart to abandon it. He was combating the debasing sophistry that there is no knowledge and no virtue, and life is a sham; and it was in the separate

---

[1] *Phœdras.*
[2] *Mystic Immanence.*

existence of the ideas that he found his proof that each soul is immortal, and that knowledge and virtue can be attained, partially in this bodily life, but fully in the spiritual life hereafter."[1] If Plato and Dr. Gow had seen that there was no reality in the material world, which was only the real world falsely seen, Plato's dogma would have been no longer 5 mysterious. He was on the very verge of the truth, anxiously reaching up and peering over the barrier of matter into the ocean of Life.

Neo-Platonism.—In this system the soul was not a single indivisible unity, but was made up of a higher divine part and a lower sensuous part, the higher part being intermovable. The Neo-Platonists taught "that evil 10 has no independent nature, no reality of its own, but merely adheres to another being; that it is nothing but an obstruction and privation of the soul"[2] (Eucken). Plotinus, the founder, taught an important truth. He said that thinking alone led to truth, and that the absolute Unity or God was above the Ideas, and could only be apprehended by man exercising 15 a kind of intuition that transcended knowledge; he then was united with the divine Being. His followers practised what is spoken of as a kind of meditative trance, instead of the study of nature, showing that he had a dawning idea of how to think. He knew too much, however, to allow them to fall into a trance. According to Maeterlinck, he had the most divine 20 intellect of any man that ever lived. In his moments of inspiration it is said that his face shone with a light not of earth.

Aristotle, 384-322 B.C.—Aristotle, the great systematiser, founded the School known as the Peripatetics. Being a biologist, he could not follow the strict lines of Plato, the mathematician, to whose school he was 25 attached for twenty years. He took Plato's Ideas, and placed them in the mind of supreme Good. He left out Number, and grouped together material bases of ends or atoms with the material ideas. Under his system he had to discover some independent source of motion, and put forward a truth, as far as any material theory can be said to be true, namely, that it 30 was the ether that, revolving in an eternal circle, supplied the movement of the material world. Aristotle therefore divided Plato's principle into two—the one, the supreme Intelligence, and the other, the source of everything in the material world. He saw that the material world, being kept in revolution by the ether, would by its own nature evolve, one after 35 another, all the phenomena of the material world—crystal, plant, animal, and man. He did not grasp that one of his two principles, namely, the ether, which appeared to be the source of everything in the material world, was simply the counterfeit of the other, the supreme Intelligence. At the same time, he taught that God was not in the material world to 40 whom it was as if it did not exist, and he looked upon qualities as realities. He dealt very fully with the material world under the heading "Physics," and then dealt with philosophy or theology, "the science of the real as real," in a series of essays, some unfinished, which he placed after "Physics." From this arose the name "Meta[after]physics." He never 45

---

[1] *A Companion to School Classics.*
[2] *The Problem of Human Life.*

12

harmonised the two portions, and evidently felt the impossibility of doing so, as he never finished this part of his system. He endeavoured to understand the reality of so-called facts.

Benevolence, or love to others, is said not to have been recognised
5 definitely by Plato or Aristotle, and to have first appeared in Cicero and the later Stoics. Plato recognised the love that is unaccompanied by any sensuous emotions, and is based on moral and intellectual affinity. He recognised that human love is only a subordinate form of this perfect and ideal love of truth "which the soul should cultivate."
10 Aristotle held that there was the supreme Intelligence and its Ideas, the matrix of matter loaded with material ideas or "form" (the hieroglyphs of the invisible Ideas caused to move by the motion gained from the Ether), and looked upon supreme Intelligence as immaterial, immovable, and invisible Essence, incapable of change and therefore an actuality. At
15 the same time, he looked upon the ether as an actuality. He rightly held that there was no evil in the eternal Actualities—that is to say, in the supreme Intelligence and its Ideas, but only in the material world. He taught that the "nous" of man was eternal and had no birth, whereas the animal soul—human mind—being acquainted with perishable things,
20 perished with them. He not only said that matter was purely negative, but that the "source of all motion was itself unmoved, and the way in which it acts can only be expressed by saying that it 'moves as an object of love.' It is pure mind, with no object but itself; it is thought, with thought as its object—pure self-consciousness, with nothing beyond. It is God." [1]
25 Like many modern advanced thinkers, he was called an atheist, and was prosecuted by the Athenians for atheism.

Eucleides, 323–283 B.C., founder of the Megarian School, and, under the name of Euclid, a terror to non-mathematical schoolboys, went beyond his master in adding goodness and wisdom to the other attributes
30 of the Deity. He looked upon goodness, virtue, etc., not only as the supreme ends, but as the only realities of life. This is true, but the virtue and goodness with which we are acquainted in this material world are only a limited sense of the real virtue and the real goodness. Another great truth the Megarian School taught, namely, that evil is only an illusion of
35 our sensuous nature and has no real existence.

Pyrrho, 360–270 B.C., founded the sect called Sceptics, recognising the untrustworthiness of the senses. He would not affirm even that snow was white; as a fact, he suspended judgment on it. "We define nothing," was the motto of his school.

40 **Stoicism,** founded by Zeno of Citium (280 B.C.) shortly after the death of Aristotle, was a pantheistic system, having matter on one side and universal Soul diffused through matter on the other. Its human soul was a single indivisible unity of part of the universal Soul.

The Stoics gave practical advice on wisdom and virtue, and the mode
45 of attaining them. Their logic was such as particularly appeals to what is

[1] *Harmsworth Encyclopædia.*

called common-sense. They thought the soul received impressions through the senses. In physics they were materialists or pantheists, and maintained that the impressions of the senses are the sole source of knowledge, and that nothing exists except what is material and can act on the senses.

The soul of the universe they described as Cause, Spirit, Reason, Nature, Fate, Necessity, Law, and God. The later Stoics, such as Seneca, preferred the use of the name God. Their God was really only so-called natural law. They taught that the soul, after death, did not die, but retained its individuality until the general end (ekpurosis). To live according to reason, they taught, was the same thing as to live according to nature, and that when the emotions could no longer be suppressed, man was to commit suicide, as Cato and many others did. They taught that the God which the individual seeks must be identical with the good of the community. This they seemed to have been the first to teach. This good, however, we now know is spiritual and tangible, not the material so-called good.

Epicurean School.—This antagonistic school, founded by Epicurus, 341–270 B.C., also endeavoured to give this practical guidance, maintaining that ethics is the proper study of man as being the path to true happiness. Both these schools, which were materialistic, teaching that the senses alone were the source of knowledge, became far more influential than previous ones.

Both the Stoics and the later Neo-Platonic School depended on the unaided strength of what they called the individual soul, namely, the human so-called "mind."

In those days there were numerous philosophers. Seneca [1] (A.D. 60), Plutarch (A.D. 100), and finally Epictetus [2] (A.D. 120) with Marcus Aurelius (A.D. 121–180), amongst the Stoics, the brilliant Lucretius (95–50 B.C.) amongst the Epicureans, and Sextus Empiricus (A.D. 250) of the Sceptics, are perhaps the best known. Some believed in the old pagan gods, demons, etc., and that God manifested himself materially. The last of the pagan philosophers, Porphyry and Iamblichus, Neo-Platonists, grouped together in various combinations the four great principles laid down by Plato, viz., the supreme Being or the Good; the system of Ideas, the real things in heaven; Number, or vibration; and matter, the manifestation of thought or vibration. With the rise of the new school of Christian philosophers, with men like Origen, Athanasius, and Augustine, ancient paganism disappeared, being extinct in enlightened centres in A.D. 420, and in A.D. 529 Justinian shut up the schools of Athens.

These olden philosophers were most of them trying to elucidate the truth, and were, no doubt, of use in their way; although Mommsen says of the Greek philosophers that "the long series of philosophical systems that had come and gone, had accumulated huge piles of intellectual rubbish," and of the Romans, that "they were simply inferior scholars of bad teachers."

[1] One of his sayings was "To obey God is freedom."
[2] It was he that said "It is not things that disquiet us, but our opinions about things."

Up to the present I have dealt with the earlier schools of philosophy, before they had begun to realise clearly the great importance of so-called "thought" and the difference between what is called objective and what is called subjective "thought." The former is a belief in that of which we are 5 conscious, being something external to our "consciousness," and material; the latter is a belief in that of which we are conscious as being only an impression in our so-called "mind," having no other existence, real or otherwise. Both now turn out to be false "mental" impressions, or ethereal vibrations, material and entirely illusive. For years, philosophers 10 have argued as to these two methods of obtaining knowledge, the subjective and objective.

Bruno, 1550.—This philosopher taught "that space is infinite, filled with self-luminous and opaque worlds, many of them inhabited, this statement being his capital offence. He was burnt at Rome in 1600. He 15 believed that the world is animated by an intelligent soul, the cause of forms, but not of matter; that this lives in all things, even such as seem not to live. He nevertheless thought that matter and the soul of the world together constituted God.

Jacob Boehme, 1574–1624, the great mystic and father of German 20 philosophy, was a working shoemaker. His keen intellect was spent in deep and original thought, and he had a marvellous knowledge of the truth. He wrote: "Blessed art thou therefore if thou canst stand still from self-thinking and self-willing, and canst stop the wheel of thy imagination and senses; forasmuch as hereby thou mayest arrive at length to see the 25 great salvation of God, being made capable of all manner of divine sensations and heavenly communications. Since it is nought indeed but thine own hearing and willing that do hinder thee, so that thou dost not see and hear God. This thy willing moreover stops thy hearing. And having brought thee hither, it overshadows thee with that which thou willest; it 30 binds thee with thine own chains, and it keeps thee in thine own dark prison which thou makest for thyself; so that thou canst not go out thence, or come to that state which is supernatural and supersensual." Of him Emile Boutroux writes: "Inner experience and reflection are, once for all, his true means of investigation. True, he was an illuminate; his meditation 35 was a prayer; his discoveries, divine revelations." [1]

Descartes, 1596–1650.—This theologian, who was also a profound philosopher and mathematician, was forced by the contradictions of knowledge gained materially—through sense impressions—to believe that the true starting-point of knowledge was subjective, that is to say, 40 in "mental" reasoning or thought. He stated that the only safe ground was the knowledge that he existed. "I think, therefore I am." Thought he regarded as without an equal, and Huxley affirmed that his system was the very soul of contemporary philosophy and science. His dream has now been realised, namely, how by thought to preserve mankind from illness 45 and disease, even from the debility of old age. To-day the *Gazette d'Anvers*

[1] *Historical Studies in Philosophy.*

would not have announced his death as it did then: "In Sweden there has just died a fool, who said that he could live as long as he wished."

Spinoza, 1632–1677, the so-called pantheist, whom Novalis calls a God-intoxicated man, claimed complete freedom of thought and belief in the interests of true piety. Hume speaks of "this famous atheist" and   5 his "hideous hypothesis." This is a very good instance of how people often jump at conclusions with regard to the ideas of those who are too much in advance of them. They may even hound them down with much yelping, regardless of the possible truth of the ideas.

Spinoza tried to look at life from a mathematical point of view and to free   10 his views from bias. "The inclusion of the finite—the illusion of sense . . . in the eyes of Spinoza, is the source of all error and evil to man. On the other hand, his highest good is to live the universal life of reason, or what is the same thing, to view all things from their centre in God, and to be moved only by the passion for good in general, 'the intellectual love of   15 God'" (Edward Caird, D.C.L., D.Litt.). To the heat of passion he had only one advice: "Acquaint thyself with God and be at peace." "Love to an object that is infinite and eternal fills the soul with a changeless and un-mingled joy" was one of his statements. He also said: "I assert expressly that the mind [the human mind] has no adequate conception either of   20 itself or of external things, but only a confused knowledge of things."

He pointed out that unless we knew God we could know nothing else. God, according to him, is Pure Being, the underlying Principle of all particular forms, containing them within Himself in their entirety. He truly said that "all limitation is negative," and that "by denying the   25 negative we reach the affirmative," the "unconditioned [unfettered] being which alone truly is." "Evil is not something positive, but a state of priva-tion . . . only in relation to the intelligence of man" (Epist. 32). When Blyenbury accused him of making God the author of evil, he answered that evil had no existence for God. Brought into contact with the idea of   30 God, all ideas, he points out, become true and adequate by the removal of the negative and false element. "Nothing that is positive in a false idea is removed by the presence of truth as such" (Eth. iv : 1). This view of his is expressed by Edward Caird as follows: "Spinoza . . . says that what ever reality is in the finite, is of the infinite. But he is unsuccessful in   35 showing that, on the principles on which he starts, there can be any reality in the finite at all" (Article on Cartesianism, Ency. Britt.). Naturally he could not do this, as the finite is a false sense of reality.

These statements had comparatively little effect in the world, because he had no knowledge of how practically to apply them and so demonstrate   40 their truth. This deep thinker presents a glaring instance of a world's misjudgment of one far in advance of his age. He failed, as he had not a purely metaphysical basis.

Locke, 1632–1704, on the contrary, in reaction, stated that the only reliable knowledge was obtained from the senses, although he believed in   45 spiritual assistance and revelation.

Leibnitz, 1646–1716, the discoverer of the Differential Calculus, who tried hard to bring about a union between the Catholic and Protestant

Churches, stated that Spirit was the only reality, and truly thought that the knowledge of the material world was knowledge of the spiritual world seen "confusedly and under disguise," and that God was "universal harmony." He believed the material world to be the best possible world, 5 and that evil merely increased the good by contrast.

In his famous theory of optimism, the world is by no means represented as perfect; it is only the best of all possible worlds, the best the Creator could make out of the materials at hand. In recent times Mill showed a marked preference for this view.

10   Leibnitz was deterred by theological scruples from accepting the theory of gravitation, which appeared to him as a substitution of the action of physical forces for the direct action of the Deity. Agassiz, who advanced along "the pathway leading to divine Science," but dropped from his summit, made the same comment with regard to Darwin. He regarded it 15 as a fatal objection to the Darwinian theory that it appeared to substitute the action of physical forces for the creative action of Deity. In his *Essay on Classification*, he regarded every organic form as a concrete thought of the Creator, interpretable by the human "mind." This shows how close in theory he was to the truth, and yet how far away he was from the know- 20 ledge of Truth as Mind and its manifestation.

Berkeley, 1685–1753, Bishop of Cloyne, whilst putting forward a metaphysical view of the world, and stating that there exists nothing but man's thoughts of things, was, as Huxley called him, a "mixed logician." Mr. Oldroyd has said that "Christian Science is Berkeleyism run mad," 25 but his system was only semi-metaphysical, practically pantheism. Berkeley wrote: "Although our sensations are wholly subjective, we do not deny an independent reality of things." He also said that there was "no substance of matter, but only a substance of mind termed spirit; that there are two kinds of spiritual substance, the one eternal and uncreated, 30 the substance of Deity; the other created, and, once created, naturally eternal." He fell from the sublime to the ridiculous by recommending tar water as a panacea for all human ills. He had not seen the fundamental Principle, that all was divine Mind, God, and not the limited human sense wrongly called mind; consequently he could not keep his practice on a 35 level with his theory.

Emanuel Swedenborg, 1688–1772, was a notable man. He took his degree of Philosophy at the age of twenty-one, and was ennobled for his distinguished engineering services on behalf of his country. In 1724 he declined the chair of mathematics at Upsala University, and spent some 40 twenty years in study and research in mining, mathematics, physics, astronomy, anatomy, etc. Some of his writings show striking anticipation of later scientific development. For instance, the nebular system of the origin of the universe, now so widely accepted by physicists, was, in its fundamental principle, first presented to the world by Swedenborg in his 45 *Principia*. Kant's great work, elaborating this theory, was not published until 1755, twenty-one years later.

In 1744, three years before he resigned his seat in the Upper House of the Legislature, he began to find that he had extraordinary powers. Kant, who was not only a great philosopher, but also a painstaking scientist, made a special inquiry into, and verified several of the remarkable instances related of Swedenborg, and published a work containing the results of his investigation.

Swedenborg was a very clever man, and in advance of his time. Although 5 he founded a sect whose theories and practice, whilst advanced, are based upon wrong principles, nevertheless, his religious views have influenced such eminent men as Goethe, Coleridge,́ and Emerson. Swedenborg was unaware that there was nothing special about his powers, which were only an absence of the limitations in certain directions that ordinary mortals 10 at present are supposed to have. With the greater development of material so-called mentality comes a greater need to the world of divine guidance and protection, or else such development must lead to greater troubles. In addition to this, Swedenborg, unknowingly, intensified wrong thoughts by dwelling on them, being ignorant of the sad results of so doing. Now, 15 by the knowledge of truth, we can destroy these wrong thoughts, and all limitations will disappear gradually and harmoniously as we learn how to pray rightly.

Hume, 1711–1776, the great historian and political economist, followed on, and showed by clear thinking that what Descartes claimed, 20 namely, that man was able to gain knowledge subjectively, was true. He showed that Locke's objective method was a failure, as we could not find either substance or cause amongst the objects of experience, and, in fact, threw doubt upon all the sciences, doubting the possibility of obtaining knowledge by the objective world altogether. He is better known as a 25 religious sceptic, because of his attack upon miracles, and has usually been considered a materialist. He recognised that "what is incorruptible must be ungenerable." In Huxley's life of Hume, he says : "It is hardly necessary to point out that the doctrine just laid down is what is commonly called materialism. But it is nevertheless true, that the doctrine contains nothing 30 inconsistent with the purest idealism."

Kant, 1724–1804.—Then came the great Immanuel Kant. He condemned the view of Leibnitz, holding that the material or phenomenal world was wholly different from the real, so that in knowing the material we did not know reality at all. He corrected Hume's scepticism, and showed 35 that the inner activity of man, properly used, made science trustworthy. He went further, and whilst denying intuitive understanding, or what Mars, a recent writer, calls "rational intuition," he showed that what we have called our sciences, however sufficiently reliable for use, were not deserving the name of knowledge in the true sense of the term. He thought 40 it essential that all knowledge gained intuitively should be tested logically to show its credentials. This test, however, is not satisfactory, owing to the human being's imperfect grasp of true knowledge. Nor is it necessary. When we are working properly and gaining our knowledge intuitively, by the realisation that God is the Principle of all knowledge, and that there- 45 fore man has all requisite knowledge, nothing but what is true comes to us whilst, or even just after, praying in this way. The only true test of knowledge is its logical results in one's life and that of those with whom

one comes in contact. In this way we can now prove practically the truth
of our purely intuitive knowledge.

Kant only recognised three-dimensional space. He, however, recognised
that time is simply one way of being conscious of "one thing going before
5 and another thing coming after something else," that is, as the consciousness of succession. Although he was close upon the truth, he did not
quite reach it. Kant writes in his "Inaugural Dissertation": "By our
sensibility we do not know the nature of things confusedly. We do not
know it at all. Apart from our subjective condition, the object, as repre-
10 sented and qualified by our sensibility, is nowhere to be found. It cannot
possibly be found, since its form as phenomenal appearance is determined by those very subjective conditions." He taught nothing to warrant
the assumption of the existence, that is to say, the permanence and therefore reality, of matter, but taught exactly the reverse; as according to him
15 the mind constructs through the imagination a sort of hybrid world, the
objects of which, while mental concepts, yet partake of a material or
sensuous character. This is the world we seem to know through our senses.
He recognised the relation between subject and object, and expressed the
belief that Mind could not be known by man the human being; stating
20 definitely that the phenomenal, or apparent, is all that we can see, and that
from the very nature of our minds, we can never know reality. Kant
wrote to the effect that against other criticisms of the doctrine of immortality, one may adduce the transcendental hypothesis; all life is essentially
only intellectual, and not subject to time changes, neither beginning with
25 birth nor ending with death. This world's life is only an appearance, a
sensuous image of the pure spiritual life, and the whole world of sense,
only a picture swimming before our present knowing faculty like a dream,
and *having no reality in itself*, for if we should see things and ourselves as
they are, we should see ourselves in a world of spiritual natures with which
30 our entire real relation neither begins at birth nor ends with the body's
death.

Fichte, 1762–1814, who was dismissed from his professional chair
at Jena under a charge of atheism, endeavoured to reconcile religion
with first principles. He got closer to the understanding of the teaching
35 of Jesus that "the kingdom of God is within," by asserting that all knowledge is of the inner self, and that whilst objective perception seems to
come from external source, it is really the creation of the thinker. He,
however, also made the mistake of Hegel in not recognising the distinction
between Mind, as perfect good, and the ethereal or so-called human
40 "mind," although he saw that subjective knowledge could not stand for
reality. Like Schelling and Hegel, he endeavoured to found a new philosophy of the absolute on the morals of Kant.

Hegel, 1770–1831, Professor of Philosophy at Berlin, endeavoured
to further develop the Idealistic School started by Kant. He correctly
45 regarded thought and thing, even thought and being, as one, that is,
matter as being materialised thought; and the so-called unfolding thought
in man as the coming to consciousness of objective (so-called) reality. He
refused to be satisfied with mere objective knowledge, and made more

practical the unknown reality of Kant, although he mixed up Mind, God, and the human mind. He said: "Of the greatness and power of Mind we cannot think too highly." He looked upon life as a progressive unfoldment of Being, the unfolding in rational consciousness of all nature and all history towards the fulness of the ultimate Idea. This word he used as 5 standing for the Reality, which is God, and looked at it as the final Cause or the end. He said that through this unfolding "the implicit unity of the subjective and objective is now realised, and this is the Idea."

Balzac, 1799–1850, in his "Louis Lambert" says that : "Specialism (seeing all) consists in seeing the things of the material world as those of 10 the spiritual world in their rational and consequential ramification," and says that it "opens to man his true career and the infinite dawns upon him and he gets a glimpse of his destiny."

Lotze, 1817–1881, Professor at Leipzig, Göttingen, and Berlin, one of whose favourite themes was the mechanical view of nature, started as 15 a scientific man, and became a great Christian philosopher. He believed as firmly as Kant in the goodness of God, and felt deeply the failure of science to explain reality.

Schopenhauer, 1788–1860, the pupil of Fichte, following upon Hegel, constructed a philosophy of life based upon the collective will as 20 cause. He looked upon the "will to live" [1] as the cause of everything, and the material universe as its "objectification." This, as far as it went, was perfectly logical. He consistently carried this to its inevitable conclusion, namely, the disappearance of the material universe with the cessation of the "will to live" in a material universe. This is an instance of how really 25 logical thinkers are much nearer to truth than is generally recognised.

This so-called "will to live" individualised is : (a) The individual human consciousness that apparently constitutes a material being, and (b) the succession of thoughts coming to this human consciousness, these thoughts being counterfeits of the true thoughts of God. Human knowledge may 30 also be expressed as thoughts coming into consciousness. As a matter of fact, there is only one thing in the material world; that is, the apparent succession of thoughts or the seeming action of thought in the material consciousness, and there is no difference between the human will to live and human knowledge. 35

Schopenhauer, as Drummond says, regarded consciousness as the hideous mistake and malady of nature. This is true of the material, illusory consciousness, the consciousness that allows the sinful thoughts to enter, but not true of the real, Christ consciousness, the true self. Schopenhauer recognised that there was something beyond mere human 40 knowledge, and discerned the value of the Christian religion to those who were able to grasp it. He envied the attitude of the Quietists, and said: "Knowledge can deliver itself from the bondage of the will and exist

[1] "The Science of Paul's declaration resolves the element misnamed matter into its original sin, or human will; that will which would oppose bringing the qualities 45 of Spirit into subjection to Spirit. Sin brought death; and death is an element of matter, or material falsity, never of Spirit" (*Miscellaneous Writings*, p. 201, Mary Baker Eddy).

12*

purely for itself [this he considered the source of art]. Further, if it reacts on the individual manifestation of the will, it can bring about self-surrender," i.e., resignation, which is, he said, "the final goal, and indeed the inmost nature of all virtue and holiness—and is deliverance from the
5 world." Schopenhauer therefore exposed material existence as the manifestation of material evil which binds its victims, alias mortals, on the Ixion wheel of desire and ennui until the "will to live" is metaphysically denied and disowned. He recognised that the material person was nothing, the mere passing phenomenon of the "will to live"; and although an agnostic,
10 he recognised that the Christian religion had something of essential value, which it was perfectly impossible for him to fit in with what he knew of material existence. His philosophy made him a misanthrope of the bitterest kind, and joy was almost unknown to him. He was so logical that the tiniest grain of truth would have turned the scale and opened his eyes to
15 the vast outlook on reality.

There are various schools of modern philosophy, of which I only refer to a few.

Hedonism, which says that the agreeable is the good.

Utilitarianism or Universal Hedonism, which is a considerable
20 advance on the above. The Utilitarian argues that it is good to be happy, that happiness is the good.

Perfectionism, another variety, argues that it is happy to be good, that perfect goodness is happiness.

Evolutionary Ethics, as propounded by Herbert Spencer, Darwin,
25 Leslie Stephen and others, has already made that of Mill and Bain out of date. It may be called the evolution of Hedonism, tracing, as it does, the rise and progress of morals to man's sense of pleasure and pain.

Pragmatism, the name coined by Professor W. James, denotes an attitude of mind towards our ultimate beliefs in the light of their
30 consequences. The following, by its founder, gives one main view of the doctrine propounded as an antidote to scepticism: "It is now seen that life and action are deeper than logical processes, that immediate premises are behind all inferences, that thought cannot begin until life furnishes the data, and that there is nothing deeper in conjunction or life than the funda
35 mental needs, interest, and instincts of the mind." This is true of the Mind that is God.

All the great men of modern days have been very close to the truth. There are so many great thinkers that I can only mention about half-a-dozen.

40 **John Stuart Mill,** 1806–1873, an admittedly earnest truth-seeker, whom Gladstone describes as the saint of Rationalism, writes: "All appearance attests the strength of the tendency to mistake mental abstractions, even negative ones, for substantive realities." At the same time believing in the reality of matter, he was faced with the belief that God was
45 not omnipotent, and wrote: "The only admissible moral theory of creation

is that the Principle of good cannot at once and altogether subdue the powers of evil. We must save God's goodness at the expense of his omnipotence." This is the position into which the belief in the reality of matter has driven one of the best of modern philanthropists, a Christian Socialist and reformer, who teaches that God is improving mankind by means of 5 matter, and that evil is not really evil, as it is necessary for the improvement, and therefore benefit, of mankind.

Huxley, 1825–1895, Professor at the Royal College of Surgeons, the Royal Institution, and the Government School of Mines, gave his life to the vigorous promulgation of what he regarded as truth, and had a 10 passion for "absolute veracity." His teachings have been completely misunderstood by many. He called himself an idealist and followed Plato in his constant endeavour to discard the shifting appearances of our senses, and find truth. He considered metaphysics and physics as complementary, saying that: "They will never be completely fruitful until one united with 15 the other." [1] At last they have been welded into one, by the elimination of physical misconceptions and the spiritualisation of semi-metaphysics. This spiritualisation is bringing forth much fruit.

It is necessary to keep always clearly in mind the difference between false and true metaphysics, the metaphysics of the pure Mind that is God. 20 You will find that human semi-metaphysics harmonise with so-called natural science, and that they are identical. This is possible, because neither is true, they are both a false sense of the real, dealing only with disappearing phenomena.

Huxley coined the word "agnosticism" which, as concerning the mortal 25 man who can never know the reality, turns out to be true. He said that the path which leads to the truth was, "that idealism which declares the ultimate fact of all knowledge to be consciousness, or, in other words, mental phenomena, and therefore affirms the highest of all certainties, indeed the only certainty, to be the existence of Mind." [2] 30

He admitted that sense and logic alone are utterly helpless, and did not make Kant's mistake, but recognised the influence of what has been shown in the female's complement of wisdom, namely, intuition, which he called mother-wit, or inborn capacity of genius.

His philosophic position he has summed up as follows: "The key to all 35 philosophy lies in the clear comprehension of Berkeley's problem—which is neither more nor less than one of the shapes of the greatest of all questions, 'What are the limits of our faculties?' And it is worth any amount of trouble to comprehend the exact nature of the argument by which Berkeley arrived at his results, and to know by one's own knowledge 40 the great truth which he discovered—that the honest and rigorous following up of the argument which leads us to materialism inevitably carries us beyond it. The more completely the materialistic position is admitted, the easier it is to show that the idealistic position is unassailable, if the idealist confines himself within the limits of positive knowledge." And he 45 adds, in conclusion: "And therefore, if I were obliged to choose between

[1] *Methods and Results.*
[2] *Ibid.*

absolute materialism and absolute idealism, I should feel compelled to
accept the latter alternative."

Fiske, 1842–1901, the well-known historian, Professor of Philosophy
at Harvard and St. Louis, was in his earlier days an agnostic. As he
5 became wiser his agnosticism disappeared, and his last work was written
to prove that science led irresistibly to the doctrine of immortality,
although he thought there was no proof of the spiritual world.[1]

He wrote as follows: "The untrained thinker who believes that the
group of phenomena constituting the table on which he is writing has an
10 objective existence, independent of consciousness, will probably find no
difficulty in accepting this sort of materialism. If he is devoted to the study
of nervous physiology, he will be very likely to adopt some such crude
notion, and to proclaim it as zealously as if it were an important truth,
calculated to promote, in many ways, the welfare of mankind. The science
15 [material] of such a writer is very likely to be sound and valuable, and he
will tell us about Woorara poison and frogs' legs, and acute mania, and it
will probably be worthy of serious attention. But with his philosophy it is
quite otherwise. When he has proceeded as far in subjective analysis as
he has in the study of nerves, our materialist will find that it was demons-
20 trated a century ago that the group of phenomena constituting the table
has no real existence whatever in the philosophic sense. For by 'reality'
in philosophy is meant 'persistence, irrespective of particular conditions,'
and the group of phenomena constituting a table persists only in so far as
it is held together in cognition. Take away the cognising mind, and the
25 colour, form, position, and hardness of the table—all the attributes, in
short, that characterise it as matter—at once disappear. . . . Apart from
consciousness, there are no such things as colour, form, position, or hardness, and there is no such thing as matter. This great truth, established
by Berkeley, is the very foundation of modern scientific philosophy; and,
30 though it has been misapprehended by many, no one has ever refuted it,
and it is not likely that anyone ever will."

He said of Kant: "His work was thus critical rather than constructive.
It was to break up the hard and crude notions that man had of a solid,
material world, wholly independent of spiritual presence, and to sub-
35 stitute for this the thought of an ideal world, which is for and of the
spirit alone."

Herbert Spencer, 1820–1903.—Spencer propounded what is called
his law of evolution. He looked upon the universe as "but the progressive unfolding and evolution of a fixed quantity of force," Infinite and
40 Eternal Energy, acting in the antagonistic forms of attraction and repulsion,
and truly stated that from the constitution of the human mind (so called),
knowledge of noumena is impossible.

Spencer, throughout all his works, regards as the All-Being the Power
of which "our lives, alike physical and mental, in common with all the
45 activities, organic and inorganic, amid which we live, are but the workings."

He believed that his synthetic philosophy was consistent with either an
idealistic or materialistic view of the universe, because we could reduce it

[1] *The Unseen World.*

to terms of mind or matter. In this he was correct as far as he went, because, as has been pointed out, all phenomena can now be given in terms of "mind" (material mentality) or in terms of matter, both being equally incorrect because there is no matter and only one Mind, God, good.

Dr. Beattie Crozier writes: "With Spencer, the universe with all it contains is but the progressive unfolding and evolution of a fixed quantity of force in the antagonistic forms of attraction and repulsion; with Hegel, it is the same progressive unfolding, only of Being or Existence in general, with positive and negative poles. The truth is the same with both, namely, 'a continuous process of differentiation and integration,' as Spencer himself defines it. Any such system basing all phenomena as being simply the multiplex and complex phases of one universal fact—the redistribution of matter and motion—must inevitably and admittedly fail to throw any light upon the great cosmical mysteries of beginnings and endings."

Haeckel.[1]—Haeckel, in *The History of Natural Creation*, gives a picture of the evolution of species from an amœba to man. In this he is unable to explain the force, which has started this evolution, except by admitting spontaneous generation, which is mathematically an impossibility, as you cannot make something out of nothing. If spontaneous generation is admitted, then the material world must be a non-reality. He is thoroughly accurate as far as he goes, as he only recognises the material world and puts forward the evolution of life from the albumenoid compounds of carbon.

According to Professor McCabe, Haeckel admits that true Intelligence is not to be found in this world of matter, and therefore we have only the untrustworthy senses to testify to their own existence. Only recognising the material, he writes perfectly correctly: "Just as the infinite universe is one great Whole . . . so the spiritual and moral life of man is part of the cosmos, and our naturalistic ordering of it must also be monistic." By "spiritual" he can only mean man's "sense of the spiritual."

Montaigne's analysis of the beliefs of philosophers with reference to God [2] is interesting. Briefly it is this:—

Thales believed God to be a spirit that made all things of water; Anaximander, that the gods were always dying; Anaximenes, that the air was God, procreated and immense, always moving; Anaxagoras the First, that all things were conducted by the power and reason of an infinite spirit; Alcmæon, that the sun, moon, and stars, and the human soul were God; Pythagoras, that God was sprinkled over the nature of all things from which our souls are extracted; Parmenides, that He was a Circle surrounding the heaven and supporting the world by the ardour of light; Empedocles, that the four elements were Gods; Protagoras had nothing to say on the subject; Democritus, that the images were Gods; Plato divides his belief into several opinions, he makes the world, the heavens, the stars, the earth, and our souls, Gods; Xenophon reports that Socrates was in perplexity, saying at first that there is one God, and afterwards that there are many; Speusippus, the nephew of Plato, makes God a certain

---

[1] 1834–1919.
[2] "*The Essays of Michael Seigneur de Montaigne*," translated by C. Cotton.

power governing all things, and stated that he had a soul; Aristotle at one time says that God is a spirit, and at another, the world; Zenocrates makes eight Gods, five amongst the planets, the sixth composed of all the fixed stars, the seventh and eighth the sun and moon; Heraclides Ponticus 5 shifts in opinion, and finally deprives God of all sense, saying that God is heaven and earth; Theophrastus wanders in the same irresolute manner; Strato said that God is nature; Zeno says 'tis the law of nature commanding good and prohibiting evil, which law is an animal; Diogenes Apollonates, that 'tis age; Zenophanes makes God round, seeing and hearing and 10 breathing, and having nothing in common with human nature; Aristo thinks the form of God to be incomprehensible; Cleanthes supposes God to be reason and various things, one the soul of nature; Perseus, Zeno's disciple, was of opinion that men have given the title of Gods to those who have been useful, and have added any advantage to human life; Chrysippus 15 reckons amongst a thousand forms of Gods the men that have been deified; Diagoras and Theodorus flatly denied that there were any Gods at all; Epicurus makes the Gods shining and transparent, fixed between two worlds, and clothed in a human figure.

" God by god flits past in thunder, till his glories turn to shades :
20   God to god bears wondering witness how his gospel flames and fades.
      More was each of these, while yet they were, than man their servant seemed :
      Dead are all of these, and man survives who made them while he dreamed "
                                                                    (*Swinburne*).

The ideas of God to-day are almost as diverse as the ideas of the old 25 philosophers. A large number of people, however, are now rejoicing in a practical, demonstrable understanding of God. These people find that this knowledge of God is an ever-present help in trouble, and capable of relieving themselves and others of all worries and troubles.

The following extract from *The Life of Paracelsus* by Dr. Franz Hart- 30 mann gives an idea of present philosophical views : " Man is a materialised thought; he is what he thinks. To change his nature from the mortal to the immortal state he must change his mode of thinking; he must cease to hold fast in his thoughts to that which is illusory and perishing, and hold on to that which is eternal. But who but the enlightened can hold on 35 to a thought? Men do not think what they choose, but that which comes into their mind. If they could control the action of their minds, they would be able to control their own nature and the nature by which their forms are surrounded. There is no god, no saint, and no man in whom we can put any confidence, faith, or trust for the purpose of our salvation, except the 40 power of the divine principle acting within ourselves. Only when man begins to realise this truth will he begin his infinite life, and step from the realm of evanescent illusions into that of the permanent truth."

Although it is interesting to note the advancing trend of modern thought, we cannot but endorse what Browning so ably expresses in the following 45 words :—

            "Oh ! The little more,
              And how much it is !
            And the little less,
              And what worlds away."

Through divine Principle, ever-active, omnipresent Mind, God's man will always be in direct touch with that individuality through which he will receive the idea he needs at any time. Hence the brotherhood of man and his perfect environment when governed by divine Principle.

ON THEOSOPHY 5

> *"Who seeks for Heaven alone to save his soul*
> *May keep the path, but will not reach the goal,*
> *While he who walks in love may wander far,*
> *Yet God will bring him where the blessed are"* (H. Van Dyke).

The Theosophical Society, a movement which has appeared in the 10 Western World of recent years, owes its vitality to the human attempt to live an altruistic life. There is a large band of theosophists, deep-thinking men and women, reaching out towards Truth and believing that there is no religion higher than the truth. The best of them recognise that there is a body of truth which forms the basis of all religions, and which cannot be 15 claimed as the exclusive possession of any. This they would call the truths of theosophy. Members of the Theosophical Society study them; when they live them they are theosophists. They recognise and endeavour to bring about the brotherhood of man without regarding race, creed, sex, caste, or colour, and believe in mutual and universal toleration. The 20 objects of the section in England, under Mrs. Besant's leadership, are also "to encourage the study of comparative religion, philosophy, and science, and to investigate unexplained laws of nature and the powers latent in man." The objects of the American branch, under Mrs. Tingley, are: "To study ancient and modern philosophy, and science, and to investigate 25 unexplained laws of Nature, and the Divine powers in man." Both base their objects upon the underlying truth in the teachings of that extraordinary woman, Madame Blavatsky.

The ideals of Theosophy are high, but theosophists have not recognised that what they term spiritual is really only an ethereal manifesta- 30 tion of human consciousness. A study and practice of the system does not develop the capacity to destroy sin, disease, and death, but rather induces and deepens the illusion of the necessity for a series of deaths, or so-called passings on into new phases of the dream of life in matter and a material universe. 35

Theosophy teaches that what is called death is a passing into an astral world, from which man advances into a second world, and so on until he reaches the highest possible state. He then begins to come back again through these different worlds, being ultimately again born upon this planet as a child, the "soul" finding itself in a new physical body! This 40 mistaken belief has grown up from facts that have been referred to, namely, that the human "mind" fits into the body and can be seen when it is separated from that body. This human "mind" is what they call the astral body, and when the theosophist speaks of working on the astral plane, this only means that he has the power of causing his human "mind" 45 to leave his human body and move about in a state of consciousness separated from it. This, so far from being an advance upward into eternal

and spiritual realities, is a dangerous and incomplete human method of working, leaving the body unprotected and liable to all sorts of accidents. The theosophists recognise this and say that the necessary preparation must always include high moral development. Even this will not prevent
5 the evil results of broken law. Working in the way Jesus the Master worked, no such danger can arise.

The following statement of Mrs. Besant in *Theosophical Manual No. II* sets out the general theosophical belief with regard to reincarnation: "The theory of reincarnation, then, in the Esoteric Philosophy, asserts the
10 existence of a living and individualised principle, which dwells in and informs the body of a man, and which, on the death of the body, passes into another body, after a longer or shorter interval." In *Reincarnation* she has written: "The proofs of reincarnation do not amount to a complete and general demonstration, but they establish as strong a presumption as
15 can, in the nature of the case, exist."

ON REINCARNATION

There is a good deal of difference of opinion with regard to details of reincarnation.

Schopenhauer, Fichte the younger, Herder, Lessing, Hegel, Leibnitz,
20 Paracelsus, Boehme, and Hume, all were in favour of the theory of reincarnation. The reason for this is that reincarnation is a little nearer the truth than the belief that when man dies he goes to hell or to heaven. The amount of truth that there is in it will be seen on pages 263–271 of this book.

I do not deny the fact that a dozen people in different parts of the world,
25 and without comparing notes, will all agree as to the identity of a given person in what they call their previous incarnation, or life on the material world. But it is clear from what has been said that if a few strong thinkers —they should really be called leading picturers—agree in any such belief the mass follows, and holds the same views. The material facts upon which
30 the doctrine of reincarnation has been built are given on the above-mentioned pages, and it will be seen that the so-called "ego" does not return to this material world, as it never has been in it, but always is in heaven.

MAHATMAS

35 Mahatmas are thought by some to be beings who, having left this world, are consecrated to the helping of suffering humanity. The belief in them is largely due to the fact that the material mind can obtain knowledge of material facts, materialise objects, etc., and if the person doing this has a strong enough belief that the objects are brought by some attendant spirit
40 who helps them, everything in connection with the appearance of the things will agree with this theory. The person in some cases will even see parts or the whole of the Elder Brothers or Masters as they are called, who are believed to bring the things. Similar phenomena are obtained by spiritualists, theosophists, witch doctors, and by many other sects in
45 many different parts of the world, all of whom have different theories to account for the results.

COUNTERFÉSANCE

I might put the position again shortly. Man is now and always has been a perfect spiritual being in heaven. He is seen falsely in this world, this state of consciousness, as a material man. When this material misrepresentation what is called dies, its human or carnal mind passes into another state of consciousness, another material world, and the material body decays in this state of consciousness. When the so-called man wakes up to find himself in another material world, he has another material body, because his mind is not changed; it still is material, and he has to work out his salvation, purifying his so-called mind by turning in thought to God, which he continues to do.

When the material thing called a man has what is called died, and has passed on into another material state of consciousness, the real spiritual man does not leave heaven, for heaven is still here then, as much as it ever was. The real spiritual man is therefore seen again here, that is, in this state of consciousness or material world, as another material being, another cinematographic-picture man; only in this case he is seen again as a little child, which grows and grows, becoming more and more like the real man, until this new misrepresentation in its turn again dies, its place to be taken by another child. This goes on until the so-called end of the world. Each so-called man passes from one state of consciousness to the next, from one material world to another, until ultimately he has sufficiently purified his so-called mind to dematerialise. That is to say, he ultimately ceases his material dream existence, and appears to wake up and find himself in heaven; that is to say, to find that in reality instead of being a material man liable to sin, disease, and death, he is a perfect being in a perfect world, governed by a perfect God.[1]

There may be a hundred or more different states of consciousness, with a hundred or more different misrepresentations of your real self, all apparently struggling through various material worlds, and gradually improving. These worlds are all here, probably interpenetrating each other. When the final end of matter comes all these fictitious worlds cease to exist at the same moment, and all these so-called human beings, these misrepresentations of your real selfhood, appear to wake up to find themselves in the one spiritual world, the world of reality, and all of them appear to merge into the same perfect spiritual being, your real selfhood, of which they have been the misrepresentation in the different material worlds. In other words, all false sense disappears.

It will be seen from the above that, unlike reincarnation, the so-called ego does not pass on from world to world, and then ultimately return and be re-born as a little child into this material world, with a future dependent upon its past; but the spiritual man always has existed perfect, in a perfect state of consciousness, and the material misrepresentation passes on from world to world, gradually improving his so-called mind through the action of God, until he ceases his dream life and appears to wake up and find his true self.

[1] See Psalms 17, verse 15.

ON SOCIALISM

"Citizens, would ye be free? First of all, love God, love your neighbour, love one another, love the general welfare; and if ye have this love and union among ye, true liberty will be yours" (Savonarola).

5 There is another great class of thinkers called Socialists. This is a bad term, because its true meaning has been clouded by the action of those, wrongly called Socialists, who have departed from the spirit of true socialism. It has been said: "I believe in the Socialism that gives; I do not believe in the Socialism that takes." This may almost be taken as a 10 definition of true and false socialism.

We can all give help through our thoughts, especially those who are not hampered with the accumulation of wealth stored up in decaying structures by ignorant selfishness. "A recognition of the fact that the real *ego* in every man is Divine would be the golden key which would unlock the most 15 puzzling of the social problems of the age" [1] (Archdeacon Wilberforce).

The only true socialist is the spiritual being in heaven, where we have true communism, the communism of divine Love, essential for our common good.

Amongst the Socialists are thousands of splendid men and, doubtless, 20 women, earnest thinkers, who are devoting and in some cases sacrificing their lives in the attempted amelioration of the lot of their fellow-men. Many of these are called agnostics and even atheists, because they are too logical to accept the orthodox view of a God who allows and therefore legalises evil, if even He does not actually create it. Nor can they accept a 25 religion which offers no infallible remedy for, or even adequate relief from, the appalling misery and terrible injustice that confront us in every class of society throughout the world.

A good instance is Mr. Robert Blatchford, whose writings have had a very large circulation.[2] Mr. Blatchford does not deny the existence of God.

30 [1] *Mystic Immanence.*
[2] Since this was written Mr. Blatchford has come more to the front, owing to articles with regard to Germany. These articles, however accurate, can neither avert nor bring on war. Any result following upon such statements, is only apparently due to them. What is liable to happen, already exists as so-called 35 thoughts, which, as the Bible shows, are predestined to come into action at their appointed time, unless they are destroyed by right thinking. Our work is to destroy these thoughts and so protect mankind. Even the attempt to do this must result in partial, if not total, reversal of the lot of those poor unfortunates whose destiny it otherwise would be to fall under the mailed fist of Assyria. The events of 721 B.C. 40 will not again be repeated in full in its final repetition in the dream, as far as its disastrous results to Israel are concerned, for when "The Lord hath performed his whole work upon mount Zion and on Jerusalem [or a body of deep enough thinkers who know how to think rightly], I will punish the fruit of the stout heart of the king of Assyria, and the glory of his high looks. For he saith, By the strength of my hand 45 I have done it, and by my wisdom; . . . Therefore shall the Lord . . . under his glory . . . kindle a burning like the burning of a fire. And the light of Israel shall be for a fire, and his Holy One for a flame: and it shall burn and devour his thorns and his briers in one day." For "Israel . . . shall stay upon the Lord, the Holy One of Israel, in truth" (Isa. 10:12, 13, 16, 17, 20). In other words, the knowledge of the 50 truth that is here presented may result in the destruction of all the evil thoughts that would otherwise appear in the from of trouble to countries at war with each other, "the rod of mine anger" (Isa. 10:5). The Rev. R. Douglas thinks that the

He states that man is essentially good in himself, and is gradually evolving into a more perfect state of being. This, he believes, will be brought about by organising society on a co-operative material basis, thus putting an end, on the one hand to large accumulations of wealth amongst a few individuals, and on the other to the frightful suffering and poverty existing amongst 5 nearly one-fourth of the total population. Mr. Blatchford's objections to the Christian religion are summed up in this statement: "If God is responsible for man's existence, then God is responsible for man's acts." This is perfectly logical and absolutely true. We have now attained to the certain knowledge that God could not have made the material, sinful man 10 as we see him. God, the Principle and therefore source of all good, cannot make a mistake or create anything unfinished or imperfect, or be capable even of thinking of anything imperfect. The only logical deduction from this is, that the material, sinful man is unreal, or of man's invention, because he is neither made by God nor of God's world. 15

> "God's in His Heaven—
> All's right with the world !" (*Robert Browning*).

The sole responsibility for the acts of the sinful, mortal man, rests therefore upon the false concept called man's thoughts. The more closely we face this most uncomfortable question, the more certain do we become 20 of the fact that each man of us, besides being his own evil genius, is also jointly responsible with all mankind for all the evil apparent in the world !

Ignorance is now no longer a possible excuse for this terrible nightmare, and prejudice and apathy can maintain for a very little while longer 25 their unworthy, selfish, and most unfortunate standpoint, for "Knowledge is now no more a fountain sealed," and darkness is being rapidly and finally wiped out in the universal noon of infinite light.

Many Socialists are Determinists. These believe that man is a creature of material heredity and environment, that he has no free- 30 will, and is not responsible for his acts, good, bad, or indifferent. This also is perfectly true, until man learns how to think rightly, and so realises only the will of God. Every evil act brings its own punishment upon the perpetrator, every bit of good equally ensures its own reward, and the evil thinker, and therefore evil doer, must be continually punished until he 35 learns how to think rightly and ceases sinning. This right method of thinking can destroy any evil hereditary tendency, and lift one out of any evil environment. It is absolutely scientific and certain in its results.

It is evident that all our troubles can only come from what is called wrong thinking; regarding as real fact what is wholly material theorising. 40 Now Socialists, individual or collective, equally with all would-be reformers, have at hand a complete and perfect remedy. A union of

Germans are men of Judah, and that the Jews are chiefly Idumeans. This shows how difficult it is to follow the early developments of nations. The only method of doing this properly is to be inspirationally led, and then to check the resultant 45 information in the ordinary way. This was written in 1910. In 1913 I stated in my lectures that the minor troubles would start in June, 1914, and the major troubles in July, 1914.

religion and science has now dawned upon the world, which will not only lift them, but all their fellow-creatures, out of the quagmire in which they find themselves, into a present happiness hitherto undreamt of.

5 We now have a religion that is practical, which helps on every forward movement of the day, and not only does this, but gives each one the power, and immense happiness, of helping one's fellow-men out of any trouble, however seemingly bad.

ON WOMEN'S RIGHTS

Another branch of the socialistic movement is now before the public,[1]
10 namely, the endeavour being made by women to obtain their rights—an equal vote with men. Let me at once say that I am entirely with them in my desire for the real result for which they are sacrificing themselves. My first public speech, about thirty years ago, was made in favour of women's rights. Thinkers must be entirely at variance with them as regards the
15 means they adopt.

If you attend a meeting in favour of women's votes you are apt to find that the major portion of the time is taken up with complaints of the action of the Government, and the cruelty being meted out to women. Instead of dwelling on women's rights, they dwell on men's imagined wrongdoings.
20 This simply intensifies the thoughts appearing, and makes things seemingly worse. Remember this apparent action of human thoughts is merely seemingly caused by the temporary but universal consent to the present-day theories—which consent constitutes the only law—of evil action. Wrong views are the cause of the wrong doings, and intensify themselves
25 on the so-called mind of the people picturing them, and so hypnotise the victims, who consequently harm others, and therefore are harmed themselves. If suffragettes would only spend an hour a day for six weeks in learning how to think rightly, and would dwell on men's rights, the divine rights, of the real men—as already mentioned, I admit no essential
30 difference between men and women—the present agitation would soon be at an end. I believe that the result would be that women would then find themselves with votes at once, because true justice would be brought about, and the influence of true womanhood is always for good. The result of the suffragettes' working in the right way would certainly be to bring
35 about what is best. This is all that the most insistent could possibly desire.

If these social reformers had seen, as I have, over two thousand people howling, and then have seen the whole of the savage wrong thoughts disappear, and happiness come into the faces within a few seconds,
40 through one individual alone turning in thought to God, and realising the actual presence of God, divine Love, filling all space, they would never again try to meet brute beast with brute beast. Instead of fighting only for a detail in a local centre, they would find that they were a power, a divine power throughout the world.[2] This power would not be limited

45   [1] This was written in 1910.
    [2] "The Lord giveth the word: The women that publish the tidings are a great host" (Ps. 68:11, R.V.).

to one direction, but would be exerted in favour of every movement that comes into the panorama of human existence, for the amelioration of the conditions of the human race. This is a present possibility. Do not lose a moment. Begin now and prove the omnipotence and availability of God.[1]

Because it is a demonstrable fact that "woman is the highest species of man,"[2] and the clearest channel for the most powerful force acting on earth to-day, it is obvious that unless rightly directed, it is the most dangerous.

In this dawn of the so-called "mental" era, accompanied as it is by greater knowledge of ethereal phenomena, that removes all restraints of material limitations as easily as a butterfly leaves its chrysalis casket, giving to each one the power and authority to "be a law unto himself," it will be quickly found that it is the female lawgiver who has to be reckoned with in the near future.

- This discovery by the mass of what is well known already to the few, will not come in consequence of any possible parliamentary position of authority; but should that position accompany this inevitable discovery, where is to be found the school in which the woman of to-day can qualify for her high office?

I unhesitatingly affirm that the school of the great Principle of right thinking can alone fit her to use aright this tremendous and newly found responsibility, and it alone can teach man how to protect himself from a new danger, greater than he has ever faced before. This Principle alone can teach man how to duly appreciate and benefit by a greater help than he has yet found, the help of true womanhood in the attaining of a perfect understanding of the one Mind. The greatest, because most scientific, stateswoman in the world in our own times has proved that "One on God's side is a majority." And it may be added in elaboration of that great scientific declaration of independence that this ONE is the spiritual offspring of a perfect union of male and female qualities. This can only be seen abroad upon earth where love and unity demonstrate the intelligent recognition of the science of the equality of the sexes, bringing mutual co-operation in higher planes of action. Under such happy circumstances, where highest spiritual intuition and love, expressed by woman, and uplifted wisdom and strength, expressed by man, are found joined in mutual obedient worship of one God, then the harmonious manifestations and demonstrations of Truth and Love will prove that the earth is in deed and in truth filled with the knowledge of God, as the waters cover the sea. With male and female qualities united and co-operating in wise rule, there will be no longer any need for material laws of limitation, for "the government shall be upon" man's shoulder, and he shall be called "the Prince of Peace" (Isa. 9:6).

ON BUSINESS

"Keeping my mind in His holy presence, and recalling it as often as I found it wandered from Him . . . I made this my business, as much all the day long as at the appointed times of prayer: for at all times, every hour,

---

[1] Since this was written in 1910, many of the leaders of the woman's movement have learnt how to think rightly.

[2] *Unity of Good*, p. 51. Mary Baker Eddy.

*every minute, even in the height of my business, I drove away from my mind
everything that was capable of interrupting my thought of God"* (Brother
Lawrence, First Letter).

It has often been said that it is absolutely impossible to carry on business
5 on a high ethical plane. This is not true. Before we knew how to think
rightly it was difficult, as, by doing what was best for another, it was often
found that he took advantage of us, and we suffered. When a man knows
how to think rightly he can safely put his fellow-man's interests before his
own. This does not mean that unscrupulous individuals will not sometimes
10 take advantage of us, but this they can only do if our knowledge of truth
is too limited. Nevertheless, however much such men may momentarily
take advantage of us, it will be found that in the long run we do not suffer,
but that they pay the penalty for their ignorance of the laws of good.[1] You
will find that on thinking a man is going to take an unfair advantage of
15 you, he will respond more or less to this hypnotic thought, and if this
wrong thinking be continued, you will soon have to be on your guard.
Being on guard means systematically guarding your own thoughts, and
regularly each day devoting a few minutes to treatment for the difficulty.
If really thinking rightly, no one can possibly take advantage of you.

20 Putting another's interests before our own does not mean always
sacrificing our own interests to his. Our first consideration must always
be to *act* in strict accordance with our highest understanding of God's
requirement of us. This demand met, Principle will decide as to how far it
is for our client's best interests that his desires should be fulfilled. Working
25 from this individual standpoint of persistent right thinking and its correlative just action, it will be found that in whatever form results may appear,
they will include the greatest good for the greatest number.

It is becoming common knowledge now amongst thinkers that to succeed in business, one must not, as was previously thought, take every
30 advantage of others where possible, but, on the contrary, one must earn
a reputation for absolutely fair and even generous dealing. This alone will
not enable a man to succeed. He must be businesslike, accurate, and
prompt in his dealings. This will follow if the thoughts are right. On the
other hand, should he constantly fear, for instance, that a merchant will
35 not supply goods to him in the time promised, he will probably find that
such accentuation of wrong thoughts will bring about the failure, and result
in a repetition of the same delay in his dealings with his own clients.
Hitherto we have thought that such a mistake was not our fault. In future,
should this take place, we shall know that it is solely our ignorance of
40 truth or incapacity to treat that is to blame.

As the false concept of matter changes, the details of business and
business methods will change. Material means for bringing about desired
results will be dropped, and a true mental method adopted, namely, the
realisation of truth.

45 In the past the fundamental principle of business has been entirely

[1] The commercial value of the Golden Rule is beginning to be recognised. In
the January, 1914, issue of the *Organiser*, a practical magazine for business men,
appears the following: " 'The Golden Rule' is truth; in the hands of intelligent
people, and joined with efficiency, it actually pays dividends."

misunderstood by nearly all. The principle upon which it has been based has been to gain good for ourselves, and incidentally, as an unfortunate necessity, to give something in exchange to others. This has to be inverted. A higher basis is thus won. The true principle of business is to give of the best to others as the necessity, while incidentally receiving in return.[1] Then we shall receive abundance with but little trouble. This is no chimerical dream, but is the natural result to the man who follows truly scientific methods. The man receiving most has the most to confer on others.

We must be willing to lay down all for truth in business as well as in all other paths of human experience. We must gradually "lay down" all thinking of the future, consideration of ways and means, thoughts of antagonistic people, all fear, anxiety, and worry, and ultimately all the old material means. We must adopt the higher and more scientific methods that progress will in any case eventually demand. Such as are willing to thus adopt Christian and scientific methods of business will of necessity be led by Principle into the best and most successful enterprises during the forth-coming period of rapid advancement that accompanies the final stages of all exchange of "goods."

One of the chief results accruing from practical right thinking is the complete protection of the individual from so-called mental science, which even to-day is unwittingly practised on a large scale. A client to whom the evil effects were recently pointed out replied that this made clear to him what had made him, on the previous day, buy a cargo of salt for which he had not the slightest use. It has already been shown how this fatal method of obtaining an apparently temporary advantage—though really disadvantage—is even now being openly taught and practised. It is time that mankind learned the scientific and unfailing method of pro-tection, the truth that makes man free from all evils.

We have to remain in business, or in such state of life as the "second coming of Christ" finds us in, until Principle clearly leads us out. The sooner this takes place the better. Gautama Buddha truly said: "I say unto thee, remain in thy station of life, apply thyself with diligence to thy enterprises. It is not life and wealth and power that enslave men, but the cleaving to life and wealth and power."

THE DIFFERENT WAYS OF LOOKING AT LIFE

It is comparatively easy to understand reality, called heaven, because scientifically we know that there can be only one cause; that cause must be good; we can never know cause, it can only be known by its manifesta-tion; and, as the manifestation of cause must partake of the nature of the cause, its manifestation must be good. This cause and its manifestation is spoken of by the religious world as God and heaven. The metaphysician speaks of it as Mind and its ideas.

If there is only one cause and its manifestation, both of which are good, whence this terrible evil that appears so very real to us? What is the cause, if any, of all this hideous misery around us? When we come to try and solve this puzzle, one of the difficulties is that each of the three great schools,

[1] See Matthew 10, verse 8; Proverbs 11, verse 24.

science, religion, and metaphysics, working along their own lines of thought, have found certain results which they attribute to something to which they give a different name; whereas all these results are due to the same thing. The scientific man speaks of the ether, the religious man
5 speaks of the devil, the modern metaphysician of mortal mind, the philosopher speaks of phenomena, and the up-to-date psychologist speaks of the unconscious or sub-conscious mind, the subliminal self, etc., he has a dozen names. All these are different names for the same thing.

There is only one statement that is true about the material world, and
10 that has now been absolutely proved; namely, that it is a non-reality. That means that it has no permanence, it is not made by God. At most it is a horrible dream, but without a dreamer.

When you come to explain how best to get out of the difficulties, that is to say, how to destroy matter and its resultant evil, so that the good appears
15 more manifest, there are four ways in which the material world can be expressed.

From the Religious Point of View.—Looked at from a religious point of view it may be said that we are tempted into all our troubles not by a person, but by impersonal evil, alias the evil thoughts that
20 unfortunately are always more or less attacking us, until we learn how to pray rightly and so protect ourselves. You can look upon evil as something brought about by wrong thinking, and you can look upon the action of God as destroying evil when man prays. The religious world looks upon evil as real. If it were real it could not be destroyed by God, because if it
25 be real it was made by God, and God cannot destroy anything that He made, as God "created all things, that they might have their being" (Wisdom of Solomon 1:14). The only devil or evil are the evil thoughts, and the only hell the mental state and experiences resulting therefrom.

If God made disease, or uses it as a method of punishing us, thereby
30 bringing us as it is called nearer to Him, we have no right to take drugs to get well. The more diseased we are the better. The ordinary religious man not only tries hard to prevent God punishing him but says that a good man at death reaches heaven. Nevertheless, nearly all good men do their very best to try and prevent God taking them into heaven, preferring to
35 remain in this hell of a material world. How full of illogical nonsense we are!

From the Metaphysical Point of View.—From a metaphysical point of view, things are just as we think. This is the covenant stated by Moses: if you think good—if you have only one God, good—you will get good.
40 So, if you think evil you will get evil. But when you want to bring about so-called good you must not think lies, and try to think that you are well when you are ill. You must not even think of the good as seen around us, as there is no real good in the material world. All the good is part of heaven, and matter merely hides it from us. Jesus himself said: "*Why callest thou*
45 *me good? There is none good but one, that is God*" (Matt. 19:17). You have to think of the absolute good. You have to think of an ideal perfect world, the highest good that you can possibly imagine, namely, to think of what has been called God and heaven. This is a mental world, the world of

reality, in which all is perfect because governed by a perfect God. The Apostle John speaks of knowing "he aletheia," which means "the absolute truth" as opposed to "aletheia" "the relative truth" or "so-called truth" of the material world.

From the Scientific Point of View.—The best way of expressing 5 the material world from a scientific point of view, is that thought is a high tension current right above the Marconi wave, and thought after thought sweeps across the mind at the rate of about twenty miles an hour, ringing out sweet tones or jangling its discordant notes. Every sin and every disease has what may be called its own cell in the subconscious mind. If the anger 10 cell is clean a million people could not hypnotise you to be angry. If on the contrary there are small electrical particles on the cell, these will damp down the cell as pitch does a tuning-fork, so that when the angry thought passes over the man's mind it will vibrate with the lower vibration of anger and the man will be angry whether he wishes it or not. The human 15 mind may be looked upon as an electrical transmitter, and bad thoughts as low vibrations, so-called good thoughts as high vibrations.

When a man knows how to think rightly, the following are the results: (a) By the denial, the evil thoughts attacking are destroyed and temporary relief obtained.   (b) By the affirmation, the action of God can be utilised 20 to completely purify any particular cell in the subconscious mind—i.e., to short-circuit the electrical particles upon it—so that the cell will never again vibrate with that particular class of wrong thought.

The Most Accurate View—Cinematographic Pictures.—This way of looking at the material world is the most accurate, as in it there 25 is the least pretence of any life, power, or reality in matter. The life of the material universe may be said to consist of a succession of groups of cinematographic pictures, which we may call a succession of different periods, each period consisting of a group of these fleeting dream pictures, and each group extending over a gradually diminishing length of time.   30

Successive Periods of History.—These cinematographic pictures are the mist that went up from the earth (Gen. 2:6), and they hide the beauties of heaven from us. As time goes on these pictures pass in review before us, each group of pictures being a repetition of the same events, false views of the real world, seen as what is called successive periods of history, and 35 recognised by students of the past. Whilst these periods are more or less different, they coincide in their main features, a steady improvement for the better in the cinematographic pictures taking place as time goes on, and each period steadily reducing in length of time.

For instance, let us take, merely arbitrarily, the first period as extending 40 from the apparent first start of the lines of force until the time they begin to roll up into electrons. This period probably extended over millions of millions of years. Then let us take the second period, as lasting from the end of the first period until the electrons commenced to mass together and form aqueous vapour, say, hundreds of thousands of millions of years. 45 The third period might be taken from the formation of this aqueous vapour up to the time when it began to revolve and to break off into separate portions, ultimately contracting and forming the separate worlds.

This may be said to last for tens of thousands of millions of years. The fourth period might extend until the production of the lowest form of mineral life, say, thousands of millions of years; and the fifth from the lowest form of mineral life, on the one hand, to the highest form of
5 mineral and lowest form of vegetable life on the other, say, hundreds of millions of years. As quoted by Professor Winchell,[1] Reade estimates 500,[2] and Lyell 240 million years since sedimentation started in Europe. Houghton puts the sedimentary age at 11,700,000, Professor Winchell at 37 million years.[3] The sixth period let us take as extending from the
10 commencement of vegetable life until animal life became apparent, say, millions of years. The seventh, the evolution of animal life up to the lowest form of distinct human life, say, hundreds of thousands of years. The eighth, from that time until now, say, many tens of thousands of years. Anthropology gives man fully 100,000 years.
15   Now, in the same manner, let us take as the last period but two the period from A.D. 1866, the date shown in the Bible as that of the second coming of Christ, to December 3, 1910, the date shown of the loosing of the devil; the last period but one from that date to December 3, 1917. The final period is unknown. I used to think that it would be only forty-
20 five hours, but this turned out to be wrong. There is nothing in the Bible to show its length.
    The above periods are purely arbitrary, but give an idea of how they keep on steadily reducing in length, as so-called time continues. Men differ almost incredibly about the length of the different periods. For
25 instance, Belt estimates that 20,000 years have elapsed since the glacial period. Hume 80,000, and Croll 240,000. Yet men have existed in more southern regions, Professor Winchell says, "in times remotely pre-glacial."
    Most people have seen the transformation scene at a pantomime. At first all is darkness and gloom on the stage. This corresponds to the period
30 when the lines of force alone were apparent, the nearest of the veils hiding heaven from us. Then one by one the intervening gauze curtains are lifted, and gradually the light from the stage behind pierces through, until we can even see dimly the appearance of something moving behind, corresponding, let us say, to the evolution of the animals. Then even the colours
35 appear, corresponding to the appearance of man; and, finally, when the last veil has lifted, we see the full beauty of the transformation scene.
    The So-called Evolution of the Material World.—Let us imagine that myriads of years ago we were standing looking at heaven, and in front of us were these numberless veils—these material cinematographic films of
40 gradually shortening lengths, each one behind the other—hiding the perfect world from us. The nearest to us would be the first period I have mentioned, and this, consisting solely of lines of force, would extend out a tremendous distance right and left, corresponding to vast æons of time. The second, which would not extend quite so far, would contain the
45 electrons, the third only aqueous vapour, and so on. As these films receded from us their length would gradually reduce, corresponding to

[1] *World Life*, p. 179.
[2] Address, Liverpool Geological Society, 1876.
[3] *World Life*, p. 367.

the reduced period of time, until the last one of all would be of a length representing only the final hours.

Whilst at first we were looking at heaven through all these many different veils, each one being down, heaven to us would be what is spoken of in the second verse of Genesis as "without form and void," as it would 5 only appear as lines of force, one impossible to distinguish from the other. When this was lifted, first the electrons would appear as "darkness," and then would be seen the aqueous vapour. These two changes could be spoken of by the words that follow: "and darkness was upon the face of the deep."   10

Intellectual Meaning of the First Chapter of Genesis.—Every passage from the Bible has three meanings—the spiritual, the material, and the intellectual. The spiritual meaning of the first chapter of Genesis is an inadequate description of reality, called heaven. The material rendering describes how the writer thought the material world was formed. The 15 third, or intellectual meaning, is a detailed description of the gradual lifting of these veils—namely, the evolution of the world from the darkness that "was upon the face of the deep," ending with the completion of the action of God in destroying all evil when "he rested on the seventh day from all his work which he had made."   20

As time went on, the film containing only the lines of force may be said to be lifted up, and we could then see heaven as something a little more defined—namely, as electrons. Then the lengths of films would go on lifting, or we may call it rolling up from the side, and we would see heaven as aqueous vapour, and later as something definite—namely, as mineral 25 life; then we would see slight movements in the form of the lowest vegetable life, and later on the highest vegetable life or earliest animal life, as they are practically the same. Later, during the mammoth age, instead of seeing the spiritual beings in heaven, in a glorious spiritual universe, we would see them as gigantic, terrible animals and horrible flying reptiles 30 —the origin of dragons—walking about, preying upon each other in a dreary, swamp-like world. Later man seems to have been seen as half human being and half animal, about twelve feet in height, one preying on another, as appears to have been the case in Lemuria, the cinematographic pictures of which have been seen by psychometrists. This is confirmed by 35 the old Irish legends of the Fomorachs, monsters in size, and hideous in shape, many footless and handless, whilst others had the heads of animals. Hence no doubt the many tales of Satyrs, Centaurs, etc., which abound in ancient literature. Then film after film would pass, and we would see everything more and more like the reality, until we came to that indicated 40 in the third, fourth, and fifth verses in Genesis, namely, conscience evolved in man, and he recognised the difference between the good, called "light," and the evil, called "night." Then, as the rolling up of the films continued, the human beings appear to have more wisdom, more activity, greater love. In time the meaning of the sixth verse became evident, and "the 45 firmament divided the waters," namely, man began to obtain spiritual understanding. As he gained the understanding of the firmament, called heaven, mentioned in the eighth verse, he began to understand what prayer was, and the eleventh and twelfth verses show how he began to obtain the results of prayer. So the view of heaven steadily improved, or, rather, ceased to be quite so bad, not so hidden, until we came to the portion of the film that represented the eighteenth century. In front of us, hiding heaven, two hundred years ago, appeared the pictures of ordinary 5 human beings, seen as cruel, delighting in bear-baiting, cock-fighting, etc.

Ultimately, as shown in verse sixteen, man gained a knowledge of the "two great lights; the greater light to rule the day," namely, the affirmation, which purifies and improves the human mind, so bringing more light to us; "and the lesser light to rule the night," the denial, which 10 destroys the night, namely, the darkness or evil. Verse seventeen shows these were set "in the firmament of the heaven to give light upon the earth," namely, to improve our spiritual understanding, and to enable us, as shown in verse eighteen, "to divide the light from the darkness," the real good of heaven from the evil and so-called good of the material world. 15 Then came the "winged fowl," as mentioned in verse twenty-one, namely, the uplifted thoughts, "holy thoughts winged with Love."

As the films continue to roll up, everything seen would steadily improve, until comparatively few films veiled heaven, as at present, when we see human beings, the majority of whom are unselfish towards their fellow-men, 20 if they can be so without prejudicing themselves. No longer is there only slimy vegetation, rank grass, and stagnant pools, but luxuriant trees, beautiful grasses, and lovely flowers; even the animal life is seen more varied, more graceful, more docile and useful to humanity. This is typified in verses twenty-four and twenty-five, where "God made the beast of the 25 earth after his kind, and cattle after their kind, and every thing that creepeth upon the earth after his kind: and God saw that it was good."

In verses twenty-six to twenty-eight we read the description of man in the image and likeness of God, who had "dominion over . . . every living thing that moveth upon the earth." This period is now coming all 30 over the world; man is beginning to recognise that he is divine, the power of God, with infinite power to destroy evil of every kind.

Finally, the last of all the veils, the one representing the final period, with rejoicing will pass away, and, freed from the mist of materiality, the mist that "went up . . . from the earth," we will see heaven with all its 35 beauties, glorious ideas of God, from the least to the greatest, the greatest being man, God's consciousness. In verse thirty-one we read: "God saw everything that he had made, and, behold, it was very good"; and in chapter two, verses two and three: "on the seventh day God ended his work. . . . And God blessed the seventh day, and sanctified it: because 40 that in it he had rested from all his work." This means that the work of destroying evil, these cinematographic pictures, is ended. The veils are all lifted, and heaven, as it really is, appears to open to the human consciousness, with the disappearance for ever of all matter, and its inevitable accompaniments—sin, disease, worries, troubles, and limitations. Then 45 all men wake up to find themselves perfect beings in a perfect world, governed by a perfect God. As Paul and John show us, man will be found to be "in Christ." This does not mean in the man Jesus, but having the Christ consciousness, God's consciousness, being the highest manifestation of God, by means of which God thinks and works.

How to Check Prophecies of the Future.—As each of these separate portions of the cinematographic film represents the same thing—namely, heaven—seen a little differently, the portion of each film through which we are looking at any one given time should have a similarity. It will be found that this is so. If you look along the films at the commencement of 5 the different periods, you find them all more or less showing the same sort of thing in a gradually improving condition as the veils are lifted. Looking along the ends of the film you see that each of the ends also shows the same kind of event. "Declaring the end from the beginning, and from ancient times the things that are not yet done" (Isa. 46:10), we can gain accurate 10 knowledge of the future, or check it when gained by what is called thought-reading, namely, seeing in advance the cinematographic pictures, or by reading Bible or other prophecies.

Confirmatory Evidence.—Pythagoras, in the fifth century B.C., one of the most wonderful men of ancient times, is said to have taught that the same 15 events recur again and again in regular cycles.

The German geologist, Edward Suess, in *Das Antlitz der Erde*, speaks of "a great and yet unknown rhythm in the evolution of living beings— a rhythm dependent on periodic changes in the inorganic environment." Another instance "is offered us by M. Lichtenberger in his study of 20 Nietzsche. One of the famous German philosopher's most famous theories, the one that he thought must paralyse the world, was the theory of the eternal return. . . . Briefly, it is that everything which happens must have happened in exactly the same way any number of times before, and he thought, will go on happening at intervals for ever." 25

The theosophists, in reading the "Akashic Records," as they call these cinematographic pictures of the past, have found that over and over again a somewhat similar chain of events occurs. Mrs. Besant speaks of these successive periods as "recurrent cycles in history," and states that rein-carnation "affords the only sufficient explanation." Now we understand 30 what they really are, and why reincarnation is as incorrect as the theory that at death we go either to heaven or to hell.

Gradually Improving Human Presentations of the Christ.—Not only do the beginnings and the ends of the films show the same kind of event, but, looking at any portion of the cinematographic pictures, you see right 35 through on each successive film also the same sort of thing. This is why we find in the Bible one man after another seen as successive dream pictures —types of someone else to follow. Abraham, Joseph, Joshua, Jeremiah, and others, have been pointed out by Bible commentators as earlier types of the spiritual being that was later materially seen as Jesus of Nazareth, 40 the highest human conception of a spiritual being possible; but, not having the necessary key, they were unable to follow the idea to its logical conclusion. Looking back, we find that the characters and groupings of events that stand out in the past successive ages of history, prefigure in an extraordinary way the characters and groupings of the succeeding ages. 45 In other words, "history repeats itself."

The earliest end of a film that I can form any idea of is the destruction of the continent of Lemuria, of which but little is known; but no doubt there were people saved from Lemuria in the way in which Noah, I

believe, was saved from the final destruction of Atlantis, when he crossed
the water in his vessel and landed on what is to-day the main continent.
This is the earliest of the commencement of the films of which there seems
to be any definite knowledge.

5	*The Commencement of Each Period an Escape from Evil.*—Some half-a-
dozen men have been now working for some time at the "Akashic Records"
—these cinematographic pictures. They tell us that there were two previous
submergences of great portions of the continent of Atlantis, the northern
portion of which reached right up to the coast of Ireland, and was the first
10 to be submerged. It is interesting, if it turns out to be the case, that Cessair,
who the early Monkish analysts said was the grand-daughter of Noah, and
lived in Ireland, arrived at the time of the final submergence of Atlantis.

Genesis 10, verse 5, gives details of the grandsons of Noah, and says:
"By these were the isles of the Gentiles divided in their lands." Smith's
15 Bible dictionary shows that the phrase "the isles of the Gentiles" would be
more correctly spoken of as the "far distant western isles." It would be
interesting, but not surprising, if it turned out that the British Isles were
divided, as stated, among the grandchildren of Noah. This would explain
why Ireland seems to have been so advanced in religious thought in early
20 days, and would clear up some of the difficult references in ancient Irish
history.

Now, if you look along the commencement of these cinematographic
films, you will recognise many known events in history, where, as in the
case of Noah, members of the human race have left behind difficulties and
25 destruction, and have crossed the water to make a fresh start. After Noah,
there was the destruction of Babel, when the children of men were scattered
abroad. Then Abraham left Haran, crossing the river into Canaan. Later,
Dan left Egypt, and crossed the water into Greece, founding, I believe,
the race of Grecian heroes. Again, we get Jacob fleeing back to Haran to
30 Laban, Rebekah's brother. A little later what we see on the film is more
striking still, as we see the Israelites leaving Egypt, and crossing the Red
Sea. Further on we see the ten tribes of Israel fleeing out of Media from
the destruction of Nineveh, when "the most High then shewed signs for
them, and held still the flood, till they were passed over." This reference
35 is to the upper waters of the River Euphrates, which we are told in II
Esdras 13, verse 44, divided to let them pass into Southern Russia. This
was referred to by Zechariah as follows: "all the deeps of the river shall
dry up: and the pride of Assyria shall be brought down" (Zech. 10:11).

Then, again, we see the flight of Joseph and Mary with Jesus into
40 Egypt, and later the flight of the Benjamites from the destruction of
Jerusalem, again crossing water. Not long after we see three of the tribes
of Israel, known then as the Ostrogoths, crossing the Danube and commencing their invasion of Roman territory, and ultimately capturing Rome.
We see the other seven tribes, under the name of the "Angles," crossing
45 the sea and arriving in England, dividing it into seven portions, one for
each tribe, and founding the Angleish, or English race. If you look at
the blessings of Moses on the twelve tribes, you will find that the
blessings on the seven tribes referred to are descriptions of the seven
portions into which England was then divided. These seven tribes you

will find are joined later by the three tribes, whose name had become changed from Ostrogoths to Normans, again crossing water, in the form of the English Channel, and entering the promised land.

Again in the present days will this be repeated, and the waters of death will be dried up until advancing man awakens to find himself already in the holy land—God's world, "for the first heaven and the first earth were passed away; and there was no more sea" (Rev. 21:1).

The Final Film.—In the final film, whatever its length, will be again repeated the start and the finish, the start being the general change of thought from a material to a spiritual basis, and the finish being the final destruction of all matter, and therefore of all evil, everything that hides heaven, when "God shall wipe away all tears from their eyes; and there shall be no more death, neither sorrow, nor crying, neither shall there be any more pain: for the former things are passed away" (Rev. 21:4).

"For, behold, I create new heavens and a new earth: and the former shall not be remembered, nor come into mind . . . and the voice of weeping shall be no more heard" (Isa. 65:17, 19).

FORESHADOWINGS OF HEAVEN

The Radiation of God's Ideas.—God's ideas never come to us singly in reality, and even in the material world a rose is apparently a combination of parts. Spiritual ideas always come to us as combinations of wondrous beauty, which we group together into further glorious combinations. These radiate out from us into infinity, giving infinite spiritual beings happiness. Now, in heaven, God, the Principle of good, being essentially ever active, has been for ever creating these perfect combinations through man, yet no combination can exist in Mind without some part of consciousness, some spiritual individuality, being conscious of it. How can this be so, when one spiritual being in the reality can no more be separately conscious of more than one group of ideas at a time than this material counterfeit? The answer can only be this. On receiving a group of ideas a man reflects it, and it is reflected from one to another until it comes to one who, needing it for building up a perfect combination, groups it together with other groups of ideas and it forms a part of a new and larger combination. These combinations again are sometimes subdivided up into their component parts.[1] Now this has been going on for ever, and thus these groups of ideas, which cannot increase or diminish in number, being infinite, increase or diminish in respect of the number of ideas of which each is individually composed. The quality of ideas of which they are composed is always infinite, giving infinite happiness.[2] By man passing them on the ideas are circulated in Mind.

[1] "This Mind forms ideas, its own images, subdivides and radiates their borrowed light, intelligence, and so explains the Scripture phrase, 'whose seed is in itself.' Thus God's ideas 'multiply and replenish the earth.' The divine Mind supports the sublimity, magnitude, and infinitude of spiritual creation" (*Science and Health*, p. 511, Mary Baker Eddy).

[2] "God expresses in man the infinite idea for ever developing itself, broadening and rising higher and higher from a boundless basis" (*Ibid.*, p. 258).

Heaven is a world of four dimensions, of which we see three, seeing it therefore all wrongly.[1] The fourth dimension is infinity, which cancels the other three, as there are no limitations of space in Mind.

Man has existed for an infinite time, and will exist for ever, as part of God's consciousness; to him have come an infinite number of perfect ideas; he has grouped these ideas into an infinite number of glorious combinations—to express it materially, has composed an infinite number of sonatas, an infinite number of poems, etc.—he has been conscious of an infinite number of spiritual worlds; he has known an infinite number of spiritual beings in the past, and will have the joy of becoming acquainted with an infinite number of spiritual worlds in the future.

Man is made in the image and likeness of God, therefore he reflects infinite Love, infinite Life, infinite Truth, infinite wisdom, knowledge, beauty, joy, etc. The only limitation, if it can be called a limitation, is, that he can never know the whole of God, because the ideas of God are infinite, continually unfolding to him, idea after idea coming into his consciousness, this constituting man's eternal life.

When first I realised that man grouped together the ideas of God, and reflected them with infinite power, the idea followed immediately that this was the action of God as the Word or Logos or Æon. "In the beginning was the Word. . . . All things were made by him" (John. 1:1, 3). Still praying, realising God as Truth, I was led to turn up the meaning of "Æon" in Webster's Dictionary, and found that it was defined as "a certain substantial power of Divine nature emanating from the Superior Deity and performing various functions in the creation and government of the universe." This is another illustration of the practical way in which knowledge is obtainable when one knows the scientific method of praying in the way the Master taught.

I since find that Archdeacon Wilberforce in *Mystic Immanence* has written: "The Logos is the quality of Originating Mind that forms, upholds, sustains all that is. 'Without the Logos was not anything made that was made. . . .' The Logos is the dominating power in the soul of man. It has always been so. The early Aryans, 1700 B.C., knew it, but generations of wrong thinking have darkened human minds to their Divine origin as possessors of the 'Logos Emphutos.'"

Spiritual Reality of Food.—The material misrepresentation of these ideas that come to us to be grouped together is the food that the material man eats, and the spiritual reality of the act of taking food is the taking in of ideas with the object of grouping them together in a new combination. The real plates and cups are therefore the spiritual man's power of mentally holding a certain number of ideas, whilst additional ideas are coming to him to be grouped together into a new and beautiful combination. The knowledge of the reality of food is of value in the treatment of troubles arising from imperfect working of the internal organs.

God as Life causes us to receive the ideas, God as Truth enables us to understand the ideas, and God as Love causes us to re-present them. It is Life that settles the order in which the ideas come to us, and there-

[1] See Ephesians 3, verses 17, 18, and Revelation 21, verse 16.

fore Life enables us to understand them. Soul gives the spiritual man
wisdom and intelligence and enables him to understand the ideas.[1]

Of Animals.—These symbolise qualities of the spiritual man, the consciousness of good, God's consciousness; for instance, the lion, moral
courage; the worm, tireless patience; the serpent, wisdom; the dog,
fidelity; the cat, watchfulness; the lamb, innocence.

This is why we have the appearance of evolution in the material world.
The so-called ancestors of the material man were animals. Binet, in the
Physical Life of Micro-Organisms, maintains that infusoria exhibit memory,
volition, surprise, fear, and the germinal properties of human intelligence. 10
The counterfeit material animal is much closer to the counterfeit material
man than most people think. Maudesley says: "There is not a single
mental quality which man possesses, even to his moral feeling, that we do
not find the germ is more or less fully displayed in animals. Memory,
attention, foresight of ends, courage, anger, distress, envy, revenge, and 15
love of kind." [2]

There is no actual line of demarcation between animal and vegetable
life, and that between human beings and so-called animals is steadily
fading away. As a matter of fact, there is no more life, intelligence, or
wisdom in the material human being than in the material animal. They are 20
both cinematographic pictures, hiding the real man and real animal from
us.

The question has been asked as to what happens to animals at death,
and whether animals exist in heaven. Heaven being a world of four
dimensions, of which we see three, there must be a spiritual reality of 25
everything we see, from a human being down to a grain of dust. As the
material animals manifest Life, that Life cannot die, because it *is* Life, or
God. At so-called death, therefore, the animals merely pass on into the
next state of material consciousness, as do human beings, where they are
seen again, practically as they are seen here. 30

What is the spiritual reality of an animal? The only thing that I know
definitely is that it is a perfect combination of God's ideas. Whether what
we see as an animal is really a spiritual being seen in a limited way, or
whether it is a lesser combination of ideas, I cannot tell.

At one time the whole of the spiritual beings in heaven were seen as 35
animals, that is to say, the mist of matter was so thick, and heaven was so
densely hidden from us, that all that could be seen was a limited number
of the good qualities of the spiritual beings. Some of them were even seen
as ferocious animals feeding on each other.

From this one might infer that what you see as your dog is really a 40
spiritual being. The recent wonderful discoveries with regard to the
capacities of animals is an argument in favour of this view.

The difficulty in looking on the animals around us as spiritual beings
seen falsely is that theoretically, if this is so, no dividing line can be
drawn, and all the smaller animals—of which there are incalculable 45

---

[1] "Life is the law of Soul, even the law of the spirit of Truth" (*Science and
Health*, p. 427. Mary Baker Eddy). Life settles the order in which the ideas come to
man, and therefore is the law that causes these ideas to be understood.
[2] *Philosophy of the Unconscious*, Vol. III.

13

numbers—would also be spiritual beings. This difficulty is not insuperable, because the real spiritual earth is a mental world, and has no limits of space; but following this line of argument, every tree is also a spiritual being, because we know that at one time the spiritual beings in heaven
5 were seen only as vegetables. Then, if you go back far enough in human sense—so thick was the mist of matter hiding heaven from us—your spiritual self was seen as a rock. Follow the line of argument still further, and we must admit that every stone is really a spiritual being seen falsely. The logical conclusion of these sequences is that every-
10 thing must be a spiritual being seen materially. This, to a certain extent, may be looked upon as possible, because all the infinite ideas in heaven together are part of man specifically, *alias* all the spiritual beings in heaven. Man is the activity or movement of these ideas, and this activity is insepar-able from the ideas.
15 Every idea, it seems to me, must reflect the whole of God, namely, infinite Love, Life, Truth, Mind, Spirit, Soul, and all the other aspects of God, because "*God saw every thing that he had made, and behold it was very good*" (Gen. 1:31). Can everything be "*very good*" if it does not mani-fest every quality of good? Every manifestation must also partake of the
20 nature of its cause, Life, Love, Truth, and each of the other aspects of God cannot be split up into fragments, and therefore each idea must reflect the whole of infinite Life, the whole of infinite Love, etc., almost as each drop of water reflects the whole of the sun, or whatever is opposite to it. Each idea is therefore perfect and complete in itself, and the infinite
25 variety in our Father's glorious world consists of the infinite combinations of these perfect ideas which themselves are infinite in number.
Each man consists of an infinite sequence of combinations of these ideas which have been continually unfolding to him, and ever will unfold with infinite variety, and man specifically, or all the spiritual beings in
30 heaven, consists of all the ideas combined together in infinite sequences of these ideas, each sequence consisting of infinite combinations of these ideas.
The question now arises: What are the details of the material universe which we see around us, some of which are seen in the form of animals? From what we first stated, it will be seen that all the ideas are perfect and
35 therefore equal in quality; for this reason the difference between the various details must be a question of number or quantity. An animal, for instance, may be:—
(1) A sequence of combinations of ideas—not an infinite sequence of combinations, as man is, but a sequence of a definite number of combina-
40 tions.
(2) An infinite sequence of combinations, each combination being of a lesser number of ideas than those of which man consists, combined together. This is not likely.
(3) Simply a combination of ideas, instead of a sequence of combinations.
45 In the material world, to sense, plants feed upon minerals, animals feed upon plants and minerals, and man feeds upon all three.
It is quite possible that each particle of mineral life we see around us consists simply of a combination of ideas. A combination of these com-binations of ideas may appear as what we call plants. (It may be a sequence

of these combinations.) An animal may be a sequence of a definite number of plants, that is, of combinations (or sequences of combinations) of ideas, and man may be an infinite sequence of animals, that is, of sequences of combinations of ideas.

At present, in treating for animals, probably the best plan would be to 5 treat for them as if they were lesser ideas of God; this is the way in which I have treated in the past, and it has been successful. When this is the case, I always keep to the method of working until I find something which I can prove to be better.

As in the case of human beings, it is important to work for the moral 10 qualities of an animal, and it will often be found that the physical healing takes place just in proportion to the amelioration of the moral qualities.

Similarly every so-called inanimate thing has its spiritual reality: oil— gladness; perfume—gratitude; wine—understanding.

Other Spiritual Realities.[1]—"*Do not let us imagine that existence* 15 *hereafter will be something so wholly remote and different that we cannot learn by the testimony of experience here*" [2] (Sir Oliver Lodge).

Let it be quite understood that to heal well it is not necessary to have this knowledge of spiritual realities; but, the greater the knowledge of the world of reality and the more accurate the knowledge of its details, the 20 easier it is to heal. In any case, this tends to greater activity of thought and a better elimination of thoughts of materiality. "As material knowledge diminishes and spiritual understanding increases, real objects will be appre- hended mentally instead of materially" (*Science and Health*, p. 96, Mary Baker Eddy). 25

Given the main lines it is comparatively easy to find out the spiritual reality of most things. Some, however, are more difficult, and have only been obtained through specific treatment, such as the spiritual reality of rain, which is the vivifying action of God on man, enabling him to be conscious of multifarious ideas. If you add the words, "and to hold the 30 ideas," then you have the reality of snow. The reality of grass is the power of being conscious of the beauty of every idea in a combination. The hair is the capacity to receive ideas from any direction. We are covered with hairs, and every hair is an embryo eye.

Almost the only seeming difficulty was to find the spiritual reality of 35 the shoulder. On turning up in the Concordance to the Bible all the references to the word "shoulder," it became clear that the shoulder is the loving support which enables man to use "the arm," that is, "the power of reflecting or passing on the ideas of God." Immediately, as usually happens, came the opportunity of proving the value of the knowledge. A 40 Christian Scientist who, for two years, had suffered with her shoulder, and who had had a good deal of treatment, asked for any idea that would be of use. The spiritual reality of the shoulder was then explained, and the con- versation, which was practically an audible treatment, ended with the following statement: "The loving support that enables you to utilise the 45

---

[1] EDITOR'S NOTE: The author of *Life Understood* has dealt in fuller detail with this subject of spiritual realities in his book, *Treatment, or Healing by True Prayer*.

[2] "Christian Revelation from a Scientific Point of View." Address delivered before the National Free Church Council, Portsmouth, March 9, 1911.

power of reflecting God's ideas never can be injured, because it is God's loving support." There was never any further trouble, and thus the truth of the statement was demonstrated.

If one wants instantaneously to get rid of really difficult troubles in the
5 seeming material world, it is necessary to understand the spiritual world. "For now we see through a glass, darkly" (I Cor. 13:12). When anything is going wrong in the material world and you turn in thought and realise with sufficient clearness what is happening in the spiritual world, this recognition of the action of God results in what is called a miracle, i.e., the
10 material trouble is put right. In this way every difficulty can be overcome. There is no limitation whatsoever. "Seek ye first the kingdom of God, and his righteousness; and all these things shall be added unto you" (Matt. 6:33).

The Christ Capacity.—The spiritual reality of the head is man's capacity, the Christ capacity that the spiritual man has of utilising in
15 various ways any of the infinite ideas, or combination of ideas, that exist in heaven. "The head of every man is Christ" (I Cor. 11:3). For instance, the spiritual reality of the eyes is the capacity of spiritual discernment, of the ears the capacity to understand any of the infinite ideas that there are in Mind, as distinguished from the actual understanding of any idea that
20 is being presented, which is done by the spiritual reality of various internal parts of the body. The foot is another power enabling man to understand, being the power of concentration.

This correspondence is correct, as the human being does not see with his eyes nor hear with his ears. Looked at from a natural science point of
25 view, sight and hearing are mental effects produced by the action of "thought" on the human mind.

The Christ is "the true idea of God and His manifestation,"[1] the consciousness or mind of Mind,[2] God. Now each of us being an individualisation of that consciousness, an individualisation of the Christ, man has the
30 capacity of being conscious of any of the ideas in Mind. This is the Christ capacity. "I can do all things through Christ" (Phil. 4:13), the "Spirit-revelator."

As one speaks of the love of Love, the life of Life, and the truth of Truth,[3] so one can speak of the consciousness of Mind. This consciousness is man
35 specifically, the infinite number of spiritual beings that have always existed in heaven. This is why there is no limitation to the power of man, the spiritual man, as he individualises the Christ, and essentially, because spiritually, is one with the whole Christ consciousness of God. Man

[1] "Blessed with all spiritual blessings in heavenly places in Christ" (Eph. 1:3).
40 "Christ is all, and in all" (Col. 3:11).
    [2] "Man and his Maker are correlated in divine Science, and real consciousness is cognizant only of the things of God" (*Science and Health*, p. 276, Mary Baker Eddy). "The answer to the riddle of the universe is God—the answer to the riddle of God is Christ" (Raymond Brucker).
45   [3] "We can by special and proper capitalisation speak of the love of Love, meaning by that what the beloved disciple meant in one of his epistles, when he said, 'God is love.' Likewise we can speak of the truth of Truth and of the life of Life, for Christ plainly declared, 'I am the way, the truth, and the life'". "Mind, joyous in strength, dwells in the realm of Mind" (*Science and Health*, pp. 319, 514, Mary
50 Baker Eddy).

individualises the power [1] or activity of God, and God is seen to work by means of the spiritual man, who is His means of expression.

Summary.—Let me sum up the conclusions arrived at regarding heaven. Heaven is a state of absolute bliss, consisting solely of God and His infinitely varied manifestation, all being spiritual. In this perfect world 5 we have:—

(1) The simple unfolding (receiving) and re-presenting (passing on) of God's glorious ideas as combinations of ideas. This is counterfeited in the material man as breathing.

(2) The arrangement of these ideas and their combinations into new 10 and perfect combinations, in order to reflect them or pass them on. This appears in the material man as the process of eating and digesting food.

(3) The intensification of a new combination of ideas, when so arranged, with the object of this new and beautiful combination being received and enjoyed with someone else. This takes place when the spiritual being so 15 grouping them together is not yet in mental touch with the being to whom this new combination is necessary to complete and make perfect the sequence of ideas that has just come to him. The individual who has reflected the last ideas to the one grouping them together, in his turn comes into mental touch with someone else, fulfilling in himself God's law 20 of perfect sequence of ideas. This intensification sometimes results in the person grouping together the new combination, becoming acquainted with a spiritual being hitherto unknown to him. This joyous meeting of what we may call "two strangers" is probably counterfeited in the material world when a child is born.[2]   25

(4) Movement from one combination of ideas to another. A spiritual being, for instance, thinks of the spiritual reality of any planet—say, Jupiter—and immediately he experiences all the effect of being there, becoming fully conscious at once of every required detail of the idea presented. He can then mentally call anyone, with the object of pointing 30 out the beauties that are delighting him. When a thought comes to the spiritual man in heaven, it is the thing itself that is presented, as God's thoughts are tangible and real. Man does not move in Mind, as he is God's infinite consciousness. It is the ideas which move and give him all the impressions of being what we have to call "at a place."   35

The day is now past when it was necessary to say : "If I have told you earthly things, and ye believe not, how shall ye believe, if I tell you of heavenly things?" (John 3: 12).

TREATMENT OR TRUE PRAYER

Roughly, the basis of treatment is to deny the evidence of the senses 40 and realise the perfection of God and man. One method, the best, I think, is to turn in thought to heaven, a perfect state of consciousness, and deny

---

[1] "Christ the power of God, and the wisdom of God" (I Cor. 1 : 24). "His eternal power and Godhead" (Rom. 1 : 20).

[2] "Though gathering new energy, this idea cannot injure its useful surroundings 45 in the travail of spiritual birth" (*Science and Health*, p. 463, Mary Baker Eddy).

one by one, the existence in that ideal world of each trouble from which the patient is suffering, following each denial by realising the perfection of the spiritual reality of the part that is affected.

Before treating it is advisable to get one's thought as clear as possible, 5 and it is well worth while to go carefully through the Scientific Statement of Being, on page 468 of *Science and Health with Key to the Scriptures*, by Mary Baker Eddy, realising what each sentence means, not dwelling on the denials, but dwelling earnestly and conscientiously upon the affirmations. Many find it very helpful, as well, to go through the spiritual interpretation 10 of the Lord's Prayer, on page 16 of *Science and Health*. This tends to uplift the thought, and to enable the person treating to get a better and clearer realisation of the spiritual realities.

Next it is an excellent thing to try to realise God, the great I AM, in His various aspects, as Life; Truth; Love; Mind, which gives all the mental 15 activity; Soul, which gives all wisdom and knowledge in the reality; Spirit, which gives all goodness and holiness; substance, which gives all permanency or entity; intelligence; and last but not least, as Principle, the Principle of good, which always acts directly we stop thinking wrongly and think rightly. Then, whilst still thinking of heaven, the kingdom of God that 20 is within, within your mental grasp, take up one by one the various troubles that you have to work against.

Jesus said, "If any man will come after me, let him deny himself, and take up his cross daily, and follow me" (Luke 9:23), follow him in thought to God. "Deny thyself" means deny that the material so-called man is 25 you, and realise that you are spiritual. Take up thy cross daily means, take up in thought every difficulty, denying one by one each difficulty. After each denial, before another denial is taken, add a series of affirmations, the opposite of what you have denied. Only one denial at a time. The affirmation is the important thing, as it is the purification of the human mind. 30 Before you can put in the affirmation, the opposite of the evil, you have to think of the evil, then, as rapidly as possible, drive it out of your mind with the denial and dwell upon the perfection of the opposite.

On page 127, line 9 onwards, I deal with the denial and affirmation, also on page 133, line 47, and page 135, line 47. Pages 127 to 138 should be 35 studied; pages 297 to 304 also help.

How to Gain a Working Knowledge of God.—When I started my investigation I came to the conclusion that I ought, whenever I had a moment or two to spare, to have something definite to realise, and I made up my mind on these occasions to think of God as Love. Then, 40 when my love towards my fellowman seemed to have advanced more than my knowledge of Truth, I changed this realisation to that of God as Truth. Later on, every day I used to think of God in all the main views as Life, Truth, Love, Mind, Soul, Spirit, cause, intelligence, substance, and Principle, the Principle of good, which includes its idea. I now know that 45 cause ought not to have been included, as it is a synonym of God, not an aspect, or quality, as the other names are.

Later, I put each of these headings on a separate piece of paper, and then tried to find all the qualities and attributes of God that I could, putting each of them down under what I thought was the proper heading. Each day I went through these, starting by thinking of heaven, and then trying to realise what each one of them meant. At one time I had on a blank bit of paper about forty qualities and attributes that I could not place under the proper heading, and not more than twenty under any one heading; but, as my knowledge of God grew, so I was able gradually to place each of these qualities and attributes under its proper heading.

I did this every day for over three years. By that time I had over two hundred and twenty qualities and attributes, and it took me about three-quarters of an hour each day to go through them. Not only had I then been able to place the whole of the forty qualities and attributes under their proper headings, but whenever I found a new one I could at once place it in its proper place. Finding no new attribute or quality for three months, I took this as the sign that I had worked in this way long enough, and ceased.

I was once told that in treatment I would find the realisation of God as Principle most effective. Trying this, so as to see whether the statement was correct, the next day an instantaneous result was obtained by merely losing all thought of the material trouble and simply trying to realise God as Principle as clearly as possible. Proving in this way that God was Principle, the love for God that I had seemed instantly to vanish. As I went on, however, obtaining a better understanding of God, my love for God gradually returned, until, in about three months, I had a far greater love for God than I had ever had before.[1]

Being trained as a scientific man, my method of treatment is what may be called "cut and dried"; that is to say, I rely upon the flat denial of the existence of the evil, with all the insistence at my command,[2] followed by as clear a realisation as possible of the exact opposite.

How to Reverse Wrong Thoughts.—The following copy of a letter written to a patient, to show him how to reverse throughout the day any wrong thoughts that came into his so-called mind, is not only the basis of right thinking, but forms a good basis of treatment, showing how to deal with the various forms of evil that have to be destroyed :—

DEAR ——,
We have to watch our thoughts continually. "Watch and pray," and "pray without ceasing," and directly we think a wrong thought,

---

[1] Mr. Edward Kimball has said: "I remember that soon after reading *Science and Health*, I found myself mourning because 'I had lost my God,' and since then I have had occasion to comfort other mourners who had come to the same strange conclusion. Alas, dear friend, what kind of a God was it that could be so easily lost? Please do not think me harsh if I say that if you have a god that can be lost, the quicker you lose it the better. The god I then had was indeed a travesty, a thing of human conception. It was simply an impossible god. Nevertheless, while I had it, it frightened me and filled me with dread and dismay. I greatly rejoice now, that it was lost, and that Christian Science dethrones all other gods that can be lost. Instead of depriving anyone of God, Christian Science reveals the true God, and abundantly satisfies him whose joy it is to know God aright."

[2] " Insist vehemently on the great fact which covers the whole ground that God, Spirit, is all, and that there is none beside Him. There is *no disease*" (*Science and Health*, p. 421, Mary Baker Eddy).

that is, even any thought that is not harmonious, we have to drive it out of our mind, and cease thinking of things material, raising the level of our thoughts until we are thinking of God and things spiritual or truly mental. This is true prayer, conscious communion with God.

5   One method of doing this is to group our thoughts under three headings:—

First.—*Turn in thought to God and heaven,* which is a perfect condition of consciousness or "divine state of mind." This is essential.

Second.—*Deny the existence in heaven* of the wrong thing thought of, 10 seen, or felt. When, for instance, you see an angry man, or feel angry, or think of anger in any way, realise with all the power, earnestness, and conviction at your command, that *there is no anger* in the spiritual kingdom, the kingdom of heaven, the reality. This is called the denial.

15   Third.—*Realise the existence of the opposite;* namely, in reversing the thought of anger, realise that in heaven, the world of reality, all is perfect peace and infinite love. Dwell on this realisation, and get it as clear as possible. This is called the affirmation. I think that, if there is then time, it is advisable to split up one's thoughts into two mor heads, 20 namely:—

Fourth.—*Realise why this is so;* namely, because God, the Principle of good, rules and governs, and heaven is the manifestation of His government. This heaven is everywhere, for there is nothing but God and His manifestation.

25   Fifth.—*Try to form as clear an idea as you can of God* and His manifestation, heaven.

Reversing our thoughts in this way all day long is prayer without ceasing, and is not only leading us continually to "abide in the secret place of the Most High," but is teaching us to recognise, clearly and 30 persistently, that all sin, disease, worry, limitations, and all other effects of wrong so-called thoughts, are non-realities, i.e., have no permanence about them. It is also teaching us to realise the truth continually, namely, that God and His manifestation are spiritual, perfect, and omnipresent. Your progress depends solely upon the number of 35 seconds during the twenty-four hours that you are thinking of this reality.

Do not take this as a hard-and-fast rule for working; it is only the way that I have found the most helpful. Let God teach you the way to work, not man. "Prove all things: hold fast that which is good." If you 40 constantly realise that God is Truth, and that you know Truth, being the knowledge or consciousness of God, you will be led, step by step, absolutely correctly, as though by a loving father and mother. You will never have to retrace your steps, but will look back with rejoicing along the straight and narrow path by which you have come, recognising the 45 pitfalls and morasses from which you have been tenderly guarded.

You may have troubles, and find the pathway sometimes rugged, but if you keep your gaze continually fixed on the goal of reality, you will find that these troubles merely spur you on to still higher attainments, and you thereby gain the uplifting joy of relieving suffering humanity, teaching them the continuous availability of God and the meaning of "the peace of God which passeth all understanding."

Yours sincerely,

F. L. RAWSON.

I start every treatment by working against the three principal evils: 5 mortal mind, thoughts of *materia medica*—i.e., false medical beliefs—and fear. For instance, I realise that there is no mortal mind, only one Mind, God, infinite good; no thoughts of *materia medica*, only God's thoughts, man knows truth; no fear, man has absolute trust in God, trust in good, there is nothing but good, and man knows there is nothing but good; man 10 is divine, spiritual, perfect, and therefore absolutely fearless.

We ought always to work for love, spiritual perception and wisdom. In working *for* things always begin by the realisation of God; for instance, God is the Principle of all wisdom, therefore man reflects divine wisdom, intelligence, and knowledge.   15

Both at the beginning and at the end of treatment for a patient, I work against fear, which John, in Revelation 21, verse 8, puts as the first of the deadly sins. This is because it is a belief in a power other than that of God, a belief in the power of evil. Moses told us to have only one God. This is absolutely scientific. If we believe in a hundred and one gods we will have 20 a hundred and one evils.

I always work against every class of wrong thought, such as malice against the truth, aggressive mental suggestion, mental assassination, mental malpractice, hypnotism, and animal magnetism. It does not do, however, to tell a man too much, it is better to let him gradually work out 25 his own method of treatment, relying on the action of God to teach him. Each of us has a different mentality. We have very little to learn, but we have a very great deal to unlearn. Each of us has different things to unlearn, and different methods of treatment suit different people.

It may help to give one or two examples. Supposing the patient has 30 indigestion, I realise that there is no indigestion, God's ideas continually unfold to man in perfect sequence, and with perfect regularity; he assimilates, digests, and understands these ideas, groups them together and passes them on; that understanding and grouping together of God's ideas can never give any pain, it gives absolute joy and absolute happiness. Then 35 in the same way I follow by working against any symptoms present, such as flatulence, acidity, heartburn, or auto-intoxication.

If a patient has a weak heart with, for instance, bad circulation, I realise that man's heart is never weak, man's heart is the reflection of God as Love, and Love is omnipotent, for Love is God; man reflects Life and has all 40 power and all strength; there is no want of circulation, man's blood is the joy that circulates right throughout the consciousness, Love is the power that causes the joy to circulate, and Love is omnipotent for Love is God.

It is an advantage between the treatment for each patient to read a page 45 or two of *Science and Health*. I used, in addition, between each treatment, to give myself a treatment for love, purity, and wisdom.

13*

LETTER TO AN ARTIST

"For God is perfection, and whoever strives for perfection, strives for something that is God-like" (Michael Angelo). (See Deut. 32:4; II Sam. 22:31; Ps. 18:30; Matt. 5:48; Eph. 4:3; Col. 4:12).

5   Dear ——,

When you are painting you are pictorially expressing a material representation of the thoughts that have come to you, and you try to make the painting as vivid a reproduction as possible of these thoughts.

You are always able to perceive that there are thoughts of which you
10 cannot make a material representation.

You must always feel that there are thoughts which you cannot quite grasp, but which are on a higher level than those you do reach and endeavour to portray.

Now what is the effect of the pigment that you put on the canvas? It
15 merely brings the people who see it, in touch with the group of thoughts that you were ethereally in touch with when you were endeavouring to express them on the canvas.

When the person looking at the picture sees it, what it conveys to him depends upon the condition of his human consciousness.

20   (1) One man will either be struck with the excessive colouring in one place, a mistake that you have made, or possibly something that he thinks is wrong, and he obtains no pleasure at all.

(2) Another man, seeing nothing but what is nice, will simply be pleased with the general effect.

25   (3) Another man will pick out beauties in your work, and see all the best of it.

(4) Sometimes a man will even see it just in the same way as that in which the thoughts presented themselves to you.

(5) Another will see all the thoughts that you felt were there, but were
30 unable to get at, and they will lift him away altogether from the picture and material surroundings, and he will be in touch with a lovely picture, and beautiful thoughts of many kinds.

(6) Every now and then there will come one who will get in touch with thoughts that you did not even feel, but which were there all the same.
35 This man will rise in thought and lose himself and his material surroundings in the realisation of God, his heavenly Father, and those around will feel an angel's presence.

Now why this difference? It is simply a question of the stage of the individual's advancement out of seeming human limitations; in other
40 words, the condition of the man's "consciousness."

The first is one deadened to all artistic feeling with a depreciative spirit, a man who, while remaining in that attitude, does very little good to anyone.

The second has a better condition, and catches thoughts that give
45 satisfaction.

The third catches all the better thoughts, deriving great pleasure therefrom.

The fourth has the same condition of "consciousness" as yourself.

Now the fifth has a higher ideal, and catches nothing but what are called good thoughts, even thoughts that you were only just able to feel.

The sixth is he whose advancement more nearly approaches that of Jesus the Master, and one whose presence is felt wherever he goes, the man to whom children run, before whom evil flees, the man who lives habitually in the presence of God. He gets a sense of the new heaven and the new earth, the glorious kingdom of God that is within.

Why is this? Because in every case they are God's thoughts, seen, felt, or thought as you may call it, materially. The first catches such material thoughts that there appears practically no heavenly tone about them. The second sees heaven a little more as it really is, and the last is, for the time, what we call in heaven, that is to say, the thoughts that he catches are so close upon the real thoughts that he feels as though he were in heaven.

Now how are you to enable those who see your picture to be lifted up by seeing it? You can do this in two ways. By denial and by affirmation. When you are working, that is to say, when you are ethereally in touch with the so-called thoughts that you intend to portray or are portraying, and you deny the existence of wrong thoughts, you are destroying material thoughts of a bad description that would act upon those looking at your picture, whose minds were in such a condition as otherwise to catch the higher thoughts. When you are affirming, that is to say, realising the reality, heaven, you are clearing your mind, and allowing yourself to catch and portray the higher thoughts that the fifth man was able to catch, but which you only dimly perceive. Most important of all, every time you so work you are altering the condition of your "mind," purifying it, so that it is permanently more like that of the sixth man.

The result of working in this way, that is to say, treating whilst you are doing your work, recording your ideals, is, that when people come to look at the painting, you have cleared away many of the wrong thoughts that would act upon them and prevent them getting hold of the highest thoughts they were capable of appreciating. This will enable them to enjoy the painting, and note beauties that otherwise would have been lost to them.

Work of this description is what is called the work of genius, but now we know of what genius consists, and any man can be a genius more or less if only he will think in the right way. When you are at work, try to think of yourself as you really are, a perfect being in a perfect world governed by a perfect God, and recognise that the work you (the real you) are doing is absolutely perfect, because it is due to the action of God, the Principle of good. When you work, God is at work, because the real man is the expressed activity of God, the instrument through which God works in the real world. "Christ the power of God, and the wisdom of God" (I Cor. 1:24).

You have work to do. You have to lift your fellow-men, so that they see that material things are not the aim and end of man; that real happiness is not to be gained by applying one's attentions to material ends, but only by obtaining happiness for one's fellow-men; and that the only way to do this is by the purification of one's so-called mind by constant right thinking, true prayer. With some men this can be done better through the canvas than verbally, and in any case the canvas that tells this story is seen and appreciated by many.

Everyone has the capacity of doing this. All that is necessary is the
5 knowledge of the detailed method of working. We must be about our Father's business. Awake and waken the world, understand your power as "equipped by God." "The power that is at work is God's law, God's power, and this is God revealing Himself through their consciousness."
"Lift up your eyes, and look on the fields; for they are white already to
10 harvest. And he that reapeth receiveth wages, and gathereth fruit unto life eternal" (John 4:35, 36). "Enter into the holiest" (Heb. 10:19). "Allow Soul to hold the control" (Science and Health, p. 30, Mary Baker Eddy). Look "towards the imperishable things of Spirit" (Ibid., p. 21).

Yours sincerely,
15   F. L. RAWSON.

THE CHRIST

"Continue in prayer. . . . Withal praying also for us, that God would open unto us a door of utterance, to speak the mystery of Christ" (Col. 4:2, 3).
20   The following definitions, to which Dr. Inge calls our attention, will show how the advancing thinkers in the Church are approaching the scientific conception of the Christ as the manifestation of God, the conception that will heal sin and sickness when realised. Dr. Inge says: "The realisation of this conception heals sin and sickness. St. Paul gives us a
25 very complete and explicit Logos-Theology, though he never uses the word. . . . I will collect the chief passages which, taken together, comprise St. Paul's teaching on this subject. In relation to God the Father, Christ is the Image (eikon) of God (II Cor., Col.). . . . An eikon . . . represents its prototype, and is a visible manifestation of it. Christ is the
30 'eikon of the Invisible God' (Col.). In him dwells bodily the Pleroma, the totality of the Divine attributes (Col., Eph.). . . . He is 'Lord of all' and 'Lord of Glory' (Rom., I Cor.).

"In reference to the world, Christ is the Agent in creation, 'through Him are all things, and we through Him' (I Cor. 8:6). . . . He is 'the
35 first-born of all creation; in Him and through Him and unto Him are all things. He is before all things, and in Him all things hold together' (Col. 1:15, 17). 'All things are to be summed up in him' (Eph. 1:10). 'Christ is all, and in all' (Col. 3:11).[1] His reign is co-extensive with the world's history. 'He must reign till he hath put all his enemies under his
40 feet. The last enemy that shall be abolished is death.' Only 'when all things have been subjected to him, shall the Son also himself be subjected to him that did subject all things unto Him, that God may be all in all'

---

[1] Mr. R. L. Nettleship writes: "Suppose that all human beings felt habitually to each other as they now do occasionally to those they love best . . . it would be
45 the consciousness of another which was also oneself—a *common* consciousness. Such would be the *atonement* of the world."

(I Cor. 15:24–28)." [1] "All is in reality the manifestation of Mind" (Mary Baker Eddy).

These and many similar quotations confirm the scientific fact that what has been called the mystic Christ, is the true idea of God and His manifestation, or God's consciousness, through which God is seen to act, "the power of God, and the wisdom [2] of God" (I Cor. 1:24); and that all the spiritual beings in heaven individualise the Christ, the divine emanation; and that you are an individualisation of the Christ and God's representative.

Jesus the Christ.—The conception of Jesus as the only Son of God was of comparatively recent years. In the early creeds the word "only" (unicum) as applied to the Son of God is absent. It is not used in the creeds of Cyprian or Augustine; nor do Tertullian, Nicea, or even Novatian of Rome, use it. Valentinus taught in Rome between A.D. 140 and 160, the time when the Apostles' Creed is supposed to have been framed, and his school seems to have recognised the difference between Christ, the only begotten Son, and Jesus the Christ,[3] drawing attention to the fact that St. John wrote: "We beheld his glory, as of the only begotten," the word "as" differentiating the two. Adolf von Harnack, Professor of Theology at Berlin University, in his pamphlet *Das Apostolische Glaübenbekanntniss*, which pamphlet went through twenty-five editions in twelve months, drawing attention to the modern compilation of the Apostles' Creed, writes thus, referring to the words "only begotten Son": "After Nicea these words came to be unanimously believed by the Church to refer to the prehistoric and eternal Sonship of Jesus, but to transfer this conception to the Christ is to transform it. It cannot be proved that about the middle of the century the idea 'only Son' was understood in this sense; on the contrary, the evidence of history conclusively shows that it was not so understood."

There is only one Christ, the spiritual selfhood of every son of God, the spiritual divine emanation. According to Harnack, primitive Christianity had two Christologies, one pneumatic, the other adoptianist. The former view was held by Barnabas, Clement, Ignatius, and the pious Polycarp. Hermas fused the two together. H. B. Swete, D.D., Regius Professor of Divinity, Cambridge, who contests Harnack's view, writes: "It is true that the pre-existence of Christ was ignored or denied in certain quarters, and His Sonship limited to the human life, or the part of it which followed the Baptism. It is also true that the earliest orthodox writers spoke of the pre-existent Christ as Spirit." [4]

When we pray to God we individualise the Christ power, and it is the Christ that heals, mentally; Christ, the true idea of reality, of Truth, Life, and Love. In other words, we merely get the human so-called self out of

[1] "The Paddock Lectures" for 1906.
[2] Spinoza speaks of "the eternal Son of God, i.e., God's eternal wisdom which is manifested in all things, but chiefly in the mind of man and most of all in Christ Jesus" (Epist. 21).
[3] Jesus was the only one entitled to the honour of being called Jesus the Christ, as he was the only man who was the Messiah or Saviour.
[4] *The Apostles' Creed: Its Relation to Primitive Christianity.*

the way, and then God acts by means of the Christ, beautifully named by Sir Oliver Lodge "the sunshine of God."

In the Apocryphal Gospel of Peter, the dying Jesus cries: "My Power, my Power, thou hast forsaken me," the "Power" being, as Dr. Inge says,
5 "The heavenly Christ, who, for a time had been associated with the earthly person of the Redeemer."

Paul saw clearly the difference between the ever-living Christ and the corporeal Jesus with his title—the Christ. Paul hardly ever refers to the human life of Jesus, to his sayings, his parables, or his works. He
10 confines himself practically to his crucifixion and resurrection. In one place he says that he wishes to know no man, not even Christ, any more after the flesh. He knew that all good things came from realising the spiritual and dwelling in thought upon God, heaven, and the infinite spiritual man. He states: "How that by revelation he [God] made known unto me the
15 mystery . . . of Christ; . . . That the Gentiles should be fellowheirs, and of the same body" (Eph. 3:3, 4, 6).

St. Augustine held that the knowledge of God within can only be imparted by God dwelling within. Dr. Inge writes: "But the doctrine of Divine immanence in the human heart never became quite the central
20 truth of theology till the time of the medieval mystics. To ascend to God is to enter into oneself and to transcend oneself."

He also writes: "I cannot now give any further account of the manner in which the medieval mystics worked out the thought that Christ himself, through the Holy Spirit, is the life of our life, the core of our being, who,
25 if we could but rid ourselves entirely of our false self-regarding self, would be the constitutive force of our personality. . . . I need not remind you that it is the foundation of St. Paul's Christianity, and the source of his strongest and most moving appeals. 'I live, yet not I but Christ liveth in me'; 'for me, to live is Christ.' These are revelations of the deepest
30 experience, the strongest conviction, which animated that Apostle in his life and labour and suffering." [1]

This was the view of the early fathers. St. Augustine says: "Let us rejoice and return thanks that we have been made, not only Christians, but Christ. Wonder and rejoice! We have been made Christ." "Union
35 with the glorified Christ is the essence of Christianity" (Dr. Inge). "The great deed that seems to emerge as the Life of Christ is the bringing into one of God and man" [2] (Professor Wallace, of Oxford). "Ye are Christ's; and Christ is God's" (I Cor. 3:23). The last words of Pope Pius X, were "Rest everything in Christ."

40   "Where the Truth always reigneth, so that true, perfect God and true, perfect man are at one, and man so giveth place to God, that God Himself is there, and yet the man, too, and this same unity worketh continually, and doeth and leaveth undone without any I, and Me, and Mine, and the like; behold, there is Christ, and nowhere else" (*Theologia Germanica*).

45   "Therefore if any man be in Christ, he is a new creature: old things are passed away; behold, all things are become new" (II Cor. 5:17).

---

[1] "The Paddock Lectures" for 1906.
[2] *Lectures and Essays* (abridged).

Let us obtain sufficient knowledge of the living Christ to raise the dead. "Men find Christ through their fellow-men, and every glimpse they get of Him is a direct message from Himself" (Henry Drummond).

The Second Coming of The Christ.—*"Some day the great and beautiful thought which hovers on the confines of the mind will at last alight.* 5 *In that is hope: the whole sky is full of abounding hope"* (Richard Jefferies). The second coming of Christ to human consciousness is the individual recognition by man that he is spiritual now, that matter is not a reality, and that the only reality is God and the spiritual kingdom. This comes to each man directly he is ready. 10

This true knowledge, the second coming of the Christ to each, is coming all over the world with lightning rapidity, "For as the lightning cometh out of the east, and shineth even unto the west; so shall also the coming of the Son of man be" (Matt. 24:27). All over the world this knowledge is surging into men's hearts without, in countless cases, a word being spoken to 15 them. When it has come, man is born anew and enters upon a fresh sense of life, a life of peace and joy, exercising his newly developed dominion over all evil, in the healing and saving of his fellow-man from the sin, sickness, and multifarious troubles that seemingly surround him. This we do by turning in thought to heaven as often as possible. "If ye then be risen with 20 Christ, seek those things which are above . . . your life is hid with Christ in God" (Col. 3:1, 3). "Upon this rock I will build my church" (Matt. 16:18).

Sir Oliver Lodge has recently said: "Let us be not afraid of an idea because it has several times striven to make itself appreciated. There must be many failures to effect an entrance before the final success. So it is with 25 the Messiah idea which is abroad in the land—and was for years before Christ's coming—but had not been recognised by more than a few."

With regard to the prophecy of what is happening now and what is about to happen, those who can read the past are able to see the fulfilment of the prophecies taking place at the present time, and to know the point 30 reached in the history of the material world. They can also know what is liable to happen, and so, forewarned and forearmed, they can help their fellow-men against the troubles that are so shortly about to attack, and by which they are liable to be overwhelmed unless they have a knowledge of the truth. 35

"Watch ye therefore . . . Lest coming suddenly he find you sleeping" (Mark 13:35, 36).

TO WHOM IT MAY CONCERN

" When one comes to the age with spiritual translations of God's messages, expressed in literal or physical terms, our right action is not to condemn and 40 *deny, but to 'try the spirits,' and see what manner they are of. This does not mean communing with spirits supposed to have departed from the earth, but the seeking out of the basis upon which are accomplished the works by which the new teacher would prove his right to be heard. By these signs are the true disciples of the Master known: the sick are healed: to the poor the gospel is* 45 *preached"* [1] (Mary Baker Eddy).

[1] *Miscellaneous Writings*, p. 171.

The following is a copy of a letter recently written to a friend, with some additions.[1] It is but an exposure, with a view to the destruction of "some of the leading illusions along the path which Science must tread in its reformatory mission among mortals."[2] Error cannot be destroyed until it is exposed, when, being recognised, all unite in destroying it. This destruction must precede the purification of God's temple.

Mrs. Eddy in *Science and Health with Key to the Scriptures*, p. 192, line 5, makes the following sweeping statement: "We are not Christian Scientists until we leave all for Christ." Obviously this can only mean that no one is a true Christian Scientist who, amongst other things, does not abandon material methods as fast as is possible, and rely upon treatment for the hundred and one duties that have to be attended to throughout the day. "Our reliance upon material things must be transferred to a perception of and dependence on spiritual things."[3] Is a man truly a Christian Scientist, for instance, who relies continually upon the time-table to catch his train, the mesmerism of regular sleep to maintain health, the study of books to obtain material knowledge, and the habitual writing of letters when he wishes to meet a friend? All these can be better done by treatment if regularly practised. "Never fear to bring the sublimest motion to the smallest duty" (Phillips Brooks). "There is nothing so small but that we may honour God by asking His guidance" (Ruskin). "The affirmations of Science must be tested by applying them throughout the gamut of human experience"[4] (Frank H. Sprague). "A real Christian Scientist is a marvel, a miracle in the universe of mortal mind. With selfless love, he inscribes on the heart of humanity and transcribes on the page of reality the living, palpable presence—the might and majesty!—of goodness" (Mary Baker Eddy).[5]

Denial of Material Intelligence is Necessary.—"*For if a man think himself to be something, when he is nothing, he deceiveth himself*" (Gal. 6:3). Jesus said: "Let him deny himself, and take up his cross daily, and follow me" (Luke 9:23). One interpretation is that a man has to deny the material counterfeit called oneself, to handle the serpent tempter, to grasp every seeming difficulty boldly, and fearlessly to advance in a possibly hitherto untrodden path, relying solely on Truth as a guide, and giving up as quickly as possible all material, so-called aids. The cup of our Lord, of which he said, "Drink ye all of it" (Matt. 26:27), is our cross, and by commemorating this cup it becomes our crown.

To those who do not know by experience the protecting power of God, this may appear to be risking one's professional status and rendering oneself open to criticism or even ridicule. "At present mortals progress slowly for fear of being thought ridiculous. They are slaves to fashion, pride, and sense" (Mary Baker Eddy).[6]

---

[1] This letter, naturally, formed no part of the original lecture.
[2] *Science and Health*, p. 129, Mary Baker Eddy.
[3] *Retrospection and Introspection*, p. 28, Mary Baker Eddy.
[4] *The Christian Science Journal*, November, 1909.
[5] *Miscellaneous Writings*, p. 294.
[6] *Science and Health*, p. 68.

Knowledge of Truth is Necessary.—*"Speak clearly if you speak at all"* (Oliver Wendell Holmes).

Truth tells. There is no time for half measures. Mrs. Eddy says: "Judge not the future advancement of Christian Science by the steps already taken." [1] Also: "Dispensing the Word charitably, but separating the tares from the wheat, let us declare the positive and the negative of metaphysical Science; what it is, and what it is not. Intrepid, self-oblivious Protestants in a higher sense than ever before, let us meet and defeat the claims of sense and sin, regardless of the bans or clans pouring in their fire upon us." [2] Material illusion is hastening with lightning rapidity to the end of its evil dream, and practically all men are ready for the truth. It is only fair under these circumstances to state the truth as plainly as possible. "The truth . . . and nothing but the truth." We dare not hesitate in obeying God's commands. God leads and governs.

Mrs. Eddy in *Science and Health* says: "Who is telling mankind of the foe in ambush? Is the informer one who sees the foe? If so, listen and be wise. Escape from evil, and designate those as unfaithful stewards who have seen the danger and yet have given no warning" (p. 571). And again: "One must fulfil one's mission without timidity or dissimulation, for to be well done, the work must be done unselfishly" (p. 483). And in *Miscellaneous Writings* (p. 213) she writes: "The Scripture saith: 'He that covereth his sins shall not prosper.' No risk is so stupendous as to neglect opportunities which God giveth, and not to forewarn and forearm our fellow-mortals against the evil which, if seen, can be destroyed."

"Now opinion is cruel, and truth is merciful: opinion is worth little, truth is priceless; and yet probably more are moved in this world by opinion than by truth, because opinions are to weak characters what truth is to strong." The leaders in the scientific world of the present day, earnest searchers after truth, know too well the difficulties under which we have hitherto laboured, to do other than ponder over what is presented to them, and carefully to see whether it helps them to elucidate the problems which they daily have to meet. "Give instruction to a wise man, and he will be yet wiser: teach a just man, and he will increase in learning" (Prov. 9:9).

Love is Necessary.—*"When loving we learn that 'God is Love'; mortals hating, or unloving, are neither Christians nor Scientists"* [3] (Mary Baker Eddy). *"For the letter killeth, but the spirit giveth life"* (II Cor. 3:6).

To such individuals as merely have a superficial knowledge of the letter of Christian Science, I should like to point out that the class of sin Jesus most condemned was Pharisaism; namely, self-righteousness, pride, criticism, etc. Love is the antithesis of all this, and love alone is the cure for it. "That only which we have within us can we see without" (Emerson).

Constructive criticism elucidates points and clears individual thought. Destructive criticism, whereby one either uproots the faith or denies the facts by means of which a man tries to get closer to God, is absolutely wrong, unless something better is given upon which to found a higher

[1] *Science aud Health*, p. 459.
[2] *Miscellaneous Writings*, p. 171.
[3] *Message for* 1902, p. 8.

idea of God. "We have not the time to be tearing down some other man's religion" (Rev. L. G. Morong).

"Let every man begin with his own conduct, and reform that; and when every one succeeds, the world will need no further reformation. But if one cannot reform himself how shall he reform the world? If a man shall sincerely take himself in hand, he will have little time to make war upon others: it is enough for one man and will last him a lifetime" [1] (W. G. Old). "He that is without sin among you, let him first cast a stone" (John 8:7).

It will be found that this period of self-reformation will bring to each man unfoldment, not only of God's plan of reforming the world, but also of his own part to be played therein. "No man is born into this world whose work is not born with him" (J. R. Lowell).

Knowledge of what the Material World Claims to be is Necessary.—*"If any man think that he knoweth any thing, he knoweth nothing yet as he ought to know"* (I Cor. 8:2).

Those who have in the past drunk deep of the knowledge of the material universe, and know scientifically the nothingness of it all, can by reversal obtain a clearer realisation of the glorious, spiritual reality, and thereby help mankind better. It is their bounden duty to do this. It is not necessary for each individual to know all about the material world, but it is essential that some know it sufficiently to thoroughly expose its false claim and destroy it for the rest. Until this is done all must suffer.

Mrs. Eddy points out that "Each individual must fill his own niche in time and eternity." [2] At the same time we must be wise. We have to be careful in sitting "at meat in the idol's temple," making use of our material knowledge. "Through thy knowledge shall the weak brother perish, for whom Christ died?" (I Cor. 8:10–11). "The servant of the Lord must not strive; but be gentle unto all men, apt to teach, patient" (II Tim. 2:24). "To remain gentle is to be invincible. Gentleness is ever victorious in attack and secure in defence. Therefore when heaven would preserve a man it enfolds him with gentleness" (Lao-Tze). (See also Galatians 5, verse 22; James 3, verse 17.)

Mrs. Eddy says in *Harvest*: "It is of comparatively little importance what a man thinks or believes he knows; the good that a man does is the one thing needful and the sole proof of rightness." In the *Message for 1902*, p. 8, she says: "We have no evidence of being Christian Scientists except we possess this inspiration [tenderness, Truth, and Love], and its power to heal and to save. The energy that saves sinners and heals the sick is divine: and Love is the Principle thereof." In *No and Yes*, p. 33, she says: "Self-sacrifice is the highway to heaven," and in her message to the Mother Church, June, 1898, we find: "Whoever demonstrates the highest humanity—long suffering, self-surrender, and spiritual endeavour to bless others—ought to be aided, not hindered, in his holy mission. I would kiss the feet of such a messenger,[3] for to help such a one is to help oneself."

[1] *The Simple Way*, note by translator.
[2] *Retrospection and Introspection*, p. 70.
[3] See Malachi 3, verses 1–3, 5; also Revelation 11, verse 19; and 15, verses 5, 6, 8.

TO WHOM IT MAY CONCERN

Whether a man understands how to pray rightly or not can be told by whether he can heal sin and sickness instantly and habitually by turning in thought to God. This is the only proof. "Ye shall know them by their fruits" (Matt. 7:16). We have no right to criticise another's work until we can prove our knowledge of truth in this way. Even then divine patience 5 alone can bring out the manifestation of that good which is omnipresent.

It is wise not to judge another's works. "If any man will do his will, he shall know of the doctrine, whether it be of God, or whether I speak of myself" (John 7:17). What has to be done is to inquire into any unfamiliar 10 statement, so as to bring out the meaning and make certain that it is really understood. "Let us get up early to the vineyards: let us see if the vine flourish, whether the tender grape appear and the pomegranates bud forth" (Solomon's Song, 7:12; Science and Health, p. 600. Mary Baker Eddy). We must not "number the people" (II Sam. 24). There should be 15 no separation in thought induced through spiritual pride, nor fear through a belief in paucity of numbers. All men are spiritual, and dwelling on supposed differences and imperfections is merely putting off the day when all will appear to wake up to this knowledge. "And they shall not teach every man his neighbour, and every man his brother, saying, Know the Lord: 20 for all shall know me, from the least to the greatest" (Heb. 8:11, and Jer. 31:34.)

Knowledge of Underground Working is Necessary.—

"Knowledge is now no more a fountain seal'd:
Drink deep, until the habits of the slave,   25
The sins of emptiness, gossip, and spite
And slander, die" (Tennyson).

The useless effort that is being made to split the ranks of Christian Scientists, by the false, so-called mental working of those who think that they are thereby helping humanity, results in criticism by those acted 30 upon, who do not properly protect themselves. This criticism is not of an elucidating, but of a destructive character, founded upon ignorance of the seeming laws governing the material world and of the laws of Christian Science. "For we wrestle not against flesh and blood, but against principalities, against powers, against the rulers of the darkness of this world, 35 against spiritual wickedness in high places. Wherefore take unto you the whole armour of God, that ye may be able to withstand in the evil day, and having done all, to stand. Stand therefore, having your loins girt about with truth" (Eph. 6:12–14). Of course, there can be no carping criticism between those who really know and love the truth. 40

When the banner of truth is raised aloft, the Pharisaical class of thoughts at once attack. Woe comes to the unfortunate mortal who from ignorance allows himself to be made a channel through whom this assault is made, the human crucible wherein the attack rages. "Woe unto them that . . . take away the righteousness of the righteous from him!" (Isa. 5:22, 23). 45 "Lord, lay not this sin to their charge" (Acts 7:60). Remember that they never made their so-called minds, and they never made the thoughts that affect them.

Such attack cannot possibly harm the standard-bearers if they rest upon the supremacy of God and protect themselves continually by the realisation of God, as has so well been exemplified in the wonderful life of Mrs. Eddy; but it expends its imaginary force upon those who through neglect-
5 ing to protect themselves sufficiently, and without any personal knowledge of facts, repeat stories, true or untrue, against those whose understanding of truth happens to be in a line somewhat different from their own. "Beware of those who misrepresent facts; or tacitly assent where they should dissent." [1]
10 This course of action is diametrically opposed to the scientifically religious teachings of Mrs. Eddy and the broad spirit of charity that without exception underlies her statements with regard to the work of all earnest searchers after truth. "Whatever enlarges man's facilities for knowing and doing good, and subjugates matter, has a fight with the flesh.
15 Utilising the capacities of the human mind uncovers new ideas, unfolds spiritual forces, the divine energies, and their power over matter, molecule, space, time, mortality; and mortals cry out, 'Art thou come hither to torment us before the time?' then dispute the facts, call them false or in advance of the time, and reiterate, Let me alone. Hence the footprints of
20 a reformer are stained with blood." [2]
If a man has apparently no great intellectual capacity, he need not be discouraged. He can more than make up for this temporary deficiency by the pertinacity with which he realises truth throughout the day. He must, however, learn to abandon all false concepts of his neighbour and keep his
25 thoughts resting on the perfection of God and man. Working in this way and realising the absolute wisdom and knowledge that he, the perfect spiritual being in heaven, reflects, he will obtain all the knowledge that is necessary for man, both real knowledge of the spiritual world and any information concerning the material universe that is indispensable for the
30 clearing up of its seeming mystery and its subsequent inevitable destruction. The intuitive simplicity of the pure child consciousness that with wondrous beauty so readily grasps the ultimate, and even proves this knowledge by instantaneous demonstrations, is yet inadequate to grapple with and reverse the myriad forms of lurid evil that to-day enslave a
35 materially "educated" world. This "network of mystery," including "spiritual wickedness in high places" (Eph. 6:12), and other such devilish practices, being deeply rooted in false material hypotheses, requires its very groundwork to be upheaved and the basic roots exposed and laid bare for destruction by the light of Truth. "There is such a thing as a holy
40 simplicity that knows little of anything but how to treat with God. At the same time commend me to holy people of good heads " (Santa Teresa).

Assimilation of Mrs. Eddy's Writings is Necessary.—There would be no personal criticism had others attained, as all will later, to Mrs. Eddy's power of being able to see what is shortly about to take place in the
45 material world. She does not belittle the work of the material scientist, but says, in *Science and Health*, p. 195: "Observation, invention, study,

---

[1] *Miscellaneous Writings*, p. 109.
[2] *Message for* 1902, p. 9.

and original thought are expansive and should promote the growth of mortal mind out of itself, out of all that is mortal. It is the tangled barbarisms of learning which we deplore—the mere dogma, the speculative theory, the nauseous fiction." Again: "Modern discoveries have brought to light important facts in regard to so-called embryonic life" (p. 548), and speaking of one such discovery she says: "This discovery is corroborative of the Science of Mind" (p. 549).

"In the present stage of human understanding, a knowledge of various branches of learning which, in their general implications, do not harmonise with the standard of absolute Science, may be indispensable. Educational, economic and social considerations frequently enforce the necessity of cultivating and perpetuating such phases of thoughts as will lead consciousness most naturally and progressively to higher levels." [1]

Mrs. Eddy observes, on page 195 of *Science and Health*: "Whatever furnishes the semblance of an idea governed by its Principle, furnishes food for thought. Through astronomy, natural history, chemistry, music, mathematics, thought passes naturally from effect back to cause. Academics of the right sort are requisite." Merely to speculate regarding the spirituality of man and the universe does not lead to an apprehension of the divine idea. The "Word" must be "made flesh" (John 1:14). "Christian Science eschews what is called natural science, in so far as this is built on the false hypotheses that matter is its own law-giver, that law is founded on material conditions, and that these are final and overrule the might of divine Mind" (*Science and Health*, p. 127).

The following quotations from an interview with Mrs. Eddy may come as a surprise to any who might be tempted to belittle an intimate knowledge of natural science and its expression in modern inventions: "What is your attitude to science in general? Do you oppose it?" "Not," with a smile, "if it is really science." "Well, electricity, engineering, the telephone, the steam engine—are these too material for Christian Science?" "No, only false science—healing by drugs." . . . "But the pursuit of modern material inventions?" "Oh! we cannot oppose them. They all tend to newer, finer, more etherealised ways of living. They seek the finer essences. They light the way to the Church of Christ. We use them, we make them our figures of speech. They are preparing the way for us" (*New York Herald*, May 1, 1901, reprinted in *Christian Science Journal*, June, 1901).

Knowledge of Language is Necessary.—Mrs. Eddy points out the "difficulty of so expressing metaphysical ideas as to make them comprehensible to any reader, who has not personally demonstrated Christian Science" (*Science and Health*, p. 115). Metaphysical terms are meaningless, in the first instance, to the natural scientist. What does he know of the constitution of a thought? Speak of a "line of force" or a high-tension current, and he at once understands what you are saying, and has a groundwork of theory into which he is ready to fit the new material facts you are about to give him, so that he can classify them, recollect them, and, rising to a higher level, turn them to practical use, reducing his late masters to the position of servants.

[1] *Christian Science Sentinel.*

Frederick Harrison writes: "Life and conduct shall stand for us wholly on a basis of law, and must rest entirely in that region of science (not physical, but moral and social science) where we are free to use our intelligence in the methods known to us as intelligible logic, methods which the
5 intellect can analyse. When you confront us with hypotheses, however sublime and however affecting, if they cannot be stated in terms of the rest of our knowledge . . . then we shake our heads and turn away."

"Every true Christian Scientist will be careful that his words are not intended to deceive, but rather to elucidate the truth. Mortals, in talking
10 to mortals about mortal experiences, must speak in terms which will be understood in the dictionary sense of the language used, otherwise they may create a wrong impression about the teachings of Christian Science and render themselves liable to be charged with having lied" (*Christian Science Sentinel*, September 18, 1909, Archibald McLellan).

15 Materialists are most readily led to God along the line of least resistance and should be shown in a way they understand most easily, that matter is not a solid, indestructible thing, but a fleeting evanescent belief, of which scientific men admit they know practically nothing, named electricity. This has now been discovered to be simply an elementary false
20 impression of the Christ, God's spiritual manifestation. They have to be shown that the material veil can be caused to entirely disappear simply by short-circuiting it, when there is nothing material left mathematically, philosophically, or logically. Mathematically we know that if a thing ever was nothing, or ever becomes nothing, it cannot possibly ever be anything,
25 however much it appears to be something. When one shows not only that matter is electricity, and merely due to action of the tension of lines of force acting upon themselves, that is to say, that matter is a manifestation of thought, or thought made visible, it is quite easy for people to understand how the only method of working with any chance of permanent
30 success is in the way that Mrs. Eddy has been pointing out for the last forty years.

The technical terms here made use of are in common usage, and appeal to the average materialist, enabling him to see that Mrs. Eddy, when speaking of matter, uses metaphysical terms in place of those that he under-
35 stands and uses. Here let me quote her words: "As a literature, Christian metaphysics is hampered by the lack of proper terms in which to express what it means." [1] "As human thought changes . . . error will be no longer used in stating truth." [2] The time for this change has surely come. Now that the constitution of matter is understood, the statements of
40 unfolding truth will become easier to express.

Once you can shake the fundamental basis upon which a materialist founds all his theories, he at once reconsiders his position and gladly turns to the study of the Bible and Mrs. Eddy's explanatory writings as the only way by which he can emerge from the seeming difficulties that he now
45 admittedly cannot solve. "I shake not the earth [the theories of the natural scientists] only, but also heaven [the ideas of the spiritual workers]. And this word . . . signifieth the removing of those things that are shaken, as

---

[1] *Miscellaneous Writings*, p. 366.
[2] *Science and Health*, pp. 125, 126.

of things that are made, that those things which cannot be shaken may remain" (Heb. 12:26, 27). "And I will shake all nations, and the desire of all nations shall come; and I will fill this house with glory, saith the Lord of hosts" (Hag. 2:7).

Knowledge of God is Necessary.—"*They shall not hurt nor destroy* 5 *in all my holy mountain: for the earth shall be full of the knowledge of the Lord, as the waters cover the sea*" (Isa. 11:9).

"The term Christian Science relates especially to Science as applied to humanity" (Mary Baker Eddy).[1] It is the Science of God and man, and the only true knowledge is the knowledge of the ideal or real world. To 10 obtain this thorough knowledge of the real world, not only is it essential that what matter claims to be should be comprehended, but the underlying causes and the forces that claim to be at work must be uncovered. "Is God the Principle of all science, or only of Divine or Christian Science? . . . All true Science represents a moral and spiritual force, 15 which holds the earth in its orbit. This force is Spirit." [2] "Science often suffers blame through the sheer ignorance of people, while envy and hatred bark and bite at its heels." [3]

Knowledge of Evil is Necessary.—"*The proper knowledge of evil and its subtle workings . . . is indispensable.*" "*To know the what, when,* 20 *and how of error, destroys error. The error that is seen aright as error, has received its death-blow; but never until then*" [4] (Mary Baker Eddy).

"Study and practical work in Christian Science speedily bring error to the surface and give a new and more correct apprehension of its nature and pretences, its asserted laws and *modus operandi*. It is necessary that 25 evil's progeny be thus recognised before it can be destroyed, and it is equally important that they be destroyed as soon as recognised" ("Watching versus Watching Out," *Christian Science Sentinel*, September 16, 1905, J. B. Willis). Mrs. Eddy, in a letter to the *Sentinel*, of the following week, emphasising the absolute necessity of careful and ceaseless watch upon one's 30 thoughts, writes: "Does not the text-book of Christian Science, *Science and Health with Key to the Scriptures*, read on page 252, 'A knowledge of error and of its operations must precede that understanding of Truth which destroys error?'"

Only by uncovering error can we thoroughly deal with and destroy the 35 evil that is at work in the material so-called world. In the words of Mrs. Eddy I would repeat to-day: "Those who deny my wisdom or right to expose error, are either willing participants in wrong, afraid of its supposed power, or ignorant of it."[5] Mrs. Eddy is most emphatic on this point. She says: "Many are willing to open the eyes of the people to the power 40 of good resident in divine Mind, but they are not so willing to point out the evil in human thought, and expose evil's hidden [so-called] mental ways

---

[1] *Science and Health*, p. 127.
[2] *Rudimental Divine Science*, p. 4, Mary Baker Eddy.
[3] *No and Yes*, p. 43, Mary Baker Eddy.   45
[4] *Miscellaneous Writings*, pp. 108, 299.
[5] *Ibid.*, p. 335.

of accomplishing iniquity. Why this backwardness, since exposure is necessary to ensure the avoidance of the evil?"[1] She also says: "The visible universe declares the invisible, only by reversion."[2] Also, "The use of a lie is that it unwittingly confirms Truth, when handled by Christian 5 Science, which reverses false testimony and gains a knowledge of God from opposite facts, or phenomena."[3]

Mrs. Eddy makes it perfectly clear that every detail of evil has to be understood and laid bare. Under the marginal reference, "Fallacious Hypotheses," she writes in *Science and Health* (p. 79): "Science must go 10 over the whole ground and dig up every seed of error's sowing." She points out the care with which this exposure has to be made, and says that it must be done sooner or later. "This uncovering and punishing of sin must, will come, at some date, to the rescue of humanity." "Have mortals, with the penetration of Soul, searched the secret chambers of sense? I 15 never knew a student who fully understood my instructions on this point of handling evil—as to just how this should be done—and carried out my ideal." "If spiritual sense is not dominant in a student, he will not understand all your instructions."[4]

She says: "Mortals must first open their eyes to all the illusive forms, 20 methods, and subtlety of error, in order that the illusion, error, may be destroyed."[5] She also has said: "Our time, means, and health are required for the fuller investigation of this subject; to teach, write, establish practices for students, or halt, perhaps, at measures to be adopted, because of persecution." Again, she says: "Led by a solitary star amid the darkness, 25 the Magi of old foretold the Messiahship of Truth. Is the wise man of to-day believed, when he beholds the light which heralds Christ's eternal dawn and describes its effulgence?"[6] The fulfilment of the above prophecies has brought the knowledge that such investigations and needful explanations could only be made as man finds his rightful dominion over 30 evil of every kind.

When a man understands evil he has no fear of it. Mrs. Eddy points out that "His [Jesus's] earthly mission was to translate substance into its original meaning, Mind."[7] We must not expect to get an accurate knowledge of the real spiritual world if we do not understand the illusive pre- 35 tence of a material world. Jesus said to Nicodemus: "If I have told you earthly things, and ye believe not, how shall ye believe, if I tell you of heavenly things?" (John 3:12). Mrs. Eddy says: "As mortals do not comprehend even mortal existence, how ignorant must they be of the all-knowing Mind and of His creations." "If you wish to know the spiritual 40 fact, you can discover it by reversing the material fable, be the fable *pro* or *con*,—be it in accord with your preconceptions or utterly contrary to them."[8] But how can you possibly expect to gain knowledge of the

[1] *Science and Health*, p. 570.
[2] *Miscellaneous Writings*, p. 218.
45   [3] *Unity of Good*, p. 36.
[4] *Miscellaneous Writings*, p. 293.
[5] *Retrospection and Introspection*, p. 64.
[6] *Science and Health*, p. 95.
[7] *Miscellaneous Writings*, p. 74.
50   [8] *Science and Health*, p. 187.

spiritual by reversing the material, if your knowledge of the material is inaccurate?

To destroy the human belief in its own theories is to strike a fatal blow at their power to harm.

To do this thoroughly, an accurate knowledge of what it claims to be is essential. Mrs. Eddy, in *Science and Health*, points out the value of understanding its false basis, that is, what it claims to be. "Mortal mind is ignorant of self, or it could never be self-deceived" (p. 186). "As mortal mind is the husbandman of error, it should be taught to do the body no harm and to uproot its false sowing" (p. 180). Speaking of the transient potency of drugs, she also says: "These lessons are useful. They should naturally and genuinely change our basis from sensation to Christian Science" (p. 370).

Mrs. Eddy says, in *Retrospection and Introspection*, p. 55: "Let us follow the example of Jesus, the master Metaphysician, and gain sufficient knowledge of error to destroy it with Truth." She also says, in *Science and Health*, p. 102: "The looms of crime, hidden in the dark recesses of mortal thought, are every hour weaving webs more complicated and subtle." These are "the rulers of the darkness of this world" and the "spiritual wickedness in high places," spoken of in Ephesians 6, verse 12. Each of us has his work to do, and it is fortunate that some are found that can handle such wickedness without any fear. These have to know "evil aright," [1] to understand every detail of its action in order to prevent succumbing to its "serpent's sting." "The diabolism of suppositional evil at work in the name of good, is a lie." [2] We have to face this evil, to have the courage of our convictions, however much we are misunderstood and reviled. God will lead us if we are doing our work properly, and no ignorance or other form of evil can check the work or harm us. "Herein is our love made perfect, that we may have boldness in the day of judgment" (I John 4:17).

Fortunately we can retire into the kingdom of God that is within, the secret place of the Most High, and there, secure in the love of God, knowing what we really are, destroy every false and lying thought that tempts us to believe in this so-called evil. John follows on after the previous quotation by saying: "Because as he is, so are we in this world."

In *Of The Supersensual Life*, Jacob Boehme says: "And then should a man wrap his soul in this, even in the great love of God, and clothe himself therewith as with a garment; and should account thence all things alike; because in the creature he finds nothing that can give him without God, the least satisfaction; and because also nothing of harm can touch him more, while he remains in this love, the which indeed is stronger than all things, and makes a man hence invulnerable both from within and without, by taking out the sting and poison of the creatures, and destroying the power of death. . . .

"Such a man gets greater favours than the world is able to bestow upon him. He hath God for his friend; he hath all his angels for his friends. In all dangers and necessities these protect and relieve him; so that he need

---

[1] *Miscellaneous Writings*, p. 108.
[2] *Ibid.* p. 334.

fear no manner of evil; no creature can hurt him. . . . Nay, but he gets the hearts of all his good friends into his possession, and loses none but his enemies, who before loved his vanity and wickedness. . . .

"For all the children of God are but One in Christ, which one is Christ 5 in all . . . So that he can have no want of spiritual friends and relations . . . These are friends worth having . . . So in like manner, those who love Truth and righteousness will love that man . . . yet they cannot resist being of one mind with him, and being united in affection, for the great regard they bear to the truth, which shines forth in his words and in 10 his life. By which they are made either his declared or his secret friends; and he doth so get their hearts, as they will be delighted above all things in his company, for the sake thereof, and will court his friendship and will come unto him by stealth, if openly they dare not, for the benefit of his conversation and advice; even as Nicodemus did unto Christ, who came 15 to him by night, and in his heart loved Jesus for the truth's sake, though outwardly he feared the world. And thus thou shalt have many friends that are not known to thee; and some known to thee, who may not appear so before the world." This took place in the past amongst the early Christians, and is being repeated to-day in the life experience of both men and 20 women in the advanced field of Christian Science. It bears on its face its tale of fear, and in these enlightened days should be a thing of the past. It can only continue until greater knowledge dispels the night of ignorance which tries to hide the truth. On the other hand, the lack of moral courage evinced by such learners, being fatal to rapid advance, should be lovingly 25 rebuked by all true friends.

"They are slaves, who dare not be
In the right with two or three" (Lowell).

Charity is Necessary.—"If thou hast anything of good, believe still better things of others, that thou mayest preserve humility" (Thomas à 30 Kempis). "Courtesy is the sister of charity, by which hatred is extinguished and love is cherished" (St. Francis of Assisi).

All of those who know the history of Mrs. Eddy, and value aright her reiterated teachings, refrain from breaking the Golden Rule,[1] and if differing from what they hear or what they read of another, "substitute silence 35 for censure" and rely upon the mental work. "Do thou hold thy tongue for one day. On the morrow see how much clearer are thy purposes and duties" (Carlyle). This silent work either destroys that which might at first appear a menace to Christian Science, or, if right, alters the first false impression of it. Shakespeare says: "Virtue itself 'scapes not calumnious 40 strokes," and those who through ignorance pass on untruths, and those who for want of sufficient protection of themselves start untruths through misunderstanding, will be helped by the following words of our leader:

"Envy or abuse of him who, having a new idea or a more spiritual understanding of God, hastens to help on his fellow-mortals, is neither 45 Christian nor Science. If a postal service, a steam engine, a submarine cable, a wireless telegraph, each in turn has helped mankind, how much

[1] Matthew 7, verse 12.

more is accomplished when the race is helped onward by a new-old message from God, even the knowledge of salvation from sin, disease, and death." [1] Jesus said: "Forbid him not: for he that is not against us is for us" (Luke 9:50). Let us honour Christianity wherever it be found, and however imperfectly presented.

5

"Whatever in Love's name is truly done
To free the bound, and lift the fallen one,
Is done to Christ. Whoso in deed and word
Is not against Him, labours for our Lord" (*Whittier*).

Whenever there is a feeling of censure, however merited, we know that 10 there is a wrong thought that has to be destroyed, and the mental work must be done in our own consciousness. It is there the evil lies.

Mrs. Eddy writes in *No and Yes*, pp. 7–9: "No personal consideration should allow any root of bitterness to spring up between Christian Scientists, nor cause any misapprehension as to the motives of others. We 15 must love our enemies, and continue to do so unto the end. By the love of God we can cancel error in our own hearts, and blot it out of others. . . .

"I recommend that Scientists draw no lines whatever between one person and another, but think, speak, teach, and write the truth of Christian Science without reference to right or wrong personality in this field 20 of labor. . . .

"We should endeavour to be long-suffering, faithful, and charitable with all. To this small effort let us add one more privilege—namely, silence whenever it can substitute censure. Avoid voicing error ; but utter the truth of God and the beauty of holiness, the joy of Love, and the 25 peace of God, that passeth all understanding. . . .

"This one thing can be done, and should be: let your opponents alone, and use no influence to prevent their legitimate action from their own standpoint of experience, knowing, as you should, that God will well regenerate and separate wisely and finally; whereas you may err in effort, 30 and lose your fruition."

Blanche Hogue writes: "If Christian Scientists in their work together dwell upon those things in which they concur, their diverging view-points concerning non-essentials will soon slip into secondary importance and unity will prevail. Upon this matter John Ruskin in 'The Mystery of Life 35 and its Arts,' uses words both plain and strong. He writes: 'Whenever in any religious faith, dark or bright, we allow our minds to dwell upon the points in which we differ from other people, we are wrong, and in the devil's power. . . . At every moment of our lives we should be trying to find out, not in what we differ from other people, but in what we agree 40 with them . . . push at it together; you cannot quarrel in a side-by-side push; but the moment that even the best men stop pushing and begin talking, they mistake their pugnacity for piety, and it is all over.'"

"There is so much good in the worst of us,
And so much bad in the best of us,
That it ill behoves any of us
To find fault with the rest of us."

[1] *Message for* 1902, p. 11.

To complain of the exposure of electrical theories, and at the same time, through fear, to systematically avoid the seemingly destructive action of electricity in a charged electric wire is a mere exposure of the ignorant assent generally given to the hidden physical working and the
5 so-called laws of matter, until their whole detail is recognised as a bald imposition.

Again, to complain of the exposure of an accurate, basic theory put forward as a necessary method of cutting away the false authority of material phenomena, an exposure essential to the destruction of a belief in
10 it, and to complain of the use of a man's knowledge of God for the better performance of every-day details, and at the same time to take advantage of every material condition, such as the electric telegraph and the electric railway, is the hypocrisy of ignorance. Such individuals, mistakenly advertising their want of knowledge, with the object of being of use to
15 their fellow-men by exposing what they think is ignorance of true science, are unaware of the danger of the intensification of material thoughts and conditions by their own seemingly harmless use and even dependence upon these material phenomena, instead of the implicit reliance, even in trifles, on God alone, up to the fullest extent of their knowledge. A tame sub-
20 mission to the seeming laws and limitations of matter is simply evidence of the mesmerised condition under which the individual labours. Fortunately, however, we live and learn, and a man's statements in the past are no criterion of his knowledge, and therefore spirituality, in the present.

Mrs. Eddy writes: "Why I loved Christians of the old sort was I could
25 not help loving them. Full of charity and good works, busy about their Master's business, they had no time or desire to defame their fellow-men. . . . . Their convictions were honest, and they lived them; and the sermons their lives preached caused me to love their doctrines."[1] "He who has suffered from intolerance is the first to be intolerant." [2] "The original
30 text [of the Bible] defines 'devil' as 'accuser,' 'calumniator'; therefore, according to Holy Writ these qualities are objectionable, and ought not to proceed from the individual." [3] "We should draw no lines whatever between one person and another" lest we be as "sounding brass, or a tinkling cymbal." "It is the healing power of truth that is persecuted
35 to-day, the spirit of divine Love, and Christ Jesus possessed it, practised it, and taught his followers to do likewise." [4] It was the self-righteousness of the Pharisees that crucified him, and this same self-righteousness is vainly beating its head to-day against a rock, the rapidly spreading knowledge of God.
40   "It is the persistent tendency to judge, criticise, and impugn the motives and purposes of others which has come down to us from the old thought, that often prevents us from meeting the demands of true ethics. We are certainly departing from true right conduct, under any rule of ethics, when we set ourselves up as the judges of the conduct or motives of others,
45 to criticise and condemn. When we are able to see scientifically the per-

[1] *Message for* 1901, p. 32.
[2] *Christian Healing*, p.11.
[3] *Message for* 1901, p. 16.
[4] *Ibid.*, p. 9.

fect man, and view our brothers' shortcomings (as we conceive we see them) as the operation of uncontrolled evil, then . . . we shall have made a great stride towards true ethics" [1] (Judge J. D. Works). "Judge not according to the appearance, but judge righteous judgment" (John 7:24).

Beware of Jealousy.—"*When the Pharisees saw Jesus do such deeds* [5] *of mercy, they went away and took counsel how they might remove him*" [2] (Mary Baker Eddy).

Jealousy is the tyrant that proved the undoing of the scribes and Pharisees in all their dealings with Jesus. "The mischief of jealousy, manifold and fruitful, extends widely. It is the root of all evils, the fountain of [10] disasters, the nursery of crimes, the material of transgressions; thence arise hatreds, thence proceed animosities.

"The mischief is much more trifling, the danger less, the cure easy where the wound is manifest. But the wounds of jealousy are hidden and secret, nor do they admit of the remedy of a healing cure, since they have [15] shut themselves in blind suffering within the lurking-places of the conscience. Whoever you are that are envious or malignant, observe how crafty, mischievous, and hateful you are to those you hate. Yet you are the enemy of no one's well-being more than your own; whoever he is whom you persecute with jealousy he can evade and escape you. You can- [20] not escape from yourself; wherever you may be your adversary is with you; your enemy is always within your own breast. Your mischief is shut up within you. You are captive under the tyranny of jealousy" (Cyprian, A.D. 250). "Beware of no man more than of yourself; we carry our worst enemies within us" (John Ploughman). [25]

How thankful we should be to realise that all that is now necessary to attain perfect freedom from this tyrant is to recognise its absolute non-reality, and open our mind to the ever-active divine Principle, Love, and so manifest love in all dealings with our fellow-man. When false thoughts attack through so-called individuals, it is merely the call to still higher [30] work in bearing our brother's burden. "For the weapons of our warfare are not carnal, but mighty through God" (II Cor. 10:4). We must both live and let live, and let God choose His own time. "The Science of man and the universe . . . is on the way . . . purifying all peoples, religions, ethics and learning." [3] [35]

All evil that comes into our consciousness has to be destroyed in that self-same consciousness. "For though we walk in the flesh, we do not war after the flesh" (II Cor. 10:3). If we fail to destroy in our own consciousness such wrong thoughts concerning individuals, we have to recognise that it is merely through want of sufficient of the love that our [40] Master and his beloved disciple pointed out as the foundation of all law. "Love thyself last: cherish those hearts that hate thee" (Shakespeare). "Draw the curtain of night upon injuries; shut them up in the tower of oblivion, and let them be as though they had not been" (Bacon).

If we are living Christian Science throughout the day, neither criticism [45]

---

[1] *The Christian Science Journal*, October, 1909.
[2] *Miscellaneous Writings*, p. 370.
[3] *Message for* 1902, p. 2.

nor untruth about us can possibly harm us in the slightest, but must
infallibly result in our additional purification and help, through the
impersonal work of all true Scientists who hear the statements of error.
"Blessed are ye, when men shall revile you, and persecute you, and shall
5 say all manner of evil against you falsely, for my sake. Rejoice, and be
exceeding glad" (Matt. 5:11, 12).

In Mrs. Eddy's letter to the General Association of Teachers, of
October 21, 1903, she says that we must "work 'midst clouds of wrong,
injustice, envy, hate, and wait on God, the strong deliverer, who will reward
10 righteousness and punish iniquity." "Work is the first chapter of human
life; God is the conclusion" (Sri Ramakrishna). "If God be for us, who can
be against us?" "All things work together for good to them that love God,
to them who are the called according to his purpose" (Rom. 8:31, 28).

"If you launch your bark upon the ever-agitated but healthful waters
15 of truth, you will encounter storms. Your good will be evil spoken of. This
is the cross. Take it up and bear it, for through it you win and [perchance
unrecognised in the house of so-called mortal "mind"] wear the crown.
Pilgrim on earth, thy home is heaven; stranger, thou art the guest of God"
(Mary Baker Eddy).[1]

20 **The Grave-Clothes of the Letter.**—"*For if after they have escaped
the pollutions of the world through the knowledge of the Lord and Saviour
Jesus Christ, they are again entangled therein, and overcome, the latter end
is worse with them than the beginning. For it had been better for them not to
have known the way of righteousness, than, after they have known it, to turn
25 from the holy commandment*" [the law of love, the new commandment]
(II Peter 2:20, 21).

The knowledge of the letter is "the sword of the Spirit, which is the
word of God" (Eph. 6:17). If the students of the letter of the great law
of Mind, eternal good, break the new commandment and are not loving
30 to their fellow-man, but imagine evil of their neighbour, being held in
fetters by "the dead body of Science,—pulseless, cold, inanimate"[2]
"their sword shall enter into their own heart" (Ps. 37:15). These we must
help impersonally when we think of them. Mrs. Eddy says: "Such so-
called Scientists will strain out gnats, while they swallow the camels of
35 bigoted pedantry."[3]

Right throughout history we find exemplified the truth of the statement "the letter killeth, but the spirit giveth life" (II Cor. 3:6). *The more
the statements of truth are enunciated without the essential spiritual realisation and consequent human sympathy, the more deadly the result* upon a
40 human being—if, through ignorance, off his guard—and upon the self-
righteous lawgiver. The reason for this is, not that the statement of truth
can possibly do any harm, but "when the mechanism of the human mind"
has not given "place to the divine Mind"[4] and the human endeavour to
enforce *what it considers* God's law by the exercise of human will-power

45   [1] *Science and Health*, p. 254.
                                  [2] *Ibid.*, p. 113.
                                  [3] *Ibid.*, p. 366.
                                  [4] *Ibid.*, p. 176.

instead of by the destruction of the evil that lies at the root of all wrong thinking and doing, then the innocent ignorant one and the Pharisaical law-enforcer both suffer, in proportion to the violence of the attack of personal evil. This is the use of the letter of truth by the spirit of evil, evil working in the name of good, producing an illusory "negative right and positive wrong." [1] Verbal statements of God's power, cloaking the wrong thoughts behind, are the "sword" of evil—counterfeiting the two-edged sword of Truth—which morally slays the individual using it, bringing on him troubles innumerable, until, learning his lesson, he bears his brother's burden by reversing all evil thoughts of man, and knowing only the truth, that man is in reality spiritual and good.

The essence of Christianity lies in the words of Jesus in the Sermon on the Mount, "All things whatsoever ye would that men should do to you, do ye even so to them: for this is the law and the prophets" (Matt. 7:12). Mrs. Eddy writes: "The teacher of Mind-healing who is not a Christian, in the highest sense, is constantly sowing the seeds of discord and disease. Even the truth he speaks is more or less blended with error; and this error will spring up in the mind [so called] of his pupil. The pupil's imperfect knowledge will lead to weakness in practice, and he will be a poor practitioner, if not a malpractitioner. The basis of malpractice is in erring human will." [2]

"Then said Jesus . . . I am the door of the sheep" (John 10 : 7). "When once the master of the house is risen up, and hath shut to the door, [3] and ye [4] begin to stand without, and to knock at the door, saying, Lord, Lord, open unto us; and he shall answer and say unto you, I know you not whence ye are: Then shall ye begin to say, We have eaten and drunk in thy presence, and thou hast taught in our streets. But he shall say, I tell you, I know you not whence ye are; depart from me, all ye workers of iniquity. There shall be weeping and gnashing of teeth, when ye shall see Abraham, and Isaac, and Jacob, and all the prophets, in the kingdom of God, and you yourselves thrust out . . . Behold, there are last which shall be first, and there are first which shall be last" (Luke 13:25–28, 30).

Take Heed.—It is unhappily needful to warn those seeking for the better knowledge of God, and that wisely come to those who rely upon the writings of Mrs. Eddy to explain the teachings of the Bible, against appealing for help to anyone who is found habitually to speak against any person or persons, or to attach evil to their fellow-man in thought or word. Whatever their claims to a true knowledge of Christian Science may be, and however much they are trying to help their fellow-man, this judgment of another stamps them as wholly disqualified to teach, or even practise, the healing of sickness with any safety to those with whom they come in contact. Mrs. Eddy says: "It is important to know that a malpractice of the best system will result in the worst form of

---

[1] *Science and Health*, p. 491.
[2] *Rudimental Divine Science*, p. 9.
[3] That is, when night cometh and no man can work.
[4] Those who have learned the scientific truth that all is Mind, and should then "bury the morale of Christian Science in the grave-clothes of the letter."

medicine."[1] She also says: "Better suffer a doctor infected with smallpox to attend you than to be treated mentally by one who does not obey
the requirements of divine Science." [2]

Results of healing in some cases apparently follow their efforts, but these
5 are due to the recognition of truth by the patient, who is healed by the
impersonal Truth. "Many will say to me in that day, Lord, Lord, have
we not prophesied in thy name? and in thy name have cast out devils? and
in thy name done many wonderful works? And then will I profess unto
them, I never knew you: depart from me, ye that work iniquity" (Matt.
10 7:22, 23). Even the formal declaration of truth on the part of the would-be
healer, met by the spiritual receptivity of the patient, demonstrates the
unfailing action of the omnipotent Principle which, when either the letter
or the Spirit is absent, merely shines as a glorious, but unrecognised,
presence over a troubled world. At the same time, the patient cannot
15 escape contamination through association with an infected human instrument. Beginners so taught, instead of shrinking with horror at this deadly
sin of attaching evil to their fellow-men, get careless, and at last actually
excuse such guilt, on the ground that they are only telling you the position,
or only letting you know about such-and-such persons, so that you can
20 keep away from them and warn others to do the same. This is exactly the
reverse of what has to be done in fulfilment of the Golden Rule, the law of
Love, and therefore the law of Life.

Not the least of the dangers threatening the would-be searchers is that,
in very human gratitude for the initial physical benefit received, they are
25 liable to be held for a further interval under this dangerous influence. "A
slight divergence is fatal in Science." [3] On the other hand, if the helper
obeys the Golden Rule in thought and word, however slight his knowledge
of the latter, some good must, and no harm can possibly, result. This
practical charity is the signet of the true and safe worker. Criticism is the
30 danger signal. Love is the beacon light that infallibly guides us into the
safe harbour of Science, where holiness, health, and happiness alone are
found. "Oh! be swift to love, make haste to be kind" (Amiel). While
the slanderer will offer many excuses for voicing evil concerning persons,
the true worker knows that this is only justifiable when in treatment the
35 evil is uncovered for the purposes of destruction, either audibly or silently,
then and there. He also knows the absolute futility of any human attempt
to oppose the action of God, and rests securely upon this knowledge.

Personality.—Personality is the bane of mental workers. Whether
40 a person is a saint or a devil, is no business of ours. We, in any case, have
to keep our thoughts off him if we wish to avoid harming ourselves, and
making things worse. "He who worships man is neither Jew, Christian,
nor Mohammedan, and cannot but become debased and degraded. He
who worships man with all his imperfections and his weaknesses, cannot
but deaden the spark of divinity placed within him by a higher power" [4]

45   [1] *Miscellaneous Writings*, p. 233.
     [2] *Science and Health*, p. 235.
     [3] *Rudimental Divine Science*, p. 17.
     [4] Sermon on "The Jewish Idea of God," preached in the Jewish Synagogue,
Sacramento, 1902.

(H. Weinstock). We have to form a right estimate of God's idea, and only Christian Science can enable us to gain this scientific knowledge. John records the reproof that followed his personal worship before the feet of the angel, which showed him the truth: "See thou do it not: for I am thy fellow servant: . . . worship God" (Rev. 22 :9).　　　　　　　　　　　5

Many have not yet recognised that when a person appears to be harming us, mentally, physically, or otherwise, it is only impersonal evil making him a channel. It is he that has to be pitied and protected. If we do our work properly the evil cannot harm us. Retaliating, or even feeling antagonistic, is not scientific. If a man threw a stone at us we would not blame 10 and punish the stone. It is the evil that has to be dealt with and destroyed— by right thinking.

Safety is at Hand.—"*Christian Science appeals loudly to those asleep upon the hill-tops of Zion*" ¹ (Mary Baker Eddy).

The time is close upon us when there will be no mistaking the true 15 worker for the false. Both may be trying to do their best, the latter often failing through want of love. " Cast not your pearls before the unwise, but with increased power and patience press on. The fight is against an effort to enthrone matter, to enthrone self. The feverish pride of sects and systems is the death's-head at the feast of Love, but Christianity is ever storming 20 sin in its citadels . . ." ² Principle will always demonstrate where the clearest channel for truth can be found. Unselfed love is an unfailing sign, and the earnest seeker can never fail for lack of right direction, if he turns solely to Principle. Mrs. Eddy also writes: "Wheresoever you recognise a clear expression of God's likeness, there abide in confidence and hope." ³ 25 And again, "Only a firm foundation in Truth can give a fearless wing and a sure reward."⁴ The Christ is made manifest by demonstration, and Love alone heals sickness and sin. "Therefore, come what may, hold fast to love. We win by tenderness; we conquer by forgiveness " (F. W. Robertson). "The divinity of the Christ was made manifest in the humanity of 30 Jesus " ⁵ (Mary Baker Eddy). Although an accurate declaration of truth is better than a declaration of error, it requires the spirit of Truth and Love to demonstrate omnipotence, and nothing less can save humanity.

We have to recognise that throughout the history of religious experiences we find that those previously persecuted when lifted into a 35 position of eminence by the action of God, if not continually protecting themselves properly by true prayer, become the target of evil "thoughts" which are always trying to find a joint in the spiritual armour. A victim of personality, they in turn become the persecutors, condemning and maligning those who put forward a more spiritual view of life and practise 40 more closely the teachings of our Master. In this fast-approaching end of evil, we cannot expect the world to be free from the Pharisaism, and its attendant envy and jealousy, that made the so-called Christians

¹ *Message for* 1901, p. 35.
² *Ibid.*, p. 2.　　　　　　　　　　　　　　　　　　　　45
³ *Pulpit and Press*, p. 21.
⁴ *Message for* 1901, p. 2.
⁵ *Science and Health*, p. 25.

14

of Constantine persecute those of Northern Africa, because they refused to accept forms and ceremonies for the worship of the one God and the realisation of the living Christ.

"The day when the cry of 'Heretic!' was potent to stir up the passionate
5 superstitions of unthinking crowds has passed away. The world is recognising that the heresy of yesterday is always the orthodoxy of to-morrow. The same spirit accused Jesus of blasphemy, dismissed Paul as a pestilent fellow, decried Wyclif as a forger of lies, and claimed Luther was a drunken friar" [1] (Frederick Dixon). What applied to the orthodox church twenty
10 years ago applies to the leading spiritual church to-day. Excommunication without the slightest chance of defence, the constant dissemination of untruths [2] of every kind, so vile, in many cases, as to be their own undoing; the warning (against persons) of beginners, up to that time aglow with the beauty and worth of the right understanding of God and man; the stop-
15 page of the teaching of others, and then even of free speech, and, finally, of access to the church edifice; the secret espionage, and later the open watching and waiting; the searching of private letters to obtain evidence of wrong statements. All these occurring to-day are only repetitions of what has occurred in the past, and, probably, until they realise this, those
20 persecuting are just as certain that they are doing what is right as the bitterest exponents of the hellish system of the Inquisition. (See John 16, verses 2, 3).

Impossible as this latter triumvirate of evil may seem, it is only a recurrence of the usual Pharisaical methods wherever the letter of religion
25 is divorced from the spirit: "And they watched him, and sent forth spies, which should feign themselves just men, that they might take hold of his words, that so they might deliver him unto the power and authority of the governor" (Luke 20:20). Even in this position we find our instructions from him who was called to meet the same injustice, and who in the
30 culminating moments of his human agony was able to say, "Father, forgive them; for they know not what they do" (Luke 23:34). "Truth needs no champions: in the infinite deep of everlasting Soul her strength abides" (J. R. Lowell).

Bearing the above facts in mind, let each one, trying to understand and
35 live Christian Science, examine his inmost thoughts and see whether there is any criticism, any thought of others not being correct exponents of truth. If you find these devilish thoughts attacking the temple of the Holy Ghost, beware! Humbly in prayer silence the lie, realise God's man, and prayerfully and tearfully turn to God, certain that this recognition of the
40 evil is its uncovering, and this uncovering is its destruction and the relegation for ever to outer darkness of such futile efforts to delay Truth's progress.

> "The arrow that doth wound the dove
> Darts not from those who watch and love" (Mary Baker Eddy).

45 [1] The Christian Science Journal, March, 1911, reprinted from Cosmopolitan Magazine.

[2] "It requires courage to utter truth; for the higher Truth lifts her voice, the louder will error scream, until its inarticulate sound is forever silenced in oblivion" (Science and Health, p. 97). See also Ezekiel 3, verses 25–27, and Luke 6, verse 22.

Whilst the leader is alive, such leader, protected by deep, systematic right thinking, bears the brunt of the unseen, so-called mental attack, and the sheep and lambs hardly recognise what is being done for them. This bearing the sin of many is the joy of all spiritual leaders everywhere. Great is the honour of such leaders, for "sweet are the uses of adversity." On the 5 departure of this leader, those most advanced have to bear this attack. Where the knowledge has been imbibed and the lessons put into practice, such attack merely lifts the worker into still loftier regions, close to God's right hand, and from the region of this holy mountain the two-edged sword of Truth ends evil's claim to reality and power. Those whose claim 10 to the title Christian Scientist rests only on the letter, find that evil gets the upper hand, and "stings and jaws and claws" are evident. Thank God they only mark the coming end of all such devilish, so-called thoughts.

The world now awakening eager-eyed, listens with bated breath and heart-throbs deep to the wondrous unfolding story of ever-living man, man 15 that is the love of Love, the love of God.

Never again can the door be closed by ignorance in an assembly of enlightened humanity. Any unchristian regulations that would infringe on the human right of free speech and free entry into and enjoyment of the services of a scientific and religious church assembly, would be obviously 20 in direct contradiction to and an exhibition of disloyalty to the teachings of the Discoverer and Founder of the Church of Christ, Scientist. "To perpetuate a cold distance between our denomination and other sects, and close the door on church or individuals—however much this is done to us—is not Christian Science." [1] 25

Strive above all things to obey our Leader's express command, and always to leave each student "free to follow upwards individual convictions," and avoid the guilt of attempting to deprive him of his divine rights of the freedom of "the sons of God," and so to unwittingly "fight against God" and cloud the glorious view unfolding, which blesses each 30 and all. Self-abnegation is demanded from us up to the last, if we would not delay the fulfilment of our own dearest hopes and reap the inevitable punishment that awaits all those who crucify the Christ idea and hold it up to scorn, leaving the dark pall of ignorance to cloud a suffering world.

Christ is the living life, the love of Love, that lifts *the church that is* 35 *within*, the love that we have to build, that is, develop, for our fellow-men, when high above all sense of vicious personality, it shines a blazing beacon light, a guide for infancy and ignorance, till, lifted up by Love's demands, all see the truth and all are free.

The Manner and Period of the End.—"*Then shall the deep pit of* 40 *judgments lie open before the region of consolation, and the furnace of hell appear before the paradise of joy.* . . . *And the day of judgment shall be equal to the space of seven years*" (II Esdras 7, Revised Version, T. J. Hussey, D.D.).

Recognising that the channel through which false thought attacks can- 45 not escape the divine penalty incurred by this crime, the true worker, leaving his opponents alone to God's fiat—material self-extinction—with " Father,

[1] *Pulpit and Press*, p 21.

forgive them; for they know not what they do," [1] will rise to a sense of his unity with the Father,[2] and knowing the only real forgiveness, will realise that we are the love of Love, and will let an overwhelming sense of his divine prerogative wipe out all traces of the devil's work. This impersona-
5 lises the error and frees the unfortunate victim. So only do we really love our brother and fulfil the whole law (Rom. 13:8), finding then that there is no attack, and consequently no channel and no victim, for THERE IS NOTHING BUT GOD AND HIS MANIFESTATION.

Should any hesitate to accept the truth put forward in this book for the
10 benefit of the world in general, the advice of Gamaliel, the Pharisee, should be prayerfully considered, "Refrain from these men, and let them alone : for if this counsel or this work be of men, it will come to nought : But if it be of God, ye cannot overthrow it; lest haply ye be found even to fight against God" (Acts 5:38, 39). "I will stand upon my watch, and set me
15 upon the tower, and will watch to see what he will say unto me, and what I shall answer when I am reproved. And the Lord answered me, and said, Write the vision, and make it plain upon tables, that he may run that readeth it. For the vision is yet for an appointed time, but at the end it shall speak, and not lie : though it tarry, wait for it; because it will surely come,
20 it will not tarry" (Hab. 2:1-3).

"As for the truth, it endureth and is always strong; it liveth and con-quereth for evermore. . . . And all the people then shouted, and said, Great is Truth, and mighty above all things" (I Esdras 4:38, 41).

[1] Luke 23, verse 34.
25 [2] "I and the Father are one" (John 10, verse 30, R.V.).

INDEX

INDEX

A

absolute and relative xii/28–37. 142/32–41. 144/47,48. 242/9–27. 357/1–4

accept 295/29. acceptance 80/13. 295/28

accuracy 318/9. accurate xii/29. 64/6. 65/3. 86/48. 161/9. 357/24

act 32/39. 138/14. 223/31. 224/38. 237/48. 286/24. 306/15

action of God 72/21,31. 76/13. 79/35. 89/38. 99/36,39. 105/17. 107/3. 111/15. 114/34. 116/45. 118/50. 127/15. 128/3. 131/18. 134/44. 136/36. 138/3,24. 149/35. 161/2,20. 204/29. 206/9. 208/41. 210/45. 211/4,14. 212/17. 220/22,37. 223/42. 224/25. 242/30. 246/29. 288/30,37. 302/33. 323/39. 356/22. 364/20. 367/29. 370/18. 378/1; due to a. of God 128/42. 148/27. 263/35. 296/3. 312/29. 375/40. action 75/11. 95/40. 115/24. 136/45. 289/11. 293/43,45. 295/20,26. 354/26. active 2/13. 36/4. 72/32. 134/40. 170/17. 245/13,15. 295/28. 363/25. actively 173/18,41. 227/34. 274/20. 309/1. activity 35/22. 133/26. 140/11. 185/39. 237/22. 296/29. 366/13. 369/1. 375/42

advanced 94/40. 134/11,23,26. 284/1. 299/44. advancement 235/7. 237/4. 267/7. 355/17. 374/40. 375/4. advancing 129/25. 286/35. 288/6. 295/42

Aeon 364/20.

affirmation 127/34. 204/29. 210/34. 215/20. 220/37. 267/24 (see also under DENIAL and affirmation)

afterwards 79/36. 309/16

agnosticism 16/24. 255/15. 343/25

aim 304/37. 375/46. aimed 186/23

alertness 286/9

aletheia 144/48. 357/3

alter vii/34. 199/20. 312/16. 375/26. alteration 173/4. 202/21. 231/23. 274/27. alterations 257/34. altered xi/42. 75/13

alternative 145/39

anger 72/24. 128/4. 130/41. 204/19. 267/10. 357/10. 372/12. angry man 72/24–31. 127–128. 130/33,43. 203/30. 267/10

Anglo-Israelites 153/31

animal 8/32. 57/10. 230/18,19. 358/10. 359/33. 360/22. 365–367. animals

57/7. 82/38. 167/24–168/12. 192/9. 193/29. 244/36. 258/25. 279/41. 365–367

application 12/25. 38/16. 54/1. 76/10. 96/41. 305/4

appointments 167/1

apportions 65/20

argue 307/17

Aristotle 84/13. 237/21. 323/9. 333. 346/1

Armageddon 304/41

armour 214/8. 264/25. 305/2

Arnold Sir Edwin 52/10. 77/22. 326/20

Arnold Matthew 205/33. 260/25. 286/27

around 211/13. 215/4. 230/20. 281/22

arrow 172/37. 327/45. arrows 234/29

artist letter to 374

ascension 25/32. 98/35. 140/10. 268/2

ask 214/39. asked 136/31. 137/4,11. 223/9. asking 79/29. 162/32. 208/6,16. 209/5,31. 212/43. asks 137/7

assent 80/15. 168/43

astral 120/30. 269/28. 347/36,44

astrology 164/35

atheism 16/24. 255/15

atom 65/24–30. 73/37. 74/45. atomic 65/24. 66/49. 88/7. 90/12. 159/43. atoms 74/23. 82/5

Atonement 39/25

at-one-ment 77/10. 233/43. 235/9. 236/6. 237/2

attack 168/18. 172–173/5. 206/14. 283/43. 293/32. 305/5. attacking 356/20

attraction and repulsion 161/23,24. 344/40. attraction 73/26. 76/36–77/10. attracts 308/26

attributes 91/27. 370/48. 371/4. 376/31

Augustine St. 17/49. 18/5. 29/27. 33/47. 35/14. 147/10. 166/47. 221/13. 224/19. 229/11. 279/36,40. 335/37. 378/17

authority 132/28. 146/27,29. 226/11–227/1. 286/11

automata 69/2. 167/24. automaton 19/31

availability 353/4. 373/1. available 79/3,11. 98/25. 125/17,28. 145/17. 221/25. 256/46. 278/13

awake 259/24. 263/7. 275/7. 376/6. awaken 205/9. awakens 272/28. 273/2. awakening 48/22. 94/26. 111/42. 148/3

B

bacteria 244/35. 301/38
balanced 231/22. 233/2,30. 235/17. 301/5
Balzac 341/9
baptism 131/21
basis scientific 7/37. 136/25. 148/37. 296/26. 315/5; false mental 19/29,37; of material world 63/18; of all evil 145/25; mental worker while still on material 238/33; basis 187/41. 281/9. 311/16. 355/4. 363/10
bath mental 301/10
battle 172/8. 261/39. battle-axe 297/42. battleground 173/13
beam 204/33. 290/14
beast 25/15. 89/11. 96/25. 230/23. 238/37. 352/42
beauty 24/31. 238. 314/16
Beelzebub 214/3
before 64/17. 77/15. 106/3,12,21. 115/23. 124/15. 143/7,31. 144/21. 171/37. 276/32. 361/24. 370/4. beforehand 166/50. 167/18. 312/11
beggar 226/12. 301/24
beginner 38/32. 125/19. 134/12,21. 136/44,46. 223/30. 283/32,36
Being 50/43. 85/29. 337/23
being
  perfect 32/34. 50/5. 99/19. 375/38
  spiritual 34/24. 36/7. 53/37. 99/31. 103/12. 108/38. 133/31. 205/40. 219/16. 273/32. 310/37. 312/34. 349/3. 369/15,23,27. 361/40
  human 21/10. 32/17. 49/11. 64/5. 68/38. 69/15. 86/34. 105/25. 111/18. 120/11. 148/28. 168/17. 221/27. 245/43. 246/24. 252/21. 253/38. 263/34. 312/37. 339/43. 359/33. 365/20
  material 310/36. 341/28
  being 99-101. 145/19. 340/45. 370/6
beings
  spiritual 100/4. 133/25. 145/27. 148/4. 288/2. 359/29. 363/24. 364/10. 365/35. 368/35. 377/7
  human 107/8. 192/21. 271/21. 277/8. 365/18
  material 63/46. 99/30. 267/4
  beings 91/22. 99-101. 270/38. 360/45
belief false 24/43. 87/1. 208/48. 263/43; human 70/17. 209/5. 226/12; better 167/22. 203/20. 279/15. belief 3/16. 17/12. 31/37,39. 69/37. 72/1. 126/28. 131/17. 136/6. 146/43. 196/43. 198/ 26,33. 208/2. 209/24. 243-246. 262/2. 264/17,39. 271/7. 280/20. beliefs false 14/20. 197/38. 245/37. 274/21; better 124/17. 302/21; human 135/42. 244/1; beliefs 14/16. 41/20. 68/33.

169/4. 204/21. 215/21. 243-246. 264/37. 271/36. 305/37. believe 18/47. 37/1. 217/24,25. 219/15. 307/16. 313/16. 314/37,41. believes 143/25. 229/9
beloved 290/26
beneficial 72/20. 187/40. 258/19. 282/43. benefit 75/20. 139/12,14. 150/38. 170/48. 210/39. 221/48. 229/5. 235/40. 252/17. 283/32. 301/21. 317/38. 353/23
Bergson Henri 19/34. 37/9. 51/22. 69/43. 75/4. 104/12. 115/39. 166/40. 193/42. 265/33. 272/45
Berkeley Bishop 13/33,36. 85/10. 338/21. 343/36
Besant Annie 123/27. 124/47. 245/42. 251/5. 268/9. 274/34. 277/39. 287/37. 288/28,48. 326/7. 347/21. 348/7
best 134/10,14. 160/38. 201/42,45. 246/30. 301/23. 302/48. 306/34. 355/5. better 48/13. 73/4. 155/2. 158/4. 240/17,18. 274/20. 302/5,38. 307/40. 312/9
bewitched 18/16,17
Bible 10/47. 148-154. 162-171. 194/14. 202/33,48. 207/33. 249/21. 255/15. 273/23. 286/17. 305/23. 315/38. 319/21. 359/12
birth 2/22. 36/10. 56/23. 87/6. 129/25,26. 167/15. 168/19. 204/21. 233/21. 264/36. 268/24,25. 270-279. birthright 144/3. 167/7. 210/36
blackmailing 134/33
blasphemy 92/1
Blavatsky Madame H. P. 251/7. 347/28
blessing 127/37. blessings 307/30,33
bliss 101/40. 210/22. 270/38. 292/17,20. 297/45. 314/22. 369/4
blood 373/41
bodies 313/13. bodily 184/8,22,28. body spiritual 25/35 54/36-55/14. 367/35-369/2; human 20/34. 25/38; material 25/30. 70/8-73/18. 137/1. 263/37-269/31. 280/27; dematerialisation of 25/30. 49/13. 125/32,35; etheric 120/18-126/20. 347/44
Boehme Jacob 155/48. 230/33. 286/47. 292/42. 298/29. 336/19. 389/36
Bon Dr. G. Le 4/46. 5/49. 24/27. 40/46. 41/14. 43/35. 44/7. 55/36,49. 58/32. 66/35,51. 68/42. 81-82, 86/40. 88/6. 90/10. 91/46. 98/14. 113/31. 203/4. 269/42
bonds 235/12. 291/29
book this 3/4. 63/16. 228/26; little b. of Apocalypse 151/20 books protection in the reading of 114/23
born anew 379/16

bound to appear 169/7. 302/28
brain 7/40. 70/24. 71/13–19. 103/34.
167/42
breathing 369/9
brethren false 318/25
bringing-up 173/46. 241/3
brotherhood 232/29. 347/3
Browning Elizabeth Barrett 52/19.
231/8. 239/41. 297/6
Browning Robert 25/1. 25/7. 38/36.
48/10. 58/35. 174/30. 206/24. 215/9.
223/26. 285/9. 287/10. 309/15,24,46.
346/44. 351/17
Buddha Gautama 173/17. 325
bugle call 219/43. 281/19
bull's-eye 179/12
burden 300/36. **burdens** 172/20
busiest 110/40. **business** teaching
God His 209/10. 302/24. business
129/16. 245/10. 300/22. 301/12. 353/
42. 376/6

C

Cæsar rendering to 236/12
calculating 119/11
call 308/10
cancer 199/24–203/10. 259/37,39
canonical writings 149
capacity 8/10. 63/3. 100/19. 133/36.
148/28. 311/28. 368/13
Carlyle Thomas 34/18. 39/43. 52/17, 25.
89/47. 145/6. 176/6,41. 237/10. 390/37
cause God as 19/19,23. 27/33,40, 39/18.
50/2. 59/12. 86/21. 145/22–29. 228/29.
288/30. 309/26. 355/36–44. 370/45;
of evil 19/10. 68/2; of disease 20/12.
198/10. 242/5. 259/29; a divided
87/28; of the trouble 134/25,26.
138/25. 144/27. cause x/13–17. 131/
17. 145/24. 355/38,44. 366/20
cells 72/7–73/6. 114/35. 128/4. 198/16.
203/26–204/32. 220/25. 227/9. 357/
10–15
certain 199/8. 242/29,40. 246/28. 351/
38. **certainty** 10/27. 69/38. 218/29.
301/41. 317/14
change viii/17–21. 13/13. 91/28. 92/22.
199/22. 207/11. 272/10,38. **changed**
73/3. 141/4. **changes** 185/27.
changing 60/14. 313/13
channel 89/37. 99/40. 160/36,37. 210/
45. 211/16
charity 390/28
chemical 71/24. 74/47. 81/15,17,45.
86/39
chemicalisation 137/16,47
child 138/40. 271/15,18,28. 274/2. 349/
18. 369/25
choice 294/43–296/17. **choose** 173/

38. 246/30. 294/35. **choosing** 246/
38. 295/26. 303/5
Christ Jesus and Jesus the C. 10/39.
140/4. 173/15. 242/38. 377/10. 378/7;
definitions and functions of the 10/40.
28/16. 35/20. 86/32. 176/16. 296/27.
368/27. 376/20–377/9,30,41. 378/
23,36; each an individualisation of
the 32/37. 35/5. 148/5. 298/10. 368/29.
377/8; union with, in, through 34/39.
378/34; the mystic 35/25,28. 377/4;
second coming of 35/31. 36/11. 90/23.
269/4. 281/20. 379/4; and consciousness 79/41. 86/32. 136/35. 341/39.
360/48. 368/27,38; and demonstration 89/23. 91/27. 137/39. 219/42.
241/43. 242/39. 299/4. 377/41. 379/1;
capacity, power 100/19. 155/5. 368/13.
377/40; only one suppositional
opposite of 138/6; standard of 173/28.
296/27; anti-christ versus 304/42;
improving human presentations of
361/33; The 376/16; only one 377/30;
is the living life 399/35. **Christ's**
285/15. 286/32. **Christs** false 248/
34
Christianity 37/42. 40/1,11. 196/42.
208/22, 218/16. 229/3,7,29. 281/32.
306/26. 315
Christian Science 221/48. 305/32.
315. 379/38–399/39
Christologies 377/32
church viii/9. 35/11. 197/3. 209/37, 40.
280/41–283/6
cinematographic (*see under* PICTURES)
circulate 101/27. **circulated** 363/40
citadel 173/43
clairvoyance 107/28. 124/10
clear 172/24. 370/4. 372/17. **clearer**
134/12. **clearing** 96/37. **clearness**
92/13. 242/33. 313/20
co-exist 196/24. **co-existent** 38/27.
143/20
collective 69/37. 93/6. 243/21
combinations 51/10,41. 99/44–101/42.
280/2. 363/19–367/4. 369/7–35
Comforter (*see* HOLY GHOST)
comfortable 133/47
communication mental 111/1. 115/
17,45. 123/2. 158/20
command 273/8,10. 286/28. **Commandment** First 28/27. 70/5. 135/45.
146/23. 241/34. **commandments**
195/37. 285/17
companionship 235/1,9,38. 236/21.
314/34
communion 128/37. 129/23. 173/20.
281/42. 372/4
completion 131/19
concept 71/9. 137/37. 138/18. 143/18.
148/16. 173/4. 209/8. 224/36. 292/35.

313/24. 351/19. concepts 97/30. 273/32. 311/35. conception 2/20. 38/20. 89/10. 129/27. 272/15. 311/11. 312/34. conceptions 114/2. 278/43. 318/4
concern to whom it may 379
condition 73/2. 167/22. 175/30. 227/ 9,18,23. 243/33. 312/1. 374/20,41. 375/26. conditions 19/47. 80/14. 94/19. 225/31. 286/14. 295/35
confidence 178/3
Confucius 206/21. 325
conscience 241/1
conscious of ideas 110/8. 364/8. 367/ 30. 368/30. 369/29. conscious 159/3. 227/34. 293/45. 295/28
consciousness
    a perfect state, heaven 11/37. 16/17. 260/19. 369/42; of God 28/20. 34/25. 71/20. 86/32. 100/23. 101/25. 105/16. 114/1. 136/35. 224/3. 360/ 36. 364/5. 368/27,34
    human c. 71/22. 72/23. 73/2. 107/31. 109/4. 111/40. 112/3. 113/4. 119/35. 121/38. 123/9. 125/30. 127/17. 136/45. 137/7. 183/38. 203/43. 255/44. 263/28,33. 267/8,19. 271/ 19. 312/2. 321/44; individual human 73/2. 87/29. 104/14. 231/26. 233/24. 235/17. 236/4. 260/37; purification of human 127/1, 128/4,17. 129/14. 131/29. 138/27. 168/31. 169/2. 172/22. 211/2. 220/24,38. 222/16. 243/18. 268/41. 299/27. 300/7. 312/6,30; own 85/32. 130/41. 137/ 36. 168/17. 172/25. 223/10. 293/8
    passing into another state of 6/21. 122/4. 135/36. 265–269. 312/27; counterfeit of true 12/12; material 64/45. 86/6. 204/37; mechanical equivalent of 68/15; moving from place to place 125/29–41; false 131/33. 138/12. 158/43. 266/36. 271/35,38; one universal material 138/8. 158/29. 293/6; never made his 293/31
consecrate 232/26. consecration 235/33. 301/26
consent 168/41. 206/32. 264/6,29,31. 352/22
consequences 242/13. 306/23
consistent 231/27. 235/7. consistently 291/3. 306/21. 315/41
contemplation 207/12. 209/42. 210/26
contest 172/44
continually 100/46–101/40. 211/12. 298/9. 300/40. 364/16. continue 143/15. 173/33. continuous 220/2. 242/40. 299/36. continuously 152/9
co-operation 90/40. 237/4. co-operative 351/3
15

correct but not true xii/29. 63/27. 161/9; basic theory 14/8
counterfeit 12/11. 15/14. 32/25. 51/4. 55/2,5. 58/14. 111/29. 209/29. 247/29. 269/31. 271/4. 273/33. 275/3. 333/39. counterfeited 51/45. 55/1 276/1. 369/8,24. counterfeits 54/35. 58/1. 63/37,43. 64/3. 77/2. 89/3. 240/7. 279/39. counterfesance 271/1. 349/1
courage 127/29. 133/32. 231/14
covenant 169/28–170/7. 238/42. 296/10. 301/13
create 68/34. created 145/40,46. creation 51/6. 88/15. 100/42. 332/14. 376/33. creator 22/3. 311/17
Crichton-Browne Sir James 7/40. 70/9. 71/10. 72/6. 73/8. 106/23. 114/22. 175/26. 177/30. 205/15
criticism 149/41. 171/41. 172/13. 234/8,12,24. 290/1. 381/42
Crookes Sir William 3/30. 57/41. 66/33. 74/20. 78/8. 83/23. 87/32. 90/11. 103/24. 112/38. 115/9. 158/21. 159/40. 249/34,37. 296/23
cross take up 132/10. 370/23
cure 187–189. 216/22. 243/17. 263/7. 282/19. 315/12
current 68/10. 127/4. 357/7. currents 65/42. 69/13. 73/20. 158/31. 160/41
cycles recurring 274/35, 278/5. 327/28. 361/16

D

daily 95/29. 131/42. 132/1. 210/31. 283/38. 293/35. 315/9
dangerous in future. More 94/20; working 115/15. 123/19. 124/33. 125/ 32. 348/1; experiments 124/33. 126/1; in more d. form 171/43; form of prayer 209/6; dangerous 126/17. 144/25. 149/5. 172/32. 230/24. 244/44. 247/29. 290/37. 291/2. 353/7. dangers 124/28. 234/26
Daniel's control 8/28. 230/21
darkest hour 93/47
Darwin Charles 9/14. 21/22. 41/5. 62/43. 167/39. 193/34. 278/33. 342/24. Darwinian 65/31. 278/26, 279/6
day 90/42. 93/25. 94/20. 124/18. 131/9. 150/30. 273/16. 294/35. 310/9. 314/29. days the last 78/40. 94/32. 129/13. 233/20; latter 141/24. 153/33. 171/26. 285/27,40; days 101/38. 157/1. 316/16
dead 30/26. 47/30,36. 56/22. 196/ 13,28,38. 218/20. 219/41. 266/5. 271/ 37. 272/8. 312/20,26. 379/1
dearest 229/35

death 6/22. 12/20. 56/24. 57/7. 87/6.
93/8. 98/20. 127/19,23. 134/3,8. 139/
41,44. 141/10. 149/48. 205/2. 233/21.
236/38,40. 245/4. 255/44. 260/26,
263/37–269. 282/46. 312/18. 313/
15,28,40
deduction 161/45. 276/38. 315/9
deep 78/28. 129/21. 138/46. 211/19.
deeper 154/32. 171/6. **deeply** 297/17
defence 174/3
Deity 27/28. 70/34
deliverance 2/34. 221/48. 294/31.
300/19
demand 134/40. 228/26. 286/32. 316/1.
demands 138/29. 229/6. 285/18
dematerialisation 25/26. 72/49. 76/19.
139/19. 200/19. 235/5. 263/27. 269/3.
313/35. **dematerialise** 299/47. 349/
23. **dematerialised** 25/30. 49/14.
52/23. 91/8. 125/32,35. 139/21,33.
253/8. 263/29. 276/13. 280/27. 302/33.
312/31. **dematerialises** 275/8
democratic 273/8
demonstrable 18/48. 39/48. 40/4.
148/43. 149/38. 162/43. 218/30. 278/
31. 309/35. 313/10. 314/37. 315/5.
demonstrably 43/38. 171/31.
demonstrate 127/20. 200/37.
224/32. 235/38. 253/32. 256/45.
demonstrated 72/7. 90/29. 91/43.
98/42. 116/46. 130/29. 148/40. 161/
45,51. 170/38. 270/45. 294/41. 303/2.
321/17. **demonstrating** 222/3. 305/
5. 321/7. **demonstration** 79/22.
91/1. 105/24. 131/8. 134/6,14. 149/8.
195/41. 196/18. 201/14. 223/32. 235/
15. 242/7. 268/45. 270/19,32,42. 279/
47. 280/36. 296/2. 299/28. 304/22.
305/46. 315/11,16,33. 318/42.
demonstrations 158/18. 272/39.
299/42. 302/23
denial and affirmation ix/31. 80/5.
130/17–135/7. 136/7. 169/1. 201/26.
210/44. 222/8–19. 223/35. 260/17.
299/25. 300/8. 305/54. 312/5. 314/3.
357/19. 360/6–10. 370/2,27; denial
92/16,21. 127/9. 138/37. 139/13, 210/
46. 233/33. 297/41. 301/44. 305/39.
370/28. 380/28. **denials** 236/4.
denied 136/2. 305/41. **denies** 161/
19. **deny** 80/18. 130/45. 131/18,
45,47. 132/10. 143/42. 242/32. 291/3.
297/10. 302/14. 314/2. 369/40,42.
372/9. 380/30,31. **denying** 131/4.
132/2. 133/12. 138/1. 243/3. 256/43.
301/8. 370/26
departed 256/6. 271/18. **departs** 271/
14
depended 173/23. **dependent** 98/18.
depends 129/38. 288/5. 299/11.
302/27

depth 89/36. 292/40. **depths** 80/19
Descartes 30/12. 43/32. 83/31. 167/37.
272/41. 336
desirable 54/18. 306/24. **desire** 51/
30. 100/24. 221/14. 229/17,18. 242/
43. 246/38. 288/27. 306/25. 342/7.
desired 155/3. 214/25. 246/30. 354/
42. **desires** 99/1. 100/21. 209/26.
287/34. 288/21,41. 354/24
destroy 65/6, 95/42, 96/8. 104/17.
113/12. 128/21. 130/5,34,36. 143/5.
162/23. 167/17. 168/46. 169/15. 200/
43. 226/8. 241/27,37,41. 256/39. 260/
15. 274/43. 286/37. 293/7. 303/45.
312/16. 351/37. 356/14. 360/31.
destroyed by action of God 65/11.
116/45. 118/50. 161/2. 162/15; unless,
until d. 69/10. 99/36. 107/3. 167/8.
169/7. 311/23,41; before they take
form 124/15; when d. good thoughts
take their place 124/17. 302/30–32.
312/8; how to tell when 124/21,22;
for all 138/7. 293/8; before evil is
202/40; when d. no future trouble
203/10; destroyed 68/29. 97/30. 108/
43,45. 133/24. 134/45. 138/15. 144/35.
188/3. 208/10. 241/46. 260/17,33,43.
261/2. 267/30. 268/25. 290/16. 293/
21,30. 303/40. 304/1. 305/41. 312/5.
destroying 96/26. 124/34. 126/43.
150/37. 171/37. 223/10. 231/10. 261/
30. 269/7. 278/17. 356/23. 360/41.
375/19. **destroys** 99/40. 114/34.
127/15,27. 132/20. 133/3. 157/34.
299/26. 301/41. 317/13. 360/10.
destruction and judgment 92/15.
293/14,41; Satan loosed for 95/44;
final 246/6. 363/11; error tends to its
own 130/1. 299/23; that is permanent
134/45; a question of praying 262/3;
destruction 64/17. 73/4. 75/21. 130/18.
139/12. 143/13. 208/45. 261/41. 263/
38. 264/32. 280/36. 290/9. 300/19.
313/37. **destructive** 220/23. 290/6
details 105/7. 149/27. 157/34. 161/36.
274/16,17
deterioration 253/37
development useless and harmful
64/45. 126/16. 191/41. 248/18. 339/11;
summary of intellectual 323
devil the loosing of the 94/42. 358/18;
in later life he was a 263/31; devil
vii/38. 15/29. 68/3. 71/40,41. 95/24.
96/12. 119/29,34. 133/5. 144/29. 158/
44. 181/14. 209/24,30. 241/31. 260/20.
293/6. 356/5,27. **devils** 15/36. 138/
40. 197/1. 212/32. 214/2. 260/20
differentiate 50/37. 210/23
difficult 304/6,9,13. 305/50.
difficulties 4/38. 6/1. 7/39. 9/1.
206/15. 229/40. 300/17. **difficulty**

help out of any 2/38; will disappear 53/4. 54/9. 202/3. 219/19. 304/23. 368/10; face a past or present 79/18; take up in thought each 136/16. 370/26
digesting 369/12
dilemma 145/33. 147/13,15
dimension 99/45. 364/2. dimensional 202/17. 243/3,5. dimensions 55/15-57/46. 58/12. 73/27. 99/44. 364/1. 365/25
direct 135/21. directed 176/18. 262/12. 353/7. directly 100/21. 135/15,23. 371/35
disappear caused to 63/34. 81/17. 161/21. 201/35. 202/7; disappear 134/31. 149/37. 271/43. 273/17. 276/15. disappearance total, final 63/20. 72/49. 89/7. 91/7. 243/7. 318/7. 323/39. 360/43. disappearance 19/28. 20/11. 25/27,32. 53/2. 143/13. 201/15. 203/1. 205/24. 220/1. 312/42. disappears 138/3. 144/13
disasters forthcoming 90/34. 93/17. 188/1
disbelief 3/16
disciples 170/47. 173/34
discovered 134/27. 154/32. discoveries 41/19. 157/17. 276/25. discovery 175/32. 316/16. 318/6
disease the cause of 20/12. 198/10; re-appearance of the 203/21. 213/8. 226/8; connection between sin and 205/17; calling attention to 263/18,21. disease 143/28. 177/21,44. 213/34. 215/21. 216/22. 226/13,23. 227/16. 243/37,39. 245/4. 259/29-261/12. 264/24. 267/27,29. 268/42. 295/36. 315/12. 356/29. diseases 187/17,21. 189/28,34. 196/35. 213/41
dispossess 286/24
dissociated 292/26. dissociation 159/43
distance 107/23. 109/4. 121/37. 123/2,5,18. 251/18,33
distribution 279/27. distributor 228/29
divination 114/4. 257/38
divine 116/27. 126/4. 146/26. 212/19. 291/12
do 302/4. 306/19. doing 231/28
doctor 195/10. 205/32. doctors 97/42. 227/15
dog 365/5
dogma 40/13. 44/6. 80/27. 142/12. 317/39. dogmas 44/7. 48/11. dogmatic 281/18. dogmatism 44/8,12
doll 52/1
dominion 48/32. 65/6. 80/24. 126/20. 167/7. 176/18,19. 226/13. 286/1. 289/32. 292/28. 314/32. 379/17

doubt 306/13
dream without a dreamer 15/15. 77/17 356/12; material world not even a 145/46; of death and after 265/8. 266/22,37. 268/16. 270/14. 271/5; pictures 271/27. 272/1. 274/25,38. 285/38. 313/27. 361/37; we must not 274/18; dream 31/45. 85/40. 86/6. 87/24. 91/14. 304/39. 349/45
drive 370/31. 372/1. driving 138/36
drug 6/13,40. 197/40. 198/25-39
Drummond Prof Henry 4/15. 46/16. 47/5. 58/28. 60/24. 264/43. 379/3
duality 31/20
dust 147/25. dustheaps 273/1
duties 286/39. duty 128/2. 172/8,42. 195/24. 228/39. 231/36. 237/8. 256/19. 261/28. 285/2
dwell 127/41. 128/43. 211/14. 213/3. 227/36. 241/35. 297/14. 299/2. 370/32. dwelling 96/38. 98/29. 157/31. 173/20. 204/10. 295/13. 298/21. dwelt 299/41
dying 134/3. 264/12. 289/21

E

ears 368/18
earth flat 18/37. 104/23. 311/4; spiritual 24/42,44. 87/10. 133/18. 270/18. 275/44. 366/2; new 139/25. 211/25; earth 88/19. 96/9. 159/32. 223/19. 265/9. 270-271. 275/37,40. 304/20
ease 242/14. 306/26. easier 162/38. 303/32. easily 97/30. easy 245/9. 304/14. 355/36
eating 369/12
ecstacies 213/27
Eddy Mary Baker 138/47. 141/21. 230/43. 276/37. 315-322. 379/38-399/39
Edison Thomas A. 66/13. 71/11. 75/32
educate 64/14. 151/22. educated 70/2. 279/13. 285/22. 384/35. education 98/5. 152/43. 239/26. 313/39. educational 241/4. 385/11
effect 69/27. 78/23. 79/15. 94/17. 129/14,20. 130/24. 169/3. 175/2. 187/8. 198/18, 203/32,37,48. 204/26. 207/14. 218/23. 256/23. 374/15. effective 94/27,28. 210/25. 244/25. 293/2. 371/16. effects 89/22. 91/47. 94/35. 149/40. 243/30. 245/12. 283/31,33. effectually 97/30
efforts 72/42. 173/12
Ego 28/3. 38/26,27. ego 348/31. 349/40
Egypt 272/22
electrical 68/30. 73/47. 74/42/ electricity 5/12. 43/46. 71/18. 75/

8,24,32. 158/28. 160/14,47. 250/37.
386/18,26. electro-magnetic 76/
37. 279/24. electro-mechanical
114/41
electron 44/35. 65/44. 73/19. 83/44.
87/23,26. 159/16. 160/43,48. 198/30.
202/25. 280/26. 313/12. 357/42
element man's natural mental 134/41.
226/28. elements 70/47. 74/38,47,
51. 81/7. 83/3. 88/7
Elijah 176/11. 202/42
elimination 32/23. 98/8. 208/47. 318/3.
343/16
Elisha 109/12,15. 202/41
Elohim 33/28,30
embodiments 287/25
Emerson 24/24. 31/31. 34/36. 36/28.
64/41. 134/20. 148/31. 166/28. 248/19.
288/7,14. 303/34. 308/15. 317/4.
339/8. 381/41
emotions 21/14. 126/22. 183/35-187/
40. 258/49
end of sin and ignorance 144/26;
eternal good the inevitable 229/1.
295/15; final e. and portal 310/10;
of treatment 373/16; manner and
period of 399/40; material things not
aim and 375/46; of matter (see under
MATTER); of world (see under WORLD)
endeavour 32/22. 206/23. 234/27.
308/8
enemy 171/33. 263/45-264/26. 305/7
energetic 36/4. 136/7. energies 171/
36. energy 13/29. 24/28. 70/21.
74/3. 80/34. 82/7,21,25. 203/8,9.
248/31. 251/9. 303/23
enjoyment 90/37
enlightened 209/39. 346/34.
enlightens 249/16
enlist 241/43
enriches 296/32
enslave 355/33
enter 138/17. 305/53. enters 379/16
environment 3/17. 73/1
epignosis 28/37. 299/32
equipped 136/3. 226/10. 231/30
era 225/15. 278/36. 353/8
error uncovering of 380/4. 387/35-
388/30; error 130/1. 137/32. 227/13.
279/14. 286/9. 297/40. 299/23.
302/14
escape 16/20. 171/25,29. 206/22. 362/5.
escaped 174/2
essence 116/24. 142/3. 145/24. 289/33.
essential 94/25. 140/12. 154/26.
173/15. 209/28. 274/17. 285/19. 315/
41. 350/17. essentially 368/37
eternal 142/6. 314/17. 346/34.
eternity 79/4. 86/47. 101/6
ether and mortal mind 11/42. 104/11.
113/1. 116/17. 118/38. 133/5. 157/30.

158/44. 180/2. 203/12,45. 328/47; and
matter 158. 160/40; no e. 280/25.
313/11; ether 4/40. 11/34. 65/38.
71/40,41. 72/48. 73/25,34. 81/32,
37. 83/38. 88/7,9. 109/6. 247/35.
250/32. 293/6. 326/46. 333/31. 356/4.
ethereal Matter in its primary form
e. 11/44; material man e. individualisation 30/23. 279/34; three dimensional only 55/30; e. form of matter
and occult results 57/3; impressions
or counterfeits 63/35,43. 64/16. 312/
43. 313/5; the so-called mind merely
71/36, 240/2. 340/39; matter merely
e. phenomena 76/5. 311/16; chart
80/1; in e. touch 105/29. 108/30, 32.
114/24. 115/17. 116/17. 138/22. 251/41.
252/14. 255/29. 374/17; " thoughts "
e. vibrations 107/2. 175/29; physical
sight an e. effect 108/26; appearance
120/24. 121/40. 125/37. 267/1; e.
things wrongly called " thoughts "
167/16; contest is with e. thoughts
172/44. 293/32; not truly mental
181/1. 191/42. 238/33. 256/34. 301/37;
e. forces called human mind 193/14;
e., material, mental 198/19; disease is
213/35. 243/35. 260/1; hypnotism is
246/23; counterfeit of consciousness
247/28; intensification of e. impressions 260; false e. law 264/7; e.
earth called matter 265/8; workshop
273/2; false e. concepts 311/35;
miscalled spiritual 347/30; ethereal
11/28-12/21. 179/42. 279/11.
etherealisation 250/37. 261/43.
etherealised 312/36. etherealism
249/33. etheric 66/10. 120/31.
ether-world 264/34
ethics 46/38
Eucharist 129/24
event 90/32. 256/22,23. 361/9. events
112/4,28. 153/23. 162/16-21. 272/18.
278/4. 361/44
everyone 98/25. 305/12
everything 87/17. 111/28. 311/15.
314/16
evidence 270/21. 315/17
evil
destruction of 15/34. 65/6. 75/21. 89/
38. 92/15. 99/41. 104/17. 108/44.
113/12. 126/43. 127/25,26. 143/13.
144/35. 150/36. 162/30. 169/15.
172/24. 194/8. 202/39. 211/1. 220/
23. 226/8,33. 256/39,46. 274/44.
278/18. 280/36. 288/8. 290/9. 293/
14,41. 300/19. 301/42. 312/3-17.
356/14. 360/10; self-destruction of
86/24. 143/26. 144/6. 145/25. 146/
28. 262/14,16. 323/37
non-reality of 16/34. 18/27. 80/6.

86/26–29. 99/27. 127/20. 143/11. 225/37. 313/22. 315/15
God and 17/18–19/36. 39/29–40. 86/27. 101/37. 143/1. 145/15–146/36. 147/6. 208/31–44. 350/24. 351/9–23
origin of 18/20. 19/10,12. 355/44
consciousness of 32/26
possibilities 62/15–22
fearless attitude essential 62/24, 80/24
power of 62/24. 70/2
uncovering of hidden 62/25. 95–96. 131/16. 387/19–389/30
good and (see under GOOD)
end of 89/47. 90/1. 96/8. 127/25. 135/40. 150/31. 154/26. 235/6. 262/48. 313/19
result of change of thought towards 93/8. 213/16
immunity against 94/10,36. 95/41. 129/4. 253/49. 269/12. 283/26. 375/6
handling 129/31–139/18. 297/36. 300/9. 301/8. 370/31. 371/32. 379/18
greatest in highest spiritual centres 140/33
of no value 142/42
impersonality of 172/30. 356/19
dominion over 176/19. 230/9. 286
evil x/28. 14/36. 23/30. 69/37. 72/43. 160/24. 168/16. 170/19. 207/12. 240/13. 241/30. 256/23. 283/14,41. 290/36. 291/2. 295/17. 311/30. 330/6. 333/10. 342/6. 359/43. 362/5. evils 146/2. 355/28. 373/5
evolution spiritual 2/26. 51/17. 86/46. 280/1; of sense of God 25/8. 89/18; evolution 2/25. 65/33. 86/36. 147/37. 207/16. 238/20. 276/20. 278/26. 312/40. 327/31. 344/38. 345/16. 358/37. 359/17. 365/7
exact 299/32. 317/1,40
example 157/47. 173/25
exceed 148/28
exception 46/44. 47/6
exchange 50/48. 100/11. 101/2,18,30. 150/4. 355/3,18
excitement 120/6,10,14
excuse 274/17,47. 351/24
exercise 146/27. 235/40. 245/42. 286/37,39. 379/17
exhaustion 139/16
exhibitions 246/11
exist 68/36. 101/25. 143/15. 145/25, 27. 148/12. 158/4. 160/42. 311/19. 323/33. 349/33. 364/4. existed 51/16. 99/34,45. 332/11. 368/36. existence apparent 11/38. 31/11. 75/17. 81/21. 87/21. 107/2. 161/31. 263/30. 295/25; true 19/7. 101/16. 134/39. 146/31. 170/37,38. 228/43. 237/1. 245/13. 294/41. 297/12. 310/20; denial of 131/45. 132/2,19. 136/38. 169/1. 172/

23. 206/6. 297/10. existence 65/37. 135/40. 146/41. 235/26. 286/13. 318/6. exists 64/13. 142/7. 310/18
exorcise 146/27
expect 302/24
experience 64/47. 70/3. 79/14. 90/13, 32. 104/36. 156/41. 159/44. 162/12, 25. 213/16. 219/31. 229/1. 234/39. 236/37. 268/32. 294/46. 295/35. experiences 71/23. 116/9. 369/28
experimental 78/39. 284/4. experiments 123/34. 156/44
explain 306/4. 307/18. 356/13. explanation 112/36. 228/7. 252/11. 274/36. 280/17
explore 101/14. explored 234/38
expose 62/20. 305/38. 316/34. 330/25. exposed 65/13. 236/39. exposes 63/17. exposing 2/28. exposure 3/38. 63/14. 65/18. 225/2. 233/28. 318/1
express 149/1. 152/9. 173/8. expressed 232/6. expresses 73/2. 111/46. expressing 91/26. expression 149/26. 176/14. 238/30,35. 239/33. 369/2
extend 64/47. extension 64/42. 218/18
external 68/33. 127/4. 251/8. 256/22. externalisation 279/8
eye 20/36. 21/3. 55/33. 107/44. 109/1. 204/33. 290/15. 367/34. eyes 238/29–239/4. 309/28. 368/17

F

face 79/17. 233/26. 239/33. 351/20
fact 14/21. 75/45. 149/12. 169/1. 204/40. 217/19. facts material, so-called 3/43. 60/14,21. 204/34. 213/15. 269/38; theories and 14/11; not a presentation of 80/8; real 98/9,29. 225/3. 243/34. 274/16; brings out 290/3; facts 37/2. 312/15. 313/2,38. 316/28
fail 134/19. 292/38. 304/12. fails 218/30. failure 160/16. 206/44. 295/24. 304/15. 305/48. 354/36. failures 295/22
faith 173/46. 177/24,26. 202/37. 212/18. 214/30. 227/44. 228/32. 281/26. 299/28. 308/26. faith-healers 247/17. faith-healing and faith cures 7/28–36. 189/31. 211/33. 218/22. 247/8–18
fall 33/33
fallacies 1/31. 2/25,28. 63/17. 305/38. 316/34. 317/28. 318/1. fallacious 65/7. fallacy 98/12. 214/49. 295/25
false 204/39. falsely 11/32. 25/37. 58/14. 63/36. 108/38. 111/28. 285/22. 349/3. falsities 4/36. 313/38

families 236/23. family 89/12. 227/4
famine 307/6
Faraday Michael 12/10. 31/32. 60/40.
66/1,39,45. 74/44
Farrar Dean 41/30
fatal 235/36. 264/27. fatalism x/34.
99/37. 162/4. 168/45. 311/39. 312/3.
fatality 75/3
Father 10/42. 28/16. 30/2. 98/36. 273/2.
Father's 366/25. 376/6
fatigue 259/21,28
fault 205/38. 206/14. 290/24. 291/47
fear No f. of evil when it is understood
62/26. 80/22. 388/31 ; a thing of the
past 69/11 ; wrong thoughts go when
f. goes 124/21 ; must not f. when
troubles gather 144/24 ; Truth does
not f. strongest light 149/42 ; recognising f. had upper hand 160/22 ;
obtaining freedom from 237/45 ; f. sin
you make something of it 241/32 ;
unconquered 241/38 ; working against
303/40. 373/17 ; prevents results
309/39 ; lay down all 355/12 ; fear
17/19. 134/15-17. 244/6. 259/47.
260/6. 261/23. 264/3. 267/15,34.
268/5. 314/31,33. 354/34. fearless
80/23. 234/15,23. fearlessness 260/
18. fears 167/6. 245/3
feel 260/38. 374/35. feeling 172/21.
286/34. feelings 184/19. 256/6. 262/
31
fellow-beings 91/33. fellow-creatures 95/27. fellow-man 2/36.
50/46. 51/35. 100/40,46. 101/29. 137/
46. 147/1. 172/31. 221/6. 227/27.
230/45. 281/15. 285/21. 295/41. 354/8.
379/18. fellow-men 51/1,41. 108/
46. 111/17. 171/3,36. 172/19. 173.
229/26. 256/17. 275/9. 283/41. 306/1.
375/45. 379/33. fellow-soldiers
172/6. fellow-worker 94/41. fellow-workers 136/5. 315/39. fellows
104/13. fellowship 291/30
female 343/33. 353/12 (see also MALE
AND FEMALE)
Fichte 288/34. 340
fictitious 68/3. 82/11. 394/32
fight 138/12. 163/28. 173/14,18,33.
207/5. 241/44. 242/14. 245/45. 283/6.
304/41
film 169/16. 274/33. 358/39. 359/21.
363/8 (see also under PICTURES)
final 149/34. 236/4. finally 170/12.
360/32
financial 136/17. 221/28
finish 131/3. 363/10. finished 98/37.
131/6
finite 146/32
fire 262/16
firmament 359/47

first 111/48. 143/7. 233/25. 293/7. 302
46. 372/7
Fiske 12/40. 21/46. 24/30. 84/34. 344
five 306/32
flesh 202/18. 317/15. 378/12. fleshly
268/24
flood 92/48. 95/30. 226/24. flooding
98/46. flood-tide 226/32
flying 126/9
foe 172/8
fog 63/10
follow 132/7,11. 173/14,25. 321/19.
followed 135/21. followers 173/
23. following 111/26
food 101/33. 150/4. 244/13,30. 364/36
fool 9/32. fooled 11/41. 99/29. foolish
243/21. fools 234/4
foot 368/21. footsteps 80/4,5. 90/41.
111/26. 229/1. 233/34. 289/17
force lines of vii/35. 66/9,39. 73/19-31.
87/15. 158/30,34. 159/20. 198/36.
202/23. 204/5. 280/25. 313/11 (see also
under THOUGHT) force 58/10. 66/34.
67/38. 68/6. 74/9,45. 76/37. 80/31,33.
82/5. 88/11. 173/22. 176/11. 198/33.
203/5. 243/21. 246/1. 248/23. 304/20.
forced 91/4. 170/11. 212/41. forces
111/39. 250/6. forcing 202/8. 315/
46
forecast 275/12. forecasts scientific
62/37. foreshadowed 261/9.
foreshadowings 363/18. fore-
shadows 162/13. foresight 163/32.
261/39. foretelling 109/17. 116/31.
162/16. 169/29. 171/23. 208/37. 285/
26. fore-vision 171/27. forewarned 171/32. forewarning 96/
27
forget 132/1. 309/16. forgetting 105/
47. forgotten 283/5. 288/35. 292/
26
forgiveness 143/38. 400/2. forgiving
131/40
form 108/40. 167/22. 266/34. 312/11.
forms 63/43. 121/40. 279/28,30.
304/4. formation 251/40
formula 138/45. formulas 98/14
found 38/16
foundation 2/17. 63/15. 67/42. 148/
38. foundationless 149/30.
foundations 80/20. 98/8. 287/44
fowl 360/15
Francis of Assisi St 70/19. 141/6.
182/18. 185/5. 210/2. 390/31
frankness 133/33. 231/15
free 95/41. 143/30. 146/29. 168/24,33.
170/12. 254/31. 260/44. 261/36. 267/
12. 299/35. 350/2. 355/28. freed
89/42. 219/44. 220/36. 223/12. 263/20.
290/16. 360/33. freedom 2/41. 72/
43. 143/30. 146/30. 159/39. 210/37.

265/4. 268/42. 283/34. 335/46. **freeing**
205/34. 306/4
free-will x/18,32. 167/20. 330/8. 351/30
friend 256/6. 270/26,27. 326/37.
friends 271/8. 291/16. **friendship**
233/32
fulcrum 8/40. 91/40. 92/4
fulfil 286/34. **fulfilled** 170/3–12,47.
295/36. 354/24. **fulfilment** 51/30.
135/46,47. 236/11. 273/12. 285/18.
fulfils 65/21
fulness 133/22. 224/11
fundamental 93/7. 166/6. 294/40.
295/10,26. 315/43. 317/12. 318/21.
fundamentals 235/26
future 78/19,22. 94/21. 96/17. 100/8.
105/32. 107/3. 113/1. 115/1. 116/31.
124/16. 144/29. 157/31. 169/29. 251/
19. 252/22. 257/42. 258/12. 260/11.
274/41. 311/18. 355/11. 361/1. 364/11

G

Gabriel 127/34. 132/15. 133/8,27.
211/2. 306/17
general 92/18,22. 94/26. 213/39,44.
generally 94/14
Genesis 359/11
genius 108/46. 118/35. 151/25. 156/25.
287/16. 343/34. 351/21. 375/35
gentleness 231/31. 235/10. 287/17.
296/31. 382/30
Gethsemane 303/36
ghosts and visions 120/18
Gibbon Edward 47/26. 119/42. 196/34
gift 217/40. 226/18. **gifts** 119/9. 208/7
give 229/14. 232/4. 236/2. 306/42.
355/3,4. **giver** 111/46
glorify 287/22
goal 372/47
God
definition of viii/26. 2/13. 27/23
the great I AM viii/26. 59/10. 370/13
and His manifestation x/7. 11/36.
70/43. 89/29. 98/32. 143/19. 176/15.
201/12,24. 227/34. 267/26. 280/31.
296/28. 310/18,35. 313/29. 368/27.
369/4. 376/22. 400/8
not a distant potentate 2/13
the mystery of 10/25 ·
one G. 10/41,43. 28/25. 69/39. 89/17.
146/23. 170/10. 209/1,3. 210/14,19.
296/11. 373/19
the only reality 11/36. 19/40. 64/19.
81/33. 89/28. 146/6. 242/11. 256/45
and material world and material man
16/23. 23/17. 24/6. 30/19–32/26.
39/29. 105/17. 145/34. 148/10.
211/4. 220/20. 310/25. 311/6. 323/
34. 351/10. 356/11

and jealousy and revenge 23/3. 39/25
208/31
the arraignment of 23/5
and the standard of good 23/34. 79/20.
242/26
and good 24/6. 35/40. 37/32. 99/27.
144/22. 240/16. 294/43. 295/12
created you and real world 24/9. 310/
22. 323/32
Hebrew names for 26/42. 39/17
in man's likeness 27/19. 38/5,6
not a personal tyrant 27/31
is All-in-all 27/31,44. 98/30,42.
145/40. 310/18
the only Person 28/2
the triune 28/16. 99/3
the presence of 29/27. 99/3. 137/35.
211/12. 217/42. 227/33. 232/1.
281/28. 299/3. 305/52
perfect 32/37. 64/7. 78/35. 99/32.
147/22. 211/13. 310/38. 375/39
and man 35/22. 38/20–27. 98/29.
136/47. 143/20. 147/1. 196/24. 296/
11. 298/4 (see also under MAN)
and individuality 38/28. 271/10
apportions to each his work 65/20
nothing impossible to 78/25. 304/12
every question that has G. in it
89/25
and devil 95/24. 119/29. 144/29
speaks 111/17,23
all, allness of 127/20. 146/39. 147/3.
253/15. 313/21. 315/15
there is nothing but 127/25. 201/22,
24. 204/38. 280/31. 310/18. 313/29.
400/8
reasons why G. should not be G.
134/18
only is self-conscious 143/44
still small voice of 176/10
anthropomorphic 208/27
no limit to 282/37. 303/27
rewarding, blessing true workers
284/4. 308/8
affords fresh opportunities 287/47
your only true friend 292/1
only one false representation of 293/5
teaches us 309/9
can never know the whole of 364/
15
God and evil (see under EVIL)
God and heaven (see under HEAVEN)
God (see also LIFE, TRUTH, LOVE,
MIND, SOUL, SPIRIT, PRINCIPLE
and under CAUSE, INTELLIGENCE,
SUBSTANCE)
God's ideas 51/31. 99/46. 100/41. 131/6.
143/44. 158/5. 204/16,38. 223/15.
287/18. 363/19. 369/8. 373/31; perfect idea 137/31,32. 252/7; existence
demonstrable 170/38

god 27/8. 28/34,35. 29/42. gods 26/17. 29/35. 34/1. 38/3. 89/17. 207/38. 208/9,11. 324/40. 373/20
Golden Rule 135/46. 273/12. 354/46. 390/33. 396/21
good law of 2/12. 90/47. 130/28,29. 236/7. 295/22,31. 315/44. 354/13; and evil 23/30. 86/21–35. 95/25. 131/25. 142/42–143/9. 144/10. 151/23. 204/17. 208/43. 240/13. 290/7. 306/36. 313/24. 330/5. 343/1. 359/42; is part of heaven 24/4,32; working for universal 28/7. 234/16; origin of 29/7. 99/27. 102/2. 360/14; absolute 37/31. 39/28. 79/20. 145/18. 204/17. 215/4. 240/13; what we call 37/31. 240/13. 241/1: reality of 52/11. 113/13. 256/44. 293/4; one millionth part known of possible 62/14; cannot cause or use pain 69/39; if he lives a g. enough life 76/10; the saving knowledge of 89/12,13. 142/29; channel for 95/23. 224/33; infinite possibilities of 98/23; man's unity with 103/15. 223/17; let g. work 124/14; God's way, will, is perfect g. 128/12. 160/39; fear that one is not g. enough 134/16; gain every bit of 144/1; evil turned to g. account 144/14; to do us harm devil sends us g. 144/31; g. follows thinking of g. 170/18,19. 296/11. 298/22. 301/14; trying with human mind to do g. 192/31; impossible to tell what is 201/46; replacing negative form of 203/20; praying if it be g. for us 214/43; cannot limit or outline 219/23. 302/23–38; human mind can do nothing g. 240/6,11; in the material world 242/16. 311/8. 356/42. 360/14; nothing will come but 246/34. 306/41; what in olden days we called 287/43; learn our capabilities for 288/2; not upon how g. we are 288/6; do right because we love g. 288/20; inevitable end eternal g. 295/16; for the greatest number 304/37. 354/27; not make neighbour but myself g. 305/18; so-called g. thoughts not of God 316/24; if it does not manifest every quality of 366/19; good 24/4. 242/19; goodness 27/29. 147/4. 238/26. 239/27. 264/20. 289/22. 343/2
gossip 302/2
governed 32/37. 64/7. 89/43. 100/22. 101/14. 105/16. 112/6. 151/7. 245/20. 295/10. 310/38. 347/4. 375/38. governing 313/20. government 132/44. 168/39. 292/28. 372/23. governs 126/2. 286/35. 294/40. 372/22
grace 166/19. 298/21

grasp mental 370/20
grass 367/31
gratitude 237/23. 307/29,34
grave 125/36. 268/33
gravity 41/4. 76/33. 88/13,20. 279/22. 280/28. 313/14
greater 304/26. greatest 301/19. 304/37. 354/27. 360/35
grief 238/1. 256/6
groping mental 98/13
group 91/24. 284/1. 363/30–40. grouping 51/9,40. 64/25. 86/46. 99/47. 100/9,42,47. 101/3,31,38. 108/47. 363/22. 364/18. 373/34
grow 172/30. growing sense of confidence 295/37; pencil g. 56/21; understanding 281/14. growth 56/23. 57/7. 131/1. 279/41. growths 201/34. 243/16
guard 146/24. 256/15. 296/29. 354/17. 372/45
guidance 228/19. 234/37. 320/42. guide 64/22. 151/13,21. 230/35. guides 304/19. guiding 233/43
gulf 79/6,9

H

habit 260/27. 272/5. 290/37. 297/1. 301/33. 302/1. habits 246/43. habitual 231/27. 280/35. 303/3. habitually 139/20. 215/7. 218/24. 227/33
Haeckel 21/33. 23/46. 28/30. 145/8. 275/20. 345
hair 367/32,34
hand 15/18. 54/37
happen 94/23. 105/31,32. 112/30. 113/10. 162/16,18. 166/37. 169/34. 251/18. 303/45
happier 143/41. happiest 101/38. 236/37. happiness 2/43. 9/9. 21/44. 51/24. 52/10. 100/27–101/42. 144/1. 146/30. 221/8,18. 229/31. 231/1,9. 232/19. 237/21,45. 241/44. 256/19. 262/32,36. 268/22. 274/45. 284/3. 285/20. 288/14,15. 291/28. 292/13. 295/23. 308/4,14. 314/21,26. 319/35. 322/1. 352/3. 363/24. 373/35. 375/46. happy xii/42. 99/43. 143/39. 144/4. 247/26. 282/48. 287/28. 305/20. 332/22. 342/20–23
hardest trying their 172/41
hard up 268/17
harm 17/8. 69/8,16,25. 95/31. 101/36. 124/24,41. 130/24. 131/26. 143/33. 144/31. 179/29. 180/48. 214/30. 230/21. 234/31. 246/40. 261/26,27. 267/36. 304/16. 352/26. harmed 69/12. 172/43. 246/32. harmful 62/20.

96/1. 124/9. 126/31. 135/23. 194/12. 246/2. 247/21. **harming** vii/31. 94/22. 116/7. 127/7. 144/3. 172/3. 294/23. **harmless** 80/12. 105/27. 215/31. **harms** 75/20. 130/25. 213/1. 234/32. 262/28

harmonious 77/3. 90/39. 235/38. 295/ 35. **harmony** 70/1. 136/12

Harnack Adolf von 150/1. 218/15. 223/45. 377/19

harvest 96/9

hastening 283/45. 300/18

hate 72/37. 205/24. 229/26,27

have 79/4. 219/6

haven 95/29. 140/34

head 1/18. 55/3. 368/13. **headache** 132/3. 209/14. 267/11

heal 7/27. 139/16. 195/37. 201/38. 203/7. 208/1. 217/38. 224/24. 227/46. 279/47. 285/14. 299/41. 316/17. 367/18. **healed** 47/30. 85/43. 133/26. 221/37. 282/38. **healer** 136/46. 137/13. 227/ 18. 243/19. 247/14,17. **healing** apparent 7/29,35. 203/2. 212/44. 213/48. 215/15. 251/35; mental 7/35. 194/13. 197/23. 200/30. 282/26; Mind 138/46; with human no-mind 179/27. 180/6; hypnotic 179/32–181/23; permanent 203/25. 207/1; divine 218/10; instantaneous (*see* INSTANTANEOUS); faith (*see* FAITH-HEALING). **healing** 7/26. 65/22. 135/37. 181/21. 186/41. 195/26. 196/9,43. 225/48. 281/49. 296/31. 301/20. 321/36. 367/11. 379/ 18. **heals** vii/37. 98/48. 224/30. 242/37. 247/19. 376/24. 377/41. **health** 90/36. 127/37. 185/46. 186/3. 215/13. 218/27. 226/21. 227/3. 237/1. 244/20. 245/1

hearer 309/5. **hearers** 232/4. 308/44. **hearing** 91/24. 109/1. 111/19. 274/10. 302/7. 368/25

heart 55/10. 287/3. 373/38. **hearts** 140/12. 172/35. 268/44

heaven perfect state of consciousness 11/37. 16/17. 49/42; knowledge of, a true mental science 12/24; not future state 16/14; we make our own 16/15. 49/29; a perfect world 18/45; the real spiritual world 25/36. 253/ 36; rising to true sense of 32/23. 298/40; here 32/27. 50/6. 131/7. 140/ 14. 201/6. 270/13. 274/16. 372/23; cannot be pushed into 48/28. 241/47; what it is and what it is not 49/1. 57/5; God and 50/2. 242/11. 355/41; what it is like in 50/40,48. 51/1,15,28. 54/17. 79/3. 99/8. 105/15. 108/37. 111/14. 131/5,11. 143/43. 145/29. 161/43. 169/12. 221/26. 228/30. 369/4. 372/22; a world of four dimensions

55/27. 99/44. 364/1. 365/24; thinking of God and 116/21. 129/39. 299/12,30; in thought to 120/15. 132/3. 201/42. 297/9. 305/55. 369/42. 372/7. 378/13 (*see also under* TURN); denying existence of troubles in 130/42. 138/2. 161/20. 242/12,34; a true mental realm 131/5; forming best concept of 134/11. 224/36; the new 139/24. 211/24; reaching out for fuller realisation of 144/22. 211/20; thinning of mist hiding 169/3–21. 206/30. 274/34. 280/23. 298/22. 313/9. 358/38. 360/1; absolute love in 229/44; perfection of 240/15,18. 242/34. 243/5; death not stepping stone into 263/44; the true harmonious consciousness 260/19; the atmosphere of love 262/37; waking up to being in 267/5; spiritual man always in 268/7. 269/5. 273/41. 275/10. 310/38. 349/14,25; same false sense of h. as before 269/34. 271/26; turning from toy imitation of 275/44; practical love the way to 291/12; matter hides 311/10; fore-shadowings of 363/18; do animals exist in 365/24. **heavenly** 128/1. 176/25. 215/5. 235/15. **heavenwards** 148/20

Hegel 75/6. 340. 348/19

hell 15/29. 26/1. 49/29,33. 168/24. 243/4. 262/37. 264/39. 356/28,35

help out of any difficulty 2/37; for neighbour and fellow-man 172/20. 173/12. 234/21. 256/17. 285/20. 305/ 46. 307/34. 308/4. 309/45. 319/34. 352/6; only way we can h. ourselves 308/6; looking for h. through special channel 160/36; intense desire to 230/7; only think and talk of others to 290/38; cannot tell whom best to 301/23; help 79/29. 123/17. 131/25. 135/38. 136/37. 147/47. 168/16. 230/ 24. 235/47. 291/40. 292/31,34. 301/39. 346/27. 350/11. **helped** 127/22. 262/ 15. **helper** 308/6. **helpers** 123/23. **helpful** 225/11. **helping** vii/28. 94/41. 131/10. 152/6. 173/2. 254/33. 256/13,19. 290/4,29. 294/23. 302/5. 307/11. **helpless** 21/5

heralds 309/45

here 87/10. 131/7. 132/5. **hereafter** 253/4

hereditary 241/3. 351/37. **heredity** 199/39. 351/30

heresies 41/20. **heresy** 40/30. 398/6

hesitation 160/22

Heysinger Dr. J. W. 10/6. 41/24. 42/14. 44/2,8. 46/36. 62/11. 67/15. 80/43. 103/20. 108/17. 250/29. 265/19 **hidden** 3/38. 95/4. 145/42. 148/29.

15*

150/10. 158/5. 232/18. 234/26. 274/12. 280/23. 360/2. **hide** 357/32. **hides** 24/43. 310/30. 311/10. 363/11. **hiding** 169/14. 311/26. 313/8. 358/40
higher 29/2. 95/39. 98/7. 220/29. 235/8. 283/35. 286/39. 288/1. 355/4, 13. **highest** 62/24. 136/41. 137/28. 140/33. 151/4. 172/15. 210/31. 227/28, 35. 230/39. 283/15. 305/32. 354/22. 360/48. 361/41
himself 94/41. 143/43. 244/29
historical 162/27. 313/6. **history** 150/29. 162/17. 171/45. 272/4,18. 274/24. 312/44. 357/31. 361/44
hold 174/1. **holding** 173/43
holiness 127/38. 129/21. 131/38. 173/25. 224/29. 319/2
holy 138/28. 211/19. 272/28. 281/12. 363/6
Holy City 297/44. **Holy Ghost** 10/42. 28/17. 92/9. 146/24. 166/21. 170/41. 223/42. 224/29. 298/46. 318/30. 398/37. **Holy Spirit** 166/21. 224/9. 298/46
Holmes Oliver Wendell 6/36. 381/2
home truths 204/39. home 288/32
homeopathy 6/41,49. 197/39. 218/32
honest 168/30. 234/22
hope 94/6. 177/24. 215/27. 243/40. 295/36. 306/28. 308/26. **hopeful** 282/49. **hopeless** 221/29. 222/1. **hopes** 229/9. 295/23
horrors viii/41. 95/26. 145/35. 171/25. 301/36
hourly 94/3. 264/28
Hudson T. J. 42/33. 103/38. 183/1. 186/24. 197/26. 198/9. 201/33. 211/39. 258/27
human capacity 8/10. 311/28; body wonderfully bad 20/34; no-mind 70/14. 179/27. 261/19; mechanism 72/28. 114/35. 173/3; experience 90/13,32. 268/32; normal h. enjoyment 90/37; footsteps 90/41; personality 99/1; appears to be marvellous being 103/9; so-called powers 104/31; must not outline h. events 112/4; substratum of h. belief 125/36; subordinating h. to the divine 126/4; broken reed of h. intelligence 131/19. 302/38; handling h. mortal self 131/45. 135/49. 136/34,47. 137/13,30; correct our h. ideas 137/46; h. illusive systems 172/45; when h. is thinking of God 224/5; love 230/38; cannot run counter to h. requirements 236/17; purest h. not really good 240/10; unhappiness of development of h. mind power 248/18; intensification of h. concepts 249/30; when you understand h. theories

261/42; goodness no protection 264/20; being and beings (see under BEING); consciousness (see under CONSCIOUSNESS); mind (see under MIND); life (see under LIFE); humanhood 310/10. **humanised** 153/3. **humanitarians** 3/1; **humanity** 1/27. 90/2. 91/21. 138/10. 146/17. 168/12. 173/42. 228/25,37. 235/40. 253/5. 264/28. 283/3. 301/22. 313/24. 318/36. 321/41. 360/23.
humanly 306/34
humble 228/17. 273/7. **humility** 119/5. 161/47. 173/25. 287/1. 303/24
humbugged 99/29
Hume 142/14. 339
hungry 309/6
husband 235/8. 236/14
Huxley Thomas 9/15. 11/35. 13/28. 42/20. 43/18. 46/1. 59/9. 60/12. 62/37. 68/14. 70/20. 76/4. 83/15. 129/26. 142/14. 152/37. 188/8. 200/29. 280/8. 325/38. 343
hypnotic 110/10. 116/26. 202/31. 206/47. 209/20. 212/46. 214/9-30. 216/16. 246/27. 262/1. 282/40. 292/34. 354/15. **hypnotism** 30/4. 69/21-26. 75/18. 99/29. 109/30. 110/1. 120/9,11. 126/29. 179/32-181/23. 193/28. 203/34-41. 212/28. 245/40. 246/20. 247/23-248/33. 262/25. 264/12. 269/26. 282/26. 318/27. 352/25. 373/24
hypotheses 83/28. 92/49. 168/43. 206/32. 226/27. 316/34. 317/36. **hypothetical** 13/29. 63/34. 66/10. 278/30. 311/19

I

" I " 240/38-44
idea man the compound 27/34. 33/42. 360/36. Christ the 28/17. 35/20. 296/27. 368/27; birth of new 36/10; man the eternally divine 38/27; know any i. of God 100/9,19. 221/26; i. after i. 101/28. 364/16; cannot outline Mind's 137/29; Principle and its 143/21. 196/25; individual, intelligent i. man 145/32; serpent struggles to destroy spiritual 228/23; every i. must reflect whole of God 366/15; God's (see under GOD); idea 27/27. 28/8. 32/45. 34/21. 35/31,36. 91/23. 137/31,32. 184/26. 229/47. 366/24. 379/23. **ideal** 32/39. 79/16. 136/35, 47. 138/23. 208/46. 313/33. **ideals** 176/25. ideas old 1/3,21. 61/13. 82/36. 280/34. 317/43; of God 4/37. 51/5. 116/19. 158/5. 201/1. 346/24; false 37/27. 150/9. 274/14. 280/19;

succession of 50/32. 77/36; perfect 50/41. 51/1,38. 100/39. 237/3. 280/2. 366/34; grouping of 51/9–17. 64/25. 99/47. 100–101. 108/47. 363/21; re-presenting the 51/11. 111/15; infinite 79/11. 101/17. 221/25. 366/11; interchanging 100–101; God's (see under GOD); ideas 27/28. 92/48. 112/5. 116/17. 145/27. 238/46. 276/16,24. 293/19,20. 355/42. 373/33
identify 32/39
idols 43/36
ignorance 2/29. 11/10. 20/21,22. 79/10. 96/1. 132/18. 144/27,28,34. 205/34. 228/33,42. 243/20,37. 261/39. 263/45. 264/3. 274/4,18,47. 295/45. 300/15. 317/12. 321/44. 351/24. 354/13,39. ignorant 135/33. 234/11,32. 264/22. 327/18
ill 135/29. 204/6. 217/23. 317/15
illogical 39/42. 143/35. 148/9. 273/4. 356/35
illusion 15/1. 18/22. 215/6. 220/22. 243/7. 268/23,33. 279/1. 297/43. 311/3. 312/16. 313/27. 323/36. 327/36. 381/10. illusionary 12/1. 58/7. illusions 11/30. 146/42. 149/36. 184/42. 268/8. 311/38. 380/3. illusive 68/36. 75/6. 87/34. 149/29. 172/45. 204/17. 267/1. 311/17. 312/36,42. illusory 19/10. 71/42. 103/26. 126/17. 188/1. 270/19
image and likeness 27/35. 91/26. 101/36. 103/14. 111/45. 113/49. 137/32. 145/32. 147/4,26. 148/11. 149/26. 273/9,11. 278/40. 289/29. 291/23. 314/25. 364/12; image 8/1. 26/22. 32/46. 269/25. images 58/26. 112/36. 269/7. 332/8. imaginary 311/31. imagination 58/40. 156/4. 179/43. 227/46. imagined 207/13. 227/12. 245/45. imaging 94/36
imitation 162/13. 213/34. 275/41,43. 279/39
immanence 147/2
Immanuel 89/23. 299/42
immortal 70/43. 83/3,4. 299/42. immortality 127/38. 241/44. 264/26, 44. 270/39. 286/10. 288/4. 330/2
immunity 90/37. 94/9. 95/40
impartial 229/32
impersonal 137/44. 223/6,10. 290/3. 356/19. impersonalise 137/32. impersonality 172/30
impinging 64/18. 109/7
importance 90/31. 126/40,42
impossibilities 146/10. 200/23. impossible 78/25. 113/20. 304/11
impressions 19/25,39. 51/4. 59/5. 63/35. 64/16. 69/9. 72/16. 77/23. 79/19. 104/19,42,43. 188/18. 229/39.

258/48. 274/30. 312/14,43. 313/5. 369/35
improve 144/19. 360/12. improved 148/13. 240/16. 246/35. 282/39. 312/12. 360/1. improvement x/22. 134/7. 220/40. 240/14. 357/37. improves 73/3. 263/34. 360/8. improving 312/29. 349/44. 361/7,33
incentive 143/6. 144/26
increase 51/17. 283/36. 363/36. increasingly 295/35
incredulity 290/20
independently 275/45
indestructible 82/4,8. 203/8
indirectly 160/11. 173/2. 305/3
individual 85/38. 237/3. 270/41. 272/39. 319/1. 341/27. individualisation 30/23. 32/36. 34/24. 35/4. 64/2. 136/36. 148/5. 298/9. 368/28. 377/8. individualise 35/21. 133/25. 368/37. 369/1. 377/40. individualised 71/20. 103/13. 105/16. individuality 38/28. 50/15. 51/14. 85/38. 98/44. 114/25. 123/19. 136/34. 137/30. 271/19. 287/38. individually 65/20. 126/40. 271/10
infinite 19/23. 27/31. 98/23. 99/44–101/42. 146/11,13,37. 310/23. 363/34–364/17; i. number (see under NUMBER)
infinitude 100/18. infinity 34/25. 55/27. 99/45. 148/42. 363/23
influence 110/11. 165/28. 232/16. 241/4. 247/16. 248/24. 253/28. 254/22. 261/34. 276/26. 282/9,19. influenced 69/26. 123/20. 135/15. influencing 120/11. 188/29. 247/25
information 115/3. 160/20
Inge W. R. 14/41. 18/36. 35/17. 38/3. 50/7. 143/38. 147/6. 166/10. 224/17. 289/43. 331/10. 376/20. 378/18,35
inheritance 98/26,27. 149/10. 204/44. inherited 126/28
injustice 168/15. 234/22. 254/20
inquirers 317/5. inquiry 149/44,46
insanity 9/40. 111/41. 119/3. 156/32, 38. 228/1. 301/39
insight 108/35. 162/7
insomnia 245/18
inspiration 113/15. 119/44,47. 148/27. 154/39. 156/40. 206/37. 320/39. inspirational 151/1,4. inspirationally 160/10. 351/45. inspired 119/47. 150/26. 274/20. 309/2. 315/37
instantaneous 2/32. 64/16. 134/6,14. 136/7. 200/37. 206/41. 219/47. 220/2. 221/5. 222/30. 223/27. 224/38. 225/43. 227/5. 230/10. 242/35. 243/15. 280/35. 299/36. 301/24. 303/3. 305/45. 371/17. instantaneously 2/36. 213/43. 218/4. 221/5. 227/6,32. 242/35.

305/34,45. **instantly** 54/5. 80/22.
100/19. 105/15. 114/33. 129/31. 210/
45. 223/35. 273/14
instrument 290/25. 375/42
intellect 37/7. 162/2,9. 317/45.
intellectual 85/13. 130/4. 136/17.
151/42. 159/33. 230/38. 232/4. 233/25.
234/40. 235/3. 236/3. 267/36. 273/24.
323/2. 359/11. **intellectually** 113/10.
220/39. 301/5
intelligence God as 27/39. 59/12. 130/
47. 370/17. intelligence 36/5. 63/44.
69/5. 71/20. 77/25. 83/22. 131/20.
150/6. 258/30,33. 261/18. 296/33.
302/39. 303/22. 345/24. 365/2,10,19.
380/28. **intelligent** 80/23. 85/39.
296/24. 315/6. **intelligently** 63/13.
79/17
intensification of thought (*see under*
THOUGHT); intensification 102/3. 215/
22,31. 243/33,36. 249/30. 256/39.
260/22. 263/4. 298/12. 352/24. 369/
13,21
interaction 63/30. 73/20,30. **interchanging** 51/2,38. 76/41. 100/33,34.
101/5. 235/25. **intercourse** 234/40,
43. 236/29
interest 232/6. **interests** 101/15.
354/8,20
interfere 149/35. **interfering** 116/45.
118/50. 123/19
international 150/33
interpenetrate 271/38. 349/31
interpretation 148/36. 149/5. 150/28.
151/3. 152/1,18. 153/27. 162/22.
318/41
intuition 38/36. 133/33. 231/15. 235/42.
343/33. 353/33. **intuitional** 24/46.
intuitive 340/2. **intuitively** 339/41
invariable 61/7. 170/18
inventing 107/31. 351/14. **inventions**
113/21. 157/17. 279/11. 385/32
invigorated 218/2
inviolable 61/7
invisible 12/18. 70/11. 238/34. 251/24
ion 73/22
irritability 221/16. 287/4
is and is not 76/28, 210/9
island 71/32
Israel 153/44. 169/29,30. 170/10. 272/
21. 362/31-42

J

James Prof. William 3/22. 63/38. 146/
35. 184/15. 249/35. 300/22. 342/28
jealousy 393/5
Jehovah 26/26. 208/12
Jeremiah 8/15. 151/5. 272/13,33. 361/38
Jerusalem 272/35. 285/39. 297/44.
362/41

Jesus life of 11/16; material form of
25/33; the Master-metaphysician 25/
41. 75/19; teachings of 27/17. 150/16;
newly discovered sayings of 27/26.
32/31. 302/11; met a felon's fate
41/6; marvellous work of 47/7; way
in which J. worked 75/19. 78/35.
125/27. 181/21. 196/21. 218/21. 219/4.
266/20; miracles illustrate mental
laws 76/7; and the night 94/37; and
greater works 97/47; demonstrated
God-likeness 98/42; saw things at a
distance 107/21; knew all things
112/30. 157/46; and instantaneous
movement 122/31; appearance of J.
when doors were shut 125/26;
miracles scientific 126/32,41; we
have to follow 132/7; and the angel
reapers 132/42; and other great
teachers 139/19; and teaching the
nations 141/1; and sin 143/37;
miracles and the New Theology 148/
15; and material steps 173/22; and
our healing power 195/26,38; and
the loaves and fishes 200/41; greatest
miracle 201/14; such a doctor was
205/32; and human picturing 207/
34; and Beelzebub 213/48; none good
but one 240/9; and death 266/39.
268/44; tempted like as we 269/1;
highest human conception 272/14.
361/40; and Nicodemus 273/21; and
two commandments 285/16; and
true unselfishness 292/23; truth
taught by 299/37
joy 24/31. 39/29. 50/47. 51/19,23. 70/1.
90/36. 100-101. 131/12. 144/2. 174/4.
230/9. 231/32. 232/20. 237/6. 256/
12,29. 286/12. 292/20. 295/47. 314/
22,30. 337/19. 364/10,14. 372/49.
373/35,43. **joyous** 36/4. 89/43. 133/
45. 134/38. 237/1,22
judge 112/3. 149/5. 392/40. **judging**
254/20. **judgment** 92/15. 174/24.
290/6. 293/11. 395/40. **just** 293/18,
20. 354/26. **justice** 134/28-34. 171/1.
293/29. 352/32

K

Kant 13/1. 49/44. 77/26,31. 84/23. 167/
33. 338/45,48. 339. 344/32
Karma 124/30. 288/42. 326/1
Kelvin Lord 1/6. 13/19. 73/32. 88/39.
153/17. 183/42
key 150/28. 151/2. 272/16. 361/42.
keynote 308/8
kill 198/24-37
Kimball Edward A. 16/36. 211/29.
221/45. 243/25. 286/6. 371/36

kind 239/30
kindled 228/36
kingdom 32/27. 49/20. 51/28. 89/30.
90/2. 224/10. 242/27. 270/13. 280/20.
288/31. 297/17,40. 305/55. 370/19
King's touch and King's evil 7/32.
183/3
know 18/48. 30/9,10. 32/28. 76/13.
100/14–21. 126/37. 134/17. 148/30.
159/4. 172/3. 215/4. 242/6. 297/29.
310/25. 330/35. 343/26. 364/15.
knowable 18/46. knowing 91/25.
105/21. 111/43. 112/29. 127/19. 146/
28. 152/10. 172/42. 202/8. 210/35.
273/10. 286/34. knowledge of God
10/29. 11/18. 12/24. 28/19,38. 29/32.
48/27. 64/46. 94/40. 101/46. 126/18.
135/17. 142/28. 158/5. 162/36. 173/45.
179/21. 210/28,31. 218/24. 219/42.
222/3. 224/3. 227/20. 232/28. 255/20.
262/20. 267/40. 274/20. 282/20. 299/
31–34. 308/7. 315/16. 317/13,40.
387/5; advancing human 37/29;
definite 56/5; of our real selves 58/33;
grows 89/11,13. 91/44,46; forced to
gain 91/4; of how to think rightly
97/31; in reality 100/14. 101/3. 111/
47. 130/48. 364/13; obtaining needful 105/7. 114/37. 148/29. 154/29.
158/23. 160/10. 364/27; gaining k.
in right way 114/31. 157/40. 304/46;
of so-called mind and Mind 135/17;
scientific 153/16. 197/25. 280/35.
296/26. 299/33; true 162/43. 270/45.
305/44; of heaven 169/21; fullest use
of 170/48; real purpose of all 220/32;
essential 228/42. 274/17; protective
264/23. 305/4; intimate k. of reality
280/32; only true test of 339/48;
necessary 381/1. 382/14. 383/23. 385/
37. 387/19. 390/28; k. of Truth
(see under TRUTH); k. of truth (see
under TRUTH); knowledge 9/23. 42/20.
43/28. 48/9. 67/11. 99/2. 116/1. 133/
22. 158/3. 163/21. 201/27. 225/11.
227/21. 228/31. 249/16. 303/2. 306/16.
319/32. 332/26. 336/10. 339/40–340/2.
341/30,35. 351/26. 379/1,34. known
30/15. 100/3. 163/23. knows 94/24.
105/15. 295/42. 306/16. 308/32

L

land promised 174/23
language 37/19. 275/31. 385/37
Lao-Tze 49/42. 139/36. 173/17. 196/31.
229/42. 288/37. 289/31. 290/31. 292/5.
324. 382/32
latent 302/28
law of Life 2/11. 265/11. 285/18. 294/42.

295/28; of physics 5/43. 15/1. 41/3.
60/36. 61/5. 82/30. 115/9. 279/22;
of God, of Mind, divine 11/11. 61/6.
100/24. 120/16. 149/33,35,40. 168/39.
179/21. 194/21. 207/14. 244/26. 273/
14. 279/26. 295/12. 315/7. 369/20;
and miracles 46/44,46. 47/9. 76/8,10.
125/27; and order 46/47. 61/8. 94/29.
196/22. 270/41; of good 130/28.
236/7. 295/21,31. 308/5. 354/13.
false, so-called 168/21. 207/35. 225/
31. 236/39. 243/27. 264/7. 272/5.
275/46. 301/43. 312/39; law 92/19.
171/1. 221/32. 226/40. 229/6. 244/29.
253/32. 276/6. 295/17. 394/44. laws
false, so called 1/31. 13/25. 207/13.
233/28,33. 259/14. 261/44. 270/33.
276/3. 295/25; natural 60/7; laws 2/8.
48/19. 65/38. 169/30. 196/21. 263/13;
lawgiver 295/2. 353/12. 394/41
Lawrence Brother 129/19. 210/4. 217/
44. 221/23. 281/29. 297/4. 354/3
lead 306/29. 355/30. leader 173/14.
320/12. 321/9. leaders 227/45. 381/
28. led 173/33. 209/25,29. 308/32.
372/41
learn 37/4. 65/5. 91/3. 94/8. 95/38.
144/16. 176/7. 223/36. 242/3. 288/17.
291/14. 296/18. 308/7. 309/8. 373/27.
learned 9/22. 214/16
lecture 220/8. 247/32. 315/18. 316/5,13.
317/32
Leibnitz 13/19. 79/46. 166/41. 337.
348/19
let 131/18. 288/30. 306/29
letter 149/23. 274/19. 305/3. 315/9.
316/37. 371/28. 374/1. 380/1. 394/20
level 222/27. 372/2. 374/12. levelment
231/26. 233/5. 235/4
lever 92/3
liability 130/37. 268/16. liable 99/30.
146/26. 209/18
liberty 75/4. 213/32. 350/4
lie 23/17. 65/13. 87/2. 142/43. 143/22.
146/6. 172/19. 202/6. 206/36. 217/23.
241/29. 263/45. 293/33. 295/29. lies
18/47. 41/11. 146/3. 214/26. 298/12.
356/41
Life Truth and Love viii/26. 2/14.
27/32,36. 28/15. 35/40. 38/34. 55/4–12.
59/11. 89/21,43. 99/3. 100/13. 139/14.
149/36. 226/9. 253/48. 273/11. 300/44.
364/13. 368/33; as, is, God 2/2. 38/29.
50/44. 55/7. 101/32. 264/23. 295/4.
301/2. 364/45. Life 2/11. 135/37, 46.
212/20. 228/43. 264/46. 268/44. 285/
18. 286/15. 294/42. 295/28. 313/32.
364/47. 373/40
life so-called 9/12. 63/43. 69/5. 76/21.
103/34. 138/17. 275/24; everlasting
and eternal 11/22. 100/18. 210/29;

belief of l. in matter 11/39. 15/38. 304/39; real 24/31. 34/38. 101/15. 219/35. 237/15,27; human 86/19. 90/47. 107/2. 275/33; truth and love 27/33. 39/28. 229/21. 279/48; ways of looking at 355/35; life 13/1. 14/43. 76/11. 84/26. 94/25. 95/24. 141/6,11. 142/20. 151/13. 177/9. 227/24,26. 235/40. 237/23. 245/33. 264/17. 265/8,10. 274/15. 285/29. 286/12. 297/7. 302/3. 306/37. 340/25. 368/33
Life Understood (see under RAWSON)
lift 162/25. 173/44. 223/17. 241/3. 262/15. 375/45
light 48/45. 62/25. 63/3,11. 64/37. 78/7. 132/20. 136/18. 138/28. 147/21. 149/42. 273/16. 309/47–310/11. 332/5. 351/28. 359/42. 360/6–14
likeness image and (see under IMAGE)
likeness 58/39. 108/44. 148/11. 268/27
limbs 54/42. 55/2. 121/20
limit 52/20. 79/4,7. 221/7. 282/37. 302/23. 303/27. limitation 89/47. 126/28. 143/6. 203/43. 208/48. 221/27. 302/26. 364/14. 368/36. limitations 2/39. 37/44. 56/40. 57/28. 77/33. 89/39. 90/28. 97/29. 98/12. 100/14. 103/10. 104/16. 105/25. 107/32. 144/20. 201/15. 221/14. 241/4. 245/30. 275/42. 278/38. 283/4. 295/39. 313/14, 25. 364/3. limited 14/38. 77/14. 88/31. 311/28. 354/11. limitless 2/18
lion 365/4
listener 302/15. 307/11. listening 176/10. 274/12
literal 37/15. 316/4. literally 282/6
literature 100/1. 226/24,32
live 48/14. 211/11. 227/26,33. 229/11. 242/26. 295/12. lived 105/34. 285/16. lives 214/16. living 101/32. 135/37. 289/21. 295/42. 296/25. 298/24. 303/39
liver 55/7
loaves and fishes 201/5
Locke 13/45. 337
Lodge Sir Oliver 24/16. 25/1. 34/26,44. 35/39. 46/28. 47/4. 50/17. 52/28. 53/45. 60/42. 62/36. 63/22. 66/43. 75/2. 121/31. 160/5. 167/32. 238/11. 249/35. 250/15. 280/42. 314/5. 367/17. 378/2. 379/23
logic 173/31. 343/31. logical 17/6. 43/35. 146/16. logically 161/44. 315/43. 339/41
Logos 28/21. 128/14. 205/44. 328/13. 364/20,30. 376/25 (see also WORD)
Lombroso Prof. 63/9. 107/45. 108/9,13. 112/9. 116/35. 119/2. 121/36. 122/7, 14. 123/6. 156/16. 168/26. 249/35,46. 250/21. 254/9,18. 255/4
looking-glasses 271/40

Lord our 111/43. 112/28. 126/3. 143/38. 258/21
lose 51/13. 162/38. 211/15. 223/14. 242/33. 292/12. 298/16. 353/3. 371/18. 374/35. loses 94/40. 119/37. 280/21. 321/6. lost 82/31. 102/1. 272/7. 292/25
Love the only power 12/13; as, is, God 50/45. 55/10. 86/30. 127/42. 172/36. 230/20. 229/32. 232/27. 237/29. 270/8. 302/34. 364/46. 370/39. 373/40,43; divine 134/39. 230/26. 307/7; is supreme cause 228/29; Love 77/2. 228/3. 232/25. 237/18–30. 285/13. 286/34 (see also LIFE, Truth and Love)
love (noun) real 24/31. 39/28. 52/5. 77/9. 100/28–32,35. 101/20. 134/32; of Love 270/9. 368/33; treating for 283/39. 373/12; l. for 140/5. 173/32. 228/37. 229/27,34. 288/20. 291/12. 300/23. 370/40. 371/21. 399/36; antithesis of 290/12; love 89/12. 133/33. 172/21,35. 173/45. 227/29. 228/39. 262/37. 289/16. 290/1. 296/29. 297/35. 327/21. 334/4,6. 353/33. 359/45. 381/34. 393/40. love (verb) 100/33. 101/1. 172/34. 193/30. 229/27. 232/18. 241/45. 285/17. 288/19. 291/10. 292/35. 400/5. loved 102/1. 232/20. 273/16. lovers 291/29. loving 127/43. 128/5. 131/39. 173/1. 229/27. 249/6. 286/32. lovingly 285/15
Lowell J. R. 137/43. 287/46. 291/36. 296/7. 303/11. 320/32. 382/13. 390/27. 398/33
loyalty 285/20
lungs 55/6
Luther 70/37. 94/7. 156/23. 171/11. 181/33,35. 272/47

M

madman 138/35. madness 156/32. 168/16. 242/6
Maeterlinck 32/1. 59/3. 239/17
magic 45/33. 258/3. magicians 257/3. magic-lantern picture 199/21
magnetism animal 135/43. 246/2. 250/37. 262/25. 373/24
Mahatmas 348/34
majority viii/20. 89/36. 92/17. 135/42. 225/26. 231/21. 243/27. 264/31. 303/10. 313/20. 353/27
male and female 73/28. 87/27. 133/20. 174/18. 231/22,25,29. 233/2. 353/29, 38
malice against the truth 373/22. malicious 135/34. 262/22

malpractice 246/3,8. 261/23. 262/22. 318/28. 375/24; **malpractise** 283/36. 298/11

man

God by means of x/38. 35/22. 111/14. 232/29. 273/8. 360/47. 363/24-40. 369/2. 375/41; perfect universe and 11/37. 145/32. 149/26; the compound idea 27/34. 33/41. 360/36; not a human being thinking of spiritual things 32/17; the true 32/27; spiritual 50/30. 99/15,18,31. 100/22. 103/14. 114/33. 135/31. 148/11. 217/23. 231/17. 268/7. 270/17. 273/39. 310/34. 349/2. 365/3. 379/8; not God, nor separate from God 33/41. 147/1; one with God 35/20. 298/4. 368/37; reflecting aspects and qualities of God 36/2. 54/47. 100/13. 130/47. 270/8. 364/12. 368/34. 399/15; coexistence of God and 38/26. 143/20. 196/24; never existed in material body 49/16; spiritual and fourdimensional 58/6; time and spiritual 77/36. 364/4; Christ and spiritual 86/32. 136/36; not liable to sin, disease, death 99/18. 146/25; see real m. more as he is 105/21; God's 137/38. 138/18. 289/29. 347/1; the individual intelligent idea 145/32; the real 224/2; never thinks of himself 287/17; and newly born child 312/36. 349/17; in his right mind 313/43; can never know the whole of God 364/15; consists of 366/27; the activity or movement 366/13; God's consciousness (*see under* CONSCIOUSNESS); power of (*see under* POWER)

is the real m. material or spiritual 30/1; and noble destiny 34/36; fills his niche 65/18; when picture m. turns to God 99/38; cannot retrograde 134/42; belief that troubles improve spiritual 148/11; reversing, you are a better 220/39; love for m. in the street 229/35; apparent duality of 240/28; two opposed concepts of 273/32; waking up 275/8. 360/45; acts independently of 275/44; never think of yourself as a material 298/11; when an antagonistic 307/34; gaining a spiritual sense, loses 321/6; to whom children run 375/6; not aim and end of 375/46

material m. x/10. 8/43. 55/1. 67/11; misconception of real 11/39. 273/34; helpless 21/5; mere brute beast 25/15. 89/10; evolution of 25/25; cajoled and hypnotised into 30/4; material or carnal m. as described in Bible 30/19; unreal 58/6. 269/6. 351/14; origin of material 86/44; appears marvellous 103/9; apparent powers 120/18; the human beast 230/23; can do nothing 287/9; never made his consciousness 293/31; a puppet 311/43; seen falsely as a material 349/4; responsibility for acts of 351/8,18

manifestation with living good as its 14/25; Christ, God's 28/17. 376/22; man not God but 33/42; cause and its 50/2. 145/26. 355/36-42. 366/19; matter and its 75/6. 76/7. 80/16. 94/15; false working to bring about 201/44; highest 360/48; manifestation 35/42. 170/18. 192/22. 243/13. 261/10. 278/40. 279/33. 303/17; God and His m. (*see under* GOD); Mind and Its m. (*see under* MIND). **manifestations** 146/2. 270/30. **manifested** 94/13. 311/36

mankind 80/17. 126/40. 135/38. 140/4,12. 142/29. 207/11. 253/2. 264/31. 296/32. 317/14

manna 232/19

Marconi 60/34. **Marconi wave** 204/2. 357/7

Marcus Aurelius 86/20. 176/47. 260/9. 335/27

marriage 233/22. 234/40

martyrs the scientific 40/36

mass 348/29. **masses** 94/28

Master 124/18. 129/22. 138/31. 140/6. 201/40. 219/4. 273/21. 393/41. 397/41

matter caused to appear and disappear 11/30. 13/21. 75/8. 76/18. 148/15. 158/31. 200/21. 251/32. 253/5; human mind is 12/11. 70/10; non-mental 12/30; manifestation of false impressions 13/16; non-reality of, no such thing as 16/34. 44/25. 64/19. 80/25. 89/28,37. 92/16. 97/29. 158/28. 159/34. 160/10. 161/12. 253/14. 344/28. 345/4. 379/8; lie that God made 23/17; hides reality 24/43. 52/21; pantheism implied by conscious 27/6; attenuated thought of 44/33; occult results concerned with 57/3; rests upon visionary basis 72/2; and electron 73/23,31; matter 74/28; supposition of Spirit's opposite 75/5; electricity 75/8. 158/28. 386/26; never moves 76/18. 313/14; and its workings 80/8; a theoretical hole 81/40; false concept, belief 83/10. 148/15. 197/34;

so-called solid 88/22; end of 89/7,31. 91/7; only a manifestation of thought 94/14; consciousness passing through 125/31; argument that all is 145/8; is vibration 153/15; disappearance of 159/9; power of Mind over 176/17; mental effect on 192/34; has no power to act 199/14; Jesus could not create 200/41; believed to be a manifestation of Spirit 243/13; power of mind over 247/13; stages in formation of 251/40; human mind endeavouring to act on 259/19; refined up to dematerialisation 263/27; self destructive 311/9. 323/37 (see also under ETHER, FORCE lines of and MIST). **material** everything m. is only delusion 15/7; so-called good thoughts and bad both purely 68/12; becomes steadily less 89/6; replacing every picture of the 136/11; wrong to form picture of the 137/4; the age seems too 140/9; partly spiritual and partly 145/10; as man becomes less 245/21. 265/10. **materialisation** phenomena of 250/34. **materialist** 104/37. 204/35. 386/15. **materiality** 130/5. 132/18. 153/34. 360/33. **materially** 58/14. 63/37. 111/28. 375/10

Maudesley Henry 103/8. 365/12

Maya 85/28

means material 173/23. 199/20. 303/9. 304/17. 354/42. 355/13; means 101/22. 123/2. 179/1. 369/2

measure 62/40. 153/18. 172/33. **measurement** 228/9

mechanism 71/45. 72/28. 108/28. 109/35. 114/35. 137/10. 157/35. 167/35. 173/3. 178/31. 198/13. 260/35. 272/44,46

medical 6/1. 29/15. 175/19. 179/30. 188/9. 190/39. 215/32. 221/33. 225/9. 259/29. 282/14,41. **medicine** 6/7. 181/36. 195/10

meditation 128/18. 210/26,35

meekness 98/35. 289/16. 296/31

meet 236/33. 270/25. **meeting** 101/19. **meeting-place** 270/34

Melito 17/40. 210/17

memoria technica xii/34. 60/7. 63/26

memory 105/3

men 48/7. 133/43. 270/36; and women 48/14. 231/30,33. 232/16. 236/29. 350/19. 352/30

mental definition of 12/6,7. 107/34; all disease is 20/21. 200/31; so-called m. effect 175/2; Mind and mental 178/30. 215/6. 225/11. 233/42. 313/37. 314/12. 370/14; all is 187/43. 293/30; ethereal not truly 191/42. 238/33;

the m. age, era 278/26. 353/8; mental 83/7. 94/26. 108/37. 115/21. 140/13. 149/28. 209/8. 225/4. 226/28. 242/31. 272/38. 279/44. 289/10. 293/45. 302/3. 366/2. 372/4. **mentality** constitute the only 19/40; basic false 19/12,42. 64/2. 71/31. 72/8. 103/21. 118/37. 133/18. 138/5,9. 157/29,33. 158/30,46. 172/26. 252/13. 267/23. 328/46; false 60/30. 70/14,35. 71/40. 86/45. 91/6. 104/15. 105/15. 133/5. 214/1,29. 273/18. 279/34. 311/16; a person's 136/44. 244/31; lenses of more spiritual 274/40. **mentally** identify yourself 32/39; moving 53/25. 102/5; to act m. on matter 97/45; work only by 116/21; playing the shot, pitching sound 178/23,47; refreshed 259/24; work m. to destroy 260/15

message the whole of this 228/20

Messiah 35/37. 129/29. 140/2. 299/4

met 100/12. 295/37. 300/41

metaphysical 3/47. 37/15. 65/22. 79/1. 90/43.187/41.356/37.**metaphysician** 5/43. 39/18. 104/38. 197/27. 204/33. 206/35.319/29. **metaphysics** 343/20

method practical 1/33. 126/43. 147/42. 156/14. 278/17. 297/46; instantaneous 2/32; only one m. of healing 7/36; right 32/22. 75/21. 94/8. 124/38. 125/17. 131/44. 187/39. 222/29. 309/40. 351/36; Jesus' method 75/19. 173/15; used by sorcerers 75/18; of practice necessary 85/14; this way instead of wrong 110/9; scientific 114/29. 138/44. 187/39. 191/17. 220/34. 247/20. 355/27; wrong, dangerous, unsatisfactory 115/16. 123/18. 125/31. 194/10. 202/10,34. 209/27; old m. of prayer 135/18; do not confine themselves to this 137/41; mistaken views of best 162/40; only m. of escape 171/25; evil as a m. of making people good 208/34; one 369/41. 371/24; work out his own 373/26. **methods** right and wrong vii/5,16,25. 139/18. 200/35. 201/30. 217/8. methods 107/32. 143/31. 234/36. 273/5. 355/13, 15. 373/29

miasma 241/39. 254/42. 272/38. 304/20

Michael 92/21. 127/9. 133/3,8,27. 210/46

might 133/42. 286/13,35

miles 68/21. 206/43. 357/8

Mill John Stuart 78/2. 89/25. 146/34. 170/36. 342

millennium 52/20. 130/10. 206/31. 226/21. 283/2

Mind the real M., God 12/22; eternal cause 19/18. 27/33; opposite of 19/40. 68/18; divine state of 49/43;

false sense of action of 65/10; and its manifestation 81/34. 145/30. 146/7. 187/45. 233/42. 279/46. 295/43. 310/24. 314/10; not in anything but everything in 83/9; be of one 92/5; and its ideas 101/16–30. 363/40. 368/16–369/35; counterfeiting the infinite capacities of 103/11; reason for study of Science of 135/33; rules and practice of M. healing 138/46; if M. knows evil 142/42; whatever M. knows is the manifestation of Truth 145/30; reflection, expression of 149/26. 231/24. 313/42; protection of 173/28; no real mind except reflection of the one 175/34; M. and mental 178/30. 215/5. 225/10. 233/42. 313/37. 314/11. 370/14; the power of M. (see under POWER); Mind 11/11. 79/3,40. 105/16. 120/17. 135/18. 211/14. 245/15. 270/27. 279/26. 301/6. 323/12

mind
open 3/9. 112/5. 160/4,35. 223/31. 242/42
human m. must be dematerialised 25/38. 49/13; fits into body 70/10. 120/19. 347/42; called the soul 70/18,33. 120/19. 240/31. 266/47; purification of 96/36. 133/13. 135/1. 173/27. 203/25. 206/10. 243/18. 266/12. 267/30,34. 268/1. 293/37. 312/30. 360/8. 370/29. 375/26; opens the 99/39; healing with 139/17. 180/6. 202/47; test of working with 218/1. 259/18; wrong use of 247/23,47. 259/18; unhappiness and human m. power 248/18; reason for acquaintance with 305/37; human m. 12/11. 63/6. 68/20. 69/11. 70/8. 73/11. 75/11. 77/34. 83/8. 103/2. 202/50. 240/5. 247/34. 260/35. 266/12. 269/29. 271/27. 276/40. 312/30
mortal 68/4. 70/29. 71/39,41. 104/11. 133/5. 138/9,12. 157/30. 158/30,44. 293/7
mechanical equivalent of consciousness 68/17
subjective, subconscious 71/38. 72/5. 103/13,21. 104/4,9,18. 105/14. 126/28. 157/30. 158/45. 172/27. 203/26. 227/10. 252/13. 280/27. 313/13. 328/46. 356/7
take away cognising 85/6
so-called conscious 126/27–30. 280/27
knowledge of action of so-called 135/17
that portion of his 138/25
sinner never made his so-called 206/13
spurious m. culture 226/29

so-called m. of healer and patient 227/18,23
wrong to keep m. free from thought 253/31
mind 12/14. 62/38. 176/48. 177/9,21, 39. 185/44. 186/3,4. 261/31. 279/34. 290/39 (see also under NO-MIND and NON-MENTAL)
minded spiritually 32/18
minute 134/3. 299/1. 354/1. minutes 160/34. 300/1
miracle the word m. 47/6,43; anyone can do a 76/9. 126/32; result of law and order termed 94/30; will take place 202/4. 368/9. miracles of Jesus 25/42. 76/7. 121/7. 125/27. 126/32. 181/19. 200/42. 201/14. 219/4. 249/17. 316/17. miracles 41/19. 46/44. 179/18. 196/47. 201/39. 219/29. 230/12. 246/38. 288/5. 321/35. miraculous 4/39. 47/38. 124/11. 181/31. 196/35. 200/39. 249/21
mirror 138/26,27
miserable 99/43. 131/9. 204/7. 268/18. misery 9/10. 98/21. 256/16. 274/45
misinterpretations 148/32
misrepresentation 30/25. 100/6. 271/12. 312/35. 313/2. 349/4. 364/36. misrepresentations 327/31. 349/29
mist thinning of 52/19. 99/41. 105/20. 169/15. 281/22; mist 3/39. 74/22. 87/32. 89/19. 97/17. 236/38. 281/19. 314/17. 357/32
mistake 65/19. 114/23. 124/11. 263/21, 24. 286/30. 351/12. 374/22. mistaken 6/17. 16/22. 95/4. 116/28. 123/22. 162/40. 172/41. 208/3. 226/27. mistakes 2/10. 101/15. 142/24. 162/47. 279/16. 298/11
mistranslation 148/39. 151/10
moment 79/6,28. 101/39. 127/7. 149/12. 167/15,18. 227/34. 241/46. 242/43. 300/43. 302/32. 306/25. 349/33. 353/4. 370/38
Montaigne 345
moral 61/9. 136/16. 147/17. 205/14,30. 209/8. 245/44. 250/13. 252/38. 253/37. 254/39. 286/8. 305/17. 321/27. 329/45. 367/10. 390/23. morality 234/41,44. 236/22. 281/4. morally 217/1. 220/39. 301/5
mortal 68/33. 135/35. 157/31. 176/25. 203/42. 265/13. 267/8. 273/38. 280/18, 20. 312/19–35. mortality 140/13. 277/1. mortals 12/17. 21/3. 145/42. 167/26. 173/44. 223/20. 269/8. 270/36. 272/38. 291/41. 386/9
Moses 8/14. 96/32. 111/24. 130/1. 139/34. 169/22. 170/26. 195/42. 202/50. 238/43. 255/40. 295/1. 299/24. 356/38. 362/47

mother 53/14. 230/39. mother-wit 343/34
motion 58/10. 76/14. 84/15. 112/24. 179/42. 280/28. 313/14. 327/36. 328/1. 334/21
motive 95/4. 125/19. 236/30,32. 245/23. 258/21. 306/31
mount 270/34. mountain 36/42. 129/3. 310/2
movement 53/20,25. 63/29. 67/12. 68/3. 76/16,22. 101/27. 121/33. 125/37. 192/35. 278/15. 311/27. 334/22. 353/1. 366/13. 369/33,34
Münsterberg Prof. Hugo 179/49. 180/33. 184/24. 187/25. 246/41. 254/46
murderer 30/30. 118/26
muscles 183/36. 184/4,6. 191/32. 192/3
music 100/1,37. 278/11. 327/6,47
Myers F. W. H. 68/22. 103/28. 109/48. 119/3. 122/42
mystery 1/32. 3/39. 4/8. 6/3. 10/25. 11/25. 62/22. 64/33. 160/24. 205/23. 249/10-25. 262/44. 318/5
mystical 152/21. 273/21. mystics 210/1

N

name 232/22. names 71/41. 153/13. 158/46. 165/30. 173/7. 198/20. 356/8
Napoleon 29/3. 165/10. 247/32
nation 263/21. 275/20. 281/2. 301/25. nations 90/39. 232/27. 296/37
natural 94/29. 100/24. 105/26. 115/21. 154/42. 155/3. 225/4. 355/7. naturally 124/12. 154/30. nature 16/28. 21/18. 58/28. 60/24,31. 64/42. 232/22. 275/17. 310/8
nearer 135/5. 341/26. nearest 94/34. 229/35
necessary 380/28. 381/1,34. 382/14. 383/23. 384/42. 385/37. 387/5,19. 390/28. necessity 94/25. 144/14. 160/35. 171/24. 253/48
necromancy 266/46
need 136/6. 222/26. 301/19. needed 91/25. 219/17. needful 105/7. needless 265/9. 270/20. 295/27. 296/8. needs 105/16,22. 159/4. 162/35. 221/27
negative 84/14. 86/22. 253/22,46. 273/47. 337/32. negatives 79/42
neighbour 229/23. 285/18. 290/34. 291/11. 300/23. 305/13-20
Neo-Platonism 333
nerves 7/44-8/1. 69/30. 180/48. 187/18. 213/34. nervous 59/7. 124/45. 260/39
net on the right side 226/19
new 42/40. 100/9. 101/20. 104/35. 271/21. 274/15. 285/15,40

New Theology The 148/1
news 8/19. 109/43
Newton Sir Isaac 41/2. 76/35
Nicodemus 273/20
night 90/42. 132/17. 245/10. 259/25. 261/38. 359/43. nightmare 86/6. 269/32. 283/5. 351/24
no-mind so-called healing with 179/27. 217/38. 220/1; no-mind 12/5. 19/37. 70/14. 103/2. 124/36. 175/30. 204/4. 220/26. 238/36. 240/2. 247/28. 261/19.
non-mental 12/5. 19/38. 68/36. 69/9. 87/16. 97/16. 107/34. 111/38. 136/4. 178/27. 181/1. 213/36. 225/8. 312/14
non-reality 18/27,31. 70/1. 143/12. 311/6. 315/14. 323/35 (see also under MATTER)
normal 90/36. 148/27. 162/19. 170/37. 270/31. 301/32
not Is 210/9; was 76/28
nota bene 310/15
nothing 17/7. 18/2. 91/8. 127/25. 137/44. 161/32. 201/22,24. 204/38. 241/29. 293/4. 304/9. 306/41. 310/18. 313/29. 400/8. no-thing 283/5. nothingness 80/34. 143/26. 147/23. 263/9. 313/28. 382/18
now 78/3. 79/26. 99/31,35. 295/8. 309/20. 310/21
number protect as large a 94/35; infinite 99/45-100/18. 364/4-11. 368/35; greatest good for greatest 304/37. 354/27; number 278/8. numbers enough not in 89/36. 92/12. 313/20; significance of 151/8. 153/13. 276/6, 7

O

obedience 135/45. 162/13. 228/26. 273/14. 285/18. 295/34. 314/9. 315/44-316/1. obey 146/22. 169/31. 282/5. 286/32. 295/11
object 229/37. 301/23. 302/5. 308/1. 316/33
occult 4/4. 43/10. 107/30. 108/16. 121/4. 123/6. 124/28. 125/4. 151/45. 249/17. 253/15,23. 254/13. 257/31. occultism 43/7. 124/35,44. 187/36 249/7
occupation 134/41. 226/22
offence 174/3
offspring 310/35. 353/28
old 36/10. 135/18. 264/16. olden 287 43. older 263/34
omnipotence 2/15. 48/41. 62/25. 98/33. 242/34. 287/16. 343/2. omnipotent 2/12. 22/3. 135/43. 146/32. 147/22. 228/40. 236/6. 294/42. 342/45. 373/40

omnipresence 2/15. 98/33. 270/31.
omnipresent 77/2. 147/4. 228/14,40
omniscience 98/33
one 26/15. 51/30. 79/25. 92/5. 133/37.
136/28. 171/41. 178/18. 231/21. 264/
30. 311/33. 353/26. oneness 35/43.
oneself 220/34. 223/11
open 112/5. 143/23. 150/37. 160/3,35.
223/30. 242/42. openly 154/26. 316/
48. open-minded 171/35. 290/5.
opens his human mind 99/39
opinion 143/22. 151/43. 335/47
opportunities 287/47. opportunity
79/37. 173/2. 367/40
oppose 295/10. 396/37. opposed 273/
32. opposite suppositional 63/37.
138/6. 311/8; contradictory 68/36.
295/3; exact, absolute 127/41. 130/39.
132/2. 136/10. 253/33. 297/12,14.
370/28,32. 372/15. opposite 65/19.
68/18. 140/12. 253/30. 295/13. 312/14.
opposition 76/9. 195/34,38. 231/32.
235/48. 270/33. 295/12,21
order 46/47. 61/8. 94/29. 162/17. 170/
22. 196/23. 270/41. 364/47. ordering
295/38
organs 54/38. 55/5. 364/44
Origen 17/34,37. 37/45. 151/45. 335/37
origin 18/20-25. 19/12. 29/7. 63/3.
228/40. 242/38. 253/5. 259/34,37.
270/8. 279/1. 332/38. original 86/22.
149/39. 276/23. 291/5. originating
86/42,45
orthodox 209/33. 350/23. orthodoxy
41/15. 45/18. 398/6
others ix/6,25. 95/43. 138/3. 172/18.
285/13. 289/45. 290/29,32. 292/15.
294/24. 355/3,5
ought 168/35
ourselves 84/31. 89/42. 91/14. 95/39-
41. 101/49. 138/3. 143/41. 286/8.
287/26. 294/23. 346/40. 355/2
outline 112/4. 137/5,29. outlined 149/
34,36. 217/17. outlines 282/45.
outlining 212/41. 246/30. outlinings
227/16
outlook 142/10. 261/37. 318/41
overcome 105/25. 131/25. 134/27.
143/14,41. 221/27. 256/46. 268/26,41.
286/22. 300/17. 368/10. overcoming
2/1,39. 107/32. 141/10
own 96/4,37. 98/10. 133/43. 137/45.
172/25. 173/26. 354/17,20

P

paganism 208/22. 229/3
pain 69/27. 94/39. 222/9,15. 237/16,17.
241/22. 256/27. 299/13. 301/47. 342/
27. 373/35

painting 108/29. 374/7
pair single 278/35. 279/31
Paracelsus 44/40-45/41. 95/5. 211/34.
214/32
Parmenides 76/27. 324/3. 328
particle 66/9. 68/31. 73/23,31. 74/2.
161/24. particles 63/31. 68/30.
72/26-36. 73/6,46. 75/36. 77/1. 83/46,
48. 87/35. 88/6. 114/35. 161/22,23.
203/11. 204/23,30. 220/25. 269/3.
279/25. 313/36. 357/12
past present and future 78-79. 105/
28-107/4. 157/31. 165/23. 252/15.
311/18; past 104/16. 107/3. 112/23.
113/1. 116/30. 171/45. 172/16. 205/37.
251/18. 275/1. 309/16-22. 357/36.
361/27. 364/10
paths 235/45. pathway 317/13
patience 235/10,42. 283/9
patient 79/28. 136/33-137/4,28. 138/
11,18. 207/4. 217/20,26. 223/6,12.
224/36. 225/13,34. 227/10,23. 244/36.
245/10. 247/14,17. 282/45,47. 396/5.
patients 139/14. 227/44. 241/21.
282/34. 301/17. 306/2
Paul St. 10/40. 111/25. 176/16. 239/45.
240/36,39. 296/12. 378/7,8
payment 307/40
peace of mind 2/42. 136/13. 173/20.
221/8; of God 245/20; false 261/39;
peace 11/24. 70/1. 95/29. 135/44.
139/15. 221/17. 232/23. 238/41. 274/
45. 284/3. 288/14. 290/42. 295/46.
296/31. 314/16
pearls 307/3. 397/17
pencil growing 56/20
people 50/3. 64/6. 101/20
perception 78/10. 130/10,45. 373/12
perfect spiritual and 145/41. 217/24.
242/13. 256/11. 269/10. 276/17;
perfect 23/48. 50/32. 89/42. 134/44.
204/16. 240/17. 268/7. 279/3. 291/22.
310/21. 349/42. 375/40. perfection
any thought but one of 130/31;
think of, realise 170/19. 243/4. 267/25.
297/14; from imperfection defining
214/46; perfection 38/25. 101/11,16.
116/20. 128/41. 144/21. 228/29. 264/
19. 287/36. 314/1. 374/2
periods 272/3. 275/5. 312/43. 313/1.
357/29
permanence 161/13. 311/2. 356/11.
362/5. 372/31. permanent 19/26.
84/19. 134/45. 135/3. 145/12. 168/31.
207/1. 240/6. permanently 71/8.
127/40. 128/5. 209/18. 220/37. 241/23.
278/17. 300/6. 314/35. 375/27
persecution 171/40. 242/15. persecutors 397/39
Person God the only 27/45; person
32/18. 103/12. 114/25. 135/14,48,49.

136/2,30. 143/18. 223/11. 236/30. 290/7. **personalise** 172/13. **personalities** 64/2. **personality** 69/4. 97/11. 99/1. 213/30. 229/36. 303/4. 396/38. **personification** 19/42
pharisaical 164/8. 383/41. 398/24. **pharisaism** 381/39. **Pharisees** 392/37. 393/9
phenomena material 2/28. 4/1. 15/13. 19/15. 62/2. 64/9. 83/15. 149/29. 199/17. 256/42. 273/17. 278/8. 280/30. 326/45. 330/27; occult 4/22. 123/6. 249/17. 253/16; mental 11/30. 160/13; matter ethereal p. 76/5; due to force 80/31; mechanical 167/38; human 184/41. 246/21; real 270/24,29. 273/13. 313/31–314/12; phenomena 19/18–29. 85/2,5. 280/23. 323/24,25. 356/6
philosopher 142/3,25. **philosophers** 36/34. 77/18. 84/9. 99/32. 142/8. 169/9. **philosophic** 9/1. 84/7. 142/2. 242/10. 323/26. **philosophy** 42/22. 43/23. 62/35. 74/27. 75/29. 85/11,22. 147/37. 251/6. 323–324. 342/16. 344
22
physically 91/48. 220/39. 260/10. 301/6. **physique** 28/9
physician 6/12. 26/9. 139/15
physics 5/44. 82/30. 343/14. **physiological** 7/39. 185/46
picture correct word 3/35; material universe a 12/44; change thoughts and see perfect 13/14; world of sense only a 84/29. 340/27; replace, translate, every false 136/11. 291/4; forming p. of person 136/46–137/15; body's appearance similar to mental 185/8; washing out magic-lantern 199/21; what they consider best 201/42; false thoughts making you 261/31; another meaningless 271/16. **pictured** a lie strongly enough 212/40; as a new person 271/20. **picturer** 202/6. 266/16. **picturers** 348/28. **pictures** cinema, cinematographic x/11. 12/1. 13/27. 63/33,41. 69/1. 76/21,24. 99/15–43. 104/43–105/36. 108/31. 144/25. 169/13–21. 199/18. 274/31–275/7. 280/24. 311/25. 312/42. 357/24; false 225/18. 231/10. 253/1. 269/26. 276/11. 313/2; dream 264/38. 271/27–272/1. 276/15,37. 285/38. 313/27. **picturing** 64/4. 69/44. 94/19,36. 124/13,40. 137/1. 202/2,8. 205/41. 206/5. 207/33. 215/19,20. 225/21. 227/14. 230/25. 260/21,40. 262/11. 273/3. 352/25
pitfalls 372/45
place 53/23. 54/6. 76/16,31. 91/23. 120/26. 251/33. 278/16. 302/27. 369/35

planchette 255/26
plane 95/39. 234/40–235/26. 271/13
planets 50/3. 88/13. 101/10. 164/25,29, 42. 278/12. 327/5
plant 253/12. 296/27,32. **plants** 87/9. 167/30. 193/22. 305/15. 366/45
plaster 287/45
platform displays 194/1
Plato 17/45. 37/17. 58/24. 59/19–60/3. 109/2. 128/1. 142/3,27. 155/12. 167/33. 176/49. 239/27. 278/24. 286/29. 288/12. 289/20. 299/21. 323/9. 324/14. 331. 345/42
pleasure 21 42. 101/13. 289/23. 314/13. 331/6. 342/27
Pleroma 376/30
Plotinus 239/17. 333/13
pocket-handkerchief to clean doorstep 247/27
poison 6/48. 186/8. 197/45. 198/23. 205/21. 243/43. 263/40
population 277/12–50
portion 138/24. 270/11. 271/26. 311/25. **portions** 105/23. 114/36. 274/33
position 101/26. 159/7. 169/6,14. 173/38. 208/8. 312/14
positively 307/12
possibilities 2/17. 36/26. 62/13. 75/27. 98/23. 130/10. 146/30. 270/23. **possibility** 38/39. 270/43. **possible** 241/36. 286/33
potent 135/14. 225/5,17. **potentialities** 281/48. **potentially** 65/34
power of God, Mind, good 7/26. 10/40. 35/22. 83/8. 125/28. 126/18. 133/25. 155/2,4. 176/10–21. 218/2. 224/4. 256/46. 263/9. 282/37. 297/46. 369/1; only p. is 12/13; man's God-given 38/39. 51/9. 65/6. 79/27. 91/22. 98/25. 116/46. 124/19. 125/28. 154/32. 155/5. 174/3. 218/18. 254/33. 262/21. 286. 301/40. 312/3. 352/5,43. 360/31. 368/36. 373/41; miracle an act of 47/48; development of mental 63/3. 126/16; motive 66/19. 166/10; of truth 91/38; hypnotic 95/10. 246/15. 247/23–248/33. 262/1; prevented from exercising harmful 126/31; and rod 132/43,45. 138/37; loses its 143/25; through consent or assent 168/41; with all the mental 136/2. 372/11; no one has p. over another 171/48; spiritual p. divinely directed 176/17; false working to retain individual 181/2; illusory, false 188/2. 305/41; sin has no 206/5. 242/7; divine 228/21. 303/24; of love 230/4,17; invincible p. of Christ 242/39; apparent p. until 276/3; of Principle 279/47; he who would have full 285/23; over material self 292/26. **powerless**

69/14. 96/40. 197/34. **powers** human 103/11. 104/31. 173/34; if he loses his ordinary 119/38; divine 126/21; powers 8/30. 32/39. 44/32. 63/46. 104/41. 105/26. 111/42. 120/5. 126/30. 162/45. 189/26. 208/12. 278/13

practice 2/31. 85/15. 123/25. 127/2. 135/32. 138/46. 225/13. 231/27. 245/34. 281/28,35. 291/42. 321/20,37. **practise** 48/17. 94/8,24. 128/13. 218/30. 285/14. 291/14. **practitioner** 98/31. 139/11. 216/14. 225/13

pray when it is known how to 144/15. 167/2. 211/5. 214/16. 217/40. 239/38. 256/18; until he knows how to 168/16; Jesus once told how to 219/5; learn to p. rightly 224/32. 296/18. 339/18; if when doubtful 306/15,33; if you forget to 309/16; work . . . watch and 321/37; pray 94/31. 143/29. 154/30. 161/40. 214/34. 227/38. 231/16. 237/18. 256/2. 299/2. 300/2,13. 302/12. 303/2,40. 304/18. 307/30. 330/29. **prayed** 79/37. 294/21. 304/1. **prayer** true viii/22. 72/22. 105/18. 119/47. 157/34. 160/15. 162/31. 167/8,18. 169/8. 220/27. 221/33. 223/42. 224/8. 229/39. 278/46. 281/42. 282/38. 301/15. 304/4. 307/36. 369/39. 376/1; and past events 78/18,24. 300/31; evolution in 89/15. 207/16. 330/31. 359/49; without ceasing 129/3,20. 372/27; aspiration towards good, named 136/25; attenuated answers to 136/26. 207/32. 300/11; rely upon 154/31. 303/17,47; suppliant's belief in result of 208/3. 209/5–27; three degrees, all good and effective 210/23–211/20; supplicatory 212/46. 214/19; hypnotic 246/27; humble but scientific 273/7; by p. alone 303/31. 304/12; prayer 124/38. 135/12. 202/34. 215/8. 223/2. 229/40. 300/25. **Prayer Book** 10/42, 44. 48/3. **prayers** viii/30. 196/41. 208/4,30, 214/35. 241/47. 301/23. **praying** if when vii/27. 224/35; when you think of God you are 32/20; use of sword, constant 131/39; we cannot be p. properly 144/5; what person p. thinks best 246/31; doing your mental work 262/4; without ceasing, so preventing 300/17; after 339/47. **praying-machine** 208/30. **prays** rightly. A puppet until he 311/43

predestination x/33. 99/35. 162/4. 166/1. 311/39. **predestined** 167/19. 261/21. 350/35. **predetermined** 99/37. 162/16. 166/48. 167/9. 169/7.

217/32. 261/47. **prediction** 112/17. 274/41

prejudice 290/6. 309/38. 351/25. **prejudicing** 291/45. 360/20

present 77/46. 78/22. 79/5,18. 85/33. 94/21. 98/30. 106/8. 114/37. 130/30. 144/29. 157/31. 165/23. 273/15. 285/19. 288/31. 311/18. 360/18. 363/4

prevent 62/23. 112/1. 119/8. 124/23. 131/3. 146/23. 149/35. 157/35. 226/8. 253/15. 302/37. **prevented** 77/14. 116/7. 126/31. 148/25. **preventing** 208/20. 300/17. **prevention** 163/26. **preventive** legislation 263/1

pride 143/41. 171/40. 289/35

Principle of Life, living P. 2/14. 38/29. 89/21. 135/37. 170/16. 207/15. 238/26. 275/48. 309/1; divine 2/18. 14/24. 27/35. 223/1. 228/41. 234/19. 306/40. 315/7. 347/1,4; of good 17/18,21. 35/41. 59/10. 145/22,43. 170/16. 214/27. 224/25. 242/29. 289/12. 293/30. 295/29. 310/25. 343/1. 351/11. 372/21; of all Science 27/39; action of 29/10. 130/30. 242/29. 304/19. 317/25; God as, is 38/33. 46/46. 61/8. 196/22. 229/45. 337/23. 371/16,20; of knowledge 114/32. 159/3. 162/34. 306/16. 339/45; God is P. of wisdom 130/46; and its idea 143/21. 196/25; based on 218/30. 321/32; this ever-acting 242/40; Principle 79/21. 85/38. 160/22,38. 161/49. 179/4. 236/31. 242/29. 268/20. 276/7. 279/47. 317/22. 353/19,22. 354/23. 355/16,30

prison lifting a man out of 292/23

privilege 128/2. 167/2. 172/9. 261/28. 265/4. 283/43

probe 80/19. 131/16

problem 11/14. 147/9. 318/6 **problems** 109/42. 157/16. 233/4,38. 234/15. 235/39. 278/16. 296/9. 316/31

progress depends upon 129/38. 211/17. 299/11. 372/34; progress 50/31. 53/16. 76/13. 98/6. 148/44. 162/26. 173/9. 234/27,43–235/40. 270/3. 287/40. 295/39,46. 296/26. 305/51. 342/27. 355/14. **progressive** 90/38. 311/27

proof men want p. of everything 48/12. 273/3; of our knowledge of heaven 52/34; practical, demonstrable 53/43. 148/40 236/28. 299/28. 305/47,48; mathematical 159/15,23. 160/14,26, 30; grain of 191/27; absolute 206/38. 219/47. 315/14; not sufficient p. of truth 219/46. 220/3; not profession 291/12. **proofs** 92/1. 294/41. 309/35. **prove** by demonstration 79/22. 89/22. 171/31. 242/6,36. 268/45. 270/25. 272/39. 279/46. 283/39. 340/1; my investigation . . . not to 200/31; for

himself 98/9. 157/45. 294/42. 313/17.
314/39; the omnipotence of God
353/4. proved 1/27. 2/8. 149/8.
170/37. 202/14. 242/38,44. proves
148/41. 149/29. 171/22,28. 295/24.
315/10. proving 286/34. 295/39.
321/34. 367/40. 371/19
prophecies of Moses 169/22; and their
individual significance 170/21; with
help of Bible 274/38; how to check
p. of future 361/1; fulfilment of 379/
30.   prophecy 62/37,42. 117/19.
140/25. 141/1. 162/16,22. 163/35.
170/39. 171/27. 217/27. 230/34. 294/
27.   prophesying 162/4. 171/13.
prophet test of true 249/4; prophet
117/47. 123/11. 169/28. 205/5. 256/4.
prophetess 140/44. prophets 94/
12. 248/35. 275/18. 285/26
proportion 134/29. 243/32. 270/41.
288/21. 305/51
protect self, others ix/24. 94/33. 95/39.
96/5,25. 114/27. 164/6. 168/46. 172/4,
9,42. 191/18. 214/6,18. 217/9. 228/22.
238/40. 243/32. 247/48. 261/27. 262/
20. 267/40. 283/20,25. 291/48. 305/4.
353/21; protect 94/10. 127/46. 263/5.
269/11. 304/19. 306/40. protected
262/45. 300/25. protection 99/3.
116/28. 129/4. 173/28. 230/20. 234/18.
264/21. 355/20,27. protective 230/
17
psychic 57/23. 110/12. 120/29. 122/
40,46. 125/6. 251/46. psychical
3/19. 250/21. psychism 10/10.
psychology 3/21,24. 62/10. 63/1. 80/
37. psychological 104/6. 185/46.
psychologists 103/25,37. 356/6.
psychometry 107/12. 257/39.
psychotherapy 179/26. 201/31
punish 28/28,36. punished 27/9.
168/21. 208/38. 241/33. 242/3,4. 261/
30. 293/33. punishment brings its
own 94/3. 143/27. 242/2. 351/33;
punishment x/25. 39/22,34. 70/4.
145/37. 168/29. 169/34,36. 171/3.
181/6. 205/13. 206/3–6. 241/45. 242/7.
262/43. 399/33
puppet 311/43
pure 138/28. 140/3. 234/10. 235/48.
293/39. purification 96/36. 131/20.
133/13. 135/2. 168/30. 172/22. 173/26.
203/24. 211/2. 243/17. 267/18–268/
2,41. 273/37. 293/37. 370/29. 375/49.
purified 29/1. 73/3. 114/18. 128/17.
129/13. 131/29. 135/1. 139/29. 241/41.
263/28. 269/2. 270/43. 300/7. 312/6,31.
purifies 204/29. 220/38. 299/26.
360/8. purify 133/12. 162/24. 169/2.
222/16. 274/44. 303/14. 357/21.
purifying 127/1. 128/3. 206/10.

220/24.   327/20.   349/10.   375/26.
purity 129/25. 210/40. 215/2. 231/1.
232/11. 236/24–26. 278/6
purpose 2/16. 64/40. 72/21. 147/17.
155/4. 220/31. 236/36. 256/26. 290/29
push 303/20. pushed 241/47
Pyramid the Great 141/24
Pyrrho 334
Pythagoras 278/3. 326. 361/14

Q

quackery 6/36. 39/43. 45/17. 187/31
qualities 87/29. 208/28. 231/13,22.
233/6,11. 235/15,41. 236/3. 370/48.
371/4. quality 167/27. 291/15. 363/
38
questions object of answering xii/37

R

radiate 100/2,49. radiating 173/44.
radiation 363/19
radium 74/46. 212/28
rain 367/29
raise 173/27. 229/34. raising from
the dead 196/11. 202/46. 266/5. 271/
37. 379/1
Rawson F. L. On Life Understood
v/1–vii/24. 2/45–3/4. 315/18–316/46;
Examination into mental healing
2/46. 65/22; My work 64/36. 157/1,15;
Time proved no barrier 78/11,25;
Early searchings for a practical
religion 110/31–41; Spiritualistic
and hypnotic experiments 116/25;
Love for the Master since right
understanding 140/5; Investigations
electrical, chemical, mechanical 156/
44; Advised on new medical discoveries 157/3,4; Mathematical proof
of non-reality of electricity, matter
160/11–161/8; Results of treatment
161/39. 178/21–179/18. 229/43. 232/
33–48. 305/32–34; Articles on golf
178/21–33; Value of investigation
into mental healing 200/30; One
failure 206/44; Standing where I do
as its humble servant 228/17; Love
of God seemed to disappear 229/44–
49. 371/19–23; Dinner with W. T.
Stead 232/33; Bill for stopping
mental malpractice 246/7. 263/2;
Work to be done for myself 261/3;
Mistake I made as young man 291/24;
Throughout religious services 301/
7–25; Read no books but 305/22–39;
On rules of conduct Mrs Eddy
points out 315/42; To these . . . I

owe benefit of all . . . 319/31; Working knowledge of God gained 370/36; My method "cut and dried" 371/24; I start every treatment by 373/5
reach 98/10. 270/13. 296/9. 305/55. reached 141/4. reaching 208/46. 234/37
reading evil effects when 114/16
real 17/5. 18/29. 24/33. 52/6,13. 63/33. 76/6. 84/19. 111/29. 143/1,15. 145/12. 146/12,22,43. 204/28. 240/6. 241/37. 242/9. 270/29. 279/49. 311/30. 314/17. 369/33. realisation within your capacity of 32/42; the r. of God 98/46. 105/20. 125/23. 134/12. 136/42. 137/33. 139/13. 155/8. 157/41. 162/38. 172/35. 173/24. 181/22. 201/12. 214/37. 229/43. 232/23. 253/14. 276/39. 281/42. 289/10. 299/12. 300/44. 370/41. 371/15. 374/36; striving a joyous 133/45. 134/38; on account of your 309/6; realisation 98/28–99/7. 105/18. 131/6,11. 134/31. 135/1. 201/28. 224/28. 292/40. 354/44. realise, make it real to yourself 127/14. 219/17; realise 52/39. 113/12. 114/32. 127/39. 128/43. 130/19,46. 132/6. 135/30. 137/32. 162/34. 204/29. 224/37. 227/30. 230/19. 243/4. 298/9. 302/14,34. 368/7. realised 179/5. 237/20. 281/22. 299/41. realities spiritual 2/21. 51/5. 52/22. 54/31. 240/15. 313/35. 314/12. 365/3–6. 367/15. 368/13–22. realities 52/25. 149/40. 267/26. 279/39. 314/34. reality the only 11/36. 19/35. 81/33. 89/28. 92/17. 242/11. 293/4; false view of 11/38–41. 24/12. 269/35. 272/3; spiritual 50/30. 57/24. 58/15 63/21. 77/2. 89/3. 121/13. 136/1,32 137/3,28. 138/34. 172/17. 223/8. 238/22. 271/4. 275/4. 364/36,38. 365/25. 367/28; prove, demonstrate, r. of God 64/19. 113/12. 256/44; all r. 146/6. 225/10; reality 24/46. 85/3. 98/10. 100/15. 128/43. 138/1,38. 139/13,21. 142/4,28. 158/5. 161/13. 162/13. 228/30. 240/21. 273/19. 275/47. 279/17. 299/30. 310/17. 355/36
reason 11/13. 78/7. 135/32. 138/4. 148/11. 155/6. 213/31. 252/11. reasoning 48/39. 63/46. 281/27. 309/27. reasons 121/7. 134/18. 270/12
receive 112/5. 219/23. 229/15. 232/8. 296/12. 355/6. 364/45. received 219/17. receiving 355/5,8. recipient 229/19
recognised 78/42. 105/17. 260/33. 263/12. 306/37. recognises 94/14. recognising 130/2. recognition

63/20. 92/18. 116/27. 159/34. 256/10. 269/5,10. 283/4. 379/8
recurrence 218/5. 226/8. 274/35. 278/4. 361/16,29
reduced 79/19. 290/8. 304/5. 357/39
reed broken 131/19. 255/24. 303/35. 308/45
refined 263/27. 276/11. refinement 133/34. 231/16,19. 235/42
reflect 286/15. 366/15. 369/11. reflected 271/10. 278/40. 313/42. 363/31. reflection 28/19. 54/48. 161/38. 175/33. 231/24. 268/28. 271/11. 373/39. reflections 271/41,43. reflects 2/18. 103/15. 130/47. 138/28. 150/13. 245/15. 309/1. 363/31. 364/12. 366/23
refreshment 139/15. 259/23
refuge 172/37
refuse 297/36
regain 300/40
reincarnation 105/33. 274/36. 288/48. 348/7–33. 361/31
reject 294/43. 295/29
rejoicing 132/10. 136/20. 144/26
relations 90/39. 150/33. 172/31.232/13. 259/5. relationship 136/3. 281/14. relative 86/35. 142/36,37,40. 144/48. 204/17. 240/13,18. 242/16. 311/20. 312/13. 357/3
release 25/47. 98/22. 229/31. 267/42. 268/8. 286/40
reliance 160/22. 179/17. 289/12. 303/9 relied 173/22. rely 134/23. 154/31 179/3,9. 291/38. 302/38. 303/17,46 304/18. relying 173/26
relief 70/6. 94/6,41. 241/23. 256/6. 268/34. relieve 2/36. 86/31. 285/25. 308/2. relieves 317/14. relieving 346/28. 372/49
religion true r. is helping fellow-man 48/25; when a man lives his 214/17. 255/18. 306/21; determined to live their 232/17; love lived is practical 237/29; unnatural 280/39; when explaining your grasp of 308/45; based on Principle 321/32,39; religion 25/9,10. 26/15. 29/35. 37/32–38/12. 39/16–40/2,32. 45/45. 136/27. 145/16,17. 147/44. 148/2. 150/8. 154/40. 171/45. 235/28. 281/13. 282/9,15. 283/16. 315/34. 316/9. 323/13. 352/1. religions 38/8. 63/8. 347/15. religious 136/24,27. 171/7. 294/25. 300/9,12. 301/7,11. 304/40. 323/23. 356/17
remain 312/25. 355/29,32
remedy 95/28. 96/24. 126/22. 134/22. 246/8. 263/4. 351/42
remember 105/12. remembered 288/36. remembrance 91/7

requirement 126/5. 236/17
repetition 25/42. 95/35. 162/18. 217/31.
  272/4,21. 354/37. 357/34
replacement 136/11. 203/20. 295/39.
  318/3
represent 50/45. 51/11. 108/34. 364/46.
  representation 293/5. 374/6,10.
  representing 51/31. 111/15. 369/7
respond 72/2. 130/37, 175/31. 234/13.
  354/15. response 74/7. 128/19.
  170/18. 209/6,25. responsibilities
  170/46. 286/40. responsibility
  168/35. 171/2. 205/45. 227/42. 293/1.
  295/41. 303/1. 351/18. 353/21
rest 128/42. 134/39. 139/15. 148/38.
  268/34. restful 134/35. 136/13. 295/
  38. resting 115/21
result proportionately better 134/9,13;
  of human picturing 207/32; of
  supplicatory prayer 208/3. 214/23;
  instantaneous 224/38. 309/37; to
  humanity 264/28,31; result 285/20.
  304/18. 309/42. 355/7. resultant
  right speaking and acting 170/1.
  results practical 53/43. 136/29.
  200/38. 236/28. 355/19; before good
  r. can be obtained 202/39; proportionately more alarming 205/12;
  outlining future 217/16. 246/30,38,39;
  different from faith-healing 218/22.
  219/29; of true prayer 220/27;
  according to law 221/32; instantaneous 222/30. 223/27. 229/43; to obtain
  good 223/13. 227/25. 245/23. 289/13.
  354/26; without slightest regard for
  288/18,24; results 2/33. 6/47. 72/7.
  94/16. 96/4. 97/32,47. 124/9. 161/35.
  187/40. 194/11. 209/9,27. 215/10.
  246/30. 301/22. 305/48. 318/28. 351/
  38. 360/1
retrograde 106/29. 134/42. 271/27.
  276/10
return 213/5. 215/23. 276/30. 307/43.
  361/23
Revelation Book of 170/33; revelation
  11/13. 31/24. 35/33. 47/20. 155/5.
  210/41. 273/20. 321/18
reverence 133/14. 140/5. 285/3.
  reverential 211/14
reversal 4/36. 54/7. 129/40. 130/6,34.
  132/12. 134/5. 135/47,49. 161/42.
  222/22. 223/1. 225/16. 274/14,21.
  297/1. 298/2. 299/13. 350/38. reverse
  14/21. 65/5. 129/31. 130/40. 133/48.
  144/12. 206/8. 220/36. 223/35. 262/14.
  291/3. 309/41. 371/28. reversed
  128/41. 135/6. 136/38. 144/13. 211/8.
  222/21. reverses 293/35. reversing
  128/21. 130/2. 137/38. 306/42. 312/4.
  330/25. 372 15,27. 388/39-389/2
revolution 92/2. 159/33. 235/35.

revolutionary 2/33. revolutionise
  2/3. 301/25. 321/40
reward 39/34. 226/20. 308/9. 351/34
Reynolds Prof. Osborne 76/24. 84/2.
  160/26
rhythm 276/20. 278/11. 299/3
right 136/31. 146/27. 227/28. 236/18.
  241/16. 288/17-20,30. 289/24. 302/47.
  306/21-26,39. 307/9. 354/33
rise 32/22. 126/17. 134/8. 149/3. 222/27.
  270/43. 298/39. 342/27. 374/35. rising
  95/39. 206/20. 208/46. rose above
  matter 139/21. 173/31
rock 296/27. 320/41. 366/7
rod 114/4. 132/23-31. 138/33. 299/24.
  301/40
Romanes 3/18. 21/29. 42/17. 150/15.
  154/46. 258/29
rose 251/40-252/10
Rouse Ball W. W. 13/47. 55/44. 57/36.
  81/36. 83/30. 84/4
rule 92/13. 116/22. 132/27. 297/7.
  353/38. ruler 248/50. rules 126/3.
  132/19. 138/45. 229/8. 235/40. 278/6.
  315/42,44. 316/2. 372/22. ruling
  294/45. 295/21,34
Ruskin 41/13. 73/18. 85/43. 270/5.
  302/20. 380/21. 391/35

S

Sabbath day observance 152/13
sacrifice 26/28. 39/26. 48/29. 140/2.
  208/8,18,32. 288/3. 289/33. 354/21
safety 95/29. 125/20. 126/19. 172/35.
  264/23. 300/24. 397/13
safeguard 96/2. safeguarded 143/22.
  173/41
salvation 39/32. 65/14. 91/28. 166/48.
  207/25. 225/5. 261/36. 306/1,5. 321/27.
  346/39. 349/10
Satan 94/6. 95/13,44. 127/27. 133/2.
  214/47. 241/25
satisfied 133/47. 287/43. satisfies
  100/25
save 96/3. 231/33. 320/8. saved 166/7.
  206/25. 221/47. saving 142/27.
  Saviour 140/4. 242/37. saviours
  174/5. 287/20
say 68/35. 302/4. 306/15,22. 307/9.
  308/44
sceptic 206/38. scepticism 3/14.
  42/10. 190/1. 290/19. 309/39. 342/31
Schofield Dr. A. T. 55/37. 103/27.
  177/42. 188/43. 189/11,26,45. 190/
  15, 43. 229/24. 247/8. 256/20
school 142/11. 283/11. 353/17,19.
  schoolmaster 220/30. schools
  36/39. 37/13. 147/38. 243/12. 355/46.
  scholarship golden 284/3

Schopenhauer 103/29. 176/28. 341. 348/19

Science 28/18. 40/1. 61/15. 138/49. 149/17,18,25. 202/19. 224/1. 264/46. 280/35. 297/42. 318/37. 321/40. **science** natural 4/6. 40/10. 44/22,31. 60/29. 61/14. 65/41. 105/22. 127/3. 142/24. 198/29. 280/10,12. 316/8,11. 343/22; and absolute beginnings and ends 9/43; moving towards the spiritual 10/21. 46/35; mental world the one certainty of 11/35; true, mental 12/25. 90/45. 215/13. 225/4. 226/7. 278/21; so-called mental 12/26,28. 29/43,45. 246/37. 305/29. 355/20; practical 14/24; word of God only absolute 40/9; and religion 45/45. 136/27. 154/40. 283/16. 323/13. 352/1; physical 60/10. 81/40. 280/5; the purpose of modern 64/40; led to doctrine of immortality 84/36; of the coming time 109/36; all s. worthy of the name is divine 127/2; to give s. and health to his people 218/27; unnatural 280/3; and peace with progress 295/46; unalterable 313/18; an exact 317/1,40; science 43/6,39,42. 75/28. 126/2. 147/44. 148/22. 216/29. 234/31

Scott Sir Walter 49/38. 105/36. 114/16. 316/45

Scriptures 149/9

scum 173/40

sect 317/40. **sects** 7/29. 104/11. 201/37, 46. 202/5,36. 221/47. 232/28

see 72/18. 76/20. 91/32. 96/7. 105/32. 110/2. 112/46. 311/15,24,28. 313/43. 368/23. 374/29

seed 65/11. 296/32

self material 11/41. 99/40. 140/7. 211/15. 292/25. 298/13,17. 325/5; mortal 31/26. 131/45; real 32/26,40. 49/8. 77/17. 103/29. 109/27. 162/38. 273/47. 292/26. 341/39. 349/29,46; spiritual 58/14. 99/40. 103/29. 108/37. 137/15; subliminal 103/29. 158/45. 356/7; self 241/25. 288/14, 289/25,29. 298/10. 301/26. 303/3. 377/42. **selfhood** 38/22. 49/9. 211/16. 349/34. 377/30. **selfishness** 135/35. 143/45. 256/18. 289/27. 292/11. 350/13. **selfless** 119/5. 288/12. **selflessness** 289/16. **selves** 12/24. 38/23. 58/33. 133/24. 314/1. **self-betrayal** 315/46. -confidence 314/31. -conscious 103/38. 143/44. -consciousness 84/17. 86/33. 143/42. 167/31. 288/3. -conducted 295/27. -deification 289/37. -dematerialisation 263/34. -destroyed 67/43. 88/32. 203/18. 270/21. 311/12. -destruction 89/3.

144/6. -destructive 19/43. 89/40. 143/16. 145/25. 207/21. 311/9. -elimination 323/37. -examination 398/35. -expression 85/39. -forgetful 237/4. -hypnotised 11/41. -imposed 226/6. -intensification 280/26. 313/12. -knowledge 241/26. -love 288/13. -made 259/14. -maintained 91/14. -protection 135/33. 187/46. -realisation 128/13. -righteous 287/44. -sacrifice 6/8. 292/19. -sacrificing 253/2

semi-metaphysical 148/2. 187/44. 323/27. -metaphysics 343/17,21

sense material 19/25. 32/20. 89/39. 161/30. 228/22; limited 24/45. 169/9. 270/44. 311/22; human 32/24. 70/37; false 65/10. 98/40. 111/18. 130/4. 138/17. 263/29. 269/31. 272/7. 273/34, 36; sense 22/9. 79/14. 92/20. 104/19. 223/15. 227/28. 229/39. 289/21. 299/21. **senses** spiritual, true 162/3. 243/6. 316/29; senses 20/31,32. 24/25. 58/13,30. 64/10. 66/16. 77/14,24,33. 78/20. 81/3,18. 104/30. 121/14. 162/1. 216/27. 369/40. **sensibility** to suffering of others 301/38

separated less likely to be 292/39. **separates** not persons but 290/7. **separation** from God a heresy 40/30; separation 136/25. 147/1. 256/14. 269/29. 270/19,27,46. 272/6. 289/18. 300/11

sequence 54/17. 94/3. 252/17. 261/21. 366/27. 369/18,21. 373/32. **sequences** 105/28

Sermon on the Mount 285/15. 395/12; sermon 205 3. 239/10

serpent 130/2. 228/22. 299/24. 365/5

servant 126/23. 280/13. **servants** 234/31. **serve** 134/30. 173/11. **service** 229/18. 292/15. **services** 301/7,11

sex 231/12,20. 236/15. **sexes** 233/1. 353/31

shadow 15/27. 59/22. **shadows** 210/5. 276/4

Shakespeare 19/17. 37/30. 84/8. 86/15. 92/25. 103/4. 107/6. 131/38. 133/41. 144/35. 155/42. 166/35. 176/37. 211/10. 229/22. 238/2. 261/23. 288/25. 291/7. 298/23

shield 173/46. 269/11. 305/4

short-circuiting 67/43. 68/28-32. 72/33. 75/15. 158/34. 161/14. 203/11. 313/35. 314/23

sickle 96/9,11

sickness will try all sorts of methods with 143/30; God's visitation 195/31; where s. is due to sin 207/4,7; healing of s. element of Christianity 218/15;

healing of s. bugle call 219/43 healing of s. not sufficient proof 219/45; heal instantaneously not only 221/4. 305/45; in many cases mere foolish belief 244/38; fear sufficient to cause 259/46; regarded as cross 281/45
sight 66/29. 107/5. 108/26. 110/6. 116/33. 238/34
sign 47/48. 249/5. 303/45. **sign-posts** 129/40. 299/8. 309/43
silence 391/24. **silent** 302/6,12. **silently** 291/3
simple 297/7. **simplicity** 236/24. 303/21. 306/27,38
sin 2/34,37. 14/45. 15/6,11. 16/21. 20/12. 72/10. 94/3,7. 130/34. 141/13. 143/9,26. 144/34. 146/22,23. 168/16. 169/35. 202/30. 203/26,40. 204/44. 205/13–207/10. 208/33–48. 213/9. 218/4,15,28. 219/45,47. 220/31,34. 221/4. 228/1. 241/16. 268/42. 289/37–43. 292/7,41. 315/14. 373/18. 379/18. **sinless** 203/43. 310/9. **sinners** 264/16
sleep 15/15. 120/4. 179/35. 245/6. 266/41. 271/24
smell 112/8. 150/2.
socialism 350/1. **socialist** 343/4
Society for Spreading the Knowledge of True Prayer ix/45
Socrates 20/21. 156/23. 167/23. 323/3. 329. 345/44
solution 11/14,25. 146/16. 268/19. 278/16. 296/8,10. 318/5
somnambulism 120/1
Son 10/42. 25/35. 27/10. 33/5. 39/26. 48/29. 140/8. 176/15. 377/17,23,44; **son** 25/35. 32/19. 286/25. 290/26. 310/36. 321/7. **sons** 32/29. 34/19. 174/4. 269/10
sorcery 75/18. 262/24
Soul God 2/14. 27/37. 28/16. 59/11. 70/42. 111/45,46. 114/32. 295/5. 365/1. 370/15; from sense to 130/4; false belief of S. in body 263/43; **soul** 70/31–42. 71/46. 103/35. 104/40. 120/19. 123/9,12,48. 151/47. 158/46. 240/31. 254/42. 266/47,49. 299/21. 347/40
sound 66/26,29. 68/28. 109/6. 110/23. 111/19,24,27. 327/7
space 9/46. 57/1. 66/22. 67/39. 68/39. 77/25,32. 79/1. 100/2,49. 159/21. 169/11. 278/38. 306/10. 364/3
speak 79/34. 295/41. 302/13. **speaking** 91/24. 152/10. 170/1. 283/41. 316/48. **speaks** 232/45. 307/9. **speech** 111/14. 230/34
species 272/10. 279/2,20. 345/16. **specific** 136/22. 367/28. **specifically** 301/18. 366/12, 29. 368/35

Spencer Herbert 10/28. 32/2. 36/8. 48/24. 58/11. 63/2. 68/7. 84/19. 126/26, 323/11. 342/24. 344
Spinoza 237/44. 337. 377/44
Spirit God 2/14. 27/37. 28/16. 38/13. 59/11. 70/42. 129/36. 133/42. 145/10,22. 146/11. 232/25,27. 243/13,14. 281/13. 295/29. 299/3. 303/39; **spirit** 214/10. 281/48
spirits 120/24,35. 186/32. 249/40. 252/19. 253/11. 254/22. 255/22,35. 257/45. 348/39. **spiritual** wrong to form outline of 137/5; partly s. and partly material 145/9; eternal because 149/28; things as good and 211/15; sixth sense 223/15. **spiritualisation** 261/43. 343/17. **spiritualised** 129/36. **spirituality** 29/16. 32/15. 38/9. 71/21. 98/44. 130/4. 227/20
Spiritualism 116/26. 247/15. 249/26. 348/4.
sponge 70/12. 120/21. 138/39
spread 69/1. 79/5. 249/15. 307/46. 308/29. 317/38. **spreading** 27/18. 65/17. 91/18. 222/2. 281/17. 296/30. **spreads** 314/24
stage 72/53. 94/5. 135/40. 162/12. 226/6. 286/35. 312/26. 374/38. **stages** 173/9. 227/16. 251/40
standard 13/14. 79/16. 149/38. 173/28. 208/47. 236/11. 242/15,22. 283/35. 296/27
standpoint 11/38. 55/31. 211/11. 226/26. 242/32. 274/15. 302/4
star 309/23
start 94/37. 363/9. **started** 129/24. 173/14. 311/37. **starting** 87/15
state 313/33. **states** 16/14. 349/28
statement 148/40. 149/2. 161/12. 201/27. 204/41. 291/4. 356/9. **statements** 145/7. 146/9. 148/38
statesman 295/1. **stateswoman** 353/26
steadily 95/28. 144/19. 239/46. **steadiness** 256/26. **steady** 283/38. 305/13
step 98/9. 111/48. 130/4. 293/9. 295/39. 372/41. **steps** 98/16. 153/34. 173/14, 22. 289/10,12
strength 62/40. 120/8. 132/29. 133/32. 42. 227/12. 231/18. 248/31. 304/28. 314/31. 353/34. 373/41. **strong** 171/47. 172/2. 262/8. 348/39. **stronger** 229/47. 245/45. **strongly** 209/19. 214/24
strife 173/40,42
strive 227/29. **striving** 133/45. 134/9, 37. 170/22. 210/31. 299/35
student 138/48. 151/22. 228/17. 318/46. **students** 234/28,35. 235/37. 283/39. 317/26. **study** 64/46. 103/17. 135/32.

138/46. 152/24,33. 153/46. 155/36. 309/40. 315/6,13,33. 318/13
subconscious (*see under* MIND *and* NO-MIND)
subjective 77/25. 336/3. 340/12,40. subjectively 128/18
substance God as 27/38. 59/11. 296/34. 370/16; substance 11/40. 12/1. 64/12. 70/20. 74/47. 81/20. 85/16. 120/48,49. 199/19. 253/1. 278/39
succeed 295/24. 354/28,32. success 197/23. 285/12. 288/14. 294/32, 34. successful 247/26. 355/16. succession 50/31,35,41. 77/28. 274/ 20. 276/37. 340/6. 341/29,33. successive 76/19. 77/35. 272/3,11,18. 274/25,32,37. 276/14. 285/37. 312/ 41. 313/1. 324/19. 327/31
suffer 243/32. 286/41. 296/8. 354/12. sufferer 6/7. 256/12. suffering ix/5. 16/20. 26/6. 69/36. 91/4. 94/8,12. 144/15,34. 205/28. 228/44. 229/1. 236/19. 243/34. 292/19. 295/27. 301/ 38. 308/2
sufficient 69/37. 76/11. 94/10. 124/23. 201/28. 210/27
suggestion 109/30. 138/36. 180/11,34. 184/46. 186/24–31. 212/27. 214/44. 215/15. 217/14. 240/14. 247/1. 253/49. 282/26,33,39. 373/23
suicidal 89/41. suicide 244/39. 268/8
summary 323/1. 369/3
summit 174/13
sun 62/25. 67/23. 88/13. 104/22. 138/ 26. 311/4. 366/23. sunlight of Truth 174/20
Swedenborg 8/18. 59/13. 115/26. 118/6. 156/19. 238/6. 338
sweep 68/20. 226/32. 290/33. 297/42. sweeping 69/10,24. 273/2. sweeps 127/5
sword ix/29. 127/41. 131/22. 210/44. 297/41. 320/9. 395/7
symbolism 140/23. 153/37. symbols 58/1. 59/6. 154/24
sympathy 231/34. 234/3. 281/5
synchronous 77/1. 118/35. 204/18. 278/11. 327/4. synchronously 72/ 14. 105/14,23. 113/6. 157/33
synonym 111/46. 370/45. synonymous 27/36
systematic ix/21. 3/48. 78/29. 129/21. 208/45. 211/19. 304/46

T

talents 134/11
talking of others 261/25. 290/36; talking 307/14
tares 133/1

teach 214/26. 217/39. 224/31. 227/45. 283/1. 302/24. 372/38. 395/41. teaches 223/17. 309/9. teaching 135/37. 209/9. 318/22,36. 319/3. teachings 11/15. 96/20. 142/18. 150/16. 167/5. 170/23. 197/3. 268/44. 282/6. 316/35,38. 317/23
telegraphy mental 115/13
telepathy 104/39,44. 110/29. 115/8,41. 121/9
tempt 172/23. temptation 72/12. 90/37. 204/6. 218/6. tempted 356/18
tenderness 229/16. 270/40. 281/5
Tennyson 24/18. 28/13. 31/19,48. 33/ 36. 88/34. 106/13. 176/38. 193/49. 223/3. 284/7. 286/30. 300/26. 383/27
tension 75/12. 158/33. 202/21
Teresa St. 213/27. 221/2
test 39/47. 218/1,3. 242/24. 249/4. 265/18. 294/41. 296/2. 339/47. tested 149/6. 234/14
thankful 305/27. thanking 101/1. thanks 291/27. 307/27
themselves 96/5. 99/29
theologian's 39/17. 148/1. theologians 36/32. 64/35. 65/33. 71/40. 104/10. theology 39/12. 46/24. 70/37. 146/10. 147/7. 148/1. 378/20
theories 2/27. 14/8. 60/22. 63/7,12,28. 72/7. 80/18. 145/22. 161/10. 167/6. 225/2. 233/33. 238/22. 273/4,6. 276/ 29. 278/30. 312/38. 317/39. 318/2. theory 1/30. 4/1. 14/8. 62/2. 63/16. 64/14–36. 67/31. 77/44. 80/19. 94/13. 160/47. 245/34. 255/2. 256/31. 278/26. 280/30
theosophy 124/29,35. 347/5,36
thing wrong 127/8. 297/10,13. things 32/17. 137/6. 211/14. 223/14. 276/2. 278/28. 281/24. 311/24. 375/46
think by the way we 16/15; rightly 21/12. 49/32. 97/31. 123/23. 130/29. 167/21. 168/25. 176/23. 204/28. 239/38. 255/24. 285/22,28. 286/24. 287/42. 291/41. 293/29. 296/25. 297/ 31. 354/5,8. 357/18; praying when you t. of God 32/20; only have to t. of anything to 54/45. 79/4; showing beforehand way to 96/27; when knowing how to 104/17. 116/44. 176/7. 237/46; scientifically 152/8. 168/40. 187/45. 220/33; think 132/4. 136/31. 137/45. 138/23. 143/41. 170/ 18,19. 210/22. 242/26. 244/49. 297/17. 298/11. 302/4. 306/22. 307/16. 336/41. 356/38. 375/37
thinker and thoughts 63/40. 79/6. 311/32; strong 199/8. 214/7. 253/21, 46; perfect 313/43; thinker 75/28. 91/41. 219/10. 303/13. 311/32. 317/1
thinkers 36/30. 39/14. 63/40. 64/27.

82/35. 146/32. 148/25. 175/27. 215/2.
234/33. 255/17. 276/26. 288/23.
293/46. 323/23. 324/35. 341/26.
354/28
thinking
strong vii/32. 75/12. 116/42
systematic 3/48. 78/29. 129/21. 211/19
right 12/25. 38/11. 48/31. 70/6. 92/4.
93/40. 94/9,24,27. 108/43. 126/30.
134/40. 144/15. 170/1,18. 176/30.
231/28. 244/25. 247/19. 273/12.
276/14. 291/42. 293/43. 295/12.
354/25. 375/49
change of thinking, thought, thoughts
13/13. 73/3. 92/22. 93/6. 141/4.
184/4. 186/2. 199/22. 207/11. 346/32
wrong 20/20. 70/7. 94/20. 96/4. 156/
36,39. 172/43. 201/46. 204/9. 206/
30. 207/34. 212/40. 247/21. 261/
15. 285/22. 290/28. 351/40. 354/16
always t. God's thoughts 32/26
results of right and wrong 48/30
so-called 64/4
of God 115/22. 116/21. 127/42. 129/
39. 148/30. 223/7. 224/5. 247/19.
299/30
God's power of 224/4
active 245/13. 253/34,48. 303/13.
309/1
rightly 291/48. 354/19
thinking 11/33. 63/46. 69/19. 135/20.
137/2. 178/6. 191/18. 209/16. 214/9.
221/28. 298/12. 301/13. 333/14.
355/11
thinks of God 37/34. 143/44; thinks
96/41. 112/39. 143/43. 204/26. 205/
41. 209/14,19. 244/32,48. 296/11
thirsty 307/10. 309/6
Thomson Prof. Sir J. J. 65/26. 66/44.
74/14
thought
and lines of force 11/47. 66/3. 68/5.
75/15. 80/21. 86/43. 158/35. 161/2,
15. 197/28. 198/42. 203/12,47.
204/4
forces 13/19. 251/5
and matter, material, materialised
13/21,25. 39/33. 70/16. 71/36. 72/
18. 94/15. 148/17. 162/13. 167/8.
204/15. 311/15
every t. followed by similar effect
14/26.
power of 65/15. 92/7,12. 138/16. 213/
45. 251/7. 264/30
high tension current 68/9. 127/3,4.
357/6
contradictory opposite 68/34
intensification 69/12,18. 95/9. 115/14.
120/12. 121/11. 124/32. 176/24.
203/31,39. 204/7,10. 209/17. 215/24.
217/9,31. 227/12. 243/35. 246/25.

252/9,20. 255/36. 256/1. 260/41
261/16. 262/8,13. 280/26. 302/37
313/12. 354/36
theoretical aspect of 80/2
majority in clearness of 89/36. 92/13,
17. 313/21
last great liberation of 95/34,37
sequences 105/28
wrong 124/27. 130/22. 137/11. 168/22.
173/43. 205/22,39. 234/32. 264/27
handling wrong t. 128/41. 129/31.
131/44. 134/44. 167/17. 169/3. 187/
38. 201/48. 211/7. 220/37. 222/21.
290/16. 293/7. 294/20. 297/8,36.
299/13. 306/3. 373/22. 371/28
in t. to God 132/7. 223/13. 269/13
(*see also under* TURN)
one t. nearer the end 134/46
human 135/49. 177/48. 244/35
effect of so-called 175/27
one right 178/19
action of 197/22
evolution of advancing 279/45
thought 62/40. 75/7. 77/15. 79/16.
84/16. 96/38. 98/32. 135/14. 149/34.
160/4. 172/20. 173/19. 175/27.
184/25. 193/28. 213/39. 220/29.
225/6. 232/31. 242/23. 252/14.
253/31. 261/20. 273/2. 292/35.
296/27. 304/4. 306/2. 317/2. 334/23.
354/15. **thought-forms** 57/22.
121/23. **-germs** 161/22. 203/15.
-reading 106/39. 112/15–118/34.
124/10. 162/44. 169/27. 170/39.
227/22. 258/4,7,42. 285/26. 361/11.
thoughtfulness 235/42. 283/41.
287/27
thoughts
devilish 15/36. 96/36. 263/32
wrong 19/47. 89/9. 114/26. 127/28.
178/2. 202/1. 254/27. 298/10. 311/
32,44
handling wrong t. 16/22. 54/8. 73/4.
79/39. 124/20,22. 130/6,22. 135/
47. 136/38. 143/8. 150/37. 171/37.
173/3. 194/7. 299/26. 302/29. 312/4
God's 19/40. 32/26. 111/18,28. 135/
26. 197/30. 217/28. 316/27. 341/
30. 369/33. 375/9
true 38/14. 207/14
material 57/25. 72/3. 77/13. 87/17,20.
108/39,43. 119/1. 121/40. 169/4.
201/3. 214/28. 242/5. 302/27,36.
311/14
good 68/11. 73/5. 124/17. 135/24. 204/
15. 214/9. 302/30. 316/24
bad 68/11. 204/14. 312/7,8. 316/26
human 68/33. 115/23. 194/3,11. 204/
37. 212/45. 261/18,46. 302/34
action of 72/23. 73/11. 172/1. 183/36.
241/40

higher 72/34. 88/26
false 94/22. 116/4,18. 124/34. 135/25.
    254/28. 261/28,30. 311/40
evil 104/17. 127/18. 129/14. 133/2.
    135/24. 213/43. 234/13. 237/47.
    262/39. 290/7. 295/13. 303/44.
    312/5. 356/19
ethereal 107/2. 167/17. 172/44. 175/28.
    243/35. 252/16. 255/29. 258/10.
    260/11,41. 261/16. 293/32. 311/41
destroyed before formed 124/15
so many t. nearer 127/22 ,
affected by 176/4
material representation of 374-375
thoughts 19/39. 28/8. 63/39,40. 78/41.
    79/7. 94/13. 95/42. 96/39. 98/47.
    108/31. 113/3. 118/50. 121/22.
    129/36. 130/18. 135/14. 137/8,45.
    138/13. 149/36. 162/23. 167/19.
    168/18. 171/40,42. 172/13,23. 176/
    46. 177/10,11,16. 184/19. 185/19.
    200/43. 201/47. 206/14. 211/6. 220/
    24. 223/18,34. 227/35. 235/26. 244/
    31. 253/48. 256/28. 260/15,38,43.
    261/35. 265/15. 278/29. 279/8,27.
    301/22.302/19,38. 341/31. 354/17,33
three points of view 36/29; stages of
    Truth 42/30; meanings of Bible 151/
    39. 359/12; phases of love 230/34;
    types of thinkers 323/22
throne 292/23
time over aeons of 69/1; at any given
    78/15. 167/13; predetermined 166/38.
    167/9. 169/7. 311/29,42; better given
    to others 307/44; time 9/46. 68/39.
    77/11. 88/10. 99/33,45. 124/27. 131/6.
    135/5. 154/31. 169/9-21. 171/16.
    196/22. 206/34. 208/8. 228/44. 241/
    20. 245/6. 270/35. 278/38. 280/28.
    302/29. 309/19. 312/39. 313/14.
    324/19. times 121/3. 161/41. 285/42
tired 101/12,16. 218/2. 259/23. 268/33.
    tiredness 245/11. 259/15. tiring
    115/16,20. 252/35
tithes 299/44
touch ethereally in 105/28-41. 108/29-
    40. 113/1. 114/24. 116/17. 138/22;
    in t. with spiritual being 108/37;
    touch 157/34. 173/44. 256/8. 259/2.
    260/46. 301/34. 347/2
trained 260/38. 282/29. 371/24.
    training 98/7
trance 119/22. 124/2. 251/47. 252/4.
    254/10
transcendentalism 81/38
transfiguration 270/30,36
transformation 16/49. 358/28
transition 2/23. 76/27,31. 269/20
translate 291/4. translated 70/33.
    219/13. translation 24/25. 47/44.
    58/31. 103/33. translations 152/25

treat 136/19. 166/20. 169/15. 300/43.
    354/40. treating 283/38. 367/5.
    370/4. 375/28. treatment personal
    136/30; impersonal 137/44; treat-
    ment 75/21. 98/28. 135/8. 162/30.
    179/1. 201/23. 225/34. 231/13. 237/42.
    267/32. 276/39. 299/45. 300/9. 306/2.
    354/18. 369/39
Trinity 28/14
trouble supposititious cause of 68/2;
    increases to last moment 94/4; cause
    of the 94/22. 114/35. 116/1. 131/16.
    134/25. 136/39. 138/25. 156/36. 162/
    24. 168/13; no t. about living 101/32;
    when thought of t. comes 131/46;
    without incentive of 143/6. 144/16;
    worse t. coming 172/12; again in
    some form of 202/27; destroyed, no
    t. in future 203/10; return of 203/23.
    213/5; wrong thought creates physical
    205/22; seventy-five per cent of t.
    is over 205/37; get out of every 221/6.
    305/46; resulting from sin 242/5;
    temporary removal of 247/21; pictur-
    ing 260/20-42; trouble 262/10. 267/
    35. 285/26. 287/9. 289/9. 292/2. 303/
    45. troubled 136/18. 260/7. 284/1.
    troubles prophesied viii/41. 285/
    25,27; at the end 93/9; minor, major
    95/41. 351/47; end of all 127/23;
    reducing the 151/16. 174/12; troubles
    vii/35. 97/32. 99/4. 141/25. 144/24,28.
    168/12. 178/1. 191/8. 209/7. 219/44.
    244/39. 267/32. 268/35. 351/39. 356/
    18. 372/46. 379/19,33
true within limits 44/29. 60/10. 280/6;
    correct but not 63/27; true 126/37.
    145/8,18. 146/3,9. 148/44. 157/45.
    217/25. 240/16. 274/22. 291/35. 316/
    11. 337/31. 339/46. 343/23. truisms
    315/9
trust 260/18. 298/17. 302/40
Truth Christ 38/34. 89/23. 91/27. 241/
    43; as, is God 39/17,28. 79/35. 114/
    34. 135/1. 145/7. 146/20. 152/10.
    162/37. 181/22. 307/9. 308/31,45;
    light of 63/11. 136/18. 143/24; action
    of 65/11. 162/15. 311/13; knowledge
    of 101/45. 142/36. 144/2. 226/1. 261/1.
    267/12. 308/2; sword of 127/41. 131/
    22. 210/45. 297/41; Truth 18/46-48.
    37/32. 38/44. 43/38. 62/27. 91/3. 92/4.
    95/17. 142/38. 145/19-32. 146/2.
    149/4,41. 172/24. 202/18. 220/22.
    229/2. 231/32. 232/45. 242/37. 262/21.
    263/46. 274/10. 276/40. 285/14. 296/
    33. 297/37. 300/8. 301/47. 305/34.
    308-309 (see also LIFE Truth and
    Love)
truth, knowledge of, viii/25. ix/9. 94/37.
    116/27. 144/36. 241/3. 285/29. 292/21,

301/4. 305/3. 379/34. 381/1; ignorance of 9/40. 11/17. 354/40; demonstrable 48/40. 268/45. 313/10. 314/37. 315/11, 33; mathematical 56/30. 269/40; knowing the 94/10,31. 95/27. 110/7. 116/5. 137/38. 140/1. 202/15. 245/12. 269/16. 283/26; realising the 114/32. 130/19. 204/29. 302/14. 354/44; absolute 134/32. 144/47. 217/21. 320/42; statements of 217/18. 299/40. 301/45. 307/12; spirit of 224/30; spiritual 270/30. 273/19. 291/5; truth 43/18. 65/19. 85/34. 91/18. 93/5. 96/3,40. 98/9,40. 105/17. 112/4. 127/ 18,41. 142/2. 145/1. 148/32. 170/12. 171/35. 206/36. 215/13. 219/15,28,46. 226/7. 236/41. 238/10,11. 239/28. 242/44. 279/48. 280/37. 290/4. 295/ 41. 297/5. 307/47. 311/2. 316/4. 319/46. 346/42. **truths** 2/7,30. 152/ 20. 162/9. 173/31. 204/39. 266/44. 294/42. 318/46. 324/1
trying 134/10. 141/13. 172/40. 397/16
tuition 78/39. 284/4
tuning fork 72/24–36. 357/13
turn 114/31. 126/41. 129/40. 132/3. 135/5. 143/11. 144/12. 213/47. 242/31. 263/35. 292/37. 297/9,36. 300/16,41. 369/42. 372/7. **turned** 143/4. **turning** vii/10. 75/14. 111/44. 116/23. 120/15. 124/12,40. 134/30. 137/37. 138/14. 143/12. 201/41. 202/14,36. 203/23. 218/7. 267/25. 283/25. 293/29. 299/9. 305/54. 312/3. **turns** 79/28. 94/5. 99/38. 143/3,31. 249/4. 279/46
two 143/20. 243/1
types 272/14. 275/16. 361/38
tyranny 89/41. 171/40. 208/25. **tyrant** 27/32

U

unbreakable 149/27
unconscious 119/46. 120/2. 245/26. **unconsciously** 179/28. 248/43
uncover 80/19. 96/2. 131/16. **uncovered** 65/10. 134/27. 249/11. **uncovering** 327/19. 387/23–389/30
understand 2/2. 62/26. 91/33. 127/1. 130/44. 147/46. 150/12. 151/3,14. 153/31. 217/20. 242/41. 287/31. 288/1. 314/41. 364/46. 368/5,21. 376/6. **understanding** right 2/2. 78/29. 140/6. 188/3. 228/24. 249/13; scientific 11/21. 171/28; of God 11/21. 78/29. 146/1. 171/28. 172/30. 210/28. 220/31. 233/30. 249/13. 264/22. 281/14. 298/ 47. 346/26; demonstrable 31/40. 346/26; better 38/21. 146/1. 152/6; perfect 51/29; clear 142/21. 149/12. higher 149/4. 235/8; practical 155/8;

spiritual 256/9. 273/17. 300/33. 359/ 47; understanding 86/33. 94/33. 98/ 42. 111/46. 135/44. 138/45. 148/41. 152/22. 161/46. 172/30,39. 202/38. 208/42. 210/28. 220/31. 229/20. 233/ 30. 245/20. 261/43. 263/46. 265/11. 268/45. 270/41. 272/39. 274/46. 281/ 14. 286/36. 288/21. 295/42. 301/15. 308/37. 316/3. 321/34. 354/22. 368/19. **understands** 76/10. 153/16. 298/47. 373/33. **understood** 78/43. 90/27. 96/41. 148/39. 151/20. 156/31. 171/34. 205/11. 218/23. 235/46. 249/18. 299/ 41. 305/49. 315/47. 321/16
unfolding 50/40. 100/18. 101/35. 237/2. 369/7. 373/32. **unfoldment** 90/38. 100/24. 149/3. 279/43
united 93/40. 135/38. **unity** 33/41. 36/9. 74/6. 79/40. 223/17. 230/9. 235/7,45. 236/6. 278/9. 286/42. 292/40. 353/30
universal 80/15. 90/39. 113/6. 138/8. 145/18. 158/29. 159/43. 168/43. 172/ 26. 226/9. 229/6,31. 235/5. 269/ 28. 272/38–273/9. 279/49. 293/5. **universally** 87/12. 273/14. 312/38. **universe** spiritual 11/37. 145/31. 149/25. 269/35. 270/13. 279/2; real 11/43. 12/45. 272/9. 313/32,34; material 12/36,44. 65/37. 87/34. 161/8. 176/11. 249/14. 276/7. 316/39. 357/27. 366/32; physical 81/1; universe 66/50. 70/43. 74/29. 82/11,23. 83/20. 85/23. 88/8. 145/41. 147/41. 218/25. 233/30. 243/2. 314/23. 315/34
unlearn 223/36
unreal 19/20. 146/4,21. 311/9,17. 351/ 14. **unreality** 77/7. 146/28. 247/14. 264/39. 273/1. 276/3,32. 311/1
unselfish 126/34. 173/32. 229/32. 281/12. 287/27. 290/40. 360/19. **un-selfishness** 76/11. 227/26. 292/4–42
untrue 146/3,21. 204/36
uplifted 98/29. 111/21,24. 270/34. **uplifting** 99/3. 230/8
use 38/38. 131/38. 134/24. 159/38. 170/48. 171/23. 172/41. 227/30. 260/ 14. 287/47. 292/2. 299/25. 305/3. **useful** 237/23. **useless** 116/28. 123/34. 247/7. **usual** 134/8. 155/2. **utilise** 69/39. 138/30. 154/32. 155/2. 229/19. 261/1. 368/14. **utilised** 2/16. 71/21. 125/28. 173/28. 316/36

V

value 7/36. 142/42. 147/45. 150/29. 152/12,18. 200/30,34. 209/21. 281/11. 283/40. 289/11
vapour 87/31. 120/28. 324/45. 357/45
veil 96/17. 226/22. 253/3. 270/42. 314/

27,28. 358/36. **veils** 358/39. 359/17.
360/32
vibrate 105/14,23. 109/7. 119/2. 222/
17. 260/38. 357/14. **vibrates** 113/5.
157/32. **vibration** 66/3,29. 67/10–14.
73/26. 77/1. 116/18. 127/6. 137/12.
153/15. 164/13. 165/16,33. 267/17.
278/8,47. 326/46. **vibrations** 11/34.
68/8–28. 72. 107/12. 112/42. 167/14, 16.
175/29. 198/10–43. 203/14–204/32.
258/8,11. 261/33. 262/3. 280/25. 357/
10–17
victim 21/5,11. 95/21. 172/3. 206/41.
243/38,41. 252/4. 262/39. **victims**
96/2–42. 164/10. 301/42. 352/26
view 36/29. 65/41. 127/3. 136/19,24.
143/18. 171/16. 204/36. 298/22. 302/3.
356/17,37. 357/5,24. **views** 80/45.
84/7. 155/4. 235/18. 265/10. 272/3.
275/6. 281/18. 352/24
virgin 129/25–26. 247/10
visible 121/14,40. 201/44. 243/36. 273/
18. 312/37
vision 79/5. 95/14. 160/4. 162/6. 297/45.
visionary 72/1. **visions** 120/18.
252/22
voice 176/10. 252/21. 268/46
volition 100/22. 168/28. **voluntary**
166/13,23

W

wake 16/16. 37/24. 86/4. 91/13. 101/45,
49. 110/7. 267/4. 283/1. 304/38. 321/
45. 349/45. 360/45. **wakens** 243/34.
266/22. **wakes** 267/14. 269/32.
349/7. **waking** 48/26
want 180/19. 219/24. 221/29. 286/8.
287/30. 292/11. 301/24
Wallace Prof. Alfred Russel 9/14. 35/
·18. 160/9. 238/18. 378/37
war 6/34. 143/39. 248/26,41. 281/3.
350/51
warning 95/27. 124/35. 194/10. 205/10.
234/34. 263/25. 318/31. 395/33
waste of time 124/25. 154/28. 165/23.
241/20. 245/6. 300/37
watch 130/7. 211/5. 223/34. 229/18.
237/39. 299/2. 321/37. 371/34.
watch-dog 211/7. **watches** 193/13.
watchword 330/35
water 296/29. 307/1. 366/23
waves 66/27. 68/13,28. 76/27. 285/25
way wrong vii/6. 112/2. 119/37. 123/31,
36. 200/36. 241/16; scientific 105/24.
126/41. 148/29. 258/21; right 114/
27,31. 136/41. 154/31. 203/11. 217/41.
218/7. 246/34. 331/1; way 96/27.
110/9. 111/43. 124/39. 128/1. 129/20.
130/6. 134/5. 136/20,28. 137/38. 138/
30. 150/31. 157/41. 160/38. 169/13.

171/29. 206/22. 218/8. 220/3. 241/2.
291/12. 292/19,31. 296/25. 306/5.
309/12. 316/16. 348/5. 374/27. **Way-**
shower 25/30. 321/5. **ways** and
means 101/22. 355/11; ways 158/20,
24,32. 200/34. 355/35
weak 171/47. 172/2. 281/4. **weaker**
246/1. **weakness** 245/2. 248/32.
281/47. 314/30
wealth 150/26. 153/30. 221/31. 228/6.
320/14. 350/12. 351/4. 355/33
weapons 174/3. 305/1
web 63/17. 68/2. 249/48
weed 305/13
weight 92/17. 276/13
well 214/11. 217/18–25. 301/2
Wesley John 48/4. 120/36. 182/6
Westcott Bishop 37/1. 142/32. 229/15
whirlpools 234/1
Whittier 38/31. 79/26. 129/11. 289/47.
294/13. 304/38. 391/9
whole 77/3. 100/15. 138/9. 142/7. 151/
12. 228/31. 237/15. 274/29. 314/23.
366/15
Wilberforce Archdeacon 28/21. 35/30.
128/16. 131/2. 207/23. 332/18. 364/29
will 61/2. 128/12. 166/11. 179/44. 213/
29. 246/36. 288/15,26. 324/39. 341/20,
43. **will-power** vii/32. 60/41. 71/17.
75/12. 176/8. 198/40,41. 261/13. 394 /
44
winnowing 64/37
wisdom 10/40. 24/31. 36/5. 38/43,45.
39/29. 100/13. 101/3. 111/47. 130/47.
133/32. 173/18. 176/16. 228/34. 231/
14. 235/43. 296/29. 303/22,24. 343/
33. 353/34. 359/44. 364/13. 365/2,20.
373/14. **wise** 228/42. 234/6. 264/47.
290/29. 307/15. 315/41
witch 7/8. 252/3. 257/47. 348/44.
witchcraft 7/16. 95/18. 262/24.
witches 4/28. 75/18. 95/7. 257/31
within 98/10. 140/14. 242/27. 260/7.
288/31. 297/18,40
wizards 257/3
woman 112/28. 159/32. 202/46. 228/23.
231/14. 233/8,26. 235/43. 320/5,8.
353/5–47. **women** men and 231/30,
33. 232/16. 236/29. 350/20. 352/30.
women's rights 352/8
Word 133/23. 364/20 (*see also* LOGOS);
word 3/35. 168/22. 236/16. 307/6.
words 37/10. 119/5. 136/14. 149/1,40.
196/21. 299/40. 330/37
Wordsworth 155/24. 167/33
work mental 69/17. 115/21. 124/14.
173/39. 217/11. 262/3. 263/8. 283/20,
38; individual and collective 92/23.
138/28; God's 98/37. 135/6. 226/10;
false non-mental 111/39; mentally
116/21; let good 124/14; incentive to

w. and rejoice 144/26; our 171/38. 174/11. 275/7. 299/1. 304/30. 350/36; actively at 173/41. 274/20; provides ample 194/8; greatest 207/15; that brings joy 237/37; w. out his own salvation 306/1; highest 308/14; work 65/20. 110/9. 124/18,23,26. 125/25. 131/3,19. 134/2. 136/37. 137/ 33,36. 172/17,21. 231/10. 242/16. 260/42. 261/3. 300/7. 303/46. 304/5. 314/38. 321/37. 373/12. 375/28–45. worker 94/39. 134/11,26. 135/41. 136/40. 238/32. 320/15. 397/16. workers 96/7. 97/48. 137/40. 171/26. 173/16. 174/4. 198/26. 201/8,38. 217/10,12. 231/9. 235/47. 247/23. 254/2,32. 281/23. 282/5. 283/1,12,19. 284/1. working mental vii/45. 124/ 29; metaphysical 3/47; false mental 62/20; scientific w. restful 134/35; non-mental ethereal 181/1; with human mind 218/1. 259/18; w. out higher problems 235/39; devilish system of 247/49; working 2/46. 115/1. 124/24,29. 134/5. 138/30. 162/ 34. 171/24,36. 212/20. 253/30. 258/ 20. 262/14. 292/30. 304/45. 306/40. 339/44. 373/5. works 76/12. 113/4. 179/19. 207/11. 232/29. 236/33. 299/ 28. 375/42. workshop 273/3

world perfect 18/45. 23/47. 35/41. 64/7. 79/34. 89/43. 99/20,32. 101/24,49. 128/43. 145/28. 162/2. 211/12. 242/34. 313/25. 375/38; of reality, real 18/43. 24/9,20. 128/42. 197/31. 275/10,47. 310/20; spiritual 19/36. 24/12. 25/20,36. 32/21,35. 87/1. 100/7,21. 101/10. 161/37. 162/36. 247/20. 270/12. 273/46. 274/12. 323/33. 349/35. 368/5,8; of four dimensions 55/15. 99/44. 243/5; a glorious, wonderful 91/14. 101/43. 281/21; God's 272/28. 322/2. 363/6 the mysteries of our 4/8; mental 11/35; of sense 13/2. 84/29; wonders of the 22/14; benefits the 75/20. 150/38. 171/1; end of 89/46–98/4. 132/37. 133/1. 171/10. 267/4. 271/42. 322/2; scientific 96/9. 187/42; this 100/27. 318/5; helping the 127/22. 138/20; all the, the whole 136/18. 141/3. 150/12; saving the 142/27; of use in 172/41. 227/31; next 269/21. 271/9 material w. Theory that accounts for 4/3. 256/42; of appearances and changes 11/29. 13/24. 199/10. 272/2; false spiritual 12/15; evil and the 14/35; a counterfeit 15/13. 51/46. 54/35. 111/29; God and the material w. 16/23. 23/18. 24/6.

39/30. 105/18. 145/35. 148/10. 211/4. 220/23. 310/25–33. 311/6. 323/34. 356/9; a lie 18/42; a false sense 24/11,19. 49/9. 111/17,20; the good in 24/33. 52/6,13. 242/16; different from real w. 49/44; if anything is wrong in 52/39. 368/5; of three dimensions 58/12; suppositional opposite 63/38. 85/40. 276/1; necessary that accurate view of 65/3; foundation of 67/42. 82/3. 203/4; nothing to do with real self 77/16; evolution of 86/37. 358/37. 365/7; end of material w. 89/46–98/4. 127/23. 132/30. 140/16. 153/ 34. 201/29. 211/4. 276/14. 293/10; correct in 144/49. 166/6; is hell 168/23; fatal contemplation of 207/13; away in thought from 223/ 14. 224/35. 242/33. 253/35. 298/ 17; wrong to think of 247/21; mechanical 275/32; entirely separate 331/15; only one statement true about 356/9; most accurate view of 357/25; material w. xii/38. 63/41. 68/38. 69/7. 145/44. 157/31. 162/48. 166/37. 168/15. 169/13. 204/16. 240/19. 274/5. 311/3,30,36. 312/13,28. 349/16. 359/ 15. 382/14

world 229/34. 234/27. 240/36. 263/5. 271/34. 283/45. worlds 51/43. 100/3–101/21. 243/1. 357/48. 364/9. world-wide 95/36

worries 2/41. 16/23. 89/39. 221/9. 283/34. 295/14. worry 245/19. 260/20. 295/23. 355/12

worse 127/7. 131/10. 195/34. 209/16. 240/18

worship 16/32. 170/10. 207/38. 208/ 5,23. 210/21. 273/16

worth 161/42. 289/24. 302/7. 308/3

wrestlings 130/5. 233/27

writings 148/24. 384/42

wrong 1/3,21. 52/39. 104/19. 105/12. 136/33. 137/6. 157/42. 194/12. 246/20. 247/21. 282/40. 283/12. 292/34. 368/7

Wyclif's Bible 218/25

Y

you 32/24–40. 53/9–19. 72/13. 131/48. 133/31. 240/20. 310/36. 323/32. 370/ 25. 375/41,45

young 263/30,33

Z

Zeno 323/9. 327. 334/40. 346/7
Zenophanes 328. 346/9
Zoroaster 325

COSIMO is a specialty publisher of books and publications that inspire, inform and engage readers. Our mission is to offer unique books to niche audiences around the world.

COSIMO CLASSICS offers a collection of distinctive titles by the great authors and thinkers throughout the ages. At COSIMO CLASSICS timeless classics find a new life as affordable books, covering a variety of subjects including: *Biographies, Business, History, Mythology, Personal Development, Philosophy, Religion and Spirituality*, and much more!

COSIMO-on-DEMAND publishes books and publications for innovative authors, non-profit organizations and businesses. COSIMO-on-DEMAND specializes in bringing books back into print, publishing new books quickly and effectively, and making these publications available to readers around the world.

COSIMO REPORTS publishes public reports that affect your world: from global trends to the economy, and from health to geo-politics.

FOR MORE INFORMATION CONTACT US AT
INFO@COSIMOBOOKS.COM

If you are a book-lover interested in our current catalog of books.

If you are an author who wants to get published

If you represent an organization or business seeking to reach your members, donors or customers with your own books and publications

COSIMO BOOKS ARE ALWAYS AVAILABLE AT ONLINE BOOKSTORES

————— VISIT COSIMOBOOKS.COM —————
BE INSPIRED, BE INFORMED

Printed in July 2019
by Rotomail Italia S.p.A., Vignate (MI) - Italy